T0367752

# Advanced Credit Risk Analysis and Management

For other titles in the Wiley Finance series
please see www.wiley.com/finance

# Advanced Credit Risk Analysis and Management

**Ciby Joseph**

WILEY

*Registered office*
John Wiley & Sons, Ltd, The Atrium, Southern Gate, Chichester, West Sussex, PO19 8SQ, United Kingdom

For details of our global editorial offices, for customer services and for information about how to apply for permission to reuse the copyright material in this book please see our website at www.wiley.com.



*Library of Congress Cataloging-in-Publication Data*

Joseph, Ciby, 1969-
Advanced credit risk analysis and management / Ciby Joseph.
pages cm
Includes bibliographical references and index.
ISBN 978-1-118-60491-5 (cloth) – ISBN 978-1-118-60488-5 (ebk) – ISBN 978-1-118-60490-8 (ebk) – ISBN 978-1-118-60489-2 (ebk) 1. Credit–Management. 2. Risk management. I. Title.
HG3751.J67 2013
658.15′2–dc23

2013008536

A catalogue record for this book is available from the British Library.

ISBN 978-1-118-60491-5 (hbk) ISBN 978-1-118-60488-5 (ebk) ISBN 978-1-118-60487-8 (ebk)
ISBN 978-1-118-60490-8 (ebk) ISBN 978-1-118-60489-2 (ebk)

Set in 10/12pt Times by Aptara, Inc., New Delhi, India
Printed in Great Britain by CPI Group (UK) Ltd, Croydon, CR0 4YY

# Contents

# Preface

The aim of this book is to present a thorough and comprehensive treatment of credit risk in a way that would be useful to everyone who is interested in credit risk analysis and management. The motivation for the book has emanated from the fact that during my two-decade-long tryst with credit risk management, I have met several people – bank officers, regulators, credit executives, credit officers, chief finance officers, finance managers and business students – who asked me to refer a good book on credit analysis. Firstly, the coverage of this book is more comprehensive, and especially describes the developments and challenges of today's credit risk environment and covers the real nature of corporate credit risk and management in depth. Secondly, the credit risk perception of many – even at top management level – is blurred, resulting in unnecessary assumption of equity risk, which invariably results in higher credit risks without corresponding return. The various events related to the 2008 Global Credit Crisis that shook the financial world are an example. The exponential growth in credit and credit products in the recent decades has proven a big challenge not only to the leaders in finance but also to the bank regulators in several countries. Thirdly, businessmen, auditors, consultants, entrepreneurs and educators also yearn for a practical reference book on credit risk analysis and management. This book will be helpful to both lenders and borrowers in understanding the nature of credit risk analysis and management and will guide them to the prudent use of credit risk products and financial leverage, which is the hallmark of any successful business.

The way corporate credit risk is analyzed and studied in this book is unique. It provides a thorough treatment on Credit Risk and discusses obligor risk, portfolio risk, capital requirement, credit pricing and Basel accords. Amongst others, this book:

- Introduces the nature of credit risk and discusses advantages of credit (Chapter 1) and discusses the historical progress and challenges of credit risk analysis (Chapter 2).
- Explains the strategic role of credit risk culture and risk appetite statements (Chapter 3) and highlights the importance of separating key credit risk variables (Chapter 4).
- Provides guidance on various external risks and the formulation of effective early warning indicators (Chapter 5).
- Discusses the impact of business cycles on the industry and analyzes industry profitability factors (Chapter 6). The chapter ends with a detailed case study.
- Studies the entity level risks, including strategy and management risks (Chapter 7). The chapter ends with a detailed case study.
- Provides in-depth treatment of financial risk analysis (Chapter 8) with several worked-out examples and a detailed case study. About 50 pages have been devoted to this important topic.

- Explains how to make integrated credit risk judgements and provides several credit risk mitigants for obligor risk (Chapter 9).
- Shows how obligor credit risk analysis is converted into risk grades and discusses how PD can drive credit decisions in a logical and mathematical manner (Chapter 10). Links the Merton Model to the traditional accounting-based credit risk analysis.
- Provides in-depth analysis of the credit risks of two common situations - Project Finance and Working Capital Finance (Chapters 11 and 12). Besides worked-out examples, both chapters end with detailed case studies.
- Explains the benefits of portfolio risk analysis and the role of systematic and unsystematic risks and credit portfolio beta (Chapters 13 and 14).
- Shows the importance of Migration Risk and how to construct Credit Loss Distribution and calculate Economic Capital (Chapter 15). The chapter ends with a detailed case study.
- Digs out the subtle issues in the Basel Accords, explains the role of external credit rating agencies and explores Kelly's formula in the context of credit risk management (Chapter 16).
- Provides various credit portfolio risk mitigants such as traditional and modern diversification, and a mathematical way of calculating sector limits, sale of credit assets and credit derivatives. Discusses the pros and cons of Credit Default Swaps (Chapters 17 to 19).
- Explains the importance of credit risk pricing, interest rate hedging and explains several pricing methods, including RAROC, EVA and NPV Pricing (Chapters 20 and 21). Chapter 20 ends with a case study.
- Elaborates the role of security as a return enhancer and credit risk mitigant. Also discusses various aspects of collateral and how systematic risks may impact collateral (Chapter 22).
- Discusses the issue of structural subordination and the importance of both financial and non-financial covenants, and how to set covenants to manage the underlying risks (Chapter 23).
- Examines the reasons for credit crises and links the credit to growth and how and when disconnect can happen, leading to credit bubbles and subsequent credit and banking crises (Chapter 24). The chapter ends with a case study.
- Explains the 2008 Global Credit Crisis and the role of the US Housing Sector, which in turn was impacted by the sub-prime market bolstered by various credit market players and new credit risk-linked products (Chapter 25).

Whilst the above provides a glimpse of the contents of this book, the readers will find that the topics have a unique and practical treatment that will enable them to look at credit risk with clarity and better understanding. There are several examples in the book which are adapted from real life and have a practical touch.

During the two decades of my career I got the opportunity to play several roles in corporate credit risk: Relationship manager, credit analyst, credit reviewer, credit project leader, and credit approver are some of them. Whilst I sanctioned credit facilities, I also participated in the development of credit risk analysis software, Basel I and II implementation and credit risk training. I extended credit advice to corporate clients and helped them to raise debt through bi-lateral or syndication deals and guided the clients in effective utilization of credit facilities. I have dealt with almost all business sectors such as Construction, Contracting, FMCG, Hospitality, Airlines, Healthcare, Education, Wholesale Trading, Retail, Imports and Exports, Ceramics, Aluminium, Steel, Petrochemicals, Glass, Utilities, Financial Services, Telecoms, Food Industry, Poultry Farms, Dairy Industry, Textile Industry, Precious Metals Industry, etc. Over and above the experience and insight from my career, considerable research has also gone into this book as well as discussions and dialogues with senior credit professionals from different parts of the world.

One of the serious issues facing today's financial world is that there is a lack of serious credit risk education, which might have been a contributing factor to the recent credit crises. A plethora of financial products are available in the market which imbed credit risk, and dealing in such products requires thorough knowledge of credit risk. For example, many issuers of Credit Default Swaps (CDS) thought of them as an insurance product; however, fundamentally they are a credit risk product. Because they equated CDS to insurance they tried to replicate 'laws of large numbers', which is successfully applied in regular insurance products, with disastrous consequences. Whilst credit markets dwarf equity markets, it is arguable that not enough academic attention is given to credit risk; equity risk analysis gets a lot of attention in academic circles. It is a welcome measure that, realizing the importance of Credit Risk in the financial market, more and more universities now offer dedicated credit risk courses or treat them as part of the curriculum. The 2008 Global Credit Crisis probably acted as a wake-up call.

I have summarized most of the lessons learnt during my two-decade-long credit career and topped it off with extensive research and dialogues with credit experts. I take this opportunity to express my special thanks to Jeff Peanick, former Senior Vice President, HSBC, New York; Christopher Lewis, former Head of Trade Finance, HSBC, Hong Kong; Roy Philip, Head of Credit (Wholesale) HSBC, Dubai; Ian Spowart former Head of Credit, Lloyds TSB Middle East; Mammad Kuniyil, Head of Risk Management, Sharjah Islamic Bank as well as my colleagues Bhupesh Bansal and Brian Yau in Lloyds TSB Middle East. Many of my friends and well-wishers in HSBC, Lloyds TSB, Standard & Chartered, Emirates NBD, National Bank of Abu Dhabi and Crowe Horwath, who prefer to remain anonymous, have provided their insights. I also take this opportunity to thank businessmen, CEOs and CFOs who shared their views on credit risk, especially Michael Boocher, a young and dynamic entrepreneur and Ahmed Al Raqbani, Managing Director of East Coast Group. My sincere thanks to Dr. (Prof.) Stephen Mathews and my father P D Joseph (ex-banker) who performed the initial review of the manuscript and provided valuable suggestions, and to Werner Coetzee and the team at John Wiley & Sons for their timely guidance on several issues related to the publication of the book. Finally, special thanks go to Dr. Teena, my wife and my wonderful daughters for their support during the rigorous (but enjoyable) process of authoring this book. Whilst the views expressed herein are the result of a lot of experience, efforts and research, with humility I seek from esteemed readers suggestions to improve the book further.

Ciby Joseph
April 2013

# Part I
# Introduction

Credit risk analysis is an art as well as a science. It is a science because the analysis is based upon established principles emanating from a body of knowledge and sound logic. Individual skill and the way the principles are applied constitute the art element.

# 1 Credit Basics

Historically credit is good, if used wisely. However, there are numerous instances where both lenders (and creditors) and borrowers (or debtors) and even global economies suffer because of credit. The main reason is traceable to poor credit risk analysis and inadequate credit risk management. The purpose of this book is to delve into the realm of credit risk analysis and management in depth so that both lenders and borrowers can make the best use of credit for the common good.

Credit prudently used can create wealth and bring overall prosperity to the economy. Accordingly, credit, nowadays, is pervasive and is a common feature of all global economies. The only places from which it would be probably absent would be among the hunter/gatherer tribes in the deep jungles of Africa, South America or Asia or in similar tribes still living in primitive conditions.

Look around, observe your newspapers, magazines, television or radio or the billboards on highways – you can see invitations to participate in credit. Manufacturers of automobile and consumer durable goods offer credit directly or through their finance subsidiaries at low interest rates or offers instalment schemes with easy repayment terms. Credit card issuers attempt to persuade almost everybody to live on credit and at least some of the credit card holders find themselves living beyond their means and almost in perpetual debt.

Individuals borrow to meet their immediate requirements of physical needs such as house, furniture, car, consumer durable goods or to meet consumption expenditure such as marriage expenses, education or holidays. Business borrows to make investments to facilitate expansion or to meet working capital requirements, amongst others. Governments borrow to keep themselves afloat and hope to repay them from future tax revenues or further loans. Central government and big businesses borrow from abroad, which if not managed properly, can plunge the debtor country into an inevitable foreign exchange crisis, as has been seen in the 1997 Far East Asian Crisis and 2001 Argentina Crisis. The sub-prime lending crisis in the US (2008) and the Greek debt crisis (2010) and Spanish debt crisis (2012) are also linked to credit risks.

While the policy makers and officials scramble to find solutions with the least impact on the economy during such crises, it may be noted that these issues are often complex in nature and reflect the incredible power of financial and credit markets to systematically affect people from all walks of life. The level of credit extended and enjoyed by borrowers has far reaching implications for the economy. The lending, credit and regulatory policies that govern the financial sector and the levels of acceptable debt by the corporate sector require not only adequate monitoring but also sound understanding of the nature of credit risk. Insufficient knowledge of credit risk or its underestimation will result in distress to both lenders and borrowers who will suffer legal cases, bad debts, losses, to name just a few of them.

No doubt credit is ubiquitous and all important in the proper day-to-day functioning of the economy. Any disruption to the credit flow in the economy will have serious consequences for the economy itself.[1] As we will see in the rest of the book, credit is the life blood of business activities and the economy. Hence, the importance of credit risk and credit risk management.

## 1.1 MEANING OF CREDIT

Credit had a role to play from the early days of civilization. Nowadays credit implies monetary or monetary equivalent transactions. However, given the more accurate and realistic definition of credit, it includes non-monetary and/or barter transactions. Roughly, we can define credit as 'A transaction between two parties in which one (the creditor or lender) supplies money, goods, services or securities in return for a promise of future payment by the other (the debtor or borrower). Such transactions normally include the payment of interest to the lender.'[2]

The second part of this definition is interesting, it shows that credit is not cost free. The creditor parts with the resources because he has the incentive – either directly or indirectly. The incentive is required because the lender has an opportunity cost – he can deploy the resources elsewhere gainfully. Accordingly, for the sacrifice of this opportunity, the lender expects a return, which is normally known as interest. Over history, how much a lender can charge as interest has been under dispute prompting certain segments of society to view interest as an evil. However, it is an undeniable fact that interest is a type of cost of capital, charged by lenders, who do not have the right to enjoy the fruits of ownership. Another way of looking at interest is that it is equivalent to rent. Just as the owner or supplier of the building will charge rent, the interest is the rent charged by the supplier of credit or debt capital. While excessive or imprudent borrowings can be catastrophic, cost of capital cannot be blamed for the imprudence.

Of course, interest rates that do not justify the underlying economic realities and result in deprival of economic assets of the borrower are exploitation and a strategy followed by bigger powers. The East India Company ensured dependency of some its vassal states in India by lending them large sums of money at exorbitant interest rates. The book *The Honourable Company* by Mr John Keay, describes loans by the East India Company to the Nawab of Arcot at exorbitant interest rates of 20–25%. This ensured not only the indebtedness of the Nawab to the company but the revenues of the Carnatic also found their way into the East India Company without all the hassle and recrimination.

The novel *Money Changers* by Arthur Hailey depicts loan sharks in the US, who charge excessive interest rates and their collection technique is purely muscle power. This category of suppliers of credit, who exist in almost all countries, do not belong to mainstream suppliers of capital and their actions do not serve any social justice or contribute to the economic progress of the public. No court of law will approve their ridiculous interest rates or their collection methods. However, the main reason for their existence is akin to the Stock Market Theory called the Greater Fool Theory. This theory refers to the buyers of stock/shares at ridiculously high prices (inflated valuations) with the hope of finding somebody who will buy them at an even higher price! Similarly are those who borrow at exorbitant rates.

[1] US President Herbert Hoover in a speech during 1932 stated 'Let me remind you that credit is the lifeblood of business, the lifeblood of prices and jobs'.

[2] Definition from *Encyclopaedia Britannica*.

The probability of using the credit productively is very low, but not impossible, at least theoretically.

So, the borrower is responsible for the debt service obligations and should be aware of the consequences of the borrowings. So the caveat is 'Let the borrower be aware'.

Naturally, a small percentage of debtors won't pay back the credit as promised, sometimes even sending the creditor into bankruptcy. But the majority of debtors meet their commitments. That is why the World Economy survives. Credit losses or bad debts occur in both finance and non-finance businesses. The reasons vary. In certain cases, if the credit is extended to crooks, it is a bad debt from inception. However, the bulk of credit losses happen because of genuine business failures. The reasons vary from increase in competition, new technology, substitutes, increase in prices, decline in demand, over-estimation of demand, over-supply position in the market, government regulations, union problems, mismanagement, death of key persons, business cycles, over-ambitious projects, financial losses, excessive leverage, concentrated exposure, defective diversification and so on. A proper credit risk analysis will bring to light the probability of credit loss arising out of genuine business factors.

There are situations where the creditor ends up losing even if the debtor settles the dues on time. Three such situations are described below:

- One instance is inflation. If the rate of inflation exceeds interest rates, the suppliers of credit are badly affected. In such situations, inflation actually redistributes money from lenders to borrowers. If interest rates are 10% and inflation is 20%, the saver will lose 10% of the real value of the savings. However, the banks and other financial intermediaries do not lose much in an inflationary situation because they in turn pass on the reduction in purchasing power to the depositors. (Moreover, the central bank of any economy will increase the interest rates, to bring down the inflationary pressure by dampening the credit off-take.)
- In the second instance of devaluation of a foreign currency, in which the debt is denominated, the creditor loses to the extent of the rate of devaluation. For instance, during the 2001 crisis, the devaluation of the Argentinian currency, the peso, had taken its toll in many banks in the US, Spain and leading exporters to that country. Accordingly, a US creditor who had a receivable of one million Argentinian pesos in early 2002 (when the peso had parity with the dollar) would find the value in dollars plunging from $1 million to $333K in a period of six months. Banks and financial intermediaries would have suffered losses if they were holding open their own exposures in Argentinian pesos.
- Another instance will be non-compliance with anti-money laundering measures implemented by the central banks of most of the countries. Money laundering is a menace of the modern day world, hence the importance of Know Your Customer (KYC) policies and procedures. In most cases the loss will be through the penalties imposed by the respective authorities if the institution aids or abets money laundering activities knowingly or unknowingly. Similarly, if sanctions are imposed on certain countries, then dealing with or lending to the customers in such countries can also spell trouble and result in losses.

Whilst the risk that a borrower (whether individual or corporate) may default on obligations is known as Credit Risk, the risk that a foreign government may fail to honor the credit related obligations is defined as Sovereign Risk. It may be noted that the legal remedies in the event of sovereign risk are limited. Hence when extending credit to a business firm located in a foreign country, it is better to ascertain the level of sovereign risk, than to study the credit risk of the business firm.

## 1.2 ROLE OF CREDIT

Idle economic resources can be effectively put into use through credit. Borrowers who do not have enough resources to pursue an activity can borrow the resources, which can be returned to the lender after having achieved the objective. There is a practical difficulty for those with surpluses to identify potential borrowers. This is where financial intermediaries come in. Broadly, banks and other financial intermediaries collect economic resources – mainly in the form of deposits – from the public and engage in intelligent lending. Financial intermediaries play an important role in any economy. From a macroeconomic perspective, the main function of the financial system in any country is to mobilize resources for economic growth. The financial intermediaries not only intermediate between savers and investors but set economic prices of capital, in line with the monetary policy of the nation.

Financial intermediaries play a vital role in making the credit available. Those financial institutions like banks who can retake the loan proceeds given to one party from another can in fact increase the credit availability in the economy. This is called 'credit creation' by banks. Please see the Appendix for details.

Prudent use of credit results in economic growth of borrowers, which in turn leads to the overall economic well-being of the society and ultimately the country. Credit stimulates both household consumption and business investment. Hence, a national credit policy is an important tool used to encourage industrial development and business investments, thereby creating employment opportunities and improving the standard of living of the general population. As purchasing power increases, people will tend to spend more on consumer goods and this will stimulate further economic growth. Remember how Allan Greenspan attempted to accelerate credit off-take, especially after 9/11, by slashing the interest rates to the lowest in the last 40 years.

Usually the state of the credit markets will reflect the relative health of a larger economy as well. Often the prevailing interest rates and risk appetite for various grades[3] of credit risk are some of the indicators of the state of the credit markets.

## 1.3 CREDIT MARKET

The credit markets dwarf the equity markets. An equity market crisis usually impacts a limited number of financial players; however a credit crisis often shakes the foundations of the economy. However, since both equity market and credit markets are part of larger capital market, sometimes both markets may move together.

A business firm or a large corporation or multinational company finds that the market can absorb even if production is doubled. But they do not have enough funds to expand the operation. What is the easy solution? Similarly, if you want to buy a car or travel abroad but you currently do not have sufficient cash in hand, what would you do? The answer is probably to approach a bank or financial institution or ask the supplier of the good or service to extend credit. Governments are also active in credit markets. Many governments act through their central bank and buy and sell credit to meet their funding needs.

The demand for credit is ubiquitous, as the economic agents feel scarcity – while pursuing unlimited wants with limited resources. Borrowers or users of credit can be classified into

[3] The credit risk varies from least risky (e.g. treasury bonds) to very high risk (e.g. junk bonds). We will examine various grades of credit risk later in the book.

different categories. Whilst classification varies depending on the context, the most commonly followed binary categorization is – Personal Credit[4] and Business Credit.

The granting of credit to commercial customers (business credit) is more complex than personal credit. This is because commercial borrowers are engaged in a much wider range of activities and their needs for credit vary according to the nature and size of their operation. Business credit is the most common, but for which world trade and the economic progress of mankind would have been impossible. Demand for business credit emanates from companies, partnerships, sole proprietorships, clubs and associations, of different nature, size and intentions. They usually obtain credit through person(s) acting on their behalf. Businesses are of different types with differing requirements depending upon the nature of their activity. Accordingly, the type of funding required by an airline is different from the funding required by the retailer in your locality. Similarly, the credit may be required for the short term, medium term or long term.

## 1.4 CREDIT – ADVANTAGES AND DISADVANTAGES

The discovery and control of fire has brought several benefits to mankind and it touches the day-to-day life of almost every human being. However, unless fire is used carefully, it can be disastrous. Like fire, if used cautiously, credit is useful to mankind. It brings benefits not only to the lender and user but to the entire economy as well. However, on the other hand, misuse of the credit will bring woes. Let us look at the advantages of credit to the borrower, which propels the demand for credit.

### 1.4.1 Merits of Credit

Successful businesses, individuals and government use credit. Usually, credit growth in the overall economy goes hand in hand with economic growth.

#### *1.4.1.1 Wealth Creation and Maximization*

Credit is a vital part of the financial management of almost all entities engaged in economic activity – whether government, business enterprises or private individuals. Whilst the purpose of this book is to deal with the credit risks of commercial credit, it seems appropriate to mention that even governments borrow money much along the lines of business credit. Such loans are expected to be repaid from future government revenue (taxation, customs and other revenue) or foreign aid. It is common knowledge that in many of the countries these

[4] The borrowing needs of individuals vary according to their financial status. The individuals may be salaried employees/self-employed i.e. people who have their own business or agriculture/professionals such as doctors, solicitors or architects etc. Their need to borrow money could be for purposes such as: buying a house/car/furniture/home appliance, repairing or improving a house/getting married/holidays/starting a new business/setting up a practice in the case of professionals/children's education etc.

In general, the demand for credit by individuals may be categorized into three types. Low-income people – the demand for credit by this group of people is often limited since they normally keep a close balance between incomings and outgoings. Conversely, they may attempt to borrow to satisfy consumption needs, which they cannot afford on limited income. This category of borrowers ought to be very cautious in using credit unless they are able to identify alternate repayment sources. Middle-income people – the demand for credit by this group tends to be much greater. This group may have significant financial assets (deposits/shares etc.), but they tend to show a preference for borrowing for the purchase of consumer durables rather than liquidating some of their savings. They have realized that borrowing can be used not only as a way of meeting emergencies but also as a means for improving their standard of living. For affluent people, credit provides additional flexibility and access to liquidity, especially if their financial wealth is locked in long-term investments, real estate or otherwise.

borrowings are siphoned off by the ruling elite and indirectly the burden falls on the shoulders of the common man in the respective countries. So, a nation can become prosperous only if the resources – including the credit (funds) borrowed – are gainfully deployed to yield a satisfactory economic return. If the borrowing nations use credit without corruption and inefficiency, it will not only result in more economic goods, enhancing the standard of living, but will ease the burden on the population for additional revenue through direct and indirect taxation.

If used wisely, credit helps in multiplying wealth much faster and beyond the existing resources of a nation/business enterprise/individual. The reasoning and logic is simple enough. While the cost of a credit facility is fixed and if the borrower/user of credit can deploy it at a return higher than the cost of credit, the difference results in wealth creation for the borrower. For example, if you borrow $10,000 @10% cost and deploy it for 25% return you end up with a wealth of $1,500/-. This fundamental concept has found its application in many financial theories of leverage. We will look more closely into it later in this book when we discuss financial risks. Productive employment of credit calls for good governance/management.

#### *1.4.1.2 Tax Planning Tool*

The cost of borrowings is tax deductible, which preserves a proportionate portion of wealth from tax. Individuals also borrow credit as a tax-planning tool. In several nations across the world, income tax legislation allows the deduction of interest and instalments on housing loans obtained by the salaried classes and self-employed.

Companies and business add value not only by value differential, but also through the tax advantage of borrowed funds. For example, suppose ABC Ltd starts operations with a project cost of $100m, fully funded by equity on which it earns Profit before Interest and Tax (PBIT) of $25m after the first year of operations. Assuming a tax rate @ 50%, the net profit attributable to shareholders would be $12.5m with a Return on Equity (ROE) of 12.5%. Think what happens if 50% is borrowed @10%. After meeting the interest costs of $5m, the PBT would be $20m on which tax of $10m to be paid. Attributable net profit to shareholders would be $10m with a ROE of 20%. Notice the sudden jump in ROE due to the leverage effect.

If individuals borrow to create assets it will improve their wealth. Most individuals who borrow to build or purchase houses or residential units, usually find that the market value of the house (after several years) has outstripped the gross repayment obligations of the housing loan.

#### *1.4.1.3 Convenience*

The owners need not bring all the funds to run the show. Often the first generation entrepreneurs who commence a new line of activity may find it difficult to amass enough funds to start and run the business. Hence, they turn to debt, which is a convenient method of raising funds, and which can be returned later.

#### *1.4.1.4 Business Control*

When confronted with the choice of type of capital, many entrepreneurs prefer debt capital because they can retain control over the business. In the case of equity capital, the new shareholders have the right to ownership privileges, effectively reducing the existing owners' control over business. Secondly, while with borrowings the existing owners can enjoy the full benefits of the business after meeting the fixed finance obligations, additional equity capital would mean that the new owners will partake in the whole benefits accrued from business.

#### *1.4.1.5 Socio-Economic Advantages*

There are many advantages to the society and the country emanating from business lending. As the business borrows more and spends, the local society/economy is benefited as more demand is created. This activity – borrowing and spending or investing by the economic participants in an economy – is self-reinforcing because the increased spending results in more income, rising profits and higher net worth of businesses which in turn results in higher capacity to borrow, which encourages banks and lending institutions to lend more, increasing the spending and investments further in the economy. All this will result in higher employment creation and improved standards of living. Overall, the business spending on credit has far reaching implications for the country's economy, which can drive up the demand for goods and services, accelerating economic growth. However, credit induced growth needs to be monitored closely by the government and monetary authorities (usually the central bank and finance ministry) as it carries bubble risk. We will discuss more about credit bubbles in later chapters.

### 1.4.2 Demerits of Credit Usage

Using credit is not without disadvantages. Major demerits are:

#### *1.4.2.1 Reduced Profitability*

As far as business credit is concerned, it is true that if the ROI exceeds the borrowing costs, leverage is beneficial to borrowers. On the flip side, when the ROI is lower than borrowing costs, the business will suffer from lower profitability.

#### *1.4.2.2 Default and Bad Reputation*

One of the main disadvantages of relying on credit is the inability of the borrower to meet the obligations on time. If the business runs at below breakeven then additional funds/cash need to be brought in from other sources to meet the interest obligations, and it is better not to speak of the principal portion. Any default will not only result in compounding of the interest burden; but most of the financing institutions levy charges such as penalty interest, etc., adding to the woes. So, instead of improving shareholder value, it can destroy value. Ultimately, the business entity will find itself out of business or with negative publicity. Trust will be lost. Unpaid financial institutions and suppliers and other non-FI creditors will take action that will bring a bad name to the obligor in business circles.

#### *1.4.2.3 Bankruptcies*

Almost all bankruptcies are caused by the creditors pressurizing the borrower to pay up. Bankruptcies are not good for the creditors either, as they cause credit losses, impacting their profitability. Nonetheless bankruptcies occur and are universal. Some famous or infamous bankruptcies are CRB Capital (India), Yokokawa Securities (Japan) Daewoo (Korea),

WorldCom, Enron, Global Crossing, Lehman Brothers (US) etc. In the environment of globalization and opening up of markets, corporate management challenges and increasing competition, along with prudent credit usage, become even more important.

#### *1.4.2.4 Propensity to Over-spend*

The main disadvantage for users of credit is the tendency to over-spend beyond their means. Many individuals, nowadays, with easy availability of credit from credit cards or other sources of credit are tempted to 'keep up with Joneses' otherwise known as the 'demonstration effect'. It is not unusual to read in newspapers about people committing suicide because of debt burden. Similarly, during times of easy availability of credit many successful businesses over-leverage themselves to diversify into riskier sectors (e.g. real estate and/or financial investments) or unfamiliar territory, and suffer subsequently during the sector downturn or failure of new ventures.

Unexpected drying up of future inflows – say loss of a job, fall in income from business, sudden delay in collection of receivables, accumulation of unsold inventories – can result in repayment defaults and associated costs such as penal interest and finally confiscation of the collateral, if any, plus the associated damage to personal prestige. Similarly, contingent and unexpected events such as earthquakes, accidents, wars, rebellion etc., can strain the cash available for repayments. Such 'black swan' events cannot be wished away. Since no accurate estimation of these events is possible, businesses/individuals/households should always be conservative while borrowing.

### 1.4.3 Is Wealth Creation Through Use of Credit Easy and Simple?

Whilst successful use of credit is common across the world, many nations and businesses have found that the 'debt trap' is too deadly. Argentina, Greece, Enron, Bear Stearns, and Lehman Brothers are a few examples during the early 21st century. Annually a number of individuals commit suicide or businesses become bankrupt because of imprudent use of credit – it reflects lack of adequate credit knowledge and skills. Excessive imprudent credit can be harmful to the economy itself.

An interesting case of business credit going beyond the limits which can be harmful to the country is Japan in the 1980s and 1990s. Too much credit will have inflationary pressures. During the mid-1980s most Japanese companies borrowed to create additional capacities, for which there was little demand. At the same time, a real estate boom flourished in Japan fuelled by bank borrowings. As the expanded companies found little demand for augmented capacity, they found the repayment of the loans taken for expansion difficult. As the real estate boom began to descend, the real estate dealers who borrowed to buy up the properties also found themselves cash strapped. In both cases, the repayment of the borrowings was tardy and sluggish, which, along with the cumulative and compounding interest burden, sent many companies and real estate dealers into bankruptcy. In turn the lending institutions had to book huge credit losses, triggering a series of collapses of banks/financial institutions, leaving thousands of stakeholders in the mire. As you might have already guessed, although credit is a useful tool for the economy and meets several needs and demands of the population, it is a double edged sword. That is why the central bank authorities of the country are always vigilant in controlling credit flow in the economy. In capital scarce countries, it is of more importance as the scarce capital has to be channelled to the priority needs of the economy.

Another interesting case is the US before the credit crisis of 2008. We will discuss more about this later in the book.

To put it briefly, whether it is business, or managing a country or personal wealth creation, the way that limited resources are managed has a significant impact. Maximization of wealth through optimal utilization of resources is the true objective of financial management, in any context. The credit has contractual obligations, however it can result in additional value to the owners/shareholders (and hence impact wealth maximization positively) if the cost of credit or borrowing is lower than the return for which the borrowed resources are deployed.

Debt within limits is safe and will definitely add value, contributing positively towards wealth maximization.

## 1.5 SUPPLIERS OF CREDIT

During a walk around the cities, towns and even some of the remote areas of a country you will see suppliers of credit such as commercial banks, non-banking finance companies, private financiers and others. The traders and manufacturers and service providers also extend credit to their buyers, normally called 'trade credit'. Whilst financial intermediaries extend money as credit with a condition to repay in money, trade credit is available in the form of goods and services, but to be settled mostly in monetary form. In any economy the suppliers of credit vary from individual moneylenders to mammoth institutions. Suppliers of credit can be briefly classified as follows:

(a) **Commercial Banks**: Commercial banks are among the important suppliers of credit in any country. They are central to the banking system and constitute an integral sub-system of the financial system and channel small savings from households for deployment in the corporate sector. Commercial banks are the largest suppliers of short-term finance for business requirements in all countries although the structure of the banking system may be different from country to country. However, the role of a central bank is important in all countries to regulate the operations of commercial banks.

Credit risk is vital to the survival of commercial banks and hence one of the primary concerns of commercial banks and regulators. Given the importance of public confidence in the banking sector governments always want to keep commercial banks in good health. So, governments are highly concerned about the credit risk exposure of the banking sector. That is why the level of bad credit assets or non-performing assets is always measured and monitored on an ongoing basis.

Usually commercial banks are less likely to extend long-term loans and financing, given the short-term nature of most of the deposits. However, in certain cases and on a very selective basis commercial banks do undertake long-term credit exposures.

(b) **Term Lending/Development Institutions**: As the name indicates, their main function is to extend term loans, project finance and meet other long-term finance needs of the corporate sector. Most governments have their own State Finance Corporations, to promote industrial development. Development institutions in Japan and Korea played a prominent role in industrializing and ushering in the economic prosperity. Realizing its importance many nations in the world have formed development institutions.

(c) **Public Debt Market**: Whilst developed countries have a matured Public Debt Market, in developing countries it is now in its growth phase. Large, established and usually listed public companies with enough credibility and financial standing bypass the banking sector and seek financing directly from the capital market, by way of bonds, debentures or commercial papers. Usually such debt issues require mandatory rating by credit rating agencies. After the debt issue, the rating agencies continue to monitor the financial position of the company. However, during the post Enron/WorldCom/Lehman Brothers period, rating agencies, especially those in the US, face wariness from the public.

(d) **Other Institutions in Credit Financing**: A host of other entities undertake credit financing, as part of their normal operations. Housing finance companies, hedge funds, non-banking subsidiaries of major MNCs (e.g. the financing arm of automobile majors such as BMW), etc. are some of the significant players in this segment. Insurance companies have a large pool of resources at their disposal, which are also deployed in a variety of lending/investment activities. Non-Banking Financial Institutions (NBFIs) also play an active role in lease and hire-purchase financing. Mutual funds also deploy varying amounts of money in credit markets depending upon its nature – e.g. Fixed Income Mutual Funds.

(e) **Trade Credit**: Another source of credit is the supplier/trader/manufacturer who offers credit for short periods, ranging from 30/120 days. Whilst in monopoly situations, the seller can impose stricter terms such as 'cash in advance', competition compels liberal credit terms, as a major source of competitive advantage. Trade credit is used by both domestic and foreign suppliers, with the latter having a tendency to protect it through letters of credit. Trade credit is one of the tools of sales promotion techniques. As we will later see in 'Industry Analysis' (Chapter 6) the credit terms prevalent in an industry are a function of the 'bargaining power' of suppliers and buyers. However the choice whether to extend credit to a particular customer is a pure credit decision.

Different categories of suppliers of international credit exist. The world of international suppliers of capital (both debt and equity) is vast and sometimes bewildering given the massive resources at their disposal. Both rich closely-held private companies (such as the Rothschild family) and multilateral institutions are active in international credit. Well known multilateral institutions include the World Bank, IMF, IDA, ADB, IFC, multinational banks and governments. Given the foreign exchange flows involved, over-reliance on international credit can bring havoc as has been proven by the repetitive instances of economic collapses around the world, in our recent memories. Whilst in the 1980s and early 1990s the whole of Latin America suffered, during 1997/98 it was the turn of the tiger economies of the Far East and in 1998/99 both Turkey and Russia had to bear the brunt. India too had a close brush with such a situation in 1991.The story of 2002 was Argentina while in 2010 it was the turn of Greece.

## 1.6 CREDIT RISK STUDY

There is a common element across all the categories of suppliers of credit discussed above – the need to study the creditworthiness of borrowers or counterparties or the need for credit risk analysis.

What is 'creditworthiness'? It denotes checking whether the prospective borrower is worthy to receive credit. It is similar to the term 'seaworthiness' of a ship, which is a normal clause in marine insurance policies. Just as a ship lacking 'seaworthiness' carries significant risk of sinking at sea, a person, or a business firm or a company who is not 'creditworthy' has a high propensity to default on credit. As we will see later, the study of creditworthiness has macroeconomic implications, which if not properly studied by the economic participants, may lead to a financial/economic/credit crisis. The perception that the risk analysis involved in credit is less difficult than the alternative investments (Equity, Venture Capital, etc.) is quickly dispelled if one understands the complexities of credit. The lessons of the collapse of banks/financial intermediaries in Japan (1990s), the US (1930s and 2008) and other countries, under the weight of bad credit assets (credit losses) highlight the significance of credit risks and the need for sound understanding of the principles of credit risk analysis and credit management.

Credit risk analysis is more than establishing creditworthiness. In fact, creditworthiness is a vague term. There are ranges of creditworthiness, the proper grasp of which is critical to understand the probability and quantum of credit losses. Secondly, just as in other return/risk relationships, the level of pricing to be charged on credit is determinable only if the underlying credit risk is properly evaluated. Thirdly, often the relationship between the creditor and borrower is long standing, especially in banks and other financing institutions. Most of the suppliers of credit are also interested in the upside business potential of the customer although the downside risk is a vital consideration of credit risk analysis.

Given the multifarious nature of credit risk the modern techniques of credit analysis deploy a variety of tools to study and understand its various ramifications. We will see the repertoire of techniques/tools useful to study credit risk in the ensuing chapters. Now let us consider the essentials of 'Credit Risk Analysis', the topic of the next chapter.

## APPENDIX: CREDIT CREATION

Banks can create credit virtually out of thin air! This is because of the fact that the credit extended by the banking system, in most cases, comes back to the banking system. Of the deposits received, banks, after maintaining the legal minimum reserves (stipulated by the central bank to ensure liquidity of the banks) the remaining portion can be extended to the public as credit. Since the bulk of the monetary transactions are routed through banks, the amount extended as credit will come back to the banking sector as deposits, which enable the banks to extend further credit, although no additional currency has been printed.

The following example demonstrates the concept better:

Example: Mr A, Mr B, Mr C, Mr D and Mr E deal only with XYZ Bank Ltd, which is required to maintain 10% reserve ratio on deposits. On 1 May 20X3 XYZ Bank received a deposit of 10,000/-. Mr A applied for credit on the same day and was provided with 9000/- after setting aside 10% as reserve ratio. Mr A used the credit to buy a TV from Mr B, who deposited the amount with XYZ Bank the next day. The bank kept aside 10% and extended credit to Mr C who applied for 8100/-, and used it to buy a stereo from Mr D, who also similarly decided to deposit it with XYZ Bank. The bank once again set aside 10% reserve on the deposit and lent 7290/- to Mr E.

As is evident from the above, XYZ Bank was able to create three credit deals totalling 24,390/- (9,000+8,100+7,290) from a single initial deposit of 10,000/-.

Although the subsequent credit facilities are reduced because of the 10% reserve requirement, it is evident that the bank can 'create credit' more than once from a one-time deposit! The chain of credit transactions and resultant deposits will continue until the reserve requirement makes it impossible to provide further credit. In this case, by that time the total credit transactions of XYZ would add up to 90,000/-, i.e., exactly nine times as large as the original cash deposits of 10,000. The following chart depicts the situation clearly.

| Serial No. | Deposits | Reserves | Advances |
|---|---|---|---|
| 1 | 10,000 | 1,000 | 9,000 |
| 2 | 9,000 | 900 | 8,100 |
| 3 | 8,100 | 810 | 7,290 |
| 4 | 7,290 | 729 | 6,561 |
| 5 | 6,561 | 656 | 5,905 |
| 6 | 5,905 | 590 | 5,314 |
| 7 | 5,314 | 531 | 4,783 |
| . | ... | ... | ... |
| . | ... | ... | ... |
| n | ... | ... | ... |
| **Total** | **100,000** | **10,000** | **90,000** |

The amount of credit the banking system can create with a single initial deposit, can be calculated by the following formula:

$$\text{Credit Creation} = \frac{\text{Initial Deposit } (1 - r)}{r}$$

where r = reserve ratio.

Although the exact credit creation by banks is determined by a variety of factors such as convention, central bank reserve requirements, general market conditions and demand for loans etc., normally the banks can create credit to the extent of 5 to 6 times their original deposits (500 to 600%).

## ✍ QUESTIONS/EXERCISES

1. What are the advantages and disadvantages of using credit?
2. Do you believe credit is the life blood of the economy? Please elaborate.
3. Which market is bigger – the equity market or the credit market – and why?
4. Who are the major suppliers of credit? Name a few international credit institutions.
5. What is meant by credit risk analysis?
6. Do you believe traders and manufacturers also require credit risk analysis before they extend credit to their customers? Please elaborate.
7. What is meant by sovereign risk?
8. What do you mean by Credit Creation by banks?

# 2

# Essentials of Credit Risk Analysis

Credit risk exists whenever a product or service is obtained without paying for it. In the business sector, credit risk is pervasive. Households also use credit extensively. For instance, individuals/households who are electricity consumers, telephone users and credit card holders expose respective suppliers to credit risks. Similarly, persons placing deposits with banks/financing companies are also exposed to credit risk.

## 2.1 MEANING OF CREDIT RISK

Credit risk can be defined as follows: 'Credit risk refers to the probability of the loss (due to the non-recovery of) emanating from the credit extended as a result of the non-fulfilment of contractual obligations arising from unwillingness or inability of the counterparty or for any other reason.' If the probability of the loss is high, the credit risk involved is also high and vice versa. The study of credit risk can be split into two, which facilitates better understanding of the term (see Figure 2.1).

A single borrower/obligor exposure is generally known as Firm Credit Risk or Obligor Credit Risk while the credit exposure to a group of borrowers, is called Portfolio Credit Risk. This bifurcation is important for the proper understanding and management of credit risk, inasmuch as the ultimate reasons for failure to pay can be traced to the economic, industry or customer specific factors. As we will see in later chapters, while obligor risk decides the fate of the overall portfolio, portfolio risk has different dynamics and plays a crucial role in determining the quantum of economic capital required, which is a function of expected credit loss.

Up to now, we looked at credit risk assuming that both obligor and creditor are located in the same country. Institutions engaged in cross-country credit transactions would argue that credit risk goes beyond the customary view of 'default to repay the principal and interest'. In such cases the credit risk may manifest itself in subtly different ways, depending on the financial transaction in question, and it is useful to distinguish between the three aspects: (i) Settlement risk arises when the conduit through which the payment is channelled fails to pay. For instance, sometimes the moneys sent from the Middle East to the US have been confiscated due to suspicion related to terrorism links; (ii) or sometimes, UN sanctions prevent dealing with certain countries and this may also result in failure of payments, even if the counterparty is creditworthy; (iii) or, the collapse of banks (e.g. Herstatt Bank in 1974[1] or Lehman Brothers in 2008) who had received payments from a number of counterparties but went bankrupt before payments were made to the other parties in the transaction. Usually settlement risk is non-existent in domestic transactions because of the centralized clearance controlled by the Central Bank, although isolated settlement risks leading to credit loss cannot be fully ruled out.

---

[1] Settlement risk is also known as Herstatt risk after the infamous collapse in 1974 of Bankhaus Herstatt, a long-established German bank. Herstatt ran into funding problems in the middle of a trading day and was immediately closed down by the Bundesbank (German Central Bank), by which time most of its FX counterparties had already issued their payment instructions for that day. Those banks never received their counterpayments on time and it took them years to recover the amounts owed.

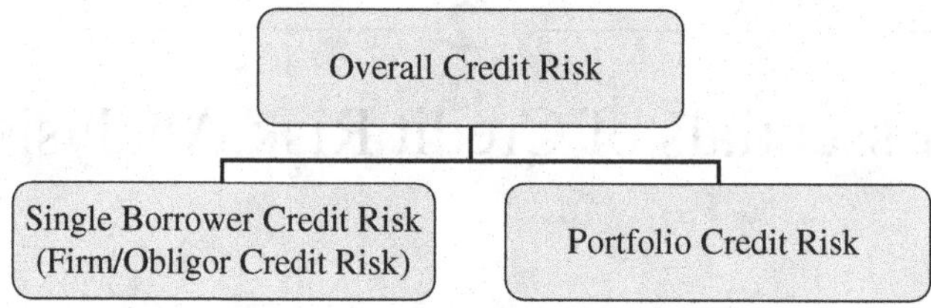


**Figure 2.1** Division of Credit Risk

On a global scale, the settlement risk is now being reduced through the initiative of the Bank for International Settlements (BIS). Another credit risk emanating from cross-border credit is sovereign risk, which occurs if the government imposes foreign exchange controls. Malaysia did so soon after 1997/98 Far East Economic Crisis while Pakistan did so after the US sanctions subsequent to their nuclear test in 1998. Whilst the obligor is willing to settle the credit, the government may not allow it. Foreign currency risk is the loss of credit value resulting from adverse foreign exchange fluctuations. Accordingly, creditors with significant exposures to foreign markets will be interested in looking at how these three risks impact the firm risk and portfolio risk.

Evaluating credit risk is a matter of information processing, which is becoming complex in line with the advancement mankind is witnessing in various areas, technological or otherwise. Certain types of and factors triggering credit risks are controllable while others are not. Understanding and differentiating between the two is highly critical for sound credit risk analysis and management.

## 2.2 CAUSES OF CREDIT RISK

Credit risk is subtle and hidden and has to be unearthed carefully, especially in view of the fact the returns (earnings) for credit risk are much lower than other kinds of investments such as equity or real estate. In fact credit risk is the product of a variety of events, some controllable, others uncontrollable. The ultimate credit risk originates from several factors with international aspects (1997 Asian Crisis or September 11 2001) or domestic issues (changes in government policy or industry) or company specific reasons (poor management, bad products, etc.).

Figure 2.2 summarizes the various triggers of credit risk:

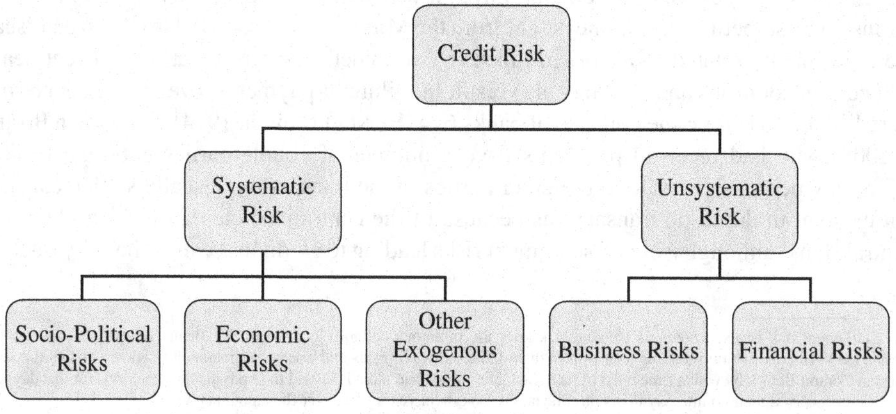


**Figure 2.2** Major Causes of Credit Risk

Both obligor credit risk and portfolio credit risk are impacted by or triggered by systematic and unsystematic risks. The ensuing chapters discuss the various levers of impact and mitigations which can be effected. Obviously, rigorous study of credit risk through meticulous dissections is the hallmark of good credit risk analysis. Not only financial intermediaries and large multinationals, but also all classes of medium-large businesses will benefit from thorough credit risk analysis as it will minimize bad debts and associated costs, such as collection charges, administration time and costs spend on follow-up, litigation costs, etc.

External forces that affect all businesses and households in the country or economic system are called systematic risks, and are considered as uncontrollable risks. For instance, if the economy is witnessing a sharp economic crisis/recession, bankruptcies will increase, triggering credit losses, while stock markets will decline due to lower corporate profits, while unemployment rises, amongst other effects. Thus systematic risks impact all in the playground (viz. economy). Similarly political risks such as a military coup, new elected government discontinuing certain policies and programmes, wars, terrorism, international isolation and hosts of other political risks can severely impact the quality of a credit asset and may lead to losses.

The second type of credit risk is known as unsystematic risk/controllable risk. These risks do not affect the entire economy or all business enterprises/households. Such risks are largely industry specific and/or firm specific. A firm can diversify these risks by extending credit to a range of customers. We will see more in Chapters 5–7. At present suffice to say that the credit risk triggered by both systematic and unsystematic factors are to be carefully handled, and a business entity ought to attempt to transfer, shift and avoid.

## 2.3 CREDIT RISK AND RETURN

The primary objective of a business firm taking credit risk is to earn a return. Whilst the financial intermediary earns commission or interest income, non-financial firms benefit in the form of enhanced sales, resulting in more profits. Economic agents involved with credit risk will attempt to (a) maximize return for a given level of credit risk and/or (b) minimize credit risk for a given level of return.

For financial intermediaries directly involved in lending or investing in bonds and debentures, the relationship between credit risk and returns is explicit, while in non-financial firms, the relationship is implicit and embedded in the profit element. However one fundamental is common to both: given the probability of default, is the return offered by the prospective credit decision attractive?

## 2.4 CREDIT RISK ANALYSIS

Credit Risk Analysis (CRA) is the study from the perspective of a supplier of credit of a present/prospective claim on another economic agent (both disaggregation/aggregation basis) in the form of debt, including trade payables, loans, public securities, amongst others. CRA is valid in a variety of decision contexts. A few such situations are discussed below:

**Banks/Financial Institutions**: What are the risks involved in extending a loan to a particular firm? Given the risk level, how should it be priced? What about its repayment capability? Is the management capable? Which economic and industrial factors will impact the performance of the firm?

**Mutual Funds/Insurance Companies**: Shall we invest in the debentures/bonds of XYZ Ltd? What about the financial position and major solvency ratios? Are the indenture provisions adequate? What are the major factors that may trigger distress and default on debt? Given the risk level, is the return acceptable?

**Manufacturer/Trader**: Should we extend credit to this customer? If so, what is the credit period to be offered? What are the financial position and bank facilities enjoyed by the customer? Is collection risk manageable?

**Hedge Funds**: Shall we buy the distressed debt of XYZ Ltd (e.g. Enron or Lehman Brothers)? Will the final recovery for the claims (under distressed debt) be higher than current prices? What is the downside to buying the distress debt/claims at current prices? Are the returns attractive?

Credit risk is embedded in these routine decision situations. Whilst the selling price and delivery terms are important for a non-financial business entity and secondary capital market considerations may weigh in the mind of a bond investor, credit risk is the most critical factor. What is the benefit, if all other factors are favourable, but credit risk is very high? The outcome is a foregone conclusion.

Besides suppliers of credit, there are other parties who have a general interest in the creditworthiness of an economic agent. This category does not engage in detailed examination of credit risk, but their decisions are influenced by the credit standing of the firm/business. For instance, a *potential customer/buyer* will check the probability of the financial distress of the manufacturer to ensure its survival so that he can be reasonably assured about the warranties and replacement parts and other services. Another interested party is the *Auditor*, who will check the probability of imminent financial distress while evaluating the applicability of the 'Going Concern Concept' of the firm under audit.

*Borrowers* are also interested parties in credit risk analysis. It will enable them to understand what the usual thoughts of banks and financial institutions are, while extending credit facilities. This will not only enable proper presentation of facts but also enable the borrower to decide about the most feasible sort of financing. Many good companies with attractive business models[2] can borrow at cost-effective rates, if they know how their strategies, decisions and action plan will impact their debt raising capacity and creditworthiness.

Mark Twain's quote on banks is famous:

> A banker is a fellow who lends you his umbrella when the sun is shining, but wants it back the minute it begins to rain.

Whilst this is a witticism, the borrower has to bear in mind that the banks accept deposits from the public and hence any symptom of deterioration in credit risk or creditworthiness is bound to trigger a panic somewhere in the credit chain within the lending institutions. Moreover, the banks operate with thin margins and hence they try to avoid credit loss at any cost (also see point 6 in Section 2.6 later in this chapter). Once the general market – suppliers, etc. – comes to know that the lending institutions are not supportive of a particular business organization, even the suppliers' credit may become tough to obtain and could trigger a chain reaction.

[2] During my credit career I have seen many good companies with sound underlying business models flounder due to the deterioration in credit risk mainly due to fund diversion – to take up new risky projects, help/promote associate concerns or similar activities. During the real estate or stock market boom times, it is not uncommon that funds are diverted into unfamiliar activities with gambling tendencies motivated by greed, which ultimately affect the core activities. We will discuss more of this risk later.

## 2.5 HISTORICAL PROGRESS OF CREDIT RISK ANALYSIS

In fact, credit risk analysis has existed for many centuries and can be considered one of the oldest established financial activities known. Throughout history, the act of lending funds has been accompanied by an examination of the ability of the borrower to repay the funds. Ancient civilizations and societies had their own forms of trading and banking activities. The medieval bankers of Europe studied the business activities of their clients and often decided the outcome of wars and the fate of monarchies while financing. They relied largely on the character and direct knowledge of the borrower. The majority of credit transactions and lending can be categorized as 'name lending'.

As modern accounting and finance developed during late 1800s and early 1900s, so did credit analysis techniques, which became more systematic and detailed. During the early days when the financial statement based approach of credit analysis was gaining popularity, the primary emphasis was on the corporation's balance sheet. Financial strength or weakness as displayed by the balance sheet depicted the ability of a corporation to withstand bad times. Sufficiency of assets and their quality and the owner's contribution to the business can be useful indicators of the soundness of the financial base. As the years went by, the emphasis began to shift to the Profit and Loss Account as the sustainability of earnings was given prominence. A large illiquid asset base with little cash generation from operations does not offer much comfort to creditors. Meanwhile the business world was witnessing major changes simultaneously. Management consulting, decentralization and newer management concepts, the development of management accounting and various other initiatives were unfolding in the business field. By the late 1970s, given the inadequacies of the Balance Sheet and P&L, Funds Flow Statements emerged, which of late have been replaced by Cash Flow Statements. Today financial analysis has become an inseparable part of credit risk analysis and almost all kinds of financial intermediaries employ finance specialists.

In recent decades, the process of credit risk analysis has been changing from routine procedure to a new generation of state-of-the-art techniques. Today credit professionals are armed not only with finance, management and mathematically related qualifications but they also undergo rigorous training to learn new skills. The Basel Committee is trying to revolutionize the way banks manage credit risks through its proposed new Accord (known as Model III and expected to be implemented within a couple of years). Progressive financial intermediaries have implemented Portfolio Theory, Value at Risk, Optimization and other techniques/models, amongst others, to manage and maximize returns from credit portfolios. Whilst most of these models are useful, over-reliance on risk models can be disastrous. The 2008 Credit Crisis is partly blamed on the use of financial models based on assumptions that differed from reality. It is beyond doubt that credit risk management is now more challenging and stimulating. Ensuing chapters will explore this further.

## 2.6 NEED FOR CREDIT RISK ANALYSIS

Credit risk plays an important role in ensuring the financial health of both financial and non-financial businesses. It directly impacts possible bad debts or credit losses. As far as banks and financial intermediaries are concerned, traditional credit measures are strained by the advent of new challenges of the 21st century and as a result a revolution is taking place in the way credit is evaluated and managed. Following the 2008 Global Financial Crisis, there has been a resurgence of interest in risk management systems and practices across the world, cutting across financial and non-financial enterprises. Credit risk management systems are no exception. Whilst 40% or more of the balance sheet of a financial institution or bank comprise of credit assets, many non-financial institutions also carry a significant level of credit assets in their balance sheet, as credit is a primary tool that adds economic value to their core business activity. New ideas, technologies and tools are being sought to enable the institutions to understand and manage the credit risk better. Let us examine why so much importance has been attached to credit risk analysis, especially by banks and other financial intermediaries, with significant credit exposure:

1. **Prudence**: Demand for credit is pervasive, given the insatiable desires constrained by limited resources, and credit is one technique adopted to overcome this problem. However, it is the responsibility of the supplier of credit to ensure that their actions are prudent because excessive credit will prove disadvantageous to almost everyone in the economy as has been evidenced by the demise of many banks in Japan during the 1990s, as the result of over-lending in the late 1980s. This was almost repeated in the US during 2008 and 2009 after the sub-prime crisis. Non-financial institutions are also impacted. The cash crunch faced by several construction contractors in the Middle East (e.g. UAE) with long delays in collecting contracting receivables during 2009/10 is one of the best examples.

   Excessive credit has an important role to play in the boom and bust of the economic cycle and is precisely one of the major reasons why many Central Bank governors attempt to put brakes on economic expansion by hiking interest rates.

   The illustrious boom can spell doom later, with copious credit being one of the major reasons. Usually all are confident during the heightened pace of economic activity and financial institutions are no exception. They lend to over-confident borrowers to expand or import or produce more goods and services for which there is little demand. Later, it turns out to be the creation of over-capacities funded by borrowings. The resultant bad debts weigh heavily which resulted in the collapse of financial intermediaries in Japan (1990s) and the US (2008). Extending credit during the boom phase is highly challenging. So is providing credit during a recession period. The only alternative left is to conduct a proper risk analysis of the credit: ascertain, measure and manage the credit risk in such a manner that it does not spin out of control.
2. **Increase in Bankruptcies**: Recessionary phases are common for the economy although timing and causes may be different for different countries. Ample examples exist from history. During a recession, bankruptcies multiply. As stated earlier, Japan is yet to recover fully from the recession that hit its economy after the boom of the 1980s, while Latin American countries experienced a rather quick succession of cycles in the past. Far East Asia had its crisis in 1997/98 while the oil-dependent middle nations faced economic slowdown in the 1998/99 period. During 2008–10, the US economy went through massive job losses, sluggish growth and suffered economic slowdown. Given the incidence of bankruptcies, the role of accurate credit analysis hardly needs to be emphasized.
3. **Increase in Competition**: With increase in competition, naturally pricing is under pressure. When margins get thinner, even the previously accepted level of bad debts would become unacceptable. In other words, as your returns get lower, technically your risk level should also reduce. So, increase in competition is yet another reason for tighter credit risk analysis.

4. **Volatility of Collateral/Asset Values**: Gone are the days where collateral offered comfort. Whilst it is no longer easy to insist on collateral, in view of the increasing competition in the market, the value of collateral also fluctuates widely as has been witnessed in the Japan (1980) the Far East (1997) and the US (2008) crises. Land and real estate prices in various parts of world have witnessed wide swings. The property/real estate prices that reached record highs during booms may not even quote half the value of the credit extended during the boom period. Similarly, as vehicle lessors would testify, if there is a sharp price reduction, many lessees simply default and return the vehicle, because they are in a position to buy new vehicle with the remaining unpaid lease instalments!
5. **Poor Asset Quality**: Non Performing Asset (NPA) is the term used to denote credit assets that are on the verge of becoming credit losses. In other words, they display high risk tendencies to become bad debts. NPA management is a major challenge for banks and non-financial businesses, where credit is extended to their customers. One of the major constraints of the competitive efficiency of banks is the propensity to accumulate poor quality assets. The level of gross NPAs was significantly high in many banks in the US and Europe during 2009 due to poor credit risk underwriting during the immediately preceding years. Whilst competing for business, effective credit risk management should check the propensity to accumulate poor quality of assets.
6. **High Impact of the Credit Losses**: It is a common perception that a small percentage of bad debt is acceptable and won't do much damage. However, unfortunately it is not the case. Even a small credit facility will hurt the business if it turns bad, especially for banks and other financial intermediaries operating in a highly competitive sector. For example, suppose a bank, which makes an average spread of 2%, suffers a credit loss of $2m, then it has to deploy $100m in further lending to recoup the credit loss ($2m/2%). Additional business to be booked to recover the loss made is 50 times the loss suffered. Minimizing credit loss is the best option rather than attempting to book 50 times business volumes, to ensure adequate returns to the shareholders.
7. **Proliferation of Limited Liability Entities**: Limited liability enterprises are among the creative inventions of mankind, and emerged as a solution to expanding world trade in the mid-1800s. Unlike in proprietorships and general partnerships, liability of the owners/shareholders of Limited Liability Companies (LLCs) is limited to their original contribution of capital. Whilst this accelerated risk taking, the new arrangement shifted the onerous burden to the creditors to ensure the creditworthiness of the business enterprises, separately from the shareholders. Accordingly, they had to satisfy the cash generation capacity of the LLC itself, unless of course they could derive unlimited guarantees from the shareholders/owners of LLC, which still falls short of the unlimited liability of unincorporated entities. Another major corollary of LLCs was the advent of public financial statements as the ownership of the LLC and management became separated. Audited financial statements, which began primarily as an instrument of communication between the shareholders and management, are now used and analyzed by several external parties, including creditors.
8. **Risk vs. Return Matching**: Different levels of risk require varying returns. As the credit risk increases, so should the returns in order to compensate for the higher risks taken. A quality credit risk analysis structure is unavoidable to understand the real risks involved when extending credit, which then should be priced appropriately. Each credit should not only be analyzed and mitigated thoroughly, but also priced adequately. In the absence of

credit risk analysis, higher risks will be undertaken for inadequate return with predictable consequences.

9. **Disintermediation**: With the expansion of secondary capital and debt markets, many creditworthy customers, especially the larger ones, access and raise funds directly from the public. Debentures, commercial paper and bonds are popular and the firms that are left behind (i.e. those which cannot access the debt capital market) rely on banks and financial intermediaries. Since credit rating is compulsory for raising debt from the public market, the firms that are not able to fulfil this requirement would be among the borrowers approaching financial intermediaries, including banks. This can result in the lowering of the quality of the credit asset portfolio. Hence, a vigilant approach by the lenders is the logical conclusion.
10. **Off-Balance Sheet Transactions**: As the business environment and nature of businesses become complicated businesspeople are in search of various risk reducing/risk transferring transactions. Derivatives of numerous shapes and categories are being used by companies to control foreign exchange exposures, interest rate fluctuations, commodity price volatility and so on. Usage of other off-balance sheet transactions such as operating leases, factoring with recourse, discounting of bills, etc. are not uncommon. The obligations arising from these off-balance sheet items can sometimes create havoc to the business and even result in bankruptcies, as has been proven by the collapse of Enron (2001) and several financial intermediaries in 2008. In-depth credit analysis is a must to unearth the real credit standing of a firm using derivatives extensively.

Credit risk should be studied thoroughly and managed. In the next chapter we will be discussing how to manage credit risk from a systemic point of view.

## 2.7 CHALLENGES OF CREDIT RISK ANALYSIS

Many businesses, especially banks and financial institutions, have collapsed due to poor selection of credit risk in their attempt to grow portfolios and maintain or improve earnings. Almost all bank failures have a common characteristic: the top management – CEOs and Boards of Directors – failed in their responsibility to understand the challenges of credit risk and manage it well.

### 2.7.1 The Art and Science of Credit Risk Analysis

Credit risk analysis is an art and a science. It is a science as the analysis is based upon established principles and sound logic. However, like law, medicine and equity analysis, credit risk analysis is not an exact science. Individual skill is the art element and the application of the principles will differ from analyst to analyst. Analysis involves research to gather important facts and data and presenting them in a coherent, logical and intelligible manner so that a specific judgement or opinion can be expressed.

The global credit crisis during 2008 triggered a lot of questions on the quality of credit risk analysis done by several banks and financial intermediaries because the credit losses suffered either pushed them into oblivion or near bankruptcy. It can be argued that this is the result of abandonment of a sound analytical approach or delusion created by the protection offered by credit derivatives. Nonetheless, it should be accepted that there are obstacles in credit risk analysis.

Major challenges in credit risk analysis are:

1. **Reliability of the Data**: In order to conduct a credit risk study, analysts require a substantial amount of data and information related to the general economy, industry and the borrower. Financial statements are one of the major sources of data. Usually the annual financial statements are audited. Deliberate falsifications of financial statements are rare.[3] However, sometimes disclosures may be limited. If the relevant information is not forthcoming, the analyst with experience can discern the subtle credit risks involved and study the impact through sensitivity analysis.

   Usually audited accounts are relied on heavily by banks, financial and credit institutions. They take comfort from the fact that the books of accounts are audited by financial experts. However, the collapse of several high profile institutions – just months after a clean report issued by their auditors – casts a long shadow over audited accounts as well. A few such cases are mentioned in Table 2.1 below:

   **Table 2.1** Collapse of High Profile Institutions

   | Name of the Company | Auditing Firm | Year of Collapse |
   |---|---|---|
   | Enron Corporation | Arthur Andersen | 2001 |
   | Lehman Brothers, US | Ernst & Young | 2008 |
   | Satyam Computers, India[4] | Price Waterhouse | 2009 |

   It is interesting to note that subsequent to the collapse of Enron in 2001, Arthur Andersen lost its licence to audit and went out of business.

   Can lenders blame the auditors, if the company fails? We will cover this in Chapter 8.
2. **Profitability/Business Considerations**: Banks and financial institutions are also commercial establishments and often profits are a key driving factor. The management team is also usually incentivized to aim at higher profits that will result in bonuses for key executives (decision takers) and dividends for the shareholders (owners). Sometimes, the over-riding focus on profitability blinds the decisions on risk taking with disastrous consequences.
3. **Unpredictable Future**: Historical analysis of the borrower is done with an underlying assumption that the past track record provides a 'rough guide' to the future. Hence, the analyst's work involves studying the past and understanding how much it is relevant for the future. An analyst's work invariably requires a future outlook based on the past. This is a big challenge because the conclusion drawn based on the past may become worthless if there are new developments in the economy, sector or within the borrower itself. How can an analyst overcome this challenge? By preparing scenario analysis, an analyst may prepare a (i) Base Case, (ii) Realistic Case and (iii) Worst Case. Among the three, worst case usually could be a default scenario, and the analyst must also identify ways to protect repayment sources through appropriate covenants and conditions.
4. **Reliability of Risk Models**: The increasing use of credit risk models to measure risk and to price assets during the late 1990s and early 2000s was heavily criticized after the 2008 Global Credit Crisis. Often, the reliability of models decreases with complexity and the assumptions based on which the models are developed.

[3] Some infamous cases of deliberate falsification of accounts are Enron (US), Satyam (India), Parmalat (Italy) etc.
[4] The statutory auditors were found guilty of professional misconduct.

This does not mean that statistical techniques or modelling should not be employed in credit risk analysis. Whilst they play a fundamental role in the risk management of banks and financial institutions, practitioners, regulators, academics and model designers must be aware of the limitations and set realistic expectations of what models can do. During the heyday of credit risk models, the individual judgement of the credit expert or credit analyst was often ignored. Based on the personal experience of the author, there were cases when the model rating was given more importance. The argument was that the model was bias-free.

## 2.8 ELEMENTS OF CREDIT RISK ANALYSIS

The aim of credit risk analysis is to find an answer to a question of whether a new credit is to be extended, or whether the current set of credit facilities given to a customer must be withdrawn. In all such questions, the following factors (known as the 5Cs of credit) will be considered, either implicitly or explicitly:

1. **Character** – This shows the integrity and honesty of the borrower to settle their dues on time. It is pertinent to say that the history of credit has recorded several instances where the borrower had the capacity to repay but not the willingness. Credit extended to a crook can be considered a credit loss from its very inception. An analyst will take an informed view about the character of the borrower through the study of ownership and management as well as his past track record. Appropriate market enquires are also needed.
2. **Capital** – A prudent lender would ensure that the borrower has a sufficient stake in business. Hence, the higher the capital contribution by the owners in the business, the better. Lenders need to ensure that a substantial interest of the entrepreneur is at stake should the business fail.
3. **Capacity** – The borrower's capacity to meet their debt service obligations must be studied. In the case of business lending this is done through the study of financial statements – i.e. financial analysis, including interpretation of financial ratios that indicate the borrower's ability to pay. Since the business is influenced by the wider economy, the study of economic conditions is also necessary to assess the capacity.
4. **Conditions** – Conditions cover the terms and covenants included in the loan or credit facilities agreement. The lender must ensure that the loan agreement clauses are legally enforceable.
5. **Collateral** – Collateral means the assets offered by the borrower to secure the credit. Whilst collateral is a prominent part of the 5Cs, it is to be noted that most of the high quality creditworthy customers – for instance AAA rated corporate – need not extend collateral in most cases. Often, AAA companies obtain credit with negligible terms and conditions. Similarly, in non-recourse project credit or factoring, the suppliers of credit cannot insist upon any collateral at all. It is a rule of thumb in credit that 'the credit must be able to stand on its own' with the support of any collateral. The collateral is just an additional comfort.

The 5Cs Model is the traditional credit analysis model. Modern credit risk analysis techniques have improved upon the 5Cs[5] Model making it more extensive and comprehensive in its

[5] The banks and financial institutions also follow 5Cs for evaluating personal credit. In such cases, the capacity refers to the personal monthly income of the individual. Even in personal credit, new PC based Credit Scoring Techniques are acting as an improvement over traditional 5Cs.

approach to credit risk analysis. A vast body of knowledge on credit analysis has been developed, which calls for in-depth study of various factors influencing the credit risk. Economic and external risks, industry and internal risks, financial and derivative risks are some of them. The modern approach enables the analyst to see the whole picture from external, industry and corporate level and facilitates effective judgement on the level of credit risk involved in a given situation.

## ✍ QUESTIONS/EXERCISES

1. What do you mean by credit risk analysis? Is it an art or science?
2. Do you believe the emergence of 'limited liability companies' has revolutionized credit risk analysis? Please elaborate.
3. Explain the major causes (sources) of credit risk.
4. Is it true that non-financial institutions also have significant credit risk exposure? Please elaborate.
5. What are the challenges of credit risk analysis?
6. What do you mean by portfolio credit risk? How does it differ from firm (or obligor) credit risk?
7. Explain how the traditional 5Cs Model is augmented in modern credit risk analysis techniques.
8. One of your friends argues that borrowers need not study credit risk analysis because it is the territory of the lending institutions. Do you agree? Please elaborate.

# 3

# Credit Risk Management

Elimination of credit risk is impossible as long as credit forms an integral part of the economy. The organization should manage credit risk in such a manner that it does not spiral out of control. In the meantime, the organization faces other types of risks too. Where does credit risk stand among them?

Let us now establish the context of credit risk, for an organization as a whole, and see how credit risk management is set up. Sound credit risk management presupposes the presence of a good system of credit analysis that will prop up the credit risks to be dealt with. An organization that manages credit risk well will succeed and attain its business objectives – this is true for both financial intermediaries and non-financial firms.

## 3.1 STRATEGIC POSITION OF CREDIT RISK MANAGEMENT

The importance of the role of credit risk management within the broad framework of an organization is a function of the credit exposure a business takes in its day-to-day operations. Financial intermediaries who are active in the credit market provide utmost importance to this function. However, even financial intermediaries who put credit risk management in the top slot are also exposed to other risks such as liquidity risks, market risk and so on. In non-financial businesses, there are other risks, which take priority over credit risks. For instance, in a pharmaceutical company, quality risk may be the most important although credit risk is a matter of concern so far as the company sells on credit. Whilst the risks of an organization vary depending upon the core operations, generally the following types of risks are common to most businesses:

- Operational risks arising from day-to-day operations. Whilst a credit of a cheque to the wrong account poses an operational risk at a bank, the pilferage of stock is an operating risk for a retailer.
- Market risks crop up from the business environment in which the firm operates. The new product launched by a competitor or the emergence of a new competitor are some of the common instances of market risks.
- Legal risk is the result of the various legally binding agreements entered into by the firm or because of contravention of the laws of the land.
- Computer/system risks arise from the information technology used and associated systems and procedures. Whilst system crashes due to several reasons can wipe out a vital database, misuse of the system through unauthorized personnel is yet another risk.
- Reputation risks emerge from factors that would lower the goodwill and reputation of the business in the eyes of the public, which impacts business prospects.
- Liquidity risks and improper balance sheet structure are among several financial risks faced by a business's entity.

In short, credit risk is one of the risks faced by business entities. The importance and relevance of credit should be defined in the overall context of all the risks faced by the business entity. If the credit risk is minimal, as in the case of cash based businesses, then the credit risk function will be given least importance. On the other hand in the case of banks with a significant credit portfolio, credit risk management is of paramount importance. All financial intermediaries other than banks also attach prominent significance to credit risk. After all, financial intermediaries are among the main pillars of any economic system and indirectly credit risk is critical from the point of view of the economy as well. For most non-financial businesses, credit risk can be considered critical and is usually regarded as one of the major risks to be monitored.

## 3.2 CREDIT RISK MANAGEMENT CONTEXT

Credit risk management cannot be isolated from the overall organizational context. The goals and strategies of credit risk management emanate from the overall mission and vision of the entity. Similarly, it is defined in relation to the other core essentials for the survival of the business, depending upon the circumstances. Whilst a profitable deposit-taking financial intermediary may forgo good credit exposure to ensure solvency, a profitable non-financial enterprise operating in a highly competitive market may extend a longer credit period to good customers. Whilst liquidity is important for any business, it is of paramount importance for a deposit-taking financial intermediary, which otherwise would be risking a run. Risk appetite is invariably linked to the corporate philosophy, culture and strategic perspective of a business organization. For instance, certain banks are known for their aggressive approach towards credit risk, while others are marked by their cautious approach. Credit risk appetite is also dependent upon the human, financial and operational resources an organization has. A SWOT analysis of credit risk management is advisable on a periodical basis.

## 3.3 CREDIT RISK MANAGEMENT OBJECTIVES

Whilst the ultimate nature of the credit risk borne by a financial and a non-financial enterprise is the same, the objectives differ. A financial intermediary takes credit risk to earn financial income in the form of interest income or otherwise. A non-financial entity takes it to enhance its revenue base. Whilst the mission and vision of an organization is stable, the objectives are subject to changes as they adjust to the dynamism of the business environment.

The best analogy might be that of a ship sailing to its destination, but the unpredictable sea conditions may force the Captain of the ship to take tough decisions – for example, the meals per day may be cut from three to two, to ensure food for everyone during the period of unexpected delay. Similarly a business which has faced certain huge credit losses in the immediate past will have the objective of ensuring maximum credit quality and may tighten credit policies – accepting only high quality credit customers, even at reduced pricing. Having attained the goal within two years, they will usually find that they have lost market share, because of the tight policy, and they may decide to be a bit more liberal to gain increased business, while ensuring that the previous bad credit experience is not repeated. This is yet another objective of credit risk management: to maintain a historical default database, which will be used on a periodical basis to conduct back-testing or stress testing of the credit quality of the portfolio.

Overall, the major objectives of credit risk management would include the following:

(a) Maximizing benefits from potential credit opportunities.
(b) Pricing credit risk adequately.
(c) Minimizing bad loans.
(d) Adherence to credit policies.
(e) Maintenance of a reliable database.

## 3.4 CREDIT RISK MANAGEMENT STRUCTURE

In order to ensure the attainment of credit objectives, various strategies and steps have to be implemented, which requires a structure with specific functions. Structure should be adapted to the strategies which emanate from the objectives. For instance, while a tight credit risk policy may result in centralization of approval powers, a lenient attitude towards risk in order to garner higher market share may require the strategy of decentralization of such powers.

Usually in financial intermediaries a high level authority – Chief Credit Officer or General Manager (Credit Risk) or equivalent – is in charge of overall credit risk management to ensure the attainment of the related goals and is usually responsible to the Chairman/Managing Director and to the Board. A talented pool of credit experts and specialists at both macro and micro levels is essential and forms one of the core essentials for effective credit risk management, which is divided among a number of departments with a clear definition of how they participate in the risk identification and management processes.

In non-financial organizations usually the top authority of credit risk management lies with a senior management team member, who generally reports to the Finance Director/Chief Finance Officer or equivalent.

## 3.5 CREDIT RISK CULTURE

The CEO and Board of Directors are responsible for a fundamental and critical element of credit risk management – an effective and strong credit culture. Unless an organization has a carefully defined and disciplined credit culture, supported by its Board, protecting it against imprudent credit and pricing decisions, it may not survive the macroeconomic challenges emanating from the dynamic business environment.

Credit culture is a set of values and beliefs shared by people in credit risk management. It encompasses the tangible written policies and procedures, and the intangibles – such as traditions, philosophies and informal standards. Credit culture is developed over time, defines the circle of competence and is passed on. The creation of the right risk aware culture goes a long way to ensuring effective credit risk management. Weak credit culture will lead to assumption of credit risks not in line with credit risk management objectives and strategies. Periodical training of credit risk management staff, a risk conscious top cadre in credit risk management, proper two-way communication, the establishment of detailed credit policies and standards and strict adherence to them are some of the effective methods to ensure a strong credit risk culture in an organization.

Having a strong set of policies and processes and an auditing and checking mechanism is not enough. It must be backed up by a strong credit culture. For example, if the culture of the bank or financial institution is low risk taking, then the policies and procedures will reflect the strict criteria with which the credit risk will be underwritten. This must be corroborated in all meetings, words, actions and communications. If the senior management of the bank began to extol the advantages of the high rewards embedded in high risk taking and to encourage such deals in the quest for extra profits, it would show a cultural breakdown or conflict, which would not be good for the organization.

A well understood credit risk culture will enable the decision takers and employees in credit risk management to take effective and intelligent risk decisions, ensuring the achievement of the credit risk management objectives. Employees can imbibe the credit risk culture in dissimilar ways. Different organizations have their own methods of achieving this. Whilst most of the banks take junior officers with a cut-off age of mid-20s, through a rigorous selection process, and train them up through hands-on jobs and mentoring, most banks are also open to credit professionals from varied environments and attempt to achieve a blended credit culture.

A strong credit culture promotes good credit decisions. Commitment to quality decisions and continuous learning is an essential element. The recent 2008 Credit Crisis has highlighted the importance of credit culture, the lack of which led to deficiencies and flaws in credit processes and decisions. Credit systems ought to have an early warning mechanism and encourage independent common sense judgements and reality checks as well a sound logical framework for day-to-day decision making.

## 3.6 CREDIT RISK APPETITE

Credit risk appetite must be established as a strong foundation, which will prescribe the type, amount, nature and extent of credit risk that an organization is willing to underwrite. Usually a credit risk appetite statement is drawn up prescribing the following:

- **Target Market**: Understanding the target market to which the credit would be offered is essential for a number of reasons: (i) it ensures strategies and products are developed in accordance with the market; (ii) the market criteria ensure that no opportunities are missed in the identified target markets and conversely they will screen out the market segments, where the organization has no risk appetite.
- **Minimum Credit Standards**: Credit risk appetite will prescribe the minimum acceptable standards of the credit risk required while building the business.
- **Sectors**: Risk appetite would require the study of major sectors to identify those which are desirable. The sectors identified with good potential would be favoured while the riskier sector would be shunned. Depending upon the sector's attractiveness the risk appetite would vary as follows:
  - 'No Appetite/Reduce' – least attractive sector.
  - 'Grow' – sector with good potential.
  - 'Selective Growth' – sectors that hold reasonable potential.
- **Products Offered**: Risk appetite would also detail the type of credit products to be developed in line with the risk appetite; while pricing the product, it would be ensured that the risk (selected based on the minimum standards) is adequately priced in.

The above is only guidance as credit risk appetite differs from organization to organization. In large multinational organizations, the credit risk appetite for each subsidiary, division or geographical area would be required. In many organizations, the credit risk appetite also requires setting up and operating a system of limits to control risk taking in the organization. This system is akin to a budgetary control system inasmuch as it monitors actual behaviour against the limits set.

## 3.7 CREDIT RISK MANAGEMENT IN NON-FINANCIAL FIRMS

In the case of a manufacturing firm, or trading firm, extension of credit is essential for sales promotion. The resultant receivables or debtors portfolio evidences the credit risk undertaken by the firm. Usually they finance the customers' purchases on an unsecured basis for periods ranging for one month to six months. Extended credit running into years is not uncommon, with the support of bank guarantees or letters of credit.

Well-established businesses have credit control systems to establish creditworthiness and monitoring of credit customers. While extending credit the supplier expects that the buyer will have enough resources at their disposal to meet the commitments. Such an assurance is the product of credit risk analysis.

The goal of the analyst in non-financial firms is to protect the investment in receivables. 'Receivables' are amounts of money owed to the firm (seller) by its customers (buyers) for goods (including raw materials and/or services) supplied. It is an integral part of credit management, which supports the sales force in their efforts to maximize sales without endangering the survival of the business.

In many companies receivables are among the largest assets appearing on the balance sheet and require significant commitment of precious working capital resources. An increase or reduction in the amount invested in receivables will usually have a significant (negative or positive) impact on the company's cash flow and on the company's cash cycle, which is the time required to convert goods into cash, from the date the company pays the costs of acquisition of the goods to the date of receipt of the cash from associated sales.

The risk of loss of a receivable and the danger it presents to the survival of the company is the primary force behind the need for analysis and its management. The loss of a large amount of working capital by way of bad debts will almost inevitably lead to the failure of a company. The credit risk management techniques discussed in this book are applicable to both financial and non-financial enterprises. Usually most non-financial entities use a credit management approach, which is generally a watered down version of the techniques used by financial firms.

## 3.8 CREDIT RISK MANAGEMENT IN FINANCIAL INTERMEDIARIES

Given the fact that most of the financial intermediaries, especially banks and financial institutions have credit assets constituting more than 40% of the total assets, the importance of the systematic study and analysis of credit risk hardly needs to be emphasized. In accordance with good credit management, all employees are made aware of the need for credit risk consciousness. The approach used by commercial lenders is elaborate and follows comprehensive credit analysis.

### 3.8.1 Stages of Credit Risk Management in Financial Intermediaries

The steps usually followed by a financial intermediary are listed below:

**Nature and Purpose of the Credit**: The purpose should be acceptable to the lender, i.e. it must be legal, non-speculative and in accordance with the lender's priorities. It must be ensured that the credit facilities are used to finance the customer's normal business activities. The amount should be sufficient for the purpose and reasonable in relation to the customer's own resources. In principle, there is little point in financing a potential borrower who cannot give a satisfactory reason for use of the credit proceeds. In today's world of escalating money laundering activities, it is vital to understand the purpose of credit facilities.

**Type of Credit Facility**: An overdraft is a facility that allows an individual to withdraw funds from his current account in excess of the credit balance up to an agreed limit. The customer is charged interest only on the used portion of the amount. Loans are a fixed amount for a fixed period of time and unlike an overdraft cannot be fluctuating. When the loan is granted, the full amount of the loan is debited to a loan account. The loans can be short-term or long-term. Another major subset of credit facilities extended by banks are known as non-funded lines, which includes letters of credit and guarantees, where no funds are provided. A revolving line of credit, working capital loan, term loan, lease financing, hire purchase, bill/cheque discounting and similar facilities are offered by banks. Another type of credit that is increasingly becoming widely available is the credit card, which can be used to purchase goods and services on credit, and to obtain cash advances. Many people apply for a card not in order to obtain credit or as a means of postponing payment for goods, but in order to have the convenience of a card as a method of payment as an alternative to cash or cheques.

**Capacity to Borrow**: The lenders ought to check the legal status of the person who obtains credit. Usually minors, undischarged insolvents, mentally incapacitated persons and in certain societies, women (sometimes married women) are disqualified from entering into contracts on their own. In such cases a guardian is necessary. Similarly, while extending credit to artificial legal persons, the lender should ensure that the persons representing such incorporated entities have the requisite authority to act on their behalf.

**Security**: Whether security is needed for a credit decision depends upon the level of creditworthiness. If creditworthiness is high and the resultant credit risk is low, the lenders will not insist on any security at all. When security is required, several factors should be considered such as adequacy, sufficiency and the authenticity of the security offered. The security can be either primary or collateral. Receivables, stock, machinery and equipment, real estate and guarantees are accepted as security, amongst others. (Please see Chapters 22 and 23 for a detailed discussion).

**Analyze Borrower's Financial Status**: The analysis of the financial position of the borrower is one of the essential preludes to the granting of credit. The fundamental question in the financial analysis is the ability of the business to generate adequate cash flows from operations to meet their commitments. Various measures to gauge solvency, liquidity, efficiency and repayment capacity, amongst others, have been developed to study financial parameters relevant from a lender's point of view. (Please see Chapter 8).

**Forecasting the Repayment Capacity**: The lender should have reasonable assurances about the ability of the borrower to meet their commitments when they fall due in future. The shorter the duration of the loan, the more predictable the repayment ability. That is why the analysis of project finance and long-term loans is different from the techniques followed for assessing the repayment ability of short-term loans. In such cases projections are insisted upon with assumptions. The achievability of projections with reference to historic performance and management track record is usually analyzed. Appropriate sensitivity analysis is also undertaken.

**Profitability**: The commercial lender incurs costs in making credit available to customers. Salaries of employees involved in appraising, granting and monitoring the credit, rent and other overheads should be recovered from the return generated from the credit besides the cost of funds – usually viewed as the interest paid on deposits. In fact the true profitability should be assessed with cost of capital. (Please see Chapters 20 and 21.)

**Structure the Credit Facility, Including Conditions and Covenants**: The credit facilities should be structured to suit the purpose for which they are intended to be used. The borrower and supplier of credit have to agree upon several issues, which should be formalized. Credit facility agreements specify mutual expectations of the borrower and lender and respective duties and obligations. Violation of conditions is tantamount to default and the lender can repossess the credit facility and other claims or start legal proceedings for repossession, depending upon the terms of agreement. The supplier of credit should avoid loopholes in agreements and should be meticulous in drafting credit facility agreements. When setting financial covenants care must be taken to build in enough headroom to avoid continuous adjustment yet without reducing the quality of the protection offered by such covenants.

**Constant Monitoring**: The credit facilities should be monitored closely through various steps including risk limits, capital allocation and periodical reports on the borrower, sector and economy. We will discuss in more depth the various risk identification factors, based on which monitoring has to be carried out later in the book.

### 3.8.2 Credit Risk Management Process

The credit risk management process tends to be elaborate so as to tackle the challenges associated with credit risk. A strict policy framework is maintained to ensure that the credit risk culture is enforced throughout the organization. The usual methodology is as follows:

- Finalize overall credit risk appetite.
- Establish objectives and strategy – decide the reward/ risk pattern, inclusive of provisioning.
- Roll out credit risk infrastructure to facilitate measurement and ownership of credit risk. Nowadays IT systems also play a key role.
- Identify the right people and ensuring proper communication, behaviour and incentivization.
- Implement appropriate credit risk models – ensure that there is no over-reliance on credit risk models.

A financial intermediary is in the business of risk underwriting. Hence, none of the financial intermediaries can be termed as risk averse. The primary goal of the credit risk management process is to ensure that the right people understand the right risks, isolating unacceptable risks and identifying acceptable risks. Thereafter, appropriate risk mitigants must also be identified and implemented.

It is pertinent to mention that a necessary skill in credit risk analysis is the ability to identify and screen out poor deals because the resources have opportunity costs. Another important skill required by the credit risk analyst or manager or credit approver/sanctioner is to ask the right questions. Right questioning can be deceptively difficult; however once mastered, the rest of the credit risk analysis is a deductive analysis to determine whether the initial hypothesis[1] is right.

[1] Many banks and lending institutions provide 'approval in principle' based on an initial hypothesis derived from the initial set of the information provided by the customer such as the financial statements summary and business profile. However, there is no commitment until the contract/agreement is signed, which will be subject to a thorough credit risk analysis/due diligence.

## ✍ QUESTIONS/EXERCISES

1. Explain the factors that decide whether credit risk enjoys a strategic position within a business.
2. What do you mean by credit risk culture? Discuss its importance.
3. Explain the importance of credit risk appetite. What are the factors to be considered while deciding credit risk appetite?
4. Explain how non-financial institutions manage their credit risk exposure. Please elaborate.
5. Do you believe credit risk enjoys a strategic position with all financial intermediaries? Please elaborate.
6. Briefly elucidate how credit risk management is done in financial intermediaries.
7. Explain whether a financial intermediary can shy away from taking credit risk, i.e. be credit risk averse? Please elaborate.
8. One of your friends states that in order to manage a credit institution, a strong set of policies and procedures are required. He dismisses credit culture as a meaningless word and emphasizes that adherence to the credit policies and procedures would ensure successful credit risk underwriting. Do you agree with this statement? Please explain with reasons.

# Part II

# Firm (or) Obligor Credit Risk

Obligor risks are studied to understand the probability of credit loss (viz. credit risk) from a single customer. The construction of a healthy credit portfolio requires careful selection of obligor risks.

# 4
# Fundamental Firm/Obligor-Level Risks

The number of risks that can affect the performance of companies is infinite. While taking a credit decision, it is vital to cover at least the most important risks that affect the fortunes of an individual business firm. As we have seen earlier, credit risks should be studied from two angles – firm level or business unit level and portfolio level. Obligor risks are studied to understand the probability of credit loss (viz. credit risk) from a single customer. Portfolio risk analysis attempts to examine credit risks on a wider scale and studies the likelihood of loss emanating from the exposure to particular classes of customers. Firm-level credit risk is relevant from the point of view of portfolio risk as well.

Just as the construction of a skyscraper requires the utmost care in placing each building block, so the construction of a healthy credit portfolio requires careful selection of obligor risks. Portfolio credit risk is the cluster of firm-level credit risks, although the study of the behaviour of credit risks at portfolio level needs a different approach. We will cover the credit portfolio risks later. In this chapter we will examine the firm-level forces impacting credit risk.

## 4.1 FIRM (OR) OBLIGOR RISK CLASSIFICATION

Firm credit risk analysis involves two parts – the study of (a) business risks or operating risks and (b) financial risks. The bifurcation of overall credit risk into two is important because a business firm can fail or default on credit due to purely financial reasons even when normal business risks remain at acceptable levels and vice versa. In credit parlance all such events impacting the creditworthiness of the obligor/borrower/counterparty are known as 'credit events'.

### 4.1.1 Business Risks or Operating Risks (OR)

Credit events of a non-financial nature are known as operating risks. Business or operating risk originates from the dynamic operating environment of the business. It is usually defined as the hazard that an event or situation will adversely impact a company's ability to achieve its business objectives and execute its strategies effectively. OR includes all risks that arise both inside and outside the company. Failure of an organization to optimize its assets – both tangible and intangible – resulting in the loss of the company's competitive edge, is also an OR. Good business risk management can enable a company to make rational business decisions when faced with the powerful and dynamic forces shaping the local or domestic and global arena. Study of OR encompasses changes in economic, regulatory, climatic, industry, demographic factors, changes in geo-political and governments, product innovations/substitutes, quality of management and other internal factors, amongst others. The events originating from the operating environment are numerous and in order to study the operating risks, it is better to structure them into three sub-components, namely (a) external risks, (b) industry risks and (c) internal or company risks. In fact the relevance and breadth of these variables are different, which is better captured in Figure 4.1:

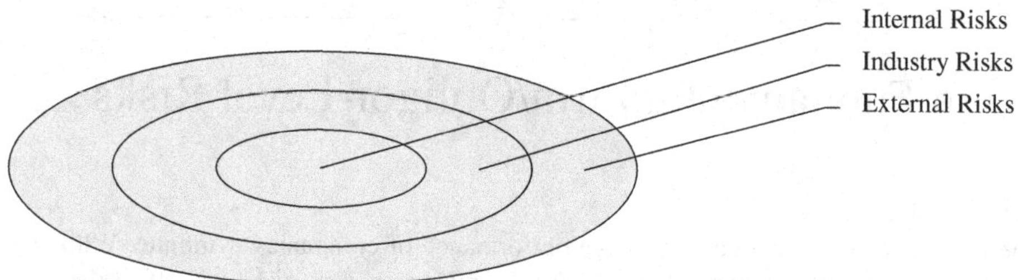


**Figure 4.1** Various Layers of Operational or Business Risks

External risks are the broadest of the three, occupying the outermost layer, and comprise national and international developments, economic, social, cultural and political factors, among others. Industry risks are specific to a particular sector or industry. Although company/internal risks are the narrowest of the three, they are more critical because entity level strategies and tactics determine the fate of a business unit as it deals with the challenges and opportunities emanating from external and industrial factors. Note that company/internal risks lie at the centre of the circular diagram above, which reflects its central role. (In the ensuing chapters, we will discuss these three risks in detail.)

### 4.1.2 Financial Risks (FR)

Credit events that originate purely from the financial aspect of the business are known as financial risks. Whilst most of them are of an internal nature, these risks are so important that if not properly taken care of they can result in the collapse of businesses. Studies have found that many businesses fail because of an inadequate finance function, i.e. financial risks can plunge a successful business into bankruptcy. Financial risks can be understood through the analysis of financial statements, which are written records of a business's financial situation and usually include the balance sheet, profit and loss account and cash flow statement. They provide business information in financial terms and are useful in credit decisions. (We will consider financial risks in detail in Chapter 8.) Before we discuss a broad overview of the relationship between operating risks and financial risks, let us summarize the discussion on firm or obligor credit risk as follows (see Figure 4.2):

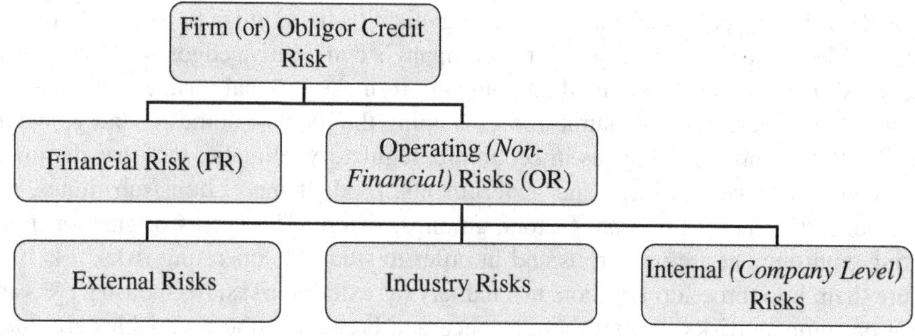


**Figure 4.2** Breakdown of Firm or Obligor Credit Risks

## 4.2 RISK MATRIX

In order to understand firm credit risks properly, both operating risks and financial risks should be studied together. The operating risks should be analyzed and ought to be linked to the financial performance of the company. Financial risks should be identified and ought to be linked to the operating environment to determine the likelihood of the financial risks triggering a crisis situation. For instance, the state of the economy and industry will influence the profit margins of a business, which will affect its financial performance. Similarly, a business operating with high financial leverage will face tough times if there is a downturn in the economy or industry.

A broad overview of the relationship among operating risks and financial risks to Credit Risk (CR) is given in Table 4.1:

**Table 4.1** Relation between Operating Risks and Financial Risks

| OR \ FR | Low | Medium | High |
|---|---|---|---|
| **Low** | Very Low CR | Low CR | Medium-High CR |
| **Medium** | Low CR | Medium CR | High CR |
| **High** | Medium-High CR | High CR | Very High CR |

This matrix depicts the relation between OR and FR and how these two levers operate upon the pure credit risks of a credit. A sound understanding of the OR and FR of the entities in which a financial or non-financial entity is taking credit risk exposure is essential because it triggers seeking of appropriate risk mitigation tools. It ought to be borne in mind that the above table does not amount to a credit rating exercise, although it is an essential part of it. The credit rating exercise is broader. We will discuss credit risk grades in Chapter 10.

## 4.3 DIFFERENT RISK LEVELS

### 4.3.1 Low Operating Risk and Low Financial Risk

The firms rated under this category have the lowest possibility of throwing up inconsistent performance or qualifying as an unsatisfactory credit asset. The credit to such firms is of the highest quality. The operating risk is low and usually characterized by stable market conditions, good management and a well-accepted product/service among its satisfied and increasing clientele. The financial position is also highly satisfactory with moderate debt usage, excellent debt service capacity and access to capital markets. Usually these firms enjoy a dominant position in the market, if they are not actually the market leader.

### 4.3.2 Low Operating Risk and Medium Financial Risk

These firms differ from those discussed above in one respect – financial risks are slightly higher. Debt usage tends to be more than moderate while financial position, profitability and cash generation, although satisfactory, are slightly lower than the category discussed above. However the quality of the management, market share, good reputation, strong brands, etc. ensure low operating risks. These firms are effectively insulated from fluctuations in the operating environment in view of their sustainable competitive advantages such as low cost base or strong brands, amongst others.

### 4.3.3 Low Operating Risk and High Financial Risk

In this category, the financial position is rather unhealthy, if not weak, and characterized by unstable financial performance, although operating risks remain low. This situation occurs when the firm ignores financial function. There are many instances where, even when the business has grown large enough for a full-time finance manager, the owner/entrepreneur will attempt to handle the finance function himself with the help of semi-skilled staff, which ultimately results in a weak finance function. Liquidity crises, high interest cost, poor collections, undue levels of stock, high cost of capital, etc. are the hallmarks, which can push the firm into bankruptcy. However, the positive element is that the sooner the finance lacuna is rectified, the sooner the problems are solvable and the firm can migrate into better classes of classification.

### 4.3.4 Medium Operating Risk and Low Financial Risk

The operating risk is medium in view of the severity of competition or strong bargaining power of suppliers/buyers. Or the market conditions may be somewhat unstable while management and the product/ service are satisfactory. The nature of business may be cyclical or impacted to a significant extent by fluctuations in the operating environment. The market presence although satisfactory cannot be termed dominant. The financial position is also highly satisfactory with low-moderate debt usage, excellent debt service capacity and access to capital markets.

### 4.3.5 Medium Operating Risk and Medium Financial Risk

This can be generally termed an average credit risk and most of the medium-type businesses fit into this category. The management at all the critical positions is satisfactory and the size of the firm tends to be around the mean size of the industry/business. The product/service is accepted in general, but the firm is not perceived as the market leader. Financial risk is medium with moderate debt usage and average debt service capability and asset quality. The profitability, solvency and liquidity positions are satisfactory although they cannot be classified as excellent.

### 4.3.6 Medium Operating Risk and High Financial Risk

These firms differ in one aspect from the class immediately above. The finance function is ignored or the balance sheet is overloaded with significant external debt and negligible support from the owners/shareholders. High leverage, liquidity problems, high cost of capital, high interest burden, unproductive and high overheads, etc. are some of the symptoms. Streamlining of finance function can help the firm to improve its creditworthiness in most instances.

### 4.3.7 High Operating Risk and Low Financial Risk

The business prospects are uncertain due to the external, industry or internal factors of the entity. However, the comforting factor is the satisfactory financial position or financial management. Potential vulnerability looms large as the high operating risks may soon erode the financial position because of the weaker performance. A good example is a company in a highly cyclical business facing recession induced low demand, projecting losses for the foreseeable future. However a strong financial position with minimum external finance may see the company through the cyclical phase.

### 4.3.8 High Operating Risk and Medium Financial Risk

As in the case of the preceding category, the business prospects are uncertain due to the external, industry or internal factors of the entity. Management is weak or dishonest requiring continual attention from the lender/supplier of credit. The financial position and financial management are also not comforting, although not as bad as other factors. Capacity to repay credit is impaired. The credit asset is inadequately protected by the net worth of the borrower/obligor. It looks as though some credit loss is unavoidable.

### 4.3.9 High Operating Risk and High Financial Risk

Any business with these features should be dropped like a hot potato. Not only are the business prospects and external environment murky with weak management, but the financial position and financial management also display vulnerability. Capacity to repay credit is so impaired that based on the overall situation the collection of the claim is doubtful and may be written off partially or fully.

More often than not, the decline in the creditworthiness of the borrower/obligor is a gradual process, which is otherwise known as 'migration' in credit/financial parlance. Credit migration (of a low risk credit asset to a higher risk level) and vice versa depend upon the change in operating and financial factors of the business firm. Hence, the supplier of credit ought to review the renewable credit or credit line on a periodical basis and/or on the occurrence of credit events.

Credit loss, which is usually the end result of a business failure, is not an abrupt process which happens overnight. However a common myth generally believed by the public and not uncommonly even by seasoned credit professionals is that business failure is a sudden phenomenon. In fact this is partly for psychological reasons. Everyone concerned with the business failure – senior management, auditors, loan managers, analysts, etc. – have good reasons to present the business failure as an abrupt event. The business failure was not their fault and they cannot be held responsible for something that is sheer bad luck or misfortune.

Several warning credit events do take place before a credit is fully written off. The credit risk analysis studies whether the company or business firm has stepped onto a path that will ultimately result in credit loss. The abovementioned risk matrix is just for guidance and is useful to monitor the risk pattern of any given business from two angles – business risks and financial risks – two broad categories of risk that can push a business entity out of business. It avoids surprises. It explains how financial risks can bankrupt a business operating in a good business environment with satisfactory growth potential and vice versa.

The firm-level risk analysis is essential to understand the business risks and financial risks. These are extremely useful, as we see later, in deciding the structure of internal ratings. The credit ratings for each customer or borrower will be different depending upon the outcome of firm-level risk analysis. We will discuss the various factors to be considered while studying the firm (or obligor) credit risk analysis in Chapters 5–9.

## QUESTIONS/EXERCISES

1. What is the difference between portfolio risk and obligor risk?
2. What is the advantage of bifurcation of the firm credit risk into business risk and financial risk?
3. Explain business risks.
4. What do you mean by financial risk? Explain the role of financial statements in the study of financial risk.
5. Explain how understanding of the various levels of operating risk and financial risk influence credit risk analysis.
6. Can operational risks influence financial risks and vice versa?
7. As a relationship manager, the fastest growing customer in your portfolio does not have a full-time qualified and experienced finance manager. Whilst profitability is acceptable, high interest cost, poor collections, undue levels of stock and high cost of capital are evident. Although the business has grown enough to warrant an experienced finance manager, the owner insists that finance is too important to be entrusted to a third party and believes he can handle the finance function himself. How would you judge the finance risk of this customer?
8. One of your friends states that the business failures of big corporates (e.g. Lehman Brothers) happen suddenly. He believes business failure is an abrupt process and a good business can fail in a few months. He cites many rating agencies which had given investment grade to Lehman Brothers just a few months before its bankruptcy. Do you agree with this statement? Please explain with reasons.

# 5

# External Risks

Almost everyone knows why the Titanic sank, in the cold waters of Atlantic on a starlit night in 1912. The tragedy of the Titanic, which was immortalized in a late 1990s Hollywood film, was the result of ignoring external threats. The ship was claimed to be the strongest and most unsinkable built to date, which led to certain unconscious decisions on the part of the people responsible for steering the ship to ignore external threats from sea and weather factors. The information on an external risk – icebergs – was taken too lightly. The confidence reposed in the strength of the ship – the best ship in 1912 – was excessive.

Similarly, in business even strong enterprises and companies have floundered because of inadequate attention to external threats. The business history of several nations tells us stories about the mighty companies that disappeared all of a sudden due to changes in the external environment. For example, the downturn in US real estate during 2007–09 wiped out several reputed business institutions in the US such as Lehman Brothers, Wachovia Bank and Washington Mutual.

In this chapter we will cover external risks, first among the three major operating or business risks. It refers to all those non-industry and non-entity factors that impact the operational and financial aspects of a business. Businesses do not operate in a vacuum. Many external factors do influence the results, actions and decisions of businesses, although diverse businesses are impacted by varied external factors in dissimilar ways. Whilst a government contractor may face a difficult situation because of delayed settlement of dues by government, a restaurant chain will not be affected to the same extent. If a bank decides to aggressively increase exposure to construction contractors towards the peak of the construction boom, it may result in serious troubles as the boom subsides. Such situations call for careful analysis of the various factors, including the economic environment, before taking a credit decision.

The real world is full of political, social and technological and other forces, which intermix and sometimes flow at cross-currents. Identification of the major external risks and awareness as to how major external variables impact the performance of the obligor is crucial for a good credit risk analysis.

The external risk factors[1] can be considered as part of 'systematic risks'. They impact the macroeconomy and would ultimately influence the success of the 'credit market' of the country. Let us discuss the major sources of possible external risks that can give rise to a risky situation as far as the entity (borrower) is concerned.

## 5.1 BUSINESS CYCLE

An economy is not static and undergoes different periods or stages of economic growth, widely known as the business cycle. Even well managed economies are not immune to this phenomenon. It is now considered an integral part of a dynamic economic system, largely capitalistic in nature. It can't be eliminated. But policy makers, with the indispensable aid

[1] These risk factors are also useful for 'Credit Portfolio Risk Analysis'. This is covered later in the book.

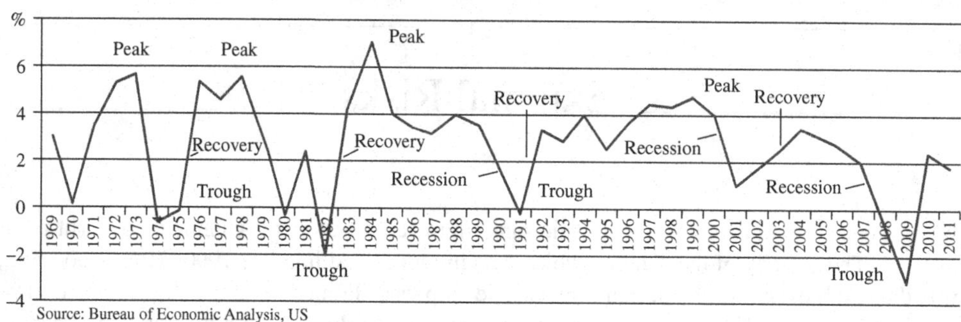


**Figure 5.1** Historical US GDP Growth and Business Cycles

of economists, have attempted to tame the viciousness of downturns. The ups and downs of a typical business cycle are evident from the chart in Figure 5.1 based on historical data for United States GDP growth.

As demonstrated above, the economy goes through different stages – Recession, Trough, Recovery and Peak. It is evident that during 1970–2010, the US economy witnessed several business cycles – a few recessions, troughs, recoveries and peaks are highlighted to elucidate the concept. It is pertinent to note that the severity of US business cycles was reduced between the 1980s and 2000, partly due to better policies. There are many who argue that the 2008 recession would not have happened or its severity could have been reduced had the Glass–Steagall Act[2] not been repealed in 1999. This change in policy resulted in retail banks entering into areas reserved for investment banks and vice versa.

The business cycle diagram resembles a mountain range. The difficulty in negotiating a business cycle and mountain range is almost identical – but with one exception. Whilst descending from the peak of the mountain can be an easy affair, in the business cycle that stage (recession) is really difficult for businesses, as described below.

**Recession**: In this stage of the cycle, economic activities slow down with rising unemployment, slowing sales and reducing corporate profits. Inflation and interest rates ought to have already risen (usually, not always) with business spending down and businessmen and corporate executives worrying about how to tighten costs. It is the widely held view that if the economic growth is negative in two quarters, the economy is in recession. During October 2008, at the onset of the recessionary phase triggered by the Credit Crisis, car manufacturers in the US and Europe announced production cuts. Similarly, major electronics giants in Japan decided to reduce production. OPEC also cut the oil production. During recession, lower economic activity leads to lower profits, usually impacting debt serviceability, especially if the business firm is highly leveraged.

Given the overall bleakness, investments are curtailed. Bankruptcies increase as weaker firms find it difficult to cope with recession. As production or economic activity reduces, the demand for resources drops. Accordingly, unemployed resources will increase including human resources. Hence, higher unemployment is common in recession. All responsible governments try to meet the recessionary tendencies of the economy well in advance by appropriate monetary and fiscal actions. Policy makers and economists, with the insight

[2] The Act passed in 1933 had prohibited deposit-taking banks from riskier investment banking and related activities.

and experience gained through previous cycles, have done much to tame the viciousness of downturns over the past five or six decades. Usually slashing interest rates, quantitative easing and fiscal stimulus are packaged together to mitigate or face the recessionary pressures. Hence, identifying the beneficiaries from the steps taken to mitigate the impact of recession would be important for maintaining or building up a quality credit portfolio during a recessionary phase.

**Trough**: Things look like they are at their worst with high levels of unemployment, general gloom, the lowest production levels in the recent history of the economy, bottomed out stock market, bankruptcies of banks and other financial intermediaries due to heavy bad loans, etc. being some of the symptoms. There is a general feeling that things cannot get any worse. The trough for most of the Asian economies impacted by the currency induced Economic Crisis, can be traced to 1998. Again, this phase can be shortened by appropriate action by governments, either with or without the help of multilateral organizations including the IMF.

**Recovery**: Things begin to look a little better, with business confidence returning and economic activity picks up. Stock prices and employment levels start rising while investments and profits increase. In the first half of an expansion, it appears that profits rise faster than wages because of increasing productivity. The periodical (monthly/quarterly, etc.) data related to the economy is full of good news with higher manufacturing growth, tertiary growth, less unemployment, less inventory level, more factory orders and so on. Sometimes the recovery can be slow, although it can be rapid as well as has been the case with Far East Asian economies hit by the cycle in 1997.

**Peak**: The economy puts up a very strong performance with low unemployment levels. Markets get heated up with price levels under pressure. Euphoric conditions prevail. Consumers over-extend their credit and spend heavily assuming steady future cash flows. The business magazines roar with positive headlines and many proponents emerge arguing this time (peak period) things are different because of technology or otherwise and predict long-term further growth. Over-confident investments are undertaken, creating over-capacity, bordering on high risk/low return business decisions. Unvigilant financial intermediaries are also pulled into supporting these ventures. Ecstasy continues till a shock sets in triggering a financial crisis culminating in a recession. Japan in the late 1980s, Far East Tiger Economies in the mid-1990s, and the US in 2007 are some of the examples.

Credit risk analysis should focus on the extent of the impact of the business cycles on obligors and assess their strengths to overcome the negative influences of cycles. It has relevance for industry analysis also, which will be taken up in the next chapter.

### 5.1.1 Benefits of Study of Business Cycles

The study of business cycles is a highly potent tool for a sound credit risk analysis – both obligor risks and portfolio risks.[3] During the recovery phase, additional investments stimulate a lot of economic variables such as additional employment, demand for finance, the creation of new assets and so on. On the other hand in a recessionary situation business confidence

[3] The risk inherent in credit portfolios peaks at the top of the business cycle. Understanding of the credit cycle, which is the expansion and contraction of credit over the course of the business cycle, is relevant for credit risk analysis, especially for credit portfolio study. During the contractionary phase of the business cycle, non-performing loans increase, profits decline and substantial losses to capital may become apparent in banks. Eventually, the economy reaches a trough and turns towards a new expansionary phase; as a result the risk of future losses reaches a low point, even though banks may still appear relatively unhealthy at this stage in the cycle. Discerning investors increase capital allocation to listed (i.e. stock market traded) banks at this stage and reap substantial gains.

erodes resulting in poor performance of most of the business entities, and this impacts the credit risk adversely.

Whilst most businesses do well in economic growth (which can be linked to the recovery and boom phase in a business cycle), economic decline (recession/trough in the cycle) causes bankruptcies and credit losses. The majority of business firms tend to do poorly in recession with the exception a few, i.e. those who have the financial means to take advantage of the depressed asset prices or non-cyclical businesses such as pharmaceuticals or the food industry or business firms enjoying the benefit of fiscal spending by the government. Bankruptcy lawyers and finance restructuring consultants perhaps also do well in such situations.

Given the serious social and political implications of recession, responsible governments will resort to appropriate monetary and fiscal actions, which will also provide opportunities to some business sectors. Usually private sector participation in a recession will remain low key and hence government expenditure ought to go up, to make up the reduction in private sector spending. Prudent governments will channel resources towards investments that will generate returns on their costs. Banks and lending institutions will have opportunities to undertake well-thought out debt restructurings in such a manner that the debt servicing is in line with income generation capability of viable borrowers. Fundamentally, both borrower and lender must ensure that income grows much faster than the debt burden.

Maintaining a close eye on business cycles would help to create and maintain quality credit assets. Whilst credit assets in cyclical industries are fine during the recovery phase, it is better to identify borrowers displaying weakness in cyclical sectors at the beginning of the recession and exit such credit assets with haste. Or credit enhancement may be sought.

### 5.1.2 Credit Risk in the Business Cycle

In fact both credit risks – obligor credit risk and portfolio credit risk – peak at the top of the business cycle, although this will not usually be realized. It is not unusual for many CEOs and top officials of banks and financial institutions to still insist on a growth strategy believing good times will continue. The resultant non-performing loans and bad debts due to the deterioration in borrowers' financial positions, emanating from declining sales and profits will become apparent during the recession phase.

Many advocate that underwriting more credit risk towards the end of the recession phase is not a bad idea. The logic behind this theory is that the economy could not sink any further down – i.e. the downside risk of the economy is limited. Whilst there is some merit in this view, this need not always be true. It depends upon the business sector and the customer. Moreover, some recessions respond to the monetary action by governments, i.e. reduction in interest rates and creating more money supply can rectify the imbalances created by the recession. However, as the experience of the 1990s in Japan shows, low interest rates need not always spur growth.

## 5.2 ECONOMIC CONDITIONS

Changes in the economy impact entire components, albeit to varying degrees. A growing economy with increased spending by consumers will result in accelerating demand; this in turn encourages production expansion, creating more demand for factors of production, and improving overall employment of resources. A sound working knowledge of critical economic fundamentals is essential for a proper credit risk analysis. One of the best ways to understand an economy is to study the National Income (NI) or Gross National Product (GDP), usually expressed as:

$$Y = C + I + G + (X - M)$$

where

Y = Gross National Income,
C = Consumption
I = Investment
G = Government Spending
X = Exports
M = Imports

### 5.2.1 Private Consumption

This is the largest component in most economies. For example, in many countries, such as the US and India, private consumption accounts for two-thirds of economic activity. What is the relevance of private consumption to understanding external risks? It can reveal lots of things. Private consumption broadly includes all type of goods consumed by the general population such as foodstuffs, clothes, cars, washing machines, home computers, cosmetics, school items, and kitchen utensils to costly interior decorating materials. Hence, changes in private consumption will definitely impact many businesses and hence constitute a risk in themselves.

Given its importance, all responsible governments actively encourage the development of various types of consumer goods and expansion of the consumer market, through budget and various other fiscal/monetary policies. Taxation policy, future expectations, income level and equality of income distribution are some of the factors impacting private consumption. Higher taxation and high levels of inequality are generally seen as suppressant of private consumption while higher future expectations and income level are considered triggers for enhancing consumption.

### 5.2.2 Government Spending

Governments spend not only on basic services such as law and order, defence, education, and social welfare activities but also endeavour to implement various infrastructure projects. Governments are usually concerned with agriculture, water conservancy, ecological environment and infrastructure projects such as railways, highways, telecommunication, power and so on. Whilst changes in government spending directly impact certain sectors such as government contractors, etc., the knock-on impact is felt throughout the economy.

This topic has earned a special significance because the involvement of government in the economy has increased, especially since the 2008 Credit Crisis. Government spending by avowed capitalist nations of the world has also increased. Fiscal spending is also considered as a countercyclical measure. Economists are concerned about the situation when government spending reduces in the economy. It may be noted that reduction in government spending is not always bad as it results in more opportunities in the private sector. Similarly, reduction in government spending enables the government to manage budgetary deficits, resulting in overall greater well-being of the economy.

Hence, the credit risk analysis must consider the impact of the increase or decrease in spending by national/regional/state/local government on various sectors and businesses. The extent to which borrowers' business is dependent on government spending must be studied. If the customer has significant reliance on government spending it may be worth understanding the contingency plans of the customer in case of reduction in spending by government. This could include trimming costs, exploring new markets, reducing inventory levels, etc.

### 5.2.3 Investment

This is one of the key economic activities in any nation and is undertaken by both private and public sectors. The investment is usually made out of savings by various economic agents in the economy. When an economy cannot save enough to meet its various investment needs, then it should seek Foreign Direct Investment (FDI) or development assistance from multilateral agencies such as World Bank and Asian Development Bank. If the gap in investment and savings is funded through foreign borrowings, it places obligations on the borrower – whether private sector and government – to service the debt on schedule. Imbalances may lead to foreign currency related problems.

### 5.2.4 Imports and Exports

Whilst trade between nations dates back thousands of years, it was Adam Smith, hailed as the father of economics, who stated that countries could benefit by mutual exchange just as a tailor does not make his own shoes but exchanges a suit for shoes. Accordingly, an oil rich desert country (Saudi Arabia) will exchange oil for rice, electronic items, automobiles, luxury goods, etc. David Ricardo's comparative advantage theory proposed that although two countries can produce the same items, they will be better off if they concentrate on items with lower comparative costs and exchange them for items with higher comparative cost to produce at home.

Without going into detail, international trade offers each country the opportunity to specialize in the production of the good in which it has the comparative advantage and then exchange it for something in which it has a comparative disadvantage. Unless carefully managed, the changes here can lead to foreign exchange problems, triggering economic crisis. This has been testified to again and again by several economic crises in Latin America, Turkey, Far East Asia, etc. Another important external risk factor will be dealt with in detail later – viz. Balance of Payments.

### 5.2.5 How to Link NI Components to the Firm

Coming back to the use of NI statistics for understanding operating risks facing a business concern, credit risk analysis should attempt to identify the contribution of the particular business segment to the overall economy. For instance, suppose you are analyzing a company engaged in the production of some kind of building material (cement, concrete admixture, waterproofing materials, etc.). It is beneficial to look at the contribution of the construction sector to the overall economy, the rate of growth in the past and that predicted in the near future.

Another way to look at NI figures is to determine the general direction in which the economy is moving. For instance, if there is heavy investment taking place in the economy, it may indicate higher industrial activity in future either for internal consumption or for exports, which will have a knock-on effect in the economy. During 1991 the GDP of South Korea was around $294 billion of which 40% represented investments. The benefits of deploying 40% of GDP into investments in 1991 were reflected in 2001, notwithstanding the Forex crisis of 1997. Between 1991 and 2001 exports soared by 123% (CARR > 12%) to $181 billion while domestic consumption (C) increased by 63% to $255 billion. The cars, computers, televisions and other electronic items manufactured in South Korea were penetrating into other world markets. Viewed against the Forex crisis of 1997/98, the improvement over a decade is remarkable. All businesses, including ancillary industries, in the sectors that witnessed growth ought to have benefited from the robust NI growth. However, on the flip side it is to be noted that excessive investment creating surplus industrial capacity will do more harm than good. In fact the South Korean chip and semiconductor industry faced the problem of surplus capacity. We will look into the factors impacting an industry in the next chapter.

Another use of NI or GDP statistics is to understand the stability of various economic activities. By comparing the contribution to the country's GDP of various economic activities and observing it over a reasonable period of time (say five years), the credit executive can identify the stable economic activities in the economy.

### 5.2.6 Benefits of Study of National Income

The study of NI components and linking them to the business entity brings out relationships, highly useful to evaluate the credit risks involved. The usefulness of NI data lies in the fact that they provide basic information for analytical purposes. Let us discuss a few important firm/obligor level variables influenced by economic conditions that can be identified from the analysis of NI components.

(a) **Revenue and Profits**: Improving consumption under economic growth will result in an increase in consumer goods – both durable and non-durable – resulting in higher sales for the firm's products and services. This in turn will trigger demand for the intermediate and basic components, essential for the production of ultimate consumer products. Overall, sales revenue will increase translating into more profits for businesses. On the other hand, in an economic recession spending will touch lower levels resulting in lower sales, which will lead to the collapse of weak businesses – those with internal flaws or bad structures.

(b) **Identification of Business Categories/Sectors**: The potential rates of growth of different sectors in the economy differ from one another. Usually the agriculture sector has a slower growth rate compared to services, trade and industry. More credit risk exposure may be taken with customers in sectors that display better prospects. As we discussed earlier (and we will discuss more in the credit portfolio risk chapters), banks and FIs categorize sectors in terms of the credit risk appetite. One of the criteria for selection is usually the NI data based sector analysis.

(c) **Business Confidence**: As demand continues to be strong and outstrip the current production level business people may decide to expand their activities. Additional investments stimulate a lot of economic variables such as additional employment, demand for finance, creation of new assets and so on. A higher level of investment activities, as we saw earlier, brings several advantages to the economy. On the other hand during recession business confidence slips resulting in the cancellation of such projects, which not only affects the individual firm's profitability but has an impact on the overall economy too.

Note that we have skipped certain pure economic terms such as multiplier effect, accelerator effect etc., which an interested reader may pursue in good economic text books. In order to facilitate better understanding of the changes in NI components, a logical approach will be adopted. This will provide sufficient detail as to the direction of the economy and risks arising therefrom.

Whilst the abovementioned expression (formula) looks at GDP from an aggregate expenditure point of view, NI can be measured using other techniques also totalling the final outputs. Real GDP is the GDP adjusted for price level changes (inflation).

Economic growth is defined as the rate of change in NI. Usually NI is divided into three sectors – Primary, Secondary and Tertiary. Per capita income is obtained by dividing the GDP by the population. Increase in per capita income is the most commonly adopted measurement for gauging standard of living.

In-depth study of various economic aspects is beneficial, for which reason many companies with sizeable credit portfolios appoint full-time economists. They occupy the highest watchtower to warn about any impeding dangers seen across the zone.

## 5.3 INFLATION AND DEFLATION

A sound credit risk analysis cannot be done without understanding the inflationary (or deflationary) pressures prevailing in the economy, the actions taken by central banks and governments and the impact on the borrower. Inflation, the term used to denote persistent increase in prices and measured by the Consumer Price Index (CPI) and Wholesale Price Index (WPI), is another trigger of external risks. Low levels of inflation, say below 3–5%, are considered normal and good for businesses as they can lead to short-term gains – viz. they can earn more profits. However higher levels of inflation will result in economic problems while hyperinflation (above 50% or 100% p.a) will lead to greater problems. Whilst the reasons for inflationary pressures are beyond our topic, it is appropriate to mention that in almost all situations where there are sudden increases in money supply, if not matched by a similar increase in goods and services, then inflation ensues. Sudden increase in demand or costs, supply shocks, deficit financing and future expectations are some of the other factors that result in imbalance in the supply of goods and money. The credit executive or banker cannot ignore the inflationary risk exposure of the obligor, mainly because of the following:

- Higher levels of inflation will persuade the central bank of the country to increase interest rates, which will usually – while other things remain the same – impact foreign exchange rates. Hence a customer having substantial foreign exchange exposure is likely to be impacted accordingly. The central bank may also take other steps to reduce money supply such as open market operations, or increasing reserve requirements.
- Higher interest rates will sharply eat into the profitability of a business relying on leverage. If the obligor is in a weak financial position with high operating risks or having internal structural defects, adverse credit risk migration is a highly likely scenario.
- Government attempts to reduce inflationary pressures not just by controlling money supply but also through increasing taxation and reducing own expenditure. As we have seen above under 'Economic Conditions' many businesses depend either directly or indirectly on government expenditure, which can have an adverse impact in the immediate future.
- Higher levels of inflation will render domestic goods uncompetitive, which may lead to lower exports. For instance, suppose a dollar buys 20 units of product X. But due to

inflationary pressures the cost of inputs increased and accordingly the producer of product X had to increase the price by 20%. At the new price the foreign buyer will able to buy only 16.67 units of product X. Given intense international competition, the foreign party may go to other competitive markets. On the flip side, higher inflation ought to be beneficial for importers as the imported items will cost less than the domestic products. However, in real life, local governments will attempt to safeguard domestic business through protection measures.

Inflation pushes up costs, which can wreak havoc on credit assets originating from customers with a weak financial position. The real difficulties of hyperinflation were experienced by many Latin American countries in the 1990s and Russia in the mid to late 1990s. For example, Brazil had witnessed average annual inflation rates exceeding 900% during the late 1980s and early 1990s. Long-term planning was difficult as businesses attempted to go long on credit period from supplies while insisting on immediate payments from buyers/debtors. Interest rates were exorbitant as the central bank attempted to control inflation. Such hyperinflation not only required frequent revisions in prices but also influenced negotiations. Renegotiations with suppliers and employees, which normally take place on an annual basis, were carried out on a monthly basis. Before concluding the discussion on inflation risks, it is pertinent to mention that the creditor loses during inflation. We discussed this point in Chapter 1.

Another threat is where deflationary pressures cause a sharp drop in price levels, putting businesses out of control. This is a situation where the majority of the goods and services produced have to be exchanged for lesser prices. Higher levels of deflation are as risky as inflation. Deflation set in in the US after the 1929 Great Crash and in Japan in the 1990s. Deflation is primarily the result of less demand leading to a drop in prices, translating into losses for businesses. This may lead to the shutdown of businesses, in turn leading to more issues such as unemployment, which would further depress demand in the economy, resulting in a vicious circle. Faced with the threat of deflation, central banks would attempt to increase the money supply in the economy – e.g. lower interest rates and open market operations – while the government would introduce fiscal policies – such as a low tax regime – to ensure adequate demand prevails in the economy.

## 5.4 BALANCE OF PAYMENTS AND EXCHANGE RATES

The impact of imports and exports and other foreign transactions such as investment flows and services, among others, is captured by the term balance of payments. It measures how much a country has to pay to the rest of the world or vice versa. It is usually divided into two – capital account and current account. Capital account is usually smaller and consists of purchase/sale of assets, loan/gold transactions, investments, repatriation of capital/dividends and foreign aid, among others. (Some authorities divide the financial assets/liabilities movements into a separate category and classify it as Financial Account.) The current account, which is the largest component, comprises trade in goods and services, repatriation of employee compensation, gifts, donations and so on. Risk lies in the management of balance of payments by governments and has close links with foreign currency rates. So it brings in another risk – volatility in foreign currency rates.

The 1997 Asian crisis had its roots in poor current account management as it resulted in massive deficits led by short-term foreign currency borrowings. When the foreigners got scared, they started to pull out the existing money and were unwilling to extend new facilities, which in turn led to the collapse of currency, which further aggravated the debt position of companies who borrowed in foreign currency, i.e. debt in local currency terms zoomed due to currency devaluations, which further deteriorated their debt service capability.

Whilst the risk emanating from adverse balance of payments and resultant movements in foreign currency rates is systematic in nature, not all businesses are affected to the same extent. Generally, the impact of local currency devaluation or appreciation has the following effect on the businesses (see Figure 5.2):

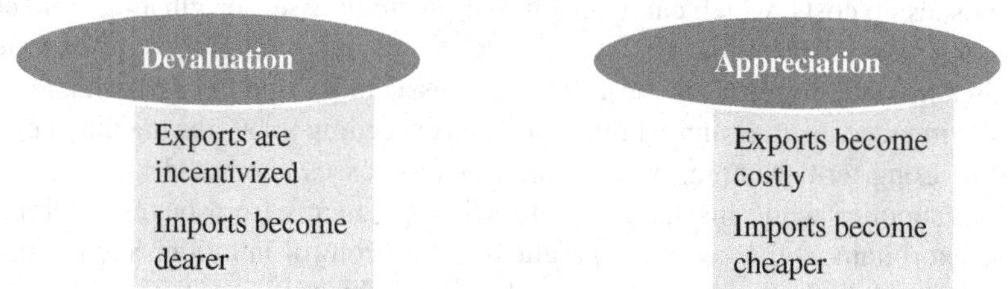


**Figure 5.2** Impact of Devaluation and Appreciation in Currencies

It is the strategy of some export-oriented countries to devalue (or keep devalued) their currencies to sell more in overseas markets.

Currency devaluation of competing nations can impact on domestic industry. The reason is that the currency devaluation of a competing nation effectively results in the appreciation of local currency. For instance, Far East Asian currencies were devalued after the 1997 Crisis. This had significant impact on the hosiery industry in India (mainly, Tirupur in Tamil Nadu) because the overseas buyers began to source goods from Thailand and other Far East exporters (instead of India). Similarly, the appreciation of the Euro in the early half of 2003 hurt exports from the region forcing the European Central Bank (ECB) to slash economic growth forecasts, evidencing the operating risk exposure of the leading exporters of the region. However, a new equilibrium would set in with adjustments to the economy and other macro variables. Credit risk analysis and decisions must take into account and understand how the life (situation) would be after this new equilibrium.

## 5.5 POLITICAL

Business is impacted by political developments, regionally, nationally and internationally. Consequently, business decisions are influenced by both political stability and business friendly policies of the political authorities. Some of the business risks emanating from political factors are confiscation, currency repatriation restrictions, limits to business transactions and legal controls. Government changes and subsequent changes in policies which may cause serious trouble for the long-term plans of businesses are yet another factor. This is why political stability is rated highly for attracting foreign investments. A second type of political risk is not directly linked to government actions but to political events caused by other vested interests. Examples are violence, terrorism, riots, guerrilla/civil wars, etc. There are a number of political events and constraints which will eventually cause loss or harm to a business operating in a foreign environment.

During early 2011, the Middle East and North Africa (MENA) region was impacted by political unrest, resulting in regime change in Tunisia and Egypt. It also resulted in a civil war in

Libya, which forced several companies operating in Oil and Gas and similar industries to invoke the *force majeure* clause in their contracts, evacuate their staff and suspend operations. This caused uncertainties related to the collection of receivables of several companies, including foreign companies, operating in Libya.

Political uncertainties will dampen investments and other spending which in turn has its own economic consequences. Terrorism is yet another political risk in many countries. For instance, during the post 9/11 period, due to terrorism fears, the number of air travellers dropped sharply causing problems for the US airline industry. Despite being one of the two largest countries with proven oil reserves, Iraq is not realizing its full potential given the wars and internal strife.

## 5.6 FISCAL POLICY

Governments use fiscal tools such as direct and indirect taxation, surcharges, disinvestments, levies, duties, tariffs, borrowings and a host of other tools to raise government revenue while government spending includes both routine and planned/unplanned expenditures. As we discussed earlier in this chapter, governments not only spend on providing basic services such as law and order, defence, education and social welfare activities but also endeavour to implement various infrastructure projects. Usually, fiscal spending is also considered as a countercyclical measure. The manner in which the government decides to raise resources and spend has business risk implications.

Annual government budgets are closely watched as they provide a fair idea about government revenues and expenses and the extent of deficits. Business risks emanating from both direct and indirect fiscal policies can sometimes be quite significant. For instance, if the budget deficit is significant, it can unleash inflationary pressures in the economy (or) if income tax levels are increased, disposable income will be lower, impacting certain categories – mostly luxury or durable goods – of business. The lowering of import tariffs, whether due to globalization pressure or otherwise, is yet another instance of business risk emerging from fiscal measures. In India, many toy manufacturers suffered and some of them even wound up their business after the flood of cheaper Chinese imports, following liberalization of import tariffs in 2002.

The level of internal and external debt and foreign exchange reserve holdings should also be tracked. Adverse movement in these variables poses an external risk. For example, it is often stated that any debt in excess of annual GDP could seriously impact economic growth while lower foreign exchange reserves are a forerunner of a foreign exchange crisis with significant economic impact, including economic downturn.

A proper credit risk analysis cannot be done without understanding how fiscal policies impact the business environment.

## 5.7 MONETARY POLICY

Government, usually acting through the central bank of the nation, attempts to control the money supply in the economy to achieve various goals such as stability in price levels and foreign exchange rates, and an economic atmosphere conducive to growth, among others. Changes in interest rates, Forex controls, buying and selling of treasury securities are some of the main tools used by central banks to achieve the desired money level in the economy.

Interest rates are generally kept high to ward off inflationary pressures or neutralize higher demand or to attract foreign investment in securities, among others.

Operating risks emanating from the monetary policies pursued by central banks are far reaching. Many economists point out that the origins of the 2008 Credit Crisis can be traced back to US monetary policy. It is often argued that the liberal (low) interest rate regime by the US Federal Reserve during the early 2000s sowed the seeds of economic (e.g. real estate) troubles in the later part of the decade. The crisis resulted in the collapse of several financial institutions and a sharp fall in stock, commodity and housing markets. The governments of several countries (including the US, UK, Ireland, etc.) had to bail out banks. We have devoted an entire chapter to discussing this Crisis, considered by many economists to be the worst financial crisis since the 1930s Great Depression.

A high interest regime is yet another risky period since demand could fall as economic agents become reluctant to buy or invest with borrowings, i.e. it would result in higher financial expenses. Certain types of industry are more sensitive to interest rates. Often it is seen that during high interest rate regimes, the automobile industry is impacted more than the food industry. While almost all businesses feel the impact, those which directly rely on leverage (i.e. external financing) such as instalment financiers, vehicle lease finance providers etc. will get jolted more during a high interest rate regime.

It should be noted that when interest rates move from 5% to 7.5% the rates have not only increased by 2.5%, but the additional financial burden in absolute terms goes up by 50%! Awareness of the current monetary policies and likelihood of their continuation, together with the ability to gauge the impact on businesses, would definitely lead to better credit decisions.

## 5.8 DEMOGRAPHIC FACTORS

Population structure and composition have immense significance for businesses because they determine most of the ultimate market. Some of its main elements are outlined below:

- A young generation with purchasing power means good times for youth oriented businesses, including sports cars, fancy two-wheelers, fashionable dress, sportswear, trendy shoes, etc.
- An ageing population on the other hand may require more health care and pension support.
- Religion determines the festivals and ceremonies associated with it, which is a good business season for most consumer goods, with knock-on effects on the whole economy.
- Similarly, ethnic mixes and their customs and celebrations provide unique business opportunities.
- Level of education. Generally, the demand of an educated population differs from an uneducated one, with better awareness of the former, translating into more demand, including knowledge related items.
- Working women in the population result in potential business for fast-cook items, time-saving household equipment, etc.
- Culture patterns determine dress codes, fashion, style, festivals as well as entertainment and other factors, having influence on businesses.

Almost all businesses are impacted – directly or indirectly – by demographic factors, which is another source of opportunities and risks. The demographic factors can be further sub-divided into vegetarians/non-vegetarians, joggers, holidaymakers, smokers/non-smokers, teetotalers, married/non-married, children (infants, school-going or college-going), heart patients, diabetics and so on depending upon the suitability to the nature of activity/business under consideration.

A rising population generally drives demand for consumer products and augurs well for the economy provided per capita income also rises. Changes in components of the population are also critical. The ageing population of Europe would drive the demand for elderly health care and migrant labour. A study of demographic factors is usually very important as far as identification of external risks and opportunities is concerned.

It is interesting to see how the challenges of external risks are managed by businesses. When a change in the food habits of the population began to impact the demand for fatty burgers, McDonalds introduced salads into their menu. However, *Punch* magazine in the UK, which had existed for over 150 years, had to close in 2002 as it didn't evolve with the demographic shift.

## 5.9 REGULATORY FRAMEWORK

The number of regulations imposed on business and penalties for non-compliance is another source of potential operating risks. They can be from customs, income tax, excise, sales tax, inspections under Factories Act, Companies Act and similar enactments by government authorities. In a modern society regulations are inevitable while excessive regulations will dampen risk taking and open doors to corrupt practices. A general understanding of regulations can indicate the potential operating risks and their possible impact on businesses.

Additionally, a proper, effective and effectual legal system goes a long way to ensuring business confidence and hence provides a suitable business environment where businesses can flourish. Absence of a good legal system or inordinate delays in legal process are potential operating risks, especially if significant disputes or legal issues threaten to emerge from business activities.

## 5.10 TECHNOLOGY

One of the main features of the 20th century was the vast number of new technologies developed, which is expected to continue with increasing momentum in the 21st century as well. If you are lucky enough to be alive and able to check 50 or even 25 years from now, you will be able to see that most of the so-called advanced technologies of today will be classified as outdated. Whilst the internal R&D of businesses can come up with new ideas and technologies, the risk is that someone else might be developing a better one! Or the cost of production under current production technology will turn out to be greater because the new technology may result in less consumption of inputs or lower process time resulting in lower cost of production or better quality products. Nowadays technology is considered a very vital source of operating risk and most of the project financing institutions insist on independent technology evaluation reports while assessing applications.

## 5.11 ENVIRONMENT ISSUES

The tradeoff between environmental protection and economic growth could provide challenges and opportunities to businesses while impacting government policy making. Given the warnings about global warming, changing climate and related issues, all governments accord the utmost importance to environmental matters. Approval from environment agencies is a must to commence various business ventures. In credit risk analysis, environmental risk is becoming increasingly important. Failure by borrowers to comply with the environment related rules and regulations is a critical credit risk. It may be noted that environment agencies have the power to enforce closure/shut down of polluting enterprises. Any such closure of the borrower's business could lead to credit loss.

Accordingly, the person conducting credit risk analysis must have sufficient knowledge about existing and emerging environment regulations to understand whether the borrowers carry significant environment risk. If necessary, the help of environment consultants may be sought. As a corollary, it may be noted that association with customers engaged in environment damaging activities or habitual violators of environmental regulations may have negative reputational impact.

## 5.12 INTERNATIONAL DEVELOPMENTS

In the ever-shrinking world, the events in other countries can sometimes have far reaching consequences in businesses operating in another part of the world as well. The best instance is the post September 11, 2001 consequences in the US, which had adverse impact on the software industry in India, although this had recovered somewhat by late 2003. After the Lehman collapse in 2008, there was an economic slowdown in the US economy. The consequent fear of less energy demand in the US and elsewhere in the world resulted in crude oil prices crashing to below US $40/- per barrel in December 2008 vs. US $140/- per barrel in July 2008, which contributed to recessionary conditions in some of the crude oil exporting nations, such as the United Arab Emirates during 2009.

Similarly at the time of writing this book, the economic situation in Greece is causing jitters in the Eurozone with speculation that Greece may exit the Euro. The Eurozone crisis has its impact across the globe – for instance, this has resulted in lower exports from China to the Eurozone, which is partly blamed for the slowdown in economic growth in China during the first half of 2012. Given the fact that China is the largest exporter in the world and accounts for a significant portion of the world's total economic output,[4] some economists highlight that further slowdown may significantly reduce imports (such as base metals and minerals) from other countries, e.g. Australia.

## 5.13 OTHERS

Several other external risks are possible depending upon the situation. For example, earthquakes may be considered as an external risk in certain countries. During 2011 there were major earthquakes in Japan and New Zealand that shook the respective economies.

Similarly, contagious diseases can be the source of external risk. For example the outbreak of Severe Acute Respiratory Syndrome (SARS) in 2003 had most significant negative effects on the Hong Kong economy till the threat faded away. During this period, consumption, exports, services, tourism and air travel were severely affected. Yellow fever and plagues have taken a huge toll on the human population and impacted economic activities in the past centuries.

[4] The International Monetary Fund (IMF) estimates that China had consumed 40% of the world's base metals – aluminum, copper, lead, tin, zinc or nickel – in 2010.

Militant unionism is yet another risk. Establishing a union and negotiating/bargaining/striking, etc. for improved employment conditions is an accepted phenomenon in today's world, although exceptions can be found in certain countries in the Middle East, Africa, etc. However, excessive unionism, disregarding the business realities, is an operating risk as it may lead to financial/operating difficulties (constant strikes, disruption of production, lower productivity, etc.), which have made many a business unviable.

## 5.14 MONITORING EXTERNAL RISKS

External risks require close monitoring. Lack of knowledge or awareness of external risk factors is a big risk in itself. It is recommended that Early Warning Indicators be prepared and tracked at appropriate levels. A threshold limit may be placed on each critical external risk factor, the breach of which must trigger action. A sample External Risk Early Warning Indicators table is given in Table 5.1:

**Table 5.1** Illustration of Early Warning Indicators

| Indicator | Trigger | Triggered? | Action / Comment |
|---|---|---|---|
| Geo-political Situation | Change in Government/ Political (in)Stability | No/Yes | If triggered an action plan to be prepared, focusing on the vulnerable areas of the credit portfolio |
| Crude Oil Price | Above $125 per Barrel | No/Yes | |
| Inflation | Exceeds 4% | No/Yes | |
| Significant Stock Correction | Exceeds 12% During Last 2 months | No/Yes | An impact paper may be prepared |
| | | | Measures may be taken to ensure Credit Enhancement, Exit or Exposure Reduction strategies |
| Significant Real Estate Correction | Exceeds 5% During Last 3 months | No/Yes | |
| Level of Foreign Currency Reserves | Satisfactory/Adequate | No/Yes | |
| Govt Debt/GDP ratio | Exceeds 50% | No/Yes | |

GDP and industrial production, currency depreciation/appreciation, stock market performance, Forex reserves (relative to GDP or foreign debt), external/foreign debt trend, balance of payments, credit growth and similar macroeconomic indicators may be tracked through the 'Early Warning Indicator' system. For example, foreign exchange reserve holding, expressed as a ratio (to foreign debt or GDP), is a good indicator of a possible foreign exchange or economic crisis.

Along with the above indicators, it may be better if corroborative indicators are also used such as (i) rail traffic, (ii) truck traffic, (iii) airline load factors, (iv) hotel occupancy, (v) electricity consumption, etc. Similarly, an eye must be kept on conflicts in the direction shown by the indicators. For example, whilst the balance of payments of the Russian economy during 1997 had shown a healthy position, its foreign reserves were going down, which finally led to the Russian financial crisis in August 1998 when the Russian government devalued the Rouble and defaulted on its debt. This led to financial difficulties for several financial institutions and the collapse of reputed firms such as LTCM.[5]

A criticism of this system is that during the 2008–09 Credit Crisis several financial institutions failed despite the presence of 'Early Warning Indicator' systems. However, it may be noted that the financial institutions that survived also had similar systems. To be effective, the system should (i) be intelligently designed and monitored, (ii) have good indicators, relevant for the business model of the bank or FI and (iii) a strong action plan and measures must be taken and implemented if triggers are breached.

The external risks are dynamic and inclusive. The above discussion, whilst it covers most of the important sources of operating risks from the external environment, is not exclusive. In other words, more external risks are possible given the circumstances of the business under consideration.

Inherent business strengths, wise strategies and timely actions can nullify or reduce the impact of external risks. This is the hallmark of good business management.

Another aspect to be borne in mind is that most of the external variables (discussed above) are sources not only of operating risks but also of opportunities. For instance, changes in demographic/social factors, the recovery phase of the business cycle, etc., among others, provide a host of business opportunities to grow, expand and diversify.

Finally, the external variables are often interlinked. For example, whilst economic conditions and political situations are two major external risks, they may be linked depending upon the circumstances. Economic problems can lead to political instability, as was the case with Argentina in 2002/03 where there were three changes of president within a span of one year. Some African countries' economies, despite mineral wealth, fail to achieve growth momentum due to the civil strife and poor political administration. Also note that business cycles, national income and monetary and fiscal policies are also closely related. Changes in one ought to impact others as well.

## ✍ QUESTIONS/EXERCISES

1. Explain the importance of business cycle analysis and national income study while conducting the credit risk analysis of a corporate/business customer.
2. Understand the current monetary and fiscal policy in your country. Discuss the reasons why such policies are followed. Investigate whether these policies are likely to change in the near future and identify the industry or sectors that would be impacted by such changes.
3. What are the demographic factors you would be interested in if you were conducting a credit risk analysis of a major consumer durable manufacturer?
4. You are a Relationship Manager in a bank and one of your customers has decided to double their manufacturing capacity. The project cost would be funded mostly by debt. What would be your views if the current economic forecast shows that the economy could face an economic slowdown? Will it be different if most of the company's production is exported? Would you be paying attention to the interest rate forecasts?

[5] The Long Term Capital Management (LTCM) Board of Directors included Nobel laureates in Economics; however LTCM collapsed during the Russian financial crisis. We will discuss more about this later in the book.

5. The Head of Business of your bank argues that after continuous decline over the last two years, the real estate sector has now stabilized, if not bottomed out. He has submitted a business case, proposing a strategy to significantly increase real estate exposure in the credit portfolio, over the next six months to one year. As Head of Credit Risk of the bank, what macroeconomic factors would you consider while studying this proposal?
6. One of your friends states that the banks contribute towards business cycles (an external risk). While the banks over-lend during boom times resulting in over-leveraged (debt burdened) business firms, they cut credit lines to business during an economic downturn, choking trade flows. Do you agree with this statement? Please explain with reasons.
7. Read any business daily (for a period of at least one month) and record the major external risks discussed in the newspaper. If you are managing a credit portfolio, you may link such external risk to the borrowers in your credit portfolio.
8. From 2010 onwards, Greece has faced a debt crisis, impacting its economic growth. Examine the government debt/GDP ratio during this period (and the immediately preceding years) and analyze whether this ratio could have acted as an 'Early Warning Indicator'.

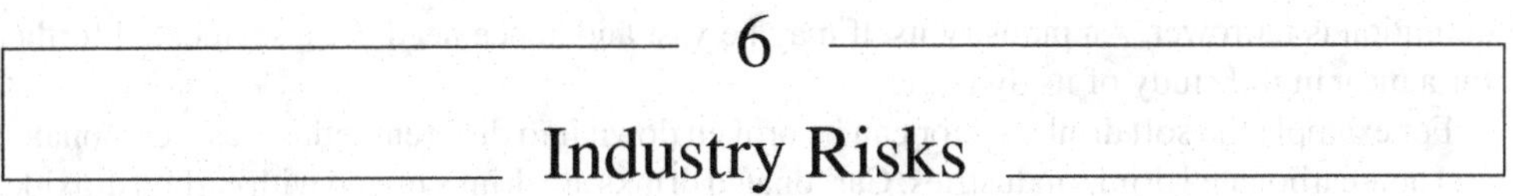

# 6
# Industry Risks

During the 1950s and 1960s, the clicking sound of typewriters was the hallmark of any office. Nowadays, you may find a traditional typewriter in very few offices. Let us look at a few industries that have vanished:

- The typewriter industry, which once prospered, is eclipsed by the computer industry.
- The pager industry, once hailed as a path-breaking new technology, is now almost non-existent, with the advent of more versatile mobile phones.
- Gramophone record players were pushed out by cassette players. Now they are giving way to compact disc players. Similarly the video cassette industry has also waned significantly.
- The dominance of US railroads dropped with the emergence of a new aviation industry in the last century.

Even within a given industry, different patterns of domination and paradigm shifts are observed, especially in technology. For example the traditional mobile phone segment faces severe challenges from the smart phones segment.

Industries decline and vanish, along with the participants in them. Hence, industry analysis is an indispensable part of credit risk analysis. The life stage, composition, nature, characteristics and structure of an industry are to be studied which will answer the following questions:

1. Why does the profitability differ among various industries?
2. What are the reasons for consistency in profitability in certain industries while others show wide fluctuations?
3. How do the operating risks differ from one industry to another?
4. What are the implications of industry risks?
5. What are the forces determining the level of competition in an industry?
6. Will an industry that performed well in one time period continue to do well in future?

Industry analysis shows how diverse and different forces act on an industry impacting its survival and profitability and indicates the fate of players in it. If industry profitability is low, it is very unlikely that the participants or players in the industry will enjoy high profitability. Given the fact that profitability is vital for survival of a business unit, insight into the various risk factors impacting industry and key profit drivers acts as a powerful tool for studying the creditworthiness of firms in that industry.

## 6.1 UNDERSTANDING OBLIGOR'S INDUSTRY OR MARKET

### 6.1.1 Sector vs. Industry vs. Market Segment

Identifying and understanding the sector and industry of the obligor is important for credit risk analysis and management. Many use sector and industry interchangeably. However there is a subtle difference between the two. The term 'sector' is more comprehensive while 'industry' definition is narrower. An industry itself may be vast and hence need to be segmented further for a meaningful study of its dynamics.

For example the soft drinks sector can be broken down into different industries – carbonated and non-carbonated drinks industries. Carbonated drinks are drinks mixed with carbon dioxide. World renowned brands Coca Cola and Pepsi belong to this industry. The non-carbonated industry is huge and includes a variety of drinks such as bottled juice, chilled juice, ambient juice, pure juice, hot chocolate, iced tea, flavoured milk, milkshakes, etc. Accordingly, this industry needs to be categorized into market segments. The diagrammatic representation of the soft drinks sector is as given in Figure 6.1:

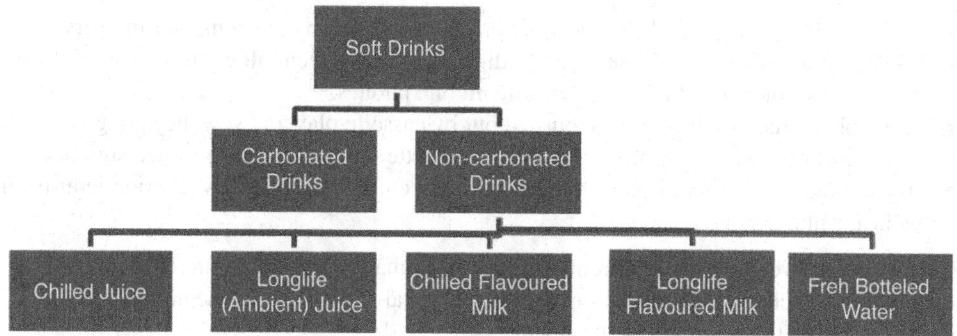


**Figure 6.1** Breakdown of Sector into Industry and Market Segments
*Note:* The above diagram is for illustration purposes. More market segmentations are possible.

An industry or market may be further classified into more meaningful sub-segments for the purpose of identifying a comparable peer group, growth drivers and related key risks. It can be based on the size of the firm or nature of the activity or any other meaningful factor as given below:

- Based on size of the firm. – e.g. the construction contracting industry has numerous players and hence is usually classified into three segments – large, medium and small.
- Based on the nature of component – e.g. wholesale trade may be segmented into different categories such as wholesale trade of clothing, wholesale trade of edible oils or wholesale trade of building materials.
- More elaborate segmentation is also possible. For example, the retail industry can initially be divided into two segments: (i) value retailing, which is typically a low margin-high volume business such as food and groceries, and (ii) luxury retailing, a high margin-low volume business, e.g. high end apparel, electronics and footwear. Further subdivision into various categories is possible e.g. (i) textile and apparels, (ii) food and beverages, (iii) electronics, (iv) toys, (v) consumer durables, (vi) home solutions, (vii) jewellery and watches, (viii) books, music and gifts, (ix) pharmaceuticals, etc.

Banks and FIs usually follow their own industry classifications or follow Standardized Industrial Classification (SIC) Codes, which have wider acceptance.

### 6.1.2 Challenges of Industry Classification

The problem of including a business entity in a particular industry is a demanding job. Although it can be easy in certain cases, there are many instances where the ideal industrial classification can have more than a single option. While it is easy to place commercial aircraft manufacturers, where do we include the manufacturers of plastic cans? Do they come within the can industry, or the packaging industry, or the plastics industry or the petrochemical industry? Similarly, as given in the above diagram we have included flavoured milk in the soft drinks category. However, aren't they a part of the dairy industry as well?

Intelligent classification of industry is vital for the study of credit risk of an obligor as it facilitates proper understanding of the peer group and industry dynamics. Hence, adequate care should be taken to ensure correct industry categorization. (The reader may refer to business dailies and compare their industry classifications.) One of the best ways to undertake industry classification of an obligor is to understand its major competitors – this can often be a good criterion for proper classification of the obligor in an industry.

## 6.2 TYPES OF INDUSTRY RISKS

Before getting down to the details of industry analysis, it is better to split the industry risks into three, as given below:

(a) **Risks Emanating from External Environment**: This type of industry risk originates from the changes taking place in the overall exterior system. For instance, suppose the government decides to lower import tariffs, causing cheaper imports from foreign producers. This impacts overall industry profitability as the competition from cheaper imports forces industry players to reduce prices. During the globalization era, industries relying on protection tariff barriers remain worried. Similarly, change in consumer preferences is a major external risk for consumer focused industries, especially fashion reliant businesses. Also a hike in interest rates by the central bank of the country would affect the automobile industry, as higher interest rates would dampen the demand for vehicles.

(b) **Industry Specific Risks**: Risks that are confined to an industry where the source of risk lies within the industry. For example, new entrants contribute to fierce competition causing retaliation from existing players in the industry, resulting in price wars, lowering industry profitability. Similarly, the bargaining power of suppliers and buyers is another industry specific risk. We will discuss this later in this chapter under 'Porter's Model'.

(c) **Risks Emanating from Industry Drivers**: Almost all industries are driven by a few key demand factors that determine the growth of the industry. Let us take the example of the construction industry. This is a key industry of any economy and plays a significant role in the nation's development. Major drivers of the construction sector emanate from demand for (a) residential housing, (b) commercial and industrial buildings and (c) roads, bridges, flyovers, ports and other infrastructure projects. Identification and understanding of the key drivers of an industry are important. Any factor that adversely affects such driver is a risk. Let us examine the key drivers of three more industries as illustrative examples:

- Crude oil prices and oil rig industry: When the oil price goes up, oil firms drill more and deeper in offshore oil fields, increasing output or exploration activity. This results in an increase in rig hire rates and boosts capital expenditure on oil-rigging assets, with favourable impact on the rig industry.
- Automobiles and tyre industry: The tyre industry is dependent on the demand for automobiles. Usually the tyre manufacturers ramp up their production capacities in line with growing automobile sales.
- Transportation and automobile industry: It is again interesting to note that the demand for automobiles is driven by other factors such as transportation demand (both passenger and cargo) and oil prices.

It is evident that the factors that contribute to the industry risks are interconnected, which sometimes results in complexities. Hence, usually large banks and FIs employ separate industry specialists for each industry where they have significant credit exposure.

## 6.3 INDUSTRY LIFE CYCLE

The US pager industry which had its origins in the 1950s witnessed a boom in the 1960s and 1970s and began its decline in the late 1980s/early 1990s as the mobile phone industry emerged. Although pagers are still used in certain specific areas, it is out of the mass market. Just as a living being moves from birth to adolescence to youth to middle age and to old age, the life of an industry can be captured by a five-stage model. However, unlike human beings certain types of industries enjoy a life cycle spanning centuries, such as shipping, insurance, banking, railways, etc. Proper industrial classification and a sound understanding of the stage through which the industry is going through are essentials. Figure 6.2 throws more light on this concept.

Let us examine the five stages of the life of an industry in more detail.

(a) **Pioneering Stage**: During this phase, the industry faces an uncertain future with modest sales growth as the market for products of the industry is small. Markets are still to be developed while prospective beneficiaries of the products are to be informed and educated; the removal of initial apprehensions/hesitations is yet another aspect of this stage. Evidently the operating risk associated with this stage is immensely high with doubtful if not negligable profitability and low sales.

(b) **Rapid Growth Stage**: Once the industry passes through the pioneering stage successfully, the next stage is characterized by increasing demand, accelerating sales and high profitability. Market is established with substantial demand for the products of the industry. The limited number of players in the industry face little competition and the increasing market ensures considerable business. The production capacities are rapidly enhanced to meet the ever increasing demand. The industry operating risks are low at this stage as sales and profits grow at over 50% (or even 100%) a year!

(c) **Maturity Growth**: At this stage the sharp growth in sales and profits vanish as demand slackens with a steady pattern emerging. Attracted by the success of the few players in the Growth Stage, many new entrants emerge in the industry, which also cause the profitability to drop to normal levels. Sales growth remains above the economy growth rate, but no longer accelerates.

(d) **Stabilization**: In this stage, which is probably the longest phase, the industry growth is almost identical to that of the economy. Whilst the sales move in tandem with the

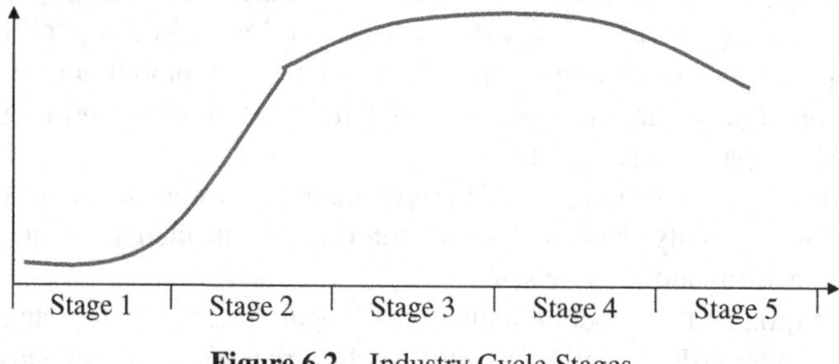


**Figure 6.2** Industry Cycle Stages

economy, the individual firms in the industry vary in profits depending upon the management capabilities. Depending upon the barriers to entry, the intensity of competition varies while the profit margins and rates of return on capital of individual firms eventually become more or less equal. Firms in the industry that earn better than industry profitability, ought to have distinct sustainable competitive advantages, which will be discussed in the next chapter.

(e) **Decline (and Death)**: The demand moves away from the industry and sales growth gives way to decline. Better and new substitutes, changes in consumer tastes and choices, and new technologies are some of the reasons for the decline and demise of industries. Whilst cassette players spelt the doom of gramophones, computers pushed the punched card industry into oblivion. Horse-driven carriages vs. automobiles, and pagers vs. mobile phones are some other examples. Evidently, operating risks at this stage tends to be on the higher side.

The industry life cycle establishes a powerful link to the overall growth pattern and establishes operating risk levels. Generally speaking, whilst the growth and stabilization stages can be considered to be low/moderate risk stages, the introduction and decline stage are high risk categories.

## 6.4 PERMANENCE OF INDUSTRY

Another useful concept in understanding industry-level risks is assessing its permanence. Industrial profitability pales into insignificance if its life is short. Similarly, an industry in the last stages of its life cycle has less permanence. In fact, the life cycle of an industry and its permanence are related in certain aspects. If the life cycle of an industry is very short, it denotes lack of permanence. Most of the fashion related industry displays this phenomenon. Another instance is where the external risks act upon the life cycle such that the industry's permanence in the local economy becomes affected. For example, due to the strict environmental laws in developed nations many chemical related industries have shifted to developing nations. Reduction in protection by local governments may cause the demise of certain industries, whether because of cheaper alternatives (imports) from countries having comparative advantages or otherwise. For instance, the ship breaking industry has shifted to nations with lower labour costs. Permanence of industry and its relative importance in the local economy should be studied for a proper credit risk analysis.

Having credit exposure to industries which are on the decline, or being phased out, involves high risk, which should be avoided unless strong mitigants are present. In today's world of rapid changes, especially in technology, the permanence of industry is of vital importance.

## 6.5 GOVERNMENT SUPPORT

The priorities of government do affect industry. Whilst governments actively protect and encourage certain industries, other industries might be facing active discouragement and no protection at all. Some industries might be treated with apathy with no signs of favour or disfavour from government. Central/State and other government authorities have different interests in adopting such policies. During the pre-independence period of colonial times, generally the colonial rulers or their dependent rulers (e.g. Rajas or Kings protected by the British Raj in the Indian Peninsula) did not encourage any local industry. On the other hand, during the post-independence period, the encouragement of industries was official policy. Certain countries such as Japan, Korea and other East Asian national governments are active supporters of industries especially those with significant export potential. Chinese government support for its various industries has enabled them to become efficient global competitors.

The second tier of government preference is with regard to specific industries. Whilst the general attitude of government towards industry as a whole (nationalization, liberalization, etc.) is important, specific industry driven policies are vital. Most governments are against the tobacco industry and devise policies discouraging smoking and other forms of tobacco consumption. The liquor industry is banned in some Middle East countries. Sometimes the government comes forward to support industries. Soon after 9/11 the US government came forward with a package worth billions of dollars to keep the airline industry in the US afloat. Similarly, after the collapse of Lehman Brothers in 2008, the US government pumped billions into the US banking industry.

Another category of operating risk emanates from the actions of foreign governments. This is akin to international development which we discussed in the previous chapter.

## 6.6 INDUSTRY AND FACTORS OF PRODUCTION

The availability of suitable factors of production influences industry. Land (natural endowments), labour, capital and entrepreneurship are the classic concepts of factors of production. Some experts identify 5Ms – Money, Man, Machines, Material and Management – as the factors of production. Risks related to the factors of production are vital as they dictate competitiveness, especially on a global scale. Natural advantages such as proximity to raw material may affect the success of industry in a particular country or area while labour conditions may be the success factor of another industry in another country. Of the factors of production capital or money is highly mobile, especially in recent times with the globalization process.

Whilst China is accepted as one of the countries with cheap labour, India is well known for its software professionals. Similarly, petroleum and petrochemical industries flourish in the Middle East due to natural endowments such as oil and gas. Entrepreneurship is at its highest in the markets of capitalist economies, where profits drive individuals (or a group) of certain abilities to take the lead and attempt calculated risks. Japanese entrepreneurship and labour productivity are stated to be amongst the top in the world, ensuring global leadership in several industries. Lack of or absence of favourable factors of production is a source of industry related operating risk.

## 6.7 INDUSTRY AND BUSINESS CYCLES

Whilst we have seen that business cycles are one of the sources of external risks, we may give a further close look to the industry context because different industries display dissimilar patterns during business cycles. In fact, most industries are impacted by business cycles, though to differing degrees. Some industries fluctuate more while others are less subject to fluctuation. Based on the sensitivity to cycles, industries can be categorized as follows:

- **Cyclical Industry**: An industry that moves in tandem with business cycles is generally known as a cyclical industry. The construction and chemical industries can be considered examples of cyclical industries. Most of the industries linked to these cyclical industries or sectors would also be impacted. However, there could be a difference as to what stage a particular industry would be impacted. For example, while the cement industry may feel the impact of declining construction in the early stages, the paint industry would feel the impact a little later as the ongoing construction of existing projects would continue to generate demand for some time longer.

- **Non-Cyclical**: These industries are not impacted by cycles. Food, utilities and the pharmaceutical industry are some of the sectors considered to be non-cyclical, the main reason being that the end products of non-cyclical industries are essentials of life. Auditing and finance consultancy and the legal profession are also considered non-cyclical. With the sharp fall in demand in cyclical downturns, many businesses will plan restructuring or downsizing and turn to financial consultants to revisit the strategies and other plans drawn up during good times. Similarly, many business deals that were inked in during a cyclical boom may no longer be sustainable, which could give rise to disputes and other legal issues as counterparties struggle or fail to perform.
- **Counter-Cyclical**: Some industries are even classified as counter-cyclical, which means that demand goes up when other industries are declining or hitting rock bottom in cycles.

A study of historical trends covering at least one full business cycle (say around ten years) will show the extent of the cyclical nature of an industry. Broadly speaking, the higher the cycle orientation, the higher the operating risk. Firms in such industries ought to have mitigants such as a strong finance structure, capable management having ample experience in taking the business through troubled waters, low operating and financial leverage (see Chapter 8) and strong shareholders, among others. Otherwise, by the time the next recovery phase happens, the business may not be there to reap the benefits.

## 6.8 INDUSTRY PROFITABILITY

In order to study and understand a firm's profit and cash generation potential, an analyst should first of all assess the potential of the industry. Profitability of various industries differs systematically and predictably over a period of time. It is the intensity of competition that determines the potential of an industry together with the following other four forces (known as Five Forces Model or Porter's Model, called after Prof. Michael Porter of Harvard University, who introduced the concept in the 1980s), depicted in Figure 6.3 below:

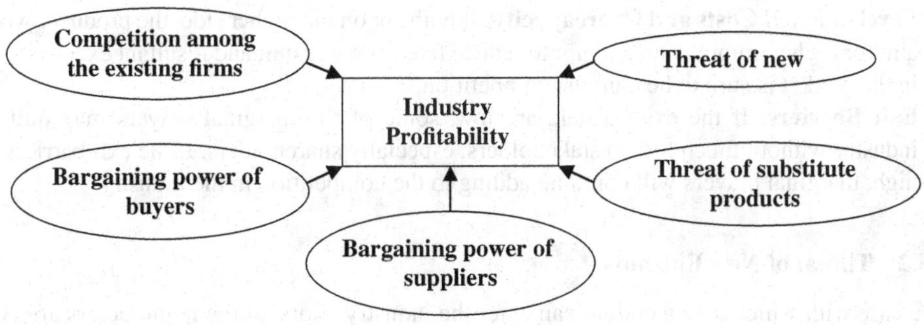


**Figure 6.3** Porter's Model

### 6.8.1 Competition Among the Existing Firms Within the Industry

Whilst there is cut throat price competition in certain industries to attract and retain customers, others compete on non-price factors, including but not limited to after sales service, brand image, etc. The main factors determining the intensity of competition among rivals within an industry are:

1. **Industry Growth Rate**: The higher the growth rate, the lower the competition as space constantly increases enabling the accommodation of all players in the industry. Accordingly, there is no need to pursue grabbing market share from others. On the other hand if the industry growth trend is negative, existing players would attempt to survive or to grow and rivals would attempt to grab market share from others by pursuing intensive competition tactics/strategies.
2. **Number of Rivals**: If rivals are few, as in the case of an oligopoly, an implicit understanding or rules of competition may be laid down to restrict competition to common advantage. The best examples are that of Cola giants, Pepsi and Coke and petroleum distributing companies. On the other hand if the players are numerous and fragmented, competition tends to be severe.
3. **Differentiation**: If products are differentiated by branding or by other means, competition tends to be less intense as each player in the field has developed or created its own target segment. For example, whilst Toyota cars are largely aimed at the middle-income group, BMW focuses on and produces cars for luxury conscious or upper class customers. Toyota itself brands certain vehicles for upper and luxury segments using a differential strategy (i.e. the Lexus brand of vehicles). Differentiation by market segment, quality, image and other means can be observed in most of the consumer oriented industries (please see the next chapter for more discussion on Differentiation Strategy). The ultimate aim of differentiation is to lessen competition by having a captive or loyal market. On the other hand, if the product is such that differentiation is impossible (viz. commodity type), prices determine the business and accordingly price competition is intense. Examples include agricultural products and other unbranded items.
4. **Switching Costs**: If the switching costs are higher, competition tends to be less intense as the consumer would prefer to continue with the same product to avoid higher switching costs. On the other hand if the switching costs are lower, competition is tough. Whilst in industrial intermediary products and capital goods switching costs are high, persuading the buyer to rely on the same source repeatedly, switching costs in consumer goods tend to be lower, which manufacturers attempt to overcome by differentiation.
5. **Level of Fixed Costs and Overcapacity**: If both are on the higher side, the producer would aim for higher output in an attempt to reduce fixed cost per unit and resultant excess supply in the market is sure to heat up the competition.
6. **Exit Barriers**: If the exit barriers are low, some of the marginal players may quit the industry without much loss to stakeholders, especially shareholders. If the exit barriers are high, marginal players will continue adding to the competition in the industry.

### 6.8.2 Threat of New Entrants

The ease with which a new entrant can enter the industry is one of the main factors affecting the profitability. If new entrants cannot enter the field despite attractive or abnormal profits in the industry, the existing players can be assured of predictable and sustainable profitability. On the other hand, if new entrants can easily enter the industry, the attractiveness of the industry will disappear, as more firms vie for market share. So the higher the entry barriers, the better for existing players; the barriers are determined by the following:

1. **Economies of Scale**: Large economies of scale act as a barrier for a new entrant because the new entrant needs to invest heavily to compete effectively on a similar scale. Accordingly, new entrants may lack capital or may not wish to risk failure by building up capacity below the optimum size. Economies of scale arise in various forms – huge production capacity of existing players, brand image (soft drinks industry), substantial investment in property and equipment (telecommunications), etc.
2. **First Mover Advantage**: Early entrants or pioneers in the industry can dominate in such a way that a new entrant cannot pose a direct challenge to the first mover. The best example is Microsoft in the household software segment. In other industries, the first mover might have tied up all the raw material supply or might have established close connections with the suppliers and other key counterparts of the industry. For example, most of the Middle East oil and gas concessions for fossil fuel are controlled by American oil giants, because of the first mover advantage.
3. **Channels of Distribution and Relationships**: High cost of developing new channels can be an effective entry barrier. Sometimes the existing strong relationships among customers in an industry make it difficult for new entrants. Examples of this kind include auditing, investment banking, advertising, etc.
4. **Legal Barriers**: These also act as an effective barrier for a new entrant, e.g. licensing, patents, copyrights, etcs.

### 6.8.3 Threat of Substitute Products

If substitute products are available, then the industry profitability is affected by the factors influencing the substitutes. If tea and coffee are substitutes, the suppliers of coffee cannot increase the price beyond a certain point as consumers will prefer tea. Thus the competition from the tea industry affects the demand and profitability of coffee industry. Railways and other means of land transportation are substitutes and it is common to see people use substitute facilities more when rates are increased in one type of transportation. Over long distances, railways and airlines may be considered as substitutes. As far as entertainment is concerned, films and TV serials and theme parks are substitutes. Ultimately, the threat from substitutes is affected by (a) relative price, (b) relative performance or the ability to satisfy and (c) customers' willingness to pay for the substitute. These differ from industry from industry and are affected by several factors. Usually, if both products serve the same identical function, price is the key determinant of choice. If one product offers more efficiency, the consumer may be willing to pay a higher price for the greater efficiency or satisfaction offered by it.

### 6.8.4 Bargaining Power of Buyers

Industrial profitability is influenced by the customers' bargaining power. In case the buyers have substantial bargaining power – as the automobile manufacturers have with spare part suppliers or computer assemblers vs. software suppliers – then industrial profitability is somewhat hampered. On the other hand, if buyers are fragmented they do not command any bargaining power: broadly, the bargaining power (BP) of buyers is as per the following table:

| Details | Yes | No |
|---|---|---|
| Price sensitivity to the buyer | BP Exists | No BP |
| Substantial % of total cost of the buyer | BP Exists | No BP |
| Is product bought is differentiated | No BP | BP Exists |
| Is quality of product important | No BP | BP Exists |
| Bargaining power – Are buyers fragmented? | No BP | BP Exists |
| – Is volume bought high | BP Exists | No BP |
| – Alternatives | BP Exists | No BP |
| – Backward integration | BP Exists | No BP |

### 6.8.5 Bargaining Power of Suppliers

As in the case of buyers, suppliers also determine industrial profitability, depending upon the extent of their influence. If suppliers have substantial bargaining power – as Coke and Pepsi have with bottlers – then the bottlers' profitability is somewhat hampered. On the other hand, if suppliers are fragmented they do not have any bargaining power: broadly, it is as per the following table:

| Details | Yes | No |
|---|---|---|
| Is product bought differentiated | BP Exists | No BP |
| Is quality of product important | BP Exists | No BP |
| Bargaining power – No. of sellers high? | No BP | BP Exists |
| – Alternatives | No BP | BP Exists |
| – Forward integration | BP Exists | No BP |

The Five Forces model, if effectively used, is a strong tool to understand the industry and its profitability. Since a discrete factor is important, the combined view of all factors is needed. The credit analyst/manager/approver ought to be able to link the findings in the Five Forces model to the obligor.

**Example 6.1**

**Application of Porter's Model**

If you study the airlines industry and try to link to a player in the industry – say Emirates Airlines (EA), the flagship carrier of Emirate of Dubai – then you must understand how the Porter's Model dynamics are applicable to the company. Your study will show that the airlines industry is cyclical and has relatively high operating leverage (e.g. high depreciation) and capital intensity, given the heavy investment in costly aircraft. Applying the model to the industry would show following results:

1. Competition from regional and international airlines (both conventional and low cost carriers) is intense.

2. Entry barriers are high due to heavy capital intensity and obstacles to getting landing rights, etc.
3. Threat of substitutes. Whilst rail or road transport can be a substitute, for long-haul passenger traffic, there is virtually no substitute.
4. Bargaining power of buyers exists as they can select from various airlines.
5. Bargaining power of suppliers exists in certain critical areas such as aircraft manufacture, e.g. Boeing and Airbus, which is almost an oligopoly in the global market.

When you apply the above findings to Emirates Airlines,[1] it is interesting to see how they overcome the challenges thrown at them by the industry. Threat of substitutes is almost non-existent for Emirates Airlines as its focus is on long-haul passenger traffic. The buyers (mainly air travellers) technically have bargaining power; the effective differentiation through superior services and punctuality results in buyers' bias towards EA. Competition from other airlines is effectively met due to the core competencies and competitive advantages enjoyed by EA, i.e. (a) it is the flagship carrier of the Emirate of Dubai, which is the only true cosmopolitan metropolis in the GCC and ideally located between East and West; accordingly whilst British Airways may struggle to get a third runway at Heathrow Airport, we can expect better support from government in the case of EA; (b) about 80% of the UAE population are expatriates and a significant portion of them are regular travellers; (c) Dubai is a tourism destination and tourists also contribute to substantial passenger traffic numbers; (d) it is a transit hub – EA takes its passengers 'anywhere to anywhere' with one stop in Dubai. Accordingly, EA has one of the best aircraft utilization rates in the industry; (e) bargaining power of suppliers is also effectively managed as the major suppliers of aircraft vie for EA orders. EA has a reputation for substantial aircraft orders – to replace the existing fleet and expand.

A detailed case study on the global oil industry is provided at the end of the chapter, where the impact of various forces in Porter's Model is discussed in detail.

## 6.9 COMPETITOR/PEER GROUP ANALYSIS

Competitor analysis within the industry analysis framework is extremely useful because the analyst can determine whether credit exposure is taken in a superior company. While deciding the peer group, consideration needs to be given to revenue/sales, assets, market capitalization, net income, profit margin, number of employees, etc. The peer group analysis highlights strengths and opportunities. Competitor analysis focuses mainly on current capacities, level of business operations, strength and strategies of the competitor.

Peer group analysis would enable the analyst to understand how the credit risk profile of the borrower compares with the rest of the industry. By selecting the best companies within an industry with good prospects, you can ensure build-up of a quality credit portfolio. It can also be seen that the best companies in an industry survive poor industry performance during

[1] A similar analysis may be attempted on South West Airlines, which is listed on the US Stock Market. Visit www.southwest.com. For more information on EA visit www.emirates.ae.

cyclical times. In fact, it is the policy of certain ultra-conservative financial/lending institutions to take exposure only with the top two players in any particular industry.

**Example 6.2**

**Peer Group Analysis (on hypothetical companies)**

ABC Constructions, a customer prospect, is compared against two peers:

| $m<br>Latest FYE | New Customer<br>ABC Constructions<br>31.03.2011 | Peer 1: Customer<br>PQR Constructions<br>31.03.2011 | Peer 2: Non Customer<br>XYZ Construct*<br>31.03.2011 |
|---|---|---|---|
| Sales | 259.7 | 458.4 | 689.7 |
| Gross Profit Margin (GPM) | 25.4% | 17.7% | 18.1% |
| Net Profit Margin | 5.63% | 6.10% | 5.9% |
| Bank Borrowings (Funded) | Nil | 50 | 147.1 |
| Provision for Bad Debts (2011) | 12.1 | 32 | 4.81 |
| Trade Debtors on 31.03.2011 | 59.7 | 160.3 | 480 |
| % of Provision to Trade Debtors | 20.3% | 20.0% | 1.0% |
| EBITDA | 22 | 51 | 87.3 |
| EBITDA Margin | 8.2% | 11.1% | 12.6% |
| Net Debt | Net Cash Position | 18 | 30 |
| Net Debt/EBITDA | N.A | 0.35x | 0.24x |
| S&P/Moody's/Fitch | BBB+ | BBB | BBB- |

* *Listed company in the stock market*

**Comments**

A comparison with two other prominent peer group companies shows that ABC is more conservative and enjoys relatively better GPM. The better margin is attributable to the careful selection of contracts and efficiency of operations. The relatively lower Net Profit Margin reflects the aggressive debtors provisioning policy adopted by ABC compared to its peers. ABC continues to be nil geared. In view of the recent construction sector slowdown, ABC and PQR Constructions had booked substantial additional provision on debtors, however ABC is more conservative. However, XYZ Construct hardly increased the provisions during 2010, despite having significant exposure to some of the troubled companies, which drew criticisms from a few equity analysts (such as Silverman Sachs), who cover this stock. Overall, ABC can be considered as a reasonably strong player in this market segment.

The techniques we have discussed in this chapter will enable one to determine industry attractiveness and risk factors. Again, the operating risk factors emanating from the industry factors need to be studied carefully. All serious risk factors must have appropriate mitigants. It is also worth ensuring that the firm has the capacity and willingness to bring in alleviative measures. For instance, industries using inflammable raw materials (such as bitumen) carry a very high risk of fire compared to other industries. While one can insure the factory and profits (loss of profits policy), additional precautions such as storing inflammable materials in a separate warehouse, locating the factory far enough from such warehouses, etc. are effective mitigants.

## CASE STUDY: ANALYSIS OF GLOBAL OIL INDUSTRY

### I. Definition of Global Oil Industry

Our first task is to get focused in order to analyze the industry in terms of Porter's Model. It is critical that the precise industry is always determined before commencing the analysis of each force in Porter's Model because each of them may well have different ramifications depending upon the component of the industry considered. A focused definition of the global oil industry might be 'design, exploration, extraction, production, refining, marketing of hydrocarbon fuels of different categories spread over and having presence in many countries'.

The global oil industry is dominated by a few major players namely Exxon Mobil, Royal Dutch/Shell, British Petroleum (BP), TotalFinaElf and Chevron-Texaco. While other oil companies also exist in the market engaged either in the full chain of extraction to marketing or some part of it, they are mostly localized and small in size compared to the big five. It is believed that more than 75% of the total market share in the global oil industry is dominated by these five major companies.

### II. Life Cycle of Global Oil Industry

The origins and introduction stage can be traced back to the mid-1850s in the US when oil drilling started on a commercial scale. While initially it was mainly used as lighting and heating oil, with the advent of internal combustion technology, leading to a new era of automobiles and coal-fired ships giving way to efficient oil-powered ones, the growth stage set in. Given the reality that crude oil is the single most important international natural resource driving the economies of world – whether it be for transportation, industry or other uses – the present stage can be defined as the maturity growth phase. Although there are times when there is an occasional drop in demand (e.g. the aftermath of the 1997 Asian Crisis or the 2008 Credit Crisis), the long-term trend is upwards.

### III. Structural Analysis of the Oil Industry

#### *A. Barriers to entry*

Barriers such as access to large capital resources, cutting-edge technology and first mover advantage in areas of proven oil reserves exist. Substantial Capital Expenditure (CAPEX) is required to enter almost all downstream and upstream activities, i.e. extraction, exploring, transportation, refining, distribution and marketing of refined products. Setting up sites for exploration, extraction and refining is expensive while the transportation/distribution of different oil products implies heavy investment in special vehicles – tankers, vehicle fleet, storage tanks and pipelines. New entrants will have to compete in all activities of the supply chain since the oil industry is driven by efficiency in handling risks such as blow-outs, while cost reduction is a priority item, resulting in a spree of consolidation. Besides, most of the oil majors have formidable economies of scale built up through decades, which is very difficult for any new entrant to replicate. Another significant entry barrier is technology and another factor is the first mover advantage enjoyed by the incumbents in the industry as they hold access to most of the proven oil reserves in the world, through concessions or otherwise. The relationship of oil companies with the countries which own the property rights to oil reserves is also crucial. It has something of a political angle as well. It is evident that these countries will allow only companies from certain preferred countries. Since most of the proven oil reserves are in the Middle East, Mexico, Venezuela and a number of republics of the former Soviet Union, their preference can also be considered as a barrier. Let us summarize the major barriers and their effect on industry profitability.

| Particulars | Effect on Profitability |
|---|---|
| Economies of scale | Positive |
| Differentiation/switching costs | Neutral *(also see Bargaining Power of Buyers)* |
| Capital requirements | Positive |
| Property rights from oil rich nations | Positive |
| Technology | Positive |
| Access to distribution channels | Positive |

As most of the seven determinants are working to increase the barriers to entry, a FULL STAR for this force because of its positive impact on retaining/enhancing industry profitability.

***B. Substitutes***

Hydrocarbons (oil), nuclear, coal, hydro and renewables (such as wind, solar, biomass, etc.) offer a choice to energy consumers. However, the limitations of the substitutes provide strengths to hydrocarbon fuels. Whilst coal and nuclear offer a strong challenge as a source of energy in certain areas (production of electricity, etc.) they cannot replace oil and gas in all fields, e.g. transportation is a field where these kinds of energy have limited application. Hydro-energy is also geographically specific and limited and primarily used for electricity generation and does not enjoy the flexibility/range of uses of oil and gas. As far as renewables are concerned, they are in early but encumbered development stages. Wherever renewables are available, price becomes an issue since these products still have relatively high production costs. The best example is solar energy cells, which are the core for solar-energy related products. Another issue is availability; not all sources of energy are available in all places. The oil and gas industry has an extensive worldwide distribution network, which cannot be claimed by any of its substitutes – except coal – which have other limitations, as discussed above. It is a long time since King Coal (the 1800s and early 1900s) abdicated the throne in favour of King Oil (since the 1930s). An additional factor is the considerable switching cost – for instance adaptation of machines, contracts with new suppliers, etc. In view of these factors, the substitute products do not pose any significant threat to the oil industry for the time being. Let us summarize the impact of substitutes on industry profitability:

| Particulars | Impact/Response | Effect on Profitability |
|---|---|---|
| Substitutes performing same function | Almost non-existent | Positive |
| Substitutes that reduce cost | Almost non-existent | Positive |
| Substitutes providing better quality | Nuclear – but dangerous | Positive |
| Consumer perception | Favourable, no alternative | Positive |
| Price of the perceived substitute | Solar, Nuclear – High | Positive |

Again a FULL STAR for this force because of its positive impact on retaining/enhancing industry profitability.

### *C. Intensity of Competition*

The intensity of rivalry among the incumbents is not low but can be considered as moderate because industry space is increasing driven by the world's economic growth along with the rising global population. Besides, they normally respect each other's markets. As we have seen, the threat of new entrants on any significant scale is absent because of the entry barriers. Each of the global majors and regional majors serves certain markets, which are rarely encroached upon by the rivals. Since all five companies are vertically integrated to a wide extent, rivalry is intense in all activities that they engage in. Whilst intensity is moderate, the major corporations are interested in gaining larger market share and increasing profits, which led to the consolidation trend that began in 1998. Let us summarize the impact of substitutes on industry profitability:

| Particulars | Impact/Response | Effect on Profitability |
|---|---|---|
| Number and size of competitors | Reduced with consolidation | Positive |
| Rate of growth in the industry | Maturity growth | Positive |
| Augmentation of oil reserves | Depleting supplies | Negative |
| Exit barriers | High | Negative |
| Surplus capacity | Not significant | Positive |

In view of the above, this force is rated at HALF STAR.

### *D. Bargaining Power of Suppliers*

Suppliers' bargaining power is one of the key factors that is shaping not only the oil industry, but maybe the world. Hydrocarbon fuels are a scarce resource concentrated in a few areas, mainly in the Middle East/erstwhile Soviet Union republics. The countries that own the property rights of crude oil reserves enjoy great bargaining power as they sell the rights for extracting oil. Oil prices are very much determined by these nations, e.g. OPEC, whose production cuts generally drive prices up. Suppliers also include the supporting and related industries supplying computer equipment, software tools, service for oil exploration and production, base map maintenance, lease data management and mapping, software for pumping and pipe flow design, pipe network analysis and many other technical solutions. However, these suppliers, unlike the nations with oil reserves, do not have much bargaining power given the availability of alternate sources. There is no real threat of forward integration, especially by oil rich supplier countries, given the entry barriers and the size and power of the oil companies present in the industry. Let us summarize the impact of substitutes on industry profitability:

| Particulars | Impact/Response | Effect on Profitability |
|---|---|---|
| No. of sellers/supply sources | A few – e.g. OPEC | Negative |
| Price sensitivity to the sellers | OPEC quotas | Negative |
| % of total sales of the seller | Significant* | Neutral |
| Is product bought differentiated | Not much – commodity | Neutral |
| Volume bought | Significant# | Positive |
| Forward integration | Negligible | Positive |

* for some countries oil dependency is very high, i.e. the main source of revenue is the sale of oil.
# off-take of large quantities for several decades resulted in a time tested bond with supplier countries.

In view of the above, this force is rated at HALF STAR.

***E. Bargaining Power of Buyers***

Buyers come from an extremely broad range and the ultimate buyers extend from individuals (such as vehicle owners) to large corporate customers engaged in an assortment of business activities. Oil is an absolute necessity in the modern world, which substantially limits the bargaining power of buyers. Oil importing nations have to continue the imports, irrespective of high oil prices. Otherwise economic activities will come to a halt. Despite the importance of oil, it is a commodity – a homogeneous product – making it difficult for the integrated oil companies to differentiate in any significant manner, especially in the retail business (service stations). Perhaps this is the only factor that gives the buyer some leverage, meaning that it is not too difficult to switch between suppliers within the oil industry. Demand from buyers fluctuates based on economic conditions impacting the performance of industries around the globe. In periods of recession, an industry will save energy because of lower production and vice versa. These limitations are almost overcome by lack of viable substitutes. No wonder somebody has said that the world runs on oil. There is no real threat of backward integration since the entry barriers are difficult to overcome and given the size and power of the oil companies present in the industry. Let us summarize the impact of bargaining power on the industry profitability:

| Particulars | Impact/Response | Effect on Profitability |
|---|---|---|
| No. of buyers | Very large (No BP) | Positive |
| Price sensitivity to the buyers | Almost Inelastic (No BP) | Positive |
| Is product bought differentiated | Not much – commodity | Neutral |
| Volume bought | Essential commodity | Positive |
| Backward integration | Negligible | Positive |

Again a FULL STAR for this force because of its positive impact on retaining/enhancing the Industry Profitability.

**Conclusion**

Overall the industry rating can be summarized as Four Star. Some may argue that given the bargaining power of a significant category of suppliers – for example OPEC – the 'Bargaining Power of Suppliers' force does not deserve any star at all. In that case the rating may be considered as Three and a Half, still an attractive rating indicating the profit potential of the global oil industry.

## QUESTIONS/EXERCISES

1. You have decided to conduct an industry analysis of major industries in your area. Explain the major areas you would focus on as part of the industry analysis.
2. The global carbonated soft drinks industry is dominated by two names – Coca Cola and Pepsi. Use Porter's Model to understand their market domination despite challenges by new entrants over the last several decades.
3. Mr Y states that all industries are interlinked. He points out that when housing construction in the US slowed down, many other related sectors such as building materials and contracting did so too and this also impacted the banking and financial services industry. Hence, he argues that there is no merit in conducting standalone industry analysis. Do you agree? Please elaborate your views.
4. What is a non-cyclical industry? Give a few examples.
5. The 'Early Warning Indicator' system of your organization shows that the housing industry may face a cyclical downturn in the short to medium term. What other industries would be impacted, either concurrently or shortly thereafter? Also elaborate on industries that won't be impacted.
6. Identify the key demand driving factors of the following industries:

   a. Telecommunications
   b. Oil rigs industry
   c. Banking and financial services industry
   d. Information technology industry
   e. Automobile industry
   f. Building materials industry
   g. Ceramics tiles industry
   h. Construction industry
   i. Consumer durables industry
   j. Pharmaceutical industry
   k. Food industry
   l. Liquor industry
   m. FMCG industry
   n. Transportation industry
   o. Aviation industry
   p. Shipping industry
   q. Tobacco industry
   r. Consumer durables industry

7. Read a business newspaper or other business publications and identify four industries that are doing well currently and four industries that are under-performing. Analyze the key reasons for the divergent performance.
8. You have completed reading a report by a recognized oil expert, who has indicated that crude oil prices will increase sharply over the next decade due to several factors such as increasing global demand as well as the increasing cost of oil extraction as the oil firms are forced to drill deeper and in harsher climates to seek out new reserves. If oil prices rise sharply, identify what would be the knock-on impact on other industries. List the industries that would be impacted favourably and unfavourably. What are your thoughts on alternate energy sources? Please explain your views.

# 7

# Entity-Level Risks

The aviation industry is a tough one – as US billionaire Carl Icahn would agree. He took exposure to the US Aviation Industry in 1985 through the purchase of Trans World Airlines (TWA) and became its chairman; however he left the company in 1993 as TWA collapsed and became bankrupt.

What are the challenges of the aviation industry? It is cyclical and has relatively high operating leverage (e.g. high depreciation) and capital intensity, given the heavy investment in costly aircraft. Moreover fuel costs, which are at the mercy of volatile oil prices, account for a significant portion of its running expenses. To remain adequately hedged against the volatility of fuel prices is in itself an immense challenge for airlines.

Whilst several global and regional airlines continue to suffer from losses, a few airlines such as UAE's Emirates Airlines and US based South West Airlines are relatively consistent in their performance and profitability.

Haven't you noticed this pattern in other industries as well? While some companies perform satisfactorily, earning reasonable profits, there are others which struggle to exist and incur losses.

Here lies the explanation as to why firms within the same industry facing exactly the same external environment perform differently. Decision-making skills, policies and competencies define certain crucial risks that can make or unmake a business enterprise. The strategies, methods, technologies, the motivation level, etc. are a few factors that are reflected in the performance and determine the survival of an enterprise. From a credit risk analysis perspective, a thorough entity-level internal analysis is essential to identify these factors and related strengths and risks. So, despite low risks emanating from external and industry factors, a badly run company implies high credit risk.

Internal analysis studies the third category among business risks – internal risks or company/firm-level risks. Internal analysis, the third level of obligor credit risk analysis, focuses on the review of the capabilities, resources, strategies, competencies, strengths and weaknesses of the borrowers or prospective borrowers. It addresses numerous questions – to understand the business model – such as:

- What are the main activities?
- What are the mission/goals?
- Are the owners and/or management passionate about the business and growth?
- What are the strategies?
- How did they do in the past?
- What are the major resources?
- How is the labour–management relationship?
- What is the relationship with suppliers and customers?
- How do they price the goods?
- How they meet competition?
- Do they enjoy or build up certain advantages over other competitors?
- How will the business environment changes impact strategies and policies?

- Are the competitive advantages built up flimsy (can be lost because of changes in environment)?
- Can it be copied by the competitors?

Internal analysis is a continuation of the two previous analyses – external environment and industry. In this chapter, we will discuss the non-financial internal risks. (Given the vastness and importance of financial risk, it will be treated in the next chapter.)

## 7.1 UNDERSTANDING THE ACTIVITY

Knowledge of the nature of business activity is the foremost element in the study of internal risks. All major activities in the business should be clearly understood. Main products, installed capacity and its utilization, major customers, major market segments, raw materials, suppliers, technology and location are some of the prime areas to be covered. The study of these variables brings out the potential operating risks. Adequate reversions to the insights gathered from industry analysis and external analysis will be required to understand the suppliers and major customers of the company. For instance, if the suppliers' bargaining power is substantial, it will influence certain company policies. The analyst should understand the strategies adopted to counter the bargaining power of suppliers and determine its suitability and success so far. A thorough understanding of the association among the external and industry factors to the operational aspects of the company is essential to conduct a SWOT analysis (discussed later), a powerful tool to unearth the operating risks involved.

Given the diverse nature of the businesses to be studied, we need a common framework applicable to all business organizations. We know that all business firms acquire economic (physical and financial) resources from the environment and perform certain activities to enhance the value (value-addition), which results in another form of economic output (finished product/service). The following diagram (Figure 7.1) shows a set of interrelated generic operating activities common to a wide range of firms.

These activities aim to create value. To be economically viable, the value created ought to exceed the cost of providing the final output (product/service). It will lead to a profit, which creates/adds value to the investors in the firm.

- **Resources acquired from environment** include all factors of production and related logistics such as procurement, warehousing and inventory control, among others. Resources such as finance and manpower are included here.
- **Processes** involve value-added activities that transform the inputs into the final product. It also encompasses research and development, process automation, and other technology used in the processes.
- **Marketing and Distribution** comprise activities required to get the finished product to the customer, including warehousing, order fulfilment, channel selection, advertising, pricing, delivery, etc.
- **After sales operations** include warranties, gathering customer feedback, providing customer support and repair services, among others.

*Resources from Environment* > *Process* > *Final Output* > *Marketing and Distribution* > *After Sales Operations*

**Figure 7.1** Interrelated Generic Operating Activities in a Value Chain

Understanding the nature of an activity is an essential part of understanding the business model and brings out certain operating risks. For instance, the perishable nature of commodities is a risk for vegetables, fruit, dairy products and similar food businesses. Similarly, business firms engaged in crude oil extraction, processing and transportation carry the risk of oil spillage and polluting the environment.

## 7.2 RISK CONTEXT AND MANAGEMENT

All business organizations take some kind of risk. The breadth, depth and pace of change faced by all companies pose many challenges and risks. Some of these risks are unexpected, but others – at least to some degree – are both foreseeable and manageable. Often a company's ability to manage its risks is evaluated on the basis of its management's track record, but previous experience alone is no guarantee that a company has sufficient risk management capability to safeguard its future success. To understand firm-level credit risk, the risk management capabilities of obligors/borrowers/debtors are important. The analyst must understand various critical risks faced by the firm and ensure that the entity has proper risk management techniques.

For example, suppose one of the customers has suffered a very significant decline in turnover – this should be a primary concern in your analysis. Determining the underlying causes of this serious weakening in turnover is of paramount importance. If it is the result of inherent business vulnerabilities, such as management, its products, or lack of market strength, then consider what corrective action management is taking. If the decline is consistent with the industry, do you expect the industry or economic conditions to improve? If so, is the business positioned to take advantage of improved conditions? Otherwise, how will the business minimize the effect of continued or worsening conditions? You should also determine what effect this deterioration in turnover growth has on the present and future ability of the business to maintain its market share and margins. If this serious decline in turnover is a continuation of a downward trend, management should have an effective plan with immediate steps in place to reverse it.

To understand the critical risks faced by a firm, the entity's goals, objectives and strategies are to be studied:

- **Goals and Objectives**: Successful organizations know what they want and usually put them down in the form of performance targets, budgets or in any other measurable form, either in quantitative terms, qualitative terms or both. This ensures the achievement of the mission and vision of the organization. Studies have proven that organizations with clear mission and vision are often more successful. Whilst the mission and vision are long term, the objectives and goals are more near to medium term. Hence, it is essential for the credit analyst/manager/approver to understand these business essentials of the customer.
- **Business Strategies**: The strategies are aimed at attaining the objectives and goals. Stakeholders – including investors and creditors – should understand the major strategies. For instance, while certain businesses follow a low price/high volume strategy, other firms might pursue a high price/low volume approach to achieve the goals. Inadequate strategies pose yet another risk. Adequacy of strategies and management capability of putting those strategies into action to achieve the goals are to be critically evaluated. Past performance is a good guide. Also, observations on how close the company came to achieving its goals and why it fell short or exceeded them provide clarity on related risks and risk mitigants. Given the importance of business strategy in the context of internal risks, the topic is covered in detail later in this chapter.

## 7.3 INTERNAL RISK IDENTIFICATION STEPS

The number of risks impacting an entity which might derail the objectives and strategies is enormous. It is not practical to identify all such risks, however it is essential to understand all material risks. A proper risk identification procedure should be developed. While there are several methods to identify risks, generally risk identification is done through (a) interviews and questioning and (b) studying market developments/peer comparison against benchmarks. These steps are detailed below.

### 7.3.1 Interviews and Questioning

Meetings with the senior corporate management and discussions are the most commonly applied method of risk identification. This includes factory visits and site and stock inspection, among others. The meetings and visits will provide information on operating/financial/marketing plans, their assessment of the competitive situation, management policies and other risk factors. Creditors need to understand their customers' businesses, a necessity best met by open and good faith explanations by the business executives concerned.

The meetings are also important for the entity. They give corporate executives and their advisors an opportunity to provide details regarding their plans as well as the company's prospects. Analysts should provide the company with adequate time to prepare a thorough presentation and guide the meeting with intelligent questioning to gather information. The person conducting the credit risk analysis must call for background material on the industry and company beforehand, which includes the following:

(a) Audited annual financial statements for five years.
(b) Latest management accounts/interim financial statements subsequent to the previous audited.
(c) Memorandum/articles of association/partnership deed/other legal or government related documents.
(d) Product brochures and other descriptive materials on the operations and products/services.
(e) Industry background and the customer's position with the industry.
(f) Industry competition factors.
(g) Order book.
(h) Corporate governance.
(i) Succession plan.
(j) Nature of activity.
(k) Competitive advantages.
(l) Critical success factors.

It goes without saying that the information provided by the obligor, to facilitate assessing creditworthiness, ought to be kept in strictest confidence by the analyst. Normal topics during a meeting are:

- Overview of major business segments.
- Comparisons with competitors and industry norms, industry prospects.
- Financial policies and financial performance goals and non-financial operating statistics.
- Managements forecasts/projections/budgets.
- Income statement, cash flow statement, balance sheet, accounting practices.

- Operating assumptions.
- Anticipated reliance on internal cash generation/external funds.
- Capital expenditure (CAPEX) plans, financing alternatives and contingency plans.
- Type of credit needed by the obligor with related terms and conditions, including repayment.

Analysts should not base their conclusions on the company's assumptions and methodology, but it forms the starting point of analysis aimed at understanding the real credit risk involved. In large banks and financial institutions, expert industry analysts, specializing in certain sectors/industries, are common. Opinions from such experts may also be sought during the assessment process.

### 7.3.2 Market Developments and Peer Comparison

The analyst ought to be a voracious (fast) reader and thirsty in gathering information. Reading of business dailies and publications, attending useful seminars and conferences, discussions with peers and networking with knowledgeable persons ought to be the habit of the analyst. Information on all factors mentioned in the previous chapters should be in the possession of the analyst. The intelligence gathered, from formal and informal sources and other secondary sources, ought to be verified as reliable, accurate and relevant. Details provided by the company are to be verified against the realities and discrepancies/differences, if any, ought to be clarified/reconciled. All these processes will enable the analyst to unearth the company level risks.

Peer analysis is yet another powerful tool to identify risks as well as relative strengths and weaknesses of the obligor. Products and processes used by others, technologies and aggressive/defensive policies pursued by them show the position occupied by the entity under analysis in the overall context. Output from competitor analysis, mentioned in the previous chapter, is useful to assess the competitors' strategies, current status and future directions, among others.

Several tools are used to understand the internal risks. SWOT analysis, understanding the strategy and related risks, evaluating the management capability and corporate governance are some of the tools or important sources that will provide information related to the non-financial risks in a business entity. The details are discussed in the remainder of this chapter:

## 7.4 SWOT ANALYSIS

Now is the time to conduct Strengths Weaknesses Opportunities and Threats (SWOT) analysis of the company. SWOT, often touted as a management tool for an overview of the current situation, is also useful for reflection and appraising risks.

**Strengths and weaknesses** are internal factors over which the entity has direct control or influence. Strengths are things the entity is good at, including its resources and capabilities that can be used as a basis for developing a competitive advantage. Examples of such strengths include: core competencies in key areas, financial power, patents, strong brand names, economies of scale, good reputation among customers, cost advantages from proprietary know-how, exclusive access to high grade natural resources, favourable access to distribution networks, innovation skills, superior technology and a favourable experience curve, among others. Weaknesses refer to things that it would like to improve. Poor R&D, weak marketing, obsolete technology/facilities and high cost structure and all factors which are the opposite of those mentioned under strengths are examples of weaknesses.

**Opportunities and threats** are external factors. As they are exogenous, an organization lacks control over them, but is in a position to respond as they appear as chances and dangers, from the world outside. Some examples of opportunities that could open doors for growth and profits are: unfulfilled demand, arrival of new technologies, loosening of regulations and removal of international trade barriers. They are opportunities to be taken advantage of provided the firm takes the necessary action. A threat is something that may cause problems if the entity doesn't act now to prevent it or limit its impact. Some examples of threats include: consumers moving away from the firm's products, emergence of substitute products, new adverse regulations, increased trade barriers.

Operating risks lie buried mainly in the weaknesses and threats, while occasionally, the strengths/opportunities may also translate into risks. For instance, suppose the strength of a company is its ability to churn out consecutive and simultaneous expansion and diversification projects, which at the same time carry the risk of project delays/cost overruns/misfired expansions. Similarly, the opportunities will not automatically result in any benefit to the entity, if it chooses inaction, which is a risk in itself.

The information output from SWOT analysis is helpful in matching the firm's resources and capabilities to the competitive environment in which it operates, based on which broad strategies can also be determined:

**Table 7.1** SWOT Based Strategies

| Particulars | **Strengths** | **Weaknesses** |
|---|---|---|
| **Opportunities** | S-O strategies | W-O strategies |
| **Threats** | S-T strategies | W-T strategies |

S-O strategies fit the strengths to the opportunities. Generally aggressive in nature S-O strategies usher in more growth, increase the asset base and profitability. Rapid growth of many national technology companies into global players can be traced to this strategy. W-O strategies are aimed at overcoming weaknesses through the pursuit of opportunities. During the 1970s one of the weaknesses of Japanese cars compared to their counterparts in the US was their smaller size. But the Oil Crisis in the mid-1970s created demand for fuel efficient small cars in the US providing opportunity for Japanese cars. S-T strategies use strengths to counter vulnerability to external threats while W-T strategies are defensive in nature. They prevent external threats from attacking weak points. Exit strategy from a loss making foreign market (weakness) in view of the emergence of a strong domestic competitor (threat) is an example of a W-T strategy.

The SWOT analysis activates a methodology to pursue the right strategy to ensure achievement of the mission and vision of the organization through the selection of the appropriate business model. For instance, most shaving products manufacturers pursue a strategy of pricing the razor at cost while the blades or cartridges carry higher profit margins.

Analysts may also use additional tools such as the Boston Consulting Group (BCG) Matrix, which studies different businesses in a multi-business group on the basis of their (i) market share and (ii) industry growth rates.

## 7.5 BUSINESS STRATEGY ANALYSIS

Strategies are the cornerstones that determine the success or failure of a business enterprise. The financial stability, profitability, satisfied customers and sustainable competitive advantages are the consequence of the effective strategies followed by firms. The strategies that are built around the core competencies yield optimum results. Whilst mergers are one of the key strategies followed by several multinationals, others build strategies on fundamental strengths. Exxon-Mobil, Chevron Texaco and Arcelor-Mittal followed merger and acquisition strategy. Apple focused on a narrow range of products where it built unbeatable competencies.

Good business strategies emanate from well thought-out strategic planning. Often strategic planning is stated to be the key factor for the success of any company, which would begin by listening to customers and delivering the performance target market's want. Well thought-out and researched business strategies help to allocate an organization's resources effectively and productively based on its core competencies and shortcomings, anticipated changes in the environment, and competition.

Business strategies are among the hot topics taught in business schools. Business managers spend a lot of resources to find a winning strategy while consultants earn a living prescribing appropriate strategies for different situations to solve diverse issues or attain goals. Let us discuss some of the main strategies followed by the business world.

### 7.5.1 Cost Leadership

In this strategy, a firm competes on a cost basis by becoming the low cost producer in an industry for a given level of quality. Often, a cost leader can be considered as the king in the industry. In the event of a price war, it can maintain profitability while the not so cost efficient competitors suffer losses. Or, the firm can start a price war to keep new entrants away or teach some of the errant competitors a lesson. Similarly, as the industry matures and prices decline, the cost leaders can remain profitable for a longer period of time. The cost leadership strategy usually targets a broad market, resulting in large volume, makes an efficient scale plant, incurring little product design/R&D cost and after sales service. The firm sells its products either at average industry prices to earn a profit higher than that of rivals, or below the average industry prices to gain market share. Some of the ways that firms acquire cost advantages are given below:

- **Economies of Scale**: A firm can bring down cost of production per unit by resorting to huge capacities. Economies of scale can also be built up in other key success factor areas as well. For instance, it is the economies of scale in technology that provide technology companies with the edge. Microsoft, with its 2,500+ highly qualified and experienced software professionals was able to release successive new versions of Windows, almost every alternate year since 1993. In companies such as pharmaceuticals, it is the economies of scale in R&D that matter.
- **Production Advantage**: Cost leadership can be achieved by having proximity to key inputs, simple design, expertise in technology or a favourable experience/learning curve, which also result in cost efficient production.
- **Low Input Costs**: Low labour cost (eg. China), low RM cost (petrochemicals in the Middle East) and similar availability of cheap key inputs enable companies to follow cost leadership strategy.

Every strategy has its risks, including the low cost strategy. For example, other firms may be able to lower their costs as well. As technology improves, the competition may be able to leapfrog production capabilities, thus eliminating the competitive advantage.

### 7.5.2 Differentiation

Developing products/services with unique attributes that are valued by customers who are willing to pay more for such special attributes, guides differentiation strategy. The firm should be in a position to charge a higher price that exceeds the extra costs incurred in offering the unique product. Most consumer products attempt to differentiate one way or another. Some of the common differentiation techniques are:

- **Differentiate the Product**: Variations in the shape and design so that not only the products look different from the competitors but among the various products of the same manufacturer. All manufacturers of consumer products (e.g. cars, TVs, computers, soap, shampoos, etc.) around the world follow this strategy religiously. Having different varieties/appearance/quality are other techniques falling under this category.
- **Differentiate the Price**: Differing prices for different market segments is another common strategy. Cinemas, hotels and airlines follow this strategy. Certain car manufacturers such as BMW/Lexus use this differentiation strategy to serve only the up-market sector. Whilst normal models of Toyota are marketed under Toyota brands (Corolla, Camry, etc.) the Lexus models are marketed without highlighting the Toyota name. The high price attracts a certain market segment. On most occasions, price differentiation strategy goes hand in hand with product/market differentiation strategies. Another strategy in the same vein is the quantity discounts offered to large buyers. Here, more quantity means lower pricing.
- **Differentiate the Promotion**: Effective sales promotion techniques are powerful tools to build perceived differentiation in the minds of consumers. Spending sizeable amounts on brand building is not uncommon in consumer products. Advertising agencies that offer better promotion techniques are always sought after by manufacturers. Superior signals of value and after sales service can also act as powerful differentiation from identical product manufacturers.

### 7.5.3 Contraction

This strategy is used when the company wants to quit certain markets or to reduce the number of products it has. For instance, soon after 9/11 Gateway declared closure of manufacturing units in Asia. Similarly, Volkswagen decided to stop production of its famous Beetle. This strategy need not be perceived negatively because contraction in certain sectors will free the company to deploy resources in areas where the potential is greater. Besides, continuation in the wrong areas will be a drag on the operations, which may eventually lead to issues such as losses, liquidity crises, low productivity, under-utilization of capacity, etc.

### 7.5.4 Market Penetration

This strategy focuses more of the same product in the same market. One of the key strategies deployed by growth firms, market penetration will be successful if the following factors are present: (a) The market ought to be growing or should have growth potential. Otherwise, existing players will retaliate with a price war or non-price wars such as promotion campaigns, etc. eventually hurting profitability. (b) In a rather mature market, penetration is possible, if one of the players leaves/shut downs operations. (c) In case the entity has certain distinct advantages, such as quality, brand power, etc., such strengths may be utilized to achieve market penetration.

### 7.5.5 New Markets

This strategy largely aims at branching out of existing markets by pursuing additional market segments or geographical regions. This strategy tends to work well if the firm's core competencies are product related, which enable it to launch successfully in the new market.

### 7.5.6 New Products/Product Synergy Diversification

Product development or new models are one of the core strategies of many businesses, especially consumer durable producers. TV technology is a constantly changing one – from picture tube to LCD to LED to 3D. Digital cameras, personal computing and mobile phones are evolving faster. Developing several value-added derivative products, based on a core product or technology, is a good example of product synergy diversification. Existing product synergies are effectively used in the new product as well. However, it may be borne in mind that the new products carry the risk of being a flop in the market.

### 7.5.7 Product/Market Diversification

Whilst attempting entry into new markets with new products is generally viewed as a riskier strategy, it can be successful provided the firm has both product and market competencies. A heavy vehicle manufacturer may enter the car market – this was done by Tatas in the late 1990s. Another area where this strategy can be successfully utilized is when the entity can bring its reputation in one area to another.

Related vs. unrelated diversification strategies are adopted in a variety of circumstances. As discussed earlier, related diversification strategies are attempted through product or market. Unrelated diversification means the firm launching into businesses radically different from the ones followed hitherto. Naturally, this is one of the riskiest strategies, although its proponents point out the benefit of unrelated diversification such as a cyclical company acquiring a non-cyclical business.

### 7.5.8 Consolidation

This strategy is followed when the firm wants to preserve its market or any of its segment or product acceptability. Various techniques are used such as branding of different products together, franchisees and licencing, among others.

### 7.5.9 Merger/Takeover

Mergers are nowadays a frequently used strategy by both large and small businesses. The guiding philosophy of most of the mergers is to attempt combining the strengths of merging firms to better face the external challenges. For instance, the merger of Exxon and Mobil is stated to bring together the strong skills in oil technology of Exxon with the salesmanship of Mobil. As mentioned above, the possibility of failure of a merger (or marriage!) exists as has been the case with the Daimler–Chrysler merger. Merging two corporate cultures is not an easy task. Takeover and acquisition are also like mergers with a difference. In a merger, both entities are considered equal, while in the other two the acquiree ceases to exist.

### 7.5.10 Expansion

This is a common strategy, whereby as the manufacturer finds that it is possible to produce and market more of the same commodity, sometimes even doubling or trebling of current capacities is undertaken. Expansion brings in economies of scale and enables the firm to grow in size and to look beyond the traditional markets. However, sometimes firms prefer to stay small for ease in managing or to enjoy the protection attached to small business, among other advantages.

### 7.5.11 Cost Control

This is yet another commonly adopted strategy to rein in costs by finding alternative cheaper suppliers or raw materials, reducing staff strength and eliminating non-essential tasks, for example. Cost cutting takes several forms, even selective buying. *Business Week* (9 April 2001) reported that Nissan achieved savings of at least $2.25 billion by dropping inefficient part suppliers and consolidating orders with the most efficient ones.

### 7.5.12 Focus

The focus strategy concentrates on a narrow segment and within that segment attempts to achieve either a cost advantage or differentiation. The premise is that the needs of the group can be better serviced by focusing entirely on it. A firm using a focus strategy often enjoys a high degree of customer loyalty, and this entrenched loyalty discourages other firms from competing directly. Because of their narrow market focus, firms pursuing a focus strategy have lower volumes and therefore less bargaining power with their suppliers. However, firms pursuing a differentiation-focused strategy may be able to pass higher costs on to customers since close substitute products do not exist. Firms that succeed in a focus strategy are able to tailor a broad range of product development strengths to a relatively narrow market segment that they know very well. Some risks of focus strategies include imitation and changes in the target segments. Furthermore, it may be fairly easy for a broad-market cost leader to adapt its product in order to compete directly. Finally, other focusers may be able to carve out sub-segments that they can serve even better.

The abovementioned strategies and their risks are for guidance only because the business world follows numerous strategies, whether to capture market share, to drive out competitors, to limit the bargaining power of suppliers/customers, to develop core competencies, to increase productivity, to automate/computerize, and so on. Some of the other famous strategies employed by companies are Kaizen and Kamban (Toyota), Just in Time manufacturing/stock control, lean production, product innovation, activity based costing, Total Quality Management and Balanced Scorecards, among others. New strategies are evolving over time from various academics and business practioners together with the change in goals and objectives of the firm and environment in which businesses operate.

Analysts should identify the strategies followed by the firm and verify its chances of success given the core competencies, strengths, weaknesses and opportunities and threats emerging from the external and industry environment. Any risk factor in the strategy is to be discussed with the company official. It is better that the credit analyst/credit manager is not involved with strategy fixing for the customer and if they are, ought to be aware that this carries a risk that the customer may claim damages for being given faulty guidance! It is essential that the strategies followed by the obligors are reviewed periodically by the analyst – annually or semi-annually or even at shorter durations, if needed – to ensure that they are working and still the best or desired approach for the company.

In order to identify the best strategy suitable for the entity and plan and control its execution, a strong management team is required. Bad management can break a good company or make a good situation deteriorate. Hence effective operations and functional management in key areas such as manufacturing, product development, marketing, distribution and customer service are essential for successful implementation of business strategies. We will examine major management risks later in the chapter.

**Example 7.1 Example of Strategy**

**Emirates Airlines**

Let us consider the main strategies followed by EA, one of the fast growing and top 10 airlines. Amongst others, the key strategies are:

- Keep ahead of the competition through innovation – Emirates' IFE system – focusing on information, connectivity and entertainment – has won the Skytrax 'Best In-flight Entertainment' award for seven consecutive years.
- Expansion – EA aims to grow the fleet through expansion, which brings in economies of scale. Also strategic tie-up with other airlines.
- Backward integration – EA has its own flight kitchen and catering arrangements.
- Maintains a 'young fleet' in its pursuit of lower fuel consumption and consequent lower costs of operation.
- Focus on 'secondary' markets – EA strategy is to enter markets in the Middle East, Asia, Africa, India and Latin America, hitherto poorly connected to the global air transport network.
- Strong marketing – EA is a big global sponsor of sports clubs and events to boost its brand, both in the UAE and in the main overseas markets it serves. It sponsors the annual 'Dubai Shopping Festival' while overseas it sponsors various events such as the Melbourne Cup (Australia's richest horse race), owns the Emirates Stadium and sponsors Arsenal Football Club (both in the UK). EA was the official airline of FIFA World Cup 2010.
- Does not allow any employee unions.
- Ensures customer loyalty through programmes such as skywards and frequent flyer miles.
- Is connected to Emirates Holidays, a major tour operator in the region.

## 7.6 PITFALLS IN STRATEGY

Let us examine some of the Strategy Risks:

1. **Stuck in the Middle**: Whenever a firm attempts multiple strategies to attain different goals, care should be taken that such strategies are compatible with one another. If a firm attempts to achieve the benefits of both differentiation and cost leadership strategies, it may not be feasible and hence may achieve no advantage at all. For example, if a firm differentiates itself by supplying very high quality products, it risks undermining that quality if it seeks

to become a cost leader. Even if the quality did not suffer, the firm would risk projecting a confusing image. For this reason, it is argued that to be successful over the long term, a firm must select only a few compatible strategies, rather than pursuing all possible strategies. Otherwise, conflicting strategies will cause the firm to get 'stuck in the middle' and will not achieve any competitive advantage.

Firms that are able to succeed at multiple strategies often do so by creating separate business units for each strategy. By separating the strategies into different units having different policies and even different cultures, a corporation is less likely to become 'stuck in the middle'. There exists a viewpoint that a single generic strategy is not always best because within the same product customers often seek multi-dimensional satisfactions such as a combination of quality, style, convenience and price. There have been cases in which high quality producers faithfully followed a single strategy and then suffered greatly when another firm entered the market with a lower quality product that better met the overall needs of the customers.

2. **Misdirected Strategy**: This covers many areas but the examples include (a) concentration on tax avoidance; (b) focus on increasing sale, ignoring profits; (c) looking for prestigious rather than profitable projects; (d) short-term fire-fighting rather than long term strategy; (e) complicating the group structure; (f) window dressing.
3. **Ethics amd Morals**: In real life many other strategies are followed which border on civil and criminal liability. The Monopolies and Restrictive Trade Practices Act 1969 (India) put restrictions on certain strategies. Industrial espionage and arson of competitors' business premises are pursued by unscrupulous businessmen.

**Example 7.2 Example of Pitfalls in Strategy**

**Air India**

Despite being the official airline of India (expected to be the natural choice of millions of Indians who travel abroad) and a fully owned government company, Air India suffers losses year after year. This is due to the pitfalls in its strategies. A few of them are given below:

- Being government owned, it seems that government comes first. For example, AI provides special protocol treatment to MPs (Members of Parliament) which adds to the cost and possible disturbance to fellow travellers.
- Poor customer service. AI is notorious for delays and flight cancellations.
- Overstaffed and aggressive employee unions.
- Misguided merger between internationally oriented AI and domestically oriented Indian Airlines created more problems than synergies.
- Ability to survive on soft loans and support from government, (which is not available for the private airlines) rather than from commercial success.

## 7.7 MANAGEMENT ANALYSIS

Good management can turn around a badly managed business or rectify business failures. In 1993, IBM was losing billions and most of the financial media were speculating over its extinction. Then Lou Gerstner took up the challenge as the CEO, and devised a new strategy to re-establish IBM's mission as a customer focused provider of computing solutions. With the support of necessary talent and capabilities IBM turned around and became a success story again.

On the other hand, bad management can break a good business in no time. Bad management is one of the biggest risks at entity level, which can cause a good business to fail, even with all favourable factors. Management risk refers to the defects, inadequacies and lack of skill and experience of the people in key positions. The degree of incompetence and unsatisfactory track record of the management team ought to suggest the magnitude of this risk. The following are some common hints, which may point to an operating risk related to the management.

### 7.7.1 One-Man Rule

It is true that a beaver-like entrepreneur who is full of energy can build up a successful business in no time, as has been proven in several cases. For instance Walt Disney proved everyone wrong by bringing out a successful media and entertainment company almost single-handedly. Once the business grew larger, his business acumen resulted in bringing in professional management to run the show. But at least some entrepreneurs do not do so. The legendary founder of Ford Motors attempted to enforce the one-man rule, which almost led the company into bankruptcy in the late 1930s. The problem with the one-man rule is that all decisions are imposed regardless of opposition, allowing no discussion and heeding no advice. The strong conviction of personal invincibility, created by previous success, directs them. Sooner or later they encounter a series of events, which initially will be covered up but which finally explodes, resulting in failure, collapse and even suicide as happened in the case of Robert Maxwell, the British media tycoon.

One-man rule exists in small, medium and large organizations. In small businesses, the owner is inevitably the ruler as he cannot take in experienced and highly qualified managers, given the lack of resources and size. Hence this risk looms large in all small business. As has been highlighted in the case of Ford Motors and the British Media group, the one-man rule exists in large corporations as well.

### 7.7.2 Joint Chairman/CEO/MGD Position

At the time of the collapse of Enron, both positions – Chairman and CEO – were held by the same individual. In a normal organizational structure, while the CEO reports to the Board, a dotted line makes him answerable to the Chairman, who also heads the Board. This puts checks on the unbridled powers enjoyed by the top-most executive authority in a business firm. Once both positions are combined, the balance is lost causing indulgent decisions. This is a very potent operating risk and as part of the credit analysis one must investigate deep into the causes and reasons for having a combined position, if such instances are encountered.

### 7.7.3 Imbalance in Top Management Team

One of the main rules of corporate governance in any developed jurisdiction is the need to have a balanced management team with an independent audit committee. Qualifications, breadth of experience, talent and skills ought to be mixed in appropriate quantities in the top management. Lack of proper balancing at the top is a significant operating risk because that may cause wrong proposals to be approved while good ones are rejected. One of the reasons for the collapse of Barings Bank is attributable to this factor. Whilst Nick Leeson entered into complicated derivative deals, the approving management team comprising of mostly merchant bankers, missed certain finer points, which would have raised eyebrows if they had been spotted early enough.

### 7.7.4 Weak Finance Function

Lack of financial monitors such as budgeting, accounting controls, timely financial information in sufficient detail (territory-wise, product-wise, period-wise, etc.) hints at a weak finance function, which can create havoc. Given the importance of financial expertise most Boards used to include experienced financial experts as an essential ingredient. Most of the term credit institutions usually put in a covenant imposing recruitment of a capable finance manager as one of the approval terms.

### 7.7.5 Lack of Skilled Managers (or Inability to Attract Skilled Managers in Key Positions)

Whilst the junior managers are fresh out of college or may have around five years' experience, the middle management may be lacking depth of experience to handle complex tasks, which will be confronted successfully by veterans in senior management. Imagine what happens if the freshers lack skills, middle management is inept and senior management lacks experience and leadership. In this fast changing modern era, skill updating is an essential task of all professionals. Such problems in senior management are a significant operating risk. Some deficiencies at middle and junior levels, although an operating risk, are not a matter of major concern provided senior management and all major functions are in capable and well qualified hands.

### 7.7.6 Disharmony in Management

Office politics and some rivalry in the management of companies, although an accepted fact, sometimes develop into a serious risk impacting operations. Usually in the case of a power struggle, decisions by one are thwarted by another causing a stalemate or ineffectiveness in day-to-day operations. A credit risk analyst ought to be concerned if such situations are prolonged.

### 7.7.7 Change in Ownership

This is yet another risk because future directions under the new management or owners need not be the same as those followed by the previous one. While a capable management team or dedicated new owners are welcome, it is a significant risk if the incoming team lacks skills, talent and experience. Accordingly, change in ownership or management may sometimes constitute a risk. The 1998 merger (effectively takeover) of Daimler Benz (Germany) and Chrysler (US) was touted as having the best synergies by industry experts; however it failed to meet the objectives. Daimler-Benz sold off Chrysler in 2007, as the synergies never materialized.

### 7.7.8 Cultural Rigidity

If the business enterprise is operating in a highly competitive and creative field like fashion, or experiences frequent model changes, a rigid and bureaucratic style is an operating risk. Many organizations which lagged behind in growth and have been overtaken by their competitors, often identified the problem as being too bureaucratic. Shedding of layers in management to speed up decisions is among the common solutions. A flatter organization with new innovative products usually results in picking up of growth momentum.

### 7.7.9 Lack of Internal Controls

Proper internal controls go a long way towards safeguarding the assets and ensuring appropriate risk taking complying with the procedures laid down. Non-compliance or laxity in internal controls is a threat, which can cause the demise of the organization itself. A credit risk analyst can often derive comfort, if the audit report is unqualified, because auditors do conduct a thorough examination of the internal controls and their implementation and ought to report back if serious inconsistencies exist.

### 7.7.10 Low Staff Morale

Employees are the dynamic resource of any organization. If almost all employees display lack of morale, it signals some serious problem with the management capability. Successful organizations usually have a satisfied workforce and are concerned about their morale, which is often taken into consideration through employee surveys and other means of feedback.

### 7.7.11 Fraudulent Management

Unscrupulous individuals in the top management deliberately mismanage affairs so as to milk the organization for personal benefit to the point of bankruptcy and possible demise of the firm. For a credit risk analysis, this can be considered as the greatest management risk and if it is identified or suspected, it is better not to extend credit at all.

### 7.7.12 Myopic Vision

Sometimes publicly held companies, especially those listed on the stock exchange, are in the media spotlight. Often top managers of such entities focus on short-term profitability, to the detriment of long-term interests. Myopic vision can happen in non-listed business entities as well for a variety of reasons – management incapability, lack of talent/experience, etc. Disregarding long-term interests will lead to critical opportunities forgone, such as loss of market share to a competitor who has decided to expand resulting in economies of scale and this may provide cost advantage to the competitor.

### 7.7.13 Big Projects

An analyst ought to be wary of big projects, because the failure of big projects has put many a good company in trouble. Accordingly, a big project – relative to a company's size – carries a significant risk that its failure could place the financial health of the company in jeopardy. Sometimes aggressive entrepreneurs get carried away by the rosy side of a new project, ignoring the risks, which include collapse of the current healthy business. Creditors should worry if the success of the project is key to the survival of the firm. As a guideline, banks should finance a new project only if the cash flows from the existing businesses are adequate to cover the repayments. All creditors who support a business that ventures into a big project are almost indirectly taking an equity risk as to whether the new business will succeed.

### 7.7.14 Inadequate Response to Change

Ideally good management will anticipate the adverse changes in the economy and industry and make suitable strategies to take preventive measures. Unawareness or the lack of response to the changes in the economy, industry environments or other external factors is a key risk. Frequently, a failed company is a long established bank customer, which slowly dies as demand for the product vanishes.

### 7.7.15 Poor Corporate Governance

Corporate governance refers to a broad set of written and unwritten processes, rules and policies in an organization that ensure the interests of the organization and its stakeholders – both internal and external – are taken care of. The first decade of 21st century witnessed several corporate scandals and accounting frauds, which calls for more introspection by corporate governance. Enron (US), Parmalat (Europe) and Satyam Computers (India) were prominent examples of poor corporate governance.

As we discussed in the preceding paragraphs, understanding the capabilities and integrity of management is highly critical for a good credit risk analysis. A rule of thumb to understand management is to look at the top. If the top management consist of individuals with commitment, passion and dedication to business with ample experience and expertise, they tend to attract similar high calibre individuals for the rest of the organization. Understanding the capabilities of management to deliver business strategies and meet the challenges to the mission and vision is very critical. Whilst management risks are important, credit risk due diligence must also focus on the underlying business model and business economics. There is a lot of sense in the following words of wisdom from Warren Buffet:

> When a management with a reputation for brilliance tackles a business with a reputation for bad economics, it is the reputation of the business that remains intact.

## 7.8 OTHER INTERNAL RISKS

1. **Financial Risks**: Several forms of financial risk exist in a company. We will discuss this in detail in the next chapter.
2. **Production Risks**: Any event that will cause cessation of production activity or loss of production falls into this category. Breakdown of key machinery, shortage of main inputs, natural calamities (fire, earthquake, flood, etc.), are some of these risks.
3. **Corporate Risks**: Risks that affect the entire company and its future direction fall under this category. Huge losses in a subsidiary may carry the risk of cash down streaming while the hostile takeover threat may cause the top management to divert attention from normal operating activities.
4. **Human Resource Risks**: Strikes and militant unionism are amongst the risks in this category. Other risks include very high staff turnover and poor motivation levels, which will lead to poor productivity levels.

5. **Product Risks**: Products with chemicals and similar ingredients can sometimes be harmful, if not used properly causing injuries to the user or environment, resulting in penalties. This can sometimes lead to bankruptcies and the collapse of companies. An example is the bankruptcies triggered by product liabilities in connection with litigation. Multinationals such as ABB and Halliburton had struggled because of asbestos litigation. Sometimes the use of certain methods or product technology can result in patent violations, inviting penalties.
6. **Customer/Supplier Concentration Risks**: Reliance on a few buyers, who can easily switch to a competitor, is a significant operating risk. This risk can be mitigated if differentiation strategy can be followed effectively. A strong relationship with customers and a time-tested track record can also be considered as mitigants.
7. **Limited Geographic Area**: Most small and medium-sized businesses operate within a specified area. They lack resources to identify and exploit opportunities available in distant markets.
8. **Key-Man Risk**: Companies that cannot function effectively without the relationships or expertise of certain executives are vulnerable, if such an executive leaves abruptly. In the case of family businesses, if such an executive is older with no clear sibling being groomed to take over, or the sibling lacks skills, this raises identical risks.
9. **Legal Risks**: Sometimes certain actions or policies or even strategies may involve infringement and may result in penalties, monetary or otherwise.
10. **Sibling Rivalry**: A visionary entrepreneur may create a formidable business entity/group, which sometimes falls into the hands of feuding siblings/successors. The person conducting the credit analysis study ought to clearly understand the succession plans, which if absent can be considered as a serious risk especially if the CEO/entrepreneur is on the verge of retirement.
11. **Image/Reputation Risks**: Instances and events that lead to the loss of consumer confidence in the products of the company etc. can lead to revenue loss and a drop in profitability.

The abovementioned risks are just for guidance purposes because in the real business world many different types of risk can crop up. Anyone conducting credit risk analysis studies ought to have a discerning eye to identify them. Some of the other risks can be: (a) adverse information in the media; (b) litigation involving top management personnel; (c) poor maintenance of factory/offices; (d) under-utilization of capacity; (e) obsolete stock; (f) extravagant spending; (g) frequent change in auditors; (h) auditors having other assignments in the company, etc.

## CASE STUDY

### Acquisition Strategy with Bank Finance

#### *Background*

The credit team of a reputed bank was presented with a transaction by their Syndication team in 2007. Sanction was sought for a short-term facility (valid for 12 months) to XYZ Ltd amounting to US$150m in a US$750m bridge loan facility being arranged by a Mandated Lead Arranger (MLA). The purpose of the bridge loan was to fund the acquisition of ABC

Ltd, a target identified by the borrower. Within 12 months acquisition finance would be arranged which would repay the short-term facility.

XYZ Ltd was a well-established, profit making marine company. They embarked upon an expansion strategy through acquisitions. The global shipping fleet was showing a growth trend since the later 1990s (see chart). The company believed that whilst shipping/ship building is a highly cyclical industry, they could take comfort in their belief that the boom phase then prevailing in the industry would continue in the medium term.

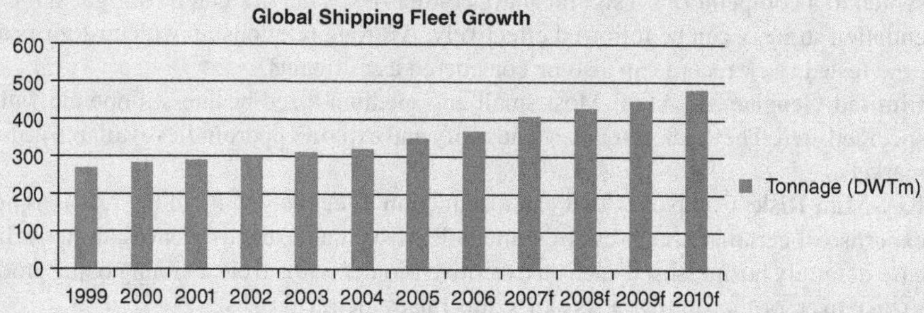


The internal studies by the company forecast that the ship building industry was experiencing a boom on the back of increasing global trade mainly in the form of (a) imports into China – and to a limited extent to India – which witnessed rapid economic growth resulting in heavy appetite for imports such as raw materials (copper, iron ore), etc. and (b) increasing oil demand, resulting in various marine vessels required not only for transportation but also for exploration and extraction in offshore oil fields.

Additional comfort was taken from the view that ship repair and ship building react to business cycles in a divergent manner, i.e. there is an inverse relationship. When the freight rates are high, ships owners postpone repairs (as the ship will be docked for weeks which reduces the revenue); however, new build orders increase. When the freight rate prices drop, ship owners catch up with repairs, although the revenue from ship building will decrease.

### *Acquisition*

XYZ Ltd identified a target company – ABC Ltd – for acquisition in a different geographical location; entirely different from the existing location of XYZ Ltd. The underlying argument was that this provided much needed geographical diversification. A reputed firm – one of the top four in the world – undertook a valuation of the target; they were also the advisors on this deal. They followed various valuation techniques – Discounted Cash Flow Method, Third Party Broker Valuation and Trading Comparable Valuation. Based on these numbers, the consultant recommended a value of nearly one billion US dollars.

### *Credit Concerns*

The credit team expressed the following concerns, amongst others:

- Cyclical business: The business is being acquired at the peak of a boom and downward correction is possible.

- Refinancing risk: XYZ Ltd is confident of completing proper long-term acquisition finance within 12 months to repay the short-term bridge finance. However it carried a refinancing risk, i.e. inability of the borrower to complete an acquisition finance deal.
- Deal risk: It seemed that XYZ Ltd was hurrying through the deal and the valuation also seemed to be on the higher side.
- Internal risks: These included the following: (i) Whilst XYZ Ltd was a well-run company, this was its first acquisition and it was also in a different geographical location. (ii) One of the activities of the target was ship building; however they had not delivered a single ship yet although they had a few orders in hand. (iii) Increasing leverage: The debt funded acquisition would increase the debt burden, interest costs and repayment commitments sharply. (iv) Post-takeover behaviour of existing management and employees of the target: Post-acquisition issues such as integration of cultural or structural differences between two businesses (which carry the internal risk of hindrance to cohesive teamwork) also existed.

Despite the above warnings, the Syndication team was able to obtain the sanction and the MLAs were able to close the deal on time for XYZ Ltd to acquire the target company.

**Aftermath**

One year into acquisition, XYZ Ltd got into financial difficulties which were reflected in the repayment of the loan. The acquisition finance did not materialize and hence the bridge loan providers had to extend the term. The 2008 Credit Crisis ended the boom times for the shipping industry. The target company, which boasted a strong order book at the time of acquisition, found that the orders were being cancelled. XYZ Ltd also faced a downtrend. In the case of ABC Ltd, the key employees had left due to differences with the incoming management while a few customers filed cases because of non-performance. All this resulted in very high credit risk and XYZ Ltd had to restructure their bank loans.

## ✍ QUESTIONS/EXERCISES

1. What is the importance of understanding the business model of a customer? Explain the essential steps and factors involved in internal risk identification.
2. Do you believe SWOT analysis of the customer is a critical step to understand the business model? Please elaborate.
3. You are the newly appointed corporate relationship manager in XYZ Bank. One of your customers has recently recorded a decline in annual turnover, in relation to its size, compared to the previous year. Overall, the business is performing at a significantly lower level of operating efficiency than its peers, as evident from the comparison with industry averages. You also notice that the total asset base of the company has increased while turnover has declined. Explain the steps you would initiate to understand the factors resulting in the drop in turnover and increase in asset base (which includes debtors, stock, investments and fixed assets).
4. Explain the importance of strategy analysis and understanding management capabilities in the assessment of internal risks.

5. You are the newly appointed corporate relationship manager in ABC Bank. One of your customers is a leading regional supermarket chain, known for the quality of its products. It is understood that the company is engaged in a strategy of rapid expansion of outlets from 38 to 80 by channelling the flow of liquidity into the investment of new stores rather than managing the present business. As a result, the company is facing stocking issues in all its stores; however the company management has assured you that this is a temporary phenomenon. Explain how you would assess the internal risks of this customer and the steps you would take to protect the interests of the bank.
6. How would you conduct management analysis of a corporate customer? What is the importance of corporate governance?
7. Do you believe weak financial function is a critical management risk? Please elaborate.
8. Read the following business biographies:
   - Lee Iacocca, who in the early 1980s rescued Chrysler Corporation – then the third largest automobile manufacturer in the world – from the brink of bankruptcy and turned it into a profitable business.
   - Lou Gestesner rescued IBM from financial crisis and extinction in the mid-1990s by implementing a successful turnaround strategy while many experts suggested breaking up IBM into several smaller companies to meet the challenges of the changing technological environment.

   Based on your reading identify (a) new strategies that led to the turnaround; (b) key management changes; (c) SWOT of Chrysler and IBM during the problematic times; (d) impact of external risks; (e) importance of in-depth understanding of the industry. Examine how the various internal risks were effectively managed. (Other business biographies, for example Sam Walton, founder of Wal-Mart etc., are also useful to understand organizational/business dynamics.)

# 8
# Financial Risks

There are several instances where businesses fail not because of lack of business opportunities, but due to poor or improper management of financial affairs. Financial risk refers to the chances of collapse of a business due to wrong financing polices/decisions/strategies such as lopsided capital structure, asset-liability mismatch, etc. Financial risks can plunge a successful business into bankruptcy, if not managed properly. Hence, it is vital for a credit decision to be preceded by an in-depth financial analysis of the customer.

Financial analysis serves mainly three purposes:

1. It digs deep and brings out the financial risks.
2. It triggers questions that lead to a meaningful operating/business analysis.
3. Thirdly, especially for financial intermediaries, such as banks, it is also useful to determine the extent of financial support needed by the prospective borrower.

This explains why financial details are given prominence, among the information called for by credit providers. Financial analysis is done based on financial statements. Credit risk due diligence relies on financial statements for financial analysis which ought to have a cash flow oriented approach. It focuses on the critical factors that affect the obligors' historical operating results and cash flows in an attempt to establish the obligors' ability to generate sustainable recurring earnings and cash flows while ensuring quality of assets.

## 8.1 IMPORTANCE OF FINANCIAL STATEMENTS

Peter Bernstein, in his acclaimed book *Against the Gods – The Remarkable Story* has stated that but for numerical skills, mankind would have never attained the technological marvels it is now proud of. Building huge bridges or sending man into space would have remained a dream, without the numbers. If we could not quantify, measure or value, we would not be able to lead our normal lives in the 21st century.

This is applicable to credit risk analysis as well, where numbers play an important role. Credit risk analysis is basically an art and a science to determine probabilities.[1] Analyzing various parameters such as sales growth, profitability, adequacy of cash flows, operating leverage, financial leverage, total leverage, breakeven point, debt service coverage, return on capital employed, debtors collection period or inventory holding period are based on numbers and these have an important role in arriving at probabilities. Hence 'number crunching' (i.e. financial analysis) is an important tool in identifying and mitigating credit risks.

Imagine a large business corporation like Toyota or Wal-Mart stating its business performance without financial figures. Without them, it would be impossible to understand the impact of what a business is doing and communicate with anyone who would like to interact with the company, such as investors, creditors or lenders. That is why accounting is aptly known as the 'language of business'.

[1] We will discuss Probability of Default (PD) later in the book.

Lenders are concerned about whether they will receive the interest payments and principal on due dates. In other words, they are concerned about the repayment capacity. Hence, lenders need to monitor the debt levels of the borrowing company and ensure that the company is generating enough cash to pay its day-to-day bills, and will have sufficient cash in the future to meet interest and other repayment commitments. The company's ability to meet its obligations ultimately depends on cash flows and profitability; hence banks, FIs and other creditors rely on financial statements to assess the financial capacity of borrowers or prospective borrowers.

Figure 8.1 explains how financial statements capture the performance of a business entity. The diagram is a general description of how financial statements evolve and capture the entire gamut of events, business decisions and actions (expressed in monetary terms) in the context of the overall macroeconomic environment. For the purposes of our analytical discussion, we refer to financial statements as those sets of information including the balance sheet, profit and loss, cash flow statement (or funds flow statement, if CFS is not available), notes to accounts and other supplementary data, provided to the reader, by statutory requirement or otherwise.

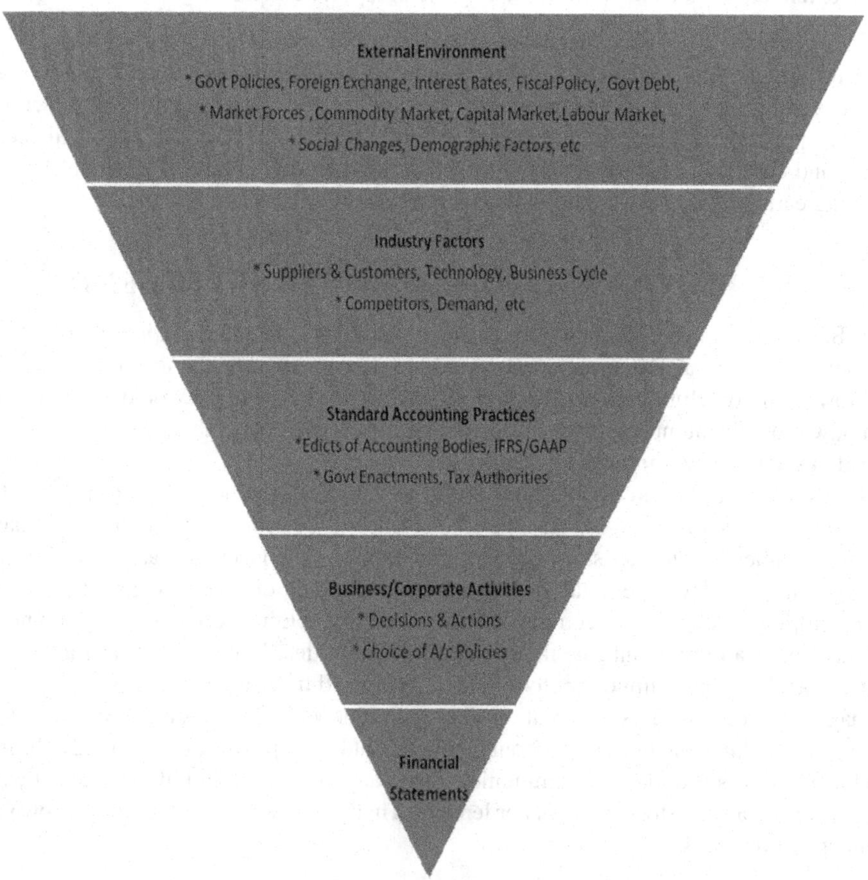


**Figure 8.1** Financial Statements in Overall Business Context

## 8.2 QUALITY AND QUANTITY OF FINANCIAL STATEMENTS

Financial statements, the end product of accounting, are viewed as proxies of economic activities and performance. Analysis of financial statements enjoys a prominent place in the assessment of the study of credit risks, lending decisions and ongoing monitoring of the lending portfolio. Financial statements are the major source of information to conduct financial analysis with because they contain data related to land, buildings, machinery, vehicles, stock, receivables, cash, bank deposits and borrowings, capital, external creditors, tax liabilities, sales, cost of sales, selling expenses, other overheads, interest costs and cash flows/funds flows, amongst others. They summarize the economic impact of the various operational and strategic decisions taken by the management.

### 8.2.1 Quality of Financial Statements

As far as possible, always use audited financial statements. An audit means that an independent professional accountant has verified the numbers and attested that the financial statements are prepared in accordance with accepted accounting practices[2] and provide a 'true and fair' representation of the financial results and financial position at a point in time. The user of audited financial statements must understand the contents of the audit report. Whilst countries such as the UK, India and Australia follow a 'principle' based system, the US follows a 'rule based' system. In most cases both systems produce identical results, although at times they can differ. Let us see what the responsibility of auditors is and what is reported in the audit report. The contents of a normal audit report are examined below:

**Audited Financial Statements Cover a Fixed Period of Time**: The auditors' report provides an opinion of financial transactions and their effects for a fixed period of time, usually one year. Sometimes it can be less than one year or more than one year. Most of the auditors' report clearly defines what type of financial statements are covered, i.e. the statement of financial position (or balance sheet) as at a particular date – say as at 31 March 20XX, profit and loss account (or statement of comprehensive income), statement of changes in owners' equity and statement of cash flows for the period (i.e. one year) then ended, a summary of significant accounting policies and other explanatory notes.

**Management's Responsibility for the Financial Statements**: Auditors' reports unequivocally mention who is responsible for the financial statements, selection of accounting policies and procedures. It is the management which is responsible for the preparation and fair presentation of these financial statements in accordance with International Financial Reporting Standards. The management is responsible for designing, implementing and maintaining internal controls relevant to the preparation and fair presentation of financial statements that are free from material misstatement, whether due to fraud or error, selecting and applying appropriate accounting policies and making accounting estimates that are reasonable under the circumstances.

**Auditors' Responsibility**: An audit can be broadly termed as an assurance or attesting function. The auditors' responsibility is to express an opinion on the financial statements, prepared by the management, based on audit procedures conducted in accordance with International Standards on Auditing (ISA). An auditor conducting an audit in accordance

[2] Includes International Financial Reporting Standards (IFRS) or country specific Generally Accepted Accounting Policies (e.g. United States GAAP).

with ISAs is responsible for obtaining reasonable assurance that the financial statements taken as a whole are free from material misstatements. ISA 240 acknowledges that due to the inherent limitations of the audit, there is a risk that some material misstatements may remain undetected, even though the audit is properly planned and performed in accordance with ISAs.

Hence, the user of audited accounts must be aware of this limitation. As is evident, the management is responsible for the preparation, presentation and integrity of the financial statements. During an audit process not all of the transactions or assets/liabilities are verified. It is a well-known fact that cleverly camouflaged frauds are not easily detectable during a normal audit. They call for a forensic audit or due diligence or management audit or some other type of assurance service. Hence, it is suggested that over and above the normal audit, a thorough due diligence exercise may be insisted upon by the lenders, on a periodical basis – say every five years. However, it is pertinent to note that nothing replaces management integrity, ethics and corporate governance.

### 8.2.2 Quantity of Financial Statements

In order to study the financial risks involved, how many years' financial statements have to be analyzed? Answers will vary depending upon the nature of business. Ideally speaking a ten year analysis is better because:

1. It captures the business performance through different economic cycles. Generally, there is a business cycle in most economies, over a period of ten years.
2. It provides more insight into the management policies and their impact in the past. Did the firm perform in accordance with strategies? How was the growth financed? Why was the firm stagnant despite spectacular industry growth? What are the important decisions made by the top management in the past? How have those decisions impacted the financial performance/position? Answers to these types of questions can provide insight into the quality of the management.

Whilst ten years' financials are ideal, at least five years' financial data are needed for a new credit prospect, unless the firm is younger than this. However, there are many banks and financial institutions who prescribe a minimum of three years' historical financial statements for new customers, which may not provide sufficient depth to the understanding of how management's strategies and actions have impacted the business. Usually some of the strategic decisions, such as expansion, entry into new markets and product diversification take at least two or more years to yield full results; hence it is suggested to rely, if possible, on five years' historical financial data.

## 8.3 ROLE OF HISTORICAL FINANCIAL STATEMENTS

Many people have often wondered why historical financial statements are analyzed, while the bank or financial institution relies on future cash flows for repayment. The answer is that the historical track record is often the best guide as far as financial analysis is concerned. Research has shown that a company's past performance record, in most cases, is the most reliable factor to understand its future course. Analyzing historical financial analysis enables one to understand the reasons for fluctuations in their past performance and provides strong guidance as to what can be expected in the future in the context of external environment, industrial trends and other company specific factors. For example, whilst a market leader in a non-cyclical business (e.g. the food industry) usually shows steady growth – exceptional years tend to be rare – the credit executive must interpret cyclical businesses (e.g. construction) based on the understanding of the business cycles, which we described in Chapter 5.

Moreover, historical financial performance also speaks volumes about the leadership and capability of management to take the company through troubled waters such as recessions, wars, civil wars, high or low interest rate environments, an inflationary or deflationary economy, political uncertainties, emergence of new competitors, changes in technology and changes in industry/market dynamics. Companies that repeatedly performed well during challenging and troubled times in the past retain a high probability of doing the same in the future.

## 8.4 FINANCIAL ANALYSIS

The purpose of financial analysis is to understand the financial strengths and weaknesses of the customer and to recognize and identify early warning signs of financial risks and suggest suitable defensive strategies and practical solutions to mitigate the risks and protect the lender from potential problems and credit losses. Financial analysis has a very important role to play in ensuring the creditworthiness of customers by enabling the lender to take appropriate timely action.

Each component of the financial statement contains numbers, pregnant with information. It is both an art and a science to read and analyze financial statements and bring out the wealth of information behind the numbers. Over the years, several techniques have evolved and are still evolving, aimed at decoding the information content in the financial statements. A financial analyst ought to use the 'why' and 'why not' style as he examines the items presented in the financial statements. Let us examine each component, beginning with the balance sheet.

### 8.4.1 Balance Sheet

The balance sheet shows the financial position of a business as at a particular date, usually the end of a period – say a year, a quarter or a month. The balance sheet is a critical tool for an effective credit evaluation. It answers a lot of questions which a financial analyst is likely to ask while ascertaining creditworthiness, such as:

- What is the capital structure of the business? Is it appropriate? Have the owners of business put sufficient capital into the business?
- What are the short-term and long-term liabilities (i.e. debt) of the business? Are they properly structured? Is it possible to relate each source of finance to a particular asset item?
- What is the credit period provided by trade suppliers? Did the suppliers alter trade terms?
- What are the taxation and other statutory liabilities outstanding?
- What is the quantum of fixed assets and are they put to optimum use?
- What is the level of stocking required and what are the stock management policies, in broader terms.
- What is the level of trade debtors?

Sometimes the financial analyst will require certain adjustments to the balances sheet variables as presented in audited accounts. This is because of the fact that the accountants and auditors prepare financial statements generally for the shareholders and many items are classified accordingly, based on IFRS or GAAP followed by each country. However, the credit executive is looking at things from an entirely different angle (as a lender), which calls for certain adjustments to balance sheet items. The following are certain instances where the financial analyst would have to recast the balance sheet, sometimes through the profit and loss account:

- **Adjusting Inventory Valuation**: An analyst may sometimes be required to perform adjustments to inventory figures. Since inventory valuation affects the cost of goods sold,[3] it has a direct impact on the net profit and consequently on retained earnings. This, in turn, can impact various financial ratios. Hence, if there is a change in inventory valuation method during a year, it is better to recast the inventory values to make the financial statements comparable. Another occasion to make adjustments to the inventory valuation would be to conduct meaningful peer analysis, if the peers follow different inventory valuation policies.
- **Reassessing the Values of Balance Sheet Variables**: If the credit executive takes the view that certain assets require more provisioning (e.g. 10% provisioning of debtors instead of 3% in the books), then the balance sheet should be adjusted to reflect the impact.
- **Converting Off-Balance Sheet Items into On-Sheet Items**: Conversion of off-balance sheet items into on-balance sheet items is yet another necessary step. Accordingly, the balance should be recast for analytical purposes by capturing the impact of off-balance sheet leases, hedges, etc. Usually while analyzing the financial statements of airlines it is practice to convert the aircraft under operating leases (shown as an off-balance sheet item) into an on-balance sheet item.
- **Dividends Payable**: In certain cases, the dividends payable may appear as part of the equity/shareholders' funds, which should be separated and treated as a current liability.
- **Intangibles**: The credit executive should deduct this from the net worth to arrive at tangible net worth.
- **Unsubordinated Shareholders Loan**: If included as part of the equity or shareholders' funds this item should be excluded, especially in the case of limited liability companies. The logic is that legally, such loans rank *pari passu* with external creditors.
- **Dues from/to Related Parties**: A close study of this item may result in adjustments. For example, the dues from related parties are sometimes used as a method of indirect withdrawal of owner's capital or funds from business. In such cases, appropriate adjustments may be made to the net worth.
- **Alternative Accounting Policy**: Where the credit executive suspects that the accounting policies used to account for certain critical items are not the best available, alternative accounting policies may be applied to the extent possible.

### 8.4.2 Income Statement (or) Profit and Loss Account

The income statement shows the revenues from operations (sale of goods or services from continuing or regular operations) costs and expenses incurred in connection with such revenues and the profit or loss resulting therefrom. As in the case of balance sheet, a credit executive may have to recast the profit and loss account to suit the purpose at hand. Some situations that require such recasting are:

- To give effect to the crystallization of a contingent liability. For example, suppose the product liability litigation, which was shown in the balance sheet as contingent liability, is now adjudged against the company.

[3] Usually Cost of Goods Sold = Opening Inventory + Purchases − Closing Inventory. Hence, a higher closing inventory would mean a lower cost of goods sold and vice versa. Sometimes, the obligors may use techniques to show a higher closing inventory for 'window dressing' purposes.

- To reverse capitalization of certain expenditures. Interest capitalization during the pre-operating period is still debated. As happened in the case of WorldCom, sometimes certain revenue expenses are capitalized. The credit executive ought to undo such gimmicks wherever suspected.
- To provide for certain omitted expenses or to make extra provisioning write-down/write-up certain asset/liability values, disclosed in the balance sheet. It is to be noted that most of the recasting will impact both the balance sheet and the profit and loss account.
- To capture results of discontinued/extraordinary operations or prior period items, if not properly classified in the P&L provided by the borrower/debtor.
- To assess the impact of alternative accounting policies.

### 8.4.3 Cash Flow Statement (CFS)

As we have seen in the first chapter, the CFS is the result of the attempt by the financial community to overcome the drawbacks of the balance sheet, profit and loss and funds flow. To a great extent, the CFS waters down the inefficiencies, if any, which have crept into the financial statements by deliberate accommodative accounting policy decisions taken by the management. It answers the questions (which cannot be fully answered by the balance sheet or the profit and loss account) such as: (a) Despite suffering losses, how has the company managed to pay dividends? (b) How is the increase in bank borrowings utilized? (c) Despite higher net profit for the period, why did the firm default the term-loan instalment?

The CFS is important because the survival and success of any business is determined not by 'accounting profits' alone but by its ability to generate cash income in excess of cash outflows. It helps the credit executive to form an opinion about the strength, stability and sufficiency of the cash flows to meet various obligations including interest, dividends, tax liabilities and repayment of term commitments and loans. Occasions for recasting of cash flows are rare, but not improbable. There are situations where the credit executive is called upon to make certain cash flow adjustments. Some instances are:

- To classify an item under the proper head. Suppose that certain investing activity is shown under operating activity. The credit executive may wish to recast it.
- To reflect the impact of certain recasting done in the balance sheet/profit and loss. For instance, if capitalization of certain expenses is reclassified, then the cash flow headings will also shift – from 'net movement in fixed assets' to the 'net result for the year'.

## 8.5 ANALYTICAL TOOLS

Financial analysis can be done in many ways, of which the four principal tools are shown in Figure 8.2 and described below.

### 8.5.1 Accounting Analysis

Unambiguous understanding of enigmatic transactions or deviations in accounting policies to boost profit or reduce losses or to show a better financial position is also one of the important focuses of financial analysis. Deliberate manipulation of accounting policies is not uncommon, and this can critically impact the solvency of companies, as evidenced by the

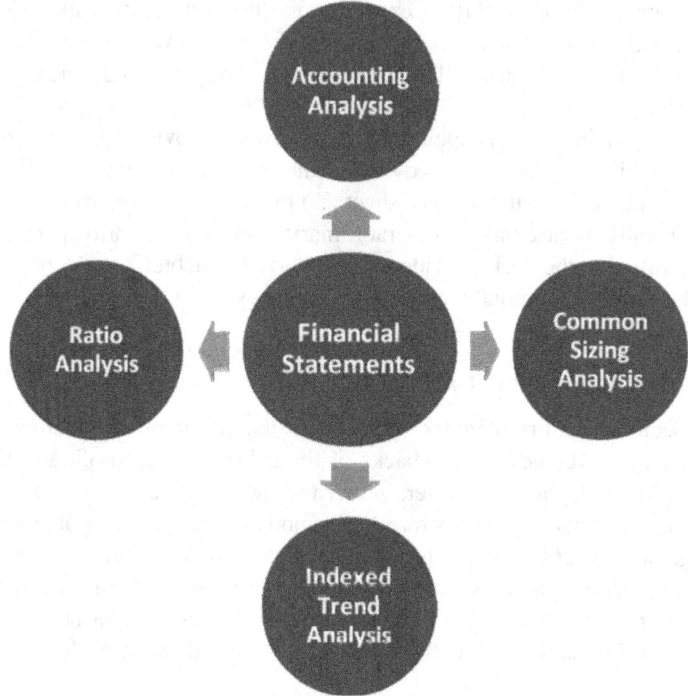


**Figure 8.2** Various Financial Analysis Tools

collapse of companies like Enron, WorldCom, Satyam Computers, etc. Hence, the analysis of accounting policies is important. The following are the major steps of accounting analysis:

(a) **Understand the Critical Activities**: Every business has certain critical factors, upon which survival hinges. For instance, for a trader dealing in fast-changing technology (mobile phones, PCs), stock management is critical. So, accounting policies used to record the stock, purchases and provisioning are decisive. Similarly, accounting policies related to the recognition of interest income on low-quality (sub-standard) credit assets and provisioning of credit losses are important for a financial institution with a large credit portfolio.

(b) **Accounting Choices**: Several accounting policies are available, which allow flexibility to account for similar transactions in dissimilar ways. For example various accounting choices for stock valuation are available (under IFRS/GAAP) such as:
   - First in First Out (FIFO).
   - Last in First Out (LIFO).
   - Average Price/Weighted Average Price.
   - Specific Identification Method.

   Similarly different accounting choices are available for various business variables such as depreciation, amortization, derivatives, hedging and investments, to name a few. Hence ideally, to the extent possible, the credit executive may identify the best method to account for the transactions, especially the critical factors, and confirm whether the accounting policies based on which the financial statements are prepared comply with substance rather than form. Knowledge of accounting standards and accounting expertise is highly desirable for the meaningful understanding of accounting of transactions. If necessary, the credit executive should not hesitate to consult accounting experts – professional accountants.

(c) **Accounting Estimates**: Several estimates are done by the firm while compiling the financial statements. Estimates of the life of fixed assets, provisions on bad and doubtful debts, slow moving stock, amortization of intangibles, termination/retirement benefits to staff, taxation liabilities, etc. are some of them. The credit executive should ensure that the estimates have been reasonably arrived at.

(d) **Judgement and Evaluation**: The credit executive should evaluate the accounting policies and estimates followed by the entity. Consideration should also be given to the off-balance sheet items and contingent liabilities. If the credit executive arrives at an opinion that the best accounting alternatives have not been followed or accounting estimates are improper, then recasting of the financial statements becomes necessary. For instance, if the life of a machinery item is assumed to be 30 years to compute annual depreciation, the credit executive ought to challenge and investigate this assumption. If it is found that the life of such machinery is 15 years, recasting of financial statements would be required (by increasing the provision for depreciation). Similarly, from the debtors ageing it can be understood whether appropriate provision for doubtful debtors has been taken. If the credit executive feels that the provision levels are low given the long outstanding over-dues, then adjustments are called for.

Why do business firms attempt creative accounting practices? There are several reasons. However, an ethical business firm would never do this. The credit executive ought to be aware of the circumstances where creative accounting or accounting manipulations or unreliable accounting estimates may be attempted. Some of them are:

- To hide business deterioration.
- To maintain the rating by external rating agencies such as Moody's, Standard & Poor's, Fitch, Crisil, etc. at acceptable levels.
- To ensure performance bonuses (for top management), normally linked to the financial results.
- To ensure compliance of financial covenants with the lenders.
- Maintenance of share prices at higher levels etc.

However, all accounting disparities need not be driven by ulterior motives; for instance, a drop in debtors provisioning may reflect the change in customer focus. The judgement and logical skills of the credit executive should be carefully employed while considering all possible explanations of accounting changes/disparities and the presence of suspicious circumstances. Whilst Merck's treatment of certain selling expenses as an addition to sales, which was later charged off as selling costs, caught the headlines temporarily, it was the accounting treatment of certain revenue expenditure by WorldCom as capital expenditure that really created a storm, along with Enron, in 2001/2002.

### 8.5.2 Common Sizing Analysis (CSA)

Common sizing of the financial statements is arrived at by converting all items in the financial statements into a percentage of the total. Thus, in order to create common size statements, each number is expressed as a percentage of total assets or total revenues. For example, each of the asset accounts may be divided by total assets. Similarly, we may also divide each of the liability and equity accounts by total assets since

$$\text{Total assets} = \text{Total liabilities.}$$

CSA facilitates easier and more productive comparisons and better understanding of financial statements. CSA is particularly useful in the following situations:

1. It facilitates meaningful comparisons between the financial statements of two firms, especially if they are different in size. For example, in order to compare oil and gas giant Exxon-Mobil with Conoco Philips, CSA would be useful. Or to compare and contrast Barrick Gold Corporation against Goldcorp Incorporated (both companies are listed in NYSE and engaged in the exploration and production of precious metals such as gold). Or to compare two steel companies – say, Arcelor Mittal listed in Europe and the US and Tata Steel listed in India.
2. It is a powerful tool for 'year on year' analysis as it brings out the changes over the period in an easily comprehensible manner.

The usefulness of CSA is evident from the following illustration:

**Problem 8.1**

The balance sheet and profit and loss accounts of ABCD Ltd for the FYE 30.09.X1 and 30.09.X0 are given below:

$ in 000s

| A. BALANCE SHEET | | | B. INCOME STATEMENT | | |
|---|---|---|---|---|---|
| SOURCES OF FUNDS | 20X1 (12m) | 20X0 (12m) | Particulars | 20X1 (12m) | 20X0 (12m) |
| **Owner's Fund** | | | Sales | 421,219.40 | 254,293.40 |
| Equity Share Capital | 10,535.60 | 10,534.90 | Mat Consumed | −302,154.9 | −178,380.40 |
| Share Application Money | 3,422.90 | 0 | Mfg Expenses | −9,880.5 | −11,734.50 |
| Reserves and Surplus | 237,409.10 | 109,411.00 | Depreciation | −28,161.40 | −15,651.10 |
| **Loan Funds** | | | Personnel Exp | −5,693.8 | −4,410.70 |
| Secured Loans | 141,888.90 | 40,684.00 | Conversion Costs | −43,735.7 | −31,796.3 |
| Unsecured Loans | 47,395.90 | 60,673.90 | COGS (sub-total) | −345,890.6 | 210,176.7 |
| **Total** | **440,652.40** | **221,303.80** | Gross Profit | 75,328.8 | 44,116.7 |
| **USES OF FUNDS** | | | Selling Expenses | −13,210 | −7,617.80 |
| **Fixed Assets** | | | Admin Expenses | −9,584 | −5,928.10 |
| Gross Block | 467,273.20 | 253,559.90 | Operating Profit | 52,534.80 | 30,570.80 |
| Less: Revaluation Reserve | − 27,385.00 | − 27,707.80 | Investment Income | 7,430.90 | 3,685.30 |
| Less: Acc. Depreciation | −150,769.20 | −118,415.30 | Other Income | 18.1 | 13 |
| Net Block | 289,119.00 | 107,436.80 | PBIT | 59,983.80 | 34,269.10 |
| Capital Work-in-progress | 15,333.10 | 5,123.80 | Financial Expenses | −18,730.10 | −12,472.50 |
| **Investments** | **38,501.60** | **67,261.10** | PBT | 41,253.70 | 21,796.60 |
| **Net Current Assets** | | | Tax Charges | −11,920.00 | −1,395.00 |
| Cur. Assets, Loans and Adv. | 196,795.40 | 91,225.10 | PAT | 29,333.70 | 20,401.60 |
| Less: Curr. Liabilities | 99,725.30 | 49,743.00 | | | |
| Total Net Current Assets | 97,070.10 | 41,482.10 | | | |
| **Miscellaneous exp. not w/off** | 628.60 | **0** | | | |
| **Total** | **440,652.40** | **221,303.80** | | | |

Please apply CSA to interpret the above details.

**Solution**

Establishing a link among various figures of two years for a meaningful comparison is a tricky exercise with the absolute numbers. However, CSA solves this, as is evident from the following table:

**Common Sized Balance Sheet and Income Statement of ABCD Ltd**

| A. Balance Sheet | | | B. Income Statement | | |
|---|---|---|---|---|---|
| Sources Of Funds | 20X1 (12m) | 20X0 (12m) | Particulars | 20X1 (12m) | 20X0 (12m) |
| ***Owner's Fund*** | | | Sales | 100% | 100% |
| Equity Share Capital | 2% | 5% | Material Consumed | 72% | 70% |
| Share Application Money | 1% | 0% | Mfg Expenses | 2% | 5% |
| Preference Share Capital | 0% | 0% | Depreciation | 7% | 6% |
| Reserves and Surplus | 54% | 49% | Personnel Exp. | 1% | 2% |
| ***Loan Funds*** | | | Total Conversion Exp. | 10% | 13% |
| Secured Loans | 32% | 18% | COGS | 82% | 83% |
| Unsecured Loans | 11% | 27% | Gross Profit | 18% | 17% |
| Total | 100% | 100% | Selling Expenses | 3% | 3% |
| **Uses Of Funds** | | | Admin Expenses | 2% | 2% |
| ***Fixed Assets*** | | | Operating Profit | 12% | 12% |
| Gross Block | 106% | 115% | Investment Income | 2% | 1% |
| Less: Revaluation Reserve | –6% | –13% | Other Income | 0% | 0% |
| Less: Acc. Depreciation | –34% | –54% | PBIT | 14% | 13% |
| Net Block | 66% | 49% | Financial Expenses | 4% | 5% |
| Capital Work-in-progress | 3% | 2% | PBT | 10% | 9% |
| Investments | 9% | 30% | Tax Charges | 3% | 1% |
| ***Net Current Assets*** | | | PAT | 7% | 8% |
| Current Assets | 45% | 41% | | | |
| Less: Current Liabilities | 23% | 22% | | | |
| Total Net Current Assets | 22% | 19% | | | |
| Miscellaneous exp. not w/off. | 0% | 0% | | | |
| **Total** | **100%** | **100%** | | | |

CSA saves time and provides an overall view of the situation and equips the credit executive to conduct further in-depth analysis. Now the reader can establish the connection between the items within a matter of minutes while an experienced eye can do it in seconds. For instance, let us sum up the balance sheet changes based on common sized balance sheets:

1. **Assets (Use of Funds)**: Investments, which accounted for 30% of the assets in the previous year have dwindled to a minor asset and form just 9% of the total as at 30.09.X1. The reason is traceable to the sharp increase in the fixed assets – increase in the Net Block to 66% from 49%, evidencing expansion. (It seems that the investments were either converted or liquidated and the proceeds were utilized towards expansion.) However, Capital Working in Progress (CAPEX) remained identical during FYE 30.09.X1 and 30.09.X0. Since doubling of fixed assets in just one year is highly improbable, a takeover/acquisition could also be a reason for the increase in the Net Block. The increase in the current assets (to 45% from 41%) exceeded the increase in current liabilities (from 22% to 23%), suggesting relatively less reliance on current liabilities to

fund the current assets. Although fixed assets are revalued, overall impact on the balance sheet is insignificant as the revaluation amounted to just 6% of the total.

2. **Sources of Funds**: The reduction in paid-up capital to 2% of the total sources of funds shows that there was a significant shift in funding pattern. The reserves and surplus percentage jumped to 66% from 49%. In view of the presence of share application money, it is evident that one of the reasons for the increase in reserves and surplus ought to be the share premium. The proportion of loans increased to 53% (PY 45%) within which the percentage of unsecured loans reduced while that of secured loans increased, suggesting stricter credit terms by the bankers/lenders. New share issue and new loans are traceable to the sharp increase in the assets – increase in the Net Block, reflecting expansion. These insights ought to trigger further intelligent questioning by the financial analyst. (Interpretation of common sized profit and loss is left to the reader, given its straightforward nature.)

### 8.5.3 Indexed Trend Analysis (ITA)

Historical financial performance can be effectively studied by ITA. It has several advantages such as: (i) it shows how the businesses performed during the business cycles; (ii) it demonstrates the financial impact of the managerial decisions taken, such as expansion, acquisition or disposal of business segments and (iii) it shows whether the business is growing or declining and of course provides a base for further intelligent questioning of the situation. The following example will clarify the advantages of ITA:

**Problem 8.2**

The five year balance sheets and profit and loss accounts of ABCD Ltd are given below.

($ Millions)

| A. BALANCE SHEET | 20X4 (12m) | 20X3 (12m) | 20X2 (12m) | 20X1 (12m) | 20X0 (12m) |
|---|---|---|---|---|---|
| **SOURCES OF FUNDS** | | | | | |
| **Owner's Fund** | | | | | |
| Equity Share Capital | 10,535.60 | 10,534.90 | 10,534.50 | 9,333.90 | 9,319.00 |
| Share Application Money | 3,422.90 | 0 | 0 | 0 | 1,879.50 |
| Preference Share Capital | 0.00 | 0 | 2,929.50 | 2,529.50 | 0 |
| Reserves and Surplus | 237,409.10 | 109,411.00 | 98,652.90 | 84,119.40 | 80,916.90 |
| **Loan Funds** | | | | | |
| Secured Loans | 141,888.90 | 40,684.00 | 59,881.10 | 54,776.40 | 27,367.80 |
| Unsecured Loans | 47,395.90 | 60,673.90 | 55,321.30 | 52,076.50 | 55,105.50 |
| **Total** | **440,652.40** | **221,303.80** | **227,319.30** | **202,835.70** | **174,588.70** |
| **USES OF FUNDS** | | | | | |
| **Fixed Assets** | | | | | |
| Gross Block | 467,273.20 | 253,559.90 | 243,309.50 | 186,503.30 | 178,483.30 |
| Less: Revaluation Reserve | 27,385.00 | 27,707.80 | 27,710.60 | 27,710.60 | 27,710.60 |
| Less: Accumulated Depreciation | 150,769.20 | 118,415.30 | 92,140.60 | 66,919.30 | 49,444.70 |
| Net Block | 289,119.00 | 107,436.80 | 123,458.30 | 91,873.40 | 101,328.00 |

| | | | | | |
|---|---|---|---|---|---|
| Capital Work-in-progress | 15,333.10 | 5,123.80 | 3,314.20 | 34,378.30 | 20,694.30 |
| **Investments** | 38,501.60 | 67,261.10 | 60,665.60 | 42,945.90 | 42,823.30 |
| **Net Current Assets** | | | | | |
| Current Assets, Loans and Advances | 196,795.40 | 91,225.10 | 78,539.50 | 84,651.80 | 51,323.10 |
| Less: Curr. Liabilities and Provisions | 99,725.30 | 49,743.00 | 38,658.30 | 51,013.70 | 41,580.00 |
| Total Net Current Assets | 97,070.10 | 41,482.10 | 39,881.20 | 33,638.10 | 9,743.10 |
| **Unamortized Miscellaneous Exp.** | 628.60 | 0 | 0 | 0 | 0 |
| **Total** | **440,652.40** | **221,303.80** | **227,319.30** | **202,835.70** | **174,588.70** |

B. INCOME STATEMENT

| Particulars | 20X4 (12m) | 20X3 (12m) | 20X2 (12m) | 20X1 (12m) | 20X0 (12m) |
|---|---|---|---|---|---|
| Sales | 421,219.40 | 254,293.40 | 178,498.60 | 126,238.00 | 115,109.90 |
| Material Consumed | 302,154.90 | 178,380.40 | 120,289.50 | 83,094.10 | 76,165.20 |
| Total Conversion Exp. | 43,735.70 | 31,796.30 | 23,414.10 | 16,440.10 | 14,559.80 |
| COGS | 345,890.60 | 210,176.70 | 143,703.60 | 99,534.20 | 90,725.00 |
| Gross Profit | 75,328.80 | 44,116.70 | 34,795.00 | 26,703.80 | 24,384.90 |
| Selling Expenses | 13,210.00 | 7,617.80 | 3,763.60 | 2,904.40 | 2,352.00 |
| Administrative Expenses | 9,584.00 | 5,928.10 | 5,659.20 | 5,020.30 | 4,190.70 |
| Operating Profit | 52,534.80 | 30,570.80 | 25,372.20 | 18,779.10 | 17,842.20 |
| Investment Income | 7,430.90 | 3,685.30 | 6,281.90 | 5,994.40 | 3,254.20 |
| Other Income | 18.10 | 13.00 | 38.70 | 115.30 | 1,323.70 |
| PBIT | 59,983.80 | 34,269.10 | 31,692.80 | 24,888.80 | 22,420.10 |
| Financial Expenses | 18,730.10 | 12,472.50 | 10,458.30 | 7,789.60 | 5,578.80 |
| PBT | 41,253.70 | 21,796.60 | 21,234.50 | 17,099.20 | 16,841.30 |
| Tax Charges | 11,920.00 | 1395.00 | 610.00 | 340.00 | 655.00 |
| PAT | 29,333.70 | 20,401.60 | 20,624.50 | 16,759.20 | 16,186.30 |

Apply the ITA and interpret the result.

## Solution

Whilst the array of absolute numbers (presented above) contains significant information, it is difficult to understand how each balance sheet variable has changed over the years from the absolute numbers. Converting the absolute numbers into an index with 20X0 as base year facilitates better comparison and comprehension of the trend, as evident from the following table:

## A. INDEXED TREND ANALYSIS OF BALANCE SHEET

| SOURCES OF FUNDS | 20X4 (12m) | 20X3 (12m) | 20X2 (12m) | 20X1 (12m) | 20X0 (12m) |
|---|---|---|---|---|---|
| **Owner's Funds** | | | | | |
| Equity Share Capital | 113 | 113 | 113 | 100 | 100 |
| Share Application Money | 182 | 0 | 0 | 0 | 100 |
| Preference Share Capital | 0 | 0 | 100 | 100 | NA |
| Reserves and Surplus | 293 | 135 | 122 | 104 | 100 |
| Loan Funds | | | | | |
| Secured Loans | 518 | 149 | 219 | 200 | 100 |
| Unsecured Loans | 86 | 110 | 100 | 95 | 100 |
| **Total** | **252** | **127** | **130** | **116** | **100** |

| | | | | | |
|---|---|---|---|---|---|
| **USES OF FUNDS** | | | | | |
| ***Fixed Assets*** | | | | | |
| Gross Block | 262 | 142 | 136 | 104 | 100 |
| Less: Revaluation Reserve | 99 | 100 | 100 | 100 | 100 |
| Less: Accumulated Depreciation | 305 | 239 | 186 | 135 | 100 |
| Net Block | 285 | 106 | 122 | 91 | 100 |
| Capital Work-in-progress | 74 | 25 | 16 | 166 | 100 |
| Investments | 90 | 157 | 142 | 100 | 100 |
| Net Current Assets | | | | | |
| Current Assets, Loans and Advances | 383 | 178 | 153 | 165 | 100 |
| Less: Current Liabilities and Provisions | 240 | 120 | 93 | 123 | 100 |
| Total Net Current Assets | 996 | 426 | 409 | 345 | 100 |
| **Total** | **252** | **127** | **130** | **116** | **100** |

**Comments**: In relation to the total index, which increased from 100 to 252 during the five year period, some items have grown more rapidly, while certain other items were either slow paced or even declined. Prominent among the items that have shown significant increase during this period are the secured loans, net block, reserves and surplus (with share premium being one of the reasons) and net current assets. Major items that have shown a decline are the investments, CAPEX and unsecured loans. Overall, the balance sheet has grown with the fuel for growth coming from both equity and debt sources. The financial leverage, liquidity, working capital management and other critical financial parameters can be further explored in the next stage of analysis.

## B. INDEXED TREND ANALYSIS OF INCOME STATEMENT

| Particulars | 20X4 (12m) | 20X3 (12m) | 20X2 (12m) | 20X1 (12m) | 20X0 (12m) |
|---|---|---|---|---|---|
| Sales | 366 | 221 | 155 | 110 | 100 |
| Material Consumed | 397 | 234 | 158 | 109 | 100 |
| Total Conversion Exp. | 300 | 218 | 161 | 113 | 100 |
| Cost of Goods Sold | 381 | 232 | 158 | 110 | 100 |
| Gross Profit | 309 | 181 | 143 | 110 | 100 |
| Selling Expenses | 562 | 324 | 160 | 123 | 100 |
| Administrative Expenses | 229 | 141 | 135 | 120 | 100 |
| Operating Profit (OP) | 294 | 171 | 142 | 105 | 100 |
| Investment Income | 228 | 113 | 193 | 184 | 100 |
| Other Income | 1 | 1 | 3 | 9 | 100 |
| PBIT* | 268 | 153 | 141 | 111 | 100 |
| Financial Expenses | 336 | 224 | 187 | 140 | 100 |
| Profit before Tax (PBT) | 245 | 129 | 126 | 102 | 100 |
| Tax Charges | 1820 | 213 | 93 | 52 | 100 |
| Profit after Tax (PAT) | 181 | 126 | 127 | 104 | 100 |

*Profit before Interest and Tax

Whilst sales increased by a factor of 3.7, the main direct expense – material consumed – has gone up by a factor of 4, possibly reflecting higher raw material costs, which may be investigated further. Conversion expenses recorded a proportionately lower increase as it comprises some fixed costs such as plant depreciation, etc. Since Cost of Goods Sold (COGS) increased faster than revenue, the increase in GP growth fell behind the sales growth. This cautions the credit executive and prompts an investigative questioning – look into the reasons behind it, is it the strategy? Or industry trend? What about the future? What is the guidance available in the market? What about the major competitors? Selling expenses shot up by 5.6 times, suggesting extreme selling efforts, reasons for which may be established. This prompts the credit executive to dig a bit into the marketing tactics and strategies. The explanation for the lower increase in admin costs is the same as that for conversion costs. As indicated by the profit parameters such as OP, PBIT, PBT and PAT, profitability growth did not catch up with sales growth. This may indicate that the company is using favourable accounting tactics to boost revenue growth – viz. including certain selling expenses as part of the sales, which are then charged off (in the P&L) under selling/other costs. An accounting analysis during the period is also suggested. Whilst investment income increased, the other income component dropped. Higher investment income may not recur as the balance sheet shows a drop in investment portfolio during FYE 20X4 because of liquidation of a significant portion of the portfolio, reasons for which may be investigated further.

### 8.5.4 Ratio Analysis

Ratio analysis is the most powerful and principal tool of financial analysis. Effective ratio analysis helps the credit executive to look behind the numbers adroitly and link the financial numbers to the business factors. Banks, term lending institutions, management, regulatory authorities, auditors, rating agencies, investors, business newspapers, magazines and many others rely on ratio analysis, depending upon their requirements. For instance, whilst the equity investors are concerned about earnings per share, a term creditor/lender is concerned about debt service ratios. For credit risk analysis, the following ratio categorization, shown in Figure 8.3, is among the best to study financial risks of a borrower/debtor, whether existing or prospective.

Ratio analysis has particular relevance to lenders in the following areas:

- Ratio analysis can provide useful insights into the state of a company's financial health, based on which further credit due diligence/research may be carried out.
- Ratio analysis enables one to assess a company's performance, profitability, efficiency and financial structure not only against previous years but also vs. its competitors.
- Ratio analysis will enable lenders to prescribe 'financial ratio covenants'[4] which enhance the lending bank's ability to manage and monitor the loan more effectively as well as to manage the credit risk.

(a) **Solvency Ratios**: These sets of ratios measure the information a creditor is most anxious to know. How is the business funded? Is there an excessive reliance on external liabilities (debt), with the owner either not willing to bring in sufficient funds or lacking the financial capacity? How good are they in servicing the existing obligations – both short term and long term? Is the company over-financed? Will the company go bankrupt? The major sub-set of the ratios under this category, as shown in the diagram, are Short Term Liquidity Ratios, Long Term Solvency Ratios, External Finance Ratios, Dividend Policy Ratios and Cash Flow Ratios.

[4] We will discuss more about Financial Ratio Covenants later in the book.

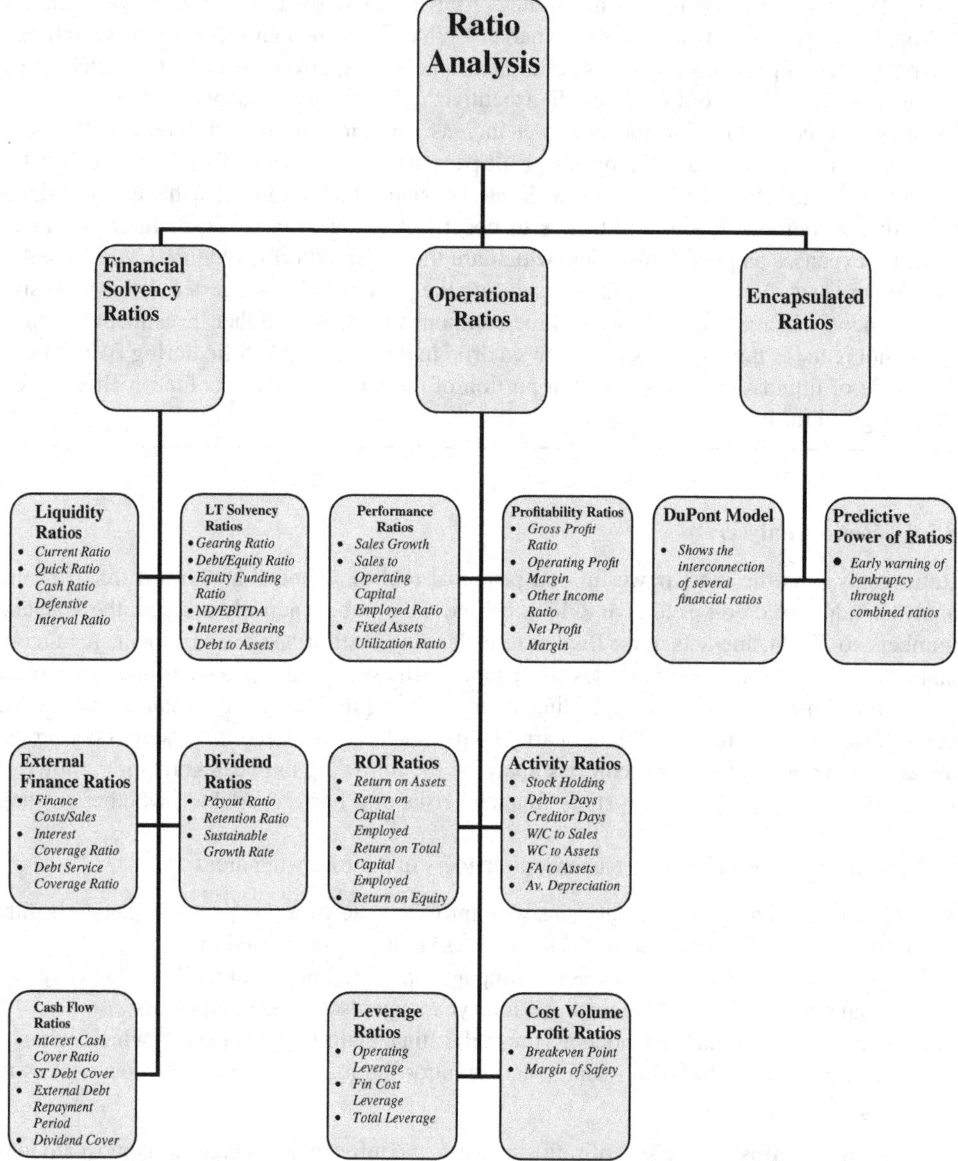


**Figure 8.3** Tools for Ratio Analysis

(b) **Operational Ratios**: Lenders and other creditors are interested to know how the business is performing. Is there adequate profitability? What is the level of various assets and how effectively they are utilized? The operational ratios are further sub-divided into Performance Ratios, Profitability Ratios, Return On Investment Ratios, Asset Management Ratios, Leverage (Operating and Financial) Ratios and Cost-Volume-Profit Ratios.

(c) **Encapsulated Ratios**: We will discuss more than 40 ratios and hence it is essential to understand how the ratios are interconnected. Given the profusion of ratios, we will discuss how certain ratios can be linked together for the following purposes, beneficial for credit risk analysis:

(i) to identify useful relationships among ratios – Dupont Model (integrated view of ratios),

(ii) to predict the probability of financial distress/default – Z Score.

We will discuss various ratios in the ensuing section. A **detailed illustration** depicting calculation of most of the ratios is given at the end of the chapter.

## 8.6 SOLVENCY RATIOS

External liabilities such as borrowings, trade credit, accrued expenses and other external obligations act as a lever to boost the earnings of a business. As we discussed in Chapter 1, financial leverage enhances ROE as long as the cost of leverage remains below the ROI (return from business). However, it increases financial risk because unlike equity, external liabilities have repayment obligations on specified due dates. The following ratios measure the financial risk involved, when a business decides to use financial leverage to boost returns.

### 8.6.1 Liquidity Ratios

A viable business can go bust because of liquidity problems, hence the importance of liquidity ratios.

(a) **Current Ratio (CR)** $= \dfrac{\text{Current Assets}}{\text{Current Liabilities}}$

CR measures the ability of the firm to meet its short-term liabilities and, generally, the higher the ratio the better. The following aspects should be borne in mind while relying on this ratio:

(i) **Industry and Nature of Business**: Low CR need not always mean liquidity problems in cash based businesses and where the business is able to negotiate higher credit terms from suppliers, covering most of the operating cycle (see also Chapter 12). However, in a normal case, low or falling ratios indicate trouble.

(ii) **Quality of Current Assets**: Just because the ratio is higher than the general norm of 1.50:1, does not automatically mean that the liquidity is sound. Satisfactory quality of the underlying current assets (such as stock, debtors, etc.) is a prerequisite. For example, even with a high CR of 5:1, a company may face liquidity problems if the entire stock becomes obsolete due to technological innovation or its debtors portfolio comprises mainly non-paying customers.

(iii) **Seasonal Nature**: Such businesses show wide fluctuations in working capital requirement impacting the current ratio. Hence the credit executive should have a fair idea about the peak and low seasons of the business. For example sugar producers procure huge stocks of raw material (sugar-cane) during the harvest season while winter cloth manufacturers and dealers stock a huge inventory of finished goods in preparation for the winter season.

(iv) **Accounting Policy**: Such changes can also boost CR – i.e. adopting a stock accounting policy that provides the highest stock valuation. For example, in an inflationary environment (or increasing prices), adoption of the FIFO method of inventory valuation would result in higher inventory valuation (compared to LIFO or average price) resulting in higher net profit. Higher inventory valuation also has a favourable impact on the CR as the total current assets would be higher (compared to LIFO or average price).

A low or falling current ratio can occur due to a variety of factors, such as (i) diversion of funds from the working capital to non-core or long-term activities; (ii) using creditors and short-term bank finance towards long-term uses, usually as a temporary measure, but this would run into difficulty if the anticipated long-term inflows do not materialize; (iii) bad working management; (iv) poor structuring of bank facilities, which allows the borrower to divert funds and (v) over-trading, amongst others. In fact CR should be studied together with working capital ratios and activity ratios because usually good working capital management means sound liquidity and vice versa.

(b) **Quick Ratio (QR)** $= \dfrac{\text{Current Assets} - \text{Stock} - \text{Prepayments}}{\text{Current Liabilities}}$

This ratio gives more a conservative view of the liquidity, by eliminating stock and prepaid expenses/other prepayments. Why do we exclude these items? (i) We exclude inventory because it is often much less liquid than other current assets. Inventory is considered to take more time to convert into cash. Time taken to convert inventory into cash varies from industry to industry. For example, a cash based retailer (e.g. Wal-Mart or Carrefour) may convert inventory into cash quickly,[5] however a car manufacturer would take a considerable time to convert the steel inventory into cash. Similarly, commodities such as gold or crude oil are more likely to be sold easily and with little loss in value than inventory consisting of perishables (vegetables or fruit) or fashion goods. (ii) Usually prepayments (prepaid insurance, etc.) are not realizable in cash under normal circumstances, due to which they are also excluded.

Whilst the usual norm of minimum QR is 1:1, all caveats applicable for CR are relevant to this ratio. If there is significant difference between the QR and CR, it means the stock is significant.

(c) **Cash Ratio** $= \dfrac{\text{Cash and Bank} + \text{Marketable Securities}}{\text{Current Liabilities}}$

This is the most conservative view of the liquidity of a business. While the denominator remains the same, the numerator takes into account only those current assets that can be immediately converted into cash. Although usually only cash, bank and liquid securities are included, other current assets that are realizable in cash immediately can also be considered for the numerator.

(d) **Defensive Interval Ratio (DIR)** $= \dfrac{\text{Cash} + \text{marketable securities} + \text{accounts receivable}}{\text{Estimated daily cash expenditure}}$

This is another way of looking at liquidity. While current assets and current liabilities represent the future inflows and outflows of cash, DIR looks at the liquidity subject to two assumptions (i) the present level of current liabilities will remain steady and (ii) there are no other cash resources such as bank finance or trade credit, owners' injection of funds or profit retention. The denominator takes into account only cash based expenses and excludes non-cash items such as depreciation, amortization and others. This ratio provides a conservative view as to how many days the business can survive with currently available quickest funds.

[5] In case stock is directly convertible into cash (say 50% of total sales are cash based), then that portion of the stock may be included in the denominator as well.

**Problem 8.3**

Hypothetical Manufacturing Ltd provides you with the following details:

- Current assets of $21.8 million.
- Current liabilities of $20.4m.
- Quick ratio of 0.95x.
- The company does not have any prepaid expenses.

Calculate (i) current ratio and (ii) the level of inventory

**Solution**

(i) Let us compute the current ratio first:

CR = Current Assets/ Current Liability = $21.8m/$20.4m = 1.07x

(ii) We know the quick ratio = $\frac{\text{Current Assets} - \text{Inventory}}{\text{Current Liabilities}}$

*where* Inventory is an unknown quantity, say *x*. We can write the quick ratio equation as follows:

$$0.95 = (\$21.8\text{m} - x)/\$20.4\text{m}$$

Solving this equation, we can find that the inventory value is $2.5m

### 8.6.2 Long Term Solvency Ratios

Various sources of capital exist – equity capital, preference capital, bonds, commercial paper, short-term loans, long-term loans, trade finance, suppliers credit, factoring, discounting of bills and so on. When a firm uses debt financing, the returns to stockholders may be magnified. This is because of the leveraging effect, i.e. the interest payments on debt are fixed. If the firm's operating profits rises, the debt holders continue to receive only their fixed interest payments and the benefit of higher profit accrues to the equity shareholders. However, if the firm suffers an operating loss, the debt holders will receive the interest payment (assuming that the firm does not go bankrupt), while the equity shareholders bear the loss (including the interest burden). Thus, financial leverage acts in favour of the shareholders as long as the business generates ROI in excess of the interest rates. In other words, leverage increases the returns to stockholders during good times while reducing returns during bad times.

Leverage ratios, discussed below, can reveal the underlying financial policies pursued by the firm – whether the firm follows an aggressive or ultra-conservative style in managing its finances.

(a) **Gearing Ratio (GR)**

$$= \frac{\text{Interest Bearing Debt}}{\text{Tangible Net Worth} + \text{Minorities} + \text{Non-Redeemable Pref. Shares}}$$

GR measures the firm's exposure to the interest bearing debt in comparison to TNW. Normally, TNW should exclude all intangibles. However, if the credit executives or analysts feel that some of the intangible assets such as trademarks, brands, etc. have real market value, then appropriate adjustments may be made, i.e. such intangibles may be included as part of TNW. Yet again it should be stressed that the conservative approach is better and all revisions ought to be based on strong logical reasoning. Similarly, if there are convertible bonds maturing in the near term, again GR may be calculated in both scenarios – one treating the converted portion of equity as part of TNW and the other not. There are situations where the numerator should be adjusted for certain items, mainly off-balance interest bearing financing. For example, in cases of leased assets and related liabilities shown as off-balance sheet items (e.g. aircraft leases by airlines), the outstanding lease payable is to be factored in to calculate the correct GR. GR differs widely across sectors. For instance, generally capital-intensive industries tend to be more highly geared than service industries, but much of their debt is usually secured on specific assets.

Usually high GR signals increased financial risk. Highly geared companies are more vulnerable to business recessions/downturns than low-geared companies, as the higher interest burden and repayment commitments literally become a burden. Interest costs become disproportionately heavier as profits decline. Secondly, high GR restricts a firm's ability to tap additional external sources. Very highly geared entities have only limited options – surrender to the conditions of the lenders or dilute the equity stake by inviting new shareholders/partners or go bankrupt. The usual reasons for the increase in GR include:

1. Disproportionately high external borrowings vs. TNW.
2. Substantial dividends taken by the owners.
3. Over-trading – see the chapter on 'Credit Risks in Working Capital' for details.
4. Erosion of TNW because of the losses.

(b) **Debt/ Equity Ratio (DER)** $= \dfrac{\text{Total Outside Liabilities*}}{\text{TNW} + \text{Minorities} + \text{Non-Redeemable Pref. Shares}}$

*including non-interest bearing un-subordinated debt from internal parties (i.e. shareholders, etc.)

DER is more comprehensive than GR. The interpretation of the ratio is more or less similar to GR. Higher ratios usually signal a riskier entity. Highly leveraged entities can meet the obligations on time as long as their ROI remains higher than the implicit and explicit costs of leverage. However, once adversity sets in due to business cycles or otherwise, the crisis is almost inevitable. The credit executive should be careful of situations where the GR and DER are moving in different directions. A drop in DER while GR records a sharp increase indicates a situation where the entity relies on interest bearing debt more, which might be a hint that non-bank creditors (suppliers, etc.) are losing faith. Such warning signs ought to be explored further to confirm or dispel the hypothesis. As the balance sheets of certain companies are complex – e.g. holding companies or large enterprises – with a differing mix of financial instruments, the denominator and numerator of this ratio may require adjustments, i.e. conversion of certain liabilities into equity or vice versa, crystallization of contingent liabilities, quantification of legal (e.g. income tax) disputes, etc. – all based on strong logical reasoning.

(c) **Equity Funding of Assets** $= \dfrac{\text{TNW} + \text{MI} + \text{Non-Redeemable Pref. Shares}}{\text{Total Tangible Assets}}$

This ratio measures the funding provided by the shareholders (including minorities) and non-redeemable preference shareholders. Immediate debt conversions into equity may also be considered for computation purposes. Tangible assets are computed by deducting intangible assets from total assets. Usually, the higher the ratio, the lower the financial risk.

(d) **EBITDA Leverage Ratio** $= \dfrac{\text{Net Debt}}{\text{EBITDA}}$

where Net Debt = Gross interest bearing term debt – Cash and Bank.

This ratio measures the term loan repayment capacity of the borrower. Earnings before Interest Tax Depreciation and Amortization (EBITDA) may be considered as the proxy of the cash flow. A higher ratio depicts a riskier situation that the firm may not be able to service their debt in a timely manner, if there is a dip in EBITDA. On the other hand, a low ratio shows that the firm can adequately service and repay debt, even if there is a fall in EBITDA. An approximate guidance is that this ratio should not exceed 2x to 3x, i.e. net debt should not be more than two or three times EBITDA.

(e) **Interest Bearing Debt Funding of Assets** $= \dfrac{\text{Interest Bearing Debt (IBD)}}{\text{Tangible Assets}}$

This is another way of looking at the level of interest bearing external finance. While the GR compares the IBD to equity, this ratio compares it to total assets. The lower the ratio, the lower the financial risk and vice versa. Any increase in the assets through non-debt sources can bring down the ratio.

(f) **Debt Service Coverage Ratio (DSCR)** = Net Profit after Tax + Interest + Depreciation
+ Amortization Interest + Instalments Arising out of Term Loan or Finance Lease

This ratio measures the repayment ability of both the interest portion and also that of the instalments. The higher the ratio, the better. An approximate guidance is that this ratio should not fall below 2x, i.e. the numerator should be at least twice the debt service obligations (interest and instalments).

**Note:** Some financial analysts prefer to use Net Cash from Operations (NCFO) instead of 'Net Profit after Tax + Interest + Depreciation + Amortization' as the former is more cash flow oriented.

**Problem 8.4**

Hypothetical Trading Company has a Debt-to-Equity (DE) ratio of 1.73 and its total equity is $3.8 million. Please calculate (i) the total debt and (ii) total assets.

**Solution**

(a) Let us find the total debt at first

We know that DE Ratio = Total Debt/Equity

*where* Total Debt is an unknown quantity – '*x*' -in this problem.

We can write the equation as follows:

$$1.73x = x/\$3.8m$$

$$\text{Total Debt is } \$\ 6.6m$$

(b) Now we can find the total assets easily because Total Assets = Total Liabilities+ Equity

$$\text{Total Assets} = \$6.6m + \$3.8m = \$10.4m$$

### 8.6.3 External Finance Ratios

Finance cost is the price of credit or relying on external economic resources, financial in nature. Whilst the external finance cost is accounted for in the balance sheet and profit and loss account on an accrual basis, CFS reflects actual cash movements. Important ratios under this category are discussed below:

(a) **Interest Cover Ratio (ICR)**

$$= \frac{\text{Profit Before Interest and Tax (PBIT)}}{\text{Finance Costs (may include both capitalized and expensed)}}$$

The ratio reflects whether the business generates enough profit to meet the interest service obligations. Traditionally, a ratio above 1.50x is considered satisfactory. The higher the ratio, the better. However, since PBIT can be influenced by changes in accounting policy, it is better to use this ratio in conjunction with the Interest Cash Cover Ratio, which is discussed later in this chapter.

(b) **Finance Costs to Sales Ratio** $= \dfrac{\text{Finance Costs (both capitalized and expensed)}}{\text{Sales}}$

A YOY comparison will show whether the external financiers are chunking away a major part of the sales value. Most businesses facing difficulty or just before applying for bankruptcy usually find this ratio disproportionately high. Hence an increasing trend in this ratio is worth examination. The Interest Coverage Ratio (ICR) is not very useful in the case of loss-making firms while this ratio is useful under all circumstances. Moreover, from an economic point of view, it shows how much of the gross value generated is absorbed by external financiers.

### 8.6.4 Dividend and Equity Ratios

(a) **Payout Ratio** $= \dfrac{\text{Dividends}}{\text{Profit After Tax}}$

All good companies pay dividends to the shareholders, who have taken the risk. A creditor is interested to know the extent of the profits paid as dividends. In case the ratio exceeds 1:1, the creditor ought to be concerned, especially if it demonstrates a continuing trend since it clearly shows that the company is paying shareholders more than it earns as net profit (PAT).

(b) **Retention Ratio** = (1 − Payout ratio)

This is the reciprocal of the Dividend Payout Ratio. All healthy and especially growing companies ought to retain a part of the profits in the business in order to augment resources. This ratio measures how much profit is retained in the business. Whilst other things remain the same, the retention leads to improvement in solvency ratios and liquidity ratios, if the retained profit is kept in current assets (or utilized to reduce current liabilities). Hence, from the creditors' point of view, the higher the ratio, the better.

(c) **Growth Potential Ratio (or) Sustainable Growth Rate** = ROE × Retention Ratio

Lenders are interested in knowing about the rate of growth of their customer's business. The interpretation of this ratio should not be rigid because dynamic external and industry factors can act upon the profitability (and, in turn, the ROE) while the firm can alter the financial/dividend policies altering sustainable growth. The importance of sustainable growth lies in the fact that it provides an idea about the funding pool internally available for doing additional business. If the firm wants to grow faster than the sustainable rate, it means that some of the drivers (payout, profitability, which can be broken up into cost/asset productivity ratios or financing policies) would have to change, providing deeper insight.

**Problem 8.5**

Suppose PQR Ltd has an ROE of 24.2% and the dividend payout ratio is 11%. Calculate its growth potential. Discuss the factors that could drag down growth.

**Solution**

The sustainable growth rate is 21.5% (24.2*(1-0.11)). The growth rate is attractive because PQR retains 89% of the net profit in the business which is deployed at an ROE of 24.2%. A higher payout ratio and a drop in ROE are the two key risks that could drag the growth rate down. ROE is further dependent upon a variety of factors discussed in this chapter, including profitability and the debt/equity mix.

### 8.6.5 Cash Flow Ratios

Cash flow ratios attempt to link various obligations and costs to understand the firm's ability to service them. Usually, the higher the ratio, the better the position is. Major cash flow ratios are discussed below:

(a) **Interest Cash Cover** = $\frac{\text{Net Cash From Operations (NCFO)}}{\text{Interest Paid}}$

We have seen that ICR is calculated under accrual assumption and can be manipulated by accounting policy changes. So, even if the ICR is above 1.50X, in certain cases the firm may struggle to meet the finance cost obligations because of cash shortages. The Interest Cash Cover Ratio overcomes the limitation of the traditional ICR and shows how much cash from operations is available to meet the interest obligations.

(b) **Short Term Debt Cash Cover** = $\frac{\text{Net Cash From Operations} - \text{Interest} - \text{Tax}}{\text{Overdraft} + \text{Short Term Loans (STL)}}$

This ratio measures the number of times operational cash flows after interest and tax cover short-term debt. The higher the ratio, the better it is. However, it is to be noted that the denominator comprises short-term debt (i.e. working capital borrowings) which usually finances the current assets such as stock, debtors, etc. Accordingly, such STLs appearing in the balance sheet are normally repaid from the liquidation of such current assets, given in the same balance sheet. So, this coverage ratio can be considered a conservative measurement basically reflecting the adequacy of cash flows and should ideally be studied for a historical trend rather than on a standalone basis.

(c) **External Debt Repayment Period (EDRP)** $= \dfrac{\text{Total Interest Bearing Debt}}{\text{Annual Free Cash Flows (FCF)*}}$

*FCF=CFO-Int-Tax-CAPEX

Unlike other cash flow ratios, the lower the ratio, the better the situation. Note that the ratio is expressed in months/years. This ratio measures, given the FCF, how long it will take to repay the interest bearing debt. Usually if EDRP exceeds five years then the credit executive should be concerned and investigate further to ensure that the situation is under control. There ought to be sustainable factors for the firm to improve FCF in future in such a way that the EDRP will decline in future years – i.e. running down of debt in future from future cash inflows (say expanded production, additional funds from shareholders), etc. This ratio should also be interpreted with care. For instance, an item of interest bearing debt appearing in the balance sheet, such as convertible bonds, does not involve any repayment, but would convert into equity.

Normally, this ratio is very useful especially from a trend point of view. A continued increase in the ratio is a warning sign. Either FCF is dwindling while debt is steady or debt is increasing faster than the growth in FCF. In such a case the credit executive should ensure that alternative repayment sources are available in the balance sheet – such as unencumbered assets – investments, freehold land, etc. A discerning lender will seek such unencumbered assets as security well in advance as the signs of trouble appear on the horizon.

(d) **Dividend Cash Cover** $= \dfrac{\text{CFO} - \text{Interest} - \text{Tax}}{\text{Dividends Paid} + \text{Dividends Declared}}$

Dividend Cash Cover checks the adequacy of operational cash flows to meet the dividends. The higher the ratio, the more comfortable the position is. If the ratio is below 1:1, it means the dividends are being paid out of external finance or similar sources and this should usually be treated as a matter of concern. This should prompt the credit executive to investigate the sources and check the dividend policy of the firm. Are the dividends paid out of bank borrowings? If so, what about the impact on the financial leverage? Are the bank facilities properly structured? Is there any business requirement – say immediate replacement of fixed assets/ expansion?

However, many experts highlight an exception – the growth companies. Because of fast sales and volume growth, additional working capital requirements of growth companies are higher, which results in negative or marginal CFO. If dividends are declared in such situations, dividend cash cover would be less than 1:1. In such cases, the credit executive should check the retention ratio (mentioned above) in the business. If sufficient retention of profits is in evidence, a dividend cash cover of less than 1:1 may be considered acceptable, depending upon the circumstances of the case.

# 8.7 OPERATIONAL RATIOS

## 8.7.1 Performance Ratios

Performance ratios are essential for proper credit analysis. The coverage ratios depend upon profits/internal cash generation, which in turn is a function of revenue and costs of revenue. Major performance ratios are:

(a) **Sales Growth/Decline** $= \frac{\text{Current Year Sales} - \text{Last Year Sales} \times 100}{\text{Last Year Sales}}$

This ratio provides the direction in which the business has moved. Other things remaining the same, sales growth/decline impacts the profits, cash needs and internal cash generation capacity. It alerts the credit executive to look for the reasons for growth, decline and stagnancy in business and a comparison with the industry to judge whether the business strategies are adequate. For bankers and other creditors, the sales growth means opportunities knocking at the door, as it usually fuels demand for further credit to finance inventory, receivables and other current assets.

(b) **Sales to Operating Capital Employed (SOCE) Ratio**

$$= \frac{\text{Net Sales}}{\text{Average Operating Capital Employed (AOCE)*}}$$

*Operating Capital Employed = Fixed Assets + Current Assets – Non-interest Bearing Current Liabilities – Non-core Assets
= Owners' Equity + Interest Bearing Debt + Non-Curr. Liabilities – Non-core Assets

AOCE is the average (viz. opening + closing/2) of operating capital deployed in the core business. This ratio captures the utilization of operating capital employed. Usually, higher ratios indicate improving performance. To understand the changes in the ratio, the credit executive should go back to the components of the operating capital and sales. Some of the factors that contribute to the improvement in the ratio are: (i) increase in sales; (ii) economies of scale; (iii) favourable change in trade terms – viz. trade creditors providing more credit period or the debtors settling promptly; (iv) new technology resulting in more efficiencies, such as lower inventory level; (v) sale and lease back of assets; (vi) management action of closing down certain branches, etc. A drop in the ratio is traceable to factors opposite to the above, such as inadequate working capital policies and ineffectual capital expenditures.

Changes in the ratio are to be interpreted carefully. Not all increases are positive and not all declines are negative. For instance, the ratio can be improved by delaying the payments to suppliers at the end of the accounting period. It can have disastrous consequences, if suppliers react. An illiquidity position may also be another indication. Liberal credit sales will improve the ratio in one year, risking bad debts provision in the following years. A fall in ratio need not always indicate a negative situation. For instance, the ratio will fall in case of a recent capacity augmentation/diversification project or similar CAPEX, the benefits of which accrue in later years. Furthermore, a business pursuing a high volume strategy will have a larger ratio than the one which follows a high margin/low volume strategy, which highlights the need to understand the nature of business as well.

(c) **Fixed Assets Utilization Ratio** $= \frac{\text{Net Sales}}{\text{Fixed Assets}}$

The higher the ratio, the better. Generally, a low ratio signals under-utilization of fixed assets. Usually, an increasing trend in the ratios indicates improving performance. However, care should be taken if leased assets are present. In such cases, sometimes the leased assets may not be factored into the balance sheet, although utilized in the business, which in turn depresses the denominator, resulting in a higher ratio, which would not have been the case otherwise. Hence, the leased assets may be added to the denominator as required.

### 8.7.2 Profitability Ratios

Profitability ratios measure how efficiently management use the company's assets to generate sales and manage the cost of operations. Profitability is the key to the survival and success of a firm. Whilst occasional short-term losses are acceptable, continual losses are detrimental and will erode the capital structure, making the balance sheet unhealthy, which will create panic, sometimes prompting creative accounting. Overall, the higher the profitability ratios, the better. Major profitability ratios are:

(a) **Gross Profit Ratio or Gross Profit Margin (GPM)** $= \dfrac{\text{Gross Profit} \times 100}{\text{Net Sales}}$

The GPM examines the difference between the sales and cost of sales in relation to the sales. The importance of the GPM is evident from the fact that a firm meets the expenses (i.e. selling, administration, finance, taxation, etc.) from the difference (margin) it derives from sales and cost of sales.

An improving ratio is always welcome and can usually be traced to (i) higher prices, (ii) increased production efficiency, (iii) lower input costs, (iv) higher volume sufficient to bring in economies of scale, (v) weakening of local currency resulting in better value realization of exports, (vi) change in stock valuation policy, such that the closing inventory value is inflated or reported at a higher figure and (vii) change in the product mix (higher margin products, etc.) amongst others. Reasons for a falling ratio are just the opposite of the reasons mentioned above. The GPM varies depending upon the nature of the business and strategy. Accordingly, the GPM of a wholesale food dealer will be lower than that of diamond merchant. Generally, the GPM under successful differentiation strategy is higher than that of a cost leader strategy.

(b) **Operating Profit Margin (OPM)** $= \dfrac{\text{Operating Profit} \times 100}{\text{Net Sales}}$

Operating profit refers to the profit after meeting selling, distribution and administration costs from the gross profit. The OPM is also impacted by business strategies. Whilst a company competing on low costs (cost leader strategy) will try to have the lowest operating costs, a differentiator has to spend more on advertising, sales promotion, branding, etc. However, even with more operating expenses, a successful differentiation strategy should result in adequate OPM, because of the price premium – viz. a higher GPM.

Nature of industry and OPM are also linked. Usually a food and provisions retailer will have a low OPM while a manufacturer needs a higher OPM, because the retailer can generate adequate return on capital by clocking in higher volume, i.e. a low OPM/high volume strategy. However, a typical manufacturing business is usually a high margin/low–moderate volume affair. If the change in OPM is in line with that of the GPM, then the reasons are the same as for variations in the latter. Otherwise changes in firms' policies and/or operational expenses are to be studied further.

(c) **Other Income to PBIT (Profit before Interest and Tax) Ratio** $= \dfrac{\text{Other Income}}{\text{PBIT}}$

This ratio indicates the level of the non-core income of the business. PBIT usually includes other income such as interest income, scrap sales, profit or loss sale of fixed assets etc. The higher the other income component, the lower the quality of PBIT. It indicates that the business is relying on non-core activity to boost the bottom line.

(d) **Net Profit Margin (NPM) (or Return on Sales)** $= \dfrac{\text{Net Profit}}{\text{Net Sales}}$

Net profit (profit available for appropriation) is the final profit to shareholders after meeting all claims of financiers and tax authorities and minorities, among others. NPM indicates whether the business is successful in ensuring positive returns to the owners. A lender financing the core activities is more concerned with operating profit ratio. However, adequate NPM in the long term is necessary to keep the owners interested in the business, which otherwise is a risk in itself.

### 8.7.3 Return on Investment (ROI) Ratios

Profitability Ratios study profits and expenses at various operating stages but do not take into account the capital deployed to meet the expenses and purchase assets. The importance of ROI ratios is that they relate the profits and the investments made to generate them. For our discussion, we rely on four major ROI ratios, each of which studies the rate of return of the business from different angles.

(a) **Return on Assets (ROA)** $= \dfrac{\text{PBIT}}{\text{Average Total Assets}}$

Some books even call this ratio ROI itself. The ratio measures profit before interest and tax (viz. profits before the settling the claims of debt holders) to total assets (viz. equity + debt). It reports the effectiveness of the utilization of the capital (or assets) irrespective of the source of capital and hence can be considered as an apt measure for inter-firm comparisons.

(b) **Return on Capital Employed** $= \dfrac{\text{Operating Profit}}{\text{Average Operating Capital Employed}}$

Operating profit is accruing from the core operations of the company. Operating capital employed means the net assets employed in the core operations of the business. For a lender, this ratio is important as it narrows the focus on the core operations of the company. What are core operations? Core operations to a lender are the operations he takes part in financing. This ratio is the product of two other ratios, which we have already discussed and the relationship is evident from the following

$$\text{ROCE} = \text{OPM} \times \text{SOCE}$$

$$= \frac{\text{Operating Profit}}{\text{Net Sales}} \times \frac{\text{Net Sales}}{\text{Average Capital Employed}}$$

Changes in this ratio can be traced back to these two ratios, and from there, the underlying reasons can be ascertained. Accordingly, ROCE is influenced by profitability (OPM) and efficiency of the capital utilization (SOCE).

(c) **Return on Total Capital Employed (ROTCE)**

$$= \frac{\text{PBIT}}{\text{AOCE i.e. Average Overall Capital Employed}}$$

ROTCE is considered a broader measure. Overall capital employed encompasses net assets plus investments (quoted, unquoted, including those in associates and subsidiaries) and other non-core current assets, capital work in progress, etc. (see the analytical balance sheet format for details). ROTCE measures the ROI from the point of view of all capital providers.

ROTCE is an important ratio because it shows the viability of the business quite explicitly. A poor ratio indicates that the company will have tough times especially in adversity caused by economy/industry/company factors. Secondly, ROTCE ought to be higher than the borrowing costs (or cost of capital, in general) for the business to emerge as successful. Otherwise, it cannot survive without outside support. The only major exception is in the case of growth companies (which expand quickly) where OCE shows an increasing trend, pushing ROTCE lower due to the sizeable investments in fixed and other assets. However, the gap between the ROTCE and Kf (Cost of funds) should ultimately narrow down with the former increasing above the latter.

(d) **Return on Equity** $= \frac{\text{Net Profit available to Equity Shareholders}}{\text{Equity Shareholders' Equity}}$

This shows the return on equity shareholders' funds and the reward for risk taking. Logically, it should be more than the risk-free return available in the economy. Whilst a low or even negative ROE is acceptable for a short period, if ROE is consistently low, it means trouble for the survival of the business unless funds are introduced into the business. However, in the private sector such a scenario is rare as prudent investors will wind up the business and with whatever capital is salvaged will try alternative investments.

### 8.7.4 Asset Management (or Activity) Ratios

The assets in any business can be broadly classified into working assets (i.e. working capital) and fixed assets. Working capital is usually defined as stock + debtors – creditors while fixed assets refers to the buildings, vehicles, plant, equipment, etc. The following ratios capture the management of key assets of a business:

(a) **Stock Holding Period** $= \frac{\text{Average Stock}^{6} \times 365}{\text{Cost of Goods Sold}^{7}}$

A credit executive is always interested in the stock policy of the company and the effectiveness of inventory management. Before deriving a conclusion based on the stock holding period, one must develop an idea about the industry stock norms. For example, a firm dealing in perishable goods ought to have a lower stock holding period compared to a jewellery firm. Although a decreasing ratio is good because it indicates that the stock is moving fast and not

[6] Year-end values may be used, instead of averages.

[7] If cost of goods sold is not available, sales may be substituted.

piling up, experience and expertise are required in interpreting this ratio, in the overall context of the firm. For instance, a firm facing a liquidity crisis might not be replenishing the stock towards the end of the accounting period, which can cause a drop in the average stock holding period, but cannot be considered as a positive sign.

Certain adjustments are suggested while calculating this ratio: (a) exclude spare parts inventory, if treated as part of stock and (b) unlike other components of the working capital, stock is influenced by the valuation policies adopted. The credit executive should ensure that the accounting policy related to stock valuation, if it has undergone change, is not done for any cosmetic purpose.

(b) **Debtors Collection Period** $= \dfrac{\text{Average Trade Debtors}^{*} \times 365}{\text{Credit Sales}}$

* year-end values may be used

If data on credit sales is difficult to obtain/estimate, the total sales may be used instead. A comparison of this ratio against the normal credit terms extended by the firm is highly useful in determining (i) the efficiency of collections and (ii) whether the stated credit policy of the company is adhered to. A decreasing ratio generally indicates efficiency and improvement while an increasing ratio is a matter of concern as it may signal impending bad debts. Some of the reasons behind a decreasing ratio are (i) incentivized salesmen, (ii) general improvement in liquidity conditions, (iii) incentives to the customer to pay up soon, (iv) a shift in sales policy to LC terms from clean (or open) sales, (v) screening away of bad and troublesome customers, (vi) general improvement in the industry, (vii) tightening of credit terms by the company etc. Common reasons for an increase in the ratio are the converse of the above. Certain adjustments are needed while calculating this ratio: (i) exclude debtors arising out of transactions other than sales – viz. core business and (ii) add back the discounted debtors, if any, with recourse.

(c) **Trade Creditors Payment Period** $= \dfrac{\text{Average Trade Creditors} \times 365}{\text{Purchases}^{*}}$

* Cost of Goods Sold (or sales) if purchases data are not available.

Trade creditors payment period indicates (i) the extent of reliance on suppliers' credit, (ii) whether they are settling their trade dues on time and within the credit period extended, (iii) an idea of the credit standing of the business in the business community or circle. Before deriving conclusions based on this ratio, the credit executive should ascertain the industry norms. Any discrepancy in industry norms and credit terms enjoyed by the customer itself call for an investigation. Usually new businesses get a shorter credit period till a reputation is established. A falling ratio may indicate that the company is becoming more liquid and less reliant on creditors, though this may also indicate poor working capital management/creditors shortening or even cancelling credit. An increasing ratio is acceptable as long as a higher credit period is allowed by the suppliers because illiquid companies also stretch the creditors' payment. *[Average payment period can be calculated for major inputs, other than material suppliers. For instance, in the case of a manufacturing company with heavy electricity consumption (such as Aluminum Furnace) then the electricity arrears should be compared with the actual annual electricity consumption.]*

(d) **Working Capital to Total Assets Ratio** $= \dfrac{\text{Working Capital}}{\text{Total Assets}}$

This ratio indicates the nature of business. Higher ratios highlight the working capital intensive nature of business. Cash based businesses such as restaurants, retailers, supermarkets, etc. will have a low ratio or even a negative ratio. Manufacturing companies will have medium to high ratios. Wholesalers, service contractors, etc. will have rather high ratios in view of their low fixed asset requirements. Generally a falling ratio indicates improved efficiency of working capital management and vice versa.

A decrease in ratio will occur due to reasons such as (i) higher reliance on suppliers' credit, (ii) an increase in fixed assets, (iii) strict credit terms to customers, (iv) improved stock management, (v) tight liquidity which pressurizes the business to squeeze working capital etc.

A higher ratio may be due to factors like (i) reduction in trade credit, (ii) sale and lease back of fixed assets, (iii) poor debtors collection, (iv) inadequate stock management, etc.

**Note**: These ratios are also relevant for Chapter 12 'Credit Risks in Working Capital'.

(e) **Working Capital to Sales Ratio** $= \dfrac{\text{Working Capital}}{\text{Sales}}$

The higher the ratio, the higher the effort needed, in terms of cash deployed in stock, debtors, etc. to generate sales. This ratio, which measures the money invested in net current assets to sales, indicates the efficiency of working capital policy in generating sales. Cash based businesses may have a negative ratio, which indicates that the credit period offered by the suppliers exceeds the stocking period whilst sales are on cash (negligible debtors). Whilst a falling ratio is always welcome as it indicates improved efficiency of working capital management there are certain exceptions such as (a) tight liquidity which pressurizes the business to extend creditors or non-replenishment of stock, which will bring down the ratio and (b) over-trading, where an under-capitalized firm seeks rapid sales growth, which squeezes working capital.

(f) **Fixed Assets (or Fixed Capital) to Total Assets Ratio** $= \dfrac{\text{Fixed Assets}}{\text{Total Assets}}$

Higher ratios highlight the significance of fixed assets for the business. It highlights the nature of the business. Manufacturing and real estate businesses have a high ratio while service industries generally have a low ratio. Generally a falling ratio may indicate fixed assets getting older as it becomes depreciated, which may suggest immediate replacement or effective maintenance of fixed assets in good working condition. The credit executive may undertake an inspection of the fixed assets, if required.

(g) **Average Depreciation** $= \dfrac{\text{Depreciation for the Year}}{\text{Fixed Assets}}$

In normal situations, this ratio should not show significant variation. Any substantial variation may signal changes in depreciation policy, the reasons for which may be ascertained.

### 8.7.5 Leverage (Operating and Financial) Ratios

Will doubling of sales always result in doubling of net profit? How can a business achieve disproportionate increase in net profit vs. sales growth?

The answers can be found by studying leverage ratios: (a) operating leverage and (b) financial leverage.

(a) **Operating Leverage** = (Sales − Variable Costs)/Operating Profit

Operating leverage measures the impact of the cost structure on operating profit. Depending upon the nature of the activity undertaken and business policies of a firm, the cost structure will differ from firm to firm. While fixed costs (FC) do not vary with sales, variable costs (VC) vary with sales. Operating leverage tends to be high for a business with high fixed costs. Increased fixed costs are risky because such costs are not compressible when demand drops and revenue streams dry up. However, at high levels of sales, it results in enhanced profitability as evident from the following:

**Problem 8.6**

Suppose ABC Ltd and XYZ Ltd are operating in the same industry with the latter relying more on automation resulting in higher fixed costs. The cost structures are given below:

$ Millions

| Particulars | ABC Ltd | XYZ Ltd |
|---|---|---|
| Fixed Costs | 3 | 50 |
| Variable Cost/Sales | 85% | 40% |
| Assets | 200 | 200 |

Please examine the impact of the cost structure under three scenarios:

(a) Sales of 50m
(b) Sales of 100m
(c) Sales of 200m.

**Solution**

Let us identify the contribution (sales – variable cost) and operating profit of both companies as given below:

| | ABC | | | XYZ | | |
|---|---|---|---|---|---|---|
| Sales – Scenarios> | Low | Medium | High | Low | Medium | High |
| Sales | 50 | 100 | 150 | 50 | 100 | 150 |
| Less: Variable Cost | 42.5 | 85 | 127.5 | 20 | 40 | 60 |
| Contribution | 7.5 | 15 | 22.5 | 30 | 60 | 90 |
| Less: Fixed Cost | 3 | 3 | 3 | 50 | 50 | 50 |
| **OP** | **4** | **12** | **19** | **-20** | **10** | **40** |

As evident from the above, the **downside risk is less for a low operating leverage** entity. On the other hand, during boom times (i.e. high demand) **high operating leverage results in a sharp jump in profits** – disproportionate increase in net profit vs. the sales growth.

In the example given above XYZ attains a net profit of $40m when sales are high but during the low sales period it suffers loss. Many managements structure their costs emphasizing fixed costs, desiring maximum profitability, which sometimes can cause problems, especially during economic downturns. OL for ABC and XYZ is calculated below:

| | ABC | | | XYZ | | |
|---|---|---|---|---|---|---|
| Sales – Scenarios> | Low | Medium | High | Low | Medium | High |
| Operating Leverage | 1.67X | 1.25X | 1.15X | NA | 6X | 2.25X |

**Sales-Variable Cost (or Contribution)/Operating Profit.*

Operating leverage is low for ABC due to the high variable cost element in the cost structure (i.e. low fixed cost base). On the other hand XYZ has high operating leverage due to the high level of fixed costs.

Key benefits of calculating the operating leverage are:

1. It captures the risk involved in the cost structure. This is especially useful in deciding the extent of automation to be implemented. Several car manufacturers have automated their production lines resulting in high fixed costs. During the boom periods, a high fixed cost structure is beneficial as high operating leverage yields better operating profits. However, during times of falling demand (e.g. recession), the high operating leverage may lead to substantial losses. This is also true of crane hire companies. Usually the crane hire companies have a high fixed cost structure. During construction boom times, the cranes will be in demand and the companies earn substantial income, however during recession times, they suffer losses as the demand for cranes dries up.
2. It explains changes to the operating profit. If the operating leverage is high, the proportionate increase in operating profit will be higher than the increase in sales and vice versa. Understanding the level of operating leverage of the borrower along with the direction of the general macroeconomic environment enables the credit executive to arrive at the appropriate credit strategy/judgement as to future profitability and cash generation of the business.
3. Operating leverage will help in a study of the impact of sales forecast errors or sudden changes in the sales forecasts – how far the change in sales forecast can impact the bottom line. In the above example, let us assume that both ABC Company and XYZ Company had the same initial sales forecast of $100 million. However, due to a sudden change in macroeconomic factors (such as the 2008 crisis), the sales forecasts were slashed to $50m, i.e. half of the initial sales forecast. From our calculations, it is evident that ABC Ltd will be relatively less impacted than XYZ Ltd, which will suffer losses in such a scenario.

(b) **Financial Leverage (FL)** = Operating Profit/Net Profit

Earlier, we discussed certain ratios (mainly the Gearing Ratio and the Debt Equity Ratio) that gauged financial risk based on the balance sheet. Financial leverage is also a ratio that links the impact of the financial policy to the bottom line. Depending upon the funding/finance policy of the company or firm, the finance cost varies. A firm depending heavily on external finance would have a higher interest burden. The situation is akin to what we discussed under operating leverage. Like fixed costs, the interest burden would remain fixed irrespective of the scale of operations. Financial leverage is high for a business with a high interest burden. A higher interest burden is risky because it is not compressible even when the firm does not make sufficient operating profit, which usually happens when demand drops and revenue streams dry up.

**Problem 8.7**

Let us continue the above example 8.6 and assume that ABC Ltd is conservative and borrows only 10% of the asset requirement while XYZ Ltd is less risk averse and funds 50% of its assets by debt. Assume cost of debt is 7.5%. Let us see the impact of financing costs:

$ Millions

| Assets Funded By | ABC | XYZ |
|---|---|---|
| Equity | 180 | 100 |
| Loans | 20 | 100 |
| **Total Assets** | **200** | **200** |

Please examine the impact of financing structure under three scenarios:

(a) Sales of 50m
(b) Sales of 100m
(c) Sales of 200m.

**Solution**

| | ABC | | | XYZ | | |
|---|---|---|---|---|---|---|
| Scenarios | Low | Medium | High | Low | Medium | High |
| Sales | 50 | 100 | 150.0 | 50 | 100 | 150 |
| Less: Variable Cost | 42.5 | 85 | 127.5 | 20 | 40 | 60 |
| **Contribution** | **7** | **15** | **22** | **30** | **60** | **90** |
| Less: Fixed Cost | 3.0 | 3.0 | 3.0 | 50 | 50 | 50 |
| **Operating Profit** | **4** | **12** | **19** | **−20** | **10** | **40** |
| Less: Interest | 1.5 | 1.5 | 1.5 | 7.5 | 7.5 | 7.5 |
| **Net Profit** | **3** | **10** | **18** | **−27.5** | **2.5** | **32.5** |

Financial leverage measures the impact on net profit arising from the external finance structure. Financial leverage for ABC and XYZ is calculated below:

| | ABC | | | XYZ | | |
|---|---|---|---|---|---|---|
| Sales – Scenarios | Low | Medium | High | Low Sales | Medium | High |
| FL | 1.50x | 1.15x | 1.08x | NA* | 4x | 1.23x |

**such situations usually indicate operating loss and hence risk is very high.*

It is interesting to see that as the operating profit increases, the FL drops. This is due to the fixed nature of the interest burden. Hence, during boom times, when operating profits are substantial, the high FL would boost profitability. However, during falling operating profits, the financial leverage would erode profitability quickly.

(c) **Total Leverage (TL)** = Operating Leverage (OL) × Financial Leverage (FL)

Total leverage is calculated by multiplying operating leverage and financial leverage. It examines the combined impact of fixed costs and fixed interest burden on the business. In other words, the determinants of total leverage (TL) are the level of fixed costs and the interest burden. During boom times, high total leverage sharply increases profitability, however during tough times, high total leverage results in a sharp drop in profitability. Higher total leverage can be considered as a risky proposition since it brings severe volatility to the earnings of the business, i.e. while other things remain the same, the presence of high fixed costs and high interest burden create high volatility to the bottom line.

If both sales and operating profits continue to increase, TL drops due to the static nature of fixed costs and interest burden and vice versa. If sales and operating profits move in opposite directions (i.e. sales increases, but operating profit drops and vice versa) or the rate of interest or capital structure (debt/equity ratio) varies, the impact on TL would be different. Overall, we can conclude that if fixed costs and interest burden are high, then the total leverage is high with predictable consequences.

**Problem 8.8**

In the example discussed above, what is the total leverage of ABC Ltd?

| | ABC | | | XYZ | | |
|---|---|---|---|---|---|---|
| Sales – Scenarios | Low | Medium | High | Low | Medium | High |
| OL | 1.5 | 1.15 | 1.08 | VH* | 4 | 1.23 |
| FL | 1.67 | 1.25 | 1.15 | VH | 6 | 2.25 |
| **TL** | **2.51** | **1.44** | **1.24** | **VH** | **24.00** | **2.77** |

**VH = very high.*

Whilst ABC Ltd is able to retain profitability with low total leverage even during business downturns, XYZ attains the best profitability during boom times. On the other hand, during low sales (or recession), XYZ suffers heavy losses while ABC is able to retain profitability due to its low relative total leverage.

### *8.7.5.1 Benefits of Total Leverage*

- If both ratios (operating leverage and financial leverage) are high, **it signals higher risks** involved with the firm or company. It has heavy fixed costs and a high financial burden, which makes it necessary to operate at higher levels to survive. A credit executive ought to be careful about such entities, unless they have strong competitive advantages such as a monopoly position, etc. or enjoy large economies of scale.

- There are several real life examples, where business firms built up cost and finance structures, resulting in high total leverage. During the boom times of 2004–08, several shipping companies bought ships on credit. Such companies faced tough times during the recessionary period during 2008–10. The airline industry is yet another industry where total leverage is typically higher and hence usually requires a relatively high level of aircraft utilization to generate profits.
- Cyclical sensitivity of the business and total leverage are also to be studied together. It is suggested that a cyclical business must avoid high total leverage because the presence of high levels of fixed costs and interest burden would aggravate earnings volatility, leading to a sharp downturn in performance and profitability during cyclical downturns.
- Expansions with a heavy focus on capital expenditure and funded mainly by borrowings require close examination as the total leverage, especially during the initial phase, tends to be high.

### 8.7.6 Cost-Volume-Profit (CVP) Ratios

As we have seen, profit depends upon a large number of factors, primarily the selling price, cost of inputs and the volume of sales. All these factors are interlinked. Analysis of these three factors enables the credit executive to understand the effect of costs on volume and the impact of price/output fluctuations. Let us examine two CVP ratios that will help the credit executive to better understand the operations of the business.

(a) **Breakeven Point (BEP)**: measures the critical level where a business entity is about to make profits. It not only shows at what level the business will be profitable, but is helpful in indicating what level of operation should be maintained to avoid losses. There are two formulae to arrive at BEP:

Formula (1) BEP (units) = Total Fixed Costs/(Unit Selling Price − Unit Variable Cost)

If selling price per unit and variable cost per unit are not available, it can be computed by the following formula. However, note that the following equation provides the breakeven in value terms (not in terms of units/output).

Formula (2) BEP (value) = Total Fixed Costs/Contribution Ratio

Where Contribution Ratio = (Total Sales − Total Variable Cost)*100/Total Sales.

Usually if fixed costs or operating leverage are on the higher side, BEP will also be on the higher side and vice versa. This does not mean that higher fixed costs are bad, as at optimum or full capacity utilization levels, higher fixed costs tend to maximize returns. For instance, most petrochemical plants are capital intensive with resultant higher fixed costs, but are of lucrative profitability, as they are operating at optimum capacity levels.

**Problem 8.9**

The fixed costs of a manufacturing company are $100,000 a year. The variable cost is $25 per unit and each unit may be sold for $75. How many units must be sold in order to break even?

**Solution**

The contribution per unit is \$50 (= 75 − 25). The breakeven must therefore be 2,000 units (= 10,000/50). If more than 2,000 units are sold then the business will make a profit, otherwise it will suffer a loss.

(b) **Margin of Safety (MOS)** = Sales − BEP Sales (or Volume in Units − BEP in units)

This is the difference between breakeven level and current level of sales (volume) if the firm is profitable. On the other hand, if the firm suffers losses, it shows the level of additional sales required to reach the safety level (viz. breakeven level).

## 8.8 ENCAPSULATED RATIOS

We have discussed numerous (40+) ratios. Given the proliferation of ratios, a user may get lost in the details, being unable to see the wood for the trees. Encapsulation of ratios provides a comprehensive picture. Two such situations are given below:

### 8.8.1 Dupont Model

This model provides an overall view of the ratios and the interconnection among them. To get an overall picture, an integrated approach is ideal along with the study of individual ratios. The Dupont Company of the US introduced a system of financial analysis interlinking the financial ratios which shows how the major ratios computed so far (except cash flow ratios) are connected by an analytical chart (see Figure 8.4):

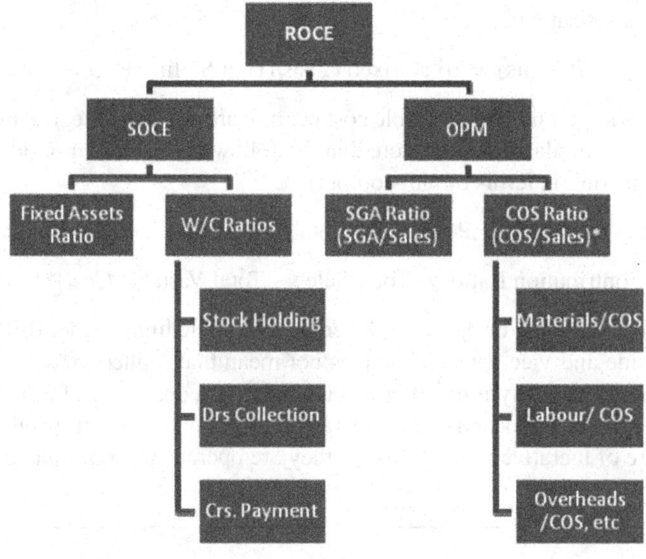


* (1-GPM)

**Figure 8.4** Analytical Ratio Chart

The left hand side of the chart is SOCE, and its component ratios have been discussed in detail earlier. Fixed assets, turnover ratio, inventory holding period, receivable collection, and creditors payment ratio, amongst others, provide a deeper insight into how changes in each category have impacted ROCE. It highlights how ROCE can be improved by pursuing different policies.

The right hand side of the chart is OPM, and its component ratios have been discussed in detail earlier. It provides insight into cost management and how cost control measures will impact on ROCE. The establishing of interrelationships among the productivity and efficiency of ROCE is useful in comparing YOY performances and inter-firm comparisons in a meaningful manner in the shortest span of time.

### 8.8.2 Predictive Power of Ratios

Do ratios have this magical power? Can they predict the future of a business?

One of the perpetual worries of a creditor is the possibility of a borrower going broke. Several studies have been conducted in this area, among which Prof. Edward I Altman's Z-Score Model is well known. Z-Score predicts the likelihood of a firm going bankrupt. Z-Score is calculated as given below:

$$Z = 1.2X_1 + 1.4X_2 + 3.3X_3 + 0.6X_4 + 0.1X_5$$

where

$X_1$ = Working Capital/Total Assets
$X_2$ = Retained Earnings since Inception/Total Assets
$X_3$ = Profit Before Interest and Tax/Total Assets
$X_4$ = Market[8] Value of Equity/Book Value of Total Debt
$X_5$ = Sales/Total Assets

The interpretation is as follows:

Z = Score > 2.8 = Low or Negligible Risk of bankruptcy

Z = Score < 1.8 = Very High Risk of bankruptcy

1.8 < Z = Score < 2.8 = Moderate Risk of bankruptcy (Altman called this region an area of uncertainty, the company can go either way. Further investigation is required to confirm the risk level).

According to Altman, the Z-Score can predict with 95% accuracy the risk of a business going bankrupt within a year and 72% within two years. Altman had studied 33 bankrupt firms along with a paired sample of 33 non-bankrupt firms and examined 22 ratios, based on which he identified the abovementioned five ratios.

The Z-Score has faced criticisms such as (a) being more useful in the US context, (b) use of total assets as the denominator, in three of the five ratios (a credit executive may exclude all intangible assets from total assets. Intangibles usually do not have value unless the firm is a going concern), (c) lack of emphasis on liquidity ratios, since it is the illiquidity that ultimately leads to bankruptcy or insolvency, (later researchers like Mr Tafflan, evolved ratio based Bankruptcy Models emphasizing current assets and liabilities, but did not seem to act

[8] If market value or market value of comparable business is not available, then book value may be used.

as any better indicator), (d) whilst 95% predictability one year ahead is fair enough, usually all troubled companies will publish the accounts quite late, reducing the practical use.

Despite these criticisms, ratio based predictions are commonly used in the financial world. While certain ratios such as Altman's, Tafflier and LC Gupta are published, there are other models[9] which remain proprietary and are not disclosed to the public. Z-score models are used routinely by most of the banks, financial institutions and accountancy firms. They may be used to (i) get an idea of the probability of trouble ahead, (ii) track a company's progress over time and (iii) compare companies of similar sizes in the same sector of industry.

**Problem 8.10**

The following ratios are computed for Lameduck Ltd for the FY 20X2.

- Working Capital to Total Assets ratio = 28% – $X_1$.
- Retained Earnings to Total Assets ratio = 30% – $X_2$.
- Profit Before Interest and Tax to Total Assets =33% – $X_3$.
- Market Value of Equity to Book Value of Debt = 160% – $X_4$.
- Sales to Total Assets = 250% – $X_5$.

Calculate the bankruptcy risk of Lameduck Ltd, based on Altman's Z-Score.

**Solution**

Applying Altman's Z-Score formula:

$$\begin{aligned} Z &= 1.2x_1 + 1.4x_2 + 3.3x_3 + 0.6x_4 + 0.1x_5, \\ &= 1.2 \times 28\% + 1.4 \times 30\% \times 3.3 \times 33\% + 0.6 \times 160\% + 0.1 \times 250\% \\ &= 3.06 \end{aligned}$$

Conclusion: Z-Score is 3.06, which is above 2.8. Hence, the risk of bankruptcy is low.

## CASE STUDY

ABCD Ltd is a diversified business group. The consolidated balance sheet, profit and loss account and cash flow statement of ABCD Ltd prepared in analytical format are given below:

| **Customer Name** : ABCD LTD | UNITS : $ THOUSANDS | |
|---|---|---|
| Financials - Date : | 31Dec2009 | 31Dec2010 |
| Financials - Type: | AUDITED | AUDITED |
| | *(12months)* | *(12months)* |
| **BALANCE SHEET** | | |
| **CORE ASSETS** | | |
| Land and Buildings | 249,572 | 249,594 |
| Construction in Progress | 2,744 | 7,592 |

[9] Banks, FIs and accountancy and audit firms can develop their own models.

| | | |
|---|---|---|
| Plant and Machinery | 189,892 | 194,166 |
| Furniture and Fixtures | 72,952 | 71,580 |
| Vehicles | 14,339 | 11,788 |
| Less: Accumulated Depreciation | (307,198) | (320,054) |
| **TOTAL FIXED ASSETS** | **222,301** | **214,666** |
| Stock | 309,806 | 272,547 |
| Trade Debtors | 366,246 | 308,547 |
| Finance Lease Receivables (Curr.) | 18,728 | 28,702 |
| Other Debtors | 27,988 | 28,357 |
| Cash and Near Liquid Funds | 31,873 | 31,623 |
| Prepayments | 8,787 | 9,763 |
| Less: Trade Creditors | (217,121) | (230,476) |
| : Other Creditors | (153,728) | (126,892) |
| Less: Dues to Related Cos | (12,299) | (16,923) |
| : Taxation | (12,189) | (8,617) |
| **OPERATING CAPITAL EMPLOYED** | **590,392** | **511,297** |
| **NON-CORE/NON CURRENT ASSETS** | | |
| LT Lease Receivable | 8,848 | 10,718 |
| Investments in Subs/Assoc | 55,226 | 55,734 |
| Dues From Related Cos | 7,547 | 4,386 |
| **TOTAL NON-CORE/ NON CURRENT ASSETS** | **71,621** | **70,838** |
| **OVERALL CAPITAL EMPLOYED** | **662,013** | **582,135** |
| **CAPITAL STRUCTURE** | | |
| Ordinary Share Capital | 20,000 | 20,000 |
| Profit and Loss Account | 98,278 | 61,549 |
| Other Reserves | 35,080 | 36,303 |
| Contribution from Shareholders | 202,248 | 202,248 |
| Less: Intangibles | (12,112) | (9,620) |
| **TANGIBLE NET WORTH** | **343,494** | **310,480** |
| Minorities | 53,422 | 62,929 |
| Provisions/Other L/T Liabilities | 61,790 | 56,445 |
| TOTAL | 115,212 | 119,374 |
| **EXTERNAL FINANCE** | | |
| Bank O/D and Short Term Loans | 203,307 | 152,281 |
| OVERALL CAPITAL EMPLOYED | 662,013 | 582,135 |
| CONTINGENT LIABILITIES | 101,000 | 131,977 |
| CAPITAL COMMITMENTS | 52,500 | 50,000 |
| **PROFIT AND LOSS ACCOUNTS** | | |
| Sales | 1,446,791 | 1,469,762 |
| Less: Cost of Goods Sold | (1,117,664) | (1,132,857) |
| **GROSS PROFIT** | **329,127** | **336,905** |
| Less: Distrib. and Selling Costs | (156,049) | (160,370) |
| : Administration Costs | (114,623) | (106,887) |
| **OPERATING PROFIT (LOSS)** | **58,455** | **69,648** |
| Share of Profit (Loss) of Ass.Cos | 2,030 | 10,059 |
| Other Income (Expense) | 24,819 | 13,703 |
| PROFIT (LOSS) BEFORE INT AND TAX | 85,304 | 93,410 |
| Less: Interest Expense | (7,619) | (4,777) |
| **PROFIT (LOSS) BEFORE TAX** | **77,685** | **88,633** |
| Less: Taxation Charge | (6,500) | (6,500) |
| PROFIT (LOSS) AFTER TAX | 71,185 | 82,133 |
| Minorities | (11,976) | (16,583) |
| **PROFIT(LOSS) AVBLE FOR APPROP** | **59,209** | **65,550** |

| | | |
|---|---|---|
| **RECONCIL. RET'D PROFITS (LOSSES)** | | |
| Profit(Loss) Avble for Approp | 59,209 | 65,550 |
| Less: Dividends Paid and Proposed | (100,000) | (101,056) |
| Adj/Tfrs (to)/from Reserves | (705) | (1,223) |
| RETAINED PROFIT FOR YEAR | (41,496) | (36,729) |
| Profit and Loss B/Forward | 139,774 | 98,278 |
| TOTAL REVENUE RESERVES | 98,278 | 61,549 |
| **CASH FLOW** | | |
| **OPERATING CASH FLOW** | | |
| Operating Profit (Loss) | 58,455 | 69,648 |
| Depreciation/Amortization Charges | 29,421 | 32,767 |
| ADJUSTED CASH FLOW FROM OP'S | 87,876 | 102,415 |
| **WORKING CAPITAL MOVEMENT** | | |
| (Inc)/Dec in Stock | (34,692) | 37,259 |
| (Inc)/Dec in Debtors | 9,421 | (7,214) |
| Inc/(Dec) in Creditors | 28,665 | (8,723) |
| Other Net Working Cap Movement | 0 | 0 |
| NET CASH FLOW FROM OPERATIONS | 91,270 | 123,737 |
| Less: Taxation Paid | (1,660) | (10,072) |
| Less: Interest Paid | (9,652) | (4,688) |
| NET FREE CASH FLOW FROM OP'S | 79,958 | 108,977 |
| Less: Dividends Paid | (105,361) | (58,087) |
| Less: Other Cash Outflow | (5,923) | (8,378) |
| NET C/F BEFORE INV. GRP AND FIN ACT | (31,326) | 42,512 |
| **CASH FLOW FROM INVESTMENT AND GROUP** | | |
| Net Cash from Fixed Assets | (21,747) | (25,562) |
| Net Cash from Investment Act | 14,746 | 13,995 |
| Net Intra-Group Funds Flow | 0 | 0 |
| Other | 30,059 | 19,236 |
| NET C/F BEFORE EQUITY AND FIN. ACT | (8,268) | 50,181 |
| **CASH FLOW FROM EQUITY AND FIN. ACT** | | |
| Inc/(Dec) in Equity | 0 | 0 |
| Inc/(Dec) in S.Term Debt | 5,766 | (51,026) |
| Inc/(Dec) in L.Term Debt | 0 | 0 |
| Other | 873 | 595 |
| NET C/F FROM EQUITY AND FIN. ACT | 6,639 | (50,431) |
| Inc/Dec Cash and Nr Liquid Funds | 1,629 | 250 |
| TOTAL | 8,268 | (50,181) |

**Additional Information**

- Turnover comprises: Equipment and Automotive $286.8m, Consumer Products $714m, Industrial Products $298m and Office Equipment $171m.
- Represents global brands such as TOSHIBA, XEROX, NESTLE, BRIDGESTONE, PEPSI, CATERPILLER etc.
- Largest inventory item was trading inventory and finished goods, which towards 2010-end, decreased to $191m ($222m as at 31.12.2009).
- Shareholders had purchased long o/s government receivables, amounting to $49m of a group company to improve its cash flows. Unused bank facilities as at 31.12.10 were $168m.
- Sales growth of 2010 is almost in line with the previous years. Trading inventory and finished goods as at 31.12.2010 was $191m ($222m as at 31.12.2009).

You may calculate major financial ratios and prepare a brief analytical report deriving the financial risk involved. Structure your report covering performance, profitability, working capital management, liquidity and cash flows.

**Suggested Solution**

The solution is derived in two steps. First the major ratios are computed. Thereafter, an analysis report is prepared stressing financial highlights and ultimate financial risk involved.

## I. RATIOS

| A. SOLVENCY RATIOS | 31.12.2009 | 3.12.2010 |
|---|---|---|
| **LIQUIDITY (SHORT TERM SOLVENCY) RATIOS** | | |
| CURRENT RATIO | 1.28 | 1.27 |
| QUICK RATIO | 0.74 | 0.74 |
| **LONG TERM SOLVENCY RATIOS** | | |
| LEVERAGE | 1.80 | 1.75 |
| GEARING | 0.51 | 0.41 |
| FINANCE COSTS COVERAGE | 11.20 | 19.55 |
| FINANCE COSTS CASH COVER | | 31.56 |
| **CASH FLOW RATIOS** | | |
| INTEREST CASH COVER | 9.45 | 26.39 |
| SHORT-TERM DEBT CASH COVER | 0.39 | 0.71 |
| DIVIDEND CASH COVER | 0.75 | 1.87 |
| EXTERNAL DEBT REPAY PERIOD | 2.5 | 1.4 |
| **B. OPERATING RATIOS** | | |
| **Performance Ratios** | | |
| SALES GROWTH | – | 2% |
| PRODUCTIVITY (SALES TO OPERATING CAPITAL-SOCE) | 2.4x | 2.9x |
| NET PROFIT GROWTH | – | 11% |
| OPERATING CAPITAL GROWTH | – | −13.1% |
| **Profitability Ratios** | | |
| GPM | 22.7% | 22.9% |
| OPM | 4.0% | 4.7% |
| NPM | 4.9% | 5.6% |
| **Return On Investment Ratios** | | |
| ROCE | 9.9% | 13.6% |
| OROCE | 12.8% | 16.0% |
| ROE | 17.2% | 21.1% |
| **Asset Management Ratios** | | |
| W/C TO SALES RATIO | 5.7% | 10.5% |
| W/C TO TOTAL ASSETS RATIO | 15.6% | 15.0% |
| STOCK TURNOVER (days) | 101 | 88 |
| DR COLLECTION (days) | 92 | 77 |
| CR SETTLMENT (days) | 71 | 74 |
| FIXED ASSETS UTILIZATION | 6.51 | 6.85 |
| **Cost-Volume-Profit Ratios** | | |
| BREAKEVEN SALES (TO COVER SG&A O/H) | 1,189,832 | 1,165,920 |
| % TO THE ACTUAL SALES | 82% | 79% |
| BREAKEVEN SALES | 1,223,324 | 1,186,760 |
| % TO THE ACTUAL SALES | 85% | 81% |

**C. ENCAPUSLATED RATIOS**

**a. Dupont**

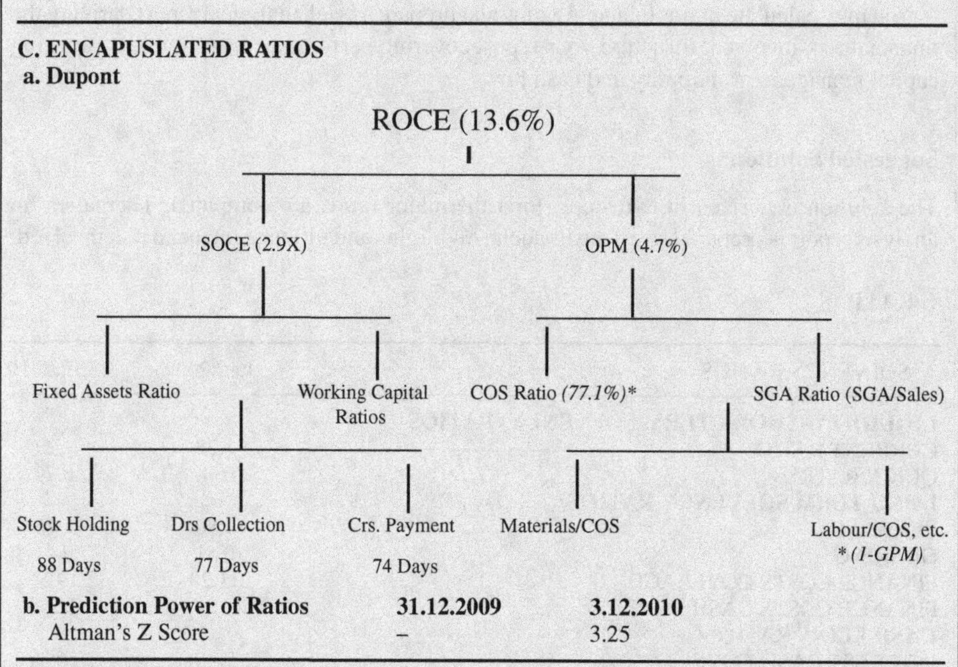


| **b. Prediction Power of Ratios** | **31.12.2009** | **3.12.2010** |
|---|---|---|
| Altman's Z Score | – | 3.25 |

*Note: The ratios are averaged, wherever applicable.*

## *II. FINANCIAL ANALYSIS REPORT OF ABCD LTD*

### *PERFORMANCE*

Breakdown of the turnover, which is characterized by moderate growth with low levels of fluctuations indicative of the relatively mature markets for many of the products manufactured/traded in by group companies, is given below:

| Particulars | 2010 | Percentage to the total |
|---|---|---|
| Equipment and Automotive | 286.8 | 19.5% |
| Consumer Products | 714.8 | 48.6% |
| Industrial Products | 298.0 | 20.3% |
| Office Equipment | 170.2 | 11.6% |
| **Total** | **1,469.8** | **100%** |

The consumer products segment was the largest and accounted for about 48.6% of the total turnover. Overall the turnover is derived from diversified activities which offer some protection against severe turnover fluctuations. ABCD entities and subsidiaries represent leading global brands resulting in 'brand captive' markets. Accounting policies comply with GAAP and accounting analysis does not indicate any major accounting policy changes.

***PROFITABILITY***

GPM remained almost identical to that of the previous year at 22.9% (22.8% in 2009), reflecting continuation of similar overall profit margins. GPM continues to be at satisfactory levels, given the diversified nature of ABCD. Marketing expenses, which increased by 3% to \$160m (2009: \$156m) are justifiable as they remained around 10.9% of turnover. However, effective cost cuts were attained in admin expenses, which reduced by 7% to \$107m (\$115m in 2009). Taken together, selling and admin costs show a reduction of \$4m. This, coupled with slightly better GPM, has resulted in an improved OPM of 4.74% (2009: 4.04%).

Sales to Operating Capital Ratio has improved to 2.90x (2009: 2.41x), which reflects improved productivity of the group. This is traceable to improved fixed asset utilization (better sales to fixed asset ratio) and favourable changes in terms of trade (see working capital management). Despite marginal improvement in GPM and volume, ROCE recorded rather significant improvement to 13.6% (2009: 9.9%), traceable to the better asset productivity (improved SOCE) and successful cost reductions (improved OPM). ROCE can be spilt as follows:

$$\text{ROCE} = \text{OPM} \times \text{SOCE}$$

$13.6\% = 4.7\% \times 2.9$ – please refer to the DuPont chart given earlier in this report also.

ABCD's share of profit in the associates stood at \$10.06m, while other income, \$13.7m includes foreign exchange income of \$1.6m (2009: \$2.1m) and interest income (mainly on instalment sales) of \$4.6m (2009: \$5m). More information is not available. Interest expenses decreased to \$4.8m (\$7.6m in 2009) due to the lower average interest rates and reduction in bank borrowings. Interest coverage ratio and interest cash cover, which improved to 11.2x and 26.4x (4.89x and 9.5x in 2009) were highly satisfactory.

After providing for the minority interest (\$16.6m vs. \$11.98m in 2009) in subsidiaries, ABCD ended FY2010 with an 11% increase in the net profit to \$65.6m compared to \$59.2m in the previous year. Improved efficiencies and productivity resulted in a satisfactory and five year high ROE of 21.1% (2009: 17.2%).

***WORKING CAPITAL MANAGEMENT***

**Stock**: comprises trading items (food items, office appliances, etc.) and inventory for the factories. Largest inventory item was trading inventory and finished goods, which towards 2010-end, decreased to \$191m (\$222m as at 31.12.2009) reducing the average holding period to 88 days (101 days in 2009). Overall, the inventory management continues to be satisfactory. **Trade Debtors**: The collections improved as evident in the decrease of average collection period to 77 days (92 days in 2009). One of the main reasons was the purchase of receivables, amounting to \$49.2m by shareholders. Overall, the average collections period is satisfactory taking into account the diversified nature of ABCD. **Trade Creditors**: Average creditors payment period of the group increased to 74 days (2009: 71 days) which indicates an acceptable level of reliance on suppliers' credit. **Short Bank Borrowings**: were reduced by \$51m, primarily from the cash flows from favourable change in terms of trade – i.e. whilst the stock holding period and debtors collection dropped, the payment period to creditors had increased.

### *LIQUIDITY AND CASH FLOWS*

Satisfactory liquidity with cash flow driven by moderate sales growth, improved operating margins and satisfactory working capital management. Current and quick ratios remained almost identical at 1.27:1 and 0.74:1 respectively (1.28:1 and 0.74:1 as on 31.12.2009) reflecting continuation of adequate liquidity. Moreover unused bank facilities as at 31.12.10 were $168m, which can be considered as a quick source of funds, if needed.

Cash flows continue to be stable and adequate to meet the business and owners' withdrawals. Most of the cash flows originate from low risk business segments such as consumer products, suggesting sound quality of cash flows. Whilst adjusted cash from operations improved to $102m due to better profitability and higher non-cash charges, the net cash from operations stood at $123.7m, as favourable changes in terms of trade released working capital. Net cash from operations is historically positive, reflecting the inherent strength of operational cash flow.

Investment inflows include dividend income of $10.4m. Dividends outflow of $58m comprise $50m to shareholders and balance to minority interests. Other major cash outflows were the net addition to the fixed assets, $25.6m and interest payments, $4.7m. Cash generation has historically been adequate to cover all priority outflows. Coverage ratios are satisfactory with interest coverage of 26x and a low external debt repayment period of 1.4 years.

### *CAPITAL STRUCTURE*

TNW declined to $310.5m ($343.5m in 2009) because of the dividends in excess of the net profit for the year. It is pertinent to note that although the shareholders brought in funds to purchase a receivable of a group entity, the dividends were substantial. Contributions from shareholders, which have been made to meet the w/c requirements of ABCD and subsidiaries, are interest free and have no repayment schedule and are subordinated to bank facilities. During 2010, gearing and debt/equity ratios declined to 0.41:1 and 1.58:1 respectively (0.51:1 and 1.66:1 as on 31.12.2009) and reflect rather moderate financial leverage. External debt usage is well controlled given the relatively stable operating environment with low CAPEX/incremental investment requirements. High dividend payout in 2009 and 2010 (169% and 155% of distributable annual profit respectively) has resulted in erosion of P/L reserves. However in view of sustainable profit margins, low leverage levels and strong competitive position this is considered acceptable.

### *CONCLUSION*

Z-Score is well above the cut-off of bankruptcy. The sustainable growth rate is negative because the dividends exceeded the profit for the year and without any retention. (Nonetheless, ABCD has debt capacity to grow by leveraging its creditors and lenders, which may be closely monitored.) Overall financial position is considered strong with good balance sheet structure and strong income statement. The outlook for ABCD is stable, given its diversified nature and strong brands. Overall **financial risk can be classified as medium** given its strong capital structure, moderate leverage, adequate profitability and quality internal cash generation although higher dividend outgoings and delay in collection of government related receivables (which forced shareholders to purchase it to provide liquidity) are matters of some concern.

## QUESTIONS/EXERCISES

1. Explain how you would conduct a financial analysis of a corporate customer/business to understand its financial strengths and financial risks.
2. Mr. X states that (i) ratio analysis is possible without accounting analysis and (ii) current ratio is a better measure of a firm's liquidity than the quick ratio. Do you agree? Explain your views.
3. Hypothetical Manufacturing Ltd provides you with the following details:
   - Current assets of $12m.
   - Current liabilities of $6m.
   - Net sales of $20m.
   - Quick ratio of 1.00.
   - Debtors collection period of 30 days.

   Calculate the level of inventory and receivables.
4. What is the importance of understanding the operating leverage, financial leverage, total leverage and breakeven point from a credit risk analysis perspective?
5. You are the credit manager of XYZ Bank. You have been provided with the following financial summary of a customer who enjoys credit facilities of US$18m.

| US$'000 | FY2007 | FY2008 | FYE 2009 | FY2010 |
|---|---|---|---|---|
| Turnover | 15,664 | 21,843 | 22,085 | 25,967 |
| Operating Profit | 987 | 1,469 | 2,441 | 1,823 |
| EBITDA | 1,531 | 2,213 | 3,158 | 2,770 |
| Profit before Tax | 1,041 | 1,688 | 2,030 | 1,228 |
| Gross Debt | 4,031 | 4,994 | 7,963 | 8,830 |
| Net Debt | 3,670 | 4,321 | 7,034 | 8,219 |
| Intangibles | 300 | 200 | 100 | 0 |
| Tangible Net Worth | 7,030 | 8,719 | 10,748 | 11,977 |
| Capital and Reserves | 7,030 | 8,719 | 10,748 | 11,977 |
| Free Cash flow | N/A | −1,154 | 1,092 | 706 |
| CAPEX | 3,985 | 547 | 1,826 | 708 |
| Gross (Net) Debt/TNW (%) | 0.57 | 0.57 | 0.74 | 0.74 |
| Net Debt/EBITDA (x) | 2.4 | 1.95 | 2.16 | 3.27 |
| Current Ratio (%) | 140% | 162% | 130% | 127% |
| Quick Ratio (%) | 136% | 156% | 125% | 124% |
| Operating Profit Margin (%) | 6.30% | 6.72% | 11.05% | 7.02% |
| Interest Cover (x) | 6.37 | 4.98 | 4.98 | 2.62 |
| External Debt Repayment Period(Years) | NA | -4.3 | 7.3 | 12.5 |

Please provide your views on (i) profitability, (ii) capital structure and (iii) liquidity. It is evident that there is deterioration in net debt to EBITDA and interest coverage. Explain your views and clarify whether you would recommend reduction in existing credit facilities.

6. As the Head of Credit of PQRZ Bank, you have just read a research report that provides a dismal outlook about the macroenvironment and warns about a possible recession. What would be your future outlook on the profitability and liquidity ratios of your customers in the credit portfolio? Based on the historical financial statements, your team has classified the credit portfolio (i.e. the customers) into the following categories:
   - Customers with very high net debt/EBITDA.
   - Customers displaying very high operating leverage, but low financial leverage.
   - Customers exhibiting both high operating leverage and financial leverage.
   - Customers with very tight liquidity ratios and high gearing levels.

   Explain the steps you would take if the above customers are engaged in highly cyclical businesses. Would your views be different if they are engaged in moderately cyclical or non-cyclical businesses? Please elaborate.
7. The following are the financial statements (along with common sized analysis) of XYZ Ltd.

**PROFIT AND LOSS ACCOUNT**

| Statement Date | 3/31/2008 | | 3/31/2009 | |
|---|---|---|---|---|
| Amounts in: US$ Millions | | | | |
| **No. of Months** | **12** | % | **12** | % |
| Turnover | 36,441 | 100.0 | 42,674 | 100.0 |
| Less: Carriage inwards | 701 | 1.9 | 822 | 1.9 |
| Less: Cost of Goods Sold | 11,005 | 30.2 | 14,443 | 33.8 |
| Gross Profit / (Loss) | 24,735 | 67.9 | 27,409 | 64.2 |
| Less: Admin Overheads | 16,469 | 45.2 | 18,997 | 44.5 |
| Less: Selling Overheads | 3,755 | 10.3 | 3,797 | 8.9 |
| Less: Depreciation | 1,652 | 4.5 | 2,150 | 5.0 |
| Less: Amortization of Intangibles | 48 | 0.1 | 61 | 0.1 |
| Total Operating Expenses | 21,924 | 60.2 | 25,005 | 58.6 |
| Operating Profit/(Loss) | 2,811 | 7.7 | 2,404 | 5.6 |
| Add: Other Income/(Expenses) | 3,027 | 8.3 | (910) | (2.1) |
| Less: Interest Payable | 734 | 2.0 | 535 | 1.3 |
| Net Profit/(Loss) before Taxation | 5,104 | 14.0 | 959 | 2.2 |
| Less: Current Taxation | 59 | 0.2 | (78) | (0.2) |
| Less: Deferred Taxation | (31) | (0.1) | (7) | |
| Net Profit/(Loss) after Taxation | 5,076 | 13.9 | 1,044 | 2.4 |

**BALANCE SHEET – ASSETS AND LIABILITIES**

| **Statement Date** | | **3/31/2008** | | **3/31/2009** |
|---|---|---|---|---|
| CURRENT ASSETS | | % | | % |
| Cash | 10,360 | 22.3 | 7,168 | 15.1 |
| Trade Debtors | 1,679 | 3.6 | 1,107 | 2.3 |
| Liquid Assets | 12,039 | 25.9 | 8,275 | 17.4 |
| Stock | 751 | 1.6 | 1,053 | 2.2 |
| Due from Related Companies | 1,384 | 3.0 | 2,070 | 4.4 |
| Advance Lease Deposits | 912 | 2.0 | 900 | 1.9 |
| Other Debtors | 1,482 | 3.2 | 1,682 | 3.5 |
| Prepayments | 1,723 | 3.7 | 1,350 | 2.8 |
| Available for Sale Financial Assets | 96 | 0.2 | – | |

| | | | | |
|---|---|---|---|---|
| Held to Maturity Investments | 216 | 0.5 | 200 | 0.4 |
| Derivatives | 188 | 0.4 | - | |
| Other Current Assets | 6,001 | 12.9 | 6,202 | 13.1 |
| Total Current Assets | 18,791 | 40.4 | 15,530 | 32.7 |
| FIXED AND NON-CURRENT ASSETS | | | | |
| Total Fixed Assets | 21,369 | 45.9 | 29,086 | 61.3 |
| Held-to-Maturity Investments | 2,048 | 4.4 | 113 | 0.2 |
| Investment in Joint Ventures | 560 | 1.2 | 441 | 0.9 |
| Loans and other receivables | 1,228 | 2.6 | 1,039 | 2.2 |
| Other Operating Non-Current Assets | 223 | 0.5 | 192 | 0.4 |
| Derivatives | 1,377 | 3.0 | 125 | 0.3 |
| Other Non-Current Assets | 5,436 | 11.7 | 1,910 | 4.0 |
| Total Fixed Assets and Non-Current Assets | 26,805 | 57.6 | 30,996 | 65.3 |
| INTANGIBLE ASSETS | | | | |
| Total Intangible Assets | 919 | 2.0 | 924 | 1.9 |
| **TOTAL ASSETS** | **46,515** | **100.0** | **47,450** | **100.0** |
| CURRENT LIABILITIES | | | | |
| Total Short Term Loans | 1,416 | 3.0 | 1,372 | 2.9 |
| Trade Creditors | 6,916 | 14.9 | 7,453 | 15.7 |
| Due to Related Parties | 56 | 0.1 | 194 | 0.4 |
| Dividends Payable | 912 | 2.0 | | - |
| Tax Payable | 162 | 0.3 | | 23 |
| Other Creditors | 5,666 | 12.2 | 4,883 | 10.3 |
| Accruals | 165 | 0.4 | 169 | 0.4 |
| Derivatives | 170 | 0.4 | 31 | 0.1 |
| Total Current Liabilities | 15,463 | 33.2 | 14,125 | 29.8 |
| NON-CURRENT LIABILITIES | | | | |
| Total Long Term Debt | 12,301 | 26.4 | 15,140 | 31.9 |
| Total Other Non-Current Liabilities | 2,063 | 4.4 | 1,774 | 3.7 |
| Total Non-Current Liabilities | 14,364 | 30.9 | 16,914 | 35.6 |
| CAPITAL AND RESERVES | | | | |
| Ordinary Shares | 801 | 1.7 | 801 | 1.7 |
| Other Reserves | 782 | 1.7 | – | |
| Retained Earnings | 15,105 | 32.5 | 15,610 | 32.9 |
| Total Capital and Reserves | 16,688 | 35.9 | 16,411 | 34.6 |
| **TOTAL LIABILITIES** | **46,515** | **100.0** | **47,450** | **100.0** |

Using the above information, complete a comprehensive ratio analysis for XYZ Ltd:

(i) Calculate liquidity ratios: current and quick ratios.

(ii) Calculate activity ratios: inventory holding period, debtors collection period.

(iii) Calculate finance ratios: gearing ratio, debt-to-equity ratio, net debt to EBITDA.

(iv) Calculate coverage ratios: interest coverage ratio, finance cost to sales.

(v) Calculate profitability ratios: gross profit margin, net profit margin.

(vi) Use the DuPont method, and after calculating the component ratios, compute the ROCE for this firm.

(vii) Calculate Altman's Z Score and appraise the bankruptcy risk.

8. Select a stock market listed company (e.g. Tata Motors or Wal-Mart) and apply the analytical techniques discussed in this chapter. Elaborate your views on the financial position of the company.

# 9
# Integrated View of Firm-Level Risks

In the today's world, as we have seen in Chapter 1, credit is pervasive and inexorable. From the local retailer/financier to multinational banks/manufacturers and multilateral financial institutions, credit holds sway. We have already seen external risks, industry risks, internal/company risks and financial risks. The credit risk model we discussed in Chapters 5 to 8 comprehensively covers all the significant components of credit risk at an entity or firm or company level. Now an integrated approach is required. Having covered all External, Industry, Internal and Financial (EIIF) risks, an integrated view is required to arrive at the correct credit risk.

## 9.1 RELEVANCE OF AN INTEGRATED VIEW

The obligor credit risk analysis calls for the critical examination or due diligence of the credit risk on a disaggregation basis (EIIF model/risks). However, the overall risk assessment is done on an 'aggregation basis' using the output derived from the study of each component of the EIIF model. The division of credit risk into EIIF risks facilitates in-depth study of the credit risk and covers all factors that impact the creditworthiness of a business firm. It should be borne in mind that it is seldom the case that a single condition causes failure, but rather it is a combination of factors. EIIF risks should be viewed together because often two or more EIIF risks work together to trigger a business collapse. For instance, the foray into new markets/ sectors in which management lacks experience/competence coupled with high leverage can be considered as almost a sure recipe for disaster. An integrated view is also important to identify appropriate tools to mitigate the risks.

## 9.2 JUDGEMENT

It is not unusual that credit risk executives, after the detection of EIIF risks, find it difficult to integrate them and arrive at a proper credit decision. EIIF analysis will bring in a lot of pluses and minuses on the creditworthiness of the business firm. Usually most of the minuses can be considered as risks. In most cases, the pluses can act as mitigants or lend comfort to the creditor, although at times they may turn into a risk, especially in a different scenario. For instance, while huge capacities bring in economies of scale, if economic recession lowers demand, huge capacities pose the risk of significant under-utilization of resources. This can plunge the company into losses as the fixed costs are incompressible despite the fall in revenue (impact of operating leverage, which we discussed in the previous chapter) and if the huge capacity expansion has been undertaken with debt, it will complicate the matter further.

Every time a spacecraft takes off, several 'mission critical' risks are involved. Whilst hundreds of space missions are completed successfully, there are occasional failed space launches, as one of the 'mission critical' risks is triggered. Likewise, in the world of credit risk too, despite all safety measures, things can go wrong. The risks of a credit decision that stare the credit executive in the face can be challenging, often impacting the reputation of the decision taker.

The approach advisable is akin to that of a judge or jury bench, who arrive at decisions (on cases) based on the 'beyond reasonable doubt' principle. The credit risk executive, after studying EIIF risks, ought to arrive at a judgement, just as a judge in a court makes a conclusion beyond reasonable doubt after weighing the evidence. The risk matrix discussed in Chapter 4 ought to provide overall guidance in this regard. If any significant risk is judged as a high risk, strong risk mitigants must be sought to make the credit of an acceptable quality.

## 9.3 IDENTIFYING SIGNIFICANT CREDIT RISKS

While evaluating various risks at hand, the credit executive ought to weigh them and segregate them between significant and insignificant ones. While this is usually subjective, some degree of objectivity can be brought in by assessing the following:

(a) **Probability (Likelihood) of Occurrence**: This can be categorized into 'Low, Moderate or High'.
(b) **Consequence, if it Occurred**: The impact can be rated 'Weak, Moderate or Strong'.

The analysis of various risks is undertaken with the purpose of prioritization – prioritize the risks and decide which risks are to be kept open and which ones are to be covered or mitigated fully or partly. The likelihood and the impact of EIIF risks can be presented in a matrix form as follows (see Table 9.1):

**Table 9.1** Risk Impact Assessment

| Occurrence/Impact | Low Probability | Moderate Probability | High Probability |
|---|---|---|---|
| Weak Impact | Insignificant Risk | Insignificant Risk | Significant Risk |
| Moderate Impact | Insignificant Risk | Significant Risk | Very Significant Risk |
| Strong Impact | Significant Risk | Very Significant Risk | Extremely Critical Risk |

Depending upon the risk categorization, credit risk mitigation measures may be sought. The following criteria could provide an approximate guidance. It may be noted that this exercise is purely judgemental and depends upon the experience of the credit executive and circumstances of the credit proposal under consideration. Usually the credit risk models[1] cannot handle this role.

1. If the risk is identified as insignificant, it may be kept open. Often it is suggested that there is no need to specifically highlight the insignificant risks in the credit proposal/ recommendation.
2. It is advisable to cover all significant risks in the credit proposal/recommendation with a justification of why it is still acceptable.
3. If the risks are very significant, it is essential that there are strong suitable mitigants.
4. If extremely critical risks are present, it is advisable not to pursue the credit.

[1] If credit risk models could make judgements, then it can be argued that even legal judgements can be modelled.

**Example 9.1**

Ms X is new to credit risk analysis. While analyzing the risks of an established airline based on the EIIF model, she identified the following risks:

1. Stagnant business growth resulting from competition from other airlines.
2. Aggressive fleet expansion, which may lead to over-capacities. There are about 170 aircrafts under order, which could also result in massive financial commitments. A comprehensive feasibility study has been shared by the company, justifying the expansion strategy.
3. Safety standards resulting in crash/disastrous hijacking.
4. Volatile oil prices. There is a risk of failure to address adequately the challenges of fluctuating oil prices. Whilst it is usually rising oil prices that hurt airlines, during 2008, several airlines suffered significant hedging losses as the hedging strategies went awry, when oil prices plummeted from $147 p/b in July 2008 to $35–40 p/b level.

Please help Ms X to classify the above risks.

**Solution**

Let us decide which are the significant ones. Suggestions are given below:

1. Stagnant business growth is of moderate occurrence or probability. The consequence, if it occurred, is also considered to be moderate. Hence **Moderate Probability/Weak Impact**. It can be kept open with sufficient monitoring of how the airline is facing the competition, including strategies and management plans.
2. Whilst fleet expansion is welcome, the risk of over-capacity looms large. The probability of this risk can be considered as low, in view of the fact that the expansion has been undertaken after thorough market study. However, if over-capacity risk turns out to be a reality, the financial strain of flying half-empty aircrafts would be hefty. Hence, the impact is high and can be classified as **Low Probability/High Impact**. It is a significant risk and advisable to introduce appropriate financial covenants, to act as early warning indicators. It must also be ensured that the airline can cancel or modify current orders without penalty, in case the external environment undergoes drastic changes, making the expansion unviable.
3. Any crash or dangerous hijacking incidents will create negative publicity, poor image resulting in a decline in revenue and similar consequences. Whilst the probability is low, the strong impact ought to force the seeking of appropriate mitigants. Hence, the impact is high and can be classified as **Low Probability/High Impact**. It is suggested to ensure the adequacy of safety systems, to establish the average age of the aircraft and if necessary, to seek the help of an external expert.
4. Oil price fluctuation is a business risk that has serious implications for the profitability of the airline business. However, since this affects almost all competitors, the impact can be considered as moderate and can be categorized as **Moderate Probability/Moderate Impact**.

## 9.4 RISK MITIGANTS

Risk mitigants are sought as a comfort to the credit risks identified. Mitigants refer to certainties which ensure adequate financial resources or means to repay the credit despite the presence of risks. Mitigants reduce uncertainty. Many mitigants can be traced to the income, assets, wealth or strengths of the obligor, some of which can be identified by financial analysis. It should always be borne in mind that the primary source of repayment should be the cash flow of the business, and analysis should focus on its sustainability. Nonetheless, strong mitigants also help. As a simple example, suppose credit analysis shows that the credit risk involved in extending credit to XYZ Ltd is high. However, if XYZ Ltd offers a bank guarantee from a first class Commercial Bank, it amounts to an adequate mitigant, which converts the high credit risk into an acceptable one.

## 9.5 TYPES OF MITIGANTS

Risk mitigants can be broadly categorized as shown in Figure 9.1:

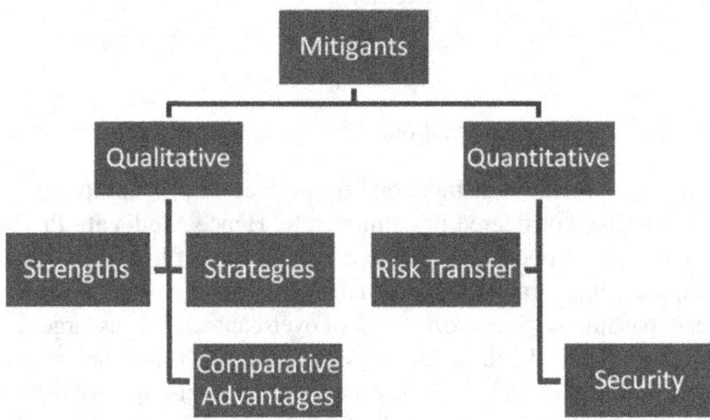


**Figure 9.1** Classification of Risk Mitigants

### 9.5.1 Qualitative Mitigants

These mitigants derive force from the factors that provide excellence or superiority to the obligor in certain areas, which ensure adequate repayment ability by ensuring sufficient volume of business or profitability. While qualitative mitigants vary from case to case, broadly they can be classified into three:

(a) **Strengths**: As we have seen in Chapter 7, SWOT analysis is one of the important components of company analysis. SWOT brings out the strong points of the obligor. In many situations these strengths offset some of the credit risks to be undertaken by the creditor. A few strengths that can be considered as strong mitigants are given below, as guidance:

- **Deep Pockets/Substantial Resources**: Since most of the business or operating risks ultimately lead to financial losses or cash hemorrhage, the higher the fund raising capacity, the better.

- **Market Leadership**: This can be considered as a strong mitigant if the obligor has adopted policies aimed at retaining the market leadership position, without considerably eroding its profitability. For example, new entrants are one of the major operating risks facing Gillette, which is the global market leader in the shaving products industry. In a relatively low barrier industry, market leadership is a strength for Gillette to effectively meet the threat of new entrants or existing competitors trying to capture the market share.
- **Natural Advantages**: Various countries have certain peculiarities, which result in some kind of competitive advantage. Whilst China currently has the cheapest labour force in the world, Indian software engineers are considered the best in the world. Whilst oil companies in Saudi Arabia, Kuwait and the United Arab Emirates enjoy the natural advantage of enormous oil reserves, the strength of Japanese companies lies in their innovation and entrepreneurial skills.

(b) **Strategies** that provide sustainable competitive advantages and core competencies are strong mitigants to some of the credit risks of an obligor. Basically these factors can ultimately be traced back to the quality of management. Capable and honest management with a proven track record go a long way as an effective mitigant as they are able to develop successful strategies. Along with the strategies discussed in Chapter 7, the following measures also act as strong mitigants, if the obligor/customer has implemented them successfully:

- **Developing Core Competencies**: Core competencies refer to the organizational skills that provide a competitive edge. The skills may be related to technical, marketing or finance factors or anything that provides a firm with the ability to introduce/create better products, achieve cost efficiencies, or serve the customer better, for example. Not all firms come to the market place with core competencies in critical areas. The missing pieces of a core competency can often be acquired through alliances and licensing agreements or recruiting capable hands. While turning around Nissan in the early 2000s, the main strategy was to focus on their core competency: technology (leading to several sophisticated models at affordable prices).
- **Identifying Alternative Sources**: Ability to switch production to another factory or outsource the interrupted activity and similar disturbances in the value chain often act as strong mitigants. The companies that report little or no disruption in the supply chain generally have two factors in common (a) alternative transportation methods from suppliers/to customers and (b) sufficient inventory or resources in channels or in alternative geographic locations. Such a risk management plan by management is a proof of sophistication. Although such contingency plans do not eliminate risk, they result in significant risk mitigation because they save the entity from losing markets/revenue from such risks. They also enable companies to quickly react to market developments.
- **Comparative and Sustainable Advantages**: Certain inherent advantages arising from proximity to key inputs, cheaper sources of supplies, captive markets, etc. are some of the advantages that can be treated as mitigants. Business firms having sustainable competitive advantages in one form or another or successfully developing such advantages are likely to face less difficulties in a business downturn. Comparative advantages are of two types: (i) one that comes from the external environment and benefits all in the industry; (ii) the second type of comparative advantage that accrues to a particular

firm. For example Tata Steel has its own iron ore and coal mines, providing a unique advantage. Another example is the size of the business, usually the higher the size, the better it is as it brings in economies of scale.

(c) **Other factors**: The mitigants are to be established on a case-by-case basis. Some of the other mitigants are (i) strategic importance of the business unit to the local economy, in which case local governments ought to come out with friendly measures and policies to ensure its sustainability. Moreover, a large business provides employment to tens of thousands and given the jobs involved, government will be interested in its survival, although it could be influenced by the policy of the government in power (e.g. Chrysler in the 1980s). In other instances, (ii) the political connections can sometimes act as an effective mitigant.

The above list is not exclusive; other mitigants are available depending upon the circumstances. Most of the qualitative mitigants depend upon the strengths of the company or the management techniques adopted by the company. Prioritizing a company's business risks is usually a matter for senior management. Ideally, the amount of management effort spent on one issue in relation to any other should parallel the perceived degree of risk that it poses to the business. The selection of a qualitative mitigant expects a close correlation between a creditor/lender's perception of a given risk and the extent to which they can control that risk, through covenants and conditions. The perceived risk would then be greatest for the factors over which the creditor has least control.

### 9.5.2 Quantitative Mitigants

Such mitigants are quantifiable and often the creditor or lender can estimate the level of comfort quantitatively. Letters of credit or guarantees provided to a manufacturer by buyers and mortgages of land and buildings by a borrower to secure a bank loan are some of the examples. Two of the common quantitative type mitigants are:

(a) **Transfer of Risks**: This is usually done by insurance, where the specifications of insurance are spelt out. Insurance covers a lot of operating risks and some financial risks. Fire, marine, theft, third party damages, loss of profits, key-man risks are some of those that can be insured. In cases where the credit exposure is large, usually the creditors (viz. banks) call for assignment of the insurance in their favour. A loss of profits policy covers financial loss risk associated with the operating risks. Another technique of transfer of risks is through the use of derivatives such as forward contracts, hedging, swaps, and options. Usually foreign currency exposures, interest rate risks and commodity price risks are mitigated by the use of derivatives. However, it is to be noted that the use of derivatives in itself is a risk, which if not properly managed and executed can bring havoc to the organization.

(b) **Security**: Tangible and intangible securities[2] are sought by the creditor/lender to mitigate the credit risks. This can take several forms. Whilst the usual intangible forms of securities include guarantees, letters of credit, letters of comfort and so on, tangible securities take the form of real physical assets such as land, buildings, equity shares of financially sound listed companies, etc. Similarly the presence of quality and unencumbered assets in the business, acceptable as security by lenders, can at times act a mitigant. Securities can be

[2] We will discuss more about security later in the book – see Chapters 21 and 22.

taken in several different forms, with varying degrees of ease in liquidating them to cover the repayment obligations. This topic is covered in detail later in the book. (See Part VII 'The Last Line of Defence – Security'.)

The above points are meant to provide an overview only. In real life various mitigants can be shaped in more dynamic and creative ways to protect or enhance credit quality.

### 9.5.3 Difference between Qualitative and Quantitative Mitigants

The essential differences between qualitative and quantitative mitigants are two: (i) the former relies on the repayment ability from within the organization while the quantitative mitigants are usually from a third party or source; (ii) another difference is that the creditor can be reasonably assured about the sum or amount in quantitative mitigants, as the name implies, i.e. they are more quantifiable. As an example, the value of land or building taken as security can be provided by a valuation expert.

## 9.6 PRINCIPLES TO BE BORNE IN MIND WHILE SELECTING MITIGANTS

1. Integrity and an excellent track record of the obligor are the best mitigants. Whilst 'willingness' and 'capacity' to repay are both important, it is willingness that is more important. If you ask an experienced banker, he/she will tell you about cases where the credit loss can be ascribed to the 'unwillingness' of the borrower, despite having the 'capacity' to repay.
2. If the credit is not able to stand alone or be justified in itself, it is often too risky to extend it just on the basis of the mitigants.
3. A source of repayment ought to be embedded in the purpose of the credit, as far as possible. This includes a first degree mitigant or qualitative type of mitigant, which we discussed earlier. For instance, when a raw material/input supplier provides goods on credit, he can be reasonably assured that the repayment will come from the sale of the inputs (sometimes after conversion) supplied. Similarly, when a financial institution provides working capital finance, the repayment ought to flow in on completion of the working capital cycle while project financing repayments ought to come from the project inflows. Procedures that enable the supplier of credit to track down and control the use of funds are part of effective mitigants.
4. Since the cash flows are the source of repayment, the mitigants should either protect the cash flows or open up another source (of cash flow) in the event of risk occurrence.
5. Always seek as a minimum two sources of repayment. One can be based on the purpose itself, as discussed above. Also identify a secondary repayment source as an additional mitigant. For instance, whilst liquidation of the current assets is the main source of repayment of working capital credit/loans, the net profit + depreciation component (e.g. Short-Term Debt Cover Ratio – See Ratio Analysis in Chapter 8) can be another source. Quantitative mitigants such as insurance, letters of credit, etc. can act as the secondary source, if the borrower/debtor fails to meet commitments.
6. Although tangible security is a mitigant, it is not the same as the source of repayment. Most of the securities, especially physical assets, take time to be converted into cash through

legal enforcement. The only exception may be the loan against fixed deposits and leasing, to a certain extent. Under leasing the assets are owned by the lessor.

7. In the case of term loans, Free Cash Flow (FCF) must be checked and if insufficient, it must be understood how the obligor will meet the repayment commitments.

## 9.7 MONITORING OF CREDIT RISK

Many credit losses occur because of lack of monitoring of credit risk. Although banks and financial institutions have systems to ensure periodical risk monitoring (usually through annual/semi-annual credit reviews), it is often considered as a passive affair. Gathering of some information from the customer and processing it through some minimal ratio analysis is frequently the way annual review/periodical review/monitoring is handled. Many credit executives fall into the fallacy that in today's highly competitive environment, it is difficult to canvass new business let alone displease the existing customer by enforcing strict monitoring. Whilst it is understandable that marketing pressures compete strongly for dilution in the rigour of credit risk monitoring, the dangers of lack of proper monitoring are serious. This will negate the extra business canvassed and the underlying credit risk may turn out to be high. Bad credit makes great demands on management time and follow-up costs can be debilitating while the probability of ultimate non-recovery of dues looms large.

Proactive management of credit risk before serious problems arise is the hallmark of sound credit risk monitoring. It requires strong awareness of the operating risks and financial risks in sufficient detail to recognize adverse developments in any of the underlying factors. Sound understanding of External, Industry, Internal and Financial (EIIF) factors impacting the obligor provide an effective framework for credit risk monitoring. Similarly the hypothesis of credit risk monitoring should be that the deterioration in the general economic and business conditions will inevitably be reflected in the performance of obligors. Frontline credit risk management officers ought to be alert to adverse developments – viz. early warning signs. The fundamental question to be answered in a credit monitoring/review situation is 'Is the obligor strong enough to justify continuation of the banking lines or credit facilities?'

Some of the essentials of a proper periodical credit risk review are given below:

1. **Follow religiously the 'Know Your Customer' principle**. A business enterprise is a dynamic entity changing as it acts and reacts to the various stimuli of the operating environment, comprising external, industry and internal factors. Hence 'Know Your Customer' needs constant updating which can be accomplished by looking at the monitoring process as if a new credit is being sanctioned.
2. **A good understanding** of the mission and goals of the obligor as well as the company culture and business practices assists in determining the focus of the monitoring. As we discussed in Chapter 7, sound understanding of the business model is essential to understand the business risks.
3. **Timely receipt and analysis of financial information**. The financial analysis must transcend rudimentary or elevator (viz. just seeing increases and decreases in the ratios and figures) analysis and focus on the real causes and its future course. Given the financial and accounting irregularities, as exemplified in the high profile instances (such as Enron, Worldcom and Satyam Computers) sufficient attention should be paid and no financial number should be accepted without understanding the underlying accounting policies.

4. **History often repeats itself**. It is especially true for business cycles and resultant economic up- and downturns, which lift and sink business enterprises in its course. Given the dynamic but volatile markets and asset prices, monitoring should focus and ensure that the repayment sources do not become illusory and that collaterals are not unstable. If the obligor is multi-banked, always ask the question 'What are the alternatives available for the obligor if other banks cut the lines?'
5. **Early warning signs** are necessary. This is often listed and published in the credit department of both financial and non-financial enterprises for monitoring the credit risk. As mentioned in Chapter 5, success seems to be mixed as evident from the plethora of credit losses and Non-Performing Assets (NPA) in many countries. This observation is not meant to diminish the traditional monitoring and warning signs, but to set the process in the proper context.
6. **Wealthy business families**. Whilst most business families have strategies to retain their wealth, there is a risk that it could have been eroded away. Hence when dealing with wealthy family connections with perceived wealth, adequate evidence by way of a statement of assets position to substantiate verbal assurances must be sought periodically preferably from credible third parties such as practising accountants. This is of particular importance when personal guarantees are relied upon.
7. **Growth plans**. Any growth/expansion strategy of the business is to be closely controlled. Appropriate Management Information (MI) must be sought to effectively monitor the position against agreed milestones.
8. **Understand the liquidity of the obligor**. Liquidity shortfall and over-trading risks should be considered as part of the review process. It must be ensured that the diversion of funds into risky ventures such as real estate doesn't happen. If the obligor is insistent upon going ahead with a project that may result in diversion of funds, it must be ensured that adequate liquidity is maintained. The debt maturity profile of the obligor must be reviewed in every credit monitoring situation.
9. **Check with other lenders**. When providing bilateral facilities, as part of the risk evaluation, the credit risk analyst/manager/approver should have knowledge of the quantum and maturity profile of facilities provided by other lenders to ensure a full understanding of the wider funding/leverage position.
10. **Conduct a suitable sensitivity analysis**. As part of monitoring or annual renewal a sensitivity analysis must be done and any potential breaches are to be fully investigated and a rationale provided if considered acceptable.

## APPENDIX – CREDIT RISKS AND POSSIBLE MITIGANTS

Common credit risks and possible mitigants are given below:

### A. External Risks

1. Foreign currency changes: Hedging/derivatives.
2. Economic slowdown: Export markets (counter-cyclical business activities).
3. Tariff structure: Usually, an open risk.
4. World Trade Agreements: Usually an open risk; if risk is too high ask for strong quantitative mitigants.
5. International trade risks: Letters of credit.

6. Sovereign risks: Letters of credit by a bank outside the subject country.
7. Civil wars/domestic disturbances: Letters of credit or insurance, as appropriate.
8. Interest rate risks: Interest rate derivatives/hedges.
9. Inflation risks: Usually an open risk – pass it on to customers.
10. Devaluation risks: Hedging/derivatives.
11. Cultural/fashion changes: Management expertise/skills/adaptability.
12. Outbreak of epidemics (SARS, etc.): Management expertise/skills/adaptability.
13. Corruption, etc.: Management expertise/skills/adaptability.
14. UN sanctioned country exposure: Comply with sanctions.
15. Terrorism: Open risk, may try for insurance cover, if available.
16. Liquidity crunch: Management expertise/skills/adaptability.
17. Environmental risks: Compliance with local regulations.
18. Sharp stock market correction: Diversified asset classes/businesses.
19. Sharp real estate correction: Diversified asset classes/businesses.

### B. Industry Risks

20. Buyers concentration risk: Strong, long, satisfactory relationship (see Chapter 6).
21. Suppliers' concentration risk: Strong, long, satisfactory relationship.
22. Intensity of competition: Strategies (see Chapter 7).
23. Raw material/key input prices: Hedging/ability to pass costs to the buyers/access to cheap sources.
24. Dumping issue: Strategies/influence govt anti-dumping policies.
25. Life cycle: Life cycle related strategies.
26. Risk of new entrants: Establish strong barriers of entry.
27. Surplus Capacity: Open risk. Explore export markets.
28. Emergence of substitute: Open risk. Start dealing in/producing substitutes.
29. Business cyclical risk: Open risk. Diversify.

### C. Internal (Company Level) Risks

At company level the decisions, policies and strategies are to be made to tackle the issues originating from the external environment and industry. In fact, as we have seen in Chapter 7 internal risks are critical because this decides how the business meets the challenges from the environment and exploits opportunities and the development of core competencies and strategic advantages, ensuring survival and long-term profitability. Some of the company level risks and mitigants are:

30. Inadequate strategies: Open risk (see Chapter 7). Change in strategies.
31. Poor management skills: Appoint qualified and experienced personnel.
32. Internal controls: Appoint external auditors/consultants to get them fixed.
33. Sibling rivalry: Succession planning.
34. Big projects: Capacity to withstand if the projects go wrong.
35. Over-diversification: Ensure necessary skills to effectively deal with new areas.
36. Non-core activities: Make a covenant in the loan agreement to prevent this.
37. Product risks: Insurance cover on product liabilities.
38. Bad debts (liberal credit): Inculcate and improve credit policies.

39. Lack of transparency: Adequate strong quantitative mitigants.
40. Boycotting of products: Strategies/proper corporate communication.
41. Local people's objection: Do.
42. Technological problems: Warranties from providers.
43. Loss of key agency: Open risk, alternate agencies.
44. Disputes with government authorities: Legal opinion.
45. Disputes with customers/suppliers: Legal opinion.
46. Concentration risk (of revenue, product, customers, suppliers, etc.): Long and time-tested track record. Diversification strategies.
47. Slow moving items: Usually an open risk. Improve stock management.
48. Employee frauds: Insurance.
49. Forward/backward integration: Open, diversified business/product portfolio.
50. Expiry of contracts: Open, possibility of renewal.
51. Key-man risks: Insurance cover.
52. Fire risks: Insurance cover.
53. Dwindling of capacity in relation to the industry: Modify business strategies, as appropriate.
54. Loss making divisions/subsidiaries: Implement turnaround strategies.
55. Size: If size is too low, cannot compete effectively, unless they enjoy sustainable competitive advantages or niche market.
56. Lack of focus of vital functions such as finance/marketing: Impose covenants for recruitment of capable and experienced professionals in respective areas.
57. Key shareholder busy with other projects: Usually an open risk, raise a concern.
58. Project delays/cost overruns: Usually an open risk, ensure project management capabilities beforehand. If not quit or ask for strong quantitative mitigants.
59. Poor corporate governance: Open risk, introduction of covenants adds some comfort.
60. Poor succession planning: Open risk, raise a serious concern.

**D. Financial Risks**

61. Liquidity crunch: Strong finance function and sound financial position of shareholders, Ability to raise funds on short notice from related parties or otherwise.
62. High gearing/leverage: Usually an open risk. Some of the mitigants are low operating leverage, market leadership position, growth company, sound shareholders. Better to include some kind of quantitative mitigants as well.
63. High operating leverage: Low financial leverage/maximum capacity utilization.
64. High total leverage: Financial covenants, to monitor/bring down leverage. Monopoly advantages/rapidly growing market, etc. can also be strong mitigants.
65. Cash down-streaming/up-streaming: Financial covenants.
66. Big projects: Financial covenants restricting new CAPEX.
67. Poor collections: Ensure the customer implements adequate steps. If not quit or ask for strong quantitative mitigants. Also seek monthly detailed debtors aging.
68. Huge dividends: Financial covenants.
69. Diversion of funds: Financial covenants.
70. Over-trading: Financial covenants (also see Chapter 12).
71. Poor stock management: Stock inspection (or stock audit). Ensure that the customer implements adequate steps. If not quit or ask for strong quantitative mitigants.

72. Unstable profitability/cash flows: Diversified business portfolio/quantitative mitigants.
73. Fluctuating turnover/business: Do.

Please note that the above list of risks and mitigants are for illustration purposes only. In real life there may be other critical risks, depending upon the nature of business and circumstances and it is up to the credit executive to identify appropriate risk mitigants to protect the interests of the bank, financial institution or lender.

## ✍ QUESTIONS/EXERCISES

1. Explain how you would initiate credit risk mitigation steps. Differentiate between quantitative and qualitative risk mitigants.
2. What are the usual pitfalls while conducting annual credit reviews?
3. Explain the importance of timely receipt of financial statements and their analysis for effective credit monitoring.
4. Having taken an integrated view of the credit risk factors (EIIF) of a customer, how would you screen out the insignificant risks? Also explain how would you identify the appropriate risk mitigants.
5. One of your friends argues that the Credit Risk Models can take effective judgement and arrive at credit decisions. Do you agree? Please elaborate.
6. You are a relationship manager in XYZA Bank and as part of periodic rotation of customers (credit portfolio) you are now in charge of Hypothetical Steel Fabricators Private Ltd. While studying this customer you observe the following:
   - Dip in operating performance. The turnover and net profit grew 12% and 8% respectively, but excluding gain on revaluation of properties, there is a net loss due to higher interest outgoings and a drop in operating profit margin.
   - Cash flow remained stretched as the company embarked upon a huge inventory purchase (using bank lines) believing steel prices had hit the bottom. However the steel prices are yet to recover while the order book is not very healthy as the demand for steel fabricated products remains lukewarm.
   - Balance sheet looks acceptable, however the gearing (gross interest bearing debt/ TNW) level is increasing and relatively high at 210% (or 2.10x).
   - The auditors have been associated with the company for a long time (11 years) and had also acted as the financial advisors, which might entail a conflict of interest.

   The key concerns identified are: constantly recurring liquidity issues, irregular and inconsistent financial information, below par financial management, lack of consolidated audited financial statements, absence of financial projections and poor corporate governance with owner/chairman making all the decisions without any real challenges from the management. This customer is already on the watch list and being reviewed on a semi-annual basis.

   Please explain the possible risk mitigants you would seek from the customer and the kind of credit monitoring system you would implement to closely track developments.
7. You are the Head of Credit Risk of PQRZ Bank. You recently attended a conference, where you have learned that a few banks have exited ABC Company, due to lacklustre performance and rumours of internal problems. To your discomfort, you find that there is no reduction in facilities in your bank; on the other hand, there was an increase in the recent past. The

relationship team reports that although there are concerns, the company has taken the right steps to rectify the situation, which has been highlighted in the recent annual review.

However, within a few months ABC Company applies for bankruptcy resulting in credit losses. You feel that the credit risk monitoring is inadequate. What steps would you suggest to improve the credit monitoring within the bank?

8. Take a credit report prepared by an external rating agency (say S&P or Moody's) on any company (or asset backed security) and understand their logical arguments and study how they factor in credit risk and relevant mitigants. Critically examine their views.

# 10
# Credit Rating and Probability of Default

In this chapter, we will discuss how the individual obligor risks are assigned risk grades based on study. We will also discuss how the risk grades are linked to arrive at the probability of default and credit loss. In Chapter 8, we discussed the 'Z-Score Model' which predicts the likelihood of a firm going bankrupt. Z-Score is quite popular and can be considered as the basic form of credit rating. The main limitation of Z-Score is that it is based on pure financial numbers; however in practice the rating exercise is more elaborate and takes into account several non-financial factors as well.

## 10.1 CREDIT RISK GRADING

On completion of the credit evaluation process – the EIIF study – a rating grade/score would be assigned to the borrower. These grades depict the degree of credit risk associated with the borrower. Updating of the grades is often the fundamental basis of the continued loan/credit risk review process in banks and financial institutions. A sound rating system is essential to generate accurate and consistent risk ratings for risk monitoring and management.

A credit rating scale can comprise different levels. The Basel Accord has prescribed that at least seven risk grades are necessary. Some banks and FIs have more risk grades, as high as 23 in some cases. For example, if the scale comprises 8 levels, levels 1 to 5 would represent various grades of acceptable credit risk while levels 6 to 8 represent various grades of unacceptable credit risk. An example of credit grades in a 20-level credit rating scale is given in Table 10.1 on page 163.

### 10.1.1 Linking EIIF Evaluation to Credit Risk Grades

How would the EIIF evaluation be converted into a credit risk grade? It can be purely judgemental (i.e. subjective) based on the credit risk officer who conducts the evaluation. Or the process can be made objective. Several types of credit rating software are available on the market which allow a mix of 'objective' and 'subjective' evaluation. Using such third party software requires adequate precautions. For example, expert modellers need to be employed or consulted while credit executives at all levels must understand the fundamentals of the model so they can ask right questions and know how each EIIF variable is weighted for rating purposes. However, as discussed in the previous chapter, we believe human judgement must have the final say in corporate credit decisions.

One of the methods of converting EIIF evaluation results into credit risk grades is to assign weights or marks to each EIIF factor and based on the outcome, a particular grade may be assigned. Let us explain this with the help of a simple example.

**Example 10.1**

Hypothetical Bank Ltd is conducting credit risk analysis of a new customer PQR & Co Ltd. As per its credit policy, each EIIF factor is assigned 25 marks each i.e. total mark of 100. i.e.

- External risk factors: 25 Marks
- Industry risk factors: 25 Marks
- Internal risk factors: 25 Marks
- Financial risk factors: 25 Marks
- Total: 100 Marks

The mapping of marks to the risk grades is given below:

| Category | Very Low Risk | | Low Risk | | Low-Moderate Risk | | Moderate Risk | | Satisfactory | | Acceptable Risk | | Moderate-High Risk | | High Risk | | Very High Risk | | Default | Loss |
|---|---|---|---|---|---|---|---|---|---|---|---|---|---|---|---|---|---|---|---|---|
| Marks | >99 | >95 | >91 | >88 | >84 | >80 | >77 | >74 | >70 | >65 | New customers are not considered at these levels | | | | | | | | | |
| Grade | 1 | 2 | 3 | 4 | 5 | 6 | 7 | 8 | 9 | 10 | 11 | 12 | 13 | 14 | 15 | 16 | 17 | 18 | 19 | 20 |

PQR & Co. Ltd scored 20, 21, 23 and 21 in EIIF evaluation. Please ascertain the appropriate credit risk grade for this new customer.

**Solution**

Let us find out the total marks scored by the new customer:

| EIIF risk factors | Maximum Marks | PQR & Co Ltd Marks |
|---|---|---|
| External Risk factors | 25 | 20 |
| Industry Risk factors | 25 | 21 |
| Internal Risk factors | 25 | 23 |
| Financial Risk factors | 25 | 21 |
| **Total** | **100** | **87** |

The total marks obtained by PQR & Co Ltd are 87. As per the credit risk grading policy, marks between 84 and 88 will get a credit risk grade of 5 (low-moderate risk). Accordingly, PQR & Co Ltd will be rated at Grade 5, for credit risk classification purposes.

The rating methodologies may range from purely expert or professional judgement taking into account only qualitative factors, to sophisticated models based on quantitative factors. Although the degree of subjectivity becomes less in models, an ideal risk rating system ought to balance both quantitative and qualitative factors, involving human judgement. Model risk is sometimes too critical and can lead to erroneous conclusions. Hence, expert judgement based on vast experience and knowledge is highly recommended while taking corporate credit decisions.

**Table 10.1** Credit Rating Scale

| Category | Credit Risk Grades[1] |
|---|---|
| Very Low Risk | 1 |
| | 2 |
| Low Risk | 3 |
| | 4 |
| Low-Moderate Risk | 5 |
| | 6 |
| Moderate Risk | 7 |
| | 8 |
| Satisfactory | 9 |
| | 10 |
| Acceptable Risk | 11 |
| | 12 |
| Moderate-High Risk | 13 |
| Moderate-High Risk (Poor Quality) | 14 |
| High Risk | 15 |
| High Risk (Speculative Quality) | 16 |
| Very High Risk | 17 |
| Very High Risk | 18 |
| Default | 19 |
| Loss | 20 |

### 10.1.2 Benefits of Credit Risk Grade System

- A well-established credit rating system provides an essential framework for the credit decision making process.
- It facilitates distinguishing between the credit risk of different credit assets in the portfolio. It also facilitates judgement on obligors' creditworthiness.
- Credit risk grades are highly useful for reporting purposes, internally or to regulators (e.g. central banks). Reporting may include portfolio breakdown by credit grade and various sub-segments in the portfolio (such as sectors, regions, etc.). This would also facilitate segment-wise trend and migration analysis and reporting.
- Risk ratings enable several portfolio/sub-portfolio level analyses, including statistical analysis.
- Risk ratings provide an insight into the credit quality of the portfolio and enable better monitoring of high risk customers.
- Risk ratings enable the calculation of PDs which in turn is useful in ensuring better credit pricing and allocation of capital.

## 10.2 PROBABILITY OF DEFAULT

After the 2008 Credit Crisis, improved credit risk measurement and management have been given more emphasis in almost all banks and financial institutions around the world.

[1] Please note that the credit risk grade is purely on the borrower. We can also have a similar risk grade on the collateral, based on the riskiness of the collateral. See Part VII.

**Table 10.2** PD Grading Scale

| Category | Credit Risk Grades | PD |
|---|---|---|
| Very Low Risk | 1 | 0.006% |
| | 2 | 0.012% |
| Low Risk | 3 | 0.024% |
| | 4 | 0.036% |
| Low-Moderate Risk | 5 | 0.048% |
| | 6 | 0.072% |
| Moderate Risk | 7 | 0.132% |
| | 8 | 0.216% |
| Satisfactory | 9 | 0.336% |
| | 10 | 0.504% |
| Acceptable Risk | 11 | 0.756% |
| | 12 | 1.200% |
| Moderate-High Risk | 13 | 1.944% |
| Moderate-High Risk (Poor quality) | 14 | 3.120% |
| High Risk | 15 | 5.040% |
| High Risk (Speculative quality) | 16 | 7.440% |
| Very High Risk | 17 | 10.440% |
| Very High Risk | 18 | 14.400% |
| Default | 19 | 68.280% |
| Loss | 20 | 100.000% |

Probability of default (PD) attains importance in this scenario. Nowadays PD is used for allocation of capital, better credit risk pricing, client selection and credit quality monitoring.

Probability of default is the statistical percentage probability[1] of a borrower defaulting, usually within a one year time horizon. PD is directly linked to the Credit Risk Grades. The PD can range from nil to 100% for a very high risk customer. In Table 10.2, we have added appropriate PDs to the 20 credit risk grades we discussed earlier. This is just an illustration and the PD values in real life can vary.

Whilst credit ratings 1–12 represent Good Quality, 13–16 comprise Risky Assets. 17–18 represent Very High Risk and 19–20 are Default cases. A PD assigns a statistical value for default. Past data, historical trends, external sources are all guiding factors in arriving at PD. Higher credit risk grades (i.e. low quality) have higher PDs, reflecting higher credit risks. For example, a credit risk grade of 12 has a PD of 1.2% p.a. It means that the likelihood of a firm rated under this category defaulting is only 12 in 1,000 per year. A high risk customer rated 16 has a PD of 7.44% – i.e. likelihood of default is 74.4 in 1,000, per year.

The chart in Figure 10.1 shows the probability of default in diagrammatic form.

Figure 10.1 is the pictorial presentation of PD. You can see that the PD zooms as credit quality deteriorates. EIIF must be able to select customers of sound creditworthiness so that the default scenario can be avoided. Higher credit quality assets have only negligible default probability.

[1] There are different methods to arrive PD statistically. Difference in credit risk pricing can be used to estimate the PD, which is discussed in Chapter 19. Another method is to use the total number of customers and defaults across grades over the past several years and use Bayesian theorem to arrive at probability of a particular grade given the default. This may be further refined using statistical tools. Structural models are also advocated to develop PD, which is discussed later in this chapter.

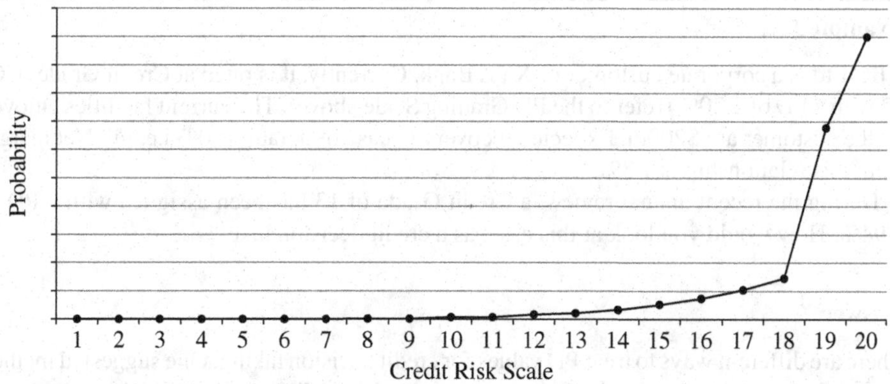


**Figure 10.1** PD Behaviour and Credit Risk Grades

### 10.2.1 Benefits of PD Values

The PD value is usually derived based on past observations and close examination and the study of various factors. The use of PD has several advantages, which are listed below:

- It is scientifically arrived at, through proper study of both internal and external data. Rating agencies such as Moody's and Standard & Poor's publish the default data from their rating universe, which also provides a benchmark to compare against the internal ratings developed by the bank or financial institution.
- The PD is also useful for credit pricing. The higher the PD, the higher the risk, hence the credit premium ought to be higher. For example, the market price of Credit Default Swaps (CDS) is driven by PDs, i.e. the PD is the main driver of CDS and a key component in deciding the credit risk pricing.
- The PD also enables calculation of the economic capital. The higher the PD, the higher the capital requirement.

Since PD is directly linked to credit rating, all the advantages of credit rating which we discussed earlier may also be extended to PD. However, the most important advantage of PD is that it quantifies credit risk.

### 10.2.2 PD Values and Credit Decisions

All credit decisions involve risk taking. While there are situations where the credit decision taker has 'table pounding' confidence about safety of the credit asset, more often such a high level of conviction may be lacking. In such cases one of the suggested methods is to utilize the probabilities embedded in the PD effectively. Accordingly, the decision hinges upon the probabilities and the extent of positive expected value, which can be arrived at based on PD. In other words, the decision taker attempts to take credit risks when he/she/the committee is confident that statistically a particular credit decision will yield an acceptable level of positive expected value. Other things being equal, ideally a credit decision taker may reject all cases with negative expected value or that fall below a cut-off positive expected value. The credit decision taker will tend to accept cases with positive expected value or above the cut-off value with appropriate conditions.

**Example 10.2**

ABC Ltd is a corporate customer of XYZ Bank. Currently, it is rated at Credit Grade (CG) 12 with a PD of 1.20% (refer to the PD Grading Scale above). The current facilities enjoyed by the customer are $200m. Expected recovery in case of default is 0% i.e. nil. Net margin from this relationship is 1.8%.

During the recent annual review, a Credit Grade of 13 has been assigned with a PD of 1.94%. How would you look at this case, as a credit decision taker?

**Answer**

There are different ways to treat PD values for credit decision taking. One suggested method is to understand the changes in the net expected value at different credit risk grades based on assigned PDs. Let us summarize the case as follows:

| Particulars (amount in million) | CG 12 | CG 13 |
|---|---|---|
| Loan amount (a) | 200 | 200 |
| PD (b) | 1.20% | 1.94% |
| Net margin (c) | 1.80% | 1.80% |
| Recovery | 0% | 0% |
| 1-PD (d) | 98.80% | 98.06% |
| Expected gain, if loan is repaid without default [a* (1+c)] (e) | 203.6 | 203.6 |
| Net expected value (e*d-a) | 1.1568 | −0.3498 |

As per the above table, the net expected value of the loan asset shows a negative value under Credit Grade (CG) 13. This is mainly due to the fact that the loss implied in the PD jumps by 62% under CG13 vs. CG12. Accordingly, the suggested credit decision is to not go ahead unless compensated by higher pricing, strong collateral and other mitigants in such a manner that the net expected value is a positive.

Usually it is not sufficient to have a positive value, there ought to be a hurdle rate. This is due to the fact that banks and FIs have to maintain a minimum capital (regulatory/economic capital) against each loan they grant based on risk weights and there is cost of capital involved. We will discuss more about this in later chapters.

## 10.3 EXTERNAL VS. INTERNAL RATING

Ratings are unique systems developed to provide an easy way to understand credit risk. Credit ratings are of two types (i) external ratings and (ii) internal ratings (see Figure 10.2). Whilst the former refer to the credit rating conducted by an external agency such as Standard & Poor's (S&P), Moody's, Fitch, etc. at the request of the obligor to facilitate tapping of the debt capital market, the internal ratings are assigned by lenders, who underwrite credit risks. Moody's (1909) and S&P (1916), are among the pioneers in external rating and over the last several decades, they have rated thousands of companies and sovereigns. Since most of the external rating agencies are considered to have expertise in credit rating and are regarded as unbiased evaluators, their ratings are widely accepted by market participants and regulatory

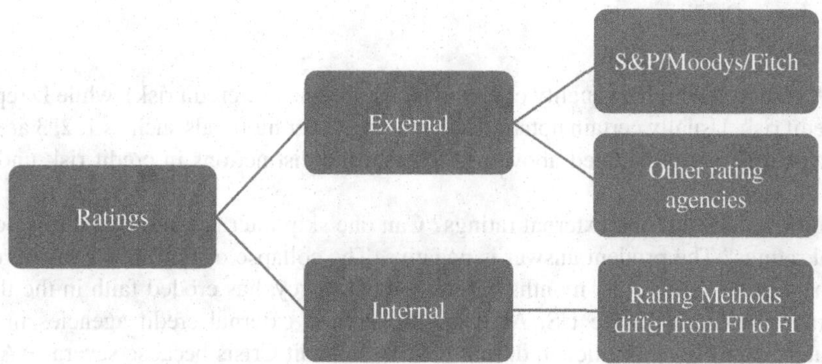


**Figure 10.2** Different Types of Credit Ratings

agencies. However, it may be noted that post the Enron bankruptcy (2001) and losses suffered by Collateralized Debt Obligations (CDO) in 2008/2009, the role of external rating agencies has come under criticism.

Internal rating systems deployed by banks and financial institutions (FIs) differ from organization to organization, but the ultimate goal and credit risk analysis fundamentals remain the same. Ratings assume more importance for banks and FIs covered by the Basel Accords. The various approaches to measuring credit risk (under the Basel Accords) actively advocate the use of credit ratings, either internal or external. While external ratings are given prominence in the standardized approach, the internal ratings are the core of the advanced approaches. (Chapter 16 discusses the Basel Accords.)

### 10.3.1 Reliability of External Ratings

A credit rating is an assessment by a third party of the creditworthiness of an issuer of financial securities. It tells investors the likelihood of default, or non-payment, by the issuer of its financial obligations. In fact external rating agencies, wherever they exist, have a very responsible role to play in the 'debt capital market' of the economy. Usually the companies that wish to approach the public 'debt capital market' ought to obtain ratings from at least two agencies. Only if the rating agencies assign a minimum investment grade, should they then go ahead with the debt issue. The agencies are supposed to keep in touch with developments associated with the debt issuer and revise ratings in the event of significant credit events. The ratings by these firms are captured by alpha-numeric notations, which are often stated to the shortest editorials that could be ever written. An example of a rating system is the *Ratings Definitions* shown below:

- Highest Quality . . . AAA
- Very Good Quality . . . AA
- Good Quality . . . A
- Medium Quality . . . BBB
- Lower Medium Quality . . . BB
- Poor Quality . . . B

- Speculative Quality... C
- Default... D

AAA represents the highest quality of credit exposure (viz. low credit risk), while D represents high credit risk. Usually certain notations like '+' or '−' or numerals such as 1, 2, 3 are affixed to the alphabeticals mentioned above to highlight the distinctions in credit risk under each grade.

But how reliable are the external ratings? Can one skip internal ratings and rely solely on external ratings? The prudent answer is negative. The collapse of Enron, which still enjoyed investment grade rating, just months before its bankruptcy, has eroded faith in the three big credit rating agencies in the US. As discussed earlier, external credit agencies in the US were subjected to severe criticism during the 2008 Credit Crisis because several AAA rated Collateralized Debt Obligations (CDO) defaulted. However, some comfort can be derived from the fact that such fiascos are uncommon and the rating agencies improve their rating methodology with every such disaster. From a creditor's point of view, unless it lacks resources, it ought to put in place a robust internal credit rating system to evaluate the credit risk. This is because of certain inherent defects in external ratings, which are explained below:

(a) Most external ratings are done at the time of debt issues by the obligors and usually to fulfil a statutory requirement. In such cases, the ratings represent the quality of the *particular* debt issue. In other words, the rating is not representative of the credit risk of the obligor/customer, i.e. external ratings need not always rate the issuer or the company in full. Accordingly, it will not be a real reflection of the issuer rating. For instance, if a debt issue enjoys sound collateral, the external rating of the debt issue would be better than that of the customer/borrower rating. External rating is debt-issue oriented rather than borrower specific.
(b) The Stock Exchange Commission (US) and similar regulatory bodies prescribe certain minimum conditions to qualify for debt issues, which screen out almost the whole of the middle or medium market and smaller business segments. Hence, the ratings from external agencies are available only for large, usually listed companies. There will not be any external ratings available for obligors belonging to entities not in a position to meet the eligibility (usually size) criteria.
(c) Conflict of interest. The agencies earn a substantial part of their income from the fees earned by providing ratings services to the corporate sector. Since the fee is paid by the same entity that gets rated, critics have always pointed this out as a conflict of interest. It is not unusual to have two agencies come out with different ratings for the same obligor.

### 10.3.2 Internal Ratings

Almost all business creditors do adopt some kind of internal rating system, ranging from crude to highly sophisticated. The denial of credit by a retailer to one of their habitually defaulting customers or the decision by a wholesaler to deny credit to a new buyer or a financial institution downgrading a borrower are all examples of internal credit rating. In businesses, where credit risk is critical, an internal rating system that provides consistent evaluation and rating facilitating coherent credit decisions across branches or divisions is essential. In banks and most FIs, the internal rating systems have been standardized and well documented, which leads to harmonious credit rating across borrowers, which on aggregation provides meaningful information of the credit quality of the portfolio as well.

The standalone credit risk of the obligor, without considering security or collateral, is vital as it brings out the intrinsic borrower level risk. Initially, it is essential to understand the borrower's fundamentals. As we have discussed under the EIIF framework, factors such as external environment, industry features, barriers to entry, growth potential, technology, market share, management competence and SWOT are studied to understand the borrower's rating. In earlier sections of the chapter, we have discussed how various EIIF factors of the borrower can be mapped to an appropriate internal Credit Risk Classification and Probability of Default. How each bank and financial institution implements an internal rating system will depend upon the circumstances of their business operations and regulatory environment.

## 10.4 PD IN CREDIT STRUCTURAL MODELS

So far we have discussed how to arrive at a credit risk rating and PD based on elaborate study of External, Industrial, Entity and Financial (EIIF) factors. Another way of looking at credit risk and PD is through the use of quantitative techniques. There are several quantitative credit risk default models, among them the widely discussed topic, the Merton Model, which is considered below.

### 10.4.1 The Merton Model (1974)

Professor Merton introduced a model which logically explains the 'default' in most cases. According to the model, the firm or obligor default occurs when the market value of the firm's assets falls to the default point (equivalent to the face value of debt). The greater the distance between the market value of assets and the default point during the credit horizon period (usually assumed to be one year) the better. A shorter distance means that the risk is higher. Once default occurs, creditors receive the market value of the firm's assets. The fundamentals of the model can be captured as shown in Figure 10.3:

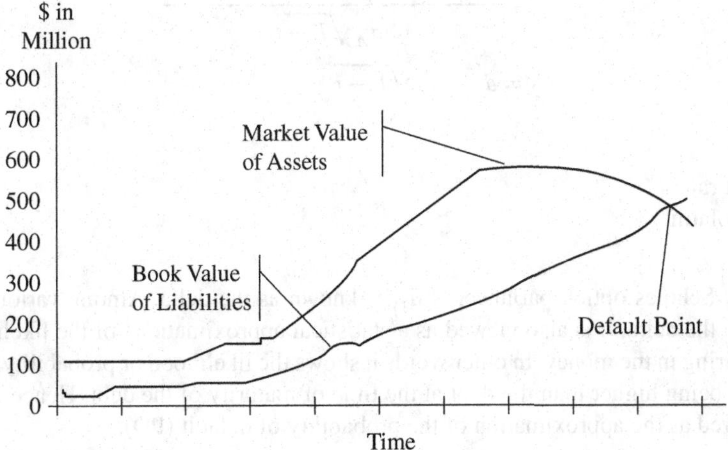


*Theoritical Representations of Firms' Default*

**Figure 10.3** Drift of Market Value of Assets and Book Value of Liabilities Over Time

In most cases, the change is gradual over time as depicted by the free curve. The higher the distance between the assets and liabilities, the lower the PD. Even the credit risk migration can be fitted into the model. Viz., if the distance gets shorter, it denotes migration risk. The default can occur when the asset value drops to the level of debt (i.e. default point), over a period of time. At this point the net worth of the borrower would be nil.

The basic Merton Model calculates the distance to default (DD) based on the Black Scholes[2] option modelling framework. Usually business firms are funded by equity and debt. The Merton Model assumes that the value of the equity in the firm is dependent upon the future value of the firm less future external liabilities. In other words the current worth of the equity of a firm is a derivative of the future value of the firm. It is pertinent to note that the Merton Model assumes that debt consists of a single outstanding bond with face value 'K' and maturity 'T'.

At maturity, the debt will be fully paid, if the total value of the assets is greater than the debt. In such cases, equity shareholders can enjoy the remainder value of assets. However, if assets < debt, it reflects a default and in such cases the creditors can apply for the business to be wound up to receive the liquidation value (equal to the total value of the value minus bankruptcy costs) but the shareholders receive nothing in this case. Accordingly, the Merton Model argues that the equity contributed by the shareholders is like a call option and the option pricing method can thus be used to identify the probability of a firm ending up with a positive TNW when repayment is due. The value of the equity in a firm is calculated as follows as per the Merton formula:

$$V_E = V_A N(d_1) - e^{-r(T-t)} D N(d_2)$$

where

$V_E$ = value of equity
$V_A$ = value of the firm
D = debt of the firm
N (d1) and N (d2) = normal distribution variable

$$d_1 = \frac{\ln(V_A/D) + \left(r + \frac{1}{2}\sigma_A^2\right)(T-t)}{\sigma_A\sqrt{T-t}}$$

$$d_2 = d_1 - \sigma_A\sqrt{T-t}$$

where

r = interest rate
Sigma = volatility
T = time

In Black Scholes option parlance, $N(d_{1)}$ is known as the delta. Among various meanings assigned to the delta, it is also viewed as a statistical approximation[3] of the likelihood of the option expiring in the money. In other words it shows the likelihood or probability of the value of the firm being higher than the debt at the time of maturity of the debt. Hence 1-N(d1) can be considered as the approximation of the probability of default (PD).

[2] Interested readers may study the Black Scholes Merton (BSM) Model in depth to understand how derivatives are valued.
[3] Although mathematical precision may be lacking.

**Example 10.3**

The current value of the assets of the firm – XYZ Ltd – is \$100m. The assets are financed by a mix of equity and zero coupon debt. The current value of zero coupon debt is \$60.65m and the final amount to be paid on maturity after 5 years is \$100m with an effective interest rate of 10%. The volatility in XYZ's asset value is 20%. Compute (i) the PD of XYZ Ltd based on the Merton Model and (ii) the impact if the volatility suddenly increases to 25% due to a sudden change in business dynamics.

**Answer**

First of all, we need to compute N (d1). We will apply the variables given in the question to the following formula:

$$d_1 = \frac{\ln(V_A/D) + \left(r + \frac{1}{2}\sigma_A^2\right)(T - t)}{\sigma_A\sqrt{T - t}}$$

Current value of the firm = \$100m
Debt of the firm at maturity = \$100m
Interest rate = 10%
Volatility in asset value = 20%
Time till maturity = 5 years

$$\text{d1} = \frac{\text{Ln}(100/100) + [0.10 + (1/2 \times 0.20 * 5)}{020 \times \text{Sqrt } 5}$$

Solving the above equation we will get 1.3418. Based on the cumulative normal value table, N (1.314) = 0.9101.

(i) Let us arrive at the PD as follows:

= 1 − N(d1)
= 1 − (0.9101)
= 9% or 0.09

It means there is a 91% chance that the total assets of XYZ will be above \$100m and thus the debt at maturity could be settled without any default. However, there is a 9% chance that the total assets of XYZ would be below \$100m after 5 years, which would result in default of the debt at maturity.

(ii) If asset value volatility increases to 25%, then the N (d1) will drop to 0.88 and hence the PD will increase to 12%.

Criticisms: Many have pointed out that the model contains many assumptions that will reduce its usefulness. The assumptions that face criticism include the applicability of normal distribution approximation, difficulty in estimating the volatility of the firm, simple assumptions on firms' liabilities such as constancy of the debt, etc.

**Practical Application**: The Merton Model – despite criticisms – has valid insights. In fact the variables used in the model can be linked to accounting variables used in credit risk analysis. The component in the formula $V_A$/ D can be linked to the leverage ratio of a firm. One way of writing the leverage ratio is debt/total assets, which shows the extent of debt usage in the business. $V_A$/ D can be considered the inverse of the debt/total assets ratio. Higher leverage will result in a drop in N(d1) and will result in higher PD.

Similarly, the difference between the market value of assets and book value of debt represents the net worth of the firm. If there is a large loss, then net worth will erode reducing the distance between value of assets and value of debt. This in turn would result in a high leverage ratio. Likewise, the volatility in the value of the assets of the firm is dependent upon its earning capacity or profits or cash generation capacity. If there is sharp increase in volatility in the profitability or cash flows (due to EIIF factors), it denotes higher risk and as we have seen in the above example higher volatility will mean lower N(d1) and hence PD will increase. Thus, it is evident that the model intuitively has links to key variables in the EIIF model; it can be treated as a rule of thumb and provides an approximate cross-check on the PD value arrived at through EIIF or the actuarial method.

Having arrived at the PD based on EIIF analysis, the credit analyst/executive many wish to conduct a sensitivity analysis of the PD by using the Merton Model if reasonable estimates of the value of the firm, debt, interest rates and volatility are available. Nonetheless, we believe the Merton Model cannot replace proper in-depth actuarial and accounting based credit risk analysis.

Whilst the Merton Model generally explains the default, the actual default need not be an inevitable consequence where debt exceeds asset value, if appropriate restructuring of the debt facilities is undertaken. If the bulk of the debt is long term and not payable in the near future, then the default may not happen because of the maturity factor. The firm can work on turnaround strategies and can make the asset/liability equation favourable by the time the debts mature for payment. Sometimes, how one looks at the market value of the assets can be vital. It could be the 'breakup' value of the assets or the 'going concern' value of the assets. Whilst in the former the selling value of each asset is considered, in the latter, the cash flows generated from the use of the assets are taken into account. For instance, the realizable value of the assets of the petrochemical plant is likely to be less than the book value. However, cash generation (or economic benefits) can be the key factor to be considered for assessing the repayment capacity. In such scenarios, the asset value may be considered as a going concern, viz. assessing the value of the business, in terms of its future. In other words, it requires a valuation of the business, which should show a favourable future for the entity. This is one of the reasons why distressed companies become targets for acquisition.

**Other Structural Models**: The Black-Cox model, Credit Metrics, the KMV Model and a few other models are also available which have been developed in the style of the Merton Model. The main difficulty, as in all structural models, lies in the underlying assumptions such as the firm value, which is an unobserved process. It is stated that the KMV Model is more accurate in predicting the default of stock market listed companies. Interested readers may pursue further information on such structural models.

## QUESTIONS/EXERCISES

1. Explain how the output of EIIF study is converted into a credit risk grade and PD.
2. What are the benefits of credit risk grades and PD?
3. Explain how PDs can help in credit decisions.

4. Differentiate external rating vs. internal ratings.
5. Are external ratings reliable? Describe the precautions to take while relying on external ratings.
6. It is often stated that the credit ratings captured by alpha-numeric notations are the shortest editorials that could be ever written. Do you agree? Please elaborate.
7. How does the Merton Model predict PD? Explain its advantages and disadvantages.
8. Mr X, one of your credit colleagues in the bank, says that he is going to rely on the external rating (of an obligor) provided by Moody's and decides to skip any separate independent assessment. He also points out that for the standardized approach under Basel II, external ratings are relied upon. He also clarifies that Moody's has rated the customer over the last ten years and knows the business model and associated credit risks better. Do you agree with this statement? Explain your views.

# Part III

# Credit Risks – Project and Working Capital

Project Finance and Working Capital Finance are among the most common sources of credit risk. Whilst it is obvious that both borrowers and lenders need to understand these risks, they are also relevant for the wider economy because unviable projects and working capital situations have socio-economic costs.

# 11
# Credit Risks in Project Finance

Successful projects by both government and the private sector usually determine the well-being of nations. Take any developed country. The number of projects initiated and completed in a developed country is usually much greater than in an under-developed country. Project has opportunities written all over it. It brings the resources of a country into productive use, creates employment, adds new products and output into the economy and a general pickup in demand ensues, which in economic parlance results in a Multiplier Effect. But a project needs capital to begin with. Project finance is a term used to describe the financing of any large capital investment that involves a longer time horizon with long run benefits. A significant part of project finance is arranged through credit.

Usually projects are funded through a mix of debt and equity because it is nearly impossible for the promoters to raise sufficient equity for large projects. The tax advantage of debt is yet another attractive factor. Also a range of suppliers of project finance exists – from regional banks and suppliers of plant and machinery to international financing institutions who are willing to fund both government and private sector projects which are viable.

## 11.1 DISTINCTIVE FEATURES OF PROJECT FINANCE

Project finance is different from other types of financing. It is this distinction that makes project financing riskier, requiring specialist knowledge. The following are some of the major distinctive features of project finance:

1. **The source of repayment is from future internal cash generation**. Working capital finance/asset finance and similar financing arrangements rely on the liquidation/inflows of the respective assets to repay the credit involved. Hence, it is possible to ensure repayment of the credit facility even in the absence of adequate internal cash generation. Asset based financing relies on the value of the physical asset financed. This is clear from the manner in which vehicle financing schemes are offered by different types of financial intermediaries. But project finance does not emphasize the value of the physical assets financed. For instance, the realizable value of a petrochemical plant is likely to be less than the cost of building it. However, the future cash inflows (or economic benefits) will be greater than the related costs.
2. **Project finance often relates to a new business venture.** It does not have a track record to be extrapolated into the future. Creditors are at a big disadvantage at this point in the absence of a proven track record. Had it been an existing concern the management capability and industry position could have been assessed from the historical data. Even if the project is started by experienced promoters, a new project is an entirely new affair.
3. **Relevance of technical study**. Technical evaluation of the project is a key element. Hence most project finance lenders have their own technical department or outsource the technical evaluation. However, with asset based financing, technical performance is not relevant or

is already a foregone conclusion. No extensive study is necessary as the asset is already in good working condition. For instance, aircraft financing or leasing of assets presupposes proper working of the asset. If the aircraft fails to make money, the fault will be with the strategy/practical situation rather than because of technical difficulties.

## 11.2 TYPES OF PROJECT FINANCE

Project financing is mainly of two types.

**Non-recourse**: In this case, the lender should obtain repayment of the principal and servicing of the debt solely from the project itself – i.e. internal cash generation by the project company and the assets owned by the project company. As is evident, this type of financing is attempted only when the lender has the utmost confidence in the project that is financed. Credit risk analysis must focus on the anticipated cash flows of the project, and is independent of the creditworthiness of the project sponsors. In such cases, if the project fails, the project sponsors have no legal obligation to repay the project debt or meet interest payments.

**Limited recourse**: This type of project finance refers to cases where the lenders retain some form of support or recourse from the promoters of the project. The nature of the recourse will be clearly established at the outset, through documentation. The project lenders ought to ensure that the sponsor's involvement is sufficient to fully incentivize the sponsor to ensure the technical and financial success of the project.

While generally lenders prefer to have the second type of financing, in reality in the case of good projects, the competitors (i.e. other project financiers) in the market will be ready to offer non-recourse project finance.

Irrespective of whether the project finance arrangement is with or without recourse, the main elements in the financing negotiations between the project sponsor/company and the lenders are likely to include the following:

- Debt/equity mix.
- Term of the debt/tranches.
- Repayment schedule.
- Provisions for prepayment.
- Drawdown schedule for both debt and equity.
- Interest rate and fees.
- Conditions precedent.
- Collateral and security.
- Reporting covenants or undertakings by the project sponsor/company.
- Financial (ratio) covenants to be maintained by the project sponsor/company.
- Representations and warranties to be given by the project sponsor/company.
- Events of default.
- Inter-creditor arrangements (where two or more lenders are involved.)
- Decisions – whether based on unanimous or majority voting.

These conditions are initially set out in a term sheet with the lenders and then incorporated into a loan agreement and related security documentation, on finalization.

# 11.3 REASONS FOR PROJECT FINANCE

Project finance is a popular concept and has been widely used to finance several government and private sector projects such as the construction of mines, pipelines, power plants, roads, railways, factories, manufacturing plants and so on. Project finance techniques can also be applied to ship, aircraft and property finance. The following are the main reasons for the popularity of the project finance.

## 11.3.1 Scarce Resources

The project promoters often lack enough capital to back the whole venture. Capital is a scarce commodity in many countries. Project financing brings the project promoters and financiers together, sometimes even cutting across the borders. It enables the entities and parties with enough funds to put them into effective use towards a worthwhile cause.

## 11.3.2 Risk Sharing

The sheer size of projects involves considerable risks, which prompt the promoters to share them with several project lenders. (Incidentally the failure of big projects funded by a single sponsor may bankrupt the sponsor.) Even when the project lender is confident of the success of the project, it is still preferable to invite other financiers to share the risk. The lenders look initially to the cash flow and earnings of the project as the source of repayment and to the assets of the unit as collateral. Some of the project risks can also be transferred to the other parties by seeking guarantee or performance undertakings (e.g. technology supplier). The end result is that the risks are shared among various stakeholders so that all will strive towards the success of the project.

## 11.3.3 Off-Balance Sheet Debt

One of the main reasons for choosing project finance is to isolate the risk of the project, taking it off the project sponsor's balance sheet, through a Special Purpose Vehicle (SPV), which is usually known as a 'project company'. Accordingly, project failure does not impact the promoters'/shareholders'/sponsors' balance sheet, and they would still be able to maintain acceptable existing financial ratios and credit ratings. At the same time the project sponsor has a stake in the project, which acts as a motivating factor to strive for the project's success.

## 11.3.4 Avoidance of Restrictive Covenants

Project finance is more complex and usually pertains to a new venture and hence the project lenders introduce a set of different covenants that do not typically apply to short-term or working capital financing. Also it may be noted that the project financed is separate and distinct from other operations of the sponsor(s), whose existing operations would be subject to a different set of covenants. The project finance structure permits the project sponsors to keep their existing and new (project) operations separate and insulates the existing operations from the restrictive covenants, such as debt coverage ratios and indentures at the project level.

### 11.3.5 Tax Considerations

As we have seen earlier, large scale projects bring in significant socio-economic benefits and governments usually extend attractive tax allowances and tax breaks to such capital investments. Such favourable tax treatments (or subsidies) are likely to improve the profitability of such ventures.

### 11.3.6 Extended Tenor

The project repayment tenor exceeds the normal corporate finance term loan and can be as high as ten years or even more in certain cases. It may be noted that large scale projects such as petrochemical plants, construction of airports, thermal power plants, nuclear power plants, oil refinery projects, etc. involve high investment costs and prefer project finance due to the extended tenor availability. For instance, Eurotunnel was completed with project finance having a tenor of 20 years. Similarly, the North Field Ras Laffan LNG project in Qatar was developed with 12 year tenor project finance.

## 11.4 PARTIES INVOLVED IN PROJECT FINANCE

Project finance transactions are complex and usually require numerous players with interdependent relationships. Major parties involved in project finance are given below.

### 11.4.1 Sponsors

Project sponsors are those who undertake the project and shoulder much of the responsibility to ensure its success. Project management, project scheduling and coordination are in their hands. Generally, they tend to be the main beneficiaries as well. The sponsor can be a government or government entity or an individual or a group of individuals – artificial legal persons or otherwise – coming together for a common purpose.

Usually for all large projects – as we discussed above – a special purpose vehicle (SPV) is created that consists of the consortium shareholders (i.e. investors). The purpose of the SPV is to build and operate the project. The SPV can be structured either as a limited liability project company or a joint venture (JV). The SPV enters into contractual agreements with a number of other parties necessary to the project. These agreements form the framework for project viability and risk allocation. If necessary, the SPV enters into extensive negotiations with government authorities to obtain all requisite licences and permits, e.g. an oil or gas exploration concession, a mining concession or a permit to build and operate a power plant.

### 11.4.2 Project Lenders

Since the projects are massive in size, multiple lenders are a common feature – this brings in the advantage of risk sharing. Usually such project finance is provided through syndication or a consortium of lenders, who come together and share the risk on a *pari passu* basis. Project finance has become a specialist area for most lenders and they have Project Finance departments employing specialists in this field. Such departments usually include finance experts and non-finance experts such as engineers and other professionals.

One of the main lenders will act as the financial advisor and undertake the preparation of Credit Memorandum, which includes project credit analysis. As the **financial advisor** the lead institution usually offers their expertise in apportioning risks and finding out what financing sources and techniques are available in the market. Normally, most of the sponsor companies might have finance departments with a high level of financial sophistication, but they still rely on advisors and consultants who are constantly in touch with the market. Commercial banks, merchant banks, term lending institutions and similar financial institutions act as the lead arranger in putting the project finance together. The **arranger** is the institution that is involved in negotiating terms and documentation and syndicates the facilities among the interested participants. Another role is to act as the **agent**. The agent is the one who is responsible for post sanction duties such as coordinating drawdowns and handling communications with all parties involved in the transaction and often holds the security. Normally the roles of financial advisor, arranger and agent are handled by the same financial institution because of the obvious synergy advantages, although these roles may be allocated to different members of the syndication, especially if one of the syndication members has specialization in any of the areas.

### 11.4.3 Project Contractors/Consultants/Lawyers/Accountants

Usually the projects are not only massive in size but complicated as well and tend to have varied technologies, sometimes new. Independent consultants are approached to clear the technical feasibility. They are also included during the implementation stage and retained for technical assistance even after the projects go on stream. Three of the usual contracts in a project are listed below:

- Engineering, Procurement and Construction (EPC) Contracts – to build and construct the project facility.
- Operation and Management (O&M) Contract – to manage and operate the facility and project during its operational phase.
- Supply contracts – i.e. contracts with suppliers to ensure an uninterrupted supply of materials (including raw materials) necessary for the project.

Lawyers and accountants are the other two indispensable parts of any project. Lawyers advise on the legal formalities to be completed to comply with the rules of the region and draft agreements to give effect to the understandings arrived at by different parties involved in the project. Accountants not only provide tax advice and tax planning techniques but conduct feasibility studies, transaction design and financial modelling, and develop hedging strategies and optimal financing strategies amongst others.

### 11.4.4 Governments

Whilst governments' (whether Federal or State) cooperation and willingness to provide an investment friendly climate are essential for any project, infrastructure projects such as roads, railways, hospitals, airports and similar projects are of direct interest to any government which may take an equity interest in such infrastructure projects.

### 11.4.5 Multilateral Agencies

Agencies across the globe may sometimes participate in the project finance arrangements, especially for mega projects. Many multinational agencies exist to promote investment and economic development on a global basis. They extend finance to big projects in the world provided they satisfy certain socio-economic-political criteria. The principal multinational agencies are:

- Asian Development Bank.
- African Development Bank.
- Commonwealth Development Bank.
- International Bank for Reconstruction and Development.
- International Finance Organization.

## 11.5 PHASES OF PROJECT AND RISKS

Unlike other financing patterns – such as lease financing, mortgage financing, etc. – project financing is more complex and poses a considerable challenge for any lending banker. Just consider for a moment some of the risks associated with a big project – say an oil refinery project – in your country. What will the price of crude oil be in three years' time? Where is it going to be located? Does the location offer convenient transportation? How is the crude oil being transported? Is it by pipelines? What about the terrorism risk? Who are the sponsors of the project? What about their track record? Has there been any track record of political instability in the country? What about labour and civil unrest?

Proper dissection and awareness of the risks involved with each project will enable a lender to understand the project better. It will lead to exploration of risk mitigants and match risks and benefits to arrive at an informed conclusion about the acceptability of the credit risk involved in the project.

Let us discuss three phases of a project and associated risks.

### 11.5.1 Construction Phase Risks

This is a critical period for any project and the stage at which project financiers part with their funds to finance materials, equipment and related costs. Since no cash inflows are generated at this stage no interest payments are possible unless these are made out of the project outlay itself, which is very rare. Engineering, installation and test run are some of the major elements at this stage. The length of the construction phase varies from several months to several years, depending upon the complexity of the case. The lenders are exposed as funds are drawn down but there is no certainty about whether the project will succeed, which is essential for future repayments.

### 11.5.2 Start-Up Phase Risks

Once construction is completed and the necessary technology is acquired, tests are to be carried out to establish whether the machinery and all components are working within the desired parameters such as temperature and pressure and are producing results well within the anticipated range. If not adjustments and technical corrections have to be performed. The start-up phase, which may last several months, will end with one or more trial runs. Several risks are involved at this stage. The test runs may not produce the desired level of output and frequent breakdowns and other technical hinges can delay the commencement of the project. As we will see later under Financial Risks, the delay can be costly as the mounting interest burdens may even lead to a liquidity crisis and search for additional financing.

### 11.5.3 Operational Phase Risks

Having completed the successful trial runs, the project is now on stream. It is beginning to generate revenue in line with the original plan. Now the risk is more related to the business and just like any other financing, the revenue streams are expected to find enough surpluses to settle the dues on time.

Awareness of the above aspects will enable project financiers to understand the level of risks that they accept. Project financing is tricky and often the commercial banks with experience in short-term credit plunge into project finance only to suffer hefty credit losses. The construction phase can be the riskiest part in certain projects such as hydro power. It is not unusual to abandon certain projects at the construction stage due to engineering or topographical reasons. In chemical and other complex metallurgical companies, the start-up phase will be more challenging. For instance, the machinery built in cold areas of the world may encounter constant breakdowns despite functioning in warmer areas. Similarly, in a highly competitive industry, with global capacity perceived to be touching optimum levels, it may be the operational phase where substantial risks lies, unless the project has specific competitive advantages. Ideal project finance should be structured in such a way that all sponsors share the risk.

## 11.6 PROJECT CREDIT RISKS

A project lender looks into the internal cash generation of the project and studies whether the cash flow forecasts justify participating in it. External environment, industry factors within which the entity is supposed to operate and the internal affairs of the new venture all require analysis, which can be effectively done through the (i) EIIF Model along with (ii) project specific credit risks and (iii) project financial viability risks. The chart in Figure 11.1 captures the different levels of project credit risk.

### 11.6.1 EIIF Risks

1. **External Risks**: The factors discussed in Chapter 5 are relevant to understanding the external risks facing a project. Economic conditions, tariff restrictions, taxes, import/export controls, foreign currency restrictions, stability of the government, political unrest, levels of corruption, environmental issues and repatriation concerns related to profits and similar items affecting the transfer of benefits abroad can be broadly grouped under this category. Political and sovereign risks are more valid for projects with international participants. Different political ideologies, sanctions and permissions by different governmental authorities involve risks, which may derail projects. In government guaranteed projects, financiers ought also to assess a government's ability to pay. *Force majeure*, which refers to events outside the control of participants impacting the success of the project, is of two types: (i) Acts of Man such as strikes, riots, wars, embargos, etc. and (ii) Acts of God or Nature such as floods, earthquakes, droughts, tornados, etc.
2. **Industry Risks**: Most of the industry level risks discussed in Chapter 6 are to be applied here. Market risk occurs, for example, when the sales price falls below the assumptions. Can the project attain the forecasted market share? How will the existing players, if any, respond? Long-term off-take agreements, which are considered to be the best antidote for market risk, should be carefully examined along with the nature of the business of the buyer to ensure absence of any conflict of interest. An escalation clause in sales contracts, wherever possible, is an effective tool to cover the input cost risks. Similarly long-term

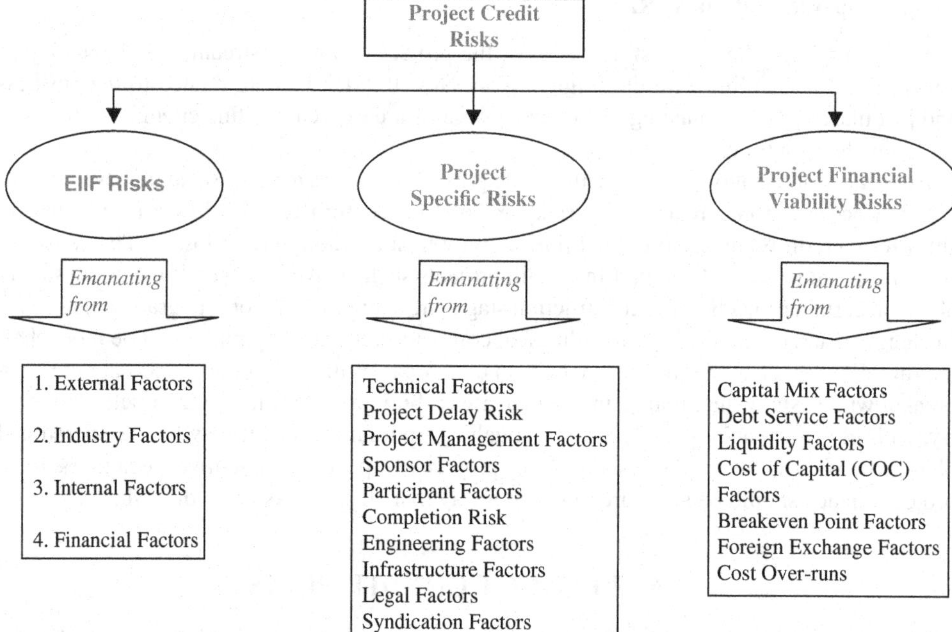


**Figure 11.1** Various Project Credit Risks

contracts with selected suppliers at optimal prices are among the best ways to ensure uninterrupted supply of key inputs. Risks to the selling price and sales volume may be covered by an in-depth market study. Porter's Five Forces Model may also be applied to understand the underlying industry dynamics.

3. **Internal or Entity Risks**: Not all factors which we have discussed in Chapter 7 may be applicable in the case of a greenfield project. Nonetheless, one should attempt to apply the core analytical tools such as SWOT, BCG Matrix, strategy analysis and management analysis to the project at hand.
4. **Financial Risks**: A project cannot be studied without the understanding of the associated financial impact of the various activities planned. A thorough knowledge and strong conceptual understanding of the financial analysis fundamentals discussed in Chapter 8 is vital for the proper study of the financial factors linked to a project. However, given the distinctiveness of a project, which renders it riskier compared to other types of finance, project creditors'/lenders' financial analysis requires a broader treatment. Accordingly, the study of financial projections is required to establish financial feasibility and identify project credit risks, and this is taken up later in this section.

### 11.6.2 Project Specific Risks

The usual unique project related risks (non financial) are described below:

1. **Technical Risks**: The nature of the technology used and the frequency of its updating are to be carefully evaluated and implemented. The financiers should take care to ensure that the technical life of the project is more than the repayment period. It is ideal to have a ratio of 2:1 between the technology life span and the funding life span. This is one of the main reasons why most project financiers maintain their own technical departments

or outsource the technical feasibility study. It is always better to ensure some sort of technology guarantee and insurance. If a novel technology is incorporated into a new project, most financiers will call for a warranty. Project financing is rarely applied to new unproven technology (venture capitalists usually take care of unproven technology ventures, which they believe would work in the market place). Project financiers examine the technical feasibility study, back up reports and assumptions and may also require sponsors or technology providers to guarantee that the technology will be supported for a period mutually agreed upon.

2. **Project Delay Risk**: The risk of delay in project implementation is a serious one, with far reaching consequences. Such delays can result in cost over-runs especially and if debt capital has been drawn down, it implies unproductive expenses creeping into the project. Cost over-run usually has a negative or inverse relationship with the debt repayment capacity. Careful planning, tight project monitoring, use of advanced project management tools, experienced project managers etc. will reduce the risks of project cost/time over-runs.
3. **Project Management Risks**: This is the key element during the project phase and operational phase. Quality of management must be ensured and it is appropriate for the financiers to insist upon a role in selecting key personnel. Financiers should also pay enough attention to medium/junior level management and other employees to ensure that they are in line with the industry standards.
4. **Sponsor Risks**: Wherever two or more sponsors are involved, the relationship and harmony among them, the extent of financial support, and conflicts of interest with their current business are among the some of the key issues to be examined. Financiers ought to consider whether all sponsors have enough of a stake to keep them interested. If project failure will not impact any of the sponsors to any material degree, it poses a significant challenge to the project financier. It is advisable in such cases for financiers to arrange for a buy-out of such sponsors. The sponsors' audited financials and credit ratings, if available, are to be studied.
5. **Participant Risks**: Usually the project involves different participants than just banks and other financiers. Joint venture agreements with foreign companies or local parties and agreements with turnkey contractors and similar key participants must be carefully documented with the help of competent lawyers. The ability of all participants to fulfil their obligations and promises should be ensured.
6. **Completion Risk**: This risk is closely linked to the project time/cost over-run risk. Sufficient attention must be given to identifying any likely disputes or conflicts beforehand. Performance guarantees from contractors are one of the best ways to mitigate this risk. Besides, the agreements ought to have provision for liquidated damages in case of negligence and deliberate sabotage of the project. Sometimes it is possible in the business arena that a project may be spoilt by one of the participants or sponsors to serve vested interests.
7. **Engineering Risks**: This is linked to design and layout and should be viewed differently from completion risk. Factory design goes a long way to reducing unnecessary movements of men and materials, which will bring in cost competitiveness. Guarantees and warranties from equipment suppliers should also be obtained and so should agreements for the supply of spare parts.
8. **Infrastructure Risks**: Lack of adequate infrastructure is a big risk for any new project. Many good projects have been shelved just because of inadequate infrastructure in the region. For instance lack of good port facilities has been highlighted as one of the main

handicaps for foreign business to establish manufacturing bases in India. Road conditions, utility supplies such as water, power and similar basic facilities are to be ensured. Whilst this may also be considered as an external risk, we prefer to treat it as an entity-level risk, assuming the project sponsors can choose a better location.

9. **Legal Risks**: Project related legal risks involve loopholes in agreements and documentation whereby the concerned parties can escape without fulfilling their responsibilities. Whilst a transparent and prudent judicial framework is essential, wherever legal risks are anticipated, a learned legal opinion should be sought.
10. **Syndication Risks**: Among the debt participants, if one pulls out or either the financial advisor or agent mis-conducts the project, the ensuing loss will be borne by all in the syndicate. Hence the credit rating and other factors of the participants in the project should be evaluated to ensure absence of any significant syndication risks.

### 11.6.3 Project Financial Viability Risks

Understanding of the financial risks is critical because as we have seen earlier, a project financier looks primarily at the project inflows rather than the assets for repayments. Hence, a proper awareness of future financial performance and the impact of each of the external/industry/entity risk factors are to be studied in detail under different scenario analysis. Project financial risk is unique because almost all project risks do have a financial angle, which has a bearing on every phase of the project. For instance project delays have financial impact as does the re-modifying of processes due to technical problems. However, there are certain pure financial risks that are built into every project because of the capital structure and cost composition. Several aspects of such project financial risks are given below:

1. **Capital Mix Risks**: An ideal mix of debt and equity differs depending upon the project at hand. Improper capital structure will reduce the flexibility to evolve with the dynamic environment and impact either profitability or solvency or both. All things being equal a project with high operating leverage or in a cyclical industry should opt for low financial leverage. Similarly, high debt content in the capital structure usually implies greater financial risks. A debt to equity ratio of 2:1 is generally considered as the threshold although capital intensive projects with stable demand can have the ratio increased up to 3:1.
2. **Debt Service Risks**: A project is expected to generate enough cash flows to repay both interest costs and the principal component from its normal operations. Unless this risk is at acceptable levels, no project financier will come forward. Usually debt service coverage of 1.5x or 2x is considered as the cut-off limit by project lenders. A host of financial ratios are used to measure the risks involved in its debt service capability, which will be discussed later in the 'Financial Evaluation' section. Sensitivity analysis also goes a long way in grasping the extent of this risk.
3. **Liquidity Risks**: Many a project faces tough times during the initial years after commencement of operations despite stable market conditions and optimum factory production. This is because of liquidity problems, which ultimately lead to rescheduling and associated issues. A liquidity crisis can occur due to several factors such as inadequate working capital envisaged at the time of planning of the project, using short-term sources to fund long-term requirements, project cost/time over-runs and initial losses. While projected liquidity ratios provide an indication of the 'would-be' liquidity situation, key liquidity factors should be identified and subjected to rigorous sensitivity analysis. Project financing experience helps to discern the probable liquidity crisis that lies ahead to prepare contingency plans.

4. **Cost of Capital (COC) Risks**: A project is feasible only if the ROI exceeds the COC. Given the dynamic nature of the financial system/economic environment, the underlying financing costs of equity and debt change over time. If COC increases and overtakes anticipated ROI during the implementation stage, deadlock can be anticipated. The risk can be mitigated by ensuring a sufficient margin of safety between ROI and COC and covering interest rate risks through derivatives.
5. **Breakeven Point (BEP) Risks**: In projects with high BEP, substantial capacity utilization is required to ensure viability. Given the fact that capacity utilization is linked to market factors, high BEP is a risk in itself unless mitigant factors exist. For instance, large capital intensive projects such as refineries and petrochemical complexes operate successfully despite having relatively high BEP. However, it is always better to optimize fixed costs so that the BEP can be held as low as possible taking into account demand conditions.
6. **Foreign Exchange Risks**: We have already seen foreign exchange controls by governments constitute political risk. Another risk is the fluctuations in Forex rates if substantial capital equipment or inputs are imported or output is exported. Forex derivatives can offer risk cover to a great extent.
7. **Cost Over-runs**: An increase in project expenditure without corresponding increase in the production level will impact the project. How project cost over-runs are financed is critical. It is always better to finance them by equity rather than debt, as the fixed commitments will increase and would have to be met from the originally forecasted output level. One technique for project sponsors to hide the real cost run is to present a revised project plan enhancing the output level and seeking additional financing for the enhanced level.

A proper financial evaluation of the project will bring out its financial viability, which is discussed in the next main topic.

## 11.7 FINANCIAL STUDY

A critical analysis of cash flows, debt service ability and their sensitivity to movements in variables such as the price of raw materials, utility costs and finished products is critical to any project. This is accomplished through a financial study of the project. A financial appraisal of any project finance has three main stages – cash flow forecasts, estimation of the economic worth of the project and assessing the creditworthiness of the project. These topics are discussed below.

### 11.7.1 Cash Flow Forecasts

In the financial analysis of projects, cash flow forecasts play an important role. Given their critical nature, the utmost care must be taken while forecasting project cash flows under different scenarios. Accounting profit, although important, does not pay dividends and meet repayment obligations, but cash does, hence its importance. Moreover, accounting profits are influenced by accounting policy decisions while cash flows are relatively independent of the accounting policies chosen. Some of the important points while forecasting cash flows are listed below:

1. **Ignore sunk costs**. Decisions should be made based on future cash flows; the expenses already incurred or investments already made are to be ignored.
2. **Include all incidental items**. A project may be influenced from many angles and the cost or benefit from all sources should be considered. For instance, while installing Automatic

Teller Machines (ATMs), the bank does not get any direct cash inflows, but ATMs will help to attract more customers who will open new accounts with the bank.

3. **Do not forget working capital requirements**. Increases and decreases in the working capital components affect the cash flows and must be included.
4. **Include opportunity costs**. Whilst the project may be utilizing a vacant land and factory building for the new factory, the project should be charged with the opportunity costs, e.g. if the land and building had been leased out to others.
5. **Ignore allocated overheads** (to the project) while any additional overheads due to the project are to be factored in. For instance, if a part of the Managing Director's salary is allocated to the new project, it need not be charged to the project, but the new project manager's salary should be.
6. **Long-term contribution (i.e. from long-term sources) to working capital** should be factored in. A portion of the working capital should always be from long-term sources. Assumption of relying entirely on suppliers and short-term bank finance has put many a viable project in trouble.
7. **Routine CAPEX** should be factored into the cash outflows of future projections. This will reduce the cash available for debt repayment and provide a more realistic or conservative picture of the cash available.
8. **Cost of capital ought to be weighted and should be post tax**. Similarly, the calculations of relevant cash flows available for project financiers should also be post tax.
9. **Project cash flows** should be prepared for analytical purposes with varying methods just as in the case of ROA, ROCE and ROE in financial analysis. Just as ROA, ROCE and ROE measure returns from the total assets, capital employed (total assets – current liabilities) and equity standpoint, project cash flows can be prepared from a total funds (or assets), long-term funds and equity point of view. Relevant cash outflows for appraisal purposes are given below:

**Table 11.1** Cash Flows from the Point of View of Different Project Financiers

| Details | Project Outflows | Project Inflows |
|---|---|---|
| **(a) Total Funds (Equity + Debt)** | Fixed Assets<br>Current Assets<br>Contingencies and Others | Net Profit (after Tax)<br>Add: Depreciation and Amortization<br>Add: Interest (Long Term and Short Term)<br>Add/Less: Working Capital Flows* |
| **(b) Long Term Funds (Equity + Long Term Debt)** | Fixed Assets<br>Net Current Assets<br>Contingencies and Others | Net Profit (after Tax)<br>Add: Depreciation and Amortization<br>Add: Interest (Long Term)<br>Add/Less: Working Capital Flows* |
| **(c) Equity** | Fixed Assets**<br>Net Current Assets**<br>Contingencies and Others** | Net Profit (after Tax)<br>Add: Depreciation and Amortization<br>Add/Less: Working Capital Flows* |

* It is a prudent measure to net off working capital movements, since it usually consumes a lot of cash. If routine CAPEX is significant, it is advisable to study the project financial viability based on FCF (CFO – W/C Changes – routine CAPEX) as well.

** To the extent funded by equity.

### 11.7.2 Estimation of the Economic Worth of the Project

The economic worth of a project can be assessed by comparing the project outflows with the project inflows. Payback period, accounting rate of return, net present value and internal rate of return are the major techniques used to study the relation between the cash inflows and outflows of a project and appraise its economic worth. A simple example is used to enumerate the concepts related to the economic worth of a project, as it will explain the financial appraisal techniques.

**Example 11.1**

Suppose a project, which costs \$40m to build, will generate \$8m cash flows for seven years and thereafter at the terminal year, the cash generation, including the liquidation of all assets, would be \$12m. The cash flow estimates are given below:

| Year | 20X0 | 20X1 | 20X2 | 20X3 | 20X4 | 20X5 | 20X6 | 20X7 | 20X8 |
|---|---|---|---|---|---|---|---|---|---|
| Cash Flow | –40 | 8 | 8 | 8 | 8 | 8 | 8 | 8 | 12 |

1. **Non-discounting Methods**: Two methods of evaluation for estimating the worth of a project that do not take into consideration the time value of money are the Payback Period and Accounting Rate of Return.
   - **Payback Period**: This is the time required to recoup the original investment. In our example, the payback period is 5 years. The original investment of 40m will be recovered in 5 years (5*8m).
   - **Accounting Rate of Return (ARR)**: This is the average rate of return during the project life. It is calculated as follows:

     = Average Annual Cash Inflows*100/ (Total Cash Outflow)

     The ARR in our example is 21.25% viz. $\{[(7 \times 8) + 12]/8\}/40$

     Both these methods have a serious drawback as they ignore the time value of money. ARR would not be affected even if all the cash inflows were postponed until the final year. The Payback Method ignores all the cash flows generated after the payback date. In fact Payback Period is popular because it shows how long it takes to recover the original investment, on an undiscounted basis. For instance where high obsolescence risks and political risks are involved, the Payback Method is a powerful tool influencing decisions. Some textbooks also advocate the use of calculation of payback period based on discounted cash flows as well.
2. **Discounting Methods**: These take into account the time value of the money invested. This is a must for three reasons. (i) All investment has an opportunity cost. (ii) Risk increases in the future. Normally, the longer the project, the greater is the uncertainty, which translates into risk premium. (iii) Inflation reduces the value of future cash inflows. Time value of money is calculated through compounding and discounting methods.

- **Net Present Value Method**: Net present value is the difference between the present value of future cash inflows less the present value of the cash outflows. It is calculated as follows:

$$= \sum_{t-0}^{n} \frac{CFn}{(1+r)^n} - I$$

where

$CFn$ = Cash Flows at the end of the year 'n'
$r$ = Discount Rate
$n$ = Period/Year
I = Original Investment

By using a discount rate of 10%, the NPV for the project is $4.5m. This shows that the present value of the future cash inflows is $4.5m. Paying $40m for a project that is worth $44.5m shows that the project makes sense.

- **Internal Rate of Return (IRR) Method**: Theoretically the IRR is the rate which takes a project NPV to zero. IRR is more popular because it is easy to understand. It is calculated as given below:

$$0 = \sum_{t-0}^{n} \frac{CFn}{(1+r)^n}$$

With a pre-programmed calculator or computer, it is easy to calculate IRR. Manually, it can be approximated (through trial and error) by establishing two rates – one that provides a positive NPV and the other, a negative NPV. Trying 12% and 13%, in our example, will provide NPVs of 1.357 and –0.105 respectively. By interpolating, we get an IRR of 12.93%. If the WACC (Weighted Average Cost of Capital) is below the IRR, then the project will result in value creation to sponsors. Hence WACC is also known as the 'hurdle rate'. In fact, the project sponsors would prefer to have a fairly large margin of safety between WACC and IRR, depending upon the perceived project risk level.

### 11.7.3 Assessing Creditworthiness – Building a Lender's Case

Usually, the project promoters approach project lenders only if the financial appraisals of the project are satisfactory. Hence, the role of project lenders is more credit risk analysis rather than the preparation of financial appraisal. But for sound credit risk analysis, a thorough knowledge of the project financial analysis is indispensable to understand the various pros and cons of the project. The usual steps followed by a project lender while assessing the project follow the pattern given below:

1. **Project Financial Modelling**: At this stage most project financiers would like to re-work the base case scenario presented by the promoters. Nowadays, it is quite easy because most financial institutions and lenders have software, facilitating projections.
2. **Derive Lender's Base Case**: The lender ought to challenge each assumption put forward by the promoters and derive its own base case. Given the long-term nature of the project,

it is extremely difficult to time and determine the quantum of cash inflows and outflows, particularly at the later stages of the project. However, all attempts should be made to take all relevant cash flows into consideration. It needs experience, sound knowledge of the customer's business and should adhere to the guidelines specified about calculation of the project cash flows mentioned earlier.

3. **Establish Debt Amount and Repayment Profile under Base Case**: Having drawn up their own base case, the project lender may find it necessary to modify the debt amount and repayment term. This is usually a period of intense negotiation among the project sponsors. As the project lender demands additional capital or subordinated loans from the promoters, the base case scenario undergoes changes. Finally, the project lender will determine the debt amount. Relevant terms, covenants and conditions will follow to cover the risks to the extent possible.
4. **Assessing Economic Worth and Debt Service Capabilities**: Various ratios are applied to the projected base case to estimate the comfort zone available. We have just discussed the major tools facilitating the estimation of economic worth. Now let us see the major ratios, which enable the estimation of debt service capabilities. They are (i) Debt Service Coverage Ratio (DSCR), (ii) Loan Life Cover Ratio (LLCR) and (iii) Project Life Cover Ratio (PLCR), which are described below (see also Illustration, later):
   - **DSCR**: This ratio brings out the ability of the project to meet the repayment obligations such as instalments, interest on term loan and other fixed obligations from the anticipated project inflows. DSCR can be either P&L based or cash based. The following are the formulas:

     P&L based DSCR = EBITDA/Repayment Obligations

     Cash based DSCR = Net Cash from Operations/Repayment Obligations

     Sometimes, for cash based DSCR – Free Cash Flows from Operations (NCFO – CAPEX) is also used. The higher the ratio, the better.
   - **LLCR**: This ratio factors the worth of the project into the repayment ability. It is computed as below:

     = PV of NCFO during the loan term/outstanding loan at the end of each year.

     It covers the extent to which the value of the project (during the term of credit) covers the loan amount. The ratio, if computed at the end of each year against the revised cash flows, based on actual performance, is a power tool to measure future repayment ability.
   - **PLCR**: This is again based on the same concept as that of LLCR, but instead of the credit term, the entire life of the project is factored into the numerator, as given below:

     = PV of NCFO during entire project life/outstanding loan at the end of each year.

     Lenders are interested to see whether the project has capacity to make repayments after the original final maturity of the debt, just in case there are difficulties in repaying all of the debt as per the original schedule. Thus PLCR factors into the entire life of the project and hence gives comfort to the lender that even if the immediate years may not be bright, the following years ought to be better, facilitating repayments, despite the risk of rescheduling in the near future.

5. **Sensitivity and Scenario Analysis**: The project cash flows are prepared to reflect the future financial positions of often complicated and uncertain projects. The project lenders should analyze how changes in various key assumptions and risk factors will affect the borrowers' future financial position. All financial appraisal ratios and cover ratios should be subjected to sensitivity analysis. All project lenders will prepare a 'worst case scenario' which shows what would happen to the project's ability to repay the loan on the basis of extremely pessimistic assumptions. A list of scenarios to be subjected to stress testing (or sensitivity analysis) is given below:
   1. Price and supply variations of major inputs (related to supplier/market risk).
   2. Price and demand variations and outputs (related to buyer/market risk).
   3. Productivity (related to technology/engineering risk).
   4. Fixed costs – operating leverage[1] (related to technology/cost risk).
   5. Debt and equity related issues – financial leverage (related to funding risk).
   6. Interest rate changes (related to funding risk).
   7. Project delay (related to management risk).
   8. FX fluctuations, etc. (related to FX risk).

   The important step in identifying which situations are to be stress tested lies in understanding the risks involved with the project. The stress tests must look at the financial impact of the various risk aspects of the project not working out as originally expected. Lenders also usually run a 'combined downside case' to check the effects of several adverse events happening at once (e.g., 6 months' delay in completion and a 20% drop in sale prices).
6. **Derive Financial Covenant Structure for Documentation**: The project agreement documents, especially in the case of syndications, run to hundreds of pages whereby the duties, obligations, liabilities and responsibilities of each project sponsor and participant are clearly stated. Various financial and non-financial covenants are to be incorporated in the loan agreements (we will discuss the various financial covenants later in the book). This is also a risk mitigation step so that none of the parties involved may raise disputes on any point. It is not uncommon for project participants to run for cover, when things go wrong, leaving others to shoulder the losses.

## 11.8 PROJECT CREDIT RISK MITIGANTS

Whilst the project credit risk mitigants differ depending upon the project in hand, in an ideal (utopian) situation all risks arising from the project study should be covered. All insurable risks should be identified and insured against with assignment to the project financiers. Marketing risk should be covered by off-take agreements with escalation clauses. Financial covenants related to cover ratios and other financial ratios should be established. Negative pledges should be obtained. If the project is too risky, strong guarantees from sponsors and/or collateral have to be obtained. Sufficient sponsor contributions must be ensured to establish their continued interest in the project. Detailed loan agreements are entered into between the sponsor and project financiers, detailing mutual obligations and duties with conditions precedent and conditions subsequent. In reality, a few risks will remain open, which the project financiers

[1] Discussed in Chapter 8.

ought to shoulder. A proper project credit analysis will facilitate an informed decision as to whether to accept those open risks. Normal project mitigants are:

1. **Technical Warranties/Guarantees**: The project sponsors usually cover the technology risk by taking warranties from the turnkey contractors/technology and machinery supplier warranties, sometimes even supported by performance guarantees from their bankers. If engineering risks are critical it may be worth trying to make the technology supplier a JV partner.
2. **Performance Guarantees**: Having performance guarantees from contractors can mitigate completion risk to a great extent. All such agreements ought to have provision for liquidated damages. Project financiers may also stipulate a condition that the project be completed by a stipulated date, failing which the project loans would become immediately repayable or attract higher interest rates (to reflect the higher risk due to project delays).
3. **Fixed Price Lump Sum Contract**: This type of contract reduces the likelihood of cost over-runs and protects the project sponsor from inflation as well. This will also incentivize the contractors to fulfil their responsibilities under the project on time.
4. **Sales Warranties**: Some of the promoters may agree to take up and sell a percentage of the output, if the sales as per the projections are not met. This is the case where Multi-National Companies (MNC) with global reach are involved as one of the project sponsors. They agree to market the product using their global distribution channels in the early years of the operational phase of the project and provide associated sales warranties. Another type of sales volume guarantee is when one of the promoters of the project agrees to purchase an agreed volume of the output that has not been sold or pay to the subject project company an amount equal to the value the project company would have received has these volumes been sold. Whilst such sales warranties mitigate the volume risk, generally they do not cover the price risk.
5. **Off-Take Agreements**: These are different from sales warranties. Whilst the sales warranty acts like an 'insurance' because the warranty provided will uplift the unsold quantities, off-take agreements are long-term contracts (firm commitment) with third parties which mitigate the sales/volume risk. The project lenders should study the counterparty risk involved and off-take agreements must be obtained and studied carefully to understand the various clauses.
6. **Cost Over-run Mitigation Measures**: Cost over-runs can be mitigated by selecting strong and experienced project partners (e.g. project turnkey contractors/technology suppliers) and entering into contractual undertakings with them. Additional commitments from equity participants as a contingency measure may be agreed upon. Similarly, standby funding agreements for additional financing or subordinated debt arrangements may also be entered into. The project sponsor may also create an escrow fund to provide liquidity in the case of cost over-runs.
7. **Insurance**: Risks related to asset quality (fixed assets, stock), protection of the profits if any (loss of profits policy), loss of the key personnel (key-man insurance), third party liabilities and similar instances are to be covered by insurance cover. Insurance is an integral part of the overall security package for project finance. Assignment of the insurance proceeds must be sought in favour of the project lenders.
8. **Hedging**: Wherever Forex transactions or interest rates are involved the respective exposures may be hedged (via options/futures/swaps/forwards).

9. **Government**: In the case of multi-billion projects of national interest it is not uncommon for governments to extend guarantees. National export agencies (usually in connection with the export of goods and/or services) sometimes extend payment guarantees, which involve a government element in addition to the commercial element.
10. **Release of Debt Finance on a Pro Rata Basis**: The project finance proceeds should be disbursed only after the full deployment of the owners' funds or on a pro rata basis.
11. **Debt Service Reserve Account**: In this case the borrower is asked to maintain a separate account to ensure that there is always a credit balance equal to at least the aggregate debt service obligations falling due in the following period.
12. **Seek Recourse**: Although most of the projects are drawn up without recourse, project lenders ought to try to have recourse to the promoters, wherever possible.
13. **First Charge on Total Assets** of the project ought to be assigned to the project lenders with a negative pledge condition.
14. **Cross Collateralization and Cross Default Clauses** to be included so that none of the creditors enjoy any undue advantage. This will ensure that the collaterals enjoyed by one of the participants are available to all while default with one will be deemed as the default of the whole.
15. **Financial Covenants** such as (a) maximum gearing and debt/equity ratios, (b) minimum shareholder equity, current/quick ratios, DSCRs, LLCRs, (c) provision of monthly/quarterly/semi-annual/annual progress reports/financial statements, (d) dividend restrictions, etc. are some examples.

The above list is not exhaustive and the project mitigants are to be understood and negotiated on a case-by-case basis.

## CASE STUDY

You have recently taken charge as the Country Head of Credit of a finance institution, and you are asked to give your views on the risks of a project finance proposal. The salient features of the proposal are given below:

### Country/Economy Details

The country is politically stable, the economy is on a growth path and the growth is likely to continue into the future. Salient features of the country and its economy are given below:

- The economy is heavily dependent on the oil sector, the driving force shaping the overall GDP of economy. In real terms, gross domestic (GDP) expanded on average by an estimated 5% annually in recent years.
- International rating agencies have provided a sovereign rating of BBB with a stable long-term outlook. The country's economy has performed well in recent years due to relatively high world oil/gas prices and robust growth in non-hydrocarbon sectors.
- Growth has outpaced population growth, thereby raising per capita incomes. Oil and gas account for around 40% of GDP, 68% of merchandise export receipts and over 60% of budget revenue.
- The manufacturing sector is also showing an upward trend (growth rate around 5.5%), but fluctuating depending upon oil prices. The country has two main steel producers –

King Steel Ltd (KSL) and Queen Steel Ltd (QSL) – who cater mostly to local demand and export to neighbouring countries.

- Economic forecasts, given below, show reasonable GDP growth for the next few years, but the main risk lies in low oil prices.

| Economic Forecast Summary | 20X1 | 20X2 | 20X3–20X9 |
|---|---|---|---|
| Real GDP (% change) | 4.8% | 4.9% | 5.1% |
| Consumer prices (% change) | 1.5% | 1.7% | 1.8% |
| **Current Account (EUR, Billion)** | | | |
| Goods: Export FOB | 55.45 | 58.41 | 56.34 |
| Goods: Imports FOB | −40.08 | −42.66 | −42.86 |
| Trade Balance | 15.37 | 15.75 | 13.48 |
| **External Debt (EUR, Billion)** | | | |
| Total Debt | 19.55 | 21.66 | 22.55 |
| Total Debt Service | 2.54 | 2.63 | 2.11 |

Overall, the country's total external debt will remain satisfactory despite the growth forecast as the government borrows to finance large industrial and infrastructure projects.

**Project Details**

22 leading business groups have floated a new company Seldom Alloys Co. Ltd (SACL) to set up a plant in the country to manufacture Silicon Manganese (SiMn) and Silicon Metal (SiMe) as an import substitution. The technology is such that the capacities are interchangeable, with the only change required in raw material inputs into the furnace. More products, e.g. Ferro Silicon (FeSi), can be added in the future, if needed. The main domestic users are expected to off-take a total annual requirement of 70,000 MT, which will absorb about 56% of the planned capacity of 125,000 MT. The balance is expected to be exported, primarily to neighbouring countries.

Project cost and means of finance are given below:

| Project Cost | | Means | Euro in Thousands |
|---|---|---|---|
| Building | 5,000 | Equity | 22,875 |
| Furnace and Machinery | 65,000 | LTL | 68,625 |
| Other Tangible Assets | 7,500 | | |
| Working Cap Margin | 9,000 | | |
| Pre-Op Exp | 5,000 | | |
| | **91,500** | | **91,500** |

**Shareholding Pattern**: The largest shareholder, among the 22 shareholders (comprising leading business groups) is Petro Holding Co. Ltd (PHCL), the leading petrochemical manufacturer in the region, with a 14% stake, the smallest stake being 2%. It is explained that many business groups in the country had shown interest in participating, hence the wide spread of the ownership. No public issue is planned now. Articles of Association state that all critical decisions must have unanimous consensus by all shareholders.

**Technical Study**: A technical feasibility study has been conducted and it has been decided to outsource the setting up of the plant to an HP, Menanessan, who has a successful track record in constructing similar plants. A technical guarantee for two years after commencement of operations is mutually agreed upon.

**Market Study**: A market study has been conducted, which highlighted the fact that there is scope for import substitution. The largest shareholder, PHCL, has a marketing company (Effiless Marketing Ltd – EML), which has offered to take up the marketing of finished goods for a 3% commission on sales. Shareholders have found that the selling and marketing costs of international competitors exceeded 3% on turnover and decided unanimously to hand over the marketing to EML, which markets a wide range of products of the PHCL group of companies, mainly petrochemicals.

**Management**: The General Manager and Finance Manager (FM) have been identified while the Production Manager is yet to be identified. The Sales Manager position does not exist as the entire production is covered by Marketing Agreement with EML. Whilst the GM is an eminent professor with a PhD in Alloys, FM is professionally qualified and has around twenty-five years' experience in manufacturing companies.

**Key Inputs**: Manganese ore accounts for about 30% of the total input while electricity accounts for 35% of total production costs. Other key inputs are electrodes, etc. No packaging is required as the finished goods will be transported in bulk. Whilst manganese will be sourced from Africa (Ghana), the electricity (power) in the country is relatively cheaper, which is one of the attractive factors that encouraged the promoters. Currently power cost is equivalent to EUR 0.05 per unit.

**Competition**: In the domestic market, the new entity will enjoy a monopoly being the first in the country. Initial talks with KSL and QSL are highly encouraging. They are eager to source from domestic producers. Internationally the competitors are SAMANCOR – South Africa, ELKEM – Norway/US, BHP – Australia, COMARGO CORREA – Brazil, FERRALLOYS –South Africa, NIKOPOL – Ukraine, PECHINEY – France, GLOBE METAL – US, XINYU – China, etc. Beyond this, most of the other competitors are highly fragmented. All these companies have the capability to switch from one product to another relatively easily. Some of the international competitors have their own manganese mines and enjoy concessionary power tariffs (e.g. ELKEM).

**Financial Summary**

The key analytical financial highlights are given below:

| | |
|---|---|
| Weighted Av. Cost of Capital (WACC) | 5.9% |
| Net Present Value | EUR 60.8m |
| Internal Rate of Return (IRR) | 23.3% |
| Payback | 4 Years and 2.5 months |
| Payback (discounted) | 5 Years and 3 months |

| | Year 0 | Year 1 | Year 2 | Year 3 | Year 4 | Year 5 | Year 6 | Year 7 |
|---|---|---|---|---|---|---|---|---|
| Overall Breakeven | | 45% | 33% | 30% | 27% | 25% | 23% | 22% |
| Cash Breakeven | | 31% | 23% | 20% | 18% | 16% | 15% | 14% |
| Calculation of DSCR (based on EBITDA) | | 1.60 | 1.86 | 1.95 | 2.04 | 2.12 | 2.14 | 2.18 |
| Calculation of 'Cash based DSCR' (based on NCFO) | | 2.00 | 2.80 | 3.22 | 3.68 | 4.19 | 4.48 | 4.84 |
| Calculation of Loan Life Coverage Ratio (LLCR) | | (0.35) | 2.10 | 2.92 | 3.35 | 3.83 | 4.37 | 4.72 |

The relationship team is very upbeat about the project. They argue that it is a 'once in a lifetime opportunity' for 22 leading business groups in the country to join hands together to start a large scale new venture. They also argue that the project has all the hallmarks of success. It has import substitution products, first in the region, about 56% captive local demand, strong promoters, projected profitability from the first year, etc. These are some of the major factors highlighted by the team. The team leader is so enthusiastic that he recommends that all project finance should be underwritten and that they should also obtain a letter of 'right of first refusal' for any additional short-term/ long-term financing in future by Seldom Alloys. The team leader is of the opinion that the shareholder guarantees may be difficult to obtain, which may result in loss of opportunity to competitor financial institutions.

As the Country Head of Credit Risk, you have to forward the proposal to the Board. Critically examine and bring out the major project credit risks. The detailed workings are given below:

| 1 | PROJECT COST AND MEANS | | | |
|---|---|---|---|---|
| | Building | 5,000 | Equity | 22,875 |
| | Plant and Machinery | 65,000 | Project Loan | 68,625 |
| | Other Fixed Assets | 7,500 | | |
| | Working Cap Margin | 9,000 | | |
| | Pre-operating expenses | 5,000 | | |
| | | 91,500 | | 91,500 |

**2 OPERATIONAL INFO**

| Capacity of SiMn* | 75,000 | MT | Year 0 | Year 1 | Year 2 | Year 3 | Year 4 | Year 5 | Year 6 | Year 7 |
|---|---|---|---|---|---|---|---|---|---|---|
| Capacity of SiMe# | 50,000 | MT | | | | | | | | |
| Capacity Utilization | | | 0% | 60% | 75% | 80% | 85% | 90% | 90% | 90% |
| Output – SiMn | | | 0 | 45,000 | 56,250 | 60,000 | 63,750 | 67,500 | 67,500 | 67,500 |
| Output – SiMe | | | 0 | 30,000 | 37,500 | 40,000 | 42,500 | 45,000 | 45,000 | 45,000 |

*SiMn = Silicon Manganese; #SiMe = Silicon Metal.

**3 PROFIT AND LOSS STATEMENTS**

| | Year 0 | Year 1 | Year 2 | Year 3 | Year 4 | Year 5 | Year 6 | Year 7 |
|---|---|---|---|---|---|---|---|---|
| Sales | 0 | 125,460 | 159,962 | 174,038 | 188,614 | 203,703 | 207,777 | 211,933 |
| Cash Operating Expenses | 0 | 86,343 | 107,499 | 116,255 | 125,319 | 134,698 | 137,392 | 140,140 |
| Cash Operating Margin | 0 | 39,117 | 52,462 | 57,783 | 63,295 | 69,005 | 70,385 | 71,793 |
| - Depreciation | 0 | 5,383 | 5,458 | 5,552 | 5,669 | 5,816 | 5,999 | 6,228 |
| - Amortization | 0 | 1,000 | 1,000 | 1,000 | 1,000 | 1,000 | 0 | 0 |
| Operating Profit (PBIT) | | 32,734 | 46,004 | 51,231 | 56,626 | 62,189 | 64,386 | 65,565 |
| - Interest | 0 | 4,877 | 3,622 | 2,868 | 2,230 | 1,593 | 956 | 319 |
| Profit Before Tax | 0 | 27,857 | 42,382 | 48,363 | 54,396 | 60,596 | 63,430 | 65,246 |
| (Tax Rate) | *35%* | *0* | *0* | *0* | *0* | *0* | *0* | *0* |
| - Income Tax | 0 | 9,750 | 14,834 | 16,927 | 19,038 | 21,209 | 22,201 | 22,836 |
| NET PROFIT | 0 | 18,107 | 27,548 | 31,436 | 35,357 | 39,388 | 41,230 | 42,410 |
| RECONCILIATION OF THE NET PROFIT | | | | | | | | |
| Retained Profit Brought Forward | | 0 | 18,107 | 41,080 | 65,654 | 89,574 | 117,524 | 147,316 |
| Net Profit for the year | | 18,107 | 27,548 | 31,436 | 35,357 | 39,388 | 41,230 | 42,410 |
| Less: Dividends | | 0 | 4,575 | 6,863 | 11,438 | 11,438 | 11,438 | 11,438 |
| Add/Less: Other Adjustments | | 0 | 0 | 0 | 0 | 0 | 0 | 0 |
| Retained Profit Carried Forward | | 18,107 | 41,080 | 65,654 | 89,574 | 117,524 | 147,316 | 178,289 |

4 PROJECT CASH FLOWS (Indirect Method)

| OPERATING CASHFLOW | Year 0 | Year 1 | Year 2 | Year 3 | Year 4 | Year 5 | Year 6 | Year 7 |
|---|---|---|---|---|---|---|---|---|
| Operating Profit | 0 | 32,734 | 46,004 | 51,231 | 56,626 | 62,189 | 64,386 | 65,565 |
| Depreciation/ Non-Cash Items | 0 | 6,383 | 6,458 | 6,552 | 6,669 | 6,816 | 5,999 | 6,228 |
| Adjusted (Gross)Cash Flow From Operations | 0 | 39,117 | 52,462 | 57,783 | 63,295 | 69,005 | 70,385 | 71,793 |
| WC MOVEMENT | | | | | | | | |
| (Inc)/Dec in Stock | 0 | −21,290 | −5,217 | −2,159 | −2,235 | −2,313 | −664 | −678 |
| (Inc)/Dec in Debtors | 0 | −30,935 | −8,507 | −3,471 | −3,594 | −3,721 | −1,005 | −1,025 |
| Inc/(Dec) in Creditors | 0 | 17,742 | 4,347 | 1,799 | 1,862 | 1,927 | 554 | 565 |
| Net Cashflow from Operations | 0 | 4,633 | 43,086 | 53,952 | 59,329 | 64,899 | 69,270 | 70,655 |
| Less: Taxation Paid | 0 | −9,750 | −14,834 | −16,927 | −19,038 | −21,209 | −22,201 | −22,836 |
| Less: Interest Paid | 0 | −4,877 | −3,622 | −2,868 | −2,230 | −1,593 | −956 | −319 |
| Net Free Cashflow from Operations | 0 | −9,993 | 24,630 | 34,157 | 38,060 | 42,097 | 46,113 | 47,500 |
| Less: Dividends Paid | 0 | 0 | −4,575 | −6,863 | −11,438 | −11,438 | −11,438 | −11,438 |
| Net Cashflow before Inv. and Fin. Act. | 0 | −9,993 | 20,055 | 27,295 | 26,622 | 30,660 | 34,676 | 36,063 |
| CASHFLOW FROM INV. ACT. | | | | | | | | |
| Net Cashflow from Fixed Asset | −77,500 | −500 | −750 | −938 | −1,172 | −1,465 | −1,831 | −2,289 |
| Other | −5,000 | 0 | 0 | 0 | 0 | 0 | 0 | 0 |
| Net Cashflow before Equity and Fin. Act. | −82,500 | −10,493 | 19,305 | 26,357 | 25,451 | 29,195 | 32,845 | 33,774 |
| CASHFLOW FROM EQ. AND FIN. ACT. | | | | | | | | |
| Inc/(Dec) in Equity | 22,875 | 0 | 0 | 0 | 0 | 0 | 0 | 0 |
| Inc/(Dec) in L-T Debt | 68,625 | −9,804 | −9,804 | −9,804 | −9,804 | −9,804 | −9,804 | −9,804 |

| | | | | | | | | | |
|---|---|---|---|---|---|---|---|---|---|
| | Net Cashflow from Eq. and Fin. Act. | 91,500 | | | | | | | |
| | Total | 91,500 | −9,804 | −9,804 | −9,804 | −9,804 | −9,804 | −9,804 | −9,804 |
| | Net Change in Cash | 9,000 | −20,297 | 9,501 | 16,554 | 15,647 | 19,391 | 23,041 | 23,970 |
| | Add Opening Cash | 0 | 9,000 | −11,297 | −1,795 | 14,758 | 30,405 | 49,797 | 72,838 |
| | Closing Cash | 9,000 | −11,297 | −1,795 | 14,758 | 30,405 | 49,797 | 72,838 | 96,809 |
| 5 | BALANCE SHEET | | | | | | | | |
| | | Year 0 | Year 1 | Year 2 | Year 3 | Year 4 | Year 5 | Year 6 | Year 7 |
| | **ASSETS** | | | | | | | | |
| | Cash and Bank | 9,000 | 0 | 0 | 14,758 | 30,405 | 49,797 | 72,838 | 96,809 |
| | Receivables | 0 | 30,935 | 39,443 | 42,914 | 46,508 | 50,228 | 51,233 | 52,257 |
| | Stocks | 0 | 21,290 | 26,507 | 28,666 | 30,900 | 33,213 | 33,877 | 34,555 |
| | Fixed Assets (Net) | 77,500 | 72,617 | 67,908 | 63,294 | 58,796 | 54,445 | 50,278 | 46,339 |
| | Capitalized Expenses (Net) | 5,000 | 4,000 | 3,000 | 2,000 | 1,000 | 0 | 0 | 0 |
| | **Total Assets** | **91,500** | **128,842** | **136,858** | **151,631** | **167,610** | **187,684** | **208,226** | **229,960** |
| | **LIABILITIES** | | | | | | | | |
| | Short Term Bank Borrowings | 0 | 11,297 | 1,795 | 0 | 0 | 0 | 0 | 0 |
| | Suppliers | 0 | 17,742 | 22,089 | 23,888 | 25,750 | 27,678 | 28,231 | 28,796 |
| | Term Debt (Current Portion) | 9,804 | 9,804 | 9,804 | 9,804 | 9,804 | 9,804 | 9,804 | 0 |
| | Term Debt | 58,821 | 49,018 | 39,214 | 29,411 | 19,607 | 9,804 | 0 | 0 |
| | Shareholder Funds | | | | | | | | |
| | Accumulated Reserves | 0 | 18,107 | 41,080 | 65,654 | 89,574 | 117,524 | 147,316 | 178,289 |
| | Capital | 22,875 | 22,875 | 22,875 | 22,875 | 22,875 | 22,875 | 22,875 | 22,875 |
| | **Total Liabilities and Net Worth** | **91,500** | **128,842** | **136,858** | **151,631** | **167,610** | **187,684** | **208,226** | **229,960** |
| | | 0 | 0 | 0 | 0 | 0 | 0 | 0 | 0 |
| 6 | KEY RATIOS | | | | | | | | |
| (a) | **Performance and Profitability** | | | | | | | | |
| | OPM | NA | 26.09% | 28.76% | 29.44% | 30.02% | 30.53% | 30.99% | 30.94% |
| | SOCE | NA | 1.13 | 1.39 | 1.36 | 1.33 | 1.27 | 1.15 | 1.05 |
| | ROCE | NA | 29.46% | 40.08% | 40.10% | 39.92% | 38.87% | 35.77% | 32.59% |
| | ROE | NA | 44.18% | 43.07% | 35.51% | 31.44% | 28.05% | 24.23% | 21.08% |

| | | | | | | | | |
|---|---|---|---|---|---|---|---|---|
| (b) **Liquidity** | | | | | | | | |
| CR | NA | 1.34 | 1.96 | 2.56 | 3.03 | 3.55 | 4.15 | 6.38 |
| QR | NA | 0.80 | 1.17 | 1.71 | 2.16 | 2.67 | 3.26 | 5.18 |
| (c) **Capital Structure** | | | | | | | | |
| Gearing | NA | 1.71 | 0.79 | 0.44 | 0.26 | 0.14 | 0.06 | 0.00 |
| Debt/Equity | 3.00 | 2.14 | 1.14 | 0.71 | 0.49 | 0.34 | 0.22 | 0.14 |
| (d) **Total Leverage Ratios** | | | | | | | | |
| Operating | NA | 1.51 | 1.37 | 1.33 | 1.31 | 1.29 | 1.27 | 1.27 |
| Financial | NA | 1.18 | 1.09 | 1.06 | 1.04 | 1.03 | 1.02 | 1.00 |
| Total | NA | 1.77 | 1.48 | 1.41 | 1.36 | 1.32 | 1.29 | 1.28 |
| (e) **Growth** | | | | | | | | |
| Sales – Value | NA | NA | 28% | 9% | 8% | 8% | 2% | 2% |
| Net Profit | NA | NA | 52% | 14% | 12% | 11% | 5% | 3% |

(E) WORKING CAPITAL CHANGES

| | (days) | Year 0 | Year 1 | Year 2 | Year 3 | Year 4 | Year 5 | Year 6 | Year 7 |
|---|---|---|---|---|---|---|---|---|---|
| Stocks | 90 | | 21,290 | 26,507 | 28,666 | 30,900 | 33,213 | 33,877 | 34,555 |
| Receivables | 90 | | 30,935 | 39,443 | 42,914 | 46,508 | 50,228 | 51,233 | 52,257 |
| Suppliers | 75 | | 17,742 | 22,089 | 23,888 | 25,750 | 27,678 | 28,231 | 28,796 |
| W/C Cycle | 105 | | 34,484 | 43,860 | 47,691 | 51,658 | 55,764 | 56,879 | 58,016 |

## Solution

Major project risks are as follows:

Whilst the project has certain advantages, the following project risks are matters of serious concern:

1. International competitiveness is to be established beyond doubt because of two main inhibiting factors (a) cost of shipping in the bulky raw materials from abroad and (b) cost of shipping out the finished goods because projected exports are expected to be around 44%, which means competing with the established international players, some of whom have sustainable competitive advantages, such as captive manganese mines, etc. Basis of exports should be logically sound.
2. Strong bargaining power of buyers and suppliers – local buyers are few and so are the key suppliers.
3. Impact of hike in power costs. Check the probability of increase in electricity prices, which is on the higher side, if the electricity companies are currently operating with marginal profitability/suffering losses.
4. Appointing EML as the marketing agency raises some concerns – their marketing expertise is in petrochemicals and not in alloys, which has an entirely different set of target markets and requires distinct strategies. Instead of paying 3% marketing commission on

local sales, SACL ought to attempt to get into long-term off-take agreements with the main two domestic customers – QSL and KSL. It appears that although the international competitors may have more selling expenses as their market geography may be wider, in SACL's case domestic marketing expenses ought to be lower, given the different market profile.

5. Sensitivity analysis should be conducted altering assumptions on input costs, volume, etc. In fact the project becomes unviable if (a) electricity cost increases to EUR 0.088/unit from EUR 0.05/unit, (b) selling prices drop by 20%, (c) capacity utilization falls below 30% from the projected level, (d) landed cost of manganese ore imports increase by 45% or more, etc.
6. A plethora of shareholders can result in a stalemate because Articles of Association prescribe that unanimous decisions are required in critical decisions. Usually the Companies Law requires only a three-quarters majority in critical matters and hence it would be a practical business decision if the Articles of Association were to drop the 'unanimous decisions' clause.
7. The relationship team ought to get shareholder guarantees, as a proof of shareholders' confidence in SACL. It is better to share the exposure with other FIs in the market, which is always a prudent measure, as it spreads the project credit risk.
8. The credit risk pricing (LIBOR+100 basis points) recommended by the relationship team and used in the financial appraisal calculation, reflects rather low credit risk perceived in the project, possibly relying on the strength of the promoters. Hence a risk of low pricing also exists, unless strong joint and several guarantees from the financially sound shareholders are obtained covering the full exposure.
9. There is a risk of local customers relying on imports, if their current suppliers abroad attempt dumping/price undercutting. Selling prices can go down – especially if the competition is from China. Competition may get tougher and local buyers may prefer imports and will be difficult to canvass for protection in the face of WTO.
10. None of the shareholders have any critical stake in SACL. In case of crisis there won't be any major stakeholder to take a strong initiative.
11. Top man (GM) of the company may prove to be a good academic devoid of rich practical business experience.
12. Risk of inadequate working capital.

## ✍ QUESTIONS/EXERCISES

1. What are the major project financing risks? How are these different from the risks involved in extending short-term facilities?
2. Name the major parties involved in a large project. What are the main contributions by each party?
3. What are the different phases in a project? Elaborate the risks under each phase.
4. How would you assess the financial viability of the project?
5. Explain the relevance of DSCR, LLCR and PLCR in credit appraisal of a project.

6. The following data represents the financial summary of a manufacturing project that is currently under consideration.

| Year: | 0 | 1 | 2 | 3 | 4 | 5 | 6 | 7 | 8 | 9 | 10 |
|---|---|---|---|---|---|---|---|---|---|---|---|
| (a) Operating Cash Flow (OCF) | | 250 | 250 | 250 | 250 | 250 | 250 | 250 | 250 | 220 | 220 |
| (b) PV of OCF | | ? | ? | ? | ? | ? | ? | ? | ? | ? | ? |
| (c) Loan Repayments | | 100 | 100 | 100 | 100 | 100 | 100 | 100 | 100 | 100 | 100 |
| (d) Loan Outstanding (year-end) | | 1,000 | 900 | 800 | 700 | 600 | 500 | 400 | 300 | 200 | 100 |
| (e) Interest Payments (10%) | | 100 | 90 | 80 | 70 | 60 | 50 | 40 | 30 | 20 | 10 |
| (f) Total Debt Service | (c) + (e) | 200 | 190 | 180 | 170 | 160 | 150 | 140 | 130 | 120 | 110 |
| DSCR | | ? | ? | ? | ? | ? | ? | ? | ? | ? | ? |
| LLCR | | ? | ? | ? | ? | ? | ? | ? | ? | ? | ? |

- Please calculate DSCR, PV of operating cash flows and LLCR and provide your views on the financial viability of the project.
- Assume cost of equity is 15% and the equity and debt mix is 50:50 and zero taxation.
- If the interest rates increase to 14%, do you think the project is still a viable proposition? Explain your views.

7. ABCD Manufacturing, an established manufacturing company, is undergoing an expansion programme. A group of syndicate lenders has come together to extend project finance. As Head of Credit, you have been provided with the following details to express your bank's interest in joining this syndication:

(a) Capacity and its utilization details are as follows:

| Particulars | Capacity (units per day) | Working Days/ Month | Monthly Production (Million Units) | No. of Months the Capacity is Utilized | | | Projected Annual Production (Million Units) | | |
|---|---|---|---|---|---|---|---|---|---|
| | | | | Base Case | Worst Case | Harsh Case | Base Case | Worst | Harsh |
| Current Capacity | 222,000 | 30 | 6.66 | 12 | 12 | 12 | 79.92 | 79.92 | 79.92 |
| Total Capacity – After Expansion | 302,000 | 30 | 9.12 | 12 | 12 | 12 | 103.59 | 95.445 | 91.755 |
| Projected Sales Under Each Scenario ($i Million) =≥ | | | | | | | 2,115.4 | 1,964.7 | 1,873.7 |

(b) Major assumptions

- Whilst turnover is estimated to grow at 62.8% in 20X6, the growth is estimated at 5.2% for 20X7 and thereafter assumed conservatively a steady turnover.
- Gross profit margin is kept in the region of 36.5%, throughout the projected period.
- Overheads will be maintained at 12.3% for the projected period and LIBOR at hedged level of 4.5%.
- No cash dividends during FY20X6. 20% dividend thereafter.

(c) Financial Highlights

| Particulars ($000s) | | FY20X6 | FY20X7 | FY20X8 | FY20X9 | FY20X0 | F20X1 |
|---|---|---|---|---|---|---|---|
| Turnover | | 2,115,449 | 2,224,906 | 2,224,906 | 2,224,906 | 2,224,906 | 2,224,906 |
| EBITDA | | 532,123 | 564,095 | 564,095 | 564,095 | 564,095 | 564,095 |
| Profit Before Tax | | 248,424 | 273,859 | 302,651 | 335,463 | 376,137 | 376,137 |
| Interest Cover | | 3.47 | 3.92 | 5.15 | 7.27 | 10.65 | 10.65 |
| Net Debt | | 1,783,704 | 1,494,881 | 1,081,864 | 588,074 | 179,955 | 179,954 |
| Covenant Compliance: | | | | | | | |
| Measure | Parameters | | | | | | |
| Financial Covenants | | | | | | | |
| a) EBITDA : Net Interest | Min 4.5x | >4.5x | >4.5x | >4.5x | >4.5x | >4.5x | >4.5x |
| Projected Test Result Ratio | | 5.3 | 6.0 | 7.7 | 10.5 | 14.5 | 14.5 |
| Covenant Compliance | | Yes | Yes | Yes | Yes | Yes | Yes |
| b) Net Debt : EBITDA | Staggered | < 3.75 | < 3.25 | < 2.5 | < 2.5 | < 2.5 | < 2.5 |
| Projected Test Result Ratio | | 3.4 | 2.7 | 1.9 | 1.0 | 0.3 | 0.3 |
| Covenant Compliance | | Yes | Yes | Yes | Yes | Yes | Yes |

(d) Term Sheet

| | |
|---|---|
| Total Facilities | $750 million |
| Syndicated | Syndicated, arranged by XYZ Bank |
| Borrower | ABCD Manufacturing |
| Purpose | • The company has expansion plans of $900m during 20X4–20X6 and the syndicate debt was raised for this purpose |
| Term | • 5 years and 3 year extension option at the discretion of the syndicate. Such extension shall be at the discretion of each lender and with the agent receiving acceptances equal to or not less than 51% of the outstanding principal balance of the Facility on the Initial Maturity Date<br>• Drawdown Availability Period: Six months from the signing date. |
| Repayment | In semi-annual instalments commencing 30 months from the signing date |
| Prepayment | Allowed without penalty |
| Voluntary Cancellation | On not less than 30 days' irrevocable prior notice, the Company may cancel the whole or part of the unused portion of the facility without premium or penalty. Amounts cancelled may not be reinstated |
| Financial Covenants | • Net Debt/EBITDA < 3.75x till 31.12.06, Net Debt/EBITDA <3.25x on 30.06.07 and 31.12.07 and Net Debt/EBITDA <2.5x thereafter.<br>• EBITDA/Interest Payable>4.5x |
| Commitment Fee | 40% of the margin p.a. payable on the unused and uncancelled facility amount during the period commencing 60 days from the signing date until the expiry of the Availability Period |
| Extension Fee | To be agreed at the time of extension |
| Participation Fee | 60 basis points flat paid upfront |
| Events of Default: | • Non-payment unless failure to pay is caused by administrative or technical error and payment is made within 3 Business Days of its due date<br>• Any breach in financial covenant<br>• Misrepresentation<br>• Cross default, subject to an agreed minimum amount<br>• Insolvency; or insolvency proceedings (including, without limitation, appointment of administrators or receivers); creditors' process; unlawfulness |

Is the above information sufficient to arrive at a decision? If not what additional information would you seek? Is the covenant suite sufficient? What would be the additional covenants you would propose? What are the major project risks you foresee from the given set of information?

8. Identify a major project in your area/country and find out the project sponsors, project lenders and consultants and discuss the various project risks and related mitigants. Discuss the socio-economic advantages of the project. If possible obtain the financial numbers and assess its financial viability.

# 12
# Credit Risks in Working Capital

Working capital is known as the blood of business. No business can survive without adequate working capital. A business without sufficient working capital is like an anaemic person. An anaemic is a person lacking sufficient red blood cells, which makes them weak and unhealthy. All interested parties will be concerned about an anaemic person, and so will suppliers of credit if their customer displays symptoms of business anaemia – viz. lack of working capital impacting the creditworthiness of customers. Working capital credit risks will lead to liquidity problems, which in turn, could result in non-settlement of bank liabilities, suppliers and other creditors.

Let us examine the nature of working capital, as the first step to understanding the major credit risks involved. Working capital is the basic requirement of any business. It refers to that part of the capital required to purchase raw materials, pay for the salaries and wages of employees, meet the movement costs of goods and similar recurring expenses. It takes into account trade credit given to customers and that received from suppliers. The timing mismatch between the transfer of title to the product and settlement of dues along with routine expenses (salaries, freight expenses, etc.) give rises to the demand for short-term funds.

## 12.1 DEFINITION OF WORKING CAPITAL

Usual balance sheet definition of working capital is given below:

Working Capital = Current Assets – Current Liabilities

**Current assets** are those assets of the business which are expected to be converted into cash within a time frame of one year (or less). Typical current assets include cash, marketable securities (sometimes also called short-term investments), accounts receivable, inventory and others, such as prepaid expenses.

**Current liabilities** are obligations that are to be settled in a year or less. These include trade creditors, interest bearing short-term loans, and the current portion of long-term debt, accrued expenses, accrued taxes and wages.

### 12.1.1 Working Capital Cycle – Finance Manager's Key Concern

All firms require a minimum amount of current assets to operate smoothly and to carry out day-to-day operations. Working capital usually revolves around the business several times during the year. This is called the working capital cycle, which we will discuss in detail later. The working capital 'cycles' around the business. On each turn of the cycle the firm or company is expected to make a profit – i.e. the goods or services should be sold for more than the cost of their production – resulting in more cash.

Working capital management involves management of current assets and their financing. It is one of the main responsibilities of the finance manager to decide the optimum balance for each of the current asset accounts (stock, debtors and creditors) and to choose the mix of trade credit, short-term debt, long-term debt and equity to use in financing them. Working capital management decisions are usually fast paced as they are dynamic.

### 12.1.2 Working Capital Cycle – Lending Bank's Point of View

Study of the working capital cycle is important for a commercial bank (and other working capital lenders), who extend working capital facilities to the business world. Usually, banks follow the normal working capital definition; however they exclude bank finance from the current liabilities. Accordingly the working capital definition can be rewritten as follows:

Working Capital = Current Assets – Current Liabilities (excluding bank finance)

Study of the working capital cycle benefits the banks in several ways, i.e.

1. To avoid over-financing the customer. For example, if the stock is already bought on a credit basis from the supplier, the banks should avoid funding the same stock.
2. To decide the usance period for letters of credit. For example, if the trade creditor provides 90 days' credit period (from the date of receipt of goods) and the time taken for shipment is 30 days, the usance period of the letter of credit may not exceed 120 days. (We will discuss more about this later in the chapter.)
3. To decide the tenor of short-term revolving loans.
4. To structure the various working capital facilities, including overdraft, short-term revolving loans, factoring, bill discounting, letters of credit and/or letters of guarantee.
5. To understand the liquidity management of the entity. The liquidity position is closely linked to the working capital management and its components (i.e. stock, debtors and creditors).

## 12.2 ASSESSING WORKING CAPITAL THROUGH THE BALANCE SHEET

As we have seen in Chapter 8, the balance sheet is a powerful tool facilitating credit risk study, which is also true for working capital analysis as well. The balance sheet shows the working capital as on a particular day and we have to assume this as the average situation for the year/period, given the dynamic nature of working capital. If the position as reflected in the balance sheet is not reflective of an 'average' situation, the analyst ought to derive a best case based on the understanding of the nature (e.g. seasonality) of business, especially its cash flows, developed through discussions/customer visits.

Let us use the following example to understand how the balance sheet can provide clarity in the working capital requirements:

**Example 12.1**

The following is the Balance Sheet of ABC Ltd.

$ in thousands

| Liabilities | | Assets | |
|---|---|---|---|
| Share Capital | 20,000 | Fixed Assets | 25,000 |
| Retained Earnings | 12,000 | Investments | 7,000 |
| Long Term Loan | 0 | Stock | 15,000 |
| Trade Creditors | 23,000 | Debtors and Others | 25,000 |
| Overdraft | 24,000 | Other Debtors | 3,000 |
| Accruals and Others | 1,000 | Cash | 5,000 |
| **Total** | **80,000** | **Total** | **80,000** |

You have been informed that the bank has extended an overdraft facility of $50m only, of which $24m is currently utilized. No other facility is enjoyed from any other bank. Calculate the following and explain your views:

1. Working capital requirement from the finance manager's point of view.
2. Working capital from a lending bank's perspective.
3. Is there any defect in the way working capital facilities are structured?
4. What is your view on the liquidity of ABC Ltd?

**Solution**

1. Let us start with the calculation of working capital from the finance manager's point of view.

   The working capital gap/requirement = Current Assets – Current Liabilities
   = (15,000 + 25,000 + 3,000 + 5,000) – (23,000 + 24,000 + 1,000)
   = 48,000 – 48,000
   = 0/–

   ***Comment:*** The working capital requirement from the finance manager's point of view is nil because the entire current asset requirements are fully funded by creditors and bank overdraft.
2. Let us now look at the working capital from the bank's perspective.

   Working capital from bank's view = Current Assets – Current Liabilities (excluding bank finance)
   = (15,000 + 25,000 + 3,000 + 5,000) – (23,000 + 1,000)
   = 48,000 – 24,000
   = 24,000/-

   ***Comment:*** Working capital requirement from the bank's point of view is $24m, which is fully funded by bank overdraft.
3. As evident from the above the entire working capital gap is covered by the bank through an overdraft facility. Overall the following defects are observed in the facility structure:
   - The bank lacks control over the facility (overdraft) utilization. In fact the undrawn facility is $26m ($50m – $24m), which may even be drawn down by the customer for non-working capital purposes (e.g. investments or as dividends). An overdraft is a kind of credit facility where the bank has least control over the end utilization. Hence, the bank should reduce the amount of overdraft and replace it with short-term loans linked to current assets – loans against stock or credit facilities against assignment of debtors may be considered as more appropriate. Appropriate controls may also be introduced in such a way that the facilities vary depending upon the level of stock or debtors.
   - Over-financing is evident. As against the working capital requirement (from the bank's perspective) of $24m, the overdraft facility extended is $50m!
   - Reduction in credit facilities is strongly recommended. While the working capital requirement (from the bank's perspective) is $24m, it is in the bank's interest to

ensure that there is some contribution from long-term sources (e.g equity capital) – known as Net Working Capital (NWC) to the working capital requirements. Hence, the bank should refrain from funding all the working capital needs. Assuming 80% is funded by the bank, the maximum working capital facilities may not exceed $19.2m (80% × $24m).

4. The liquidity position is not very comfortable as is evident from the current ratio and quick ratio, which are computed below:
   - Current Ratio = Current Assets/Current Liability, i.e. 48,000/48,000 = 1:1
   - Quick Ratio = (Current Assets – Stock)/Current Liability, i.e. 33,000/48,000 = 0.69:1

     As we discussed in Chapter 8, the usually accepted levels of current ratio and quick ratio are 1.50:1 and 1:1 respectively. Viewed against this, both ratios reflect the tight liquidity position of the business.

## 12.3 WORKING CAPITAL RATIOS

Before looking into the working capital cycle in detail, let us examine a few important working capital ratios. These ratios also bring out the efficiency of working capital (w/c) management and hence are of particular interest to creditors, banks and other lenders, who provide working capital finance. The usual ratios used to study w/c management of a business are:

- W/C to Total Assets – links working capital to the total asset base.
- W/C to Sales – links working capital to the business activity.
- Stock Turnover Ratio – shows the stocking requirement.
- Debtors Collection Ratio – shows the credit period extended to customers.
- Creditors Payment Period – shows the credit period obtained from the suppliers.

Please refer to the financial analysis (Chapter 8) for details on these ratios. Now let us see some examples, how ratios bring out the working capital efficiency.

**Example 12.2**

Following are the figures extracted from a retailer's (supermarket) balance sheet.

$ in million

| *Particulars* | *20X1* | *20X2* | *20X3* |
|---|---|---|---|
| Sales | 25,135 | 24, 046 | 23,765 |
| Cost of Sales | 19,122 | 17,663 | 17,790 |
| Stock (a) | 3,286 | 2,885 | 2,796 |
| Trade Debtors (b) | 236 | 157 | 195 |
| Trade Creditors (c) | 2,545 | 2,513 | 2,529 |
| Working Capital Finance | Nil | Nil | Nil |

Calculate w/c ratios and interpret the w/c efficiency.

**Answer**

***Calculation of Working Capital Management Ratios***

| | | | |
|---|---|---|---|
| Working Capital (a+b-c) | 977 | 529 | 460 |
| Stock Holding Period | 63 | 60 | 57 |
| Debtors Collection Period | 3 | 2 | 3 |
| Creditors Payment Period | 49 | 52 | 52 |
| WC to Sales | 3.9% | 3.1% | 2% |

**Comments**: As the retailer mostly sells on a cash basis, the debtors are almost nil, which is reflected in the low average debtors collection period. It has only very few credit customers, probably some large customers who regularly buy from the supermarket, hence the credit. Debtors' policy has remained the same for the last three years as is evident from the relatively steady collection period. Stocking policy shows that the supermarket stocks goods for about two months. Stock policy also did not undergo any substantial change although stock management appears to have improved as shown in the six days' reduction compared to the previous years. At the same time the business appears to have negotiated better credit terms from suppliers as is evident from the average payment period. Consequent upon the reduction in stock level and slightly higher trade credit, the w/c gap dropped by 53% to $460m over a three year period with a narrowing cash cycle of 8 days (57 + 3 – 52) compared to 17 days (63 + 3 – 49) two years ago. Overall the quality of working capital management is satisfactory. The customer does not rely on working capital borrowings as almost the entire requirement is met from the trade credit.

**Example 12.3**

The following is the working capital information related to a manufacturing company. Assess the quality of the working capital management:

$ in 000s

| *Particulars* | *20X0* | *20X1* | *20X2* |
|---|---|---|---|
| Sales | 459,861 | 481,753 | 514,128 |
| Cost of Sales | 310,152 | 324,694 | 342,391 |
| Stock* | 94,004 | 124,315 | 85,482 |
| Net Trade Debtors | 61,578 | 70,476 | 74,081 |
| Trade Creditors | 31,182 | 57,902 | 45,746 |
| Working Capital Finance | 65,125 | 72,136 | 55,642 |
| Total Assets | 327,227 | 415,192 | 432,992 |
| **Stock: Raw Material and Packing* | *55,229* | *70,974* | *43,369* |
| *Stock: Work In Progress* | *1,210* | *1,480* | *730* |
| *Stock: Spare Parts* | *7,459* | *6,806* | *6,929* |
| *Stock: Finished Goods* | *31,754* | *46,149* | *35,659* |
| *Less: Provision for Slow Moving* | *–1,648* | *–1,094* | *–1,205* |

**Answer**

**Calculation of Working Capital Management Ratios**

| | | | |
|---|---|---|---|
| Working Capital | 116,941 | 130,083 | 106,888 |
| Stock Holding Period* | 102 | 132 | 84 |
| Debtors Collection Period | 49 | 53 | 53 |
| Creditors Payment Period | 37 | 65 | 49 |
| WC to Sales | 25% | 27% | 21% |
| WC to Total Assets | 36% | 31% | 25% |
| WC to Bank Borrowings | 56% | 55% | 52% |

* *without spare-parts as they are not stock-in-trade.*

| | | | |
|---|---|---|---|
| *Raw Material and Packing Holding* | *65* | *80* | *46* |
| *Work In Progress period* | *1* | *2* | *1* |
| *Stock: Finished Goods(FG)* | *37* | *52* | *38* |
| *Less: Provision for Slow Moving* | *−2* | *−1* | *−1* |

**Comments**: Overall, w/c management is satisfactory. While stock (both raw materials and finished goods) increased in 20X1, by 20X2 they have been brought down. Moreover, there was a commensurate increase in the trade creditors as well in 20X1, which part-funded the increase in stock. Whilst bank borrowings also support the working capital requirement, this is reasonable and amounts to around 55% of the working capital gap. The relatively low work in progress period reflects the relatively fast conversion time – from raw material to finished goods.

## 12.4 WORKING CAPITAL CYCLE

'Working capital cycle' refers to the time taken for the business activity (or operation) to complete its course. For example in the case of a manufacturing entity, the working capital cycle denotes the time period between the point at which raw materials are bought and the point at which finished goods (made from those raw materials) are converted into cash. Generally, the shorter the working capital cycle, the more efficient the company's use of working capital. A company with an extremely short working cycle requires less cash, and can survive even at relatively lower margins. Conversely, a business may have fat margins; however if it has a lengthy working capital cycle, it may struggle to grow even at a modest pace.

Let us see the various components and the functioning of the working capital cycle of a trader:

M/s ABC Co, a trading firm enters into an agreement with the supplier and places an order on a particular day and receives the goods after 30 days. The supplier, who usually extends 30 days' credit period, is settled on time. The goods are kept in the warehouse for 45 days, when they are sold on credit to XYZ Ltd, which usually enjoys 60 days' credit from ABC Co. XYZ Ltd pays on time, completing the trading activity or trade cycle of this particular transaction. We can summarize these events as follows:

| Day | Activity |
|---|---|
| 0 | Place the order |
| After 30 days | Receipt of goods on 30 days credit |
| After 30 days | Settle the supplier |
| 45 days after the receipt of goods | Sales on credit of 60 days |
| 60 days thereafter | Collect the dues from the debtor (i.e. XYZ Ltd) |

The operating cycle usually starts from the date of receipt of goods and not from the date of placing the order, because the supplier may not supply the goods and there is a possibility of cancellation by mutual understanding or the agreement may provide for certain situations when the transaction may not happen at all. (Some variations are possible in real life. If advance payment for goods is required, then the working capital cycle starts from the date on which money is advanced.) Coming back to the example, the operating cycle starts with the receipt of inventory and ends with the collection of the money from XYZ Ltd. In the balance sheet, we can see the progress of the operating cycle from inventory to trade debtors to cash.

At this point you may have a doubt – why we are not speaking about the trade creditors, who are extending 30 days' credit? Well, in the strict sense, the operating cycle does not take the trade creditors' period into account, but 'cash cycle or working capital cycle' does. (In the case of letter of credit issuance, the time period from the date of order placement may also be factored in while computing operating cycle. Please see Section 12.11.)

- Cash cycle/or working capital cycle = operating cycle less average trade creditors payment period.
- Where operating cycle = average inventory holding period[1] + average debtors collection period.

The above working capital cycle can be depicted as in Figure 12.1:

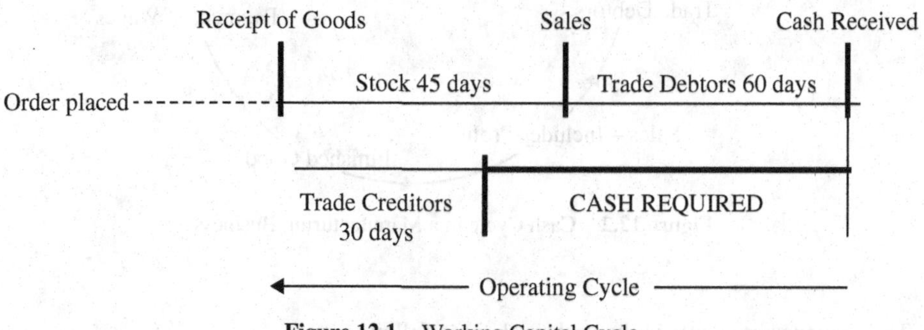


**Figure 12.1** Working Capital Cycle

[1] In the case of manufacturing entities, the inventory holding period can be further subdivided into average raw material holding period, average work in progress period and average finished goods holding period.

In the case of M/s ABC Co., the operating and cash cycles are calculated as follows:

- Operating cycle = inventory holding (45 days) + debtors collection period (60 days) = 105 days.
- Cash (or w/c) cycle = 105 days – creditors settlement period (30 days) = 75 days.

As discussed earlier, if a letter of credit (LC) is required, then the the operating cycle will include the time from order placement. Suppose the supplier insists on LC, in which case the period from the date of the order is to be included in the operating cycle. Let us assume that a usance LC is negotiated with the supplier. In this case the usance LC term will be 60 days (i.e. the time period between order and receipt of goods, 30 days and credit period allowed by the supplier after the receipt of goods, 30 days). Also see Section 12.11, later in the chapter.

The above example considers just one trading activity by ABC Co. In reality, during the course of a year, ABC will be entering into hundreds of similar transactions, and we use activity ratios (i.e. stock holding period, debtors collection period and creditors payment period, derived from financial statements) to get an idea about the average working capital cycle and operating cycle.

We can depict the operating and working capital (cash) cycle in a different manner as well. Figure 12.2 shows the operating and working capital cycle of a manufacturing business:

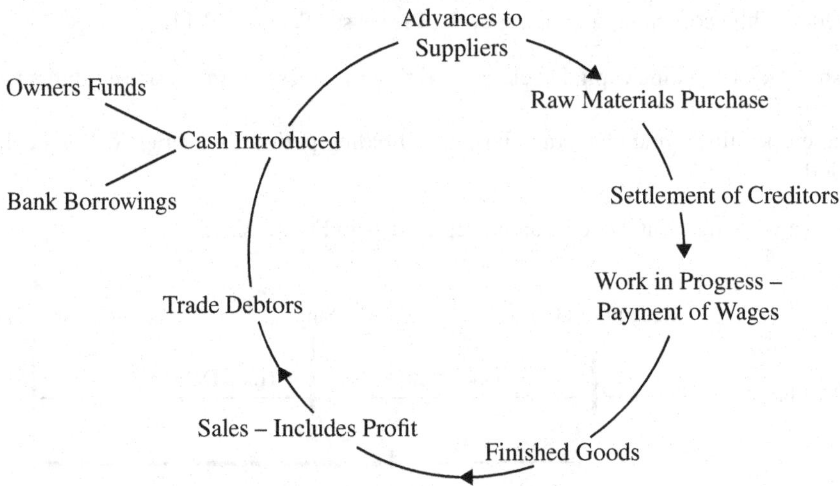


**Figure 12.2** Cash Cycle in a Manufacturing Business

The sequence of events in the cash cycle is as follows:

- The firm gets the funds to be deployed in the working capital or cash cycle from equity funds or bank borrowings.
- The firm uses cash to pay for a cash advance (usually a percentage of total purchase price) to the suppliers and thereafter obtain the raw materials on credit. After some time, the creditors are settled in cash.

- Thereafter, cash is paid for wages (to skilled and unskilled labourers) as the cost of converting the raw materials into finished goods (i.e. working capital needed to pay conversion costs).
- The finished goods are held in the warehouse until they are sold at a reasonable profit.
- The sales are usually on credit terms to the firm's customers.
- As the final step in the cycle, the debtors settle their dues, resulting in cash inflows.
- This cash is then either utilized to settle the bank borrowings or reinvested in raw materials and the cycle is repeated. If a firm is profitable, the cash inflows increase over time.

Looking at the above working capital cycle, a reader may have a doubt or a query: 'what is the harm if the firm relies fully on bank borrowings throughout the working capital cycle?' Although it may look appealing, the business realities are different. Business firms fully reliant on banks to fund their working capital carry a significant liquidity and solvency risk. Due to the changes in market dynamics, if the stock movements slow down for a few months or debtors delay the payments, a firm fully dependent on banks will run out of cash to settle the bank dues on time. Delay in settling bank dues/obligations carries not only reputation risk, but also higher interest outgoings due to penal interest clauses and possible higher risk categorization of the customer (by the bank). If the banks lose trust in the customer's ability to manage the business properly, they may even call back the entire facility, putting further pressure on liquidity.

**Example 12.4**

ABCD Ltd, one of the important customers in your bank's credit portfolio, is a manufacturer of ceramic tiles. The Head of Credit of your bank would like to know how efficiently the company's working capital is managed. He is particularly interested in the length of time it takes ABCD Ltd to collect cash from debtors, total operating cycle and working capital (cash) cycle. He is also keen to see how ABCD Ltd's cash cycle compares with the industry average of 75 days. The following information is given:

| Account | Closing Balance |
|---|---|
| Inventory | \$1,050m |
| Accounts receivable | \$1,121m |
| Accounts payable | \$ 793m |
| Net sales during the year were | \$3,770m |

**Solution**

Let us calculate the inventory holding period, debtors collection period and creditors payment period. In the absence of cost of sales, we use sales figure to calculate both inventory holding period and creditors payment period. The details are given below:

Inventory holding period: $1{,}050/3{,}770 \times 365 = 102$ days
Debtors collection period: $1{,}121/3{,}770 \times 365 = 109$ days
Creditors payment period: $793/3{,}770 \times 365 = 77$ days

Therefore, the response to the Head of Credit's query is as follows:

- Time taken to collect the dues from debtors: On average, it takes 109 days or 3.6 months (109/30 days).
- Operating cycle = inventory holding period + debtors collection period or 102 + 109 = 211 days.
- Cash or working capital cycle = operating cycle − creditors payment period, i.e. 211 days − 77 days = 134 days. Thus, about 4.5 (134/30 days) months pass between the time ABCD Ltd pays for its inventory (cash outflow) and the time it collects cash for the sales of finished goods (cash inflow). Thus ABCD Ltd has to finance its operations for over 4.5 months.
- Although 4.5 months may appear reasonable, compared with the industry's average cash cycle, ABCD Ltd is doing badly in this area. The ABCD Ltd cash cycle is on the higher side. ABCD Ltd's cash (working capital) cycle takes about 134 days against the industry average of 75 days. They could stand to improve the cycle by lowering the inventory or taking steps for faster collection of debtors while negotiating better credit terms from suppliers.

## 12.5 WORKING CAPITAL VS. FIXED CAPITAL

Those who are involved in corporate finance, finance management or financing of business know that working capital problems are different from fixed capital problems. Whilst it is relatively easy to understand fixed capital requirements, calculation of working capital requirements is somewhat difficult. A company can easily compute the total cost of the plant and machinery, computers and vehicles it wants to buy and know how much it should raise in funds.

However, many believe understanding the working capital requirements – especially those of trading and manufacturing entities – and its management is easy. This false belief has got many into trouble. First of all, nobody can calculate the working capital requirement exactly, because working capital is dynamic. For instance, while a manufacturing company will not alter the number of vehicles, or P&M, every day, the stock will vary. The company will be accepting new truckloads of raw materials, while sending finished goods to buyers. Some debtors might delay payments while suppliers pressurize for speedier payments. These factors explain why working capital is dynamic. While a conscious decision to buy a fixed asset is easy to predict and anticipate, it is challenging for a company to fully predict the working capital and related financing requirements, especially if the trading circumstances undergo rapid changes e.g. sharp volatility in raw material prices.

Working capital is constantly changing and this is due to a number of factors, depending upon the business circumstances. Accordingly, a company can only make an estimate of their working capital requirements. As we have discussed earlier, the balance sheet approach to working capital estimation is a reliable method.

## 12.6 WORKING CAPITAL BEHAVIOUR

Major factors that influence the working capital are given in Figure 12.3:

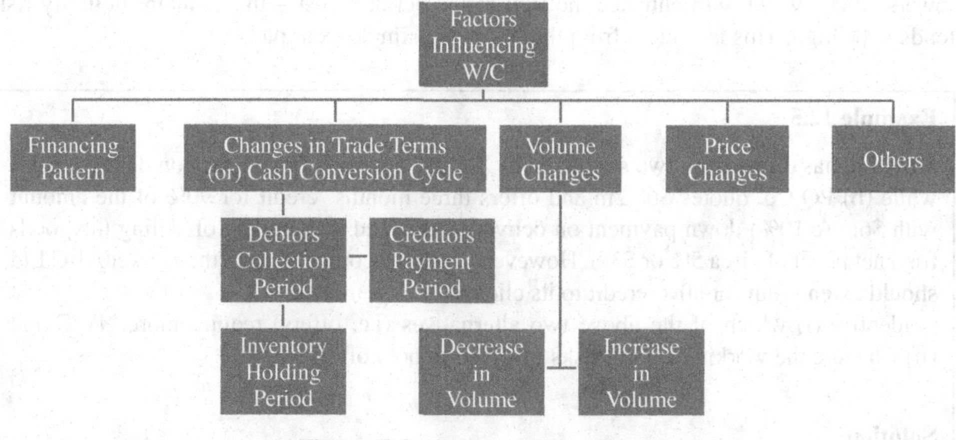


**Figure 12.3** Working Capital Drivers

### 12.6.1 Availability of Finance

Equity and bank finance are the usual sources of working capital finance. All other things being equal, a business will invest more in working capital for growth. The availability of finance decides the extent of funds invested in working capital. For example, a finance manager may decide to take advantage of falling interest rates to rely more on the bank borrowings to invest more in stock or extend liberal credit terms to customers in an effort to increase sales. During the 2008 Credit Crisis, many finance managers were caught off-guard as the banks slashed working capital lines, which forced them to change trade terms or reduce business volume.

Whilst the working capital gap can be funded by relying on short-term bank borrowings, it is strongly recommended to have some funds from long-term sources invested in working capital, which offers a cushion to the working capital management and liquidity of the business. Funds invested in working capital (from long-term sources) are known as long-term contribution to working capital or Net Working Capital (NWC). As we will discuss later, in credit based businesses NWC has an important role to play in reducing the working capital risks.

NWC is required mainly because of two reasons:

(a) To maintain business at a minimum level, a certain level of minimum current assets (such as minimum inventory, etc.) is required. It is better to fund this part from long-term sources with no link to current liability as it will obviate any external creditor pressing for immediate payment. The higher the long-term contribution to working capital, the higher would be the current and quick ratios, which reflect positively on the liquidity conditions of a business firm.

(b) Secondly, financing all current assets from current liabilities carries a risk. In case some of the current assets do not convert into cash on time, the business may face difficulties in settling corresponding current liabilities. A liquidity crisis looms large which could be avoided if part of the current assets is funded by NWC.

But deploying equity funds in working capital is not that attractive, from a profitability point of view, if the requirements can be met through credit. Higher credit in the working capital lowers NWC, which will enhance the ROI ratios but at a cost – the resultant liquidity risk tends to be high. This is evident from the following simple example:

**Example 12.5**

ABC Ltd has offers from two suppliers (a) XY Co. quotes \$60m on cash on delivery basis while (b) PQ Co. quotes \$60.2m and offers three months' credit for 90% of the amount with \$6m (c.10%) down payment on delivery. ABC Ltd is confident of selling the goods for a net profit of circa 5% or \$3m. However, given the competition in the market ABC Ltd should extend four months' credit to its clients.

Identify (i) which of the above two alternatives (i.e. offers) require more NWC and (ii) what are the working capital risks involved in both offers?

**Solution**

- **First Offer**: Return On Investment (ROI) for four months would be 5%, (\$3m/\$60m) as the entire amount is contributed from owners' funds. ROI on an annualized basis would be 15%[2] because the working capital cycle is four months. Although there are no creditors around to press for payment, profitability is low (compared to the other offer). In this case the NWC is \$60m, fully funded by the owners'/shareholders' equity with nil external liabilities.
- **Second offer**: ROI would be 50% (\$3m/\$6m) for four months while annualized ROI would amount to 150%. The trick lies in the minimum own investment by ABC Ltd. Here the NWC is just \$6m and the balance (\$54.2m) is from trade credit. However, it carries certain risks – while the supplier should be settled in three months, the payment from debtors is realizable only after four months. In other words, the second option carries high liquidity risk. (There is a one-month gap, i.e. the difference between the debtors collection period of four months and the creditors payment period of three months. If the customer is creditworthy the banks may provide short-term working capital finance to overcome such situations.)

Accordingly, the financing pattern of the working capital is an important financial decision. Long-term contribution to the working capital is important to ensure the short-term solvency of the business; and would result in higher current and quick ratios, although the profitability would have to be compromised.

### 12.6.2 Changes in Trade Terms

The working capital requirement is impacted by terms of trade. As we have discussed above, the stock holding period, debtors collection period and creditors payment (settlement) period are critical components in working capital and its cycle. The longer the working capital cycle, the higher is the working capital requirement. Whilst the working capital requirement has a direct relationship with stock holding and the debtors collection period, it has an inverse

[2] 15% = 5%x (12 months/4 months).

relationship with the creditors payment period. Let us summarize the impact of the changes in terms of trade on the working capital below.

(a) **Change in suppliers' terms**: If the suppliers reduce the credit period, then the working capital requirement will increase and vice versa. For example, if the trade creditors increase the credit period to 120 days from 60 days, the working capital requirement would drop. (The banks financing the working capital gap should be cautious about this situation because imprudent finance managers may use the excess liquidity for non-core or long-term purposes, which may trigger a liquidity crisis later.) Alternatively, if the suppliers tighten the credit terms, the working capital needs would go up while other things remain the same.

(b) **Change in the stock holding period and debtors collection period**. Any reduction will reduce the working capital requirement while any increase will result in a higher working capital requirement.

### 12.6.3 Changes in Business Volume

The changes in the business volume have a significant impact on the working capital requirements of a business. Let us examine this with the help of the following example:

**Example 12.6**

The following is the Balance Sheet of ABC Ltd.

(Amount in $)

| LIABILITIES | | ASSETS | |
|---|---|---|---|
| Share Capital | 20,000 | Fixed Assets | 26,000 |
| Retained Earnings | 16,000 | Investments | 2,000 |
| Long Term Loan | 10,000 | Stock | 16,000 |
| Trade Creditors | 16,000 | Trade Debtors | 18,000 |
| Accruals and Others | 6,000 | Cash and Others | 6,000 |
| **Total** | **68,000** | **Total** | **68,000** |

Discuss the working capital requirements. Also explore the liquidity situation. What would be the working capital situation if the turnover doubles without change in the current terms of trade?

**Solution**

$$\text{The working capital gap} = (\$16{,}000 + \$18{,}000 + \$6{,}000) - (\$16{,}000 + \$6{,}000)$$
$$= \$40{,}000 - \$22{,}000$$
$$= \$18{,}000/-$$

This working capital situation is expected to continue into the immediate future. At any time during this period, ABC Ltd needs $40,000/- in current assets. ABC Ltd can manage trade credit and other creditors of $22,000/-, i.e. the current assets are partly financed by current liabilities. This leaves a gap of $18,000/. This is funded by contribution from long-term sources or NWC. The total long-term sources (share capital + retained earnings + long term loan) amount to $46,000/- while the long-term uses (fixed assets and investments) absorb $28,000. So the long-term contribution to the working capital is $18,000/-, i.e. $46,000 – $28,000.

As we discussed earlier, NWC or long-term contribution to working capital is important to ensure the short-term solvency of business. The higher the long-term contribution to working capital, the higher would be the current and quick ratios, which reflect the liquidity conditions in a business firm.

The current ratio and quick ratio of ABC Ltd would be 1.81:1 ($40,000/$22,000) and 1.09:1 ($24,000/$22,000) respectively. Both ratios are at acceptable levels denoting satisfactory liquidity.

If ABC Ltd doubles sales on the same terms and conditions, the stock, debtors and creditors will also double in accordance with the volume growth. Accordingly, stock, debtors and other debtors would become $32,000, $36,000 and $12,000 respectively while trade creditors and accruals would be $32,000 and $12,000/-. What is the working capital gap now? $32,000 + $36,000 + $12,000 – $32,000 – $12,000 = $36,000/-. But, the current long-term contribution (i.e. NWC) is just $18,000/-. So, there is a shortfall[3] of $18,000/- ($36,000 – $18,000). Since the suppliers and other creditors will not increase their payment (i.e. credit) period, the options are (i) the owner must bring in the funds or (ii) rely on bank credit. Most businesses prefer bank credit, despite sufficiency of funds by the owners, because of the higher profitability or inherent tax advantages of the borrowing.

It is evident that changes in the scale of operations will require additional w/c funding. However, it should be borne in mind that not all businesses will need additional working capital funding with higher volumes. In the case of predominantly cash based businesses such as retailers, where the suppliers extend liberal credit while the entire sales are on a cash basis, higher volume will mean more cash! This is clear from the following example of a textile retailer, who sells on cash:

**Example 12.7**

Balance Sheet of PQR & Co. Textile Shop

Amount in $

| | | | |
|---|---|---|---|
| Capital | 200,000 | Long-term Market Investments | 380,000 |
| Reserves | 80,000 | Stock | 300,000 |
| Suppliers Credit | 600,000 | Trade Debtors | 110,000 |
| | | Cash and Bank | 90,000 |
| **Total** | **880,000** | | **880,000** |

The turnover of the textile shop is $3,650,000/- (i.e. $10,000 per day). Find out the working capital requirement of PQR & Co. Please discuss the liquidity ratios – current and quick ratios – of the firm. Suppose the partnership is in a position to double sales on the same terms and conditions. Would PQR & Co then require more working capital? Please explain.

[3]The company's level of profitability or loss will have an impact on w/c – we will discuss this later in the chapter.

**Solution**

$$\text{Working capital} = 300{,}000 + 110{,}000 + 90{,}000 - 600{,}000$$
$$= -100{,}000\text{/- i.e. negative working capital}$$

This is the average working capital situation for the customer, which is expected to continue in the immediate future. At any time during this period, ABC Ltd needs $500,000/- in current assets while the trade creditors extend $600,000/-, i.e. the current liabilities exceed current liabilities. Hence there is a negative working capital gap!

The current ratio and quick ratio of PQR & Co would be 0.83:1 and 0.33:1 respectively. Although the traditional current and quick ratios are below the accepted norms, the firm's liquidity is satisfactory, because of the nature of their business. Moreover, the firm is not reliant on any short-term bank borrowings. (It should be borne in mind that the interpretation of ratios[4] should be done in the context of the nature of the business.)

The trick lies in the nature of business and its impact on the current assets and liabilities. As we know, the turnover of the abovementioned textile shop is $3,650,000/- ($10,000 per day). Then the average collection period, stock holding period and creditors payment period would be 11 days (Debtors/Sales*365), 30 days (Stock/Sales*365) and 60 days (Creditors/Sales*365) respectively. Although the balance sheet shows that the creditors are $600,000/- against which only current assets of $500,000 is available, the company can easily meet the current obligations because of the cash nature of the business. If this is not clear, let us provide more explanation as follows:

It means PQR will have to make the payment to creditors on the 60th day while the stock will be sold in 30 days and the debtors will be collected in 11 days. That means PQR enjoys a float of 19 days (60-30-11). Considering the daily sales of $10,000/- the cash float would be $190, 000/-. (In the balance sheet the cash and bank is $90,000. It means the balance ($100,000) is reflected under long-term marketable investments.)

What will happen if this textile retailer doubles the volume on the same terms and conditions?

Suppliers, stock and debtors would become $1,200,000, $600,000 and $190,000 respectively. Now the total cash float would be $380,000! It will enjoy an additional cash float of $190,000 when the volume doubles! In situations like this the business does not require any cash funding from banks. These types of business, if shrewdly managed, will result in utilizing cost-free funds for expansion as well. It is well known that in the US (and other countries), certain chains of restaurants and supermarkets use the liquidity generated by one retail store to fund the establishing of the next store and so on! However, it must be noted that the cash management is critical in these types of 'cash float' businesses. If the short-term cash floats are blocked in long-term assets, it may lead to a liquidity crunch as the business would struggle to settle the trade creditors on time.

Now, let us summarize the discussion on the impact of changes in the business volume on the working capital as follows:

- Usually in businesses where the trade credit does not cover the entire current assets, then higher volume means a greater working capital requirement. An increase in short-term debt levels due to higher working capital borrowings to support the growth in turnover and/or

[4] This again underlines the importance of understanding the business model, as we discussed in Chapter 7.

one-time build-up of inventory or debtors is a normal phenomenon in the business world. On the other hand, if there is a drop in volume, the working capital requirements would also reduce.

- In the case of businesses where a cash float is available (i.e. trade creditors > current assets) volume changes do not create any additional working capital requirement.

### 12.6.4 Price Changes

Another instance of variation in working capital requirement normally occurs when the price of raw materials or trade wares changes. Price increases will result in more cash outlay for the same quantity of goods, resulting in higher inventory and debtors, which in turn results in higher working capital requirements. However, again the nature of business is important. The impact of changes in business volume on working capital is as follows:

- The increase in the price of materials would result in a higher working capital requirement in all businesses where the trade credit does not cover the entire current assets. It is not uncommon where the businesses depend on working capital borrowings to meet the additional funding needs due to the inflationary pressures or price increases. On the other hand, if there is a drop in material prices, then the working capital requirements would also reduce.
- If the nature of business is such that a cash float is available (i.e. trade creditors > current assets) then the price changes do not have any material impact on the working capital needs, i.e. it does not create any additional working capital requirement.

### 12.6.5 Others

Given the dynamic nature of working capital, it is impacted by several causes other than the major factors we discussed above. Nature of business, as we have already seen, is an important criterion. Whilst cash based business does not have any significant working capital needs, those businesses with a long working capital cycle require substantial outlay in working capital. The following are some of the other factors that may influence working capital, depending upon the business:

- Financial policy. Whilst conservative financial policy would finance the entire working capital requirement from NWC, an aggressive financial policy would see maximum dependence on external sources, including trade creditors and bank borrowings.
- It can be seen that supply chain management and lean management systems focus on efficiencies which result in lowering working capital requirements. For example, Adidas, one of the world's leading footwear manufacturers (factories in 60 + countries), launched a lean management programme in 2002 to reduce the 'order cycle'[5] from 90 days to 60 days. On successful implementation, whilst net sales increased 10%, inventories were down 12% from a year earlier. No wonder they were able to reduce net debt by 10%, as the working requirements dropped.
- Similarly, if conversion costs (e.g. labour cost) are a significant cost component, the values of work in progress, finished goods and debtors would be impacted by the changes in the conversion costs, ultimately impacting working capital.

[5] Number of days from initial request for a product to the date of delivery to any part of the world.

- Changes in profitability also will impact the working capital requirements. Other things remaining the same, assuming full retention of the profits in the business, broadly we can conclude that the increase in profits reduces the working capital requirements and vice versa.
- Last, but not least, the seasonal nature of business (e.g. winter cloth or ice cream) will also impact the working capital requirements.

## 12.7 WORKING CAPITAL, PROFITABILITY AND CASH FLOWS

Working capital movements are an important part of cash flows and in fact account for the bulk of cash movements. 'Audited financials' captures the 'net movements in the working capital components' as an essential part of the cash flow statement. The impact on cash flows of the various situations is summarized below:

(a) **Increase/Decrease in Working Capital Components**: An increase in current asset components such as stock, debtors and other current assets and reduction in trade and other current creditors results in absorption of cash and hence results in additional cash requirements. A decline in current assets and increase in current liabilities have the opposite effect.

(b) **Change in Volume/Input Prices**: As we discussed earlier, whilst other things (e.g. profit margins and trade terms) remain the same, usually an increase in volume and/or input prices results in additional cash requirements and vice versa.

(c) **Change in Trade Terms**: Favourable changes (e.g. lower credit period to customers/ higher credit from suppliers) in trade terms reduces the cash requirement while an adverse change in trade terms increases it.

(d) **Changes in Profitability**: Although higher volume necessitates additional cash injection into working capital, if profitability improves, the additional cash requirement due to the incremental volume (of operations) would be proportionately lower. Similarly, whilst reduction in volume releases working capital, the losses or reduction in profitability may not fully translate into reduction in cash requirements.

Whilst the working capital impacts (a), (b) and (c) are straightforward, (d), i.e. that of profitability, is bit circuitous, which is explained by way of the following example.

**Example 12.8**

PQR Ltd has sales of $1,000m. The cost of sales (COS) is $700m. The admin expenses, including depreciation ($30m), are $250m. Accordingly, the net profit for the year is $50m ($1,000m – $700m – $250m) with a net profit margin (NPM) of 5%. Trade terms are: (i) stock holding period @ 30 days, (ii) debtors collection @ 90 days, (iii) creditors payment period @ 60 days. Ascertain the impact on the cash flows if:

(a) Volume increases by 50% (admin expenses at $375m).

(b) Volume increases by 50% while NPM also improves to 14% (admin expenses at $350m).

(c) Volume declines by 30% and NPM drops to negative 26% (admin remains at the base case level i.e. $250m).

**Solution**

The impact on the cash flows (CF) is calculated below:

| Particulars | Case I<br>*Vol. Increase @50%*<br>*NPM @ 5%* | Case II<br>*Vol. Increases @50%*<br>*NPM @ 14%* | Case III<br>*Vol. Declines*<br>*NPM – 26%.* |
|---|---|---|---|
| Net Profit *(see Working Note a)* | 75 | 205 | −180 |
| Add: Depreciation | 30 | 30 | 30 |
| **CF before w/c changes (i)** | **105** | **235** | **−150** |
| *Movement in w/c Components: (See Note b)* | | | |
| *Change in Stock* | −29 | −20 | 6 |
| *Change in Debtors* | −123 | −123 | 74 |
| *Change in Creditors* | 58 | 40 | −12 |
| ***Net Working Capital Changes (ii)*** | **−95** | **−103** | **68** |
| **Net Cash from Operations (i + ii)** | **10** | **132** | **−82** |

**Comments**

As is evident from the above, while maintaining the same trade terms (stock holding period, debtors collection period and creditors payment period) the profitability changes and variations in volume impact the cash flows. The findings can be summarized as follows:

- **Case 1**: Due to the 50% growth in the business, there is an increase in stock and debtors (vs. base case – see working notes) resulting in cash outflows, shown in negative figures above. A higher volume of business results in higher creditors, which has a positive effect on cash flow to the extent of $58m and hence the net cash impact because of changes in the working capital components is $95m cash outflow. However, the 50% increase in volume improves the net profit to $75m which along with depreciation of $30m results in a net cash surplus of $10m from operations.
- **Case II**: In this case debtors remain the same as in Case 1; however mainly because of the sharp improvement in the net profit to $205m, there is a substantial net cash surplus of $132m from operations.
- **Case III**: A drop in volume results in lower cash outlay in inventory and receivables, which mainly drives the net cash release from working capital of $68m. However, the erosion of profitability and consequent losses result in the cash deficit from operations of $82m.

**Working Notes**

***(a) Calculation of Net Profit***

| Particulars | Base Case | Case I *Vol. Increase @ 50%* *NPM @ 5%* (A) | Case II *Vol. Increases @50%* *NPM @ 14%* (B) | Case III *Vol. Declines* *NPM – 26%.* (C) |
|---|---|---|---|---|
| Sales | 1,000 | 1,500 | 1,500 | 700 |
| Less: COS | 700 | 1,050 | 945 | 630 |
| Less: Other Expenses* | 250 | 375 | 350 | 250 |
| Net Profit | 50 | 75 | 205 | –180 |
| NPM | 5% | 5% | 14% | –26% |

*includes depreciation and other non-cash charge of 30 K.

***(b) Calculation of W/c Components – Changes in Accordance with the Volume***

| Particulars | Base Case | Case I *Vol. Increase @ 50%* *NPM @ 5%* (A) | Case II *Vol. Increases @ 50%* *NPM @ 14%* (B) | Case III *Vol. Declines* *NPM – 26%.* (C) |
|---|---|---|---|---|
| Stock (30 days)* | 58 | 86 | 78 | 52 |
| Debtors (90 days) | 247 | 370 | 370 | 173 |
| Creditors (60 days)* | 115 | 173 | 155 | 104 |

*based on cost of goods sold.

## 12.8 WORKING CAPITAL RISKS

Whether trade credit or bank finance, the provider of working capital facilities is exposed to credit risk, which necessitates credit risk analysis to understand the risk being undertaken. However, working capital, because of its uniqueness, has certain exclusive risks, which are discussed below and depicted in Figure 12.4.

### 12.8.1 Over-trading

As the name implies working capital difficulties emerge from the fact that the business entity tends to do business beyond its capacity. The entity expands volume excessively in relation to the finance provided by the owners. The impact of expanding 'too much too quickly' is that it will be impossible to generate funds from own operations quickly enough to meet the working capital demands of the business. Consequently, the firm relies on external finance heavily, either by over-stretching creditors or higher bank borrowings. Given the fact that the creditors won't provide support beyond a certain limit and are reluctant to assume risks involved in extending credit disproportionate to owners' funds, a liquidity crisis follows.

As the firm focuses on volume growth there are other perils such as drag on margin, low quality debtors, etc., which will further worsen the liquidity situation. Besides tarnishing its business image, the business entity will struggle to settle bills, pay wages and other expenses or would be forced to raise money from costlier sources or would have to offer exorbitant discounts to debtors to speed up collection. Fall in inventory levels due to lack of creditors' support and increased purchase costs (loss of discounts) could be further fall-out of over-trading.

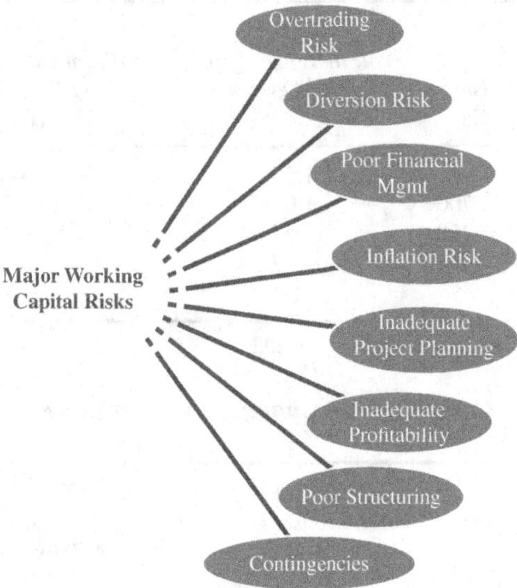


**Figure 12.4** Working Capital Risks

The financial statements reveal whether a firm is over-trading or drifting towards this malaise: (i) If balance sheet variables such as stocks, debtors, creditors or short-term borrowings show sharp increase with dramatic increase in turnover usually without any increase in profitability, that requires further investigation. (ii) Examination of certain financial ratios such as Operating Profit Margin (OPM), Sales to Operating Capital Employed (SOCE), current ratio, quick ratio, working capital/sales ratio, gearing, leverage and interest rate cover can indicate the stage of over-trading. Over-trading symptoms, at the initial stages, can be cured easily, while at the later stages, a thorough reorganization would be the only option – such as sale of certain non-core/fixed assets and/or additional equity injection and/or reduction of the scale of operations.

**Example 12.9**

The following financial highlights have been extracted from Hypothetical Steel Traders Ltd, one of the borrowing customers. Does this customer display the over-trading malaise?

| $ '000s | FY 20X9 | FY 20X0 |
|---|---|---|
| Turnover | 145,109 | 245,300 |
| Operating Profit | 10,283 | 6,803 |
| Profit Before Tax (PBT) | 8,503 | 1,572 |
| Gross Debt | 19,713 | 54,010 |
| Capital and Reserves | 25,651 | 27,004 |
| Net Cash From Operations (NCFO) | 441 | (9,274) |
| Gross Debt/TNW (Gearing Ratio) | 77% | 200% |
| Current Ratio | 1.4x | 1.0x |
| Acid Test | 1.1x | 0.4x |
| Operating Profit Margin (OPM) | 14.9% | 2.8% |
| Interest Cover | 3.8x | 1.2x |

**Solution**

Deteriorating profitability as reflected in the OPM and PBT[6] and liquidity squeeze evident in the current and quick ratios coupled with negative NCFO are matters of concern. Further the sharp increase in bank borrowings (possibly to fund the higher inventory and debtors) and decline in the interest cover ratios adds to the discomfort. Prima facie this customer shows symptoms of 'over-trading'. A meeting with the customer is required to understand whether the customer is blissfully ignorant about the troubles that lie ahead in their enthusiasm to drive up volume. The working capital cycle and changes in the stock holding period, debtors collection period and creditors payment period are also to be investigated.

### 12.8.2 Diversion Risk

Diversion risk refers to the use of working capital funds for non-working capital purposes. Usually all funds – long term and short term, profits or owners' funds or external liabilities – come first into the working capital pool. Hence, a clear distinction and an awareness of the nature of funds is a must and considered as the hallmark of good financial management. All changes in working capital components and the cash movements in long-term items (such as long-term loans, sale/purchase of fixed assets, etc.) are normally reflected in working capital. For instance, when a share issue is launched to finance an expansion, initially the moneys will be placed in a bank account, which is a current asset, a working capital component. Thereafter it will be used to fund long-term assets such as acquisition of fixed assets, technology, etc.

Many firms confuse or ignore this distinction ending up using the working capital funds for other purposes, resulting in diversion, which ultimately leads to a liquidity crisis, defaulting on bank loans, stretching creditors with resultant costs and ultimately gaining a bad name in business circles or even business collapse.

Diversion can occur in two ways: (i) diversion to non-working capital purposes, within the business and (ii) diversion of the working capital funds, out of the business. Whilst the former is traceable to the aggressive expansion or investment in non-core activities or non-working capital purposes, the latter is a case of withdrawal of funds from the business, either directly or indirectly. Indirect means of withdrawal include advances to related parties, accommodation with third parties, over-invoicing of the purchases, under-invoicing of the sales, etc. For example, assume ABC Ltd is a gold wholesaler and retailer with hundreds of retail jewellery outlets. Being in retail business, they have a negative working capital situation (we have covered 'negative working capital' earlier in the chapter). ABC Ltd has a sister concern PQRY Ltd engaged in real estate business. As PQRY identified a lucrative short-term real estate investment opportunity, ABC Ltd advanced cash to the sister concern for investing in real estate activity. However, this investment soured due to a downturn in the real estate market. Unable to liquidate this investment, PQRY is not in a position to repay the advance from ABC Ltd, which could put ABC Ltd into liquidity troubles. The author is familiar with several such instances of diversion of funds into real estate or financial investments, where the subsequent drop in real estate or financial investment values resulted in miserable situations.

The remedy lies in awareness of the importance of cash to be deployed in working capital to keep the business running. Long-term funding requirements should be met from long-term sources. Similarly, indiscriminate withdrawals should be avoided.

[6]Net Profit (before tax) Margin may be calculated, i.e. PBT/Sales.

### 12.8.3 Inadequate Financial Management

As we have seen earlier, working capital is dynamic and not fixed. A clear understanding of the working capital needs of the business and maintaining adequate funds in working capital without diverting it to other activities is yet another hallmark of efficient working capital management. The dynamism is also traceable to the underlying activities such as purchase of materials and meeting related material handing expenses, selling and associated costs, collection skills, buyer/supplier/bank rapport, negotiation skills, stock management techniques, etc. are all part of working capital management. If the skills are lacking, it may lead to antagonizing major customers, suppliers, bankers, government authorities, etc. whose actions can result in working capital problems. Additionally, the finance manager should be talented in raising sufficient financial resources, their proper allocation (respecting the maturity principle – i.e. financing long-term needs with long-term sources) and funds flow management along with reasonable financial forecasting skills.

### 12.8.4 Inflation Risk

As we have seen in Chapter 5, inflation risk is one of the potent external risks faced by business firms. One of the areas it impacts is working capital. The impact is more serious if inflationary pressures on expenses outpace sales, which is true for businesses experiencing strong competition as rivals attempt to retain market share. This inevitably impacts cash flows. In such cases, cash outflows increase with higher costs while cash inflows will not increase proportionately, impacting the working capital pool.

### 12.8.5 Inadequate Provisioning of Working Capital in Original Project Costs

Without the necessary working capital the entire investment in plant and machinery may come to naught. Working capital assumptions should reflect the market with contingencies. For instance if the average credit period in the market is two months, at least for the initial one year period the working capital should be based on three months' assumption for the new project. The author is familiar with cases where the owners insisted on sticking to the original plan despite suggestions to be more liberal in working capital estimation and their contribution, only to find them facing severe working capital shortages once the project went on stream. As the project had many shareholders, additional shareholder funding was delayed since it had to go through several legal and routine procedures of shareholder meetings and presentations to convince the hesitant shareholders to put more money into the project. This resulted in a delay in utilizing the additional working capital lines by banks. Such situations result in lost business and tight liquidity, which finally lead to the rescheduling of term loans as well. Had sufficient working capital been provided in the original project cost, these hassles could have been avoided.

### 12.8.6 Losses and Reducing Profitability

This is yet another source of putting businesses in working capital difficulties. Massive losses make the working capital vanish in no time while profits add to working capital. This can be illustrated by a simple example. Suppose a firm buys on credit goods worth $10,000 and sells for 25% profit. The resultant debtor and creditor of this transaction are $12,500 and $10,000 respectively. The liquidity ratio is 12,500/10,000 = 1.25:1 showing comfortable liquidity and hence minimum working capital risk, other things remaining the same. On the other hand, see what happens if the firm is forced to sell at 25% loss. Then the debtors' collectable would be just $7,500/- while the firm has to meet the liability of $10,000/-. (Also refer to Case III in Example 12.8 earlier in the chapter.)

Any drop in profitability that can be captured by profitability ratios (i.e. gross profit margin, operating profit margin and net profit margin as discussed in Chapter 8). Low profits result in less internal cash generation and in the event of wafer thin margins or losses the business may require external support. Whilst this may be acceptable in the short run, the long-run scenario demands reasonable profitability for proper working capital management.

### 12.8.7 Inadequate Structuring of Facilities by Banks

Often banks/financiers must share the blame for creating working capital problems and the risks associated with it. It clearly shows the need for banks to understand the business and the working capital. One example would be the short-term facilities (letters of credit, short-term loans, etc.) extended by the bank assuming a working capital cycle of 120 days, while in reality the cycle is 180 days. When banks arrive at the working capital requirement of customers, a lot of variables such as shipping time, lead time in the case of documentary credits, conversion cycle of raw material into finished goods, stocking period, credit terms to customers, etc. are to be factored in. This emphasizes the need for sound understanding of the customers' business by the lending/credit executives in the bank. 'Know Your Customer' should be strictly adhered to by banks and FIs in all respects. Any misunderstanding on any critical point can result in wrong structuring of facilities causing difficulties to both parties.

### 12.8.8 Unforeseen Contingencies

Equipment breakdown, riots, floods, etc. cause unexpected expenses absorbing working capital. For instance suppose that major repairs to a key machinery item had to be done and the business utilized the one month's collections from debtors (and bank overdraft facility) towards it. In such cases, it is evident that the current assets will dwindle without a corresponding drop in current liabilities. Unforeseen contingencies can deplete working capital or halt the proper movement of the working capital components.

## 12.9 IMPACT OF WORKING CAPITAL RISKS

The abovementioned list of working capital risks is not a complete list, i.e. other types of risk are possible depending upon the circumstances. In all cases, liquidity is impacted as the size of the working capital pool and associated elements is impacted resulting in a liquidity crisis, usually in the form of lack of sufficient resources. Payment of dues to employees, suppliers and other creditors, repayment of loans and all imaginable short-term liabilities become problematic with associated costs and difficulties. Massive discounts to debtors for prompt collection, paying penal interest to banks on the over-dues, threats of legal suits, defaults on due date and damage to reputation in business circles are not desired by any good businessman.

From the creditors' point of view, working capital risks enhance credit risk, given the insufficient liquidity to meet the commitments on time. Hence, the best strategy for creditors is to avoid credit exposure to customers showing working capital risks unless they can be mitigated.

A liquidity crisis, triggered by working capital risks, is like a vicious circle as it chokes up further working capital flows, i.e. possible tightening of credit terms by suppliers or cancellation of credit lines by banks. This could result in non-replenishment of stock, harassing the debtors to pay up or displeasing the creditors by inordinate delay in the settlement of dues.

Usually at firm level, several tricks and crisis management tactics are used to overcome liquidity problems. It is better for the credit executives to be aware of such measures adopted by the obligors, because such measures will themselves sometimes act as warning signs. This includes the following:

- Large discounts to buyers.
- Selling more on a cash basis – not only finished goods, but a part of the raw materials as well.
- Sale and lease back of fixed assets.
- Rigorous collections.
- Selling debts to a factor, at somewhat unfavourable terms to the customer.
- Making only essential purchases.
- Scramble for short term funds.

## 12.10 WORKING CAPITAL RISK MITIGANTS

The following are some of the mitigants which, if introduced, can avoid potential working capital risks.

### 12.10.1 Covenants

Working capital related covenants can ensure that adequate funds remain invested in the working capital. The covenants must be designed in such a manner that the business will be compelled to keep adequate current assets to support current liabilities with sufficient NWC. The usual financial covenants include a mix of (i) minimum current ratio, (ii) quick ratio, (iii) profit retention ratio or maximum dividend payout, (iv) minimum tangible net worth, (v) maximum capital expenditure, (vii) working capital to total assets, etc.

Proper implementation of covenants can mitigate working capital risks. For instance, a minimum current ratio covenant of 2:1 ensures a double level of current asset vs. current liabilities (adequate current assets to meet current liabilities) while a CAPEX covenant restricts the investments in projects/capital assets (prevents/mitigates diversion risk). Dividend restricting covenants ensure prudent financial management by retaining sufficient profits in the business.

### 12.10.2 Cancellation/Tightening/Temporary Freeze of Facilities

One of the methods of avoiding working capital risk is to cancel fully or reduce the credit facilities involved, which ought to alert the customer to the business realities and avoid working capital mismanagement. Accordingly, the manufacturer can refuse to supply goods to its erring customer except on a cash basis or with appropriate mitigants such as letters of credit/guarantees. Banks can similarly refuse credit lines unless fully secured by acceptable collateral. Alternatively, a temporary freezing or reduction may be implemented so that the obligor feels the pinch, which could improve working capital related behaviour.

### 12.10.3 Increase Pricing

Both financial and non-financial businesses can use the pricing policies effectively as a mitigant to manage the credit risks involved in working capital facilities. If the risky obligor still wants the credit, they can have it at a higher price or seek an alternative supplier. However, it is to be noted that once credit is granted the supplier is taking exposure to a relatively poor quality credit risk and it is always advisable to adopt a cautionary approach (seek other credit enhancement measures) while using pricing as a mitigant.

### 12.10.4 Liquidation of Non-Core Assets

As highly stressed working capital risks impact liquidity in a debilitating manner, one of the actions to infuse liquidity is to find resources within the organization. Liquidation of all non-essential assets of the business is one of the best ways to find the additional liquidity that is badly needed.

### 12.10.5 Owners' Injection/Strengthening Net Working Capital

If there are insufficient non-core assets to liquidate, then the only alternative left is to seek out funds from the owner to bolster the liquidity conditions. This has many positive sides compared to relying on further short-term borrowings, such as (a) there is no commitment of due dates and (b) it inspires confidence in creditors as they view this as evidence of owners' support and interest in the business.

### 12.10.6 Improvement of Working Capital Management

Appointing good finance managers can really make a big difference. Whilst poor financial management can ruin a good situation, a capable finance manager can tide over even difficult working capital situations with ease, anticipating and planning cash flow movements in the light of seasonal variations or the impact of external/industry risks in a proactive manner. One of the hallmarks of good financial management is the understanding of the need for matching the asset/liability maturity pattern and having sufficient long-term sources at hand to invest long term. Creditors – especially banks and FIs – may make appropriate conditions (e.g. appointment of capable finance managers with the approval of the lending bank) while extending working capital facilities.

### 12.10.7 Insure against the Risk from Unforeseen Contingencies

Most of the contingencies (e.g. loss of stock by fire) that absorb liquidity can be covered by proper insurance coverage – e.g. stock insurance, credit insurance of debtors, etc.

The above suggestions are just for guidance and in real life the mitigants must be sought depending upon the nature of the business and/or the underlying risk. The major factor in determining the successful implementation of the mitigants will be determined by integrity, honesty, commitment and capability of the management team of the obligor.

## 12.11 WORKING CAPITAL FINANCING

Banks and other short-term credit institutions are the major suppliers of working capital finance. Working capital financing occupies a very prominent position in the world financial system. Banks compute working capital financing in depth as they are in the business of credit 'risk taking' while non-finance suppliers extend credit as a corollary to their main business.

**Working capital finance** refers to an entire spectrum of financing instruments developed by commercial bankers over time to fund and control the proper end utilization by borrowers – mainly trade and manufacturing businesses. A properly structured working capital finance facility goes a long way in reducing the credit risk and is often preferred by banks over an overdraft. Letters of credit, factoring, bill finance, import and export finance are some of the major categories. A sound understanding of the operating cycle of the business goes a long way in ensuring proper structuring of short-term working capital facilities. Let us link the various common working capital financing methods to the operating cycle, which we described earlier in this chapter.

Sound understanding of the working capital cycle of the customer enables the bank to structure proper facilities. Based on the operating cycle (Figure 12.5), the following facilities may be considered:

1. A customer can seek a usance letter of credit (90/120/180 days) to cover the time period until the suppliers are settled.
2. If the customer does not have funds to settle the trade creditors (i.e. suppliers) funds may be extended against the goods or materials bought from the supplier. This facility is known by different names in different countries or regions (stock loans, clean import loan, key loan or trust receipts usually represent the credit facilities extended to settle the supplier).
3. Once the sales take place, the stock gets converted into trade debtors. At this stage various credit facilities secured by the debtors can be considered. Bill/invoice discounting, factoring, loans against the assignment of debtors, etc. are examples of such facilities. If the debtors are covered by L/Cs issued by other first class banks, then it acts as a very strong credit risk mitigant, i.e. collection risk is fully alleviated.
4. All working capital facilities, including stock loans and loans against debtors, are rolled over several times during the year i.e the borrower has to repay the working capital loans at the end of the working capital cycle; however, they will draw it again at a later date. In real life, it may be possible to accurately match the roll-over of working capital facilities to the operating or working capital cycle; it is undisputable that structuring of the working

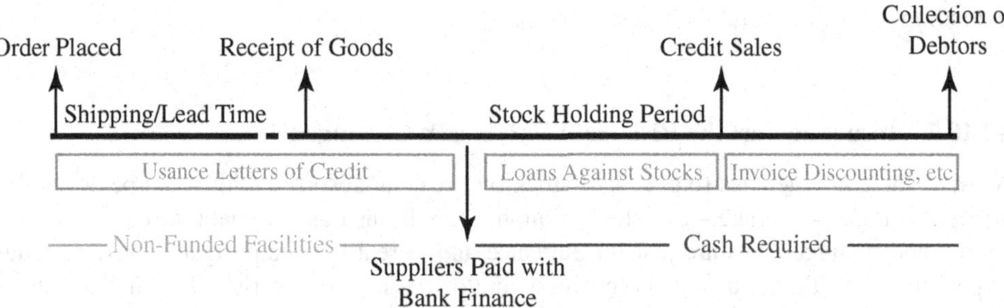


**Figure 12.5** Non-Funded and Funded Facilities in an Operating Cycle

capital facilities along the operating cycle facilitates close control over the credit utilization and minimizes the diversion risk. It is worthwhile mentioning that ignorance of the proper operating cycle by relationship/credit managers can be taken advantage of by unscrupulous customers/borrowers to obtain over-financing, with predictable consequences.

Sometimes, the creditors will demand payment when the title to the goods[7] is handed over to the customer. In such cases, 'At sight letters of credit' are to be opened in which case the following may be suggested as one of the possible means of facility structuring. In such cases, the operating cycle and possible credit facilities would appear as depicted in Figure 12.6:

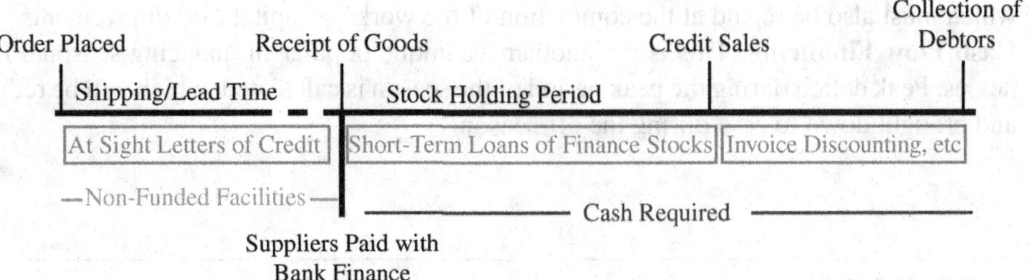


**Figure 12.6** Operating Cycle for 'At Sight' Letter of Credit

Commercial banks and other financial institutions play a major role in working capital financing and have devised various forms of lending, a few of which are described briefly below:

- **Asset Financing**: Banks sometimes prefer to finance a particular item of working capital on a standalone basis. This ensures more control over the purpose of the facility extended, which translates into lowering of credit risk. In several countries, working capital finance has been traditionally linked to current assets such as stock and debtors with prescribed margins, ranging between 20 and 30%. However, this has two drawbacks: (i) the focus on current assets often results in overall financial standing being overlooked; (ii) the suppliers' credit can be often downplayed by the borrower, as the banks inspect the books maintained by the customer – e.g. stock and stock register. The borrower is in a position to manipulate the stock position by not recording (or postponing the entry of) a purchase transaction[8] in the accounting books, but including those goods in the warehouse stock register. This is also the case with goods sent to the customer by the supplier on an 'on consignment' basis. Ascertaining of the suppliers' claim on the stock lying in the premises of the customer, although not impossible, is fraught with difficulties. Moreover, bankers may lack the time and skill set to properly evaluate the asset values or to understand the existence of double-financing. In such cases, it may be appropriate to call upon the external expertise of consultants e.g. a stock inspection by a bank-appointed consultant or auditor.
- **Short Loans**: This refers to the specified amount extended for a definite period of time. From the credit risk point of view, banks generally favour loans because (a) loans are easier

[7] Interested readers may refer to Uniform Customs and Practice (UCP) 600 to understand the internationally accepted norms of letters of credit.

[8] For readers with advanced accounting knowledge, in such cases the customer would delay (or skip) the following entry in the books of accounts 'Debit Purchases and Credit Suppliers'. However, the goods received would be taken into the warehouse and the warehouse stock register would show the goods as part of the stock in hand.

to monitor and control than overdrafts and (b) loans are granted for a specific purpose, and the repayment period and source of repayment are usually made known to the bank by the borrower at the time the facility is agreed upon.

- **Overdraft**: A facility whereby the customer can overdraw the current account up to an agreed limit. The customer can at any time deposit money into the account to reduce the outstanding balance or he can draw out money whenever he needs it as long as he does not exceed the limit. But the management of the credit risk of the overdraft facility is relatively difficult for the lender, in view of the lack of control over the end use. Hence, a working capital financier ought to minimize the overdraft limits, say to meet the incidental expenses related to working capital components – e.g. to meet the freight charges or insurance costs, which must also be repaid at the completion of the working capital cycle/movements.
- **Cash Flow Financing**: This is yet another technique popular in financing seasonal businesses. Peak deficit during the peak period of the season is calculated, which will be reduced and brought down to zero during the off-season.

## CASE STUDY

The credit department of XYZ Bank is worried about the poor performance of APC Ltd in FY 20X2. Summarized financial statements of APC Ltd are given below.

### Summarized Balance Sheets

$ thousands

| Assets | 31.12.20X1 | 31.12.20X2 | Liabilities | 31.12.20X1 | 31.12.20X2 |
|---|---|---|---|---|---|
| Net Fixed Assets | 114,102 | 113,102 | Paid up Share Capital | 70,000 | 70,000 |
| Current Assets – Stock | 24,751 | 20,773 | Retained Earnings | 8,485 | 1,080 |
| Trade Debtors | 9,734 | 6,768 | Long Term Loans | 66,126 | 59,135 |
| Cash and Bank | 1,077 | 1,839 | Current Liabilities - Trade Crs. | 4,820 | 4,050 |
| Other Current Assets | 1,279 | 805 | Short Term Loans | 1,556 | 4,164 |
| Investments in a JV | 5,000 | 5,000 | Other Creditors | 4,956 | 9,858 |
| | | | Non-Current Creditors | - | - |
| **Total Assets** | **155,943** | **148,287** | **Total Liabilities** | **155,943** | **148,287** |
| **Summarized Profit and Loss Accounts** | | | **Summarized Cash Flow Statement** | | |
| **Particulars** | **FY 20X1** | **FY 20X2** | **Details** | | **FY 20X2** |
| Sales | 73,749 | 51,462 | Operating Profit | | (2,843) |
| Less: Cost of Sales | (56,946) | (47,687) | Add: Non Cash Expenses 10,125 | | 10,125 |
| Gross Profit | 16,803 | 3,775 | Chg. In Stock | | 3,978 |
| Less: Admin Expenses | (6,384) | (6,618) | Chg. In Drs | | 2,966 |
| Operating Profit | 10,419 | (2,843) | Chg. In Crs | | (770) |
| Less: Interest | (2,307) | (4,562) | Chg. In Other CA/CL | | 5,376 |
| PBT | 8,112 | (7,405) | **Net Operating Cash Flows** | | **18,832** |
| Less: Tax | - | - | Less: Dividends | | - |
| PAT | 8,112 | (7,405) | Less: Interest and Tax | | (4,562) |
| **Reconciliation of Profits** | | | Net Investing Cash Flows – Fixed Assets | | (9,125) |
| Opening Retained Profits | 2,344 | 8,485 | Net Inflow from Other Items | | - |
| Less: Dividends, etc. | 1,971 | - | Net Financing Cash Flows | | (4,383) |
| Closing Retained Profits | 8,485 | 1,080 | **Net Chg. in Cash/Liquid Funds** | | **762** |
| **Other Information:** | | | | | |
| Depreciation/Non Cash Exp. NA | | 10,125 | | | |

Having understood that the year FY20X2 was going to be difficult; the top management had taken a proactive decision early in the year to skip dividends for the year. Moreover, the management was careful to continue the same working capital policy and retained the same trade terms with suppliers and customers and maintained same stock policy. Management is very open in disclosures with the lending banks.

However, it is observed that despite the proactive steps taken by the management, cash flows were tight with higher reliance on short-term bank facilities. It is worrying to note that the current and quick ratios halved compared to the previous year. The credit department of the bank seeks reasons for increased borrowings and the drop in the ratios despite the proactive measures adopted by the company. Please bring out the major credit risks in working capital management. Also identify and suggest risk mitigants and the next steps to be taken.

**Solution**

***1. Movements in working capital pool and relevant ratios:***

| Working Capital Pool Movements | | Ratio Analysis<br>Profitability Ratios | 31.12.20X1 | 31.12.20X2 |
|---|---|---|---|---|
| | **FY 20X2** | GPM | 22.8% | 7.3% |
| **Opening WC** | **25,988** | OPM | 14.1% | –5.5% |
| Add: Net Profit | (7,405) | **Working Capital Ratios** | | |
| : Depreciation/Non-Cash | 10,125 | Working Capital | 25,988 | 14,438 |
| Less: Dividends | – | Stock Holding Period | 159 | 158 |
| **Net Pool** | **28,708** | Debtors Collection Period | 48 | 48 |
| Change in Fixed Assets | (9,125) | Creditors Payment Period | 31 | 32 |
| Change in Term Loans | (6,991) | WC to Sales | 35% | 28% |
| Change in Bank Borrowings | 2,608 | WC to Total Assets | 17% | 10% |
| Change in Cash and Bank | (762) | **Liquidity Ratios** | | |
| **Closing Working Capital** | **14,438** | Current Ratio | 3.25 | 1.67 |
| | | Quick Ratio | **1.07** | **0.52** |
| | | **Capital Structure Ratios** | | |
| | | Debt to Equity Ratio | 0.99 | 1.09 |
| | | Gearing | 0.86 | 0.89 |

***2. Interpretation***

As is evident, the turnover (activity) ratios remained the same, evidencing the similar stock, debtors and trade creditor policies. But the inflows into the working capital pool dried up because of the net loss of $7.4m. However, the cash profit stood at $2.7m (net loss $7.4m + depreciation $10.1m) resulting in the working capital pool of $28.7m. Given the inadequate cash generation (due to net loss) for the year, the repayment commitments and routine CAPEX were met from this reduced working capital pool. The squeezing of working capital is evident in the increase in the 'other creditors' component (usually including accrued expenses such as salaries and this may reflect stress on liquidity forcing the company to delay paying salaries, etc.) while the short-term bank borrowings increased by $2.608m. We can conclude that the short-term bank borrowings were channelled to meet the repayment/CAPEX needs because there was no increase in the working capital components (stock and debtors); in fact both declined. Diversion of short-term borrowings for long-term purposes is evident.

***3. Overall the working capital risks are:***

(a) Diversion of working capital mainly towards CAPEX.
(b) Inadequate w/c mgmt. Further squeeze in working capital ought to be curtailed.
(c) Poor profitability (inadequate working capital might be a reason for low sales).
(d) NWC shrinkage (NWC dropped compared to the previous year).
(e) Increasing leverage.
(f) Current and quick ratios dropped due to the diversion of short-term funds along with the losses and increase in other creditors.

***4. Suggested mitigants/next steps are:***

Overall the situation requires close monitoring and control. Positive steps are to be initiated to bring the business back into profitability and to ensure proper working capital management and utilization of short-term bank borrowings. The following comforts/mitigants are available/suggested:

(a) Despite the increase, the leverage is still moderate.
(b) Non-core investments can be liquidated. Alternatively, a charge over the non-core and unencumbered assets of the company may be taken by the banks.
(c) Introduce covenants – current/quick ratio covenants and debt/equity or tangible net worth covenants may be introduced.
(d) Stipulate more long-term sources (injection of equity/long-term loans) to enhance NWC.
(e) If possible, convert a portion of the short-term borrowings into a medium-term working capital loan.
(f) Understand the turnaround strategy and ensure it is viable.
(g) Reduce the working capital lines in line with the reduction in turnover. Try to ensure that the working capital facilities are linked to the underlying trade transactions and are self-liquidating.
(h) Place the account under close monitoring. Monthly performance and financial information to be insisted upon. Further diversion of short-term funds to long-term uses must be prevented. Additional equity injection to be insisted upon.

## ✍ QUESTIONS/EXERCISES

1. What is the difference between operating cycle and cash cycle?
2. How do the following changes in working capital terms affect the cash conversion cycle: (a) favourable credit terms that allow the firm to pay its trade creditors more slowly, (b) increase in inventory turnover and (c) decrease in accounts receivable turnover?

3. What do you mean by negative working capital? Explain with examples.
4. What are the mitigation measures available to a bank to prevent (i) over-trading and (ii) diversion risk?
5. XYZA Private Ltd calculates that its operating cycle for last year was 98 days. The trade debtors amounted to $460,000/- on sales of $2.21 million. Calculate the inventory holding period.
6. Calculate operating cycle and working capital (cash) cycle from the following information:

| a. Account | Opening Balance | Closing Balance |
|---|---|---|
| b. Inventory | $21m | $19m |
| c. Accounts receivable | $23m | $22m |
| d. Accounts payable | $18m | $20m |
| e. Net sales during the year were $80m while cost of goods sold amounted to 70% of the sales. | | |
| Interpret the cash conversion cycle if the industry average is 90 days. | | |

7. Mr X has recently joined as Relationship Manager of PQRZ Bank. As he was going through the latest financial statements of Hypothetical Manufacturing Ltd, he found the following information:

   *$ in millions*

| Particulars | 31.12.20X8 | 31.12.20X9 |
|---|---|---|
| a. Average stock holding period | 75 days | 140 days |
| b. Average debtors collection period | 90 days | 187 days |
| c. Average creditors payment period | 92 days | 29 days |
| d. Tangible net worth | 25m | 11m |
| e. Bank borrowings | 12m | 27m |
| f. Profit for the year | 7m | 0.5m |

   Is there any deterioration in the working capital cycle during the year ended 31.12.20X9? Do you believe the credit risk has increased? Have the owners of the Hypothetical Manufacturing Ltd withdrawn funds from the business as dividends? Explain your views and possible mitigation steps, if required.
8. (a) Take a walk around the major business neighbourhood in your home town or city and identify the major features of the working capital cycle of a few businesses – for example, bakery, grocery, airlines, manufacturing company, retail trader, wholesale trader, etc. (b) Obtain the audited annual reports of a few listed (in the stock market) companies engaged in different business activities and calculate the operating cycle, working capital cycle and explain how the working capital requirements are funded.

# Part IV

# Credit Portfolio Risks

Awareness of credit portfolio risks facilitates construction of strong credit portfolios with minimal overall risk for a given return or maximum return for a given level of risk.

# 13
# Credit Portfolio Fundamentals

The modern day credit executive – banker, finance manager, financier, for example – cannot do justice to their profession unless they know Portfolio Credit Risks. Ignoring portfolio credit risks can have catastrophic impact, even resulting in bankruptcies. The failure of many banks and financial institutions across the world can often be traced also to poor credit portfolios. The credit portfolio is critical to all business enterprises having sizeable credit exposures. Most modern day businesses cannot exist without a credit portfolio. Proper understanding of credit portfolio risk is a key success factor in enterprises with significant credit assets.

## 13.1 CREDIT PORTFOLIO VS. EQUITY PORTFOLIO

Most of the portfolio management techniques evolved in the equity arena first, and were then adapted by other areas like commodities, foreign exchange and credit markets. Portfolio management techniques such as portfolio theorem, swaps, options, etc. are some of the prominent examples. Large financial institutions are devoting considerable resources to developing new models for portfolio management. With advances in technology, the efforts of many brilliant researchers in large financial institutions, and the accumulation of significant bodies of knowledge on credit experience and analysis, credit portfolio management tools are likely to become more sophisticated in years to come. Since portfolio techniques have mostly originated in the context of equity, it is better to make the distinction between equity portfolio and credit portfolio and proceed. The major similarities are (i) that credit and equity are two popular forms of capital and (ii) that both portfolios are impacted by both systematic and unsystematic risks.

The major differences are given below:

(a) **Whilst concentration of the equity portfolio[1] in a few names may be an acceptable risk, such action is not recommended for the credit portfolio**. As we will see later in the book every effort must be made to avoid any sort of concentration in a credit portfolio. The reason is that, unlike the equity portfolio, concentration is expensive for credit portfolios because of the small upside and large downside risk. Hence, wide diversification is a must in a credit portfolio.

(b) **Divergent risk/reward pattern**. The return (interest, commission charges, etc.) on a credit portfolio is fixed while that of the equity portfolio is unlimited depending upon the profits generated. The equity can participate in the entire profits after meeting other obligations. Hence, the probability of substantial returns exists in the equity portfolio, which is not the case with a credit portfolio.

(c) **Credit enjoys a prior claim on the assets of the business**. In the case of secured credit the priority increases and enjoys higher ranking as far as repayment of principal and interest is concerned. However, the equity holder will get their principal back only after satisfying all creditors. Equity has the lowest ranking in the event of liquidation of the business.

[1] Warren Buffet is famous for his quote 'Wide diversification is only required when investors do not understand what they are doing'.

## 13.2 CRITICALITY OF PORTFOLIO CREDIT RISKS

We have seen details about the individual firm credit risk and its components under the External, Industry, Internal and Financial (EIIF) risks model and how to evaluate them. Now it is time to focus on portfolio risks. While firm-level credit risk analysis attempts to establish the creditworthiness at obligor level, credit portfolio risk analysis focuses on a broader approach to credit risks and studies the credit risk behaviour of homogenous groups of obligors/credit assets.

No one can manage a credit portfolio efficiently unless the underlying portfolio credit risks are known. Portfolio management requires detailed knowledge not only of obligor credit risk exposures, but also portfolio specific risks. The portfolio perspective allows the credit risk management to adopt a top-down approach and understand the key drivers impacting the portfolio risk profile. Amongst others, it answers following questions:

1. Which are the correlated sectors within the portfolio?
2. Is there any concentration risk in the portfolio? If so, how can it be managed down?
3. What are the risky areas in the portfolio, in view of the changes in macroeconomic environment?
4. How much credit risk can the institution absorb?
5. Does it have adequate capital to take such a level of portfolio risk?
6. Which types of credit risks should the institution avoid?
7. What are the credit risks the institution is willing to underwrite?

These are all critical questions for the survival of an institution and proper answers are available only from the study of portfolio risks. Having understood the portfolio risks, appropriate risk mitigation measures can be taken to minimize the portfolio risks.

## 13.3 BENEFITS OF CREDIT PORTFOLIO STUDY

The study and examination of credit assets from the portfolio perspective is highly useful. Consequently, many enterprises, especially financial institutions, are increasingly measuring and managing the portfolio credit risks. The main benefits of credit portfolio risk analysis are given below.

### 13.3.1 Active Credit Portfolio Management

Credit assets are nowadays amenable to proactive management. Instead of holding the credit assets till maturity, they can be offloaded or sold during the intermediate period. Syndicated loans can be sold to other participants or a newcomer while the availability of credit derivatives and securitization has opened new doors for active credit portfolio management.[2] Assuming the credit risk of two assets is the same, if the low-return asset can swapped for a higher-return asset, then the credit portfolio's return will improve with no addition to risk. For all credit subportfolios with a given level of risk, the lender will select the one with the highest return. To take advantage of such opportunities, the following portfolio level questions are important:

(a) What is the portfolio risk – before and after the intended transaction?
(b) How does the change in portfolio mix impact the risk level?
(c) In the changing environment, which credit assets are to be bought and sold?

[2] Please see Chapters 18 and 19 for details.

One of the major benefits of a portfolio approach to credit risk management is its active management, which will enhance return and possibly reduce the overall credit risk. This type of portfolio level decision presupposes sound understanding of various portfolio dynamics.

### 13.3.2 Overall Credit Risk Reduction

The aggregation of all firm credit risks in a portfolio does not equal portfolio risk. In fact, proper risk management can reduce the portfolio risk below the total or average of firm credit risks. Whilst EIIF credit analysis looks at individual credit, increasing global/regional pressures, including competition among others, demanded a broader view of credit risk resulting in the portfolio approach. Firm credit risk, as discussed in Chapter 9, can be classified into different grades, denoted by alpha-numerals such as AAA, A1, BBB, B1, B2 etc. Unlike firm credit risk, portfolio credit risk is also impacted by certain other factors such as distribution of the credit exposures among industry, region, etc. The fundamental concept is roughly explained by the following example:

**Example 13.1**

A financial institution (or a large multi-product manufacturing company) has a portfolio of 100 credit customers enjoying short-term credit facilities. After strict credit assessment, the firm credit risk of all 100 obligors/customers is graded as 'medium'. What would be the portfolio credit risk in the following scenarios?

1. All concentrated in the same region/locality.
2. All from the same cyclical industry.
3. The portfolio is equally distributed between two different regions or countries separated by 2,500 km distance.
4. The portfolio is equally distributed among three different industry segments that are not related to each other.
5. The portfolio is equally distributed among different ten different regions or countries and from ten unrelated industries.

**Explanation**

Although all 100 customers are of acceptable credit quality, from a portfolio credit risk perspective scenarios (1) and (2) imply higher[3] portfolio credit risk with (5) being the least risky. The other two cases lie in between. More discussion on portfolio risks is taken up in later chapters.

The distribution, composition and dispersion of the portfolio components have significantly different ramifications as is evident from the dissimilar portfolio credit risks under the different circumstances mentioned above. Covariance or correlation of firm credit risks has a significant impact at portfolio level, which is one of the key topics in credit risk study at portfolio level. A clear idea about the aggregate behaviour of varying categories of credit assets and their overall impact on the portfolio is critical.

[3]Mainly because of higher concentration risk.

### 13.3.3 Optimizes Liquidity

Take the balance sheet of any bank or financial intermediary or any large business enterprise. A sizeable debtors/credit portfolio is a usual feature in most balance sheets. Liquidation of the receivables/debtors portfolio is a major source of cash flows to meet various commitments. Better liquidity is ensured by proper handling of the credit portfolio, which calls for understanding of portfolio credit risks.

This is critical if the credit assets are leveraged – viz. created with a significant amount of external obligations. This is most important for banks and financial institutions, where the lenders themselves are borrowers with high levels of leverage. An unexpected drop/deterioration of portfolio quality has destabilized, decapitalized and destroyed lenders. In the case of a credit crisis, a liquidity crunch is almost inevitable, especially if the underlying credit portfolio lacks quality. For example, during the 2008 Credit Crisis, several banks, finance companies, insurers, investment banks and lessors faced a liquidity crunch.

Banks create credit assets out of deposits from public or from inter-bank borrowings, all of which have contractual obligations. It results in an inevitable link between the solvency, maturity profile and quality of credit assets. The study of portfolio credit risks for assessing liquidity of a bank/financial institution/enterprise has become a necessity rather than an option.

### 13.3.4 Assists Sales and Marketing

The credit department, through portfolio analysis, can help Sales and Marketing understand where the best opportunities may exist to grow the business. Constant measuring and monitoring of portfolio risk not only ensures that the aggregate risk is managed within an acceptable range, but also influences portfolio composition/business development decisions. For example, if the sales team targets 25% growth of its current customer base, the portfolio manager can furnish valuable information on how the resulting credit exposure can be achieved with minimal increase in portfolio risk.

The opportunity to take on a slightly greater risk at 'firm' level becomes acceptable if the 'portfolio' risk (viz. overall risk pool) stays within an acceptable tolerance level. As the need to capture more markets in the face of increasing competition continues, the portfolio perspective attains more importance.

### 13.3.5 Insights into Sectoral Risk Exposures

Different sectors and industries in an economy display dissimilar behaviour patterns due to a wide range of factors. As we discussed in Chapters 5 and 6, the business cycles, external risks and industry risk affect the obligors. A large number of obligors in a portfolio is of no consolation, if the portfolio suffers over-exposure to shaky industries. It is too risky, as the obligors will definitely be impacted by a downturn in that industry, which would turn satisfactory firm credit risks into unsatisfactory ones, within a short span of time, impacting the portfolio.

It is well accepted that the overall credit risk changes with evolving changes in the macro economy. Hence, the credit portfolio risk ought to be understood in the context of possible impact to the various portfolio components in the face of changes, such as cyclical upturns and downturns, political risks, interest rate movements, tariff changes, global developments, foreign exchange fluctuations and so on.

These factors and prior bad debt experience will guide the portfolio managers to identify vulnerable sectors and accordingly certain industrial and economic sectors of the portfolio ought to be designated as high risk. In such instances, it is necessary to establish separate policies and procedures to limit/restrict the extent of such portfolio exposures.

### 13.3.6 Solves the Capital Dilemma

It is now becoming accepted that the quantum of capital should be linked to the risks undertaken, especially in banks and financial institutions. A bank balance sheet reflects its financial condition. Assets are the income-producing assets, e.g. loans. Liabilities like deposits and inter-bank borrowings along with the equity capital fund the assets. By definition, the capital of the bank equals assets minus liabilities. In banking, the term 'capital' is used instead of 'tangible net worth', which is usually used in accounting. These terms are synonyms.

**Example 13.2**

The following are simple balance sheets of two banks of identical size. Highly leveraged Bank A and low-leveraged Bank B have a total asset base of $1,000m. Both suffered a credit loss of $125m. However, the impact is very different. The details are given below:

| Bank A | | | | Bank B | | | |
|---|---|---|---|---|---|---|---|
| Liabilities | | Assets | | Liabilities | | Assets | |
| Deposits | 900 | Loans | 1,000 | Deposits | 600 | Loans | 1,000 |
| Capital | 100 | | | Capital | 400 | | |
| **Total** | **1,000** | **Total** | **1,000** | **Total** | **1,000** | **Total** | **1,000** |

**After credit loss of $125m**

| Bank A | | | | Bank B | | | |
|---|---|---|---|---|---|---|---|
| Liabilities | | Assets | | Liabilities | | Assets | |
| Deposits | 900 | Loans | 875 | Deposits | 600 | Loans | 875 |
| Capital | −25 | | | Capital | 275 | | |
| **Total** | **875** | **Total** | **875** | **Total** | **875** | **Total** | **875** |

In the case of Bank A, the capital is negative, which shows insolvency – i.e. the capital has fallen below zero. The bank's assets are not enough to repay its depositors. As it is insolvent, it would have to cease operations, unless recapitalized or bailed out by another healthier institution or the government. On the other hand Bank B continues to be solvent and can continue its operations. It is evident that high leverage is a risk. Since banks operate on thin margins (mainly the difference in margins between deposits and loans), in order to create value for shareholders, some amount of leverage is a must (i.e. unavoidable in banking business). Bank regulators, who are concerned about the cascading impact of bank failures on the overall economy, tend to prefer more capital (i.e. less leverage than the bank management, who prefer more leverage to add more value to shareholders). Accordingly, the bank regulators usually prescribe a minimum level of capital to be maintained by banks and financial institutions, which is the basis of 'Regulatory Capital' concept in the Basel Accords.

The credit portfolio has a critical role to play when deciding the amount of capital to be held by a bank. Accordingly, if a business enterprise wishes to pursue higher credit risks, a higher capital cushion is called for. This is especially true for banks and financial intermediaries, who are active in credit markets. Capital is relevant from a risk management perspective because it is a measure of owners' funds at risk in the business, which is expected to provide an incentive towards good governance as well. Calculation of the 'risk based capital requirement' is done in two ways:

**Regulatory Capital**: The central banks all over the world welcome more capital in banks' capital structure and have prescribed a minimum requirement in this respect, which is commonly known as Capital Adequacy Ratio/Regulatory Capital under the Basel Accords. The minimum level of regulatory capital is stipulated at 8% of the risk portfolio. We will discuss more about it later in Chapter 15. To put it briefly, regulatory capital aims at ensuring adequate resources available to absorb the losses. The higher the credit risk of the credit portfolio, the higher the capital required. Accordingly, a financial intermediary that comes under some kind of capital regulatory requirement ought to reduce the proportion of high risk credit exposures in the portfolio if it does not wish to maintain a higher level of capital.

**Economic Capital**: Economic capital is decided by each bank's (organization's) own internal plans. The calculation of economic capital is stated to be more scientific than regulatory capital as it focuses on prudent behaviour from the point of view of a single institution. Regulatory capital is put in place to ensure the stability of the banking system as a whole, rather than what constitutes prudent behaviour from the point of view of any single institution. Economic capital, which can be more or less than the regulatory capital, is usually calculated by statistical methods and is based on historical experience. Given its complexity, economic capital is computed only by sophisticated financial institutions, which are able to deploy resources towards advanced techniques. (Please see Chapter 15 for more elaborate discussion.)

### 13.3.7 Portfolio Management Strategies

A credit portfolio is a bunch of credit assets of different risk grades, belonging to different regions or countries and probably scattered among different industry/economic sectors. Against the backdrop of the macroeconomic environment and capital constraints, the portfolio manager ought to determine portfolio strategies such that the portfolio risk does not spiral out of control. Such strategies will provide preparedness to face all uncertainties through the construction of a balanced portfolio. This includes the study of the impact on portfolio credit risks due to changes in portfolio mix or external stimuli.

One of the unique advantages of the portfolio approach is the ability to identify where the potential of enhanced returns lies. For instance, business enterprises with well-defined portfolios having detailed sub-portfolio classifications (such as industry, region and customer sub-segments etc.), find it easy to identify which sub-portfolios provide the best credit returns. The portfolio managers in turn can devise strategies to realize the full potential of each sub-portfolio.

Another advantage of the portfolio approach is that appropriate risk management strategies can be devised. Hence many financial institutions invest resources to develop and implement sophisticated portfolio approaches to manage the credit risk. Awareness of portfolio risks enables identification, monitoring and control of risk concentrations and correlations, on an ongoing basis. Periodical review of the credit portfolio is to be undertaken, to consider portfolio risks such as:

- Growth or contraction in credit portfolio size.
- Vulnerability to any major external stimuli.
- Industry/borrower concentrations.
- Credit grade movements.
- Adequacy of provision for doubtful credit assets.
- Derivative exposures.
- Other related or current credit issues.

We believe that heavy concentrations in a credit portfolio are best avoided, however a few authorities consider industry concentrations to be a plus, arguing that specialization promotes better quality loans by developing the bank's expertise in a few industries. We believe that this is an inherently risky proposition because heavy concentrations in industries cause problems, especially during a general economic slowdown or downturn specific to those industries where risk is concentrated. However, at the same time over-diversification must be avoided – i.e. in the zeal for diversity, expansion into industries or geographies where the lending institution lacks experience and expertise may bring in challenges increasing the credit risk.

### 13.3.8 Credit Quality Issues

To monitor the credit quality of the loan portfolio, knowledge of portfolio risks is a must. It requires awareness of specialized industry exposures with higher risks, which ought to be managed carefully. Similarly, centres of expertise in specialized industries can be established pursuant to a portfolio approach in credit risk analysis. Some banks assign loans to credit officers by industry (consumer goods, media, health care, real estate and so on), allowing them to become experts in the respective industries within the credit portfolio. Where necessary, it is necessary to establish caps or manage down concentrations, which are considered to be excessive. It is better if banks operate within industry/sector/geographic thresholds, limiting and controlling credit exposures to attain the best mix of individual credit assets and portfolio safety. This process also includes the identification and tackling of potential vulnerabilities in the portfolio. Sound understanding of credit portfolio risks is indispensable to fulfil these tasks aimed at maintaining maximum credit quality.

All modern businesses with a sizeable credit portfolio seek to achieve optimum diversification to maintain and optimize credit quality. As we will discuss later in this book, diversification does not mean simply increasing the number of customers/obligors in the portfolio. Advanced diversification is a scientific function of identifying various credit asset correlations and minimizing the overall portfolio risk through intelligent diversification. In-depth knowledge of the portfolio credit risks is a prerequisite for the creation of an optimum diversified portfolio.

## 13.4 PORTFOLIO ANALYSIS

To undertake proper portfolio credit risk analysis, the portfolio representation in analytical format is of paramount importance. Usually the portfolio of banks, financial institutions and large companies has thousands of customers. Then for proper portfolio management of credit risk it is essential that the aggregate portfolio is sub-divided into appropriate sub-portfolios. Within the portfolio each sub-category represents a different level of risk and opportunity.

A sub-portfolio consists of credit assets with common characteristics such as similar size/industry/geographic location and so on, but may have different credit grades or probabilities of default (PD). Whatever sub-portfolios[4] are generated, credit risk grades may be superimposed on them to reflect the credit risk of the sub-portfolio. Accordingly, the portfolio representation might be done in such a manner that a homogenous cell further groups the exposures in a sub-portfolio having same credit risk grade.

**Example 13.3**

An example of a sub-portfolio matrix, which is based on two parameters – economic sector and risk grade – is as follows:

**Sub-portfolio Based on Economic Sector and Credit Risk (Grade)**

| Particulars | Grade 1 | Grade 2 | Grade 3 | Grade 4 | Grade 5 | Grade 6 | Grade 7 | Total |
|---|---|---|---|---|---|---|---|---|
| Government Sector | 32 | | | | | | | 32 |
| Banks and FIs | 56 | | | | | | | 56 |
| Farming/Agriculture | | | 6 | 19 | 1 | 3 | 3 | 32 |
| Manufacturing | 22 | 44 | 202 | 97 | 54 | 12 | 8 | 440 |
| Mining | | | 6 | | | | | 6 |
| Electricity | | 17 | 19 | 10 | | | | 46 |
| Hotels | | 19 | 21 | 22 | 5 | 2 | | 69 |
| Traders | 10 | 105 | 250 | 40 | 15 | 11 | 15 | 446 |
| Transportation | | 6 | 25 | 10 | 5 | 3 | 3 | 51 |
| Food | 7 | 35 | 80 | 40 | 5 | 4 | 2 | 172 |
| Construction | | 11 | 102 | 118 | 100 | 44 | 4 | 379 |
| Pharmaceuticals | | 10 | 52 | 32 | 22 | 5 | 11 | 130 |
| **TOTAL** | **127** | **247** | **761** | **388** | **207** | **84** | **46** | **1859** |

The highlighted cell is a homogenous cell, which shows that the largest concentration of credit is with traders and with credit grade 3. It accounts for more than 50% of the total traders' exposure. The homogenous cell of Construction is the largest among credit grade 4, which is a matter of concern. It appears that the sector risk is on the higher side with grade 4 and lower grades accounting for about 40% of the total sector exposure. The Electricity and Mining sectors are strong with all credit grades below 3. Whilst exposure to Government and Banks enjoys the safest rating, the profitability from the credit exposure need not be high compared to other sectors. A sub-portfolio of 'Economic Sector and Profitability' may be prepared for necessary answers. The advantage of the sub-portfolio approach is that it triggers questioning and provides a broader view and insight about the portfolio components and characteristics. (The reader may think about more possible angles to derive greater insight and information from the above table.)

In this way, the entire portfolio can be segmented into different sub-portfolios, by using appropriate criteria, as required. Some of the criteria are: (i) region/country; (ii) salesmen or

[4] A credit portfolio of a bank or large financial institution has different 'sub-portfolios' such as large corporate, listed corporate, middle market, small business, commercial real estate and so on.

relationship or account officers/managers; (iii) departments; (iv) exposure and profitability; (v) credit losses/bad debts/provisioning, etc. Fragmenting the total portfolio into various sub-portfolios and homogenous cells can be based on any logical criteria. Analyzing the portfolio data through charts and statistical tools will provide a lot of insight to craft facts into solutions.

The advantage is that it not only clearly displays the portfolio structure but it also enables further portfolio manipulations and calculations. From a historical perspective, credit risk migration tendencies, default/recovery patterns, impact of changing environment on the sub-portfolios and return on the sub-portfolios are some of the crucial areas which provide valuable insights to the portfolio managers. Based on the insights, portfolio managers can decide on appropriate strategies to enhance return or reduce risk or both at the portfolio level. It highlights dissimilar risk behaviour tendencies among various sub-portfolios and performance, amongst others. It also facilitates strategic decision taking by bringing out the potential areas within the portfolio to further business development and improve profitability.

## 13.5 CREDIT PORTFOLIO RISK VS. RETURN

All business enterprises undertake credit risk with a desire to earn a return. Is it more important to aim at enhancing return or reduce credit risks at portfolio level? In fact, in most cases the latter is the prudent decision in the context of credit risk. During the second half of the 20th century, several quantitative techniques were developed after Markowitz's pioneering work in 1950. (We will discuss the application of Portfolio Theory for credit risk management later in the book.) The aim of these methods is to maximize the return of the portfolio while minimizing or keeping the risk within an acceptable range. This requires a balancing of return and risk within the credit portfolio, asset by asset, sub-portfolio (group of assets) by sub-portfolio.

Credit portfolio risk management should give priority to the reduction of risk and then seek higher return. Whilst return is important, and is covered in a later chapter (on Credit Risk Pricing), it should be noted that the upside potential of a traditional credit asset is limited. Although the traded credit assets such as bonds can have capital appreciation (as well as depreciation), usually it is much lower than that offered by equity markets. Hence, simply pursuing higher return is meaningless or it will lead to inadvertent shouldering of equity risks without matching benefits, as occurred during the run up to the 2008 Global Credit Crisis.

Whilst the portfolio approach definitely can focus on profitability, it is safe for the credit portfolio managers to set the primary goal as the minimization of portfolio risks. It can be argued that the maximization of credit returns deserves only a secondary role. One essential fact which should always be remembered in credit is that a safe dollar is much better than a risky dollar. The portfolio managers strive to rein in portfolio risks by shuffling the portfolio, reducing credit limits to obligors, requiring altered collaterals, and other credit quality or portfolio enhancement measures. It is to be noted that a thorough understanding of the characteristics of the credit portfolio and the causes of portfolio risks is essential in selecting realistic portfolio goals and attaining them.

## APPENDIX: ORGANIZATIONAL CONFLICT IN CREDIT RISK MANAGEMENT

Usually, the firm credit risk analysis will be done at originator level – say a relationship management team; however, the portfolio credit risk analysis will be done by another team in charge of overall portfolio credit risk. For internal control purposes, the originators will not have the approval authority and this could lead to organization conflicts. The credit approval authority often rests with the portfolio management team.

Pressure tactics on the credit approvers is not uncommon, who may be called 'business stoppers' 'non-commercial' and 'unconstructive' by the frontline. It may be noted that both functions are complementary. Effective firm credit risk analysis and portfolio risk analysis are prerequisites for efficient credit risk management. It is interesting to note that sometimes there are situations when these two functions (origination and portfolio management), essential to ensure credit quality and hence the solvency of the financial institution, result in organization conflicts. It is sometimes argued that this conflict may be deliberately introduced so that healthy debates between both functions occur in order to arrive at better credit decisions. Two situations of possible organizational conflicts in credit risk management are given below:

**Case 1**: Bank XYZ suffered losses in a financial crisis. Accordingly the capital base is reduced to \$800m from \$950m. Assuming 8% capital adequacy, the risk assets Bank XYZ can hold are now \$10bn (\$800m/8%). However, the risk assets already held in the books exceed \$12bn and therefore Bank XYZ embarks upon a mission of reducing the credit book (instead of seeking more capital, which is not favoured by the shareholders and management, in view of the market conditions). In order to reduce the credit book, Bank XYZ can follow different methods:

- Exit customers from undesired sectors or that do not fall within the new strategy of the bank.
- Choose less risk weighted assets.
- Prefer non-funded assets to funded assets (i.e. lower risk weighted assets).
- Raise additional capital, so that it can continue with the current credit book (however, as stated above, this route is not preferred in this case).

The portfolio manager has been given the task of identifying assets to exit based on the strategy of reducing the credit book with strict deadlines. Imagine the portfolio manager tells a remote zonal office/branch to exit one of its large high profile customers. The relationship management team at the zonal office/branch resists highlighting several reasons and accuses Head Office (HO) of lacking understanding. This is an example of not uncommon organizational conflicts among the executives managing firm-level and portfolio-level credit risks.

**Case 2**: Mr Jain, a front line credit executive of Compliance Bank, visits his customer, ABC Ltd, a company with sound financials and a proven track record. During the discussions with the Finance Manager (FM), they express the desire to remove the CAPEX Covenant specifying a maximum \$15m as CAPEX p.a. FM highlights the following: (a) none of the four other banks have imposed such a covenant; (b) the covenant was introduced five years ago when the turnover and net profit were around one-third of the present; (c) as in the previous two years, the company would be reluctant to provide this information; (d) if the bank is bent upon having a covenant at all, then it should be fixed above \$30m, giving room for an annual depreciation charge of \$19m. Jain is eager to maintain this profitable relationship and knows that the customer is being courted heavily by several other competitor banks.The request put forward by Jain has been declined by the appropriate authority in credit portfolio management, as has been recommended by HO Credit Risk Department. Their reasoning included the following: (i) the existing covenant of \$15m is a tool to understand the potential diversion of funds from working capital facilities and hence cannot be waived and (ii) the sector risk is increasing and hence, such a covenant trigger may be kept in place to gauge the CAPEX plans of the customer. Jain complains that HO Credit portfolio management at head office is too conservative and wishes one of them would convey the message back to the company. Such instances of friction are to be avoided and such conflicts, if any, point to the need for better mutual understanding of the bank's goals and objectives as far as credit risk management is concerned. Both front line and portfolio executives should be supportive of each other in attaining the objectives. Credit risk managers ought to have two strengths – strong analytical skills and good communication skills so that they can tactfully explain their positions.

## ✍ QUESTIONS/EXERCISES

1. Discuss the similarities and differences in managing a portfolio of equity investments and credit assets.
2. Discuss the relevance of the portfolio approach to credit risk management given the fact that the banks and financial institutions themselves are borrowers with high levels of leverage.
3. Do you believe a study of various characteristics and features of the credit portfolio in a bank or financial institution would be beneficial for credit risk management? Explain your views.
4. Explain how the credit portfolio study would facilitate or assist the liquidity management of the financial institution or bank.
5. One of your credit colleagues argues that a bank needs to specialize and concentrate on lending to a few non-cyclical industries. The risk of concentration is mitigated by the non-cyclicality of the industries. Do you agree with this view? Please elaborate.
6. Explain how the credit portfolio approach is reflected in the calculation of regulatory and economic capital.
7. Hypothetical Bank Ltd's credit portfolio comprises only two customers. Customer A is a large dominant player in a non-cyclical food industry while Customer B is a conglomerate with multiple business interests. The credit portfolio manager of Hypothetical Bank argues that although there is some concentration risk, it is fully mitigated by the non-cyclicality of Customer A and the well diversified nature of Customer B. Do you agree? Explain your views.
8. Obtain the audited and detailed annual reports of large banks and financial institutions, listed on stock markets. Examine and identify their credit portfolio management practices.

# 14
# Major Portfolio Risks

The critical nature of portfolio credit risks is widely recognized. The portfolio approach to credit risk is one of the central themes of Basel Accords, which began in 1988. (Please see Chapter 16 for the Basel Accords.) During 2008, many US banks who stuffed their credit portfolio with sub-prime or sub-prime linked assets, watched helplessly as their credit portfolios failed.

Many financial institutions and banks in the Western world acquired entities as part of their expansion strategies; however this resulted in increased portfolio risk, which later proved disastrous. For example, during 2006, Wachovia Bank acquired Golden West Financial Corporation of Oakland, California for approximately $25 billion. One of the reasons for acquisition was to take advantage of exposure to the California retail banking presence. However, it added about $120 billion of residential mortgages to Wachovia's credit portfolio. Almost the entire Golden West mortgage portfolio consisted of Adjustable Rate Mortgages (ARM). ARMs suffered heavily during the sub-prime crisis and added to the woes of Wachovia Bank.

Similarly, the acquisition of Halifax Bank of Scotland (HBOS) during late 2008 brought a variety of credit portfolio level troubles to Lloyds TSB Bank (LTSB), a well-run conservative UK based bank. Subsequently, as the losses from HBOS accumulated, the merged entity had to rely on UK treasury support, resulting in 41% ownership by the UK government.

Understanding of portfolio risks is inevitable for proper management of credit risk. Credit portfolio risk is usually bifurcated into two as shown in Figure 14.1:

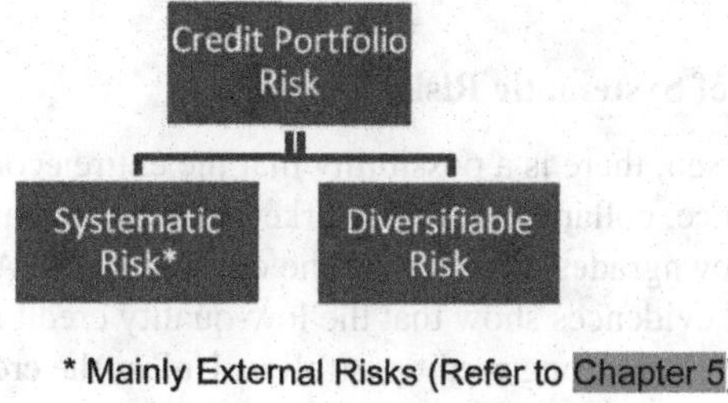


**Figure 14.1** Credit Portfolio Risks

## 14.1 SYSTEMATIC RISK

Systematic risk is the risk common to the economy or country as a whole and cannot be eliminated by combining the assets in a large and well-diversified portfolio. Hence, it is also known as non-diversifiable risk. Systematic risk is called systemic risk[1] or undiversifiable

[1] Some authorities make a distinction between systematic risk and systemic risk. Systematic risk means risk that cannot be diversified away and therefore affects most, if not all, market participants – e.g. business cycles. Systemic risk refers to the breakdown, mainly, of the economic system which could seriously impact national or international economic security or safety. In other words,

risk. Systematic risks originate in several forms, sizes and in severity. Systemic risk may apply to a certain region or country or to the entire global economy, as a whole. For example, the 2001 Argentina Crisis was mainly country specific while the 1998 Far East Asian Crisis impacted the entire region. On the other hand, the 2008 US Sub-prime Crisis almost impacted the entire global economy.

What is the relevance of systematic risk? If triggered, such risks can set off economic recession impacting all economic participants across the board.

### 14.1.1 Triggers of Systematic Risk

The external risks covered in Chapter 5 could be the triggers for such crises although a new set of triggers are also possible. A look at the major economic crises or disasters during the last two decades is a good guide. A number of global/regional crises happened during the 1990–2010[2] period spanning Asia, Europe and Americas. A few instances are:

- Japanese Crisis – late 1980s and early 1990s, main triggers included real estate and equity market issues.
- Latin American Crisis – 1990s, mainly due to hyperinflation, foreign exchange and debt issues.
- Far East Asian Crisis – 1997, mainly triggered by foreign exchange issues.
- Russian Crisis – 1998, mainly triggered by various factors leading to sovereign debt defaults.
- Argentina Economic Crisis – 2001, mainly caused by foreign exchange and debt issues.
- US Sub-prime Crisis – 2008, caused primarily by sub-prime assets and inflated real estate prices.

Whilst economic shocks and foreign exchange crisis have created problems in the past in many nations, it was war or political instability that contributed to risks in other countries.

### 14.1.2 Consequences of Systematic Risk

As systematic risks[3] worsen, there is a possibility that the entire economy would be shaken – drop in business confidence, collapse of stock market, increase in bankruptcies, sharp drop in asset prices and credit downgrades are a few of the consequences. As far as credit portfolios are concerned, empirical evidences show that the low-quality credit assets collapse first. This underscores the importance of strong credit portfolios. Unless the credit portfolios are strong, macroeconomic meltdowns may result in a series of successive and cumulative losses by banks and financial institutions or other market/industry participants and/or it may cause substantial volatility in asset or market prices leading to sharp drop in in banking sector and corporate

systemic risk focuses on risks to the financial system. For our discussion purposes, the impact of both on the credit portfolio is largely similar and hence we will use them interchangeably.

[2] Economic history is replete with similar instances as we travel back in time to the 1980s and prior decades when regional/global imbalances unleashed systematic risks, e.g. US loans and saving crisis (1980), Oil Crisis (1974), Second World War (1939–45), Great Depression (1929), etc.

[3] Sometimes systematic risks can be managed by proper financial governance by the concerned governments. For instance during 1991 India was on the brink of a sovereign default and foreign exchange crisis, which however was managed well by then Finance Minister Dr Manmohan Singh by raising secured loans in international markets pledging the gold reserves of the country and devaluation of the Indian Rupee. On the other hand, devaluation of the Thai Bhat finally led to the 1997 Far East Asian Crisis. The Argentinian sovereign debt default during 2001 was similar. It is pertinent to note that the US Fed averted a systemic crisis by rescuing LTCM in 1998.

liquidity. In a worst case scenario, bank bankruptcies will have severe repercussions on other interconnected market participants and would further dent the confidence in the economy.

A portfolio approach is essential to identify such specific and vulnerable sectors and credit asset categories, which may face catastrophic impact in such scenarios. This in turn will enable the portfolio to be balanced adequately such that the severity of differing macroeconomic meltdowns (systematic risks) is reduced.

The systematic risks provide a broad view that enables portfolio managers to be warned about how the dynamic environment and various forces acting therein are likely to impact the credit sub-portfolios. Determining exactly how the level of credit risk will be impacted by the evolving state of the macro-economy is a challenging task. Many countries have experienced a financial crisis after a period of strong economic growth, rapidly increasing asset prices and satisfactory economic statistics. The credit risk often appears low under boom conditions, but in reality, serious imbalances were building up. An in-depth awareness of systematic risks impacting credit portfolio risks ought to provide useful information to design appropriate policies to protect and enhance the quality of the portfolio, ensuring adequate returns.

## 14.2 DIVERSIFIABLE RISK

Diversifiable risk, also known as non-systematic risk or specific risk is the risk that may be eliminated by holding a large diversified credit portfolio. Theoretically the specific risks of all major firms (industrial, internal and financial risks) can be diversified. For example, the asbestos industry, especially in the US, encountered severe product liabilities, which made many a company in this industry bankrupt. A bank that had prudently diversified its credit portfolio and held not more than 2% of its equity capital in this industry would not have suffered because of the bankruptcies compared to a financial institution that took excessive (concentrated) exposures to the asbestos industry.

Figure 14.2 depicts the major firm/obligor and other portfolio risks that can be diversified away.

It may be noted that all good credit portfolio managers would suffer some credit loss during their careers. However, bad credit portfolio managers crash their portfolios which may cause substantial losses or even bankruptcy of the bank or institution. As we will discuss later, awareness of diversifiable risks facilitates proper diversification, which is one of the best ways of virtually crash proofing the credit portfolio.

A properly diversified credit portfolio would have a large number of credit assets. As the number of exposures in a credit portfolio increases, the risk of the credit portfolio declines, as shown by Figure 14.3.

As evident from Figure 14.3, the total credit portfolio risk equation can be represented as given below:

$$\begin{aligned}\text{Total credit portfolio risk} &= \text{unsystematic (diversifiable) risk}\\ &\quad + \text{systematic (undiversifiable) risk}\end{aligned}$$

On the right hand side of Figure 14.3, we have shown a typical bank's credit portfolio. It has achieved some diversification, although more risks can be diversified away. The bottom segment of the bar represents systematic risk that could not be eliminated through diversification. When one speaks of the 'beta' of a credit portfolio, one is referring to this portion of a portfolio's risk.

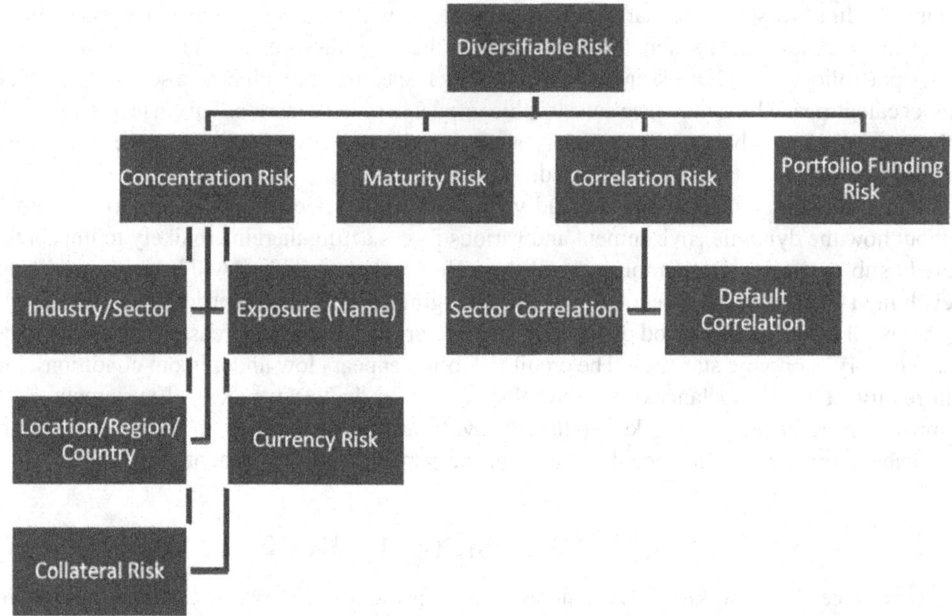


**Figure 14.2** Major Diversifiable Risks

Many academics believe that the reward for credit risk from the portfolio angle is the return for systematic risks undertaken by the lender (because all non-systematic risks can be diversified away). After achieving this challenging task – diversifying all non-systematic risks away – the portfolio manager may balance the portfolio adequately such that the severity of macroeconomic meltdowns (systematic risks) is reduced.

Let us conclude this discussion by stating that while managing credit portfolios two issues require attention: (i) monitoring systematic risk that could lead to business cycles or macroeconomic shocks and (ii) applying portfolio analytical tools and strategies to minimize the diversifiable risks (or hedge risky positions) in the credit portfolio. Periodical portfolio stress testing to measure the credit portfolio's vulnerability to economic downturns and other adverse systematic events must be applied on a routine basis.

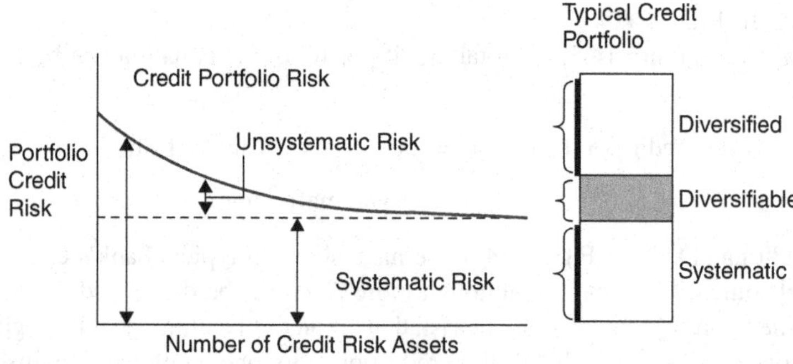


**Figure 14.3** Relationship Between Diversifiable and Systematic Risks

**Example 14.1**

Hypothetical Bank Ltd in the US has a credit portfolio of $10 billion. The key portfolio features are given below:

- The largest sector exposure is in construction which accounted for 20% of the credit portfolio (other sectors in the portfolio include cement/steel manufacturers, building material distributors, real estate developers/builders, automobile manufacturers, tyre manufacturers and investment banks).
- The two largest customers account for 30% (they belong to the construction and building materials sector).
- All obligors in the credit portfolio are within the US.
- The credit products offered by the bank include both short and long term – but the majority are long term exceeding one year, accounting for 60% of the portfolio.
- Most of the funding sources are short term – i.e. short-term deposits and inter-bank borrowings, which accounted for about 75% of the total funding requirements.
- Although entire lending was in dollars, 45% of the short-term deposits were in non-dollar currencies.
- The only collateral it accepts is real estate.

Discuss the portfolio level risks in this portfolio. Is there any significant undiversified risk in this credit portfolio? If so, suggest how further diversification can be achieved.

**Answer**

Significant portfolio risks exist in the portfolio, as given below:

- Construction sector – currently constitutes 20% of the portfolio – concentration is high – it has to be reduced to say 5% of the portfolio. The portfolio is vulnerable to any sectoral downturn, i.e. significant losses are possible if there is a downturn in the construction sector. Since banks are highly leveraged and operate on thin margins (as we have discussed in earlier chapters) such risks carry a potential risk that may put the bank out of business.
- There is also name concentration – two customers account for 30% of the portfolio. Again it is not comforting that the major names are in the construction and building materials sectors. It is well known that the building materials sector is strongly correlated with the construction sector. Whilst ensuring that these names are of top credit quality (AAA category), efforts must be taken to reduce name concentration to, say, 5% of the portfolio. Also credit assets from other non-correlated (if possible, negatively correlated) sectors may be pursued.
- Currency risk is significant because of the liability in the form of non-dollar deposits. Appropriate hedging may be attempted because the entire assets are denominated in local currency, i.e. US dollar.
- Maturity risks are evident because 75% of the deposits and inter-bank borrowings are short term, while the short-term credit assets only represent 40% (i.e. long-term credit assets make up 60% of the portfolio). This serious maturity mismatch could spell trouble if there is any trigger on liquidity in the market. Matching of maturities is important.
- The collateral concentration is also not advisable.

The intelligent efforts of the portfolio manager of this bank can mitigate all these diversifiable risks in such a manner that there is no serious threat to the bank's survival. Then the major focus is on systemic risk. Even systemic shock can, to a great extent, be absorbed by the firm with a well-diversified portfolio.

Since diversification provides a way of eliminating non-systematic risk, it is reasonable to argue that the only type of risk that should be rewarded in the credit risk should be systematic risk. This is the goal into which every portfolio manager would like to drive his/her portfolio so that he/she focus on and devise strategies to tackle movements in systematic risk factors.

Let us now discuss the major diversifiable risks impacting a credit portfolio.

## 14.3 CONCENTRATION

Concentration in credit portfolios is a critical aspect of portfolio credit risk. Concentration risk is the aggregation of exposure risk within the portfolio and would result from credit facilities to one borrower or one industry or similar concentrations. A bank or financial institution must understand the various concentration risks and define acceptable portfolio concentrations for each aggregation. History is replete with examples where concentration risk in credit portfolios caused bank distress. Portfolio concentrations decide the magnitude of problems a financial institution would experience under adverse conditions. Concentration can happen in different ways. The major concentration risks are discussed below.

### 14.3.1 Industry or Sector Concentration

Excessive exposure to a single sector or industry can be dangerous from the portfolio perspective. History has proven that sector specific downturns are not uncommon. Some of the sectors are inherently cyclical. Whilst some sectors are cyclical, it is to be borne in mind that sensitivity to business cycles varies from industry to industry.

The chemical industry, building materials, advertisement, recruitment, real estate and construction are cyclical. For instance, it is often observed that after a building boom the construction sector slows down and this results in financial problems for many participants in the sector such as construction contractors, building material manufacturers and suppliers. Any build-up of excessive exposure to the sector may appear attractive during boom times; however, it could spell trouble when the boom subsides.

During 2008 many retail banks and investment banks in the US had a weak point in their portfolio: concentration risk, i.e. too many sub-prime-asset related financial products such as Collateralized Debt Obligations, Collateralized Loan Obligations, etc. linked to the US real estate sector which caused untold miseries and bankruptcies (e.g. Lehman Brothers and Bear Stearns).

Sector correlation is also important. Some sectors are interconnected in such a manner that if a particular sector faces a downturn, there may be a lagging impact on other sectors. For example, the furniture industry will witness sharp growth in a booming residential/commercial construction market. In case of a construction downturn, the furniture industry would also drop as it is correlated to the construction activity in the economy. We will examine the correlation aspect later in this chapter.

Hence, an ideal portfolio ought to be balanced, with a mix of different industries. Diversification can be achieved by two methods – traditional and modern. Under the traditional method, an assortment of different sectors is selected for diversification, based on internal studies. Modern methods determine scientifically the type and extent of diversification required in the portfolio, drawing upon Portfolio Theories (PT), amongst others. We will see more of this later in the book.

Another important aspect is to classify the sectors based on riskiness. (See also 'Credit Risk Appetite' in Chapter 3.) Credit risk appetite will result in conscious avoidance of certain sectors while the sectors with an acceptable risk profile may be preferred. At the same time, care must be taken to ensure that it does not result in concentration on a few attractive sectors, inviting sector concentration risk. As we have discussed earlier, the sector or name concentration can pay off in the equity portfolio but not in the credit portfolio.

### 14.3.2 Exposure or Name Concentration

The amount exposed to credit risk is termed exposure risk. Even when the firm credit risk is acceptable, concentration of exposures in a few customers can spell doom. Once this weakness is identified, diversifying away from the few concentrated exposures must be given priority. For example, ABC Ltd has 100 customers in its credit portfolio totalling \$200m. However, the exposure to one customer alone accounts for \$160m with the balance of \$40m spread across the remaining 99 customers across diverse industries. Exposure concentration is evident here. There is too much reliance on a single customer, who accounts for 80% of the total portfolio. A portfolio approach is necessary to detect, manage and mitigate similar exposure risks.

### 14.3.3 Region/Location/Country Concentration

Different geographical regions – especially for relatively large countries – display different economic characteristics and their participation or contribution to the overall economy may differ. Rather than focusing the credit assets on a particular region, a portfolio scattered over a wide area offers comfort from a portfolio point of view. It ensures that the vagaries of a particular region will not impact the portfolio. Again, as in the case of sectors, it is worthwhile to have a classification of regions/countries based on riskiness.

Country risk and sovereign risk arise where a bank or financial institution in one country grants credit facilities to obligors in different countries by way of loan or otherwise. Accordingly, the banks, financial institutions and businesses of an international nature and which take cross-country credit exposures may find it necessary to achieve dispersion among various countries in their day-to-day business.

### 14.3.4 Foreign Currency Concentration

Where the credit assets and related liabilities are denoted in local currency, currency risk does not arise in any significant manner. However, if the liabilities and obligations are to be met from the realization of credit assets denoted in different currencies, currency risk exists. Any concentration of foreign currency which is subject to market fluctuations can be problematic. As was experienced by certain Far East Asian businesses in 1997/98, reliance on cheap foreign currency loans to finance local credit assets may not be ideal even if the currencies are pegged. The sudden devaluation of local currencies caused serious crises for several businesses in the

Far East Asian economies which translated into credit losses for banks in the region. Both diversification and hedging can be considered as mitigants to the currency risks.

### 14.3.5 Collateral Risk

Many creditors, especially banks, accept collateral as security to mitigate the credit risks. But at portfolio level it can be a risk. Imagine a situation where the creditor accepts only one kind of security – real estate with a 50% margin. In the event of a sharp fall in the property market beyond the 50% level, the comfort of the portfolio disappears. During the late 1980s and early 1990s, Japanese banks faced a similar situation where they financed against real estate and during the recession that followed found that the liquidation of the collaterals was insufficient not only to cover loans extended, but in certain instances did not even meet the interest obligations, let alone the principal. Many such instances ultimately led to banking collapses. The 2008 US sub-prime crisis is also traceable to the sharp fall in real estate assets held as collateral. Hence the moral is (i) concentration risks of the collateral portfolio may be avoided, (ii) values of collaterals also peak and collapse, (iii) the market value of collaterals may be positively correlated to business cycles and (iv) if the collateral value has a strong positive correlation with an obligor's creditworthiness, this is a significant source of risk which is usually known as 'wrong way correlation'. The US sub-prime crisis during 2008 has parallels with what happened in Japan in the late 1980s. We will discuss more about this later in the book.

### 14.3.6 Maturity Risks

Maturity risks are yet another important portfolio level risk. Usually the credit assets in the portfolio have different maturity dates. The maturities of the portfolio should be effectively managed in order to avoid any liquidity problems. The asset tenor (i.e. loan or investments) in a bank vary from a few days (overdrafts) to 15–20 years (e.g. mortgages or project finance). However, the deposit tenors are relatively shorter (i.e. usually up to five years). Tenor mismatch is evident. Hence, managing the tenor mismatches is a vital function with liquidity implications. Banks and financial intermediaries have to manage their balance sheets so that they can lend for long periods without compromising their ability to meet potential depositors' demand for cash. How do banks and financial intermediaries do this? They rely on money and capital markets to borrow and lend when necessary, for short periods. Shutdown to the access to money and capital markets during a crisis can be devastating for institutions that carry maturity risks.

Given the importance of liquidity, excessive portfolio exposure of lengthy credits is often not advisable unless matched against long-term funds. During the 2008 Credit Crisis, worries about the strength of US banks or financial institutions caused the money and capital markets to freeze, resulting in troubles for institutions who relied on these markets to manage maturity mismatches. Accordingly, Basel III focuses on this risk which has strong liquidity implications. As we will discuss in the Chapter 16, Basel III introduces a Net Stable Funding Ratio (NSFR), which is expected to ensure that sufficient long-term sources funds are available.

Maturity risks exist beyond the financial sector. The suppliers of machinery and capital goods tend to give longer credit terms. If a credit portfolio comprises lengthy credits, it is to be matched against long-term funds. Otherwise prolonged average portfolio maturities would lead to liquidity problems. Let us see a few examples where a non-banking business could face problems because of maturity risks in its credit or debtors portfolio.

- For instance, the government contractors may find that the settlement is inordinately delayed because of the usual red tape of budgetary constraints. Whilst the receivables are good for collection, they take a long time to collect, which means the maturity of such portfolios tends to be on the longer side. This can lead to liquidity problems.
- Although originally the credit might have been extended short term as in the case of a wholesale trader who expect the bills to be settled in less than, say, three months, they could experience delay in the settlement and, especially during times of economic crisis, the delay may even exceed a year. Effectively, the short-term credit becomes medium term or long term.
- Another example is of a trader of consumer durables who has two types of credit sales: (i) 30 days' normal credit period and (ii) instalment credit where 24 monthly instalments are allowed to settle the dues. The cash flow impact of the two types is different. In the case of the first category, the credit exposure is just 30 days; however in the case of latter category, the credit exposure (sales price plus interest) is spread up to two years. The trader ought to strike a balance between the two types of credit sales so that an adequate cash flow position can be maintained. In normal circumstances, the longer the term, the higher the risk.

### 14.3.7 Funding Risk

A corollary to maturity risk at portfolio level is the funding risk. How a bank funds its credit portfolio is equally important. A sound credit portfolio is sustainable only with a sound funding policy. A balance between asset maturity and liability maturity must be ensured. The funding risk is best illustrated by the crisis faced by Northern Rock Bank in the UK during 2007.

During July 2007, there were signs that the US sub-prime crisis was beginning to influence the short-term funding market, resulting in a halt in inter-bank lending. During August 2007, BNP Paribas closed three investment vehicles with exposures to US sub-prime mortgage assets. This resulted in a fear about the quality of investments in the financial sector with exposure to the US sub-prime market. Hence, the investment vehicles that tapped short-term financing had begun experiencing difficulties in rolling over their short-term borrowing.

Northern Rock had heavy reliance on non-retail (or institutional) funding. During 2007, only around 23% of its liabilities were in the form of retail deposits. The rest of its funding came from short-term borrowing in the capital markets. As market liquidity froze, Northern Rock found that the institutions were reluctant to refinance or fund their balance sheet. This development was attributed mainly to two reasons:

1. Banks became more concerned about potential counterparty risks.
2. Concern about their own potential liquidity requirements and that of their own subsidiaries if the funding problems in the wholesale markets became worse.

Northern Rock informed its regulators, the Financial Services Authority (FSA) during mid-August 2007 about its funding problems. As the news of problems faced by Northern Rock spread, there was a run on Northern Rock by the depositors forcing nationalization of the bank during September 2007.

The main lesson from Northern Rock's bankruptcy is the importance of having a strong and diversified funding structure that is sustainable even during fast-changing market conditions.

It is generally advised that banks should avoid concentration of funding sources and might also consider buildup of specific reserve buffers to counterbalance potential liquidity shortages.

### 14.3.8 Correlation Risks

Correlation is a highly useful tool in statistics and has been widely used in various fields including science, sociology, economics and finance. Its applications in various fields of finance such as equities, derivatives, currencies and interest rates are well known. It is also useful for credit portfolio study. However, it is still evolving. Basel II and III have recognized the importance of correlation in credit portfolio risk management.

Mathematically, correlation is denoted by the Greek letter $\rho$ ('rho') and the usual formula to compute the correlation is given below:

$$\rho = \frac{\left|\sum_{i=1}^{n} (X - \bar{X})(Y - \bar{Y})\right.}{\sqrt{\sum_{i=1}^{n} (X - \bar{X})^2}\sqrt{\sum_{i=1}^{n} (Y - \bar{Y})^2}}$$

where

X and Y = observations of two types of assets or sectors or regions or any other related variables
$\bar{X}$ and $\bar{Y}$ = mean of each variable
N = number of observations

The correlation value is between +1 (perfect positive correlation) and –1 (perfect negative correlation) while 0 shows absence of any correlation. Perfect correlation means both variables are moving together and could be impacted by the same underlying factors or causes. Negative correlations show that both variables react opposite to the external stimuli.

Now, coming back to the significance of correlation to credit portfolio risk management, historical evidence shows that there is correlation in credit risk that varies over business cycles and across firms. Also the credit risk correlation becomes higher during economic recessions. Hence, from the systematic risk point of view it is safe to conclude that overall **credit risk is positively correlated to economic downturns**. This knowledge ought to be useful while designing a credit portfolio. Since non-cyclical sectors are less impacted by economic downturns, such sectors have lower correlation to the economic downturn. On the other hand cyclical sectors such as construction, the financial industry or real estate have relatively higher correlation, suggesting that economic turmoil affects such sectors more heavily. Correlation studies can be split into different categories, as required; for instance, sector wise correlation and default correlation are given below:

- **Sector correlation**: Other things being equal (i.e. satisfactory obligor credit risk) sectors having negative correlation are the best possible choice while constructing a credit portfolio. (See also the chapter on Diversification.)
- **Default correlation**: If the obligor credit risk is high, sector correlation becomes irrelevant. As the obligor credit risk deteriorates, irrespective of the sector diversification, the risk of default is higher. Hence the default correlation is high as the credit rating approaches lower quality. This shows the importance of obligor credit risk analysis, which we discussed in detail in the previous sections of the book.

## 14.4 CREDIT PORTFOLIO BETA

Portfolio beta is a gauge of a portfolio's volatility and in a credit portfolio it means the losses it can suffer due to external stimuli or external risk. It measures the rate of change in portfolio quality (say measured by average credit grade of the entire credit portfolio) in response to the change in systematic risk factors – e.g. business cycles. As discussed, an intelligent credit portfolio manager or credit team will diversify away the risks in such a manner that only systematic risks remain a matter of concern. A well-diversified portfolio will have very low portfolio beta and can survive the hardship of an economic downturn, triggered by a systematic risk. A three-dimensional graph, depicting the impact of business cycle on a credit portfolio depending upon the degree of diversification, is given in Figure 14.4:

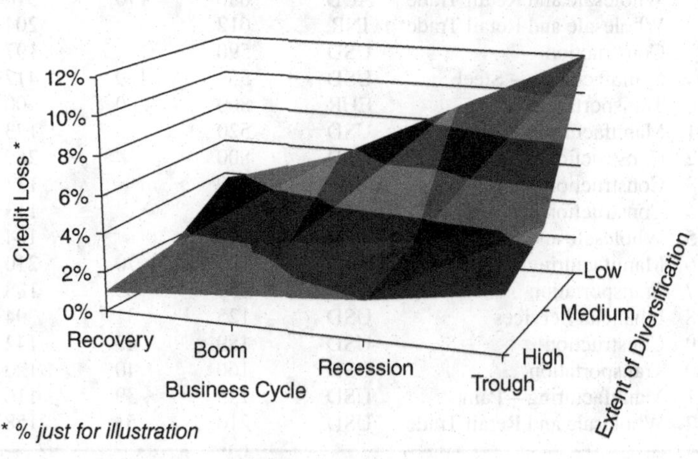


**Figure 14.4** Credit Loss in Credit Portfolio with Varying Degree of Diversification

The higher the diversification, the lower the probability of credit loss for a given (acceptable) level of obligor credit risks. Portfolio beta will be relatively high for portfolios with low diversification, i.e. the rate of deterioration in the credit quality of this portfolio would be higher than a well-diversified portfolio.

One important rule of diversification is to combine assets that are negatively correlated or less correlated or with zero correlation. How do banks, financial institutions and lenders ensure diversification? Chapter 17 discusses diversification in detail.

## ✍ QUESTIONS/EXERCISES

1. What is the difference between systematic and unsystematic risks? Is it true that regulators are more interested in systematic risks while individual banks give equal importance to both? Please share your views.
2. Explain credit concentration risk. What is its relevance for credit portfolio management?
3. What is maturity risk? Describe some of the ways in which this risk can be managed by financial intermediaries. Also explain its link with funding and liquidity risks.

4. Do you agree with the statement that sector or name concentration pays off in equities but not in credit? Explain with reasons.
5. What do you mean by country risk in the context of a credit portfolio?
6. What is the relevance of correlations from a credit portfolio risk management perspective?
7. The following is an extract from the credit portfolio of Hypothetical Bank:

| CUSTOMER NAME | INDUSTRY | Currency | Exposure – millions | Less than 1 year | Less than 2 years | More than 2 years |
|---|---|---|---|---|---|---|
| Customer 1 | Construction | USD | 3,500 | | 1,167 | 2,333 |
| Customer 2 | Building Materials | USD | 1,200 | 300 | 900 | |
| Customer 3 | Construction | GBP | 1,100 | 275 | 825 | |
| Customer 4 | Wholesale and Retail Trade | USD | 790 | | 263 | 527 |
| Customer 5 | Manufacturing – Cement | EUR | 780 | 195 | 585 | |
| Customer 6 | Wholesale and Retail Trade | AUD | 680 | 170 | 510 | |
| Customer 7 | Wholesale and Retail Trade | INR | 612 | | 204 | 408 |
| Customer 8 | Construction | USD | 590 | | 197 | 393 |
| Customer 9 | Manufacturing – Steel | USD | 556 | 139 | 417 | |
| Customer 10 | Transportation | EUR | 800 | 200 | 600 | |
| Customer 11 | Manufacturing – Auto | USD | 520 | | 173 | 347 |
| Customer 12 | Construction | USD | 800 | | 267 | 533 |
| Customer 13 | Construction | GBP | 400 | | 133 | 267 |
| Customer 14 | Construction | USD | 340 | | 113 | 227 |
| Customer 15 | Wholesale and Retail Trade | USD | 312 | | 104 | 208 |
| Customer 16 | Manufacturing – Cement | USD | 280 | 70 | 210 | |
| Customer 17 | Transportation | GBP | 250 | 63 | 188 | |
| Customer 18 | Financial Services | USD | 125 | 31 | 94 | |
| Customer 19 | Construction | USD | 189 | 47 | 142 | |
| Customer 20 | Transportation | USD | 160 | 40 | 120 | |
| Customer 21 | Manufacturing – Paints | USD | 155 | 39 | 116 | |
| Customer 22 | Wholesale and Retail Trade | USD | 210 | 53 | 158 | |

Identify the portfolio risks inherent in this portfolio. Explain your views and possible solutions to solve or mitigate the portfolio issues identified.

8. Obtain the audited and detailed annual reports of banks listed in stock markets. Examine and identify the credit portfolio risks and the steps taken by them to mitigate the risks.

# 15

# Firm Risks to Portfolio Risks and Capital Adequacy

In this chapter we will discuss more about PD and consider LGD and EL, which are covered from both the obligor and credit portfolio perspectives. We will also discuss the quantum of capital to be maintained by a lending institution with sizeable credit portfolio.

## 15.1 OBLIGOR PD AND PORTFOLIO PD

Study of both individual PD and Portfolio PD is necessary for effective management of a credit portfolio. If we know the individual PDs and LGD of all constituents in a portfolio, we can arrive at 'portfolio-level PD and LGD'. At portfolio level, the calculation is complicated as it is impacted by the correlation between the various credit assets or obligors. However, it may be noted that if the credit portfolio is well diversified, then the inherent sector or similar correlation risks ought to be insignificant.

Once a customer defaults, the probability of credit loss zooms. Usually, the banks and financial institutions include high risk customers in the watch list and monitor them closely, probably on a weekly or monthly basis. Sometimes, even better rated customers are included in the watch list, provided there are serious business developments that could harm repayment capacity – for example a massive fire in one of the main factories of a borrower.

Most of the default situations trigger negotiations with the obligor with the aim of full settlement. Whilst all defaults do not lead to credit loss, the probability of credit loss in the event of a default is very high, inasmuch as the default itself mostly highlights the liquidity crisis of the obligor. If the default continues beyond a reasonable period (say 90 days since the due date), then it is appropriate to downgrade the risk rating. Such situations also warrant the asset being classified as 'substandard' or 'doubtful'. If full recovery appears unlikely, then appropriate provisioning may also be considered. Finally, if nothing is recoverable, it is a full loss situation.

As we discussed in Chapter 10, the probability of default is asymmetric, as shown in Figure 15.1.

Figure 15.1 is a diagrammatic presentation of PD. One can see that the PD zooms as credit quality drops. Awareness of the stages through which the PD of a credit asset passes is a good guide to effectively understand how various firm credit risks and portfolio credit risks impact overall credit risk management. Naturally, some of the credit risks will turn bad and result in credit losses. The understanding of the road to credit loss is critical to manage credit portfolio risks and put monitoring devices in place to reduce/avoid losses. The major milestones in the road are:

- Migration of PD to higher levels, highlighting higher credit risks.
- Default by the obligor, which triggers calculation of loss given default.
- Assessing credit loss and provisioning and write offs.

Let us examine the migration risk.

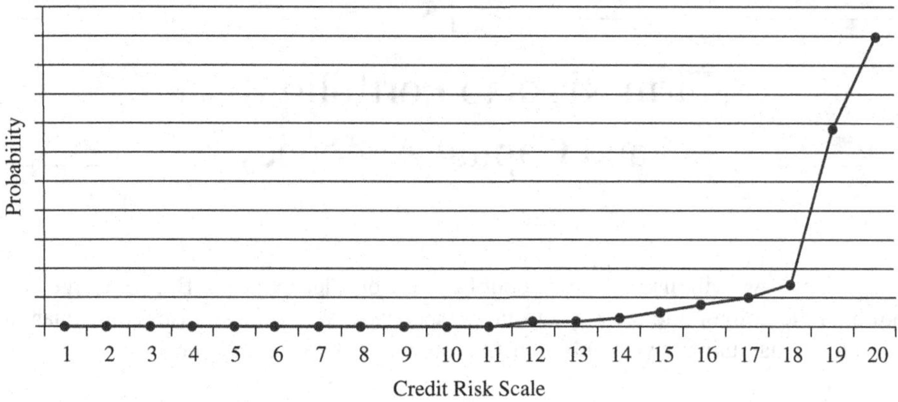


**Figure 15.1** PD Asymmetry

## 15.2 MIGRATION RISK

Migration risk means the tendency of a single customer or group of customers to move towards a lower risk grade. It signifies the deterioration in creditworthiness and highlights the increase in credit risk. Migration risk can be studied from both portfolio and firm levels.

### 15.2.1 Firm Credit Risk Migration

Firm credit risk is dynamic. Often, it undergoes changes, during the course of time. So, a 'low' credit risk can become 'medium' or even 'high' over time. The reason is the impact of dynamic EIIF risk factors. As we discussed earlier, the entire obligors are classified based on a rating scale, represented by alpha-numeric numbers, which captures different levels of their creditworthiness. A table can be prepared to capture how different credit grades behave over time. This is usually known as a Transition/Migration Matrix, which describes the probabilities (of a borrower or obligor) of being in any of the various grades.

Usually, a one year transition horizon is standard for the study of migration of credit risk exposures. A historical data of migration matrices, or a transition study exceeding one year, if undertaken, may prove useful to study the medium/long-term impact of business cycles and other systematic factors. Besides, the matrices over longer time periods offer the advantage of less noise inherent in the data, as short-term noise cancels itself out over longer horizons.

A tentative one year Credit Migration Table (on a 7-level rating system) is as shown in Table 15.1:

**Table 15.1** Credit Migration Table

| | Grade 1 | Grade 2 | Grade 3 | Grade 4 | Grade 5 | Grade 6 | Grade 7 | Defaults |
|---|---|---|---|---|---|---|---|---|
| **Grade 1** | 91.93% | 7.24% | 0.77% | 0.04% | 0.04% | 0.00% | 0.00% | 0.00% |
| **Grade 2** | 6.06% | 91.01% | 2.27% | 0.27% | 0.10% | 0.10% | 0.19% | 0.00% |
| **Grade 3** | 0.48% | 3.75% | 90.21% | 4.26% | 0.61% | 0.28% | 0.37% | 0.04% |
| **Grade 4** | 0.08% | 0.60% | 3.11% | 87.18% | 7.75% | 0.46% | 0.75% | 0.24% |
| **Grade 5** | 0.04% | 0.06% | 2.19% | 5.87% | 81.48% | 6.95% | 2.43% | 1.01% |
| **Grade 6** | 0.00% | 0.12% | 0.25% | 1.02% | 7.29% | 73.80% | 12.13% | 5.45% |
| **Grade 7** | 0.00% | 0.02% | 0.01% | 0.17% | 1.11% | 3.96% | 60.45% | 34.41% |

A unique feature of this matrix is the high probability factor on the diagonal. Usually, the obligors are most likely to maintain their current rating. Given the initial rating, the second largest probabilities of possible ratings are usually in the direct neighbourhood of the diagonal. Generally, the further away a cell is from the diagonal, the smaller is the likelihood of migration to that cell. Although a typical migration matrix is concentrated along the diagonal, the observation density diminishes rapidly as we move to the right side of the table. For instance, only about 60.45% of Grade 7 customers will continue at that grade. A significant part thereof (34.4%) would default (and possible write off) while about 5.14% would be upgraded. But none of them attain the Grade I category, although there is an instance in Grade 2. Such cases usually happen consequent upon the takeover of the troublesome customer by a sound business group. The relatively high volatility in Grade 7 is attributable to two factors: (i) some of the high risk (CCC-rated) firms are 'do-or-die' type firms. Their very risky nature makes them highly default prone, but if successful, they have a significant chance of moving their way to higher ratings and (ii) creditors can know the fate of the credit asset belonging to this category sooner than that of higher grades. Either the payment is realized or has to be written off or fully provided for.

**Example 15.1**

ABC Ltd is a lending institution and during the recent Board meeting took a decision that it would like to raise the credit standards on all new customers. Based on the Credit Migration Table (above) the Board wants to minimize the migration risk of new customers. The Board puts a criterion that not more than 5% of the new customers should fall to Grade 4 or below (i.e. worse rating) in a one year horizon. Using the Credit Migration Table, please suggest the minimum initial credit rating required for new customers to comply with the criteria laid down by the Board.

**Solution**

For any new customer, the probability of them dropping below Grade 4 is arrived at by totalling across the row of possible initial credit ratings up to Grade 4 (i.e. Grade, 1, Grade 2, Grade 3 and Grade 4). The calculations are given below:

| Criteria | Total Migration Probability to Grade 4 and below | Total |
|---|---|---|
| Probability of **Grade 1** dropping to Grade 4 and below | 0.04%+0.04%+0%+0%+0%+0% | 0.08% |
| Probability of **Grade 2** dropping to Grade 4 and below | 0.27%+0.10%+0.10%+0.19%+0% | 0.66% |
| **Probability of Grade 3 dropping to Grade 4 and below** | **4.26%+0.61%+0.28%+0.37%+0.04%** | **5.56%** |
| Probability of **Grade 4** dropping to Grade 4 and below | 87.18%+7.75%+0.46%+0.75%+0.24% | 96.38% |

An initial rating of Grade 3 matches most closely to the criteria laid down by the Board. Hence the institution should target new customers with ratings of Grade 1, Grade 2 and Grade 3 only.

### 15.2.2 Portfolio Risk Migration

The risk of change in portfolio/sub-portfolio credit quality is real given the dynamic environment of today's world. The migration risk due to systematic factors is a constant matter of concern as it could result in portfolio-wide default. The degree of impact to the portfolio differs from year to year as changes in macroeconomic factors vary in a dissimilar manner across years. Recessions usually witness the highest downgrades. Hence, at portfolio level the migration ought to be linked to systematic risk factors. Study of portfolio migration risk can often be linked to the different stages of the business cycle – boom, bust and normal times. Such linking is logical because it provides a clear guide to the portfolio managers to understand the impact of various economic scenarios on portfolio credit risks. Usually downgrades increase in an economic contraction while upgrades surpass the downgrades in times of economic expansion.

The propensity of a homogenous group's susceptibility to downgrade is captured by portfolio migration risk. Periodical portfolio study (say monthly) must involve the entire portfolio constituents and is undertaken to understand the changes in migration risk, if any. For instance, some of the portfolio-level targets fixed by a financial institution may include the following:

- In boom times, 95% of the credit portfolio should comprise BBB or higher rated credit only.
- In recessionary times, 85% of the credit portfolio should comprise BBB or higher rated credit only.
- In normal times, 90% should be the goal.

Migration study, especially on sub-portfolios, highlights the risky and stable areas of the portfolio. It provides information about the behaviour of various sub-portfolios (pools of credit assets) over time. For example, a bank with large exposures to US mortgages (in real estate sector) during the early 2000s might find that the sub-prime sub-portfolio (within the overall credit portfolio) is of acceptable quality. Let us assume that the credit grades[1] of this sub-portfolio were as follows:

- 10% of the sub-portfolio rated at Grade 3
- 80% at Grade 4
- 10% at Grade 5
- 0% at Grades 6 and 7

However, by the late 2000s, the sub-portfolio was impacted by several external stimuli, such as a fall in real estate values, skyrocketing foreclosures, etc. Accordingly, numerous downward rating revisions occurred in the sub-prime sub-portfolio. Hence the portfolio risk migration occurred, which would be reflected in the credit grades as follows:

- 0% at Grade 3
- 40% at Grade 4
- 30% at Grade 5
- 20% at Grade 6 and
- 10% at Grade 7

[1] Grade 1 = Very Good Quality, Grade 2 = Good Quality, Grade 3 = Satisfactory Quality, Grade 4 = Average Quality, Grade 5 = Below Average Quality, Grade 6 = Low Quality, Grade 7 = Default.

A historical database of migration tables through a business cycle (say 10 years) would provide banks/FIs with insight into the behaviour of various sub-segments and sub-portfolios vulnerable to specific external/systematic risks.

### 15.2.3 Benefits of Migration Risk Study

Migration study (study of downgrade risk) is significant because of the following reasons:

- It avoids surprises and provides an idea about the credit asset/portfolio's future credit quality.
- It facilitates the decision taking on credit quality related issues.
- It facilitates pricing decisions – adjust pricing to factor in migration risks.
- It facilitates active portfolio management– sell/reduce assets, if necessary, to reduce migration risk.
- It optimizes regulatory/economic capital needed.
- It indicates the provisioning requirements, among others.

## 15.3 DEFAULT RISK

We have seen how we analyze credit risk through EIIF model and arrive at credit rating and probability of default (PD) when credit facilities are granted to a customer. Whilst we try to minimize the PD, at times there are defaults. Let us now examine various types of defaults from both firm and portfolio perspectives.

### 15.3.1 Firm-Level Defaults

As the name implies the obligor defaults on due date and this could potentially lead to partial or full loss of the credit asset. Major default situations are as follows:

(i) **Simple default** is another term often used to denote the failure to pay. Whilst in banking circles it is commonly stated as past dues, in other business sectors it is often stated as overdue. Both connote the same event. The obligor did not pay on the maturity or due date. Default is treated with seriousness in all businesses. If it persists for more than a minimum number of days (say 30 or 60 or 90 days), usually banks and financial institutions downgrade the credit asset concerned to the watch list or even non-performing category. However, if the obligor is able to settle within a reasonable period, the asset continues to be performing, although repeated instances (may indicate poor liquidity conditions) call for an investigation into the causes and appropriate downgrading, if needed.

(ii) **Restructuring** is yet another instance of default. The fact that the facilities are restructured shows that the borrower/debtor/obligor is not in a position to meet the dues.

(iii) **Declaration of bankruptcy** is yet another instance of default. Similarly, application to legal authorities for protection from creditors (such as Chapter 11 under US Bankruptcy Laws or application to the Board for Industrial and Finance Reconstruction in India) also can be treated as a default. All these instances highlight the payment difficulties faced by the obligor, enhancing the probability of credit loss.

Another related concept is 'technical default'. In this case, whilst the creditworthiness and capacity to repay the obligation remains satisfactory, the obligor may be held under technical default. This happens usually in connection with breach of covenants and conditions.

Default risk is the uncertainty surrounding a firm's ability to service its debts and obligations. All defaults need not result in the loss of the entire credit outstanding. The loss suffered by a lender in the event of default is determined largely by the credit structure and collateral. If covered by sound collateral, the actual loss can be minimized. This issue will be covered by 'Loss Given Default' discussed as the next topic.

### 15.3.2 Portfolio-Level Defaults

Portfolio/sub-portfolio default risks pertain to a situation where all credit assets in a particular portfolio or sub-portfolio default together. Such a situation, where most constituents of the portfolio default, is usually triggered by systematic risks. For instance, during the 2008 Credit Crisis, mortgage portfolios and sub-portfolios of many financial institutions in the US were hit. The impact was so huge in some portfolios that the entire institution (e.g. Wachovia, Lehman, etc.) collapsed under the burden of sub-prime assets. Portfolio default risks trigger 'Portfolio Provisioning' which is taken up later in this chapter.

## 15.4 LOSS GIVEN DEFAULT (LGD)

When a default occurs, the immediate concern is how much is recoverable. It is better if the credit asset is recovered to its full book value in which no credit loss will arise. However, in the event of default, unless fully secured by top quality collaterals, some credit loss is usually inevitable. LGD is calculated as below:

$$\text{LGD\%} = 1 - \text{recovery rate}$$

Recovery rate[2] can also be termed Value Given Default. It refers to the recoverable part of the credit asset. Whatever remains after the expected recovery should be fully provided for. Recovery rates vary from 0% to 100%. Recovery rate is dependent upon various factors such as (a) nature and purpose of credit facility, (b) facility structure, (c) product type, (d) priority of rights in case of bankruptcy, (e) realizable value of collaterals (if any) and (f) possible liquidation of the unencumbered assets in the balance sheet of the customer, evoking guarantees, integrity of the obligor, etc. In fact, it is not easy to compute/predict the recovery rate and hence some assumptions about recovery rates will have to be made. Past data, history of credit losses and impact of systematic variables on credit assets are all guiding factors in arriving at recovery rates.

Usually it is the collateral that provides recovery if the underlying business of the borrower fails. Hence, collateral selection is important. While accepting collateral, consideration must be given to the following factors:

- Nature – cash is the best form of collateral.
- Liquidity – easily marketable collateral to be given priority.
- Market value – must be ascertainable at any given time.
- Risks associated with collateral – it must be ensured that environment and other liabilities do not pass on from the customer to the lender.

[2] Banks and FIs usually link the expected recovery rates to facility grades. Please refer to Part VII for a detailed discussion on collateral and facility grades.

- Quality of the charge – the type of charge (pledge, hypothecation, mortgage, etc.) must be legally enforceable.

Please refer to Part VII of the book where we have covered the collateral security in depth.

**Exposure at Default (EAD) and Maturity Factor**: LGD depends on how much the creditor is actually exposed to at the time of default and hence EAD is important. EAD represents the expected level of usage of the facility utilization when default occurs. Theoretically, as the maturity increases, risk increases, hence the probable credit loss also increases.

## 15.5 EXPECTED LOSS (EL)

Having arrived at the PD and LGD, we can estimate the Expected Loss (EL). As we discussed, each credit asset has a PD, arrived at through appropriate credit risk grades, based on EIIF study. If it defaults, a certain percentage of its value will be lost, known as LGD. If we multiply the PD times the LGD, the result is the asset's EL. This is what we would expect to lose on average over a long period of time on such credit risk grades. EL is considered as the cost of doing business. Since the EL is part of the cost of doing business, the credit pricing must absorb the EL, i.e. the higher the EL, the higher the pricing.

### 15.5.1 Obligor EL

The basic ingredients of a credit loss (firm-level) calculation, exposure, PD, and recovery, are given below:

| | | |
|---|---|---|
| Exposure at Default (EAD) | What will the customer owe the bank or FI in the case of a default? | EAD x |
| Probability of Default (PD) | What is the probability of counterparty would default? | PD x |
| Loss Given Default (LGD) | In case of a default, what would the bank or FI lose? | LGD x |
| Maturity factor (M) | What is the maturity of the exposure? | M = |
| **Expected Loss (EL)** | **As of today, what is the anticipated loss from this customer?** | **EL** |

$$\begin{aligned} \text{EL} &= \text{PD} \times \text{EAD} \times \text{LGD} \times \text{M} \\ &= \text{PD} \times \text{Exposure} \times \text{LGD} \times \text{Maturity factor} \\ &= \text{PD} \times \text{Exposure} \times (1 - \text{recovery rate}) \times \text{M} \end{aligned}$$

### 15.5.2 Portfolio EL

Portfolio EL is the aggregation of the ELs of the portfolio components. For a portfolio of N customers, the Portfolio EL is:

$$\text{Portfolio EL} = \sum_{i=1}^{N} \text{PD}i \times \text{EAD}i \times \text{LGD}i \times \text{M}i$$

where $i$ represents the credit assets in the credit portfolio.

Any loss over and above the EL is known as Unexpected Loss (UL). A bank and FI are supposed to hold sufficient capital to withstand unexpected loss in order to ensure solvency. If the unexpected loss exceeds the capital of the bank or FI, an urgent recapitalization is required, otherwise, the institution would be bankrupt. During the 2008 Credit Crisis, many banks and FIs had faced such a situation, which were either recapitalized or taken over by stronger entities or bailed out by the government.

## 15.6 PROVISIONING

Unexpected losses occur due to actual defaults. Most of the default situations trigger negotiations with the obligor with the aim of full settlement. Whilst all defaults do not lead to credit loss, the probability of credit loss in the instance of a default is high, inasmuch as the default itself mostly highlights the liquidity crisis of the obligor. The provisioning is of two types – (i) firm-level or specific provisions and (ii) general or portfolio-level provisions.

### 15.6.1 Provisioning – Firm Level

If the default continues beyond a reasonable period (say 90 days since the due date), then loss provisioning is highly recommended. Many financial institutions maintain specific provisions if the payment of principal is in arrears beyond 90 days. However, in the case of corporate and commercial loans provisioning is to be determined on a principle or judgement basis and not necessarily on a rule,[3] such as number of days delinquent. For illustrative purposes, the provisioning guidelines can be as follows:

| Type | Criteria | Provision guidelines |
|---|---|---|
| Normal | Good asset – no default | Nil specific provision. Portfolio-level provisions, as applicable |
| Watch list | Some problems are observed – however no default threat | Whilst close watch will be maintained, no specific provision is required. Portfolio-level provisions, as applicable |
| Substandard | Payment of principal is in default beyond 90 days or other judgemental factors | Specific provision required – say 25% of the net EAD |
| Doubtful | Based on the analysis, a full recovery is doubtful or other judgemental factors | Specific provision required – say 50% of the net EAD |
| Loss | No hope of recovery – exhausted all methods of recovery | Specific provision required – say 100% of the net EAD |

Booking of credit loss is inevitable if the credit asset is not worth its face value. In case recoveries (value given default) are possible, the remaining portion is the loss. When the credit

[3] Provisions for retail exposures are rule based.

asset is ultimately judged uncollectable, it is either written off directly against the income statement or charged off by reducing a previously created provision (or loss reserves/loss allowances). The critical question as to when the write-off/provisioning of credit asset should be done is more or less a judgemental matter. Management is responsible for establishing appropriate provisioning/write-off policies, documenting their methodology and defining the roles of senior management, including the Board of Directors.

Regulators – central banks – also play a significant role by providing guidelines on provisioning to the banks and financial institutions. The regulators review the provisions level held by banks and financial institutions on a regular basis. The regulators will address its concerns, if any, with the bank's or financial institution's top management as well as their external auditors. The regulators have the authority to direct the bank or financial institution to make additional provisions, if necessary.

Provision methodologies should conform to generally accepted accounting principles. Interest recognition, if any, should be on a cash basis. International Accounting Standard 39 (IAS 39) provides guidance on accounting principles for dealing with credit losses.

### 15.6.2 Portfolio-Level Provisioning

Many financial institutions maintain general provisions on portfolios well in advance, as a prudent measure, towards future possible credit losses, where a customer account or a specific credit asset is yet to be identified. The provisioning requirement varies depending upon the credit rating category. Normally, the provisioning is arrived at having a study of the past performance of the credit portfolio. High quality credit categories require lesser provisioning compared to riskier grades. The general macroeconomic outlook, historical experience assimilated through historical data and the nature and size of the portfolios are among the other considerations while arriving at the provisioning requirement. An example of such provisioning by a finance institution is as follows:

Portfolio Provisioning Rules

| Details | Positive Economic Outlook | Stable Economic Outlook | Negative Economic Outlook |
|---|---|---|---|
| AAA | 0% | 0% | 0% |
| AA | 0.10% | 0.15% | 0.20% |
| A | 0.20% | 0.35% | 0.50% |
| BBB | 0.40% | 0.60% | 0.80% |
| BB | 0.60% | 0.90% | 1.20% |
| B | 1.00% | 1.50% | 2.00% |

For instance, if the economic outlook is stable, it will require nil provisioning on AAA (Very Low Credit Risk) rated customers. AA rated customers would require 0.15% provisioning by way of debit to the profit and loss account. The charge to the profit and loss account signifies that the expected loss is the cost of giving credit. It is the cost of doing business. Since it is viewed as cost (usually called loss reserve/provision), it is booked into the P&L like any other expense. And the credit risk pricing must cover this cost, to the extent possible. As we have seen earlier, the main portfolio defects – concentration risk and correlated assets along with poor asset quality – also carry the risk of higher credit losses.

To the extent possible, personnel independent of the underwriting, monitoring and collection functions should conduct the loss provisioning. Also, whilst the specific lines of reporting depend on the complexity of organizational structure, it is better if the personnel making the final determination of the loss allowances/provisions report to a level that is independent of the credit process. Periodical portfolio study (say monthly by a committee comprising senior credit officials and bank's top management) must consider entire constituents and understand the level of migration risk, default risk and possible write-offs, if any, in the credit portfolio. The credit portfolio managers must always attempt to retain these risks at a specific level so that overall quality of the portfolio remains satisfactory.

## 15.7 CREDIT LOSS DISTRIBUTION

We have discussed EL, which is considered as the cost of doing business. We have also seen how Unexpected Loss (UL) is taken to the P&L through provisioning. A higher amount of provisions would result in net losses which in turn will erode the capital base of the bank or FI.

A bank and FI is supposed to hold sufficient capital to withstand UL in order to ensure solvency. If the UL exceeds the capital of the bank or FI, an urgent recapitalization would be required, otherwise the institution would be bankrupt. During the 2008 Credit Crisis, many banks and FIs faced such a situation, and were either recapitalized or taken over by stronger entities or bailed out by the government.

A credit portfolio comprises several individual credit assets or obligors. All credit assets are selected through strict criteria based on the EIIF model. As we have seen, the EIIF model facilitates credit risk grading, which in turn can be mapped to an appropriate PD. And for each credit asset appropriate LGD can also be arrived at mainly based on the collaterals. If we know the PD and LGD of each portfolio constituent, we can arrive at individual EL. By combining the PDs and LGD of all constituents in a diversified credit portfolio, we can arrive at the portfolio-level PD and LGD. Similarly, aggregation of EL for each exposure provides the portfolio EL, which may be converted into a credit loss distribution.

Monte Carlo simulation is one of the methods to generate a credit loss distribution. In order to capture the behaviour of credit portfolios in a more realistic manner, Monte Carlo simulation is used. Since we need to take into account diverse and dissimilar movements of various risk factors (including EIIF factors), which drive PDs, exposures, LGD, concentrations and correlations, probably, Monte Carlo simulation is the best choice to generate a credit loss distribution. Once we apply Monte Carlo simulation on the whole credit portfolio, we obtain a distribution of credit losses. (Please see Appendix for a worked out Case Study.)

The portfolio must be designed in such a manner that the higher losses are avoided at all costs. This can be done by giving adequate attention to the selection of credit assets by choosing satisfactory firm-level credit risks (using EIIF screener), sound periodical monitoring and maintaining a well-diversified credit portfolio.

### 15.7.1 Characteristics of Credit Loss Distribution

A smooth flowing diagram of a credit loss distribution is given in Figure 15.2:

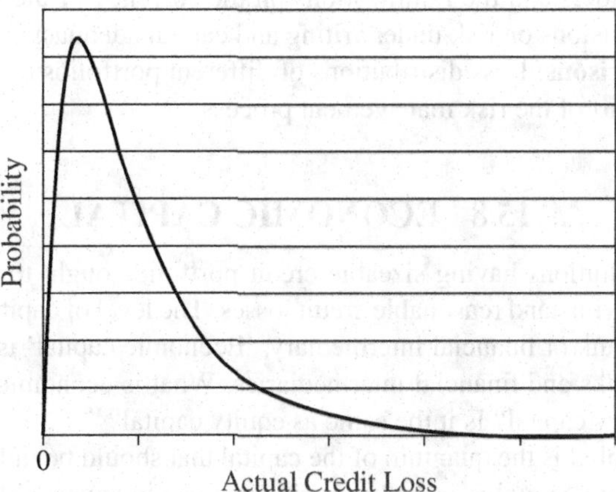


**Figure 15.2** Typical Credit Loss Distribution

The main characteristics are: (i) it is an asymmetrical distribution/diagram, (ii) it is highly skewed. The distribution is more concentrated toward small losses, with very few chances of large losses and (iii) the distribution has lengthy tail. As discussed earlier, a credit loss distribution of a credit portfolio is a function of the number of credit assets in the portfolio, their credit ratings, the exposure amount, PDs, LGDs, concentrations and correlations among credit assets in the portfolio. Please see the case study as it shows an example of Credit Loss Distribution.

### 15.7.2 Benefits of Developing a Credit Risk (or Loss) Distribution

Credit risk probability distributions are useful in the analysis of portfolio risk factors. Hence it is recommended that as far as possible, a credit loss distribution may be fitted to reflect the underlying credit portfolio loss behaviour. Credit risk (or loss) distribution is useful in many ways as given below:

**Determines adequacy of capital**: The expected loss and unexpected loss is depicted by the distribution. This will enable the financial institution to decide upon the capital required and to what extent it should leverage the balance sheet, without impacting its solvency. We will discuss this further under 'Economic Capital'.

**Credit risk pricing**: If the credit loss distribution displays a higher risk profile of the portfolio, then pricing must be high to compensate the higher risk, unless the risk level can be brought down within a short period.

**Manage the risks at portfolio level**: As we have discussed earlier, the objectives of portfolio management must ensure that the credit losses remain small and remain within the range of EL. With this as the target, proper management of critical variables (such as N, PD,

LGD, etc.) as well as the awareness of the scenarios when the higher losses could occur ought to enable proactive portfolio management.

**Portfolio stress tests**: The outcome of each portfolio-level stress test, under different scenarios, may be displayed in the form of credit loss distributions. This in turn would enable us to understand the ramifications on the solvency of the institution and to take appropriate decisions on risk underwriting and capital adequacy.

**Portfolio comparisons**: Loss distributions of different portfolios or sub-portfolios may be compared as part of the risk management process.

## 15.8 ECONOMIC CAPITAL

Banks, FIs and institutions having sizeable credit portfolios ought to ensure that they have sufficient capital to withstand reasonable credit losses. The level of capital is based on the risks underwritten by a bank or financial intermediary. 'Economic capital' is the buzz word that is now common in banks and financial intermediaries. What is economic capital? How does it differ from regulatory capital? Is it the same as equity capital?

The economic capital is the quantum of the capital that should be linked to the credit risks[4] undertaken. Economic capital is intended to absorb large unexpected losses, and protect the depositors and other creditors, which in turn will provide confidence to external investors and rating agencies on the financial health of the bank or financial institution. It may be noted that under an economic capital approach a number of other factors – such as correlation, sector concentration and name concentration risk – are also considered over and above PD, LGD and EAD. Economic capital[5] addresses two principal issues concerning the management, shareholders and other key stakeholders.

- **Solvency**: All stakeholders of a bank or FI are concerned about the solvency of the institution. As we have seen earlier, the underlying business model of a bank or FI presupposes the use of funds from depositors or other modes of leverage. A bank or FI will always enjoy leverage, which is based on the belief of solvency of the institution at all times. Economic capital measures the capital required based on the underlying economics of the credit portfolio, i.e. various risks/assets underwritten by the institution. This enables the institution to take proactive measures and seek additional capital if there is an increase in the level of risks due to changes in the risk characteristics of the portfolio.
- **Profitability**: If higher credit risks are pursued, a higher capital cushion is called for with associated costs. Economic capital also forms the basis for computing the Risk-Adjusted Return On Capital (RAROC) or Economic Value Added (EVA) for a bank or FI. We will explore these details later in the book.

The efficient use of capital presupposes sound understanding and knowledge of the risks underwritten. This re-emphasizes the importance of risk management by the banks and financial institution.

---

[4] The economic capital concept can also be extended to other risks such as market risk, trading risk, operational risk and so on. Since our topic is credit risk, the largest or principal risk in banks and financial intermediaries, we limit our discussion to the economic capital requirement in the context of credit risk only.

[5] Also useful for strategic planning, capital budgeting, performance measurement, risk based pricing, limit setting and customer profitability analysis.

### 15.8.1 Regulatory Capital vs. Economic Capital

Whilst it is acknowledged that capital is relevant from the risk management perspective for banks and financial intermediaries, we need to become familiarized with regulatory capital requirements and economic capital. Central banks across the world, also known as regulators, want to have adequately capitalized banks which will prevent bankruptcies in the financial sector. Accordingly, regulators prescribe minimum owners' capital that will be at risk in the banking or financial intermediation business. This, in turn, is expected to provide an incentive towards good governance. The minimum levels of capital prescribed by regulators are known as regulatory capital and this is influenced by the Basel Accords, which attempt to harmonize global standards as far as regulatory capital is concerned. As we have seen earlier, economic capital reflects the economic realities of the business.

Let us have a quick comparison of both in Table 15.2:

**Table 15.2** Regulatory Capital vs. Economic Capital

| Regulatory Capital | Economic Capital |
|---|---|
| Mandatory. Banks must regularly calculate regulatory capital requirements | Optional. Banks may or may not calculate economic capital. However, economic capital has emerged as 'language of risk' at major FIs/banks |
| Regulators or central bank often prescribe minimum level of regulatory capital – usually 8% of the risk weighted credit portfolio | Differ from case to case. When economic capital is calculated, it forms the basis for making a wide variety of intelligent decisions |
| Regulatory capital is often defined in terms of accounting terms and being balance sheet driven | Economic capital is more a reflection of the underlying economic impact of the various risks (mainly credit risk) on the portfolios of the bank |
| Regulatory capital aims at ensuring adequate resources available to absorb the losses | This is true for economic capital; although much broader in scope (than regulatory capital). Economic capital is decided by each bank's (organization's) own strategies and internal plans |
| The higher the credit risk of the credit portfolio, the higher the capital required | This is true for economic capital also – although much broader in scope |

Both regulatory and economic capital is evolved from a financial institution's risks. Hence, ideally the two kinds of capital ought to be equal. This is the ideal scenario and we hope the future will see new rules to bring regulatory capital more in line with the bank's or FI's economic capital. Since many banks and FIs are currently required to comply with regulatory and not economic capital, it gives rise to some interesting situations.

Let us have a hypothetical example – suppose a bank has two new credit assets under consideration:

Loan 1: It requires economic capital of $10k but regulatory capital needed is $5k.
Loan 2: It requires economic capital of $5k but regulatory capital needed is $10k.

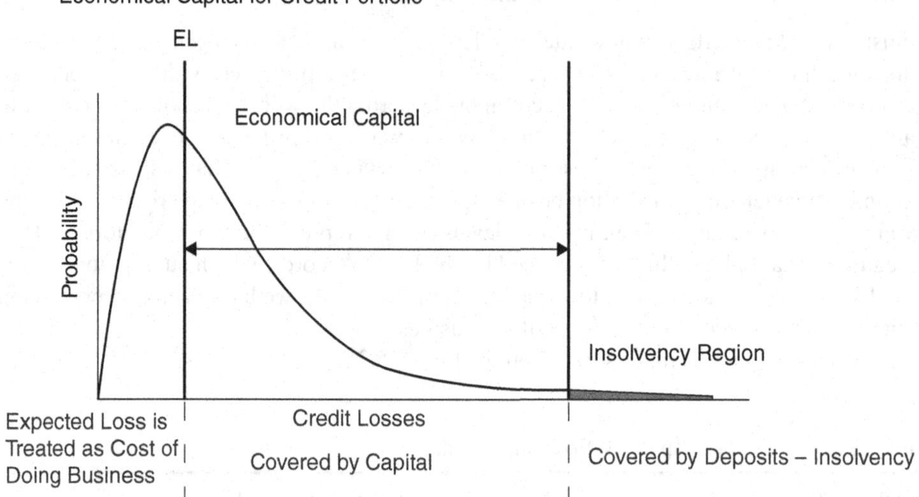


**Figure 15.3** Estimation of Economic Capital based on Credit Loss Distribution

Assuming the pricing and profitability is the same for both loans, which loan would the bank prefer?

One could argue that a bank that is required to comply with regulatory capital calculations would prefer the loan that requires least regulatory capital and would prefer Loan 1. On the other hand, a credit institution that is not subject to regulatory constraints would prefer Loan 2 as it requires less economic capital. These types of situations are akin to 'Regulatory Arbitrage' facilitated by the Basel Accords, which provided scope for banks to circumvent the rules by actually reducing their capital requirements without the corresponding reducing of risk.

### 15.8.2 Measuring Economic Capital

The economic capital is called 'economic' capital because it calculates risk based on economic realities rather than accounting rules. Economic capital can also be viewed as the amount of capital required to capture potentially large losses (i.e. unexpected losses) in a bank or FI. In this context, it is therefore important to know the underlying distribution that produces the values of unexpected losses. Whilst several options for converting a credit portfolio into a risk distribution are available, the Case Study (see Appendix) is based on Monte Carlo simulation.[6] Once the distribution is established, the process involves converting the risk distribution to the amount of capital required to support the underlying risk of the portfolio. As previously discussed, one of the uses of credit risk is to enable the estimation of the economic capita (see Figure 15.3).

[6] In practice, the decision on appropriateness of a distribution may be finalized in consultation with a competent expert.

The economic capital concept does not cover the expected loss, which is the cost of doing business. The economic capital will cover Unexpected Losses (UL). If this exceeds the economic capital, the depositors will suffer as the bank or FI would become bankrupt, i.e. the entire equity would be wiped out. Since UL is also derived based on PDs and LGDs, etc., it is important to know the risk factors of the underlying credit loss distribution (that produced the UL). It may also be noted that the credit risk variables (PD, LGD, etc.) fluctuate over time in response to external stimuli, e.g. changing economic conditions, and hence UL would also fluctuate. Hence ideally, the economic capital must be sufficient to cover the worst case scenario.

Based on the credit loss distribution, an institution can arrive at economic capital depending upon the desired level of confidence. Capital adequacy means having sufficient equity in the business that would enable the bank to survive even the worst case defaults. This is an important factor in the debt rating of banks by external rating agencies such as Moody's. The capital adequacy can be interpreted or linked to a corresponding probability of bankruptcy (or default probability). For example we can say that an AA-rated bank typically has a default probability of less than 0.05%. In other words, we can say that the bank must maintain capital adequacy at such levels that the probability of the bank staying solvent (even in the worst case default scenario) is 95%.

It is the credit risk team of a bank or FI which plays an important role in ensuring that the credit risk variables remain at satisfactory levels. It is suggested that the internal data on PD, LGD and other variables be periodically audited by external experts. Regulatory authorities often find this task challenging given the resource constraints – i.e. limited man power as well as expertise by regulatory authorities in view of the increasingly complex nature of banks and FI's lending activities. This is essential to ensure that the internally generated data is free of any potential manipulation, in pursuit of minimizing capital requirements and maximizing profits.

### 15.8.3 Optimizing Economic Capital

Primarily by varying and adjusting the PD (riskiness of credit assets), LGD (recovery rates), correlation (diversification effect) and exposure levels, the institutions can manage economic capital requirements. The lower the risk, the less capital is required and vice versa.

It may be noted that under an economic capital approach a number of other factors – such as correlation, sector concentration and name concentration risk – play a role in determining the capital over and above PD, LGD and EAD. Whilst other variables remain the same, the lower the PD and LGD, the lower would be the economic capital requirement. If both PD and LGD can be lowered together, this would generate a very conservative credit loss distribution and accordingly the economic capital requirements would also be lowered. The goal of the portfolio risk management team would be to implement the portfolio risk mitigants (discussed later in the book) and minimize PD and LGD to the extent possible.

## CASE STUDY

Hypothetical Bank has a credit portfolio of 18 individual credit assets with a maturity of one year. Credit limits (exposure), credit risk grade, and Probability of Default (PD) assigned to the grades are given below. Loss given default is assumed to be 90%. Expected Loss (EL) is also calculated, and is given below:

| CUSTOMER NAME | Exposure $million | Credit Risk Grade | PD | LGD | EL |
|---|---|---|---|---|---|
| Customer 1 | 700 | 13 | 1.94% | 90% | 12.22 |
| Customer 2 | 600 | 11 | 0.76% | 90% | 4.10 |
| Customer 3 | 600 | 11 | 0.76% | 90% | 4.10 |
| Customer 4 | 550 | 12 | 1.20% | 90% | 5.94 |
| Customer 5 | 500 | 10 | 0.50% | 90% | 2.25 |
| Customer 6 | 450 | 14 | 3.12% | 90% | 12.64 |
| Customer 7 | 400 | 10 | 0.50% | 90% | 1.80 |
| Customer 8 | 350 | 10 | 0.50% | 90% | 1.58 |
| Customer 9 | 300 | 11 | 0.76% | 90% | 2.05 |
| Customer 10 | 250 | 10 | 0.50% | 90% | 1.13 |
| Customer 11 | 200 | 13 | 1.94% | 90% | 3.49 |
| Customer 12 | 150 | 13 | 1.94% | 90% | 2.62 |
| Customer 13 | 100 | 13 | 1.94% | 90% | 1.75 |
| Customer 14 | 50 | 11 | 0.76% | 90% | 0.34 |
| Customer 15 | 350 | 13 | 1.94% | 90% | 6.11 |
| Customer 16 | 200 | 10 | 0.34% | 90% | 0.61 |
| Customer 17 | 150 | 19 | 64.32% | 90% | 86.84 |
| Customer 18 | 100 | 10 | 0.50% | 90% | 0.45 |
| Total | 6,000 | Portfolio Expected Loss -> | | | 150.02 |
| Expected Loss % (Exposure at Default × PD × LGD) | | | | | 2.5% |

The total portfolio value is $6 billion on which the portfolio expected loss is 2.5% (or $150.02m). The managing director is satisfied with the portfolio EL of 2.5%, in view of the current economic conditions. EL has been factored into the credit pricing of each customer. However he would like to know what the credit loss distribution looks like given the uncertainties associated with the behaviour of PD, LGD, and EAD over the next year, especially if the general economic conditions deteriorate. He suggests the following scenarios for each variable:

1. EAD can vary between $1 billion to $ 6 billion. Maximum utilization cannot exceed the limit.
2. PD can vary between 0.006% and PD is 100%.
3. LGD can vary from 0% to 100%.
4. Correlation is zero.

Please provide your views and explain, as necessary.

**Answer**

Let us use Monte Carlo simulation to derive credit loss distribution of the above portfolio. Based on these assumptions, we have subjected the above portfolio to a Monte Carlo simulation of 5,000[7] iterations to assess situations when the expected loss of $150.02m would be exceeded. The resultant Credit Loss (CL) distribution and loss probabilities are given below:

| CL Observations | Frequency | Cumulative Frequency | Loss Probability | Cumulative Loss Probability |
|---|---|---|---|---|
| **0–150** | 1,048 | 1,048 | **21%** | **21%** |
| **150–300** | 636 | 1,684 | **13%** | **34%** |
| **300–450** | 496 | 2,180 | **10%** | **44%** |
| **450–600** | 418 | 2,598 | **8%** | **52%** |
| **600–750** | 357 | 2,955 | **7%** | **59%** |
| **750–900** | 301 | 3,256 | **6%** | **65%** |
| **900–1,050** | 253 | 3,509 | **5%** | **70%** |
| **1,050–1,200** | 201 | 3,710 | **4%** | **74%** |
| **1,200–1,350** | 195 | 3,905 | **4%** | **78%** |
| **1,350–1,500** | 139 | 4,044 | **3%** | **81%** |
| **1,500–1,650** | 111 | 4,155 | **2%** | **83%** |
| **1,650–1,800** | 116 | 4,271 | **2%** | **85%** |
| **1,800–1,950** | 119 | 4,390 | **2%** | **88%** |
| **1,950–2,100** | 87 | 4,477 | **2%** | **90%** |
| **2,100–2,250** | 69 | 4,546 | **1%** | **91%** |
| **2,250–2,400** | 53 | 4,599 | **1%** | **92%** |
| **2,400–2,550** | 52 | 4,651 | **1%** | **93%** |
| **2,550–2,700** | 58 | 4,709 | **1%** | **94%** |
| **2,700–2,850** | **42** | **4,751** | **1%** | **95%** |
| **2,850–3,000** | 39 | 4,790 | **1%** | **96%** |
| **3,000–3,150** | 32 | 4,822 | **1%** | **96%** |
| **3,150–3,300,** | 38 | 4,860 | **1%** | **97%** |
| **3,300–3,450,** | 29 | 4,889 | **1%** | **98%** |
| **3,450–3,600** | 22 | 4,911 | **0%** | **98%** |
| **3,600–3,750** | 25 | 4,936 | **1%** | **99%** |
| **3,750–3,900** | 21 | 4,957 | **0%** | **99%** |
| **3,900–4,050** | 16 | 4,973 | **0%** | **99%** |
| **4,050–4,200** | 5 | 4,978 | **0%** | **100%** |
| **4,200–4,350** | 7 | 4,985 | **0%** | **100%** |
| **4,350–4,500** | 3 | 4,988 | **0%** | **100%** |
| **4,500–4,650** | 4 | 4,992 | **0%** | **100%** |
| **4,650–4,800** | 5 | 4,997 | **0%** | **100%** |
| **4,800–4,950** | 1 | 4,998 | **0%** | **100%** |
| **4,950–5,100** | 1 | 4,999 | **0%** | **100%** |
| **5,100–5,250** | 0 | 4,999 | **0%** | **100%** |
| **5,250–5,400** | 0 | 4,999 | **0%** | **100%** |
| **5,400–5,550** | 0 | 4,999 | **0%** | **100%** |
| **5,550–5,700** | 1 | 5,000 | **0%** | **100%** |
| **5,700–5,850** | 0 | 5,000 | **0%** | **100%** |
| **5,850–6,000** | 0 | 5,000 | **0%** | **100%** |
| **Total (N)** | 5,000 | | | |

[7] More iterations are possible.

The above represents the typical credit loss pattern. Small losses are more common while a large loss is infrequent. The highest probability of loss is between $0 and $150m (21% probability). Approximately there is a 79% chance (100% – 21%) that the credit loss may exceed the EL. Any loss over and above the EL is Unexpected Loss (UL) and the bank is supposed to hold sufficient capital to withstand UL in order to ensure solvency. The loss distribution can be diagrammatically presented as shown in Figure 15.4:

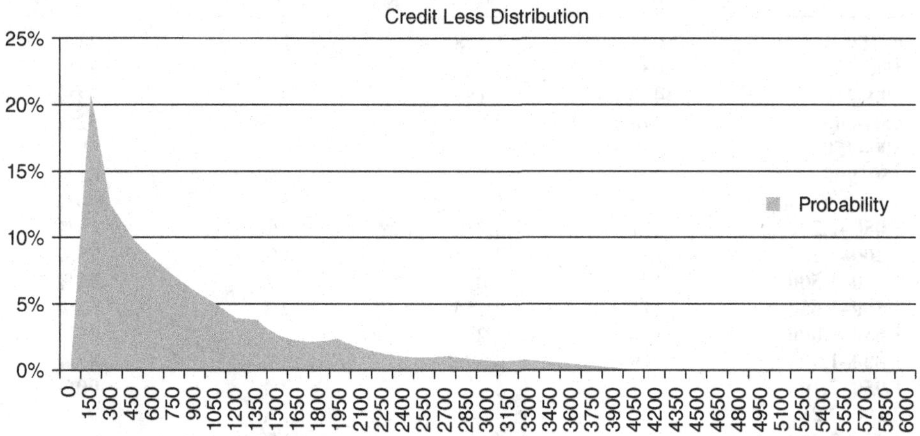


**Figure 15.4** Possible Credit Losses and Probabilities

In case of an economic downturn, the impact of the portfolio would far exceed the EL of $150.02m. One of the main reasons is that the credit portfolio has a serious limitation of name concentration. The largest exposure is $700m and comprises 11.6% of the credit portfolio while the top five names account for approximately 50% of the portfolio. Given this concentration risk,[8] any distress in the top customers would impact the portfolio significantly. The risk would be higher if the top customers belong to cyclical or identical sectors with strong positive correlation. Hence, this portfolio requires more diversification while each portfolio constituent must be monitored through regular EIIF assessment and an appropriate covenant suite. We also do not agree with the assumption of zero correlation as various portfolio constituents ought to have some degree of correlation, especially given the concentration risk. (The above credit loss distribution can also be considered for further processing to calculate economic capital.[9])

## ✍ QUESTIONS/EXERCISES

1. Explain how the Portfolio PD is calculated.
2. Explain migration risk. How does the Merton Model explain migration risks?

[8] The Basel Accord recommends additional capital in the event of concentration risk through the ICAAP Process.

[9] For illustrative purposes, by maintaining an economic capital of $2,850m, the bank can remain 95% solvent (see cumulative loss probability column) of the time – this would mean capital adequacy of 47.5% ($2,850/$6,000). However, this level of capital adequacy may have practical difficulties and hence the bank management must implement strategies to obtain more favourable credit loss distribution. Amongst others, strategies that would reduce the PD (firm credit risk screening), LGD (collateral selection and facility structuring), and other factors (proper diversification, etc.) may be pursued to reduce the economic capital requirements. For example, if we run the simulation assuming LGD of 20% economic capital at 95% the confidence level would be $600m or 10% in the above Case Study. This is because lower LGD would translate into lower credit losses, hence lower capital is sufficient.

3. How would you compute economic capital for a credit portfolio?
4. Explain PD, LGD, and EAD. How are they related to the expected loss of a credit asset? Also explain the factors influencing PD and LGD.
5. What is unexpected loss? Explain the steps required to minimize unexpected loss.
6. Explain how effective firm credit risk analysis and portfolio risk analysis ensure efficient credit risk management.
7. Theoretical Bank Ltd is conducting credit risk analysis of two new customers (i) XYZ & Co Ltd and (ii) ABCD & Co Ltd. As per its credit policy, each EIIF factor is assigned marks as follows:

   External Risk factors: 20 Marks
   Industry Risk factors: 20 Marks
   Internal Risk factors: 30 Marks
   Financial Risk factors: 30 Marks
   Total: 100 Marks

   As per the bank's credit policy, the marks are mapped to the credit risk ratings as follows:

| **Category** | Very Low Risk | | Low Risk | | Low-Moderate Risk | | Moderate Risk | | Satisfactory | | Acceptable Risk | | Moderate-High Risk | | High Risk | | Very High Risk | | Default | Loss |
|---|---|---|---|---|---|---|---|---|---|---|---|---|---|---|---|---|---|---|---|---|
| **Marks** | >95 | >90 | >85 | >80 | >75 | >70 | >65 | >60 | >55 | >50 | >45 | >40 | No new customers at these levels | | | | | | | |
| **Grade** | 1 | 2 | 3 | 4 | 5 | 6 | 7 | 8 | 9 | 10 | 11 | 12 | 13 | 14 | 15 | 16 | 17 | 18 | 19 | 20 |

   XYZ & Co Ltd and ABCD & Co Ltd scored 12, 15, 25 and 22 and 15, 18, 20 and 20 respectively in EIIF evaluation. Please ascertain appropriate credit risk grades for these new customers. By referring back to Chapter 10, explain how PD is assigned to credit risk grades.
8. What is the role of Credit Loss (CL) distributions for credit portfolio management? Explain the benefits of developing a CL distribution. Also elaborate the characteristics of a CL distribution. Elucidate how CL distributions enable us to assess capital requirements.

# 16

# Credit Risk and The Basel Accords

The Basel Accords place a heavy emphasis on credit risk. In fact Basel I, rolled out in the late 1980s, focused purely on credit risk. Subsequent Basel Accords began to include market risk, liquidity risk, leverage risk and concentration risk, amongst others. However, credit risk still occupies a place of paramount importance in the Basel Accords because credit risk is the most important of all risks faced by banks/FIs.

The major cause of serious banking problems and bad debt issues can be directly attributable to ineffective credit standards, weak risk management infrastructure, or a lack of flexibility to react quickly to changes in economic or other external circumstances that lead to a deterioration of credit assets. The 2008 Credit Crisis is a stark reminder – inadequate credit risk management can have far reaching impacts of systemic proportions. The mismanagement (or lack of awareness) of both obligor and portfolio credit risks is identified as one of the major reasons for the collapse of banks and financial institutions in this crisis.

## 16.1 BASEL ACCORDS

After the failure of two high profile international banks[1] in 1974 – Herstatt Bank in Germany and Franklin National Bank in the US – the central banks of major economies in the world recognized the need for broad supervision of banking globally. Thus the Basel Committee was formed in 1974 to formulate broad supervisory standards and guidelines of best practice in banking supervision.

It may be noted that all guidelines are recommendatory in nature and it is up to the member countries to implement them. There was also a realization that banks were becoming global in their operations and there was a need for a regime to ensure that all banks are adequately regulated and that banks held sufficient capital to protect the global financial system as well as their depositors. The general consensus for broad supervisory standards gave rise to the Basel Accords. Amongst other things, the Basel Accords provide guidance on risk management and minimum capital ratios to be implemented in the banks and financial institutions.

The Basel Committee on Banking Supervision (BCBS) is a committee of central banks representing all the G-20 and other major economies in the world. The list is given in Table 16.1.

Typically the Committee meets at the headquarters of the Bank of International Settlements (BIS) in Basel, Switzerland. However, the BIS does not participate in the policy deliberations of the Basel Committee. The decisions of the Committee are developed after extensive consultations with the banking/FI industry, mainly at national levels. The Committee formulates broad supervisory standards and guidelines before recommending statements of best practice in banking supervision. Their overriding objective is to promote sound business and supervisory standards through comprehensive risk management.

The Committee does not have the power to enforce recommendations; however, most member countries (and some non-member countries) tend to implement the policies.

[1] Both collapsed due to excessive risk taking which resulted in crippling losses.

**Table 16.1** Major Central Banks in BCBS

| | | | |
|---|---|---|---|
| Argentina | Hong Kong | Mexico | Sweden |
| Belgium | India | Netherlands | Switzerland |
| Brazil | Indonesia | Russia | Turkey |
| Canada | Italy | Saudi Arabia | United Kingdom |
| China | Japan | Singapore | US |
| France | Korea | South Africa | |
| Germany | Luxembourg | Spain | |

Recommendations are enforced through national laws and regulations. The Basel Committee is responsible for the Basel Accords.

## 16.2 BASEL I (1988) – FIRST BASEL ACCORD

In the case of banks, traditionally, they have more leverage. The equity capital represents just a small fraction of their assets. Such leverage levels are considered unacceptable for non-finance institutions. It may be noted that 100% equity funded banks are not feasible or practical. The high leverage of banks is one of the main reasons why banking is among the most regulated industries, the world over.

Basel I established a uniform system of capital adequacy standards (for banks) which came into effect from January 1993. The main principle stipulates a minimum of 8% of capital to support the value of the risk weighted assets of a bank. The prescribed formula is as given below:

$$\frac{\text{Capital (Tier 1 + Tier 2)}}{\text{Risk Weighted Assets}} = \text{Capital Ratio (Minimum 8\%)}$$

**Capital**: A distinction was made between Tier 1 and Tier 2 capital. Tier 1 capital, the more important of the two, consists of paid-up share capital and disclosed reserves (less goodwill) and Tier 2 capital, also known as supplementary capital, comprises undisclosed reserves, loan loss allowances/reserves, asset revaluation reserves, hybrid capital instruments (such as mandatory convertible debt, etc.) and subordinated debt. Also the Tier 1 capital should be at least 50% of the total capital.

**Risk Weighted Assets (RWA)**: Assets in the balance sheet of a bank are assigned different risks under Basel I, based on their inherent risk. While government and central bank obligations carry nil (0%) risk those of the private sector carry full risk (100%). The risk weighting is shown in Table 16.2:

**Table 16.2** Risk Weights for On Balance Sheet Items in Basel I Accord

| | Risk Weighting | | | |
|---|---|---|---|---|
| Counterparty/Assets | 0% | 20% | 50% | 100% |
| Cash, Central Bank, and Government Exposure | X | | | |
| OECD Govt Debt/Claims Guaranteed by Central Banks | X | | | |
| Multilateral Development Banks (ADB, IBRD, etc.) | | X | | |
| Banks in OECD/Claims Guaranteed by Them | | X | | |
| Residential Mortgage Backed Loans | | | X | |
| Private Sector Entities | | | | X |

The minimum level of capital would be determined with regard to the risk profile of a bank's portfolio. Another important aspect of the 1988 Accord is that it recognized the credit risks involved in the off-balance sheet items, which are converted based on appropriate conversion factor, extending from 0% to 100%. The summarized risk weight scale is shown in Table 16.3:

**Table 16.3** Risk Weights for Off-Balance Sheet Items in Basel I Accord

| | Risk Weighting | | | |
|---|---|---|---|---|
| Off-Balance Sheet Risks | 0% | 20% | 50% | 100% |
| Transaction Related Contingencies (Bid Bond, etc.) | | | X | |
| Direct Credit Substitutes – Guarantee of Indebtedness | | | | X |
| Letters of Credit, Collateralized by Underlying Shipments | | X | | |
| Certain Commitments that are Cancellable Unconditionally | X | | | |

Excluding Japan (which was in no position to adopt Basel I's recommendations due to the severity of their own banking crisis), all Basel Committee members implemented the recommendations by the end of 1992. Japan subsequently harmonized their policies to be consistent with Basel I in 1996 and other developing market economies (who were not participant members) also adopted the recommendations.

### 16.2.1 Criticisms of Basel I

Whilst the Basel I approach of assigning risk weights to specific assets was evolutionary in banking, Basel I was not without shortcomings. Hence Basel 1 Accord received a number of criticisms; the major ones are described below:

- **Basel 1[2] considered only credit risk**: Other risks such as market risk, operational risk, liquidity risk and concentration risk were not factored into the risk weighting. A partial amendment to the Accord was made in 1996, requiring banks to allocate capital to cover market risk (i.e. losses from movements in market prices on market sensitive assets).
- **Overly simplistic approach**: Basel 1 adopted a 'one-size-fits-all' method while prescribing the calculation of minimum regulatory capital requirements. It did not consider many differences among banks in different countries, where the methods of measuring capital might differ.
- **Rigid weightings**: It was stated the rules were too rigid and unrealistic in certain instances. For example private sector counterparties would attract a 100% weighting regardless of their underlying strength. Corporate lending to counterparties with credit ratings of AAA and B were assigned 100% weighting while it was evident that AAA was less risky than the latter.
- **Regulatory arbitrage**: The different weighting provided scope for banks to circumvent the rules by actually reducing their capital requirements without the corresponding reduction of risk (in fact they could even add to their risk profile). Banks became much more sophisticated in their operations and risk management and were increasingly finding ways to circumvent the rules, which has been known as 'regulatory capital arbitrage'. For example, whilst an on-balance sheet credit asset (e.g. mortgage) would require 100% weighting and securitization of the asset through a Special Purpose Vehicle (SPV) and converting it into an off-balance sheet item would require lesser weightings. Similarly, there was an incentive to securitize

[2] In 1996, Basel I was amended to incorporate 'Tier 3 capital' which introduced some market risk capital requirements. A provision was also introduced which allowed the banks to use an internal model for computing the amount of capital set aside for market risk.

low risk assets and hold on to relatively higher risk ones in the balance sheet since both required same capital adequacy, although with differing returns.

- **Lack of encouragement for diversification**: The rules also failed to discourage concentration risk and encourage risk management by diversification – an identical quantum of capital needs to be maintained in respect of one large loan and five similar loans to different borrowers – this provides further scope for dysfunctional behaviour.

## 16.3 BASEL ACCORD II (2006)

As the weaknesses of Basel I were becoming more evident, calls for an improved version became stronger. The credit derivatives market and securitizations also experienced explosive growth and there was evidence to suggest that banks were taking advantage of shortfalls in Basel I's simplistic risk weightings. In general banking, risk management techniques, external challenges and financial markets had undergone significant transformation. The Basel Committee decided in 1999 to propose a new, more comprehensive capital adequacy accord. This was formally known 'A Revised Framework on International Convergence of Capital Measurement and Capital Standards' and informally as 'Basel II'.

Basel II presented a more sophisticated approach to the calculation of minimum regulatory capital and introduced a three-pillar infrastructure that seeks to align regulatory capital with economic capital. Whilst Basel I was initially restricted in its focus on credit risk and market risk to a limited extent, Basel II introduced a comprehensive spectrum of credit risk approaches and, for the first time, there was a requirement to set aside capital for operational risk. Operational risk is defined as 'the risk of loss resulting from inadequate or failed internal processes, people and systems or from external events'. This requirement seeks to ensure that banks establish a strong risk culture with risk management at the heart of the organization.

**Pillar I – Minimum Capital Requirements**: The first pillar consists of similar risk capital ratios as per Basel I, albeit with the incorporation of operational risk. The fundamental ratio for minimum capital requirements is:

$$\frac{\text{Tier 1} + \text{Tier 2 Capital}}{\text{RWA (Credit, Market \& Operational)}} = \text{Capital Ratio (Minimum 8\%)}$$

The new framework allowed an array of approaches from (i) basic (standardized approach) to (ii) sophisticated (internal ratings based approach) methodologies for the measurement of credit risk, market risk and operational risk in determining capital levels. It provides banks with flexibility to adopt an approach that best fits their (i) size, (ii) activities, (iii) level of sophistication and (iv) risk profile.

**Pillar 2 – Supervisory Review**: Pillar 2 is meant to identify risk factors not captured in Pillar 1, giving regulators the ability to adjust the capital requirements calculated under Pillar 1. It addresses the role of the national supervisors – it sets out specific oversight responsibilities for the Board and other senior personnel, thus reinforcing the principles of internal control and sound corporate governance. Basel II stresses the importance of bank management to develop robust Internal Capital Assessment Procedures[3] with targets that

[3] The Internal Capital Adequacy Assessment Process (ICAAP) creates a basis to have an informed view on capital requirements to assert the Bank's position on capital adequacy. It also acts as a key document for the Bank to explain to regulatory authorities about its internal capital adequacy assessment methods, which includes the following six key features: Board and Senior Management Oversight, Sound Capital Assessment and Planning, Comprehensive Assessment of Risks, Stress Testing, Monitoring and Reporting, Robust Internal Controls. The ICAAP is expected to be an integral part of risk management and also to reflect how it is managed in practice.

correlate to their particular risk profile and control environment. This would be subject to supervisory review and intervention – supervisors may force banks to immediately raise capital should they believe that capital levels maintained are insufficient. Hence banks are incentivized to hold a buffer level of capital above the minimum levels.

**Pillar 3 – Market Discipline**: Pillar 3 aims to promote market discipline through enhanced disclosure by banks by setting out detailed disclosure requirements and recommendations in a number of areas. This includes disclosing how a bank calculates its capital adequacy and its risk assessment methods and therefore Basel II has also given cognizance to the requirements of various national accounting standards. By providing timely and transparent information, it should be possible for the market to better understand the business and respective risk of banks.

A diagrammatic presentation of Basel II and alternate approaches to credit risk weighting are given in Figure 16.1:

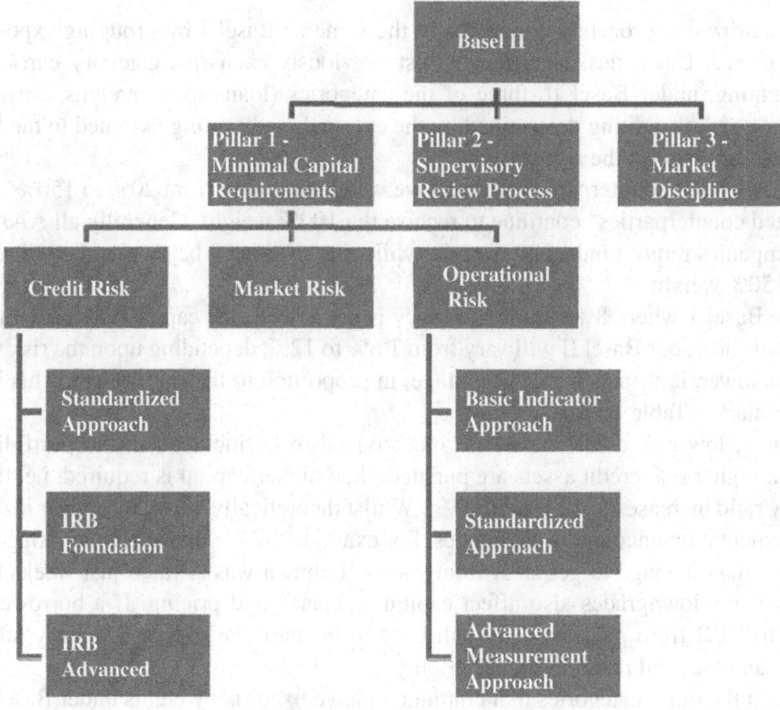


**Figure 16.1** Basel II Diagram

### 16.3.1 Alternative Approaches for Credit Risk in Basel II

Basel II provides banks with three approaches for the calculation of minimum capital requirements necessary to cover credit risk, all of which require an increasing level of sophistication:

- Standardized approach – a modified version of the Basel I approach.
- Internal ratings based approach, foundation.
- Internal ratings based, advanced.

**Table 16.4** Risk Weights in Basel II – Standardized Approach

| | | Assessment (Based on External Rating) | | | | |
|---|---|---|---|---|---|---|
| Counterparty | Unrated | AAA to AA− | A+ to A− | BBB+ to BBB− | BB+ to B− | Below B− |
| Sovereigns | 100% | 0% | 20% | 50% | 100% | 150% |
| Banks (Note 1) | 100% | 20% | 50% | 100% | 100% | 150% |
| Corporates | 100% | 20% | 50% | 100% | 100% | 150% |
| Retail-Mortgage | 35% | | | | | |
| Other retail | 75% | | | | | |

*Note 1:* Risk weighting based on risk weights of sovereign in which the bank is incorporated, but one category less favourable. Or alternatively the risk weighting can be based on the assessment of the individual bank. Claims on banks of an original maturity of less than three months generally receive a weighting that is one category more favourable than the usual risk weight on the bank's claim.

#### *16.3.1.1 Standardized Approach*

The standardized approach is conceptually the same as Basel I by grouping exposures into a series of risk categories. However, whilst previously each risk category carried a fixed risk weighting, under Basel II, three of the categories (loans to sovereigns, corporate and banks) have risk weighting determined by the external credit rating assigned to the borrower. Table 16.4 summarizes the risk weights.

Externally rated counterparties will receive weights ranging from 20% to 150%. However, the unrated counterparties[4] continue to receive the 100% weight. Generally all AAA and AA rated companies require only 20% weight while that of B- and below rated credit exposures require 150% weight.

Unlike Basel 1 where 8% capital adequacy is prescribed, the capital adequacy ratio of the credit portfolio under Basel II will vary from 1.6% to 12%, depending upon the risk weight. If the risk is lower, it attracts lower weightage, in proportion to the risk weight. This is evident from the chart in Table 16.5.

Evidently, low risk credit assets are incentivized to be included in the portfolio. In the event that higher risk credit assets are pursued, then higher capital is required, i.e. the capital adequacy ratio increases to 12% (150*8%). Whilst theoretically, this may appear ideal, practical implementation encounters challenges. For example, by hoodwinking the rating agencies, corporates may manage to get an A rating – e.g. Lehman was A rated just weeks before its collapse. Such downgrades also affect capital adequacy and pricing. If a borrower's rating changes to BBB from AA, the bank will have to increase the capital adequacy ratio on the borrower and this will result in higher pricing.

Amongst the other categories that continue to have fixed risk weights under Basel II, loans secured on residential property carry a risk weight of 35% (effective capital adequacy ratio of 2.8%, i.e. 35 × 8%) provided the loan-to-value ratio is below 80%. If the LTV is more than 80%, then a risk weight of 75% (effective capital adequacy ratio of 6%, i.e. 35 × 8%) becomes applicable. Since higher capital adequacy means more capital, the pricing[5] will be affected.

---

[4] An inherent weakness is evident. Instead of attracting a BB rating, the borrowers can withdraw from the rating in which case 100% weighting is possible instead of 150%.

[5] This may encourage the borrowers to obtain a property valuation in such a manner that the LTV is below 80%.

**Table 16.5** Effective Capital Adequacy for differing Risk Weights under Basel II

| Risk Weights | 20% Weight | 100% Weight | 150% Weight |
|---|---|---|---|
| Capital Adequacy | 1.60%* | 8%* | 12%* |

* RWA × 8% capital adequacy.

#### *16.3.1.2 Internal Ratings-Based (IRB) Approach to Credit Risk*

IRB allows banks to use their own internal estimates of risk to determine capital requirements, with the approval of their supervisors (i.e. Central Banks). Whilst the Standardized Approach (SA) is mandatory, a bank can choose IRB, subject to supervisory approval of the bank's internal credit rating systems. IRB are of two types:

1. **IRB Foundation (IRB-F)**, where the banks are required to provide their own internal estimates of Probability of Default (PD) and use predetermined regulatory inputs for Loss Given Default (LGD), Exposure at Default (EAD) and a factor for maturity.
2. **IRB Advanced (IRB-A)**, where all inputs to risk weighted asset calculation –PD, LGD and EAD – are estimated by the bank itself, subject to regulatory satisfaction.

As is evident, IRB presupposes advanced and sophisticated risk management systems in the bank. The adoption of an IRB approach requires empirical data, the main components of which are as follows:

**Probability of Default (PD)** defined as the statistical percentage probability of a borrower defaulting within a one year time horizon. PD is directly linked to the Customer Rating, based on the EIIF model. We discussed this topic in detail in Chapters 10 and 15. The PD can range from 0.00% for a zero risk customer to 100% for a very high risk customer.

**Loss Given Default (LGD)** is the estimated amount of loss expected if a credit facility defaults, calculated as a percentage of the exposure at the date of default. The value depends on the collateral, if any, and other factors that impact on the likely level of recovery. LGD estimates are to be based upon historical recovery rates and stress tested for economic downturns, among other things. Whilst in IRB-F, LGD values are to be supplied by the supervisor, banks following IRB-A can assign their own LGD values, subject to the approval of the supervisors. (See Chapter 15 for more on LGD.)

**Exposure at Default (EAD)** represents the expected level of usage of the facility utilization when default occurs. This value does not take account of collateral or security (i.e. ignores credit risk mitigation techniques with the exception of on-balance sheet netting where the effect of netting is included in EAD). Whilst EAD values are prescribed by supervisors or regulators in IRB (F), in IRB (A), banks can assign their own EAD values – but the process of estimation should meet the minimum standards.

EAD may vary depending upon the type of facilities. For instance overdraft facilities tend to be overdrawn in the case of defaulting customers, hence the exposure at default may be assumed as 110% (or a higher percentage depending upon the historical experience) of the overdraft limits sanctioned to the customer. On the other hand, in the case of reducing balance term loans, the exposure at default may be assumed as 95% because the customer is expected to meet some of the instalments before default.

In the case of non-funded facilities, the effective exposure (or credit equivalent) is calculated by assuming exposure at default at 20% or 50% depending upon the nature of the non-funded facility. In the case of derivative exposures with embedded credit risk (e.g. interest rate swaps and other OTC derivatives) the Basel framework stipulates methods[6] for determining exposure at default (EAD).

Correlation and maturity are also important for the IRB approach. All borrowers in a credit portfolio are linked to each other by a single systematic risk factor, i.e. the general state of the economy. As we discussed in an earlier chapter, in a well-diversified portfolio all unsystematic risks are diversified away. Hence, the correlations (R) could be described as the dependence of the asset value of a borrower on a key systematic risk, i.e. the economic conditions. Maturity adjustments (M) can be interpreted as anticipations of additional capital requirements due to possible downgrades in the future. Hence, the higher the term of the credit, the more capital is required, and accordingly the maturity is tweaked.

Fundamentally, under the IRB approach, a bank estimates each borrower's creditworthiness and the results are translated into estimates of a potential future loss amount, which form the basis of minimum capital requirements, subject to strict methodological and disclosure standards. Under both the foundation and advanced IRB approaches, the range of risk weights is far more diverse than in SA, resulting in greater risk sensitivity. If a bank can at least produce reliable PD empirically, then it can adopt IRB beginning with the foundation approach. The expected credit loss from an exposure is the main driver for determining the credit rating in IRB. LGD is dependent upon the collateral while EAD is the amount of credit extended. The three main elements of IRB – namely PD, LGD and EAD – are logically connected to determine the level of Expected Loss (EL) based on the formula we discussed earlier, i.e. EL = EAD × PD × LGD.

Whilst the distinction between borrower risk and transaction risk is one of the prerequisites of Basel II compliance, all elements should be viewed together to arrive at credit ratings. Interaction among PD, LGD and EAD is evident as illustrated in the following example:

**Example 16.1**

Suppose three customers, X Ltd, Y Ltd and Z Ltd, approach a bank for a credit facility of $100m with a maturity of one year. Based on EIIF study, the bank assigns following borrower/customer rating to the three prospective customers:

| Customer | Customer Rating |
|---|---|
| X Ltd | AA |
| Y Ltd | BB |
| Z Ltd | CC |

Customer ratings of AA, BB and CC are assigned probabilities of default of 0.5%, 2% and 75% respectively. LGD assigned to facilities secured by real estate is 40% while fully cash secured facilities are assigned 0%. Whilst X Ltd does not offer any collateral, Y Ltd offers real estate as collateral and Z Ltd offers full cash security for the credit facilities. Please rank the customers and assign credit ratings based on the expected credit loss.

[6] The Basel methods include (i) Basel Current Exposure Method (CEM), Basel Standardized Approach (SA) and Basel Internal Model Method (IMM). Please refer www.bis.org for details.

**Answer**

Ranking is as follows: the least risky credit will be the one extended to Z Ltd, followed by X Ltd and last would be Y Ltd. The following table summarizes the credit ratings:

| Customer | Credit Rating | PD | Collateral | LGD | Exposure | Expected Cr Loss* |
|---|---|---|---|---|---|---|
| X Ltd | AA | 0.50% | NIL | 100% | \$100m | \$0.5m |
| Y Ltd | BB | 2% | Real Estate | 40% | \$100m | \$0.8m |
| Z Ltd | CC | 75% | Fully Cash | 0% | \$100m | 0 |

* PD × LGD × Exposure (EAD).

### 16.3.2 Risk Weighted Assets (RWA) and Capital Adequacy in Basel II

RWA calculation under the standardized approach is more or less akin to the first Basel Accord, however with more granularity in weights. RWA calculation in IRB-F and IRB-A is complex. It includes (i) computation of PD, LGD and EAD, (ii) which is then adjusted to the correlation and maturity of the portfolio and (iii) computation of the capital requirement (K) as per the formula laid out in the Basel Framework. The formula for K is given below:

$$K = \left[ LGD \times N \left\{ \sqrt{\frac{1}{1-R}} \times G(PD) + \sqrt{\frac{R}{1-R}} \times G(0.999) \right\} - LGD \times PD \right] \times \frac{1 + (M - 2.5) \times b(PD)}{1 - 1.5 \times b(PD)}$$

where

N = normal distribution variable
R = correlation
G (PD) = inverse of cumulative normal distribution variable for the PD value
G (0.999)[7] = inverse of cumulative normal distribution variable for 99.9% statistical confidence (or 3.09)
M = maturity or term of the credit asset
b(PD) = maturity adjustment with PD.

Having arrived at K, we can calculate RWA by multiplying K with EAD and the reciprocal of the minimum capital ratio of 8%, i.e. by a factor of 12.5, i.e.

$$RWA = 12.5^{*}K^{*}EAD$$

Basel II imbeds risk-sensitivity into the framework. Hence less capital requirement for less risky assets. While Basel I prescribed 8% capital adequacy across the board, the standardized approach prescribes a capital adequacy range (say 2–12%). The capital adequacy requirement under Basel II IRB allows more granularity – i.e. provides for a wider range of capital adequacy, as evident from the chart in Figure 16.2.

[7] The confidence level was fixed at 99.9%, i.e. an institution is expected to suffer losses that exceed its level of Tier 1 and Tier 2 capital on average once in a thousand years.

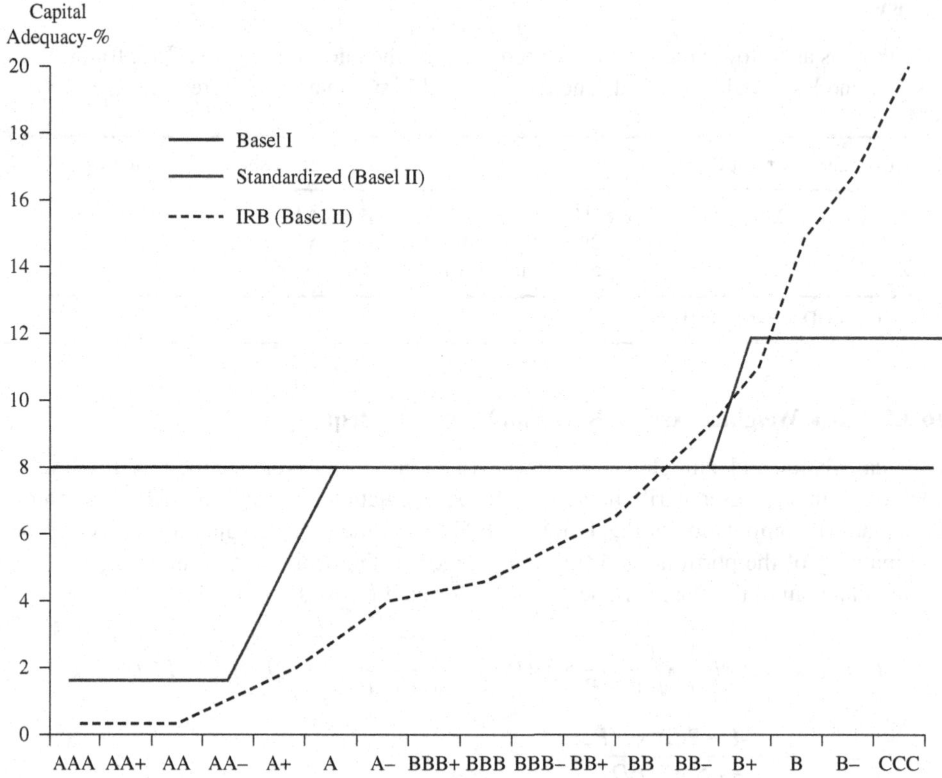


**Figure 16.2** Capital Adequacy under Various Methods of the Basel Accords

Among the three approaches, the IRB approach has greater risk sensitivity. IRB is more detailed than the Basel I and standardized approaches and in order to implement the IRB approach, the financial institution or bank ought to have a sophisticated risk management infrastructure that will capture the changes in the credit risk of the underlying portfolio components proactively and vary capital adequacy requirements accordingly. Thus IRB methods require lesser capital adequacy for AAA and A rated customers than in the Basel I and standardized approaches. At the same time, the risk sensitivity of the IRB approach attracts higher capital allocation for BB and below rated customers. One important aspect of the IRB approach is that the regulators are also supposed to have the same level of sophistication to monitor the IRB approaches to ensure that the approaches are utilized by the banks and financial institutions in such a manner that it does not result in underestimation of credit risk, in their quest to underwrite more business on less capital.

### 16.3.3 Do Higher LGD and PD Always Translate into Higher RWA under the IRB Approach?

Under normal circumstances, higher LGD and PD will result in higher RWA. However, this need not be true always. Depending upon the credit products dealt in (which impacts EAD), correlation and maturity, RWA calculation under the IRB approach can result in identical RWA even if underlying LGD and PD are different. Suppose there are two finance institutions with differing PD and LGD – say 1.6% and 45% and 2.1% and 60% respectively. Under normal circumstances, the finance institution with higher PD and LGD ought to have higher RWA. However it is interesting to note that both institutions can have identical RWA depending upon the variables such as EAD, correlation and maturity.

### 16.3.4 Criticisms of Basel II

The 2008 global financial crisis has required central banks around the world to bail out several banking giants and has been described by Federal Reserve Chairman Ben Bernanke as 'the worst financial crisis in global history'. On 15 September 2008, the investment banking giant Lehman Brothers went bankrupt, sending shockwaves around the global financial markets. Bank and financial institutions in several countries collapsed and governments had to intervene to avoid a systemic collapse. No wonder questions were raised about the efficacy of the Basel Accords that were put in place to bring stability into banking. As with Basel I, Basel II has been subject to significant criticism and there have been suggestions that it might have contributed inadvertently to complicating the financial crisis.

1. **Insufficient attention to liquidity risk**
   Many studies have pointed out that the weak liquidity profile of banks is among the important catalysts of the crisis. Adequate focus on liquidity standards to address short-term and long-term liquidity mismatches was not given. This often resulted in under-estimation of the liquidity risk. Basel II left the measurement of the liquidity risk and its management to each bank and financial institution.
2. **Increased pro-cyclicality and higher leverage**
   Riskiness of credit assets varies over the business cycle and Internal Ratings-Based (IRB) systems tend to reflect this, i.e. banks will act in a way which is pro-cyclical to the business cycle. In other words, during cyclical peaks, the borrower ratings tend to be better and hence low risk weights are applied. This anomaly typically results in the bank's setting aside less capital (allowing banks too much leverage) at the top of the cycle, effectively under-estimating their risk. Therefore Basel II can be perceived as making banks less capitalized and hence more vulnerable to failure during a downturn (depending on diversification and concentration to respective sectors).
3. **Questionable correlation assumptions**
   Basel II correlations are mostly static values. However in reality, correlations are dynamic as the underlying behaviour of credit assets is impacted by several dynamic forces such as financial product innovation, shifts in economy/markets, etc. as evidenced by the 2008 Credit Crisis. In certain cases, Basel II assumes that correlations decrease as a function of PD (i.e. that the correlation values for higher PD or lower quality obligors is lower). However, empirical studies have proven that this need not be true and that the correlations can be higher for higher PD borrowers, contrary to the Basel II assumptions. Similarly, empirically derived correlations vary geographically, suggesting that the Basel II assumption of applying the same correlation values for different geographies might not be appropriate.
4. **Over-reliance on external ratings**
   Basel II brought in a more prominent role for external ratings and accordingly, their ratings had begun to impact capital adequacy. The demand for AAA and AA rated securities (such as Collateralized Debt Obligations or CDO) were higher as Basel II required lesser capital adequacy on these categories (please see the chart in Section 16.3.3 above) and this might have acted as an incentive to get CDOs rated at AAA although inherently they

were more risky. Sometimes credit decisions were primarily based on external ratings as it enjoyed the tacit support of Basel II. However, there were serious questions about the accuracy and value of credit ratings that played such an integral part to Basel II.

Another severe criticism was that the external credit rating agencies[8] were not able to provide ratings which reflected the actual underlying risk and provided the markets with warning indictors of financial difficulties. The financial crisis saw swathes of downgrades and credit ratings agencies were criticized for allowing their own commercial interests to cloud their rating judgement.

5. **Usage of questionable risk management systems**

   Basel II is stated to have provided scope for less vigilant banks to systemically underestimate risk and loss allowances with a knock-on effect on capital adequacy. This enabled banks to pursue risky growth ambitions. The global financial crisis does reveal a serious flaw in the approach to risk management/capital adequacy as advocated by Basel II.

   Yet another criticism is that whilst Basel II factored in the asset correlation risk, this risk was underestimated. Similarly, allowing the use of risk models (based on normal distribution and related models) to estimate the underlying risk in marketable credit instruments is often highlighted as one of the major reasons for inadequate risk management in banks and financial intermediaries.

Insufficient attention to risks posed by securitization and derivatives is also highlighted as yet another lacuna of Basel II. Overall, the facilitation of unbridled credit growth (due to the ability to reduce risk weights by banks/FIs and reliance on external agency ratings) is often highlighted as the unintended consequence of Basel II.

In view of the shortfalls of Basel II, a revised Accord has been finalized – Basel III. This is the latest update of the Basel Accord designed to address a number of the underlying weaknesses existing under Basel II.

## 16.4 BASEL III

The 2008 Credit Crisis has demonstrated how large and sudden significant changes in asset values can quickly eradicate bank capital. Too-big-to-fail institutions took on too much risk which highlights a failure in the previous regulation. Basel III overwhelmingly focuses on initiatives to reduce the probability of future crises – although it cannot eradicate this risk. Basel III is also expected to promote financially prudent and conservative policies in the banking and financial sectors to build the capacity to absorb shocks, irrespective of the source. Some of the aspects of Basel III are expected to be effective from 2013 while others will be phased in over several years.

At the time of writing this book, Basel III requirements are in the final consultation phase and, as with previous accords, this will be subject to a deliberation period and it is likely to undergo amendments prior to implementation by financial centres around the world. The gradual phasing-in of the requirements is important to allow transitional costs to be managed and ensure this can be undertaken in a controlled manner.

In order to enhance the banking and financial systems' shock absorbing capacity, Basel III prescribes more liquidity measures and buffers along with tighter control on leverage. The Basel III regulations will affect all banks; however the impact may differ across types and sizes

[8] External rating agencies do not underwrite credit risk although they rate the customer, unlike a bank or FI. Unlike banks/FIs they get paid (i.e. fees) to rate a customer or an obligor.

of bank. Implementation of Basel III will result in increase in quantity and quality of capital, liquidity and improved leverage ratios, amended Pillar 2 and capital preservation. As Basel III evolves, interested readers can revert to the relevant BIS website for the latest proposals (http://www.bis.org/list/basel3/index.htm). The Basel III structure retains the Pillar I, Pillar 2 and Pillar 3 approaches; however Pillar 1 has several new features aimed at improving and strengthening the capital position of banks and FIs. Basel III can be diagrammatically approximated as shown in Figure 16.3:

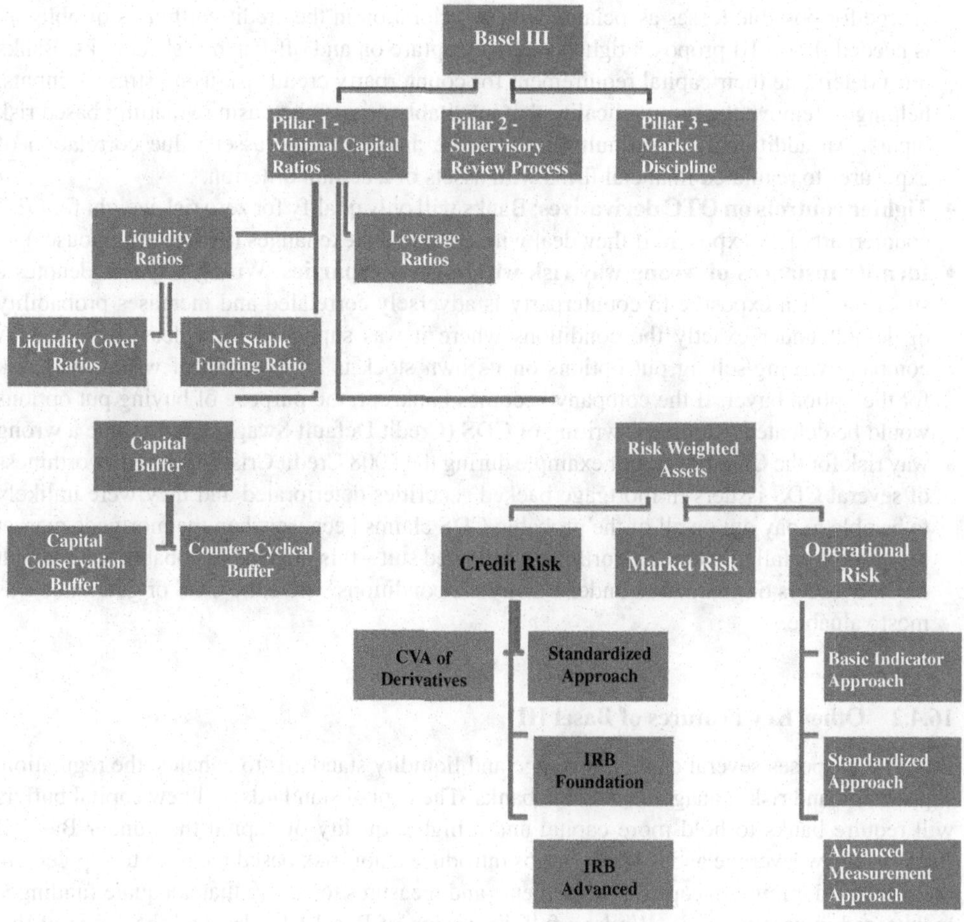


**Figure 16.3** Basel III Diagram

### 16.4.1 Credit Risk Measurement in Basel III

Credit risk measurement approaches in Basel III are almost the same as in the previous Accord (Basel II). However, based on the experience since the implementation of Basel II, a number of modifications have been incorporated in Basel III to plug loopholes and make the risk measurement techniques more robust. Major changes are discussed below:

- **Introduction of CVA (Credit Value Adjustment)**: CVA is the adjustment to the value of derivative products to account for counterparty credit risk. Many banks and FIs choose to actively manage counterparty risk through CVA trading. Basel III introduces a requirement for banks to hold regulatory capital against their CVA position.

- **Use of stress-tested PD**: Whilst PD estimates in internal ratings-based (IRB) will continue to drive capital requirements, the PD estimates will be more conservative. It will be arrived at by using the PD estimates for a bank's/FI's portfolios in downturn conditions. Accordingly, current PD estimates will not be used for capital purposes, but the stress tested PD for worst case scenarios.
- **Strengthens the requirements for the capital against credit risk**: An additional capital charge for possible losses associated with deterioration in the creditworthiness of obligors is needed. Basel III proposes tighter rules to capture on and off-balance sheet risks. Banks must determine their capital requirement for counterparty credit risk using stressed inputs, helping to remove the pro-cyclicality that inevitably arises when using volatility based risk inputs. An additional 1.25x multiplier is to be applied to the asset value correlation of exposures to regulated financial firms with assets of a certain criterion.
- **Tighter controls on OTC derivatives**: Banks will only qualify for zero risk weight for OTC counterparty risk exposure if they deal with centralized exchanges (i.e. clearing houses).
- **Identify instances of wrong way risk within counterparties**: Wrong way risk denotes a situation when exposure to counterparty is adversely correlated and increases probability of default under exactly the conditions where it was supposed to be least expected. A company writing/selling put options on its own stock is an example of wrong way risk for the option buyer. If the company becomes bankrupt, the purpose of buying put options would be defeated. Similarly, writing of CDS (Credit Default Swaps) can become a wrong way risk for the CDS buyer. For example during the 2008 Credit Crisis, the creditworthiness of several CDS issuers in mortgage backed securities deteriorated and they were unlikely to be able to pay out on all of the probable CDS claims because when the mortgage market went into freefall, their creditworthiness followed suit – this increased probability of default of CDS issuers or guarantors under exactly the conditions where the CDS or guarantee was most valuable.

### 16.4.2 Other Key Features of Basel III

Basel III proposes several capital, leverage and liquidity standards to enhance the regulation, supervision and risk management of the banks. The capital standards and new capital buffers will require banks to hold more capital and a higher quality of capital than under Basel II rules. The new leverage and liquidity ratios introduce a non-risk based measure to supplement the risk based minimum capital requirements and measures to ensure that adequate funding is maintained in case of crisis. Whilst a full discussion of Basel III is beyond the scope of this book, a few highlights are given below:

1. Raising the quality, consistency and transparency of the capital base.
   - Tier 1 Capital will consist of going concern capital in the form of common equity (common shares plus retained earnings). Tier 2 Capital is simplified and tightened up – there will be no sub-categories of Tier 2 Capital while Tier 3 Capital (allowed under Basel II) is abolished.
   - Additional capital is required in the form of a 'capital conservation buffer', which is designed to encourage banks to hold more capital than the minimum stipulated by the Accord or the national regulator. This will allow the banks to meet severe credit losses during periods of stress or crisis because they can utilize the capital buffer. During the

stressful period, if the capital buffers have been drawn down, the banks must immediately rebuild them, otherwise it will attract restrictions imposed by the national regulator on dividends, staff bonuses, etc.

- Additional capital is also required in the form of a 'counter-cyclical capital buffer'. The counter-cyclical capital buffer is expected to put brakes on rapid credit growth, which was evident in the run-up to the 2008 Credit Crisis. Accordingly, Basel III stipulates that the national regulators, at their discretion, may include a provision requiring banks to employ an additional capital buffer (above and beyond the capital conservation buffer) in economic boom times. The recommended ratio for this buffer is 2.5% of the risk weighted assets, although the final decision about the percentage belongs to national regulators, which have discretion based on the circumstances of each individual country's economy. To arrive at an appropriate ratio, regulators may consider factors such as the credit-to-GDP ratio.
- When you add up all of the numbers, Basel III stipulates that banks must hold at least 5% extra capital (over and above the normal capital adequacy ratio of 8%) to face bad times. See Appendix for Kelly's Formula which can act as a sense check on the capital buffer requirement.

2. Leverage Ratio

   The Committee is introducing a leverage ratio to help prevent the build-up of excess leverage that can lead to the de-leveraging 'credit crunch' situation.

3. Pro-cyclicality

   A series of measures are proposed to deal with pro-cyclical factors:

   - Apart from modification of calibration of the PD within risk models, it promotes forward-looking provisioning and encourages this to be based on expected (rather than the current or incurred) losses of banks' existing portfolios.
   - Banks should hold buffers of capital above the regulatory minimum – large enough to remain above the minimum in significant downturns. The buffer system may be used in a macro prudential framework to restrain credit growth – this mechanism would therefore act in a counter-cyclical manner.

4. Global minimum liquidity standard

   The Committee is introducing a global minimum liquidity standard for internationally active banks which includes the following:

   - 30-day Liquidity Coverage Ratio or LCR (highly liquid assets/net cash outflow over 30-day period) requirement underpinned by a longer term structural liquidity ratio, known as
   - Net Stable Funding Ratio or NSFR (available amount of stable funding/required amount of stable funding).

### 16.4.3 Can Basel III Prevent Future Financial/Credit Crises?

One of the major questions now being asked by concerned parties is whether Basel III can prevent the next possible financial crisis or banking sector collapse. The quick answer is negative. The 'black swan' nature of the risk triggers would lead us to conclude that that all possible risks and impacts cannot be covered through a framework of 'within the box' solutions. No amount of regulation and guidance can substitute prudent risk management by the bank. Hence, we can conclude that it is the quality of the risk management of a bank that will decide its future survival and profitability and not the procedural compliance with Basel III guidelines.

# APPENDIX

## Can the Kelly Criterion be applied to arrive at capital buffer?[9]

As we have seen, the main purpose of the Basel Accords is to ensure adequate capital of the bank to survive difficult times. Basel III has introduced several steps in this direction and seeks additional capital in the forms of buffer. Whilst at least 8% capital on risk assets is to be maintained, it is seen that the calculation of risk assets may become a challenge resulting in undercapitalization. Kelly's criterion is simple and can act as a 'sense check' or 'rule of thumb' to decide how much capital to be risked in a credit portfolio, given the overall portfolio risk measure, say portfolio PD. In other words, Kelly criterion cannot replace the Basel calculations, but can supplement it.

Let us see what Kelly Criterion is. John Kelly, who came out with the formula in 1956, was a Bell Labs scientist. The formula is a corollary to a Bell Lab application for information theory's ideas which were developed to facilitate a higher information rate for a given channel capacity (of Bell Lab projects). The genius of Kelly understood that the insight of the application is good to solve the uncertainty element of gambling or risk taking. If you have an edge in a probabilistic outcome, Kelly formula would show how much capital to put at risk to maximize long term gains.

The formula[10] is as follows:

$$\text{Capital to be committed} = (1\text{-PD}) - (\text{PD/edge ratio})$$

where

PD = probability of default at portfolio level
Edge ratio = the ratio between the net income[11] to the maximum credit loss.

Let us use a simplified example to elucidate its use in arriving at the capital to be risked for a credit portfolio.

### Example 16.2

A lending institution has a credit portfolio of \$6,000m with an average portfolio PD of 1.5%. The net income or margin is 2.5% or \$150m. If the portfolio collapses about 50% recovery can happen. Hence, maximum loss would be \$3,000 (50% x \$6,000). Hence, roughly the outcome shows a gain of \$150m vs. a loss of \$3,000, so the edge ratio is 1:20. From the PD we know that Pw = 98.5% and Pl = 1.5% or 98.5:1.5 probability. The institution maintains 8% capital adequacy and the portfolio exposure or RWA, i.e. \$6,000m. Based on the Kelly criterion, how much capital buffer should the lending institution maintain?

[9] For a detailed discussion, please refer to an article published by the author in the December 2012 newsletter by the Global Association of Risk Professionals (GARP), US.

[10] The original Kelly's Ratio for calculation of capital to be committed = Pw-(Pl / edge)
Where

Pw = probability of winning
Pl = probability of loss
Edge = the win ratio i.e. winning amount/ losing amount.

[11] After meeting all expenses, including expected loss (EL), but excluding any unexpected loss.

**Answer**

As per the adapted Kelly Criterion, the amount of capital to be risked is given below:

Capital to be committed = (1-PD) – (PD/edge ratio)
= 0.985 – (0.015/(1/20))
= 0.69 or 69% of the capital can be invested

If 8% capital adequacy is followed and assuming risk assets = $6,000m, the capital adequacy would be $6,000 × 8% = $480m. Kelly's Criterion says that this is to be equal to 69% and hence the actual capital would be $701m ($480m/69%). Hence, the capital buffer required would be $701m – $480m = $221m.

**Calculation of Capital required and Capital Buffer based on Kelly Formula**

| $, m | Base Case |
|---|---|
| Basel Accord Capital ratio | 8% |
| RWA | 6,000 |
| Net Income | 150 |
| PD | 1.5% |
| Max Loss | 3,000 |
| Pw (1-PD) | 98.5% |
| PD | 1.5% |
| Edge (Net Income/Max Loss) | 0.05 |
| Committable Capital – Kelly Formula (a) | 69% |
| Basel Accord Capital – 8% of RWA (b) | 480 |
| Capital Required – Kelly c= b/a | 701 |
| Hence Buffer Required d = c-b | 221 |
| Capital Buffer (as % of RWA) | 3.7% |

If there is deterioration in portfolio PD or LGD, or a reduction in net income, the impact on the capital buffer would be apparent i.e. exceed 5%. Under the static ratios prescribed in Basel III, the capital buffer will remain identical, because it is RWA driven. Kelly's formula, in contrast, provides more dynamism. The application of Kelly's formula is suggested not as a replacement for Basel III capital buffer rules, but as a supplement, just as successful hedge funds use it as a successful supplement to their investing or trading decisions.

Before trying this in a real life situation, the formula is to be mastered and its limitations understood as well. Just like any other methodology used in the business world, Kelly's formula has faced some criticisms. However, many businesses today (including several hedge funds that modified the formula to suit their requirements) are using it for capital allocation. Several hedge funds are using the Kelly's Criterion formula with appropriate modifications to suit their circumstances. If applied to a single deal, many recommend adopting half or even quarter of the capital computed by the criterion.

To know more, please refer to the original 1956 article, 'A New Interpretation of Information Rate' by John Kelly. Although there are critics of the above formula, successful hedge fund manager Edward Thorp is a strong supporter. Edward Thorp is also the author of two successful books related to investment and risk taking. In his books, Thorp explains the attractive features of Kelly's system. The most important is that Kelly's formula ensures that the chance of ruin is 'small'. Using Kelly's formula, in fact, it is theoretically impossible (assuming money is infinitely divisible) for a bank to lose all of its capital. Since a complete capital wipeout during a stressful scenario or crisis is one of the major concerns of banks, any formula that minimizes this threat is welcome.

## QUESTIONS/EXERCISES

1. What are the main differences between Basel 1 and Basel II?
2. What are the major defects of Basel II? Do you agree that that Basel II encouraged pro-cyclical policies?
3. What do you mean by Pillar II and III under Basel II? Do you believe ICAAP measures are adequate?
4. Discuss the major changes proposed under Basel III? Do you believe the latest version of the Basel Accords (Basel III) can prevent future financial crises similar to the 2008 Global Credit Crisis? Explain your views.
5. What are the major differences between the standardized and IRB approaches recognized in Basel Accords II and III?
6. One of your credit colleagues mentions that one of the major drawbacks of the Basel Accords is the excessive reliance on ratings (AAA, AA, BBB, etc.) by external rating agencies to decide the risk weighted assets and hence influencing the quantum of capital to be maintained against such assets. Since external rating agencies have no direct stake in the deal, he argues that it is not logical to commit vast amounts of funds into riskier transactions based on third party ratings. If the Basel Accords want an external rating, it must be done by a rating agency established and supervised by the Basel Committee. Do you agree with this view? Explain your views.
7. One of the main features of the financial sector in the 21st century is the ever increasing prominence of various types of derivatives. Discuss whether Basel III sufficiently equips the financial system of a country to cope if a bank with a large derivatives book does end up declaring bankruptcy without catastrophic effects.
8. Visit www.bis.org and see the latest update on Basel III.

# Part V
# Portfolio Risk Mitigants

Credit portfolio risks can be mitigated by deploying various tools such as caps, uncorrelated diversification, risk transfer and removal of the credit asset from the portfolio, all aimed at creating a 'shock-proof' portfolio.

# 17
# Credit Risk Diversification

History is replete with credit institutions – mainly banks – suffering immense losses or collapse due to an unbalanced portfolio structure. The London based early gold (smith) banks of the 1800s failed not because they were actually bankrupt but because they became illiquid due to improper portfolios, resulting in inability to convert assets into gold, consequent upon maturity mismatches. The recurrence of such instances resulted in the Bank of England (Central Bank) taking responsibility as re-discounter and lender of last resort.

As the 19th and 20th centuries wore on, Central Banks began to introduce several tools and measures to ensure stability by controlling credit risks of banks, paramount among which were credit portfolio risk mitigants. The Basel Committee, too, focuses on credit portfolio risk mitigation while prescribing capital adequacy norms. Even now, bank and financial institution crashes and problems created by illiquid or unbalanced portfolios due to inherent portfolio risks are not uncommon. A few such instances are given below:

- Many banking crashes in Japan in the 1990s were traceable to the concentration (or over-exposure) of the portfolio in real estate.
- The collapse of Barings Bank was also the result of the concentration of the portfolio in derivatives.
- Northern Rock, in the UK, ran into difficulties due to the concentration of wholesale funding.
- During 2008, several institutions in the US failed or were bailed out – Wachovia Bank, Lehman Brothers, Washington Mutual, Bear Stearns, Countrywide Financial, etc. were a few of them. Over-exposure to the real estate market was one of the main reasons for the crisis.

Unless suitable portfolio risks mitigants are implemented, such events are likely to continue. Only mega credit disasters attract the media limelight. Numerous situations do exist where portfolio credit risk results in bad performance of financial and non-financial institutions. Small scale/medium scale bankruptcies due to bad credit portfolios go unreported in the media while the inevitable consequences are borne by the hapless stakeholders.

Several tools have been under development, especially during the latter half of the 20th century, to tackle portfolio risks. Initial experiments were in equity portfolio, which later were adapted by portfolio categories such as Forex, Commodities, Credit and so on. Over time it has been established that many of the equity portfolio risk control techniques can be adapted to rein in portfolio credit risks as well.

Let us discuss how diversification contributes to managing and mitigating portfolio credit risks.

## 17.1 TRADITIONAL DIVERSIFICATION

All unsystematic risks mentioned in Chapter 14 can be diversified. One of the main reasons for the collapse of banks and financial institutions is concentration risk. Traditional diversification focuses on reducing the concentration risk by dispersing the portfolio among as many variables as possible so that a large and diversified portfolio is obtained. In fact the idea of traditional diversification is very old. It was mentioned by Shakespeare in the 16th Century in *The Merchant of Venice*

'My ventures are not in one bottom trusted
Nor to one place, nor in my whole estate
Upon the fortune of this present year
Therefore, my merchandise makes me not sad.'

It is quite logical that carrying all your eggs in one basket is not a good idea. If the basket is dropped conceivably all would be lost. Based on this principle banks, FIs and many business organizations manage credit risk concentrations by diversifying across obligor names, industry sectors and sub-sectors, geographic regions and countries, and product types. Various types of traditional diversification are discussed below.

### 17.1.1 Industry Limit

Credit risk exposures may be grouped according to industry or sector or market segment. Many banks usually restrict the exposure to each industry at a specified percentage, say 10% of the total portfolio. Normally financial institutions avoid concentration of exposure in any one sector of the economy. They aim to ensure that the credit portfolio is well spread across a broad mix of business sectors. Portfolio managers are alert to the risks relating to exposures in those sectors which are vulnerable to sudden changes in economic conditions or profoundly reliant on random factors/events such as government support. Porter's Model discussed in Chapter 6 is one of the useful tools to screen industries based on their attractiveness.

Figure 17.1 summarizes how the industry risks and industry life cycle (also see Chapter 6) impact the portfolio selection.

Most of the credit portfolio managers would attempt to avoid Stage 1 and Stage 5 companies given the higher risks involved. Within Stages 2–4, the choice of the industry may be carefully made based on the factors we discussed in Chapter 6. Once industries or sectors are studied, they may be segmented as discussed below.

**Target Industries/Sectors**: These industries hold promise for the future, the reasons for which can extend from good growth to inevitability to the infrastructure of the economy. Given the potential, these types of industry are highly desirable. Further increases in the credit portfolios will focus on the target sectors. Front line office units will have to tune their

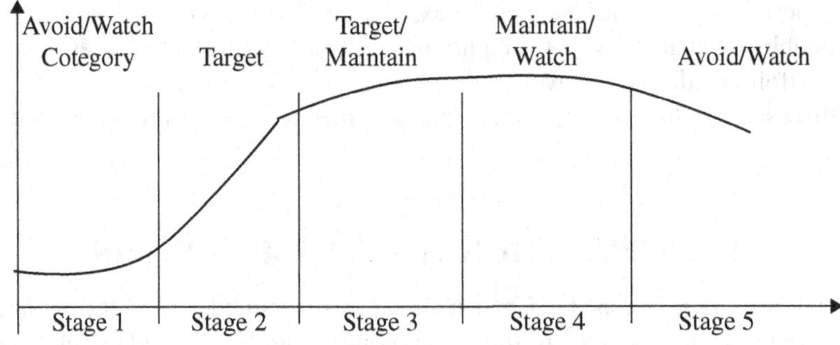


**Figure 17.1** Industry Life Cycle and Risk Appetite

business development efforts on the identified 'target' sectors. Depending upon the region and economy, multi-sector conglomerates, reputed business names, core industries in the area (e.g. petrochemicals in the Middle East or large trade houses in Hong Kong or Singapore, etc.) usually come under the target segment, which are also considered as low risk areas. Each country or region would have competitive advantages providing a tactical edge to certain types of industry in that region compared to other areas.

**Restricted (or Maintain) Sectors**: These sectors are susceptible to any possible slowdown in economic conditions or operate in a highly competitive environment. Most players in the market vie for market share resorting to cut-throat competition practices with differing attendant risks such as liquidity crisis, growth in non-collectable debt, poor inventory management and so on. However, a few players will continue to do well due to inherent strengths, which we have covered in Chapter 7. Accordingly, not all business units in the sector are shunned, but a cap is placed to ensure that only outstanding customers are accepted and up to a certain limit. For example, it is possible that automobile spare part dealers have a cap of 2% of total funded imposed and 3% of total non-funded advances.

**Avoid (or Watch-List) Sectors**: The sectors where a financial institution wishes to develop its exposure very cautiously and by very low risk lending are called watch-list sectors. Such areas are highly vulnerable to a downturn in the economy in general or to specific sectoral pressures such as delays in realization of dues – especially true for government sector reliant businesses. A sector with a low margin and requiring a professional understanding of cash flows, stock requirements, rental costs and above all trends may fall into this category. Given the low barriers of entry, new entrants are common, adding heat to a tough competitive environment. Only firms with successful differentiation strategies and competitive advantages can survive. A creditor, bank or FI or any enterprise ought to be watchful when accepting credit exposure from watch list sectors. Adequate mitigants such as strong collaterals or sustainable competitive advantages, etc. may be sought.

### 17.1.2 Counterparty Limit

This is primarily done in financial and non-financial institutions with significant credit risk exposure. Most groups look at single-name concentrations, by aggregating exposures to a borrower and related entities. A related entity is usually defined based on legal and/or control relationships. Sometimes a close business relationship between borrowers such as companies that do a very high share of business with one another may also be subjected to this criterion. In the case of banks, the central bank of the country itself stipulates a maximum credit limit to a specific party. Usually it is linked to the TNW of the bank/financial institution/creditor. For instance, it may be stipulated that a single credit exposure to any counterparty should not exceed 10% of the net worth of the creditor. In such cases, diversification across customers is attempted. Insurance companies also measure concentrations of credit risk to re-insurers and attempt diversification, as necessary.

### 17.1.3 Region-Wise Restriction

Obligors may be grouped based on country and geographic location. Too much credit exposure to a volatile region or country does carry higher risk. Hence, creditors attempt as much regional diversification as possible. However, small banks and localized manufacturing entities may not be able to diversify much on the region, which is of acceptable risk as long as local stability conditions remain. Moreover, the risk management capacity may be retained by ensuring an adequate capital cushion to meet any contingencies while ensuring that only quality obligor credit risks are underwritten and other diversifications are built into the credit portfolio.

### 17.1.4 Size

Banks and financial intermediaries seek to diversify across different type of customers segmenting into them Large (Corporate), Large-Medium (Commercial) and Small businesses (Small and Medium Enterprises or SME). Large companies may grab headlines, however, SME form the foundation of the global economy. Some studies have established that more than 90% of the world's businesses are SME.

Whilst we have mentioned four parameters – Customer, Sector, Industry, Geography and Size – as the basis of diversification, diversification can also be achieved by focusing on Product, Ratings, Asset Class, Business Units, Lending Office, Origination Teams, Duration, etc., depending upon the circumstances of the institution. The complexity of product offerings and activities of the institution along with the sophistication of systems, management and staff play an important role in successful diversification. It is often possible to decide on fixing a maximum limit based on an appropriate category such as industry, country, geography, etc.

**Example 17.1**

The Head of Risk of XYZ Bank Ltd wants to revise the cap on the construction sector as reports suggest a downturn in the near future. The Head of Risk does not want to lose more than 2% from the exposures to this sector. Based on a study, it is learned that the loss rate for this sector is set to increase to 25% (from 20%) in the near future. Current credit policy and risk appetite has fixed the construction sector cap at 10% of the total credit portfolio. Please advise what changes are to be made in the construction sector cap.

**Answer**

Calculation of the Sector Limit

| Parameters | Existing | Suggested |
|---|---|---|
| Max loss (a) | 2% | 2% |
| Loss rate (b) | 20% | 25% |
| 1-Loss rate (c) | 80% | 75% |
| Sector concentration limit [a*(1/b)] | 10% | 8% |

**Comments**: The Head of Risk may wish to reduce the concentration on the construction sector and accordingly revise the sector cap to 8% of the total portfolio. This may involve reduction in credit exposures to existing portfolio components and it may be necessary to pursue an exit strategy in a few cases. This can be accomplished by identifying the high risk customers within the construction segment of the credit portfolio.

Should all credit assets suffer default together, the portfolio loss would be the sum of all simultaneous losses. However, in the case of a reasonably spread portfolio of credit assets carefully chosen, we can expect the following:

- Not all firm credit assets will default at the same time. As we discussed, in a typical well diversified credit portfolio, a small number of losses is much more frequent.
- The portfolio risk is not the sum total of firm risks. The beauty of portfolio credit risk is that by intelligent diversification, it can be lowered below the average or total risk of the individual credit risks.

## 17.2 MODERN DIVERSIFICATION OF CREDIT PORTFOLIO

A portfolio's performance is the result of the performance of its components. The traditional diversification is successful as the portfolio risk is spread among various entities such that poor performance of certain sectors and entities will not incapacitate the portfolio. However, the traditional approach can be improved upon by studying the interrelationships among the portfolio components. For example traditional diversification is satisfied when it includes cement, paint and waterproofing industries in its credit portfolio. However, these three industries have a strong interrelationship because they are linked to the construction activities in the economy. This interlinking is often ignored by traditional diversification. In a downturn of the construction sector all three industries will be impacted together. On the other hand, suppose the credit portfolio comprises the food, paint and tyre industries, which are driven by different external factors – food is considered a non-cyclical item depending on population growth, paint depends on construction and tyres on the number of automobiles. In this case, the portfolio risk tends to be lower as a downturn in any specific sector will not pull down all the constituents of the portfolio. Statistically speaking, in this instance the industries are not perfectly correlated.

Traditional diversification can be improved upon by studying (i) behaviour patterns and co-variance among various assets, industries, sectors, etc. and (ii) portfolio composition. This idea is derived from the insights of Portfolio Selection Theory or Modern Portfolio Theory (MPT).

### 17.2.1 Portfolio Selection Theory

The role of correlation in a portfolio has been one of the cornerstones of innovative Portfolio Selection (PS) Theory put forward by Nobel Prize winner Markowitz. Correlation is a measure which studies the relation between two or more variables. Correlation coefficients can range from $-1$ to $+1$. The value of $-1$ represents a perfect negative correlation, which means the variables move in opposite directions while a value of $+1$ represents a perfect positive correlation. It denotes that both variables move in tandem. A value of zero represents a lack of correlation.

PS is widely held to be the scientific way of managing a portfolio. Initially PS was aimed at the stock market, however it later found applications in several other areas wherever portfolios were involved, including credit portfolios. Among other things, PS stated that as you diversify your portfolio the portfolio risk reduces depending upon the correlation of portfolio components. Variance or standard deviation has been considered as the proxy of risk and the following formula has been prescribed to calculate portfolio risk:

$$\sigma_p^2 = \sum_{i=1}^{n} \sum_{j=1}^{n} x_i x_j \rho_{ij} \sigma_i \sigma_j$$

where

$\sigma_p$ = Portfolio variance
$x_i$ = Proportion of total portfolio invested in asset i
$x_j$ = Proportion of total portfolio invested in asset j
$\sigma_i$ = Riskiness (i.e. standard deviation) of asset i
$\sigma_j$ = Riskiness (i.e. standard deviation) of asset j
$\rho ij$ = Correlation between assets i and j
n = Number of assets in the portfolio

#### *17.2.1.1 Criticisms*

There are criticisms of PS. The major ones are that (a) PS attempts to replace intuition with measurement and prescription and if intuition comes up with better alternatives, the whole exercise is a waste; (b) PS uses past data to look into the future – PS requires statistical variables such as standard deviation, variance and other numbers based on past historical data; (c) whilst risk is defined as volatility or standard deviation, it is often argued that risk is not adequately represented by volatility; (d) correlations between assets are assumed to be fixed and constant

#### *17.2.1.2 Benefits*

Despite criticisms, the contribution by Markowitz is outstanding and the ideas of PS can be extended to many other areas such as commodities, foreign exchange and credit, wherever portfolio risk plays an important role. Whilst some of the assumptions may not be valid under all circumstances, the insights are adequate to improve portfolio risk diversification. Core fundamentals of PS concepts can also be effectively applied to the credit portfolio by studying the (i) proportions and (ii) the correlation characteristics of the portfolio components. Let us see an example from the credit portfolio context.

### 17.2.2 Application of PS in Credit Portfolio

The variance of the portfolio is not a linear combination of component variances. Understanding portfolio variance is the essence of understanding the mathematics of diversification. As you diversify your portfolio the portfolio risk reduces depending upon the correlation of portfolio components. Let us examine a simple example.

**Example 17.2**

Suppose the two assets in a hypothetical credit portfolio have an identical credit risk grade and hence the same probability of default.

| Details | Cr Asset 1 | Cr Asset 2 |
|---|---|---|
| **PD** | 0.0216 | 0.0216 |

However, the assets are from two different sectors, Sector A (Cr Asset 1) and Sector B (Cr Asset 2). A study of external risks points out that there is a potential external risk which may impact the portfolio. Hence there is a risk of downgrade (migration risk) of portfolio components if this external event occurs. However, the risk is higher for the obligor from Sector B, i.e. 6% vs. 5% for Sector A. Correlation between both sectors is stated to be 0.50.

| Details | Cr Asset 1 | Cr Asset 2 |
|---|---|---|
| **Variance Risk** | 0.05 | 0.06 |
| **Sector Correlation** | 0.50 | |

A portfolio manager plans to completely exit Credit Asset 2 to minimize downgrade risk. Do you agree?

**Answer**

For a two-asset portfolio (viz. N = 2), the PS portfolio risk calculation formula would be

$$\sigma p = [(Xi\, \sigma i)2 + (Xj\, \sigma j)2 + 2Xi\, Xj\, \sigma i\, \sigma j\, \rho ij]^{1}/2$$

By applying the formula, we arrive at the following chart and table, depicting portfolio migration risk for different proportions of Credit Assets 1 and 2.

| Details | Cr Asset 1 | Cr Asset 2 | Portfolio risk |
|---|---|---|---|
| Portfolio Mix 1 | 0% | 100% | 6.00% |
| Portfolio Mix 2 | 10% | 90% | 5.30% |
| Portfolio Mix 3 | 20% | 80% | 4.74% |
| Portfolio Mix 4 | 30% | 70% | 4.31% |
| Portfolio Mix 5 | 40% | 60% | 4.01% |
| Portfolio Mix 6 | 50% | 50% | 3.85% |
| Portfolio Mix 7 | 60% | 40% | 3.81% |
| Portfolio Mix 8 | 70% | 30% | 3.91% |
| Portfolio Mix 9 | 80% | 20% | 4.14% |
| Portfolio Mix 10 | 90% | 10% | 4.50% |
| Portfolio Mix 11 | 100% | 0% | 5.00% |

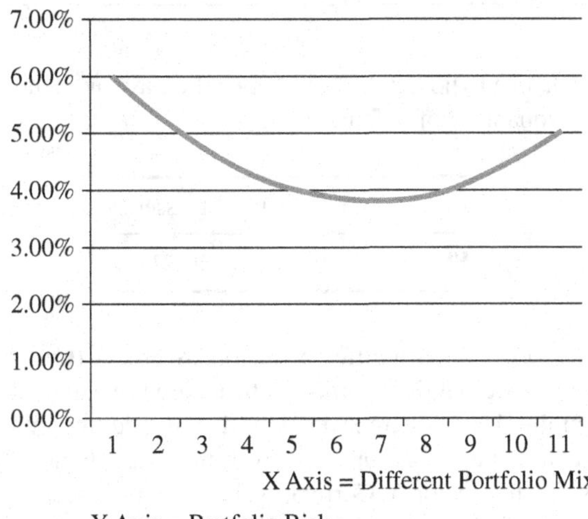


Having Credit Asset 2 alone results in higher portfolio risk of 5% while combining both assets 60:40 shows a portfolio risk of 3.81% only. It is clear that if credit policies permit, it is better to select Credit Asset 1 and Credit Asset 2 in the 60:40 ratio as it provides the least risky credit portfolio. Theoretically, it is possible to achieve even a nil risk portfolio by combining assets with perfectly negative correlated assets. In our example, if both assets have a correlation of −1, then the portfolio risk can be zero. If there is a perfect correlation of +1, the diversification does not have any benefit.

As is evident from the above, portfolio risk is not the total of obligor-level risks, but is a function of how firm risks tend to react to different economic and other systematic stimuli. To the extent possible, the portfolio should be filled with credit assets that move in different directions rather than in a single direction, so that a minimal risk portfolio is obtained. The critical factor is the understanding or knowledge of the behaviour pattern of industries.

The above example exemplifies the role of correlation and proportions in a portfolio. The idea conveyed contains an undeniable truth. As you diversify your portfolio the portfolio risk reduces depending upon the correlation of portfolio components. This conceptual model applies to the credit portfolio as surely as it applies to other portfolios, such as equity portfolios.

The lower the correlation, the lower the portfolio risk. Combining two assets with perfect negative correlation reduces the portfolio risk. Since there is no great benefit in combining assets with perfect positive correlation, the portfolio manager should prefer less correlated assets or groups of assets. Accordingly, while constructing or maintaining a portfolio, the following principles would enable us to design a relatively shockproof credit portfolio:

1. **Understand the correlation among various assets, industries, sectors, regions, etc.**: Understanding the covariance or correlation among the various credit assets and the respective sectors to which they belong is essential for effective management of portfolio risk. At the portfolio level, when considering a new addition to the portfolio, its correlation to the

existing assets and the impact of its addition ought to be recognized. The main objective is to select credit assets having negative correlation among themselves. In the above example, if the correlation is 1, diversification will not result in the reduction of portfolio risk.

Combining credit assets with less than perfect correlation tends to reduce the overall portfolio risk. However, when applying this technique, two conditions should be satisfied:

- As far as possible, the risk class, relatively at higher grades (BBB and above) of the credit assets ought to be the same. At lower grades (say BB and below) despite dissimilar industry features, due to inherent firm-level defects (either internal or financial) the possibility of joint collapse of credit assets exists. This is called Credit Quality Correlation (see below). In such cases, the common factor of a higher level of firm-level defects weighs more than the industry or other macro factors.
- Another aspect to be borne in mind is the maturity of the credit assets. Although the credit assets need not have exactly the same maturity, some semblance is desirable. As such, a long-term credit asset and short-term credit asset may not be tied together while combining assets under this technique.

While it is relatively easy to calculate variance and correlations for two credit exposures, as the number of credit exposures increases the calculation gets complicated. However, with the massive computing ability of computers, the challenge can be tackled or appropriate modifications may be made with the help of external consultants.

2. **Understand the impact of proportion of portfolio components**: The proportion of various components in a credit portfolio is the result of a strategic decision on credit asset allocation and is influenced by the credit policies. Even if the assets have low correlation, unless they are mixed in correct proportion, the full advantage of diversification may not be realized. Accordingly, while dividing the portfolio on a percentage basis among different categories – sector, industry, geography, size, etc., attention ought to be paid to ensure the most appropriate proportion. Just having low correlation will not be sufficient, their proportion is also important as is evident from the following example.

**Example 17.3**

Refer to the earlier example. Suppose the correlation is –1, i.e. perfect negative correlation. Let us see how the portfolio variance risk behaves:

| Details | Cr Asset 1 | Cr Asset 2 | Portfolio risk |
|---|---|---|---|
| Portfolio Mix 1 | 0% | 100% | 6.00% |
| Portfolio Mix 2 | 10% | 90% | 3.92% |
| Portfolio Mix 3 | 20% | 80% | 2.29% |
| Portfolio Mix 4 | 30% | 70% | 1.09% |
| Portfolio Mix 5 | 40% | 60% | 0.33% |
| Portfolio Mix 6 | 50% | 50% | 0.01% |
| Portfolio Mix 7 | 60% | 40% | 0.13% |
| Portfolio Mix 8 | 70% | 30% | 0.69% |
| Portfolio Mix 9 | 80% | 20% | 1.69% |
| Portfolio Mix 10 | 90% | 10% | 3.12% |
| Portfolio Mix 11 | 100% | 0% | 5.00% |

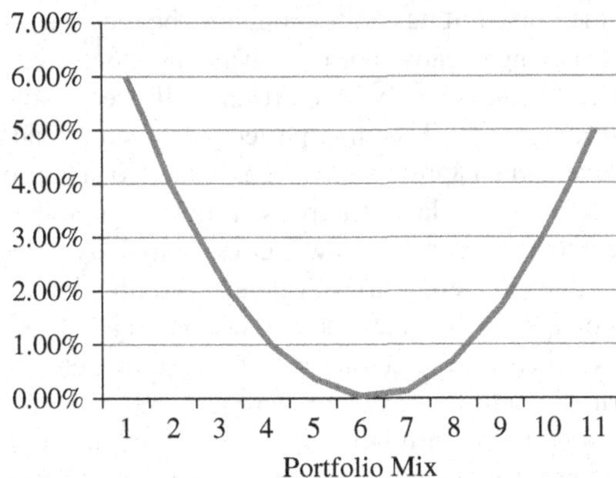


It is evident that the proportions matter – if the correlation is perfectly negative, combining the assets in a 50:50 ratio minimizes the portfolio variance risk while if the correlation is 0.54 the best proportion is 60:40.

3. **Monitor the correlations of portfolio components**: Whilst the degree of correlation of various portfolio components is expected to remain stable, it need not be the case always. The following aspects are highly relevant:
   - Correlations can change dramatically as was experienced in the 2008 Credit Crisis, when various asset classes, believed to have low correlation, behaved differently. The problem of 'correlation breakdown' during periods of greater volatility is well known.
   - Correlation in credit risk is counter-cyclical. Accordingly, it is lower during boom times but gets higher during economic downturns.
   - Similarly correlation is relatively higher among firms with low (poor) credit ratings than among those with high credit ratings.

### 17.2.3 More Tools to Study Diversification of Portfolio Risks

The interrelation of credit risks in a portfolio can be looked at from angles other than sector correlation, as given below:

1. **Credit quality correlation**: As is evident from the exposition given above, industrial/sectoral diversification is useful to minimize portfolio risk by mixing components that tend to move in opposite directions. In the example given above, theoretically the portfolio risk can be brought to nil. However, as far as credit risk is concerned, sectoral/industrial diversification is meaningful only if the credit risk grade of credit assets belonging to differing industries is the same and satisfactory.

   While industrial correlation (viz. the more correlated the sectors, the less risk can be diversified) is useful to scientifically diversify among industries, default (or credit quality) correlation is also important. It shows the propensity of the credit assets (especially low quality) to default together in the event of macroeconomic adversity. Intuitively, two credit assets from negatively correlated industries offer the best sort of diversification at industry level. But if both have a credit risk grade of 'C', the chances of both defaulting and becoming credit losses are not remote but closer. The ideal solution is to have effective screening through the EIIF method. A suggested solution is to identify the industries with low correlation, and then select only highly acceptable credit assets/credit customers from such industries.

2. **Conditional probability**: Conditional probability means an event (credit loss) will take place if a given scenario takes place. For instance, if the economic situation of a country deteriorates, the default probability of a major part of the portfolio constituents increases. On the other hand, if an industry is hit and performs badly, only the particular homogenous group – a part of the portfolio – is impacted. What is the difference between correlation study and conditional probability as far as portfolio risks are concerned? While the former studies the relationship among all the constituents, the latter focuses on a specific (and significant) event, which conditions the probable credit losses. Conditional probability is useful to study the impact on the credit portfolio in differing situations such as business cycles, interest rate changes, government policies, change in government, droughts, earthquakes, etc.
3. **Joint probability**: In this case, instead of studying just one event conditioning credit loss, more events are studied, and their joint probabilities are derived to understand the extent of probability of credit loss. For example, it can look at the probability of drought and changes in government policies occurring at the same time. Statistical analytical tools are being increasingly deployed in credit risk study at portfolio level. This is logical. Statistics deal with databases and the credit portfolio itself is a database – a bunch of credit assets.

## 17.3 CORRELATIONS IN CREDIT RISK MODELS

Various credit risk models are available which attempt to predict the credit risk of an obligor depending upon certain characteristics such as sector, size, financials, etc., where correlations are considered as an important input. However, given the difficulties involved in estimating the correlations of credit assets due to lack of complete market data (which is available for traded equity stocks) the credit risk models use proxies to arrive at asset correlations in a credit portfolio. A few instances of how the credit risk models attempt to capture correlation are given below:

- Derive it from the observed behaviour of stock market assets or sector variables.
- Use conditional probability and link correlation, i.e. understand the default rates or behaviour of a sector to the changes in GDP or other macroeconomic variables.

## ✍ QUESTIONS/EXERCISES

1. What do you mean by diversification? Explain the need for diversification in credit portfolios.
2. Explain traditional diversification. What are the various parameters of traditional diversification?
3. Do you believe the proportion of different categories of credit assets affect the quality of the portfolio?
4. Explain how the main tenets of the Markowitz Portfolio Theorem are applied in credit risk management. What are the limitations of applying Modern Portfolio Theory (MPT), especially in credit portfolios?

5. What do you mean by default correlation?
6. The Head of Credit of PQR Financials wants to revise the cap on Crane Hire Companies as reports suggest that the prospects of the crane hire business are no longer rosy. The Head of Credit does not want to lose more than 1.5% from the exposures to this business category. He believes that the loss rate would increase to 30% in the near future. Please suggest a suitable cap for this business segment.
7. MPT basically studies the correlations between the return of assets of various classes. However, the overriding concern of a credit portfolio manager is to minimize the default correlation because the interest income is relatively fixed in the case of credit assets. Do you believe this fundamental difference nullifies the use of MPT principles in credit portfolio management?
8. Exercise: Identify a large bank or a large corporation listed in the stock market. Go through the publicly available information to gauge how effectively the diversification is used to mitigate the credit portfolio risks.

# 18
# Trading of Credit Assets

Portfolio risks can be managed by buying credit in desired sectors, regions or asset classes and selling credit in undesired areas. Secondary markets for credit assets (loans) facilitate this. During the late 20th century the development of an active secondary market for loans and credit assets resulted in altering the school of thought in banks and financial intermediaries of 'originate to hold till maturity' to 'originate to sell'. (Whilst 'originate to sell' is a good business model, the 2008 Credit Crisis brought out instances where the originators did not care sufficiently about the credit quality of the asset originated while some investors acted irresponsibly without studying the credit risks properly.)

Why do banks and FIs want to trade in the credit assets? The major reasons are given below:

- Managing the credit risk.
- Selling of credit assets enables reporting of current income quickly (fees, etc.). Interest income takes time to accrue.
- Meet the capital ratio/adequacy requirements by filling the denominator with appropriate credit assets (capital/risk weighted assets).

The purchase and sale of credit assets have their own role to play in the credit markets. There are different methods to acquire and dispose of credit assets, an overview of which is provided in the rest of this chapter. A chart is shown in Figure 18.1 for a quick glance:

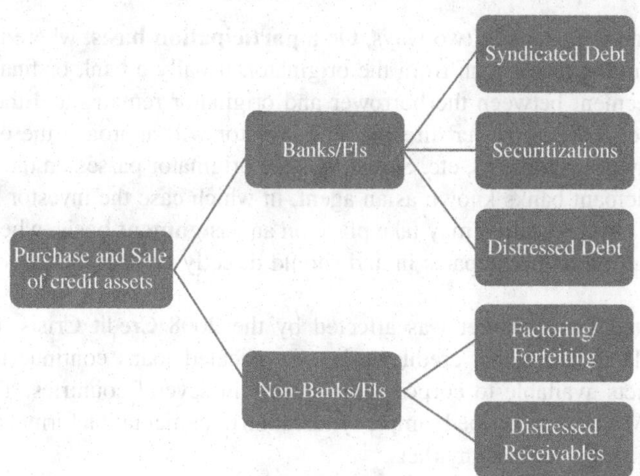


**Figure 18.1** Major Categories of Credit Asset Transactions

## 18.1 SYNDICATED LOANS/CREDIT ASSETS

The secondary loan market is common for syndicated facilities rather than bilateral facilities. Syndicated loans refer to the participation by a group of banks to provide a package of credit facilities to a corporate borrower. In addition, institutional investors such as insurance companies, mutual funds, hedge funds, bond funds, pension funds, insurance companies and other proprietary investors also participate in this market. Syndicated loans to major corporate borrowers are sometimes rated by external credit rating agencies such as Moody's or Standard & Poor's. Syndicated loans are often created through joint effort by several banks and financial institutions. A general overview of the steps involved is given below:

- The corporate borrower (issuer) negotiates with the arranger bank on the type of facilities they need and the purpose. Sometimes, before awarding a mandate, the issuer might solicit bids from arrangers.
- The arranger will outline their syndication strategy and terms, including loan pricing and various fees – arrangement fees, commitment fees, underwriting fees, etc. If there are several arrangers, then one or a few banks would act as Mandated Lead arrangers.
- Once the mandate is awarded, the syndication process starts with invitations sent out in the financial (money) market to interesting potential participants, which will include banks and financial institutions.
- The arranger will prepare a confidential Information Memorandum (IM) in conjunction with the issuer (borrower) describing the terms of the transactions. The IM typically will also include the investment rationale, risks, terms and conditions and a financial model.
- Once the offer is closed and each participant fulfils their commitment, a syndication agreement will be drawn up and signed by all parties. This will be a legally enforceable document.
- A bank or a financial institution that missed the participation opportunity can seek to purchase the credit asset from the secondary loan market. Similarly, if any one of the participants wants to sell its participation, it can make an offer in the secondary market.
- Depending upon the credit quality, the credit asset (i.e. syndicated loan participation) is either offered at a premium or discount.

Usually syndication is done in two ways. On a **participation basis**, where the investor buys or participates in the larger loan from the originator, usually a bank or financial institution. The credit agreement between the borrower and originator remains and the participant has limited recourse to the borrower directly. The investor will approach the originator on any issues, say delay in instalments, etc. Sometimes the originator passes on the agency duties to one of the participant banks known as an agent, in which case the investor should approach the agent bank. Or syndication may take place on an **assignment basis**, where the investor is assigned the portion he participates in and should directly contact the customer and not the originator.

The syndicated loans market was affected by the 2008 Credit Crisis, but continues to play a vital role in the global credit market. Syndicated loans continue to be one of the key debt products available to corporate borrowers in several countries. The Loan Market Association (LMA) has prescribed sample syndication documentation formats for both primary and secondary syndicated loan markets.

## 18.2 SECURITIZATION

Securitization is a revolutionary concept in credit portfolio management. Securitization refers to the act of aggregation of several discrete credit assets into a 'pool' managed by a separate trust, which issues bonds and securities, with appropriate documentation linking the underlying 'pool' of credit assets or loans to the bonds or securities issued. Accordingly, the periodical interest payments and principal repayment of the bonds will come out of the 'pool'.

It has some similarities to syndicated loans, which we discussed above. Both operate more or less on an 'originate to distribute' model. A bank or financial institution would originate the loan, which is then securitized. In this process the originator may fully sell off the credit asset and take his fees, such as arrangement fees, processing fees, etc. The basic idea is that loan 'origination' is decoupled from 'holding' of credit assets and consequent risks.

A bank has several incentives to securitize the loan book. Major ones are: (i) it brings liquidity to otherwise illiquid credit assets of the bank; (ii) it transfers risks to the investor, and accordingly reduces the risk assets and hence leads to lower capital adequacy requirements; (iii) it helps to manage the maturity mismatch and (iv) it also helps to reduce interest rate risk to an extent.

The growth in the credit market was tremendously aided by securitization. Several types and different classes of securitized products are available. We will discuss two of the most popular securitized products below – Asset Backed Securities (ABS) and Collateralized Debt Obligations (CDO).

### 18.2.1 Asset Backed Securities (ABS)[1]

ABS is a type of securitized loan, i.e. a bond backed by credit assets. In an ABS transaction, the bank grants several loans (for example, vehicle loans) to different borrowers. Once the loans become sizeable, the bank pools them together and sells to a Special Purpose Vehicle (SPV) or to a trust, to recover the funds deployed for providing loans. The SPV then issues a series of bonds based on the underlying loan/credit assets. The SPV may choose to issue different types of bonds based on the same pool that may vary in yield, duration and payment priority. Usually rating agencies such as Moody's and Standard & Poor's are asked to rate the bonds or bond classes. The rating agencies assign different grades of investment grade (AAA/Aaa through BBB-/Baa3) to below investment grade (BB+/Ba1 through B-/B3). The riskier tranche is kept by the SPV or bank itself. Since AAA rated assets required less capital charge in Basel II, the demand for such assets was generally strong from banks and financial institutions, even outside the US. Investors who have bought the bonds get interest every month if the borrowers who took the loan pay interest. Initially the AAA rated bond holders will get the interest, then the next in the hierarchy. Principal repayments are also made according to the same priority.

### 18.2.2 Collateralized Debt Obligations (CDO)

CDO is a structured security where the 'credit asset pool' is segmented into different tranches with a different risk/return matrix and sold to investors with appropriate risk appetite. The 'senior' tranches are considered the safest securities while junior tranches carry high risk. The senior tranches have usually been rated AAA by the rating agencies. In the case of CDOs too, AAA rated assets were in demand as they attracted less capital charge in Basel II. Interest and principal payments are made in order of seniority and accordingly the junior tranches enjoyed higher coupon rates as a compensation for the higher risk embedded therein.

[1] The boom of securitization immediately preceding the 2008 crisis was led by mortgages such as Commercial Mortgage Backed Securities (CMBS) and Residential Mortgage Backed Securities (RMBS). They also follow the methodology similar to ABS. In an RMBS transaction, the bank grants several mortgage loans of varying size, property type and location to different borrowers (i.e. who buy the property with bank mortgage loans).

Usually the major parties in securitization are:

- **Originator or Sponsor**: Usually the traditional bank or financial institution which initiates the act of securitizing its own loans or receivables of other institutions is known as the originator or sponsor of the securitization. The originator has usually created an SPV to conduct the securitization, i.e. the originator sells the assets to the SPV who in turn sells it to the investors.
- **Final Investors**: This category is the final purchaser of the securities.
- **Trustee and Custodian**: They have the responsibility to safeguard the interests of the final investors. The custodian holds the physical documentation – related to collateral[2] or otherwise – in safe custody.
- **Rating Agencies**: Standard & Poor's, Moody's and Fitch are the major rating agencies who rate CDOs and other securitized loans in the US. Some argue that there is a conflict of interest for rating agencies because they are paid by CDO sponsors.
- **Law Firms**: Law firms provide legal advice on the documentation.
- **Insurers/Credit Derivatives**: The role of insurers is twofold. (i) The insurer of the underlying collateral, say house or building. For example, in the RMBS the homeowner purchases insurance to protect the home, which in turn protects the bank/investor from the loss/damage of underlying collateral. (ii) Secondly, the insurers providing Credit Default Swap (CDS), provide insurance on the counterparty risk. (See Chapter 19 on Credit Derivatives for details.)

A typical structure of CDO is shown in Figure 18.2:

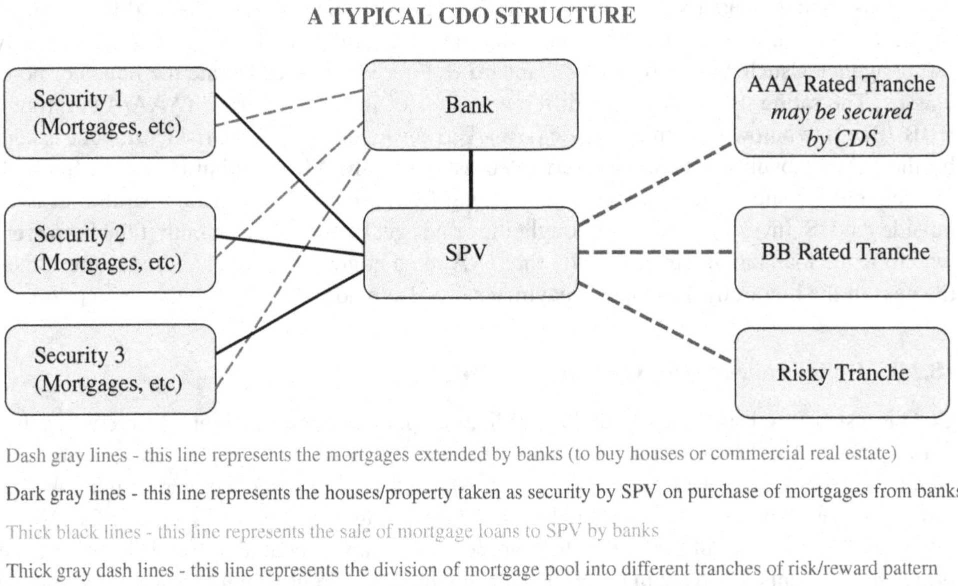

A TYPICAL CDO STRUCTURE

Security 1 (Mortgages, etc)
Security 2 (Mortgages, etc)
Security 3 (Mortgages, etc)
Bank
SPV
AAA Rated Tranche *may be secured by CDS*
BB Rated Tranche
Risky Tranche

Dash gray lines - this line represents the mortgages extended by banks (to buy houses or commercial real estate)

Dark gray lines - this line represents the houses/property taken as security by SPV on purchase of mortgages from banks

Thick black lines - this line represents the sale of mortgage loans to SPV by banks

Thick gray dash lines - this line represents the division of mortgage pool into different tranches of risk/reward pattern

**Figure 18.2** A Typical CDO Structure

[2] Collateralized bond obligation (CBO) has bonds as the collateral assets. Collateralized loan obligation (CLO) has loans as the collateral assets. Synthetic CDO does not invest in any asset, but exposure is created by selling CDS.

At the peak of the CDO boom, the demand for CDO-able assets was high. Banks and investment banks who took months to create a critical mass of CDO-able assets, with one stroke removed these credit assets from the balance sheet, which not only reduced regulatory capital and economic capital but resulted in improved profitability and liquidity as well.

Concentration risk can be mitigated by CDOs. This product enabled banks to invest in a large portfolio of credit assets sometimes with a bit of concentration risk, however quick securitization through CDOs allowed banks to diversify their portfolio and mitigate the concentration risk. However, as we will discuss later in this book, when the 2008 crisis hit, many investment banks and banks were saddled with unsold structured (securitized) products. This resulted in concentration risk and its accompanying problems.

### 18.2.3 Downfall of CDOs (and Similar Securitized Instruments)

Whilst CDOs were heralded as a path-breaking financial innovation and boomed to record levels in 2006 and 2007, post the 2008 Global Credit Crisis, global CDO issuance fell sharply. During 2009, CDO issuance was just a small fraction of its peak in 2006. CDOs are blamed as one of the main catalysts that caused the 2008 Global Credit Crisis. Critics say that they contributed to artificial demand, especially for mortgage backed properties, which the bankers and brokers were eager to securitize and sell to yield-hungry investors during the low interest rate regime which prevailed then. We will examine more on this later in the book, when we discuss the Credit Crisis. Nonetheless, if may be noted that overall securitized products are good for diversification of credit portfolios, if used prudently.

## 18.3 DISTRESSED DEBT

Distressed debt denotes the external borrowings owned by companies who have filed for bankruptcy or have a significant chance of filing for bankruptcy in the near future. Banks and FIs are willing to sell distressed assets that have fallen in credit quality and sometimes provisioned. This is to avoid headaches associated with the legal hassles involved in managing the distressed debt. For instance, during the 2008 Credit Crisis, the lender to a distressed company charged impairment provision of $44m against a credit asset with an original lending value of $100m. With future interest payments in doubt and the hassles of legal proceedings in a different jurisdiction, the lending bank jumped at the opportunity when a hedge fund specializing in distressed debt agreed to acquire this asset at 66 cents/$. As far as the lending bank was concerned, this resulted in the following:

- A write-back of $10m of the $44m (66 – (100 – 44)) impairment already charged against this asset.
- Deploying the cash received immediately in other good assets.
- Being free of the headaches of legal acrimonies related to such problem assets.
- Easing of the pressure on capital adequacy because distressed debt usually requires higher ratios to be maintained and
- credit executives' time could now be focused on good assets where interest and other ancillary income was assured.

Why do investors buy distressed debt? The reasons are many. Such investors are often specialists in this field and are able to bring the deal to a quicker conclusion than banks and often with better realization rates. In certain cases, the investor may have counterbalancing exposure to the distressed company. If the once-distressed company emerges from bankruptcy as a viable firm, the distressed debt will turn into a good asset, involving substantial profits. Hence, it is not unusual that distressed debt investors closely work with management to work out different options.

## 18.4 FACTORING

Non-banking companies are also active participants in the sale of credit assets or receivables. Usually the buying party will be a financial intermediary. Non-recourse factoring transfers credit risk to a third party known as a factor, which normally is a financial institution or bank. The seller has the advantage of removing the credit asset or receivable from the balance sheet and gets cash immediately. The rate of discounting varies primarily according to the credit risks involved and the market rate of risk-free return. It may be that factoring is used by non-financial firms which have a substantial trade debtors portfolio.

Non-recourse factoring essentially is the sale of the receivables and transfers the ownership of the receivables to the factor, who obtains all rights and risks associated with the receivables. The factor collects the payments from the debtor directly and carries the risk of bad debts, if any.

## 18.5 DISTRESSED RECEIVABLES

As in the case of banks who dispose of distressed debt to investors such as hedge funds, the companies can also sell the sticky debtors to third parties Such debts or dues are usually made up of real estate receivables, trade dues, commercial lease rentals, etc. and there are willing buyers of such debt at a deep discount (e.g. 15 cents to the dollar), in case of insolvency or near bankruptcy of the debtor.

## ✍ QUESTIONS/EXERCISES

1. What is securitization? Explain the advantages and disadvantages.
2. Explain syndicated debt deals. Who are the usual parties involved in structuring a syndicated debt deal?
3. Explain how CDOs are structured.
4. What is the nature of ABS? Explain the role played by external rating agencies in ABS deals.
5. Who are the major parties in a securitization transaction? Explain the role of each party.
6. Can concentration risks be reduced via CDOs? Please elaborate.
7. Explain distressed debt. Why do institutions prefer to sell distressed debt?
8. What do you mean by factoring? What are the advantages and disadvantages of non-recourse factoring?

# 19
# Credit Derivatives

Most financial intermediaries view credit portfolio management as comprising a strategy of portfolio diversification backed by limit caps, with the occasional sale of a credit asset in the secondary market. The advent of credit derivatives has been heralded as a path-breaking innovation that enables institutions to manage credit risks differently with more flexibility. We will discuss the various aspects of credit derivatives, how they contribute to credit risk mitigation and the need for credit risk analysis expertise by both parties involved in a credit derivative.

## 19.1 MEANING OF A CREDIT DERIVATIVE

Credit derivatives enable banks and other institutions to hedge credit risk or to guard against deterioration in the value of their credit portfolio. A credit derivative is a bilateral contract that transfers the entire (or specific aspects of) credit risk on a specified debt obligation to another party. There are two parties to a credit derivative:

1. **Protection buyers** are those who seek to protect the credit asset (e.g. loan or bond) they have or intend to acquire.
2. **Protection sellers** provide the protection or insurance on credit risk for a premium. Credit derivatives can be structured either as unfunded or funded contracts that transfer credit risk between two parties without actually transferring the underlying asset.

Credit derivatives allow holders of credit assets or fixed income securities to trade off some (or all) of the credit risk on the assets held (known as 'reference assets'). With credit derivatives, holders of credit assets can diversify their credit exposures for their portfolios and/or hedge their concentrated risks. No wonder credit derivatives have become popular in a short span of time.

Protection sellers are underwriting credit risk and hence must conduct a thorough credit risk analysis. The protection buyer transfers credit risk from the obligor to a third party. Although credit derivatives are compared with insurance, fundamentally protection sellers are underwriting credit risk.

Let us examine the advantages these derivative instruments bring to the protection buyer and the protection seller.

1. **Advantages to the protection buyer**
   - It enables credit risk transfer to a third party, significantly reducing the credit portfolio risk.
   - As the overall credit risk reduces, the protection buyer may underwrite more, i.e. increase credit capacity.
   - The asset remains on the balance sheet of the protection buyer earning income.

- In some cases, where the bank or financial institution reduces its overall credit risk through credit derivatives, it has a favourable impact on the regulatory capital, i.e. reduces the regulatory capital requirements.

2. **Advantages to the protection seller**
   - It offers the opportunity to earn unfunded income.
   - The investment remains off-balance sheet and actual cash needs to be deployed only if the 'credit event' is triggered.
   - The overall return could exceed (i.e. be more than) that of the direct investment.
   - Overall transaction cost tends to be relatively lower than the cash or direct investment.

### 19.1.1 Credit Event

As a tool of credit risk management, credit derivatives enable the transfer of credit risks to other parties who would compensate, in the event of specific losses being incurred. Such events are termed credit events.

When is the payment under a credit derivative made? It depends upon the trigger of the credit event which denotes the deterioration in credit quality impairing the repayment capacity of the obligor or the underlying or the reference asset significantly. The credit event can be mutually agreed upon by the protection buyer and seller. It usually includes the following:

- Default.
- Restructuring of the debt.
- Cross default clause triggered credit event.
- Rating downgrades/migration of the rating to unacceptable levels.
- Bankruptcy or moratorium.
- Failure to pay.
- Any other mutually agreed upon event.

Payout on a credit derivative is usually activated by the occurrence of a credit event that affects the credit status of the reference asset. Other events may be considered as credit events sufficient to crystallize the derivative, depending upon mutual agreement by the parties. The notion of 'materiality' is a key element in the definition of a credit event. It is intended to preclude either of the parties involved in a credit derivative from declaring a credit event when the event itself does not materially influence the value of the reference asset.

It is pertinent to note that the credit derivative can be taken on a single credit asset if sufficiently large or on a collection (pool) of credit assets. Both are significant in the portfolio risk management context. Transferring the credit risk of large exposures could have a favourable impact on the overall credit portfolio. If the credit risk on a pool of credit assets can be transferred, the impact will be similar.

Figure 19.1 shows the major types of credit derivatives.

## 19.2 CREDIT DEFAULT SWAP (CDS)

The Credit Default Swap (CDS) is the most common credit derivative. CDS allows the creditor (or the protection buyer) to transfer credit risk to another party by paying a fixed amount (premium), either in one lump sum or at regular intervals. The other party (the protection seller) makes a termination payment if a credit event – as per the agreement – is triggered.

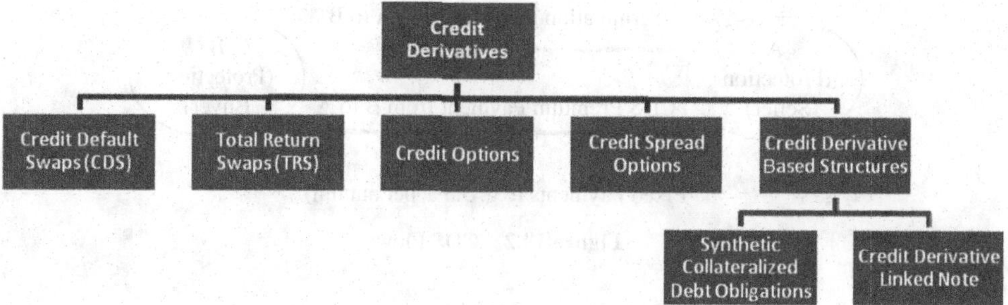


**Figure 19.1** Major Categories of Credit Derivatives

Accordingly, CDS allows the protection buyer, for a fee, to transfer the default risk on the reference asset to the protection seller. The protection period need not match the maturity of the underlying reference asset. A firm holding a credit asset (e.g. a bond) which fears default or desires to get rid of the credit risk, for whatever reason, can make use of CDS. The firm can enter into a CDS with another party who will compensate (make a termination payment) if there is any default on a bond or on the occurrence of mutually agreed credit events. The International Swaps and Derivatives Association (ISDA) have prescribed sample CDS formats.

As discussed above, the parties concerned can mutually agree on the credit event, but the typical credit events are bankruptcy, insolvency, a credit downgrade or failure to make a required scheduled payment.

**Role of Probability of Default (PD)**: PD is a critical element in CDS and determines the premium. CDS premium is a function of creditworthiness (PD) of the obligor or the credit assets issued by the obligor. If there is an improvement in creditworthiness the premium will reduce while if there is deterioration in creditworthiness, the premium increases.

The **termination payment** is the vital part of the CDS. It determines how much money can be recovered from the protection seller (or insurer) in the event of a credit event. One aspect of the termination payment is that it is a contingent event. The contingency factor is determined by the credit event. The contingent termination payment is commonly based on a formula such as:

$$\text{Termination payment} = \text{Notional amount} \times (\text{Initial value} - \text{Recovery value})$$

**Recovery value** (akin to value at default, discussed in Chapter 15) is the estimated market price of the collateral (or of the financial instrument) when a credit event has been declared. **Initial value** may be any one of the following:

- Face value (exposure amount)
- In the case of a financial instrument, the market price of the reference asset at the start of the swap
- Some agreed percentage of par, say 98.50% (so the amount paid is subject to a deductible of 1.50% in the event of a claim).

The calculation of the fixed payment is typically expressed as a percentage per annum of a notional amount. The structure of a CDS is shown in Figure 19.2:

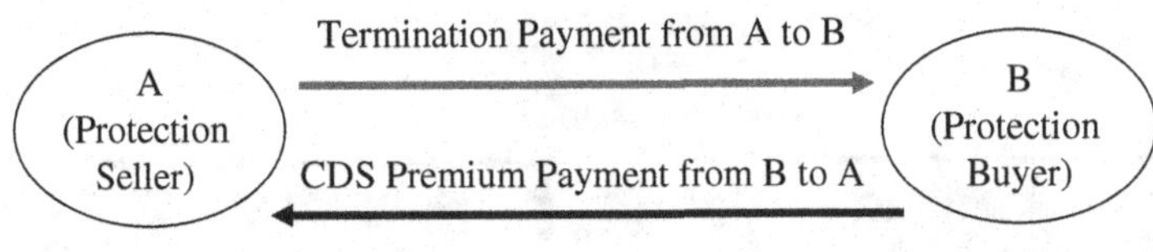


Fixed Payments (e.g. 3.5% per annum)

**Figure 19.2** CDS Flows

**Settlement of the termination payments**: In the case of a credit event, the termination payment can either be settled in cash or in physical form, the agreement again playing a key role:

- In cash settlements, the protection buyer receives a cash payment proportional to the severity of the loss on the reference asset (i.e. initial value – recovery value). One problem with cash settlement is that there may not be enough market liquidity – or market price – in the reference asset to assess its recovery value in the midst of a credit event.
- In physically settled cases, the protection buyer hands over the asset in default and receives its initial value in cash.

### 19.2.1 Is CDS an Insurance?

CDS has several similarities to insurance. It involves an insurer (credit protection seller) and the insured (credit protection buyer) and an insurable asset (underlying security). In exchange for shouldering the risk of default, the insurer gets a premium. However CDS and insurance differ in the following aspects:

- The buyer of CDS need not always own the asset. However, in insurance, only the owner who has an 'insurable interest' can buy insurance protection.
- In the event of loss, the insurance covers the 'actual loss' assessed by the insurance surveyors. In the case of CDS, a pre-determined sum is paid when a credit event is triggered, irrespective of the actual loss. Insurance relies upon the fundamental 'principle of indemnity' and holds that the insured cannot recover more than the true loss, which may not necessarily be true for CDS.
- Insurance companies are usually regulated by insurance regulators in most countries. Amongst other things, the insurance regulators take steps to ensure the solvency of the insurance underwriters. However CDS does not have any such specific regulator. Whilst some form of regulation exists in some countries through the banking regulator (Central Bank) it seems insufficient. It is likely that in the future, fully empowered credit derivatives regulators will be required given the increasing sophistication of credit instruments and credit risk management.
- An insurance contract is a 'contract of utmost good faith' and hence insurance contracts presuppose full disclosure of risks by the insurance buyer. In CDS contracts often there is no such requirement.

We can conclude that CDS is a complex product with two risks embedded in it (i) credit risk and (ii) insurance risk, although credit risk dominates this product. Hence, CDS is to be handled carefully and if not priced properly, could have disastrous consequences, as American

Insurance Group (AIG) realized in late 2008. After the Lehman collapse in October 2008, AIG suffered massive losses on various CDS written by its Financial Products Division.

### 19.2.2 CDS and Speculation

CDS can be bought by anyone even in the absence of an 'insurable' interest. In other words, the CDS can be bought by persons who hold the underlying and by those who do not hold the underlying. The latter group of buyers can be termed speculators in CDS: they speculate on the direction of creditworthiness of obligors or reference assets. 'Naked CDS' is a term used to denote the buyers of CDS without any underlying asset. Depending upon the outlook, a person may decide to speculate on CDS on an obligor/credit asset issued by the obligor.

- **Speculative Buying of CDS**: The speculator might buy CDS protection on an obligor (company or country) if the outlook is a deterioration in creditworthiness and probability of default increases. The maximum risk is limited to the premium paid (as in the case of an option premium) while the gain can be much larger, up to the maximum of the amount protected.
- **Speculative Selling of CDS**: Alternatively, the speculator may sell CDS protection if it thinks that the creditworthiness of the obligor (company or country) is improving.

**Example 19.1**

A FI believes that ABC Ltd will default on its debt. Therefore, it buys $20 million worth of Naked CDS protection on ABC Ltd's debt for one year from PQR Bank at a premium of 500 basis points (5%) per annum. Explain the scenarios of (i) default or (ii) no default. Assume nil recovery rate.

**Answer**

- **Default Scenario**: If ABC Ltd defaults then the FI receives $20 million against the $1m premium paid. This gives rise to a speculative profit of $19m while PQR Bank suffers losses, unless it is hedged.
- **No Default Scenario**: If there is no default, then the CDS contract will yield a profit of $1m for PQR bank, which will be a loss for the FI.

Studies conducted some time back have shown that about 75% of CDS are in the naked category leading to public demand to ban naked CDS and restrict CDS buying to those who actually have credit exposure to the referenced asset or obligor. It may be noted that several hedge funds profited during the 2008 Credit Crisis through naked CDS.

### 19.2.3 Uses of CDS

CDS is the most popular of the derivatives. The following are major areas where CDS can contribute towards reining in portfolio credit risk:

(a) **Credit Risk Diversification**: Diversification of portfolio credit risk is possible through CDS. CDS allows the transfer of credit risks associated with a credit asset to a third party.

It is not uncommon for banks and FIs to partake in subscriptions to loans and other credit risk exposures in view of long-term relationships with obligors. For instance, suppose ABC Bank gets an invitation to participate in the Bond Offer by SATA Steel, a long-standing customer. But ABC Bank does not wish to increase exposure in the steel industry. Neither does it desire to annoy one of its main customers by declining the invitation. Such credit exposures are more out of obligation/relationship than any real risk appetite on the part of banks/FIs. Besides, many credit assets held by commercial banks are non-transferable. Buying protection through CDS allows the lenders to reduce their credit exposures discreetly, without having to sell or assign the underlying loans or antagonizing customers which whom they have a long-standing relationship.

(b) **Buying Credit Risk**: Conversely, there may be investors who wish to take on credit exposures to given names, but lack the ability to acquire the necessary assets (due to competition, funding limitation, etc.). They are natural protection sellers. For instance, continuing the abovementioned example, suppose XYZ Finance Corporation wishes to take exposure with SATA Steel, but is hindered by competition or limiting factors. It can, through a CDS deal, buy the credit risk it desires.

**Example 19.2**

BCD Ltd has a deposit base on which it pays, on average, 4.8% interest. Being ultra-conservative, most of these funds are currently placed with other banks and institutions at 5%. It would like to diversify its portfolio into government backed entities; but lacks a sufficiently broad customer base in the region to create a well-diversified portfolio.

PQR Bank Ltd is a south based bank with a large branch network in the south and other main cities. A substantial part of the bank's credit portfolio is concentrated in loans and securities issued by southern government-guaranteed entities. These credit assets yield on average 7% p.a. which it funds at 5.2%.

PQR Bank Ltd would like to reduce its exposure to government sponsored entities. After negotiations, BCD Bank offered PQR Bank a CDS structure on the following terms:

| | |
|---|---|
| Operative date: | 01 January 20X4 |
| Term: | 5 years |
| Notional amount: | $100m |
| Early termination: | 20 days following the occurrence of a credit event |
| Termination payment: | 99% of the notional amount of reference assets |
| Reference assets: | State Public Corporation loans maturing 23 February 20XX, coupon @7% p.a. |
| Protection buyer pays: | 3% p.a. |
| Major Credit Events | Bankruptcy, default, restructuring of the debt, etc. |

In this transaction, PQR is the protection buyer and BCD is the protection seller. In fact both parties benefit.

- PQR shifts the default risk of $100m to BCD.

- BCD obtains diversification without the hassle of marketing credit and receives 3.00% p.a. from PQR. Again this is an unfunded[1] income for BCD.
- With the transfer of credit risk, PQR enjoys 4% p.a. almost[2] risk-free return, which is attractive assuming government Treasury bonds carry much lower yields.
- If the credit event (as per the contract between PQR and BCD) is triggered, only 99% of the notional amount is to be paid to acquire the underlying asset.

### 19.2.4 Sovereign CDS

Sovereign CDS is now common. This CDS market has focused on the segments where the reference assets are sovereign obligations. The movements in sovereign CDS reflect the underlying sovereign risks. Table 19.1 shows the movement of 5 year CDS of Greece over the 2009–11 period.

It is clear that the CDS premium on Greek (sovereign) debt increased between 2009 and 2011. This was the reflection of increasing probability of default on Greek debt and accordingly, the cost of insuring Greek debt increased.

Whilst the increase in CDS rates reflects increasing concerns on default risk, the improvement in the credit quality of sovereign obligations will result in a drop in CDS rates. For instance, the cost of protecting 5 year Dubai debt against default stood at 655 basis points (bps) during November 2009. However, by June 2011, 5 year Dubai CDS improved to 324 bps, reflecting the improving sentiment on Dubai's debt.

### 19.2.5 Criticism of CDS

CDS is popular as it is considered as insurance on credit default. However, its critics are many. It has been stated that one of the catalysts of the 2008 Credit Crisis, which began in the US, was the misuse of CDS. The volume of CDS transactions increased from around $600 billion in 2000 to $47 trillion by 2008. The sharp increase was due to the entry of a wide range of players – hedge funds, insurance companies, banks and other financial intermediaries – into this lucrative market. As mentioned earlier, many such CDS transactions were naked, i.e. without any assets to protect. The overdose of naked CDS is stated to be systemic risk, risk which threatens an entire market as the effect of default reverberates across various financial market participants (who however do not have direct exposure to the default) is impacted due to the exposures to naked CDS.

Many participants who dealt in CDS prior to the 2008 Credit Crisis sold protection through transactions now identified as speculative deals. CDS played a significant role in the collapse of financial giants such as AIG (the largest insurance group in the US in 2008) and the leading investment bank Merrill Lynch. Whilst AIG was bailed out by the US government, Merrill Lynch was taken over by Bank of America. We will examine the 2008 Credit Crisis later in this book.

It is also argued that CDS and other similar products resulted in 'moral hazard', i.e. the possibility of an increase in 'risky behaviour' since you know that your risky behaviour will

[1] Sometimes, the protection buyer may insist on some cash margin (collateral), in which case this may be treated as partly unfunded.
[2] PQR now has a counterparty credit risk exposure on BCD.

**Table 19.1** Major Time Lines of Greece Sovereign Credit Crisis till early 2011

| Time Period | CDS Rates* | Remarks |
|---|---|---|
| Sept 2008 | Below 200 bps | Lehman collapse |
| May 2010 | 300–400 bps | Greece budget deficit exceeds 12.7% of GDP. A rescue package of Euro 110 bn agreed |
| Mar 2011 | Above 1,000 bps | Increasing concerns on Greek solvency and effectiveness of austerity measures. |

*5 year Greece CDS.

not result in any loss to you. CDS could provide encouragement to risky behaviour, when insurance companies ought to discourage it. Many argue that this is exactly what happened in the 2008 Credit Crisis. AIG and similar institutions offered credit insurance, such as CDS. The ability to get credit insurance also acted as an incentive to 'sub-prime lending'. The banks and mortgage providers began to offer credit facilities to people who were not creditworthy because they thought the credit insurance would protect them if the borrowers were unable to pay. It resulted in a lowering of credit standards – a moral hazard.

## 19.3 TOTAL RETURN SWAP

In this type of credit derivative one counterparty (total return payer or protection buyer) pays the other party (total return receiver or protection seller) the total return of the underlying in return for a flexible (LIBOR, etc.) rate based return. The transaction simply allows the participants to go long or short on a particular credit-sensitive asset. Figure 19.3 depicts a representation of a typical TR swap structure:

**TOTAL RETURN (TR) SWAP**

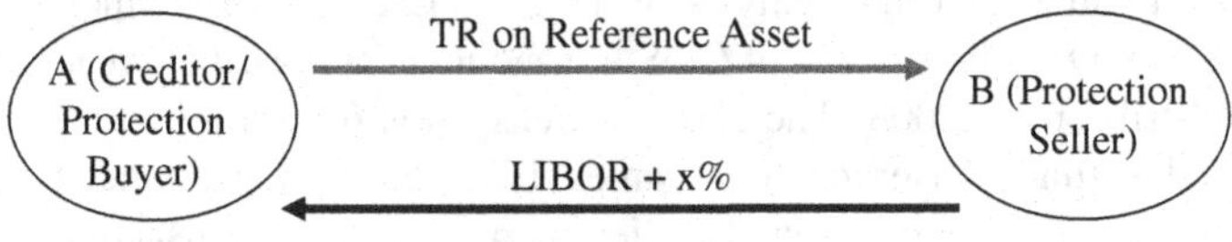


LIBOR (etc) + Spread (e.g. LIBOR + .025% per annum)

**Figure 19.3** TRS Flows

The total return swap is a swap transaction in which a party (protection buyer) agrees to pay the total return on a particular reference asset (for e.g. a traded credit asset i.e. bond issued by a corporate or a basket of such assets), and agrees to receive a rate such as LIBOR+1%. The total return includes any interest payment and capital gains over the swap settlement period. Usually, there is no exchange of principal. A party holding a bond issued by a private borrower can promise to pay its total return, thereby stripping off the risk associated with credit downgrades or defaults during the life of the bond. Thus the features enjoyed by the protection buyer are outlined below:

- Owns reference asset(s)
- Pays total return of asset(s)

- Receives LIBOR +/– spread
- Gets 'insurance' protection – receives payments to offset any capital losses/default
- Accepts interest rate risk (linked to LIBOR or other floating rates)
- Removes asset return risk.

Large institutions such as commercial banks, investment banks, insurance companies, etc. are the usual protection buyers, who are interested in insuring against capital losses for a reasonable return.

The other party (protection seller) seeks returns on the reference security without buying the asset, i.e. the protection seller does not want to purchase and hold the asset on its balance sheet. This party 'sells protection' by taking a synthetic long position in the asset(s) and enjoys the total returns without much capital outlay. Thus the features enjoyed by the protection seller are outlined below:

- Does not own or invest in the reference asset(s)
- Receives total return of asset(s) and provides 'insurance' against capital losses
- Pays LIBOR +/– spread
- Takes on asset return risk
- Also exposed to interest rate risk, depending upon the circumstances.

Protection sellers are usually hedge funds, specialty asset managers, etc. They seek maximum returns by taking synthetic long positions to generate higher returns, while avoiding the transaction and administrative costs associated with buying the assets.

Note that the market risk is not eradicated since movements in a broad market rate such as LIBOR can influence the swap related payments, which are usually settled on a quarterly basis. Suppose a bank/FI lends to a major corporate through fixed rate debentures. The credit risk on the debenture, which is publicly traded, might be linked to the rating by an external agency. If the rating is downgraded, the market price of its existing fixed rate debentures would decrease. A bank/FI that purchased credit protection for these bonds using a Total Return (TR) swap would be compensated for the amount that the bond's value had reduced.

Although there is no exchange of principal initially, the protection seller is responsible for compensating the protection buyer in the event of default. If two parties enter into a TR swap on a credit asset and if default occurs during the life of the swap, the TR receiver would make a final payment to the TR payer equal to the difference between the notional value and recovery (e.g. market value) of the credit asset. A TR swap agreement will include terms related to various payments and asset valuation steps required upon default. There will usually be an exchange of cash or physical delivery of the defaulted bonds.

### 19.3.1 Uses of TR Swap

Like other types of swap, total return swaps are commonly used for the following purposes:

- To get artificial exposure to asset returns in situations where it is either impossible or uneconomic for a party (total return receiver) to acquire the asset itself.
- To hedge an existing exposure to an asset (reference name) without physically having to dispose of the reference asset.

**Example 19.3**

XYZ Finance, a London based institution specializing in fixed income bonds/loans, wishes to acquire credit exposure to Japanese quasi-government domestic bonds/loans. However, XYZ Finance lacks the administration systems necessary to originate or settle transactions in the domestic Japanese market.

Through enquiries, it is understood that ABC Bank offers a TR swap on Japanese credit assets. The terms are as follows:

| | |
|---|---|
| Effective date: | 4 November 20×4 |
| Termination date: | 5 November 20×6 |
| Calculation amount: | GBP 10 million |
| Early termination: | Credit event for reference name |
| ABC Bank pays: | Total return on the reference asset |
| Reference asset | Japan Savings Authority 8.73% (Yen-denominated bond maturing on 16 May 20Y0) |
| XYZ pays | GBP 6 month LIBOR + 1.40% |

In this case, XYZ is the total return receiver while ABC is the payer. Both parties are happy because the TR swap enables them to get the desired positions. Whilst XYZ undertakes credit exposure in the Japanese market, ABC enjoys diversification. (As a corollary it may be noted that XYZ gets a fixed rate in Japanese Yen while ABC is exposed to floating LIBOR based rate. This means both are exposed to foreign currency movements while ABC returns are subject to the LIBOR movements as well. However, these issues are not linked with credit and hence let us assume that the foreign currency/LIBOR movements are acceptable to both parties.)

## 19.4 CREDIT OPTION (CO)

A call/put option represents the right, but not the obligation, to buy/sell. CO is a credit derivative that applies the principle of option to reduce credit risks. Like equity options, credit options may be either American or European style. A CO allows the protection buyer to be protected against any credit loss arising from any predefined credit events. If the credit event does not occur during the contracted period, then the protection buyer would let the option lapse. However, on the other hand if any of the credit events are triggered, the company/bank (the protection buyers) would seek compensation (termination payment) under the option. In exchange for these benefits and protection, the protection buyer will pay a fee upfront known as a premium.

It is very similar to CDS but with one major exception. Whilst in CDS the protection buyer makes a series of fixed payments, with the CO, the payment is upfront in full and the option period is usually shorter than that of CDS. Credit event and termination payment calculations are along the lines of the CDS.

## 19.5 CREDIT SPREAD OPTIONS (CSO)

The Credit Spread Option (CSO[3]) is an option on the credit spread *or* provides protection to the credit spread. CSO is appropriate in situations where the credit spread is a matter of concern.

What is a credit spread? As we know, corporate credit assets such as bonds pay a higher interest rate than treasury securities issued by government. If the yields are the same, a lender would prefer treasury securities. The difference that attracts the lenders/investors to corporate bonds is the credit spread, i.e. the difference in yields depending upon the credit risk. The higher the credit risk, the wider the credit spread. In an economy, if the spread widens faster, it is considered a sign of worsening economic conditions.

Since the credit spread changes with the credit risk, it has wider implications especially for traded debt securities. A bond downgrade will result in the fall of its (bond) prices, leading to losses to the bond holders. An investor who believes that a corporate credit rating may change, thereby affecting its credit spread over another benchmark rate (say treasury rate), which in turn will affect the face value of the credit asset (say debenture) can use CSO. The protection seeker/buyer can buy a credit spread option to mitigate the risk of a credit upgrade/downgrade. The option buyer ought to pay a premium, either as a lump sum, or amortized over the term of the option. In turn, the option seller agrees to compensate in case the credit spread (of the credit asset) moves over the agreed threshold.

For example XYZ Mutual Funds have investments in fixed rate corporate bonds. A rise in interest rates will reduce the market value of the bonds, which, in turn, means losses when the bonds are marked to market. The fund manager can cover this risk through CSO – buying an option, which will compensate the fall in portfolio value if general (treasury rate) interest rates increase.

## 19.6 CREDIT DERIVATIVE LINKED STRUCTURES

Credit derivatives were often used to structure complex products. Structured credit products can be either funded or unfunded or hybrid deals or transactions and credit derivatives to allow investors to access a diversified portfolio of assets. Two major credit derivative-linked structured credit products are discussed below.

In the Credit Derivative Linked Note (CDLN) funding is involved. It is nothing but CDS with movement of funds between the protection seller and protection buyer. The main differences of this type of credit derivative (linked notes) with other derivatives discussed so far are:

(a) In the case of CDLN, the principal (either in full or at a discount/premium as mutually agreed) is moved. As a rule of thumb, it can be stated that whenever a credit derivative is mentioned with the words 'linked note' it means that funds movement between the parties is involved, at the beginning of the contract itself, equivalent to the principal, either at par/discount/premium). In normal credit derivatives, no principal movements are involved.

[3] It may be noted that there is a different type of equity/commodity credit spread used by option traders. It involves buying and selling (writing) options on the same underlying/index in the same month, but at different strike prices. These are also known as vertical spreads.

(b) In 'linked notes' if there is no default, the principal is returned on maturity and in case of default the entire principal/a major part of it is not returned. On the other hand, in non-linked derivatives, the protection seller will compensate the buyer as per the terms in case of default. If there is no default, the maturity date passes by without any sort of principal payment. The latter is more like insurance.

## 19.7 FUTURE OF CREDIT DERIVATIVES

Credit derivatives are here to stay and play an important role in modern day credit. Various types of credit derivatives exist, tailor-made to the circumstances, within the basic structure of derivatives – viz. options, forwards and swaps. Credit derivatives can be structured to suit the needs at hand. Almost all credit derivatives are over-the-counter instruments. The beauty of the credit derivative is its flexibility and it allows creativity and the ability to apply fresh ideas. The transfer of credit risk can be effected for the whole life of the credit asset or for a shorter/limited period. Either the entire credit risk or a part of it can be transferred. The delivery can be structured in an insurance form or as linked notes (i.e. with funding). Similarly, one derivative agreement may cover a single credit asset or a group of credit sensitive assets. The flexibility is vast and depending upon the participants' requirements, various structures can be created.

## 19.8 CREDIT DERIVATIVES AND OVER-THE-COUNTER (OTC) MARKETS

OTC derivatives constitute a significant part of the world of global finance. OTC derivatives are privately negotiated between two parties, without going through an exchange. All derivatives which are not traded or settled through an exchange or clearing-house can be classified as OTC derivatives. The OTC derivatives markets are large and have grown exponentially over the last two decades.

Credit derivatives are OTC derivatives, i.e. they are privately negotiated between two parties. In the past two decades, the major internationally active financial institutions have significantly increased the share of their earnings from derivatives activities. These institutions manage portfolios of derivatives involving tens of thousands of positions, including credit default swaps.

## ✍ QUESTIONS/EXERCISES

1. What is a credit derivative? Why is it becoming increasingly popular?
2. Is it necessary for a credit protection seller to have expertise in credit risk analysis? Please elaborate.
3. What are the major types of credit derivatives?
4. What is CDS? Explain its benefits.
5. One of your friends argues that credit derivatives are dangerous and highlights the role of CDS in the 2008 Credit Crisis. Do you agree? Please share your views.
6. What is TRS? Explain its advantages and disadvantages.
7. Explain the difference between the credit option and the credit spread option.
8. Can credit derivatives be bought and sold in (stock) exchanges like listed equity derivatives? Please elaborate.

# Part VI
# Credit Risk Pricing

Inappropriate credit risk pricing is tantamount to a systemic risk.

# 20 Pricing Basics

Banks and financial institutions are in the business of underwriting risks. In order to survive as a viable enterprise, it is not only essential to have appropriate risk identification and mitigation strategies, but an adequate risk pricing mechanism is also vital. A financial institution engaged in multiple lines of risk underwriting must ensure that every risk is priced adequately, based on the type of risks underwritten. Appropriate risk pricing is key to the success of all risk underwriting business irrespective of whether it is credit risk, derivative risk, insurance risk or equity risk.

Credit risk pricing can often be challenging. Modern day credit products are becoming complex, hence the pricing of various types of structured products such as CDO, credit derivatives and credit risk insurance products requires in-depth understanding and analysis. For example, AIG, the largest US insurance company earned just 15% of total revenue from its Financial Products Division during 2008. This division primarily offered CDS, i.e. credit insurance and collected premiums. CDS is a complex product where both credit and insurance risks are involved and, if not priced properly, could have disastrous consequences. AIG had inappropriately priced in the credit risk element in CDS, which ultimately led AIG to the brink of bankruptcy during 2008.

As we have seen in Chapter 1, a bank/FI enjoying an interest margin (net spread) of 2%, if it suffers a credit loss of $1m, will have to deploy $50m ($1m/2%) to recoup the loss. In other words, 50 times the money lost (credit loss) needs to be deployed to recoup the loss. Hence, suppliers of credit ought to very careful while identifying and pricing a credit asset.

## 20.1 CREDIT PRICING FACTORS

While pricing credit risk, several factors need to be considered. The credit default risk is most critical. However, there are also other factors to be considered, for example, cost of funds. Figure 20.1 shows the major factors to be considered while pricing a credit asset. It may be noted that the diagram is only indicative and additional factors – for example liquidity or migration risk – may also need to be considered depending upon the circumstances.

Let us examine each factor in detail:

### 20.1.1 Credit Risk Premium

As with the generally accepted classic case of risk vs. return, the higher the credit risk, the higher should be the return and vice versa. When considering credit risk pricing, credit executives should ensure that the credit risk is not only thoroughly analyzed and understood but also priced adequately. The following simple rule is sometimes forgotten (by credit professionals) in the real world as higher risks are underwritten for low prices.

Figure 20.2 illustrates the direct relationship of credit risk pricing with probability of default. PD plays an important role in arriving at the credit risk premium on various credit derivatives such as CDS and CSO.

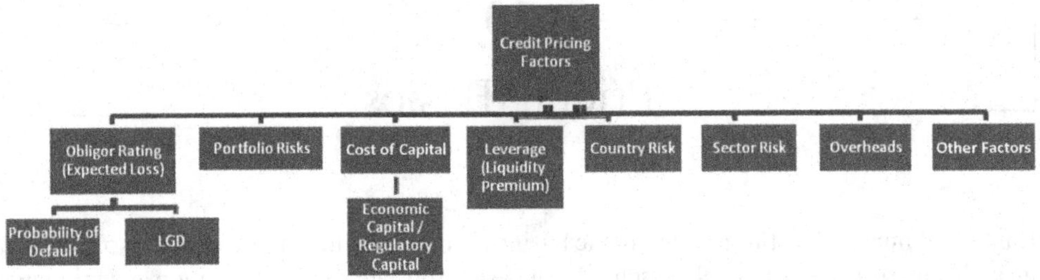


**Figure 20.1** Credit Pricing Drivers

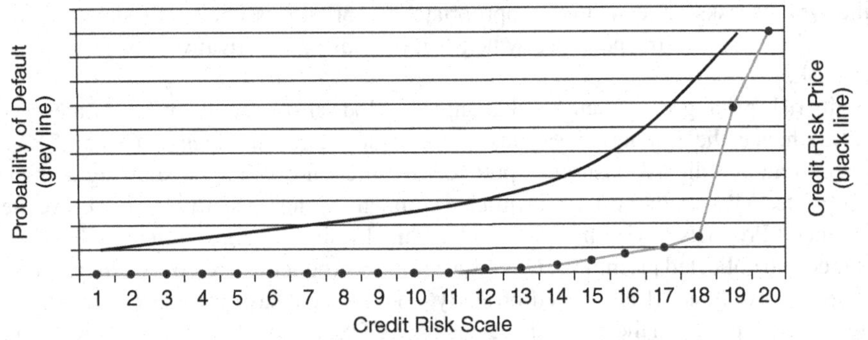


**Figure 20.2** Relationship between Credit Pricing and PD

How is PD factored into pricing? The higher the PD, the higher the credit premium, as we have seen in the case of CDS. This is the reason why corporate credit assets have a higher yield than government or treasury securities. Corporate debt is costlier than treasury bills because the latter are considered to be risk free.

It is evident that theoretically credit risk pricing and PD have a positive relationship; however there is an exception – if the LGD is low, then the credit risk pricing may not strictly have a direct relationship. As we discussed in Chapter 15, Expected Loss (EL) is a function of PD and LGD. EL is the cost of doing business and, accordingly, it will be factored into the pricing. The higher the EL, the higher the credit pricing; and the higher the PD, the higher the EL unless LGD is zero or near zero (i.e. backed by strong collateral).

**Example 20.1**

The Head of Corporate of ABC Bank is negotiating pricing with a customer who insists on an interest rate of 11% on the proposed short-term credit facility. He is interested to know the implied PD in this rate if the one year treasury bill rate is 8%.

**Answer**

Corporate debt is costlier than treasury bills because the fundamental assumption is that the treasury bill has zero PD, i.e. will be repaid on time. Hence, it is implied that the additional risk in corporate debt ought to be reflected in the credit risk pricing. By comparing the pricing, we can understand the implied PD on the corporate debt. The calculation is as follows:

$$PD = 1 - \frac{(1 + \text{treasury rate})}{(1 + \text{loan rate})}$$
$$= 1 - (1.08/1.11)$$
$$= 1 - 0.973$$

Hence the PD is 1 − 0.973 or 0.027 i.e. there is a 97.3% probability that the credit asset will be repaid on time. There is a 2.7% probability that the credit asset will default. Hence the implied PD is 2.7%.

PD is also useful in the calculation of multi-year credit assets, i.e. credit assets that mature in more than one year. In such cases it is necessary to know the credit asset's or borrower's marginal probability of default over the entire period.

**Example 20.2**

The Head of Credit Risk of ABC Bank is considering approval of a three year credit asset (term loan) with a bullet repayment at the end of the term. The credit asset shows marginal probability of default of 1.7%, 1.9% and 2.1% for each of the three years. He is interested to know the cumulative probability of default (PD) over the three year period for pricing purposes.

**Answer**

The cumulative probability can be arrived at by understanding the probability of the credit asset surviving without default, i.e.

$$= 1 - (1 - \text{Pd year 1}) \times (1 - \text{Pd year 2}) \times (1 - \text{Pd year 3})$$
$$= 1 - (1 - 0.017) \times (1 - 0.019) \times (1 - 0.021)$$
$= 0.057$ OR 5.7% over three years, which may be considered for pricing.

### 20.1.2 Portfolio Risk

The relationship between credit risk and return ought to be recognized not only at firm level but at portfolio level as well. The credit portfolio should be managed in such a manner that it meets the targeted portfolio return and accounts for portfolio risks.

We discussed in Chapter 15 (Section 15.6) how the portfolio risk is calculated depending upon the macroeconomic outlook. High quality credit categories require less general provision. On the other hand, the riskier components of the portfolio will attract higher general provision. The general macroeconomic outlook, historical experience assimilated through historical data and the size of the sub-portfolios are among the other dynamics considered while arriving at the provisioning requirement. If the general portfolio provisioning is higher, the pricing also ought to reflect that.

### 20.1.3 Cost of Capital

When a credit asset is created, it involves investment of funds or capital, which in turn results in cost of funds/capital. Hence, the return on credit should not only cover the cost of capital and related administrative charges but leave sufficient margin to satisfy the shareholders as well. Cost of capital is one of the important considerations to be taken into account when pricing credit risk. There are other factors also to be considered, which will be discussed later. But capital is more critical, especially in regulated bodies such as banks.

With the introduction of capital adequacy norms, the credit risks are linked to the capital. Consequently higher capital is required to be deployed if more credit risks are underwritten. The decision whether to (a) maximize the returns on possible credit assets with the existing capital or (b) raise more capital to do more business (underwrite more credit assets) invariably depends upon pricing. If more capital is required for a particular credit asset, naturally the associated cost of capital (in absolute terms) will also be more (higher), which in turn would require a better return, hence the need for higher credit pricing.

Economic capital based pricing is expected to ensure that the 'higher risks' are rewarded with higher returns. As we have discussed earlier, economic capital is a function of variables such as PD, LGD and the confidence level required by the bank. Accordingly, PD and LGD influence credit pricing in two ways. First directly, as PD and LGD determine the expected loss which is directly priced in. Secondly, PD and LGD play an important role in determining economic capital, which in turn will influence credit pricing by way of cost of capital.

### 20.1.4 Cost of Leverage

Banks and FIs operate with high leverage. Since they depend on external funds – mainly deposits from the public and/or inter-bank (wholesale) market – to create credit assets, they always carry a refinancing risk. There is a risk either that the refinance may not be available or, if available, that it will be at a higher cost. Refinancing is mainly a function of market liquidity and creditworthiness of the borrowing bank and FI.

It is generally seen that the bank with higher leverage attracts a lower credit rating pushing up the cost of refinancing. Higher dependence on leverage itself brings its own headaches, especially in times of economic crisis. History has proven that often banks and FIs will not be able to survive such contingencies without the liberal support of central banks. Hence, there is always a risk that refinancing may be costlier because of market illiquidity and so the bank may prudently add an appropriate liquidity premium into the credit pricing.

### 20.1.5 Sector Risks

Pricing should reflect the underlying risk associated with the sector. Certain sectors are more risky than others and, as a consequence, the constituents of such sectors may become defaulters while the constituents of a stable sector will continue to perform well.

Similarly, concentration risk, if any, which has crept into any part of the credit portfolio must also be priced in.

For example, Bank XYZ has the sector cap as shown in Table 20.1:

**Table 20.1** Sector Caps

| Particulars | Sector Caps | RAG Status | Pricing |
|---|---|---|---|
| Ideal | Up to 8% of the portfolio | Green | NA |
| Acceptable | Between 8–9% of the portfolio | Amber | 0.25% |
| Acceptable | Between 9–10% of the portfolio | Amber Plus | 0.75% |
| Unacceptable | Beyond 10% | Red | Strict Cap |

Accordingly, the maximum exposure to any sector must not exceed 8% of the total book. It may be internally decided that all credit proposals seeking additional limits to this sector will carry additional risk pricing of 0.25% or 0.75%. Beyond 10%, no lending is allowed. Such controls by credit risk management will dissuade the credit originating team from recommending credit assets that will increase the concentration risk.

### 20.1.6 Overheads

Institutions have to spend time, effort and resources (including human expertise) to appraise, monitor and control the credit and related operations. The overheads are usually classified under two heads – direct costs and indirect costs. Direct costs are those which can be easily identified with a credit asset. Indirect costs are those which are more general in nature.

### 20.1.7 Other Factors

It may be noted that the abovementioned factors are non-exclusive. Depending upon the nature of credit risk underwritten, there could be other risks, which must also be priced in. A few such factors are mentioned below:

1. **Country risks**: Cross-border lending involves country risk. Suppose Bank XYZ lends to customers in two countries – Country A and Country B. If the perceived country risk of Country A is higher, then the credit pricing on the credit asset in Country A ought to be higher, *ceteris paribus*.
2. **Security**: If appropriate and adequate security is offered as the mitigant to the credit risk, downward adjustments in pricing can be considered, if necessary, from normal pricing. Pricing should be negotiated upward in consideration of the discharge of an existing security or dilution of the bank's security position. (Please see Part VII for details.)
3. **Liquidity risk premium**: Liquidity premium is also a cost factor especially when tight liquidity conditions prevail or are anticipated in the economy.
4. **Ancillary business**: In the case of adequate and compensating additional business in some other area, the creditor may relax pricing. For example, banks price credit following the loss-leader strategy if the investment or foreign exchange income from a customer is substantial. Similarly, if the customer maintains high deposits with a bank, the bank will sometimes extend interest-free credit facilities of small amounts.
5. **Compliance with conditions/covenants**: The terms and covenants of a credit facility may be structured in such a manner that in case of non-compliance, higher pricing will be triggered. This also reflects the higher credit risk involved because of non-compliance or lack of financial discipline.

6. **Inflation**: As we have discussed in earlier chapters, inflation eats into the value of a credit asset and hence it should be compensated through pricing.
7. **Exit strategy**: Often, higher pricing of facilities is used as a strategy to cease dealings with a particular customer. Realizing that the price is higher than what is offered by competitors in the market, the customer ought to prefer other suppliers of capital. However, one important aspect to be remembered is that this strategy should be applied well in advance, before a sharp deterioration in the creditworthiness of the customer.

## 20.2 PRICING STRUCTURE

Interest on advances being the main source of a financial institution's revenue, credit executives must ensure that the rate of interest on credit provides a satisfactory return. However, usually there are accepted ways of deriving income (usually one-off) other than interest income, which are intended to remunerate the financial institution for services, whether connected with the credit or not. The following are the major sources of income which determine pricing:

1. Interest rates
2. Non-interest income (commission and fees).

### 20.2.1 Interest Rates

As we have seen in the first chapter, interest represents the time value of money and the compensation for forgoing other opportunities of deployment and consideration for accepting credit risk. Banks apply interest on all credit facilities while non-financial entities load the interest factor into the price of goods/services, if they are sold on credit. The interest rate margin varies primarily depending upon the credit risk (i.e. PD). A lower margin is fixed for less risky advances while the smaller and more risky advance usually attracts a higher margin. International credit by multinational banks and similar institutions is often quoted by reference to LIBOR (London Inter-Bank Offered Rate).

#### *20.2.1.1 Fixed or Variable Interest Rate*

Usually interest rates are set by adopting a fixed interest method or a variable interest method. A **fixed rate** of interest is one that will be applied right through the life of the advance. Changes in the base rate will not affect fixed rates. For example, if the loan is extended at 10% fixed rate for five years, this rate remains whatever happens to the base rate. The interest is deducted from the proceeds when the advance is granted (e.g. in the case of a discounted bill). Alternatively the total interest is added to the amount advanced, which is then converted into equal instalments (e.g. EMI) agreed between the lender and the borrower (e.g. in the case of most personal instalment loans and hire purchase finance).

A **variable interest** rate is fluctuating and moves with the base rate or reference rates such as LIBOR. Since there is uncertainty as to the interest rate, the charging of interest on the outstanding amount of the advance takes place periodically, e.g. monthly or quarterly. For example, if a loan is granted at 2% above LIBOR and the current LIBOR is 5%, then the interest rate would be 7%. If the LIBOR changes to 7%, the interest rate will automatically increase to 9% (i.e. 7% + 2%).

### 20.2.1.2 Interest Rate Swaps (IRS)

A swap is an agreement to exchange cash flows based on certain circumstances at specified future times according to pre-agreed rules. The primary function of the Interest Rate Swap (IRS) is to minimize interest rate risk by hedging against fluctuations in the interest rate. A risk averse corporate customer or a financial institution prefers certainty in the budgeting process, as far as interest rates are concerned. IRS can also be structured in such a manner as to earn a profit, which is common in financial intermediaries such as banks. This is usually based on the difference between the amount it pays to one party and the amount it receives from another in different IRS agreements. Working as an intermediary, banks are in a good position to find counterparties for several IRS deals which would balance out. IRSs are of different types:

- In many countries, the most common IRS is the plain vanilla swap, where one party exchanges a fixed-rate coupon stream for a floating-rate coupon stream.
- IRSs can also be entered into in such a manner that the interest rate swap involves the exchange of one floating-rate coupon stream for another.
- Usually IRSs are structured in the same currency. However, they can be structured in such a manner that more than one currency is involved. In such cases the swap can be fixed-for-fixed, floating-for-floating or fixed-for-floating across the different currencies.

An IRS is a negotiated contract, and the party who enters into a swap deal must find a second party that is willing to take the other side of the swap under terms and conditions acceptable to both parties. Interest rate swaps are the most common OTC derivative in today's world. (We will discuss OTC derivatives in detail later in the book.) Since the need to hedge interest rates arises due to borrowings, the bank is generally the counterparty in most of the IRS deals. Banks also enter into IRSs amongst themselves.

In an IRS a bank agrees to pay the counterparty a period fixed rate (or floating rate) on a notional principal over the tenor of IRS against the receipt of a floating rate (or fixed rate). Both payments are to be in the same currency and hence only net payment is exchanged. Most IRSs use LIBOR as the reference rate for the floating leg of the swap. IRS is common between banks or between banks and corporates mainly to hedge interest rate risks or reduce interest rates.

**Example 20.3**

XYZ Ltd is paying a fixed rate of interest at 7% on its long-term project finance of $100m. The general market conditions signal a possible reduction in interest rates within a year which will continue for the medium term. Current rate of LIBOR is 5% which is expected to drop, going forward. Accordingly the CFO of XYZ Ltd is interested in swapping the fixed interest rate into a floating one. ABC Bank has offered an Interest Rate Swap (IRS) solution. The IRS agreement as per ISDA standards requires XYZ Ltd to receive from ABC Bank a fixed amount of 6.8% on a notional principal of $100m, while XYZ Ltd pays ABC Bank on the basis of 3-month LIBOR+200 bps for the same notional principal. Explain the impact on XYZ Ltd in the following two scenarios: (i) LIBOR drops to 3% and (ii) LIBOR increases to 6%.

**Answer**

Let us see the flow of transactions of XYZ Ltd, depicted in the following diagram:

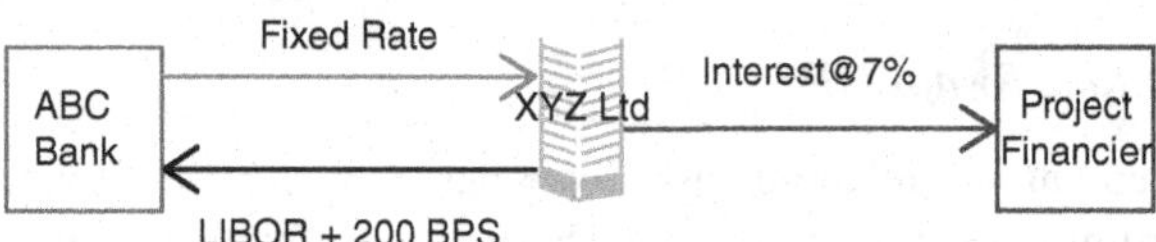


In this case, XYZ Ltd will continue to pay project finance as per the loan agreement, i.e. 7%; however by entering into an IRS with ABC Bank, XYZ Ltd can realize the goal of taking advantage of floating rates. The impact of the two scenarios is explained below:

- **LIBOR drops to 3%**: XYZ will continue to pay 7% on to the project financier, i.e. $7m ($100m x 7%). However it will receive 6.8% on the same amount from ABC Bank under IRS while XYZ will pay LIBOR +2% or 5% (i.e.3% + 2%) to ABC Bank. Accordingly, the net interest cost to XYZ Ltd is only 5.2% (i.e. 5% + (7% – 6.8%)). Thus IRS has enabled XYZ Ltd to reduce the interest costs by $1.8m ($7m – $5.2m) p.a.
- **LIBOR increases to 6%**: XYZ will continue to pay 7% on to the project financier, i.e. $7m ($100m × 7%). It will receive 6.8% on the same amount from ABC Bank under IRS while XYZ will pay LIBOR +2% or 8% (6% + 2%) to ABC Bank. Accordingly, the net interest cost to XYZ Ltd is 8.2%. Thus IRS will result in higher interest costs of $1.8m ($8.2m – $7m) p.a.

**IRS Risk**: If there is an adverse move (as in the case of Scenario 2 above) in interest rates, IRS will result in higher interest costs. If the interest rates move against the IRS position it can result in loss. Hence, if the interest rates increase, IRS will not result in any gain to XYZ Ltd; on the other hand it will result in higher interest costs.

It is evident that IRS is a directional bet on the direction of interest rates and can reduce finance costs, if interest rates move in the predicted direction. However, as we have seen above, IRS may result in higher interest costs if the interest rates move against the original direction in which IRS is entered into.

### 20.2.2 Commission and Fees

Commission is the charge collected on services rendered to the customers. For instance, when the bank negotiates a bill or provides non-funded limits such as bank guarantees or letters of credit, a commission is usually charged. Arrangement fees, processing fees, management fees, extension fees, amendment fees, etc. are some of the fees charged by creditor enterprises, while making the credit available to the customers. Banks and financial institutions usually have several sources of non-interest income.

Sound understanding of the relationship between credit risk and return is an essential ingredient for intelligent credit risk management. This relationship ought to be recognized not only at firm level but at portfolio level as well.

## 20.3 CREDIT RISK PRICING MODEL

Normally a financial institution, when pricing credit, follows a model more or less similar to the one given below:

= Cost of raising funds + Overheads (salaries, etc.) + Credit risk premium + Profit margin

- **Cost of raising funds**: When funds are raised for extending credit, the financial institution and other suppliers of credit do bear a cost. For instance, when a bank extends a loan, the necessary funds might have been obtained through customer deposits or the funds raised inter-bank. Banks are usually highly leveraged entities and hence the debt is often about 10–12.5 times (8–10% capital adequacy) of the capital. In such cases, the interest paid on deposits and the return expected by shareholders on capital are major ingredients of the cost of funds for the bank. This applies to non-financial institutions as well because the funds blocked in the receivables do have cost of capital, which is usually the weighted average of cost of various sources of capital. In the case of banks and financial institutions, on certain occasions the cost of raising funds will be substituted by the base rate/reference rate obtained from the market.
- **Overheads**: The salaries, rent and other overheads (stationery, communications, electricity expenses, etc.) related to the credit department (both front and back offices) are also to be recovered from the pricing.
- **Credit risk premium**. We have seen that various grades have differing PDs. The higher the PD, the higher the premium to be loaded into the pricing. One rough method is to factor in the default probability as the credit risk premium. Besides PD there could other risk premiums that may be required to be loaded into the pricing – e.g. (i) country risk premium and (ii) liquidity risk premium, etc., as we discussed earlier in this chapter.
- **Profit margin** is the real earnings of the credit institution. All other variables discussed above cover the costs. Profit is what motivates the credit institution to underwrite credit risks.

## 20.4 PRIME LENDING RATE

The Prime Lending Rate (PLR) is the rate of interest at which banks lend to the most creditworthy customers, i.e. those with a high credit rating. While calculating PLR, financial intermediaries apply the credit pricing model mentioned above; however the variables may differ. (For example, the percentage of liquidity ratio[1] to be maintained by banks with the central bank will also influence the credit pricing by banks.)

The PLR runs above the central bank rate, i.e. the rate charged by the central bank when lending to the banking sector of the economy. For example, the Fed funds rate is the primary tool that the US Federal Reserve (through the Federal Open Market Committee) uses to influence interest rates in the economy. Similarly, the Reserve Bank of India uses its Repo rates to influence the interest rates charged by the banking sector in the country. Usually, the PLR is approximately 200–300 basis points higher than the central bank rates.

The PLR is influenced by central bank rates. The changes in central bank rates have far reaching effects by influencing the borrowing costs of banks, and subsequently the returns offered on bank deposit products such as certificates of deposit, fixed deposits, savings accounts and call accounts. This in turn influences the PLR and rate of interest charged on credit cards, mortgages, personal loans, auto loans and business loans.

Since PLR is the rate that is offered to the most creditworthy customers (for example AAA rated), the financial intermediaries charge more to the customers who enjoy lesser

[1] Statutory Liquidity Ratio (SLR) or Cash Reserve Ratio (CRR).

ratings. For illustrative purposes, the following might be the differential pricing structure based on PLR:

| Customer Credit Rating | Pricing |
|---|---|
| AAA | PLR + 0% |
| AA | PLR + 1% |
| A | PLR + 3% |
| BBB | PLR + 5% |
| BB | PLR + 8% |

## CASE STUDY

A hypothetical lending institution provides you with the following particulars:

- Funds arranged through (i) local currency bonds, (ii) foreign currency bonds, (ii) deposits from local and foreign financial institutions are $36,650k, $1,660k, $374k and $54k with annual rates of interest of 4.07%, 4.82%, 5.48% and 4.44% respectively.
- The credit department consists of credit managers, credit analysts and credit assistants, drawing salaries of $300k, $200k and $100k respectively p.a. Normal transactions processed during a year number around 20,000. Overheads allocated to the department for utilities, postage, stationery etc. stood at $300k p.a.
- The credit risk premium varies depending upon the grading assigned – Grade 1, Grade 2, Grade 3, Grade 4 and Grade 5 are charged a premium of 1%, 2%, 3% and 5% respectively.
- Normal Profit Margin is 2%.

(a) A customer has been approved a credit of $4,000k – under Credit Grade 3. What would be the pricing of this credit facility under the following scenarios:

*Case A*: The number of transactions processed through the department is 80?

*Case B*: Continuing the previous example, what would be the pricing, had the number of number of transactions numbered 2,000.

*Case C*: Assume the Credit Risk Grade is 1, viz. Very Low Credit Risk. What would be the pricing?

(b) Please share your views on the credit pricing model. Can it be improved further?

**Solution**

(a) The pricing of the credit facility of $4m under various scenarios is given below:

**Case A**: The credit pricing ought to be 9.86%. The calculation is as follows:

| | | |
|---|---|---|
| Cost of Funds (Note 1) | 4.76%*4,000,000 | 190,359 |
| Overheads (Note 2) | 80*50 | 4,000 |
| Credit Risk Premium | 3%*4,000,000 | 120,000 |
| Profit Margin | 2%*4,000,000 | 80,000 |
| Total Price of Credit | | 394,359 |
| **Credit Pricing (%)** | (394,359k/4,000,000) | **9.86%** |

**Case B**: The credit pricing ought to be 12.26%. The calculation is as follows:

| | | |
|---|---|---|
| Cost of Funds (Note 1) | 4.76%*4,000,000 | 190,359 |
| Overheads (Note 2) | 2,000*50 | 100,000 |
| Credit Risk Premium | 3%*4,000,000 | 120,000 |
| Profit Margin | 2%*4,000,000 | 80,000 |
| Total Price of Credit | | 490,359 |
| **Credit Pricing (%)** | (490,359k/4,000,000) | **12.26%** |

**Case C**: The credit pricing ought to be 7.36%. The calculation is as follows:

| | | |
|---|---|---|
| Cost of Funds (Note 1) | 4.76%*4,000,000 | 190,359 |
| Overheads (Note 2) | 80*50 | 4,000 |
| Credit Risk Premium | 0.5%*4,000,000 | 20,000 |
| Profit Margin | 2%*4,000,000 | 80,000 |
| Total Price of Credit | | 394,359 |
| **Credit Pricing (%)** | (394,359k/4,000,000) | **7.36%** |

As is evident from the above, the credit risk pricing is influenced by several factors. In a competitive market, the credit providers would attempt to compete on pricing as well. Competitive credit pricing can be offered by controlling overheads, number of transactions and profit margins and by the selection of lower risk credit assets. Although the cost of funds is usually determined by external factors, ability to identify cheaper sources of funds can also definitely lead to lower pricing.

(b) The credit pricing model needs improvement. It does not factor in the equity and its costs. Similarly, it is also ignoring other relevant factors such as sector risk, country risk, foreign currency risk, portfolio risks, etc. Another important method to improve the pricing, especially in the case of banks and financial institutions, is to introduce Return on Risk Assets (RORA) or Economic Profit (EP) based calculations. We will take up these topics in the next chapter.

**Working Notes**

**1. Calculation of Cost of Funds (Amt in 000s)**

| Details | Amount | Cost | % |
|---|---|---|---|
| Bonds | | | |
| - Local Currency | 36,650 | 1,490 | 4.07% |
| - Foreign Currency | 1,660 | 80 | 4.82% |
| Fund/Deposits from Financial Institutions | | | |
| - Local Currency | 37,400 | 2,050 | 5.48% |
| - Foreign Currency | 5,400 | 240 | 4.44% |
| **Aggregate** | **81,110** | **3,860** | **4.76%** |

| **2. Overhead Costs Related to Credit** | | **(Amt in 000s)** |
|---|---|---|
| i) Salaries in Credit Function | Period 201X | |
| Credit Manager | 300 | |
| Credit Analyst | 200 | |
| Credit Assistants (100*2) | 200 | |
| Total Salary | 700 | |
| ii) Overheads Apportioned | 300 | |
| **Total Costs (i+ii)** | **(a)** | **1,000** |
| No. of Credit Requests Handled | (b) | 20,000 |
| Hence Cost per Credit Request | a/b | 50 |

## QUESTIONS/EXERCISES

1. Explain the importance of credit risk pricing. What are the various factors influencing credit risk pricing?
2. Explain how the credit risk pricing factors in different underlying PDs.
3. ABCD Bank enjoys an interest margin (net spread) of 2%. It suffers a credit loss of $100m. Calculate the amount of additional credit assets to be created to recoup the loss.
4. The CFO of XYZ Ltd has taken a 5 year term loan of $300m at 8% per annum. After studying recent central bank policies and economic conditions, the CFO is of the opinion that interest rates should fall and accordingly the 8% interest rate will soon be higher than the going market rate. Having failed to renegotiate the rates with the current bank, the CFO has the choice to go another bank, which will be a time consuming process. Having heard about IRS, he is curious to know how it will help him. A financial institution has agreed to enter into an IRS for LIBOR+2%. Could you please share your views with the CFO? Explain the advantages and disadvantages of IRS.
5. What is PLR and how it is related to credit risk pricing?
6. Recently ABC Bank has approved a short-term loan at an interest rate of 10%. Calculate the implied PD if the one year treasury bill rate is 8%.
7. A bank entered into a one year interest rate swap for a notional amount of $400 million, paying a fixed rate of 7.5% per year and receiving LIBOR annually. At the end of the first year, the annual LIBOR rates were 7% per year. Calculate the net payment to be made or received by the bank.
8. Obtain the details of the credit risk pricing followed by banks and financial institutions in your area and compare them. Investigate and identify the reasons for the difference in interest rates charged by various banks and financial institutions. Do you believe that tight control on overheads will enable a bank or a financial institution to be price competitive?

# 21 Pricing Methods

What method should be adopted while pricing a credit? If the price is too high, good quality credit would be hard to come by. On the other hand, if the credit risk is underpriced, not only does the value addition suffer but it also means that the risk underwritten is not appropriately compensated for.

Pursuing risk-adjusted profitability is a tough job. Nowhere is this harder than in large corporate lending, where, by most accounts, adequate risk-adjusted returns are hard to achieve, given the competition in the market for creditworthy accounts. To control credit risk exposures while ensuring adequate return to shareholders who have risked their capital (in creating credit assets), institutions must accurately measure the value delivered by a loan, bond or any other credit contract. Credit providers who are deficient in this vital capability are essentially trying to run a business without knowing how to price credit commensurately with the underlying credit risk. Most institutions today use rudimentary credit risk pricing procedures. The consequence is that the credit providers originate or acquire many credit assets that they should not, while turning down those they should have accepted. The basic pricing model, described in the previous chapter, that stresses the recovery of costs and a reasonable profit for the shareholders, can be applied by different methods discussed below, starting with RORAC:

## 21.1 RORAC (RETURN ON RISK-ADJUSTED CAPITAL) BASED PRICING

RORAC, also known as RAROC (Risk-Adjusted Return On Capital) or ROCAR (Return On Capital At Risk) attempts to link the returns to the underlying risks involved. The basic principle of RORAC is that not all assets are equally risky. First the assets are converted on the basis of the risk involved, i.e. RWAs or risk assets. Then the Return On Risk Assets is calculated by using the following formula. RORA may be defined as being the percentage net return on risk assets deployed.

$$\text{RORA} = \text{Net profit before tax (or net return)/Risk assets}$$

The relevance of the RORA method lies in the fact that all banks and lending organizations attempt to maximize the return to the shareholders, but the risks taken should be reflected in the returns. This means that, as far as possible, a bank should go for acceptable levels of credit risks, which provide maximum return on capital. If the credit institution follows a predetermined leverage ratio, it can maximize the ROE by maximizing the Return On Risk-Adjusted Assets. This has two advantages: (a) the return is always commensurate with the riskiness and (b) the leverage can be maintained so that it does not spiral out of control. RORA refers to the return on weighted risk assets and not the return on gross assets. We have seen earlier that in banks and lending institutions, capital has an important role to play – a bank or FI is supposed to hold sufficient capital to withstand unexpected loss in order to ensure solvency.

RAROC calculates whether the RORA ensures sufficient return to the capital providers, i.e. shareholders. Let us exemplify the concept of RORAC:

We know ROC (or) ROE = ROA (Return on Assets) * leverage.

Substituting ROA with Return on Risk Assets (RORA), we can modify the formula as follows:

RAROC = RORA * leverage
= (Net Return/Risk Assets)* leverage

In this case, it is pertinent to note that higher leverage meant more profitability.

Since the credit risk of each asset is different and enjoys different credit grades, ROA is modified by weighting it with different risk weights depending upon the credit risk involved. As we have seen under the Basel Accords, the credit risks are variously weighted at 100%, 150% or 50% etc. based upon the credit rating.

RORAC (or RAROC or ROCAR) measures the net return differentiating the assets based on the risks involved. The most critical part is the accurate measurement of the risk involved in an asset. (We have discussed how banks differentiate the risks of various categories of assets in an earlier chapter dealing with the Basel Accords and Credit Risk.)

In the case of banks with capital adequacy of 8%, the RORAC = RORA*12.5. Assuming no change in leverage, what should be done to maximize ROE – viz. shareholder returns? Maximize the RORA.

**Example 21.1**

ABCD Bank has two assets (let us call them Credit Asset A and Credit Asset B) and a choice to deploy EUR1 million. Capital Adequacy is 8%. Net Final Return from both credit assets is estimated to be the same, i.e. EUR15K. However, risk weighting is different – Credit Asset B requires 50% weighting while that of Credit Asset A is 100%. (a) Compare the return of both credit assets. (b) If both are not equally attractive, suggest steps to improve the less profitable credit asset so that both are equally attractive.

**Solution**

Calculation of RORAC on Credit Assets A and B:

| Particulars | Credit Asset A | Credit Asset B |
|---|---|---|
| Loan Amount (d) | 1,000,000 | 1,000,000 |
| Risk Asset Weight | 100% | 50% |
| Risk Asset Amt (a) | 1,000,000 | 500,000 |
| Capital Employed (b) (8% of Risk Assets) | 80,000 | 40,000 |
| Net Final Return (c) | 15,000 | 15,000 |
| Return on Assets (ROA) (c/d) | 1.50% | 1.50% |
| Return On Risk Assets – RORA (c/a) | **1.50%** | **3%** |
| Leverage -1/8%* (e) | **12.5x** | **12.5x** |
| ROE/RAROC (c/b) *or* (RORA × e) | **18.75%** | **37.50%** |

*Reciprocal of capital adequacy ratio.

**Comments**

From the above, it is evident that from the net return point of view there is nothing to choose between Credit Assets A and B. However, when ROE is taken into consideration, Credit Asset B scores over the former credit asset. This is due to the better RORA of Credit Asset B. Moreover, the capital employed in the latter asset is lower because 50% is fully secured by time deposits (i.e. the lower the credit risk, the lower the capital required and vice versa). In this case, the preferred credit asset is the second one – viz. Credit Asset B. The ROE of Credit Asset A can be improved as follows:

(a) Increase the pricing in such a manner that the RORA of the Credit Asset A becomes 3%.
(b) From the credit risk pricing model discussed in the previous chapter, we know that better profitability can be achieved by controlling costs or increasing the risk premium or margin. Accordingly, the profit margin (net final return) can be improved by reducing the cost of raising funds/overheads.
(c) Another alternative is to reduce the risk weighting to 50% or below by asking for appropriate risk mitigants. One of the ways to achieve this is to obtain an AAA or AA rating from an external agency on Credit Asset A (see Basel Accord standardized approach).

## 21.2 MARKET DETERMINED

Basically the forces of demand and supply also exert an influence in the credit market. In this case, the credit institution is highly influenced by the pricing of competitors. Usually the suppliers of credit offer homogenous products and the competition exerts pressure on pricing, which is a common phenomenon in almost all countries which follow relatively free market policies. Most creditworthy customers usually invite price quotations from different credit providers before arriving at a final decision. The market should be respected in negotiating credit and loans in an increasingly competitive credit/loan market. Most participants in the large corporate market focus primarily on the credit spread and fees offered and less on subtle structural features.

However, blindly following the market carries the risk of inadequate pricing. Whilst the market is important, cost and credit risk are critical. If the competition offers interest rates not commensurate with the credit risk, it is better to refrain from the compulsion to follow the market and underprice the credit risk. The market cannot underprice the credit risk for long.

Another technique is to follow a 'broad band pricing' with competitors. In this case, the pricing need not be exactly the same as that of the competitors, but fixed taking into account the factors which we have discussed in the previous chapter. However, the price charged will not be completely out of context with the market and an inbuilt flexibility (pricing linked to LIBOR, etc.) will be provided so that the price does reflect the market by linking it to a market benchmark.

## 21.3 ECONOMIC PROFIT BASED PRICING

The basis of the concept of economic profit (and similar terms such as economic value added, etc.) is the result of the persistent search by the business community for a measure which reflects the excess return they get for the risks they have undertaken. It is commonly accepted that certain investments are relatively risk free while others are riskier. There is a great deal of difference in investment in the fixed deposits of a reputed bank and investing in a business.

Looking from an investor's point of view, the shareholders (investors) seek a better return for the risks they are taking and would attempt to measure it against some benchmark – say return on risk-free investments, commonly referred to as return on treasury bonds, government securities, etc. Another benchmark is the cost of capital, which is the minimum return expected by the shareholders. In simple terms

$$\text{Economic Profit} = \text{Normal Earnings Attributable to Shareholders} - \text{Cost of Capital}$$

Either one rate of cost of capital can be applied to all credit assets of the enterprise or the cost of capital can be differentiated across various sub-portfolios. For instance, establishing cost of capital by business lines to differentiate between different levels of industry risk is possible. In case of riskier sectors a higher cost of capital may be charged, while less risky sectors may be assigned a lower cost of capital according to the discretion of senior management of the business enterprise. In multinational businesses, the cost of capital can be differentiated across countries as well. For instance, higher cost of capital on credit assets in a country that enjoys lower international rating (say from Moody's, Standard & Poor's, etc.).

**Example 21.2**

Suppose ABCD Bank has a customer who enjoys a Short-Term Loan (STL) and a letter of credit (at sight) of $100m and $20m each. The net final return – after providing for cost of funds and all overheads – for the year is $1.5m. Risk weightage of LC at sight is 20% while that of the STL is 100%. Cost of equity capital (or required minimum return, to justify the capital) is 12.5%. (a) Calculate Economic Profit (EP) and (b) What if the net return happens to be just $0.9m?

**Solution**

(a) Calculation of Economic Return

| Particulars | Facilities (a) | Risk Weight-age (b) | Risk Assets (axb) |
|---|---|---|---|
| STL | 100m | 100% | 100m |
| LC | 20m | 20% | 4m |
| **Total** | **120m** | | **104m** |
| Net Final Return | | | 1.50m |
| Less: Cost of Capital (See working note below) | | | 1.04m |
| **EP** | | | **0.46m** |

**Interpretation**: The excess return (or value added) for the extra risk taken by the bank's shareholders is rewarded by the EP of $0.46m. The shareholders have been rewarded for taking the risk as they have been provided with an economic profit in excess of the cost of capital.

(b) If the net return is only $0.9m, the economic loss suffered by the shareholders is $0.14m. Steps should be initiated to improve credit returns. Whilst the easiest route is to increase the interest rates, a creative relationship manager would explore ways to improve ancillary and other income from the customer. If there is no possibility of enhancing the return, it may be better to exit the relationship and pursue a new one.

**Working Note**

Risk weighted assets 104m
Capital adequacy 8%
Therefore, capital required 8.32m (RWAx capital adequacy)
Cost of capital 12.5% or 1.04m (8.32*12.5%)

Some studies have shown that companies that earn EP can command a premium in the stock market, as evidently such companies ought to be highly profitable. From the operational side of any business, the concept of EP enables the decision takers to focus/concentrate on really profitable opportunities, which add value to the shareholders.

We may link economic profit pricing to economic capital discussed in Chapter 15. It is clear that in certain situations the economic capital requirement will be higher than the regulatory capital. It is suggested that in such cases economic capital may be used as the basis for arriving at economic profit. If economic capital is high, then the profitability (ROE) will be impacted. Hence in order to maintain the required rate of return, higher pricing will be required. In this way, the risks related to correlation, concentration and other factors may be adequately priced in through the adoption of economic capital and the economic profit pricing method.

## 21.4 COST PLUS

All businesses are influenced by costs and an enterprise extending credit is no exception. The credit production costs should be recovered so that the entity survives. The basic pricing model we discussed in the previous chapter is an example of taking into account all the costs and adding a mark-up for profit. The attractiveness of this kind of pricing is that it is fairly simple and straightforward. It ensures that the costs will be recovered from pricing, provided unduly large credit losses do not occur, which is a function of proper credit risk analysis. However, the drawback is that it does not take into account market needs.

This is evident in the pricing of private sector banks and public sector banks in India. The former usually have higher pricing because the cost of funds also tends to be on the higher side. Private sector banks usually have to offer higher rates to attract deposits. This naturally pushes up the cost base.

## 21.5 STRUCTURED PRICING

In this category, the same debtor will be charged differing pricing for credit. Each credit structure is priced differently. The two best instances are given below:

(a) In the case of a manufacturing entity, if the customer provides a guarantee or letter of credit, the pricing will be lower compared to the open credit terms. The reason is that in the case of the latter, the credit risk is higher, hence the higher pricing. For example (i) goods may be priced @ $120/- per piece on open credit for 90 days and (ii) if LC is provided the price may reduce to 117/- per piece for 90 days' credit. The lower pricing in the case of the latter is due to the significantly lower credit risk involved.

(b) A bank may extend clean credit facilities at a higher pricing to the same customer who enjoys lower credit pricing for a secured facility. It is not uncommon where borrowers enjoy lower pricing for secured credit (e.g. finance leases/term loans covered by primary assets and collaterals) while clean credit to the customer (unsecured short-term loans) attracts higher pricing.

## 21.6 GRID PRICING

Grid pricing refers to different pricing of the same facility depending upon certain credit risk parameters. The pricing is dissimilar for perceived difference in credit risk. Usually the grid is attached to compliance with certain conditions or covenants. It is clear from the following example.

**Example 21.3**

The pricing structure of a credit facility of $100 million is given below.

| | | Pricing (p.a) |
|---|---|---|
| If Net Borrowings/EBITDA | with GTEE | w/o GTEE |
| - Greater than 3.5x | PLR+300 bps | PLR+450 bps |
| - Greater than 3.0x but less than 3.5x | PLR+240 bps | PLR+350 bps |
| - Greater than 2.5x but less than 3.0x | PLR+180 bps | PLR+280 bps |
| - Greater than 2.0x but less than 2.5x | PLR+120 bps | PLR+215 bps |
| - Less than 2.0x | PLR+80 bps | PLR+150 bps |

Mr Y who is new to credit risk analysis seeks explanation of this structure.

**Answer**

In the above example, the lender links the credit pricing to the Net Borrowings/EBITDA ratio and encourages the customer to maintain the ratio at 2x or below. This will attract the lowest pricing because (while other factors remain satisfactory) credit risk is supposedly low. If there is a strong guarantee from the parent, then the risk is considered one notch lower and hence the pricing is improved further. As this ratio goes up, it implies increasing credit risk, which attracts higher pricing. However, under conditions of satisfactory guarantee cover, the pricing is again differentiated.

## 21.7 NET PRESENT VALUE (NPV) PRICING

Currently, the NPV approach to pricing a credit is rarely used, but several academics believe it makes sense theoretically. Under this approach, a credit contract is profitable as long as it provides a return in excess of the minimum required rate of return or market norms. The credit/loan inflows are discounted at a specified rate to arrive at an appropriate net present value, which forms the basis for arriving at a host of decisions. Some decisions taken under this category are given below:

(a) Pricing of credit. Choose a level of price that will result in a minimum specified NPV. If the NPV of the credit turns out to be negative, it is a rejection case unless the pricing is improved such that an acceptable NPV is reached.
(b) Choosing among various credit options. If many credit asset options are available, choose credit exposures that provide maximum NPV, since it maximizes shareholder return.

However, the use of the NPV technique to price the credit is scattered with certain stumbling blocks, such as (a) rating migration. As we have seen in the Credit Migration Matrix in Chapter 15, there is a probability that the ratings will undergo changes. This suggests that the grades connote different amounts of risk at different times. Different grading requires varying credit risk premiums and hence it is not easy to anticipate smooth cash flows. (b) An option to pre-pay the loan will reduce the time frame. (c) Performance based grid pricing or structured pricing make it difficult to predict the cash inflows. (e) Loan covenants also add to the uncertainty because, in the event of non-compliance, the lender or the creditor can demand repayment or charge higher pricing, depending upon the credit contract. (e) Other difficulties in effecting a sophisticated NPV approach pertain to the need for calibration on loss factors by collateral type, credit spread volatilities by rating, term and sector, etc.

## 21.8 RANPV (RISK-ADJUSTED NPV) PRICING

Some academics believe a breakthrough in NPV related pricing techniques – especially Risk-Adjusted NPV – is where the future lies and may ultimately replace RAROC, which is currently in vogue in many financial institutions. RANPV is nothing but the NPV, which is arrived at by recognizing the underlying credit risk. One method of arriving at RANPV is to adopt discounting rates that vary with the credit risk grades of the credit assets. Some of the advantages of RANPV over RAROC are that whilst the latter mainly looks at the one year perspective, RANPV will focus on a period exceeding a year. Additionally, RANPV looks at the market return while arriving at the present value of the future returns of a credit asset.

## ✍ QUESTIONS/EXERCISES

1. What are the different pricing methods available? Which is the most popular?
2. Explain the RORA method of credit risk pricing.
3. Explain the EP method of credit pricing and highlight how it differs from the RORA method. Which one is better?
4. ABCD Bank has two assets (Credit Asset A and Credit Asset B) of \$10m each. Capital adequacy is 8%. Net final return from both credit assets is estimated to be the same – \$150,000/-. However, risk weighting is different – Credit Asset B requires 50% weighting while that of Credit Asset A is 100%. Calculate economic profits for both assets if the cost of capital is 10%.
5. Explain cost plus pricing. What are its advantages and disadvantages?

6. Do you believe that market driven pricing can sometimes result in mispricing of risks? Please elaborate.
7. Explain the reasons why NPV pricing is not commonly used, despite its strong theoretical foundations.
8. What are the differences between structured pricing and grid pricing?

# Part VII

# The Last Line of Defence – Security

A good security is an ideal credit enhancement tool that shields against credit loss.

# 22
# Security Basics

1815 was a crucial year for Europe. It ended the first attempt to create a European Union (Empire) by Napoleon, who lost the Battle of Waterloo. Napoleon would have won, but for the last line of defence of General Wellington. The Allied Army (the English Army under General Wellington and the Prussian Army under General Blucher) planned to put up a combined front against Emperor Napoleon, who was desperately trying to defend his Empire. Napoleon stole a march on them, defeated Blucher's Prussian Army at Ligny and pursued Wellington's English Army. With no choice, Wellington withdrew his forces with an urgent request to General Blucher to reunite with any remaining forces. Finally Napoleon engaged Wellington at Waterloo. The English Army was on the brink of defeat, but the last line of the English defence held till the Prussian Army contingent arrived and the rest is history.

Likewise, in credit risk, if everything fails or is likely to fail, a creditor's last line of defence is the security, if available. In the previous sections, we discussed how to defend against credit loss by ensuring that the credit facility will be repaid from the internal cash generation of the business. Analysis of the external environment, industry, company and financials, as well as the study of systematic and unsystematic risks and techniques to mitigate both portfolio and obligor risks, were all intended to minimize credit risk and defend against possible credit losses. Still there are situations when creditors wish to have some kind of security as the last line of defence.

## 22.1 NEED FOR SECURITY

As we have seen in previous chapters, it is important that every good loan should stand on its own, i.e. repayment should be ensured from the activity for which the loan or credit is intended to be used. Even in consumption lending, the regular source of cash flows or income should be identified as far as possible. Hence, a good credit risk analysis calls for ensuring repayment capacity, without considering the security aspect. If credit is to be granted against security in the knowledge that the security might be relied upon later to recover the debt, it is better that credit should not be extended in the first place.

Strictly speaking, no security is needed in business lending if the repayments are possible from internal cash generation. However, cash generation is contingent upon several factors and impacted by both business risks and financial risks. Whilst favourable changes that positively impact internal cash generation will result in improved creditworthiness, adverse changes will dry up the cash inflows affecting the repayment capacity negatively. In such cases, creditors need some sort of security and better protection. Without the protection of security, the unsecured creditors would be just one notch above equity investors, which is unfair as equity investors have the right to partake in the upside potential of business, whereas the unsecured creditor cannot partake beyond the agreed amount.

A large number of bank loans are backed by security, especially since the 2008 Credit Crisis. In fact certain credit facilities imply underlying security such as mortgages, financial leases and vehicle loans. Similarly, most of the inter-bank OTC deals are carried out on a collateralized basis to mitigate credit risk. This is often done through the daily margining process, i.e. daily changes to the mark-to-market value of the derivatives are balanced via collateral accounts. Security backed credit (fully secured credit) is prevalent for the following reasons:

- It provides some sort of insurance against bad credit risk analysis, i.e. the risk of inadequate credit risk analysis can be covered by security.
- Security allows credit risk pricing to reach the required level. (See Section 22.4 for details.)
- Other things being equal, secured debt may attract lower interest rates than unsecured debt.

## 22.2 MERITS AND DEMERITS OF A SECURITY

As has been discussed, every credit extended to a customer involves a certain degree of risk due to unexpected events that might adversely affect his financial position. The following advantages can be derived from security in cases where the credit analysis provides a medium to high risk rating:

### 22.2.1 Advantages to the Creditor

- The major advantage is that strong collateral lowers default risk and reduces loss in the event of default. In case the primary source of repayment dries up, realization of security provides recovery of interest and principal, either in full or in part. Regardless of ranking, the lenders of a secured credit facility enjoy the benefit of the security until they are repaid in full.
- It ensures that the borrower will strive to ensure repayment so long as the borrower desires to take back the security. Studies have shown that the element of security alters the borrower's behaviour. It transforms borrowers' incentives, alters the risk for the lender and, accordingly, some sort of tangible or intangible security is strongly suggested when granting credit facilities. Studies conducted by Smith and Warner (1979) state that 'the issuance of secured debt lowers the total cost of borrowing by controlling the incentive for stockholders to take projects that reduce the value of the firm'. Similarly another study by Stulz and Johnson (1985) indicates that in some cases the recourse to secured debt may permit the lender to finance projects that otherwise would not be financed.
- Security ensures that the borrower has a stake or equity or risk capital in the transaction the lender is asked to finance. Accordingly, banks insist upon a cash deposit/margin covering a portion of the letter of credit facility it grants to a customer. The case of a mortgage of own property – e.g. an office building – as collateral is similar.
- Strong security is also cited as a powerful mitigation tool that solves the problems related to information asymmetries in credit markets to a great extent.

### 22.2.2 Disadvantages to the Creditor

- Too much focus on security will result in lost business. Many lending opportunities are good even without any security provided the cash flows are stable, adequate and strong. Asking for security in such cases will have the effect of driving away your business to competitors.
- Secondly, as discussed above, no security is foolproof. The value of security can fluctuate and may reduce in future, sometimes even falling below the credit extended. This was

experienced by US real estate lenders in 2008 who found that the value of the property they financed was just a fraction of the loan after the collapse of real estate prices in the US.

- Thirdly, some of the securities may require maintenance and insurance, which add to the costs of monitoring. In some cases, the responsibility to ensure that the assets offered as security are maintained properly rests with the creditor who relies on it for debt realization. The legal documentation should be perfect. Moreover, certain types of security carry environmental hazards. For example, lenders in some countries are reluctant to accept petrol stations as security as the secured lenders may also be held responsible if there is any environmental and related damage that can lead to legal claims on the lender.
- Availability of strong collateral has a moral hazard as it may affect lenders' incentives to conduct in-depth credit evaluation. Just having a security does not ensure repayment on time – the security has to be realized and it has operating risks associated with it. For example, a bank provided a 180 day Letter of Credit (LC) facility to a poorly rated corporate customer with very high PD against 100% cash deposit. However, due to the discrepancy in maintaining the lien on multiple deposits maintained by the customer, all cash deposits were released before LC fell due for payment. Due to insufficient funds the bank had to meet the LC on the due date from its own funds, without having any recourse to the customer. Such operating risks can nullify the advantage of having a strong security.

### 22.2.3 Advantages to the Borrower

- Whilst the borrower, being the person familiar with the business/transaction, is confident of successful utilization of the borrowed funds, the banker might not have been convinced about the intricacies. In such cases, a security can bridge the gap of understanding of the business. And with the passage of time the creditor will become convinced of the borrower's business skills and develop more understanding about the business, when the borrower can obtain release of the security originally provided for.
- Other things being equal, a lender is expected to offer more advantageous terms to the borrower – e.g. a reduced interest rate – on a secured credit than an unsecured credit facility.
- A source of additional funds. A business may not wish to sell the assets although it is in immediate need of funds. In such cases, offering the assets on hand as security will meet the objective. Borrowing from banks against land or building are examples.

### 22.2.4 Disadvantages to the Borrower

- A major disadvantage is that the creditor obtains an interest in the asset offered as security diluting the stake of the legal owner of the asset offered as security. Once offered as security, there is a risk of being taken over/liquidated by the creditor to settle the dues. Hence most borrowers attempt to obtain credit without security.
- Secondly, once offered as security, it is very difficult to get this released, unless the borrower can identify another lender who is willing to lend without collateral. Often, creditors are reluctant to part with the collateral and it usually requires considerable effort from the borrower to make a convincing case.
- The legal protection and priority accorded to a secured creditor may dissuade other lenders from offering unsecured credit as it means that unsecured creditors will now fare worse in case of bankruptcy of the borrower. Or they may demand terms that are less advantageous for the borrower – for example, high interest rates.

- Last but not least, it can affect the borrower emotionally. For example, if the borrower has collateralized his sole house against a business loan and the business fails, this could have severe consequences for his personal and family life. Such instances have led many people to commit suicide. Hence, lenders have a moral and social responsibility to educate the borrower as to what they may offer as security.

## 22.3 ATTRIBUTES OF A GOOD SECURITY

A good security is one which, in case of need, enables the creditor to recover either partly or in full the dues – both principal and interest. Accordingly, a good security should have certain features that would enable the creditor to realize it easily and recover the amount lent if the borrower defaults:

- **Valuation**: The value of the security should be readily ascertainable and reasonably stable over the years, providing a sufficient margin for depreciation. The safest security for a creditor would be a fixed deposit with a reputed banking institution because the value is not only certain but will increase by accruing interest. On the other hand, quoted equity shares are not equally protective because of the risk of wild swings in the market price of shares and hence sufficient margins are to be taken.
- **Realizability**: If the security is not realizable or realizable only with much cost and trouble, it does not serve the purpose of security – viz. it offers no protection. A good security should be readily realizable in all conditions and transferable without undue cost or trouble. As far as realizability is concerned quoted shares/mutual fund units are best as they can be sold within hours on the stock exchange. But the sale of a house or other building usually requires a longer period of negotiation.
- **Marketability**: Although securities may be realizable, they may not be marketed easily. For instance, suppose a certain piece of plant and machinery is offered as security. Although the asset may be realizable, there is no ready market available like that for a quoted share. The creditor may have to place advertisements and use other marketing techniques such as tenders, etc. to create demand. Wherever marketability is difficult, an appropriate margin of safety should be taken.
- **Margin**: As has been discussed above, a good security should provide a sufficient safety margin. This will ensure that even if the value of the underlying security undergoes adverse changes the net realizable value – viz. net of realization expenses – remains sufficient to cover the amount of money lent and any accrued charges for the time value.
- **Title**: Even if a security satisfies all of the above, if the title turns out to be bad, then the security is of no use. Hence, the creditor should ensure safe and unquestionable title without undue trouble or expense. Difficulties in ensuring a clear title differ from security to security. It is possible to establish the legal pledge of shares much more easily and cheaply than a legal mortgage of land and buildings.

## 22.4 SECURITY AND PRICING

There is a perception that if there is strong collateral, interest rates will be low, although this need not always be the case. Pricing is a function of risk and if the risk is low due to security, it may be reflected in the pricing as well. This is because of the fact that a good security can lower LGD. The security position along with other variables (such as underlying credit risk, country risk, sector risks, etc.) should be reflected in the pricing (see also Section 10.2.2).

From the point of view of the secured creditor, strong collateral/security lowers default risk and LGD. The security is most valuable with risky borrowers and if there is credit quality deterioration, additional security is usually insisted upon, while the credit risk pricing may remain high to reflect the high associated risk. It means that in the case of high risk borrowers, a lower credit pricing may considered only if the collateral security makes the LGD nil (i.e. LGD = zero).

For the release of existing security or dilution of the security positions, the lenders may ask for higher pricing. Similarly, higher pricing should be charged, wherever possible, by credit institutions to customers with incomplete security. This should incentivize the customer to comply with the security terms and conditions.

Security also allows credit risk pricing to reach the required level. Accordingly, the presence of security can improve RAROC.

**Example 22.1**

A lending institution has a RAROC hurdle rate of 30% on all lending deals. The amount lent to XYZ Ltd is $12.5m. The risk weight is 100% with capital adequacy of 8%. Accordingly, the capital required for the $12.5m loan is $1m; hence the target RAROC (as per the bank's credit policy) would be $0.3m or 30% ($1m × 30%). However, due to the pricing issues encountered in real life (discussed earlier in Chapter 19), the net margin earned on the loan is $0.25m. The customer is willing to offer deposits as cash margin/security up to 10% of the facility amount and this can be deployed at 2% net margin by the lending institution. Please explore whether this will result in meeting the RAROC hurdle. If not, please suggest alternative solutions.

**Answer**

In order to improve and attain the target RAROC, a 10% cash margin (interest free) may be insisted upon. The calculation is given below:

| Details (Amount in $, m) | Current Scenario | Security Adjusted |
|---|---|---|
| Loan (a) | 12.5 | 12.5 |
| Cash Deposit as Security (b) | 0 | 1.25 |
| Net Lending (c = a – b) | 12.5 | 11.25 |
| Capital Adequacy (d) | 8% | 8% |
| Capital Requirement (e = c × d) | 1 | 0.9 |
| Net Margin on Loan (f) | 0.25 | 0.25 |
| Additional Margin on Deposits* (g) | 0 | 0.03 |
| Total Net Margin (h = g + f) | 0.25 | 0.28 |
| **RAROC (h/e)** | **25%** | **31%** |

*1.25x 2%

With the cash security at 10% of the facility amount, the RAROC hurdle is met. This is because of the fact that the cash security results in a lower capital requirement, while there is additional income from the cash deposits because the lending institution can deploy it in business at 2% net margin (difference between cost of fixed deposits and interest rate at which it is lent). If the cash deposits are interest free, it could provide even more attractive RAROC.

It may be noted that all securities may not result in meeting the RAROC hurdle. Securities that can result in lowering capital adequacy requirements or that can be gainfully redeployed in business may have an influence on RAROC.

## 22.5 IMPACT OF SYSTEMATIC RISKS ON SECURITY

We have seen that the security is expected to reduce LGD as it facilitates recovery of the debt by way of realization of security. However business cycles and other systematic risks impact the security. Collateral values are particularly sensitive to economic downturns for three reasons:

1. Direct effect of systematic risk exposure.
2. Indirect effect if distressed obligors cut back on asset/collateral maintenance and control and
3. Indirect effect if distressed creditors dump assets/collateral in fire sale liquidations.

One of the main reasons that margins are insisted upon when taking security is to tide over this risk. Margin on security is also known as the LTV, i.e. Loan to Value ratio. The lenders will not lend the full value of the security in order to cover the risk of value of the security going down or the loan amount along with the accrued interest exceeding the security value. Accordingly, the lenders fix a margin or LTV. For example, if you want to borrow against a land and buildings valued at $10m and the lender is willing to extend only $5m as loan, then the margin or LTV is 50%.

Not all assets offered as security would be impacted to the same extent. While equity shares and real estate are most volatile, a cash deposit is the safest provided the credit and the deposit are denominated in the same currency.

When a volatile collateral asset is provided to secure the credit, its value may fluctuate in accordance with systematic risks. Accordingly, the recovery rate of the collateral assets may also drop in an economic downturn and accordingly the recovery will also suffer. As we have discussed in Chapter 17, due to this factor it is better if the credit portfolio does not have too much concentration of collateral assets, unless they are cash or cash equivalents.

## 22.6 FACILITY GRADES

Facility grades are directly linked to LGD. Depending upon LGD, various facility grades can be provided. A sample system is given in Table 22.1:

- If LGD is 0%, Grade 1 is assigned. This is the best case and usually this is supported by cash collateral. In this case the expected recovery in the event of default is 100%. However, in the case of an overdraft, the cash collateral must be at least 110% of the facility because an overdraft tends to be overdrawn in the event of default.
- As the LGD becomes higher, different facility grades are assigned.

**Table 22.1** Sample Facility Grading System

| Loss Given Default (LGD) | Facility Grade |
|---|---|
| 0% | 1 |
| 1–15% | 2 |
| 16–30% | 3 |
| 31–45% | 4 |
| 46–60% | 5 |
| 61–75% | 6 |
| 76–100% | 7 |

Facility rating is basically concerned with the assurance of the secondary source of repayment. (The primary source is often internal cash generation.) Some of the interesting factors related to recovery rates which influence facility grades are given below:

**Size of the firm/obligor**: Even in the absence of security, it is often found that when big institutions collapse, the recoverability of at least a portion of the moneys lent is possible. If TNW and turnover of the collapsed company are sizeable, then recovery rates are relatively better than for small firms. Once the biggest US energy trader, Enron Corporation, went bankrupt in 2001. By 2011, the unsecured creditors were able to recover about 53% of the dues. Empirical studies have shown that such recoveries improve during boom times.

**Low credit quality firms vs. high credit quality firms**: As we have observed in the transition matrix in Chapter 15, the probability of default by high quality firms is very low. In the case of top-rated credit assets, it is 'human nature' to take things lightly and often no additional security is available; consequently the failure of such borrowers can result in more loss to the creditor. In contrast, relatively high risk firms are thrown into default by only slight declines in asset values or performance. Accordingly, the creditor will be more conscious of problems with the high risk credit and hence take appropriate action, including adequate security, outside the business as a possible source of repayment in case of default. Accordingly, the recovery rates of low credit quality firms, in case of distress, tend to be higher than recovery rates in high credit quality firms. That is, low credit risk firms must experience abnormally large negative shocks to asset values to enter the default region and therefore the value of their collateral, if any, is quite impaired. However, the pertinent factor is that if the top rating is assigned after a thorough credit risk analysis and confirmed through periodic reviews, there is little chance of being taken by surprise – i.e. a highly rated credit exposure turning bad all of a sudden.

**Presence of strong collateral**: Availability of strong collateral always improves recovery and hence results in lower LGD. Weak collateral security does not help much in a distress situation. A well-collateralized facility offers comfort even if the borrower rating is unsatisfactory. It will ensure recovery in the event of default – e.g. a finance lease, where the title of the asset remains with the creditor till the last instalment is paid.

**Example 22.2**

ABC Finance Corporation has granted a loan of $10m to PQR Ltd secured by a portfolio of blue chip shares with a current market value of $18m. As per the policy of the bank, a 50% margin is required on collaterals of equity shares. Please provide an appropriate facility grade, assuming ABC Finance Corporation follows the FG table given above.

**Answer**

For LGD calculation, a security value of $9m (50% of $18m) is factored in. Accordingly, LGD would be 10% [($10m – $9m)/$10m]. Hence, as per the above table, Facility Grade 2 is to be assigned because LGD is 10%.

## ✍ QUESTIONS/EXERCISES

1. Is collateral required for all credit facilities? Please explain.
2. What are the qualities of a good security?
3. What are the advantages and disadvantages of having security, from the point of view of a lender?
4. Explain facility grading. How is it linked to LGD?
5. What are the advantages and disadvantages of extending security, from the point of view of a borrower?
6. A lending institution has a RAROC hurdle rate of 35% on all lending deals. The amount lent to ABC Ltd is $30m. The risk weight is 100% with capital adequacy of 10%. The net margin earned on the loan is $0.88m. The relationship manager is confident that he can seek cash deposits as cash margin/security, which the lending institution can deploy at 2.5% net margin. Please provide guidance to the relationship manager as to the extent of cash collateral to be sought from ABC Ltd.
7. One of your friends argues that if some collateral is offered to the bank, the interest rates will be always lower even for a very high risk borrower. Do you agree with this view? Please substantiate.
8. Conduct research into the recovery rate extended to the secured and unsecured creditors of Lehman Brothers, which collapsed in September 2008.

# 23
# Collaterals and Covenants

In the previous chapter, we have discussed how collaterals can help in improving LGD as well as RAROC. In this chapter, we will examine the various collateral securities available and the different ways of taking security and we will discuss the importance of financial and non-financial covenant.

A creditor can take the security in many forms, which can be broadly divided into two groups.

## 23.1 TANGIBLE SECURITY

Tangible securities are, as the name implies, tangible – physical, real and in some kind of material form. They are the material assets of the borrower held in the creditor's name or possession and in most cases they can be realized or sold at the creditor's discretion if the customer fails to settle the credit obtained. Some of the major tangible securities are as follows.

### 23.1.1 Deposits (with Banks, Financial Institutions, etc.)

Cash deposits are a very satisfactory form of security. Such deposits do not depreciate in value and in case of default the creditor can realize the security without much hassle, legal issues or expense. For example, the chairman of a company may place a cash deposit in an account in his own name to secure a credit extended to the company. If the cash deposits are with a third party, before disbursing the credit, a confirmation should be obtained that a lien over the deposit has been recorded and that the deposit funds will be freely transferred if required.

### 23.1.2 Stock and Shares

Shares quoted on a stock exchange can be sold easily and hence are favoured by banks as security and valuation can easily be obtained from the daily newspapers or from sharebrokers. Given the volatility of capital markets, a margin should be allowed to cover any future fall in their value. The LTV or margin will depend upon the share's market performance, the standing of the borrower, the amount of the advance and the nature of the shares, e.g. a greater margin may be required for building contractors' shares than blue chips. Partly paid and unquoted shares must not be accepted as security. For the greatest protection, the lender should transfer shares which are held as security for advances into the name of its nominee. By doing so the lender obtains a perfect title and can realize them in case of default by the borrower.

### 23.1.3 Property/Land

Land, buildings and other real estate properties are often used to secure credit facilities. Valuation by an approved valuer should be undertaken while a search should be made at the Land Registry to verify the borrower's title to the property and to check whether there are any encumbrances. A substantial LTV or margin should be provided for because in case of default and forced sale, the property may not recover full value from which legal and other selling expenses should be deducted. A legal mortgage is the best way of securing an advance because it provides the power of sale to the lender upon any default. An equitable mortgage is created by a simple deposit of the title deeds by the borrower together with a memorandum of deposit in which the borrower acknowledges that the title deeds are to be held by the lender as security for the debt and agrees to execute a legal mortgage over the property if called upon to do so. Sometimes, the creditor may also insist upon an irrevocable power of attorney so that the security can be realized without resorting to a full course of legal action.

### 23.1.4 Goods

Goods may be taken as security for advances. In most cases, the security is not taken by accepting physical delivery of the goods, but by taking possession of the documents of title to the goods. Documents of title include bills of lading, godown/warehouse warrant (e.g. LME – London Metal Exchange – Warrant), delivery order and any other document used in the ordinary course of business as proof of possession or control of goods. A proper hypothecation or pledge may also be taken over the goods as well.

### 23.1.5 Gold or Other Precious Metals

In most cases, the security is taken by accepting a pledge and physical delivery of the goods. Gold and precious metals are a very satisfactory form of security because in case of default the creditor can realize the security without much hassle, legal issues and expense. A suitable LTV or margin is required to cover any future fall in their value.

### 23.1.6 Bank Guarantees/Letters of Credit

A guarantee is a written undertaking whereby a guarantor undertakes to pay if the debtor/borrower defaults. There are three parties to a guarantee:

1. The creditor.
2. The debtor.
3. The guarantor.

The debtor has the primary obligation to pay the creditor. The guarantor only becomes liable to pay if the debtor defaults. Special care needs to be taken while extending credit against guarantees because the worth of a guarantee as a security depends on the financial stability of the guarantor. Hence an evaluation of the creditworthiness of the guarantor is also needed. Letters of Credit (LC) issued by banks are also akin to bank guarantees as the bank undertakes to pay the supplier of goods provided all LC terms are complied with. Therefore, only guarantees from first class banks are usually considered as tangibles. Other types of guarantees are to be treated as intangible.

## 23.2 INTANGIBLE SECURITY

The main feature of intangible securities, as the name implies, is that they are not physical assets but generally represent documented rights of action that are held by the creditor. These rights are either issued in favour of or assigned to the lender/creditor as security against the moneys lent. In case of default, the creditors can recover the outstanding amount by executing the rights under the document held. Major examples of intangible securities are:

### 23.2.1 Unregistered Charges

Usually, whenever assets are taken as security, the charge should be registered with the appropriate authority. For example, as we have seen above, the equitable mortgage and legal mortgage when properly registered are considered as tangible security. In almost all other cases, wherever the deposit of title deeds is not registered, it amounts to intangible security only. An unregistered charge provides some comfort but does not provide protection to the extent of registered charges.

### 23.2.2 Assignment of Debtors

An assignment is a transfer of a right on a claim (related to a sum receivable) to another person. The integrity and ability of the customer, and the third party, from whom the assigned payments are expected are critical. Hence the creditors should ensure the creditworthiness of the counterparty (third party) from whom the sums are receivable. A legal assignment should be obtained with a notice of the assignment to the debtor in writing. Registration (or notarization), if required by law, must be undertaken. The borrower should instruct the third party to pay the creditor all sums due under the assignment and it is better for the creditor to have irrevocable assignments.

### 23.2.3 Corporate Guarantee

Often the parent company or associate companies provide the guarantee to the creditor that in the event of default they would step in and settle the dues. If a group concern or holding company or another associate company offers support to the borrower, then the credit risk should be viewed as a combination of both the borrower and the supporting entity. This sometimes also results in a risk known as 'Structural subordination risk' that is associated with a group of companies.

For example the holding company may have several second-tier holding companies and third-tier operating subsidiaries. In such cases, it must be clearly understood who is providing the corporate guarantee and the lender must take appropriate covenant protection on the guarantor as well. If credit facilities are extended to a holding company, it is in the best interests of the lender to obtain guarantees from the key operating subsidiaries, who enjoy significant cash flows and own substantial assets. Appropriate covenant protection may also be sought to prevent asset stripping and to protect cash flows from such key operating subsidiaries.

Credit evaluation should be applied to gauge the creditworthiness of the supporting entity/parent/group. Assuming the EIIF study proves the sound financial strength and creditworthiness of the supporting entity/parent/group, the following tiers of group support can be envisaged:

1. **Strong**: The supporting entity/parent/group provides an unqualified and legally enforceable corporate guarantee to meet the obligations of the borrower. In such cases, the creditor may even substitute/swap the rating of the borrower with that of the supporting group. Technically, in such cases the lending to the borrower should be equivalent to lending to the supporting entity/parent/group. This is the reason why the credit rating of the borrower is substituted for that of the guarantor.
2. **Moderate Support**: Non-legally enforceable written agreements such as letters of comfort or letters of awareness, financial covenants, etc. fall in this category.

### 23.2.4 Letter of Comfort (LOC)

This is a letter from the parent company to the creditor advising that the facility is obtained with their knowledge and that the parent company will see that sufficient funds are available with the subsidiary to settle the claims by the creditor. Wordings may be different, but the spirit is the same. The parent company offers support falling short of a guarantee. The letters of comfort may be legally enforceable depending upon the legal system; however they are not equivalent to a guarantee. Letters of comfort are of two types – the weak letter of comfort and the strong letter of comfort. In the case of the latter, the support of the parent is more persuasive than in the former. A letter of comfort falls short of a guarantee and under an LOC the creditor cannot claim payments directly from the parent company.

### 23.2.5 Letter of Awareness

A letter of awareness is a letter from the parent company to the creditor advising that it is aware of the facility granted to its subsidiary and confirming that it will maintain the shareholding at the current level in the subsidiary and will advise if there are any changes. Also it will include wordings as mutually agreed upon which will cause the subsidiary to be operated and maintained in such a way as to be in a financial position to repay its obligations from time to time. This security is weaker than both the guarantee and letter of comfort. However, by mutual agreement the letter of awareness can be made legally enforceable. The comfort is that the parent company, which ought to be highly reputed, once it becomes aware of the credit facilities obtained by a subsidiary, will see that the subsidiary functions properly in such a manner that the dues are settled. Otherwise, the image or reputation of the parent company may be affected.

### 23.2.6 Letter of Negative Pledge

When debt is extended to a borrower, the lender will look into the current level of unencumbered assets in the possession of the borrower, which offer some comfort. Under a negative pledge, the borrower agrees that they will seek the prior written consent of the lender, before the borrower creates or attempts to create or permit to subsist any mortgage, debenture, charge, pledge, lien or other encumbrance upon the unencumbered assets of the borrower. A negative pledge clause prevents the borrower from issuing any secured debt in the future which would jeopardize their current priority claim on the borrower's assets.

## 23.3 METHODS OF TAKING SECURITY

The manner in which security is taken is important. Unless it is properly taken, legal enforceability may not be possible. The creditor should get a good title. The person offering security should have proper ownership and the methods of taking security are often characterized by whether the ownership or the possession of the particular security is transferred from the customer to the lender. In this context, ownership and possession should be clearly understood. The person who has possession may not have the title and vice versa – this situation is not uncommon.

Ownership means that the person who owns a property has a legal right over it, i.e. he/she has the right of possession, the right to sell and the right to appoint a receiver. The owner can part with possession without surrendering ownership, e.g. by renting a house. Possession means that someone, although not the actual owner, has physical control of a property. Since he is not the actual owner, he has no right to give, sell or charge the property to anyone else. Sometimes the creditor bank may opt for ownership of the security while on other occasions the creditor will be satisfied with possession with or without the option to convert it into ownership. The following are common ways of taking a security:

### 23.3.1 Mortgage

A mortgage is the creation of an interest in an immovable property as security for the payment of a debt or for the discharge of an obligation. The borrower is called the 'mortgagor' and the creditor the 'mortgagee'. Usually land, buildings and permanent and immovable assets are subject to a mortgage. Mortgages are of two types – legal or equitable mortgages.

- In a legal mortgage, the creditor acquires the ownership of the asset – be it property, shares or a life policy – and it is registered in his name. Possession of the goods may remain in the hands of the borrower (e.g. the mortgagor of property) or be held by the creditor (e.g. the mortgagee of shares).
- In an equitable mortgage, the relative title deeds and legal documents are deposited with the mortgagee but the ownership of the asset remains with the mortgagor. Thus although the creditor is in possession of title deeds, he does not acquire ownership of the asset.

The mortgagor is the person who mortgages or charges his property in favour of a party who has lent him money while the mortgagee is the person in whose favour a mortgage is given. Residential and commercial mortgages are very popular. As we have seen earlier, Mortgage Backed Securities (MBS) have risen to prominence and were extensively used in innovative financial products such as Collateralized Debt Obligations (CDO), mainly in the US.

### 23.3.2 Pledge

When a borrower makes delivery of goods or documents of title to goods to the creditor as security for a debt it is known as a pledge. The borrower is also known as the pledgor while the creditor is called the pledgee. The pledged item is to be returned to the pledgor when the credit is settled. Whilst possession of the goods or documents of title to goods passes to the creditor, ownership remains with the borrower. Usually, the pledgee has the right to sell the pledged item in the event of default on the due date after serving a written notice to the pledgor. Precious metals such as gold are usually pledged with the lender.

### 23.3.3 Hypothecation

The main feature of a hypothecation is that possession remains with the borrower while through an agreement the creditor gets a charge over goods, or over the documents of title to goods. In the absence of possession, the creditor can call upon the owner of the goods to hand over possession, which is often done in the event of credit default or non-compliance with credit terms. Usually stock, vehicles and buildings are hypothecated to the lender.

### 23.3.4 Lien

A lien is the right to retain property of another person until a debt due from the owner of the property (the borrower) to the possessor of the property (the creditor) is paid. The interesting part of the lien is that often there is no written agreement required to enforce it. A lien usually arises in the ordinary course of business without any express contract between creditor and debtor. But the creditor under lien usually does not have any power of sale. It is an informal form of security and usually gives the right only to retain possession. However, it can be agreed upon in writing in which case the creditor can get the right to sell. Often a banker's lien on deposits provides a right of appropriation to settle a credit facility with or without reasonable notice to the customer, depending upon the terms of agreement.

## 23.4 REALIZING SECURITY

Wherever security is taken, an express power of realization without reference to the borrower or the person who has deposited the security is usually documented in all agreements. Nonetheless, as far as possible, it is better (and ethical) to serve a formal written demand for repayment of the credit plus interest and other charges, and in the event of failure steps may be taken to realize the security. Normally, the demand notice is in writing and sent by registered post or other means where the acknowledgment by the debtor (or the one who provided the security) is ensured. If the borrower fails to comply with the demand for repayment one of the following actions may be taken as appropriate:

1. Sell the security.
2. Invoke the guarantee held.
3. In the case of hypothecation, initiate steps to acquire physical possession of any stock of goods and raw materials charged.

In the event of a floating charge (in debentures, etc.) a court-appointed receiver may be needed. The most important aspect of realizing securities is to ensure that the best possible price is obtained and not that merely sufficient to cover the debt. An independent valuation should be obtained before the sale. Auction is a better route to dispose of securities and, if planned, the reserve price should be set as high as possible to correspond with the current market value.

Once the goods/securities are sold, the proceeds of sale should be utilized to deduct the following:

- The outstanding credit along with interest accrued and other direct charges.
- All legal fees and liquidation/realization expenses.

The moneys, after meeting the above, belong to the debtor or the one who offered it as security and hence should be repaid at the earliest. On the other hand, even after applying the realization proceeds, if there is still an outstanding debt, appropriate legal action/arbitration may be undertaken.

## 23.5 COVENANTS – A TRIGGER TO SEEK ADDITIONAL SECURITY

Covenants aim to prevent excess liabilities and borrowings and ensure creditworthiness by insisting that the key ratios are kept within the acceptable range of a healthy business. Given their contribution to preventing credit losses, covenants can be considered as part of security. If not complied with, financial covenants also serve as a warning sign. They should trigger questions and investigations, highlighting what is wrong with the customer. If the breach is serious and impacts credit quality, additional security may be sought.

All covenants ought to have a purpose. Covenants should not be introduced just for the sake of it. Covenants ought to cover some risk. For example, a dividend restriction covenant is relevant if the company is liberal in dividends despite lacklustre performance and enhanced debt usage. Another example is the case where the enthusiastic entrepreneur undertakes constant expansion, even with short-term funds, causing a liquidity crisis. A covenant imposing maximum capital expenditure, which should not be exceeded without the prior permission of the bank/lender/creditor, will provide the latter with a prognosis, based on which appropriate decisions can be taken, including advice to the borrower on how to structure facilities for the new expansion, without impacting liquidity. An additional minimum current ratio covenant will also make the covenant structure strong.

The covenants can be classified as shown in Figure 23.1:

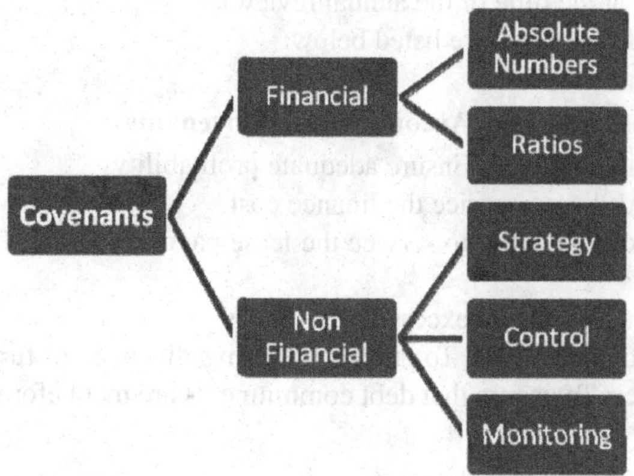


**Figure 23.1** Major Categories of Covenants

### 23.5.1 Financial Covenants

We have covered financial analysis in Chapter 8. Various financial numbers and ratios mentioned there are useful not only for analytical purposes, but also as powerful tools for controlling or monitoring credit risk. By agreeing with the customer the financial parameters which the customer agrees to maintain at specified levels, the parties concerned can take comfort with regard to the safe conduct of the business at best and, as a minimum, this can act as an early warning sign. The financial covenants prevent the parties concerned having an interest in the business of another, either as lender, banker, term lender, FI, debenture holder, etc., from helplessly standing by while the customer's business weakens. If the financial covenants are breached remedial actions can be initiated/demanded.

**Financial covenants based on absolute numbers**: This category of financial covenants specifies the actual amount to be maintained by the business, either as caps or floors. Caps refers to the maximum allowed amount, for instance, CAPEX. Usually CAPEX financial covenants stipulate the maximum amounts that can be spent by a company during a financial year. Accordingly, the covenant would appear as follows: 'CAPEX should not exceed $50m per annum without written permission ... '. Floor financial covenants refer to cases where minimum amounts are to be maintained. For instance, 'TNW not to fall to below $10 mn' is an example of a floor financial covenant.

**Ratio financial covenants**: In order to conduct effective monitoring the absolute figures often fall short of the goal. It often becomes necessary to look at the combined impact of a group of absolute numbers. For example, to control the short-term liquidity of a business, it is not sufficient to look at any current asset item in isolation, but if a covenant is based on current ratio or quick ratio it is more effective. Again, the ratio can be capped or fixed as a floor ratio. For instance whilst a minimum current ratio covenant of 2:1 is a floor ratio, D/E ratio not to exceed 2:1 is an example of a cap ratio financial covenant.

The main advantage of ratio financial covenants is that being a relative ratio, they would grow (i.e. provide flexibility) with the customer unlike absolute number financial covenants (based on a fixed amount), such as minimum TNW, which will need to be modified on a regular basis.

Once established, financial covenants should be reviewed from time to time and at least annually (preferably at the time of the annual review).

A few of the usual covenants are listed below:

### Cash Flow and Profit and Loss Account Based Covenants

1. Return on capital employed: Ensure adequate profitability.
2. Interest cover: Ability to service the finance cost.
3. Fixed charges cover: Ability to service the lease payments, finance costs and other fixed charges.
4. Dividend payout: To prevent excessive dividends.
5. Directors/intercompany dues: To prevent excessive diversion of funds.
6. Management fees: To ensure that debt commitments are met before management fees are paid.

### Balance Sheet

7. Net working capital: To ensure minimum long-term contribution from LT sources.
8. Current ratio: To ensure adequate liquidity.
9. Quick ratio: To ensure adequate liquidity, before factoring in the stock.
10. DSCR: To ensure repayment capacity of the instalment and debt.
11. Debt to equity: To prevent excessive total outside liabilities vs. net worth.
12. Gearing: To restrict interest bearing loans.

13. Minimum TNW: To ensure adequate capitalization.
14. Debt restriction: Not to raise debt without prior permission.
15. Capital commitment: Future expansion and related large capital commitments, only with prior notice.
16. External debt/EBITDA ratio: Ensures adequate EBITDA generation vis-à-vis the debt.

#### *23.5.1.1 When to Set Financial Covenants*

As far as timing of imposition of financial covenants is concerned, it should be done when times are good. Financial covenants are imposed to monitor and announce a major change in credit standing before disaster level is reached. So the sensible time to impose financial covenants is when the company is doing well so that the financial covenants can warn the lender and the company itself of a decline.

#### *23.5.1.2 How to Set Financial Covenants*

In deciding which ratio to set, the credit executive should consider each transaction as unique and decide what key issues he wishes to address. All covenants ought to have a purpose and ought to be linked to the key issues. Covenants should not be introduced just for the sake of it. Covenants ought to cover some risk. In the case of financial ratios, a working capital ratio, interest coverage ratio and a D/E ratio or TNW ratio are the most common, although what constitutes an acceptable D/E ratio will vary considerably depending on the industry/market norm. Once established, financial covenants should be reviewed from time to time and at least annually (preferably at the time of the annual review).

Financial covenants should be set based on year-end and projected data and strike a balance between allowing the customer sufficient room to operate and yet protecting the bank's interests.

#### *23.5.1.3 The Testing of Financial Covenants*

The difficulty in testing financial covenants is that the performance of a business is dynamic and may fluctuate significantly throughout the year. Whilst financial covenants are normally measured upon receipt of audited financial statements, it is prudent to test them as often as monthly or quarterly as and when financial statements are made available. Although an interim test may not be totally accurate, it does reveal a trend, especially when comparing prior years' performance and it then allows the lender to measure the customer's response to any adverse developments.

#### *23.5.1.4 When Financial Covenants are Breached*

Action should be taken if a covenant is breached. The breach must be investigated and should trigger a review of credit risk, if necessary through the reworking of all the EIIF factors and possibly higher pricing to reflect the higher risk and the breach. Steps to remedy the breach of covenants are to be initiated. Breaches of financial covenants should never be taken lightly. Firstly, the breach of the covenant should be considered as a symptom of an underlying problem and secondly, and more importantly, a breach constitutes 'an act of default'. How credit executives should react to a breach should be determined by a number of issues:

- Is the covenant critical?
- Is the covenant correctly set?
- Is the customer striving to correct the breach?
- Is the customer being uncooperative?
- Is the customer able to rectify the breach?
- Do we wish to continue with the relationship?
- Is the bank's position likely to be prejudiced by waiving compliance with the covenant?

In the case of a good customer, who is profitable to the lender, who is doing his best to comply with the covenant and likely to rectify the breach, the credit executive may perhaps continue to support the customer for a reasonable period. At the very least though, a breach should be treated as a time to review the grade of the account and pricing.

### 23.5.2 Non-Financial Covenants

We have discussed the importance of the management and strategy of the borrower in Chapter 7. Any riskier strategies and unfavourable changes in management are matters of concern for creditors. Hence, covenants related to these aspects are not uncommon in credit markets. A few examples are given below:

**Monitoring**

- Periodic inspection: Allows the creditor to inspect the assets/books and records of the debtor.
- Periodic valuation: Covenants to value stock, buildings, etc. by an independent valuer/auditor.
- Periodic management reports: Provide quarterly/semi-annual etc. accounts, status reports, ageing.

**Asset Preservation**

- Insurance: Agrees to insure the assets.
- Depreciation rates: Agrees to depreciate the assets to the satisfaction of the creditor.
- Sale of assets: Agrees not to sell assets without the prior knowledge/permission of the creditor.
- Negative pledge: Agrees not to provide any of the unencumbered assets to other creditors as security.

**Strategy**

- Ownership/management: Agrees not to alter ownership/management without the permission of the creditor.
- Acquisition/divestments: Agrees to seek permission before venturing into new acquisitions or divesting.
- Rights/new share issue: Agrees to obtain permissions, etc. from the creditor.

The list of covenants (both financial and non-financial) given above is not exclusive and should be treated as guidance. Covenants reflect the parameters within which the customer agrees to operate and based on which the creditor effectively agrees to continue its support.

Accordingly, if covenants are not complied with technically the creditor could withdraw/exit from the credit. In the case of financial covenants, it will often not be a specific breach of the covenant that initiates action, but rather the trend with regard to covenant achievement over time. For instance, a deteriorating D/E ratio, which has yet to constitute a covenant breach, should prompt the lender to initiate discussions with the customer about the worsening trend.

It should also supply an answer to the question of whether compliance can be ensured, going forward. The ideal time to introduce covenants is when there are declining trends or deterioration in the key financial ratios or figures.

It is important for all parties involved in covenants to have a clear understanding of what they mean. The requirement is especially important because various ratios and financial numbers often have different meanings, especially across countries and customs. For instance, whilst usually the audited balance sheet shows the advances to directors separately, a lender (bank) may prefer to calculate tangible net worth after deducting advances to directors. The same principle applies to the treatment of goodwill and other intangible assets.

#### *23.5.2.1 Breach of Non-Financial Covenants*

Action should be taken if a covenant is breached. The breach must be investigated and should trigger a review of the credit risk, if necessary. Higher pricing may be negotiated to reflect the higher risk and the breach. Steps to remedy the breach of covenants are to be initiated. Firstly, the breach of the covenant should be considered as a symptom of an underlying problem and secondly, and more importantly, a breach constitutes an 'act of default'. As in the case of breach of financial covenants, additional collateral may be sought, as appropriate, especially if the breach is an indication of deterioration in credit quality, which must also trigger a re-rating exercise through EIIF study.

## QUESTIONS/EXERCISES

1. What are the usual types of collateral securities?
2. Explain different methods of taking securities.
3. What is structural subordination risk?
4. Is credit evaluation of a corporate guarantor required? Please elaborate.
5. What is the importance of covenants? Explain different forms of covenants and their limitations.
6. How are financial covenants fixed?
7. What are the remedial steps if the covenants are breached?
8. One of your friends argues that collaterals are meaningless. He points out that during the housing sector boom in the US in 2004–06, several credit products (MBS, CDO, etc.) were innovated with the backing of collateral such as real estate. However, during the 2008 Credit Crisis the collaterals did not offer much comfort and many banks and financial institutions suffered losses on such products. Do you agree? Please elaborate.

# Part VIII
# Credit Crisis

Often a credit crisis is termed as a 'black swan' event, which need not be true.

# 24
# Road to Credit Crisis

As we have seen in the Chapter 1, credit is akin to fire and if it gets out of control can be devastating and create catastrophic damage to the finances of individuals, organizations and governments. However, used reasonably, it is a great tool offering immense advantages and brings prosperity to all economic agents in an economy.

## 24.1 CREDIT AND GROWTH

Prosperity comes through increased production and exchange of goods and services and value addition. For instance, the backward economies of the Middle East experienced prosperity during the second half of the 20th century as they exchanged their newly found oil and gas with the rest of the world for goods and services. Similarly, China began its fascinating economic growth journey in the 1980s as the economy was freed from the tight control of government, who then encouraged private enterprises and risk taking. India started its accelerated growth path in 1991 when it abandoned its 'licence raj' and opened up its economy, allowing freer production and exchange of more goods and services among the various economic participants in the economy.

A high level of economic activity is often accompanied by a rise in domestic lending activity. Accordingly, the total loans extended to several sectors of the economy would record faster growth. The growth in loans would be supported by the banking sector's high liquidity levels – it allows banks high financial flexibility. The Loans-to-GDP ratio and Loans-to-Deposits ratio are often used as indicators to gauge the extent of growth in loans/credit in the economy.

Strong credit flows in the economy act as a strong catalyst for growth. It is to be noted that credit is not a substitute for the creation of goods and services. The growth in credit in the economy can create prosperity. History reveals two types of credit-led prosperity:

- **Credit expansion supported by strong fundamentals**: Whilst real economic growth comes from the addition of goods and services into the economy, credit acts as a strong catalyst. Used wisely, credit gives the power to experience prosperity by providing purchasing power immediately. However, the basic premise is that the borrower has the ability to bring in value addition (say to create equivalent goods and services), which will enable the borrower to meet obligations under the credit facility. When 30 year mortgage loans are extended to creditworthy salaried persons or business people to buy residential properties, the borrower is expected to use his skills to create value, which he can exchange for money, a part of which will be used towards the repayment of the loan. If these mortgage loans are securitized, based on which CDOs are issued, such credit assets ought to be strong as they are backed by strong fundamentals.
- **Credit expansion supported by poor fundamentals**: If the credit flows within the economy rise quickly but add little value or result in lopsided incentives, this can lead to credit bubbles. For example, sub-prime loans in the US relied on the increasing real estate values for repayment rather than the creditworthiness of the borrowers. Such credit expansion was not sustainable.

Secondly, unbridled credit flow into over-capacity build-up is also dangerous and will also result in credit bubbles. Prior to the 2008 Credit Crisis, the credit flow into the real estate of the US, Spain and several other countries resulted in over-capacities. The case of Japan in the late 1980s was similar – Japanese multinationals borrowed to create additional capacity, for which there was no demand, and this impacted repayments. Likewise, the 1997 Far East economic crisis has been blamed on lopsided short-term foreign currency credit expansion. It may also be noted that lopsided credit flows into a few entities in the economy can also spell macroeconomic trouble (see the Case Study later in this chapter). Credit bubbles result in over-leverage, which in turn leads to imbalances in the finances of individuals, business organizations and nations. Often credit expansion results in asset price inflation and a rather painful de-leverage process once the unsustainable credit bubbles burst.

Central banks have the weapons to control credit flow and credit expansion in the economy. Strong central bank governance can ensure that credit growth is supported by fundamentals. It is often highlighted how the Indian Central Bank controlled the credit flow into the real estate sector during the mid-2000s, which enabled the Indian economy to be less impacted by the 2008 crisis. On the other hand, central banks in other countries, where the 2008 Credit Crisis had a severe impact, were accused of lacking oversight of the credit flow resulting in lopsided credit expansion.

## 24.2 ROLE OF BANKS

Banks are important for the smooth functioning and growth of any economy. Banks and financial intermediaries fulfil a vital economic function, as we have discussed in Chapter 1. They amass the surplus economic resources from the public – mainly in the form of deposits – and engage in intelligent lending to creditworthy borrowers. Financial intermediaries intermediate between savers and investors and set economic prices of capital, in line with the monetary policy of the nation. From a macroeconomic perspective, the main function of the financial system in any country is to mobilize resource requirements for economic growth and this function is mainly carried out by banks and financial intermediaries. During boom times, lending to the private sector would show faster growth demonstrating active credit creation in the economy.

Banks and financial intermediaries are in the business of taking various risks and conducting detailed study of the risks they undertake to ensure that these are adequately mitigated. As we have seen in earlier chapters, this is done through probability study, analysis of historical (including statistical/financial/industrial) information, logical reasoning and sound judgement. Banks and financial intermediaries are supposed to be good at this. Otherwise, they go out of business and become a social burden because the deposits (i.e. savings) of the general public are entrusted to them. Often in such cases, responsible governments will intervene and try to protect the interests of depositors, which is yet another social burden as tax payers indirectly foot the bill.

### 24.2.1 Credit Creation

As we have discussed in Chapter 1, banks have the power of 'credit creation',[1] which adds to the money supply. How do banks create credit? It is driven by deposits. The public place deposits in banks and FIs based on the confidence they have in the banks and in the financial system. If deposits are withdrawn substantially from the banks, there could be trouble.

[1] Please see the Appendix of Chapter 1 for details.

The majority (reportedly more than 65%) of the money supply in an economy is created by commercial banks through credit creation. The collective decisions of banks determine how much credit money is created, who gets the newly created credit money and how it is deployed and this plays a major role in the health of the financial system of a country, underscoring the importance of banks and their responsible behaviour.

Hence, careful bank lending is of the utmost importance in economy as the lending practices of banks account for a significant part of the economy. Each layer of credit creation results in layered leverage in the economy. If the credit is used for speculative or high risk activities in the economy it could take the shape of a Ponzi scheme or bubble, which is unsustainable and would collapse, resulting in economic hardship. Thus, it is vital to understand the ultimate use or purpose for which credit creation is used.

### 24.2.2 Confidence in Banking

The banking and financial system survives on confidence. Any incident in relation to the solvency of a financial intermediary unsettles the financial markets. Let us examine the intricacies of the banking system:

- The banks depend heavily on deposits, which are mostly short term. This results in the tenor mismatches inherent in banking. The tenor of the borrowing varies from a few days (overdrafts[2]) to 15–20 years (e.g. mortgages or project finance). Similarly, the deposit tenor varies, but is mostly short to medium term (i.e. usually up to 5 years). Overall, the tenor of deposits is shorter than that of the loans. Hence, managing the tenor mismatches is a critical function.
- Banks and FIs have to manage their balance sheets so that they can lend for long periods without compromising their ability to meet potential depositors' demands for cash. How do banks and FI do this? They rely on money and capital markets to borrow and lend. This ensures that there is sufficient liquidity and banks and FIs have access to sufficient funds to meet the cash needs of depositors. So the reliance on inter-bank borrowings and refinancing is also significant in the financial system.
- In order to ensure smooth short-term inter-bank liquidity transfers, confidence in the solvency of counterparties is essential. If there is a collapse of confidence – triggered by worries about the financial health of banks or financial institutions – this causes the money and capital markets to stop working properly. It dries up risk appetite and the banks, financial intermediaries and other investors become reluctant to lend to each other. As liquidity dries up the cost in refinancing increases. As a consequence of low liquidity in the inter-bank market and higher costs, the banking sector cuts down its lending activity and whatever lending takes place will be at a higher cost.
- Usually, under these circumstances, it is not uncommon for the banks to witness a surge in depositors (worried about the bank's health) demanding their cash. This will cut down lending further in the economy as banks stash away cash to meet the potential increased withdrawals by the depositors. A sharp reduction in lending activity will cause problems for the smooth functioning of the economy. This, in turn, lowers investment and spending by businesses and households and consequently results in a weaker economy. This could potentially turn into a vicious circle because the weaker economy will further reduce confidence in the banking and financial sectors.

[2] Bankers know that, once sanctioned, most of the overdraft becomes a permanent feature.

Banks and FIs earn interest on the lending, which in turn is passed on to the depositors, after meeting expenses and taking the profit margins for the risk banks and FI undertake.While banks and FIs share the interest income on loans with the depositors, they do not pass on the risk of bad and doubtful debts. Hence, the management of credit risk is critical in the banking and financial sector of any economy.

As a corollary, the government and central bank have the moral responsibility to ensure that the financial system is functioning smoothly. If they fail to monitor activities and leave it to 'market forces' alone, the consequences can be serious as the market is profit driven and will underwrite risks disproportionate to the return. There are arguments and counterarguments about the role the US government and the Fed played in the 2008 Credit Crisis. Whilst the US government encouraged real estate construction in order to ensure accommodation for all, the Fed followed a cheap monetary policy and did not adequately cap the credit flows into the real estate sector. Market forces led to innovative financial instruments such as CDOs, which created a win-win situation for all. When the cheap money ended, the health of financial intermediaries came into doubt, resulting in a crisis of confidence. The US Central Bank and government helped a few institutions; however they refused to do so with Lehman Brothers, and the rest is history.

It may be noted that there is merit in the argument that the government cannot bail out all failing institutions. Whilst we do not want to get into a discussion on the merits and demerits of policies and decisions, it is worthwhile highlighting that proper micro and macro credit risk management is important and highly relevant from the macroeconomic perspective and could avoid situations similar to the 2008 Credit Crisis.

### 24.2.3 Ultimate Use of Credit

Excessive use of credit can be dangerous. Broadly, the end utilization of the credit can be classified as follows:

1. **Consumption purposes**: Loans or credit facilities taken for all types of spending (e.g. travel, holidays, weddings, etc.) can be classified in this category. The borrower expects to meet the loan obligations from the sources of income other than the purpose for which the loan is utilized.
2. **Short-term business purposes**: These loans are obtained by businesses to meet short-term cash flow mismatches. This type of loan or credit facility is the most common and commercial banks are specialists in this type of activity. Businesses borrow short term to meet working capital requirements and the source of repayment is the working capital inflows. (Individuals also sometimes borrow short term to meet their cash flow mismatches.)
3. **Long-term business purposes**: Medium-term (1–5 years) and long-term (5 years+) loans are usually taken for investment purposes, say to expand or to commence a new line of business or to acquire real estate properties or financial investments. The repayment is derived from the project or investment for which the loan is used. (Individuals borrow long term mainly to create long-term assets such as residential houses, purchase of land or property and similar investment purposes.)
4. **Speculative purposes**: Speculation is the activity which aims to make quick profits from anticipated price movement in various asset classes including stocks, commodities and real estate. During times of stock market boom, often credit facilities are diverted towards the stock market for quick short-term profits. Speculation is highly risky; mixing credit

with speculation is extremely dangerous and credit executives should be vigilant about such situations. Sound analytical skills are required as the speculators usually approach the banks disguising their real (i.e. speculative) purpose, and hence it is critical for banks to understand the customer, and the purpose of the credit facilities, clearly.

## 24.3 FORMATION OF CREDIT BUBBLES

This is the most difficult part as credit expansion is normal in a growing economy where more goods and services are produced and exchanged among various economic agents. During the course of the fundamentally supported credit expansion, the underlying activity sometimes becomes detached from the basics and acquires speculative features. This transformation often goes unnoticed by most of the economic agents, who would logically justify further expansion. Given the optimism reflected in the overall economy, the lending standards also become relaxed, especially if the central bank (or regulators) misjudges the situation or leaves it to market forces, without sufficient supervision.

One of the best examples is Japan in the 1980s. Japan, after enviable economic growth in the 1970s and 1980s, witnessed a fast rise in real estate, the stock market and all asset classes fuelled by cheap credit. Usually all are confident during the heightened pace of economic activity and financial institutions are no exception. They lent to over-confident borrowers to expand or import or produce more goods and services for which there was little demand. This turned out to create over-capacities funded by borrowings. The resultant bad debts weighed heavily resulting in the collapse of financial intermediaries in Japan.

Another example is the US property boom in the early 2000s, fuelled by debt. The easy credit facilitated an unprecedented growth in sub-prime assets, which were packaged into complex securities and sold to various investors. Massive growth in sub-prime assets (i.e. high risk assets) funded by debt acquired bubble or speculative features towards 2006–07. With the increase in interest rates, the delinquency of sub-prime loans increased resulting in enormous foreclosures and the consequent collapse of US property market, contributing to massive losses of investors in such high risk assets, which included world renowned banks and financial institutions in the US and abroad.

During this period, many homeowners, who found their home values skyrocketing in boom times, approached banks for 'equity release'. This represented an additional mortgage on houses and the proceeds were often used for consumption or for additional investing in property, which further fuelled the property bubble. No wonder US banks were stated to be guilty of lax credit standards.

Often the speculative element will be hidden in the purpose of the borrowing and it requires experience and knowledge to understand the real (i.e. speculative) purpose[3] vs. the stated purpose of the borrowings. Herein lies the importance of market knowledge, proper understanding of the customer and the purpose of credit facilities.

[3] For example, residential/commercial mortgage loans are considered long-term credit facilities to acquire assets. However they have often been used for property speculation or 'property flipping'. In such cases people buy apartments, villas or commercial properties off plan or at the time of launch and pay 5–10% to the developer from own funds and the balance is tied with a mortgage loan. After paying couple of instalments, they will sell the property for short-term gain and close the mortgage loan. The second buyers also approach the same bank or another bank and remortgage the property and flip again. By the time the property reaches the hands of the ultimate investor/buyers, it will have flipped through several hands and the purchase cost of the property will have multiplied several times. If this property is taken as security or collateral by the bank, the risk of over-valuation is evident. The credit funded flipping of property was a common feature in some Middle East property markets, which underwent severe correction as the debt fuelled property expansion (bubble) halted soon after the 2008 global financial crisis.

## 24.4 TYPES OF CREDIT BUBBLE

Disproportionate credit creation results in more credit/money supply chasing a limited amount of assets, goods and services, resulting mainly in price inflation and asset value inflation. The impact of reckless credit creation is far reaching – it results in credit bubbles. We can link it to the end use of credit and accordingly credit bubbles manifest in different ways such as:

1. **Excessive consumption** – easy availability of credit fuels consumption, however the individuals in the economy get into a debt trap. A good indicator is the debt/income ratio. Higher ratios evidence over-leverage and are therefore unsustainable. In such cases, loss of income, either because of unemployment or for any other reason, would impact the debt servicing capacity of the borrower. US household debt as a percentage of income stood at an alarmingly high ratio of 130%, just before the 2008 Credit Crisis.
2. **Real estate and property speculation** – cheap credit propels speculative deals in real estate causing asset price inflation. Many households, corporate and even semi-government agencies invest in property markets, due to the availability of easy credit driving up prices. Demand for properties drives a construction sector boom, unleashing demand in several other industries such as cement, steel, construction, chemicals, paints and a host of other business segments. A unit increase in construction expenditure has a multiplier effect and capacity to generate income multiple times (estimated to be as high as five times). Whilst this translates into strong economic growth, once the credit flow is interrupted, demand vanishes, the backlog of unsold properties accumulates and construction activity drops sharply.
3. **Financial speculation** – credit creation can cause excessive financial speculative deals, just as cheap credit does in relation to real estate prices. The stock and bond market boom. Equity prices and equity issues increase sharply. Again, whilst these are normal for a growing economy, if it attains unsustainable levels, it means that the prices have reached bubble territory. There are a few indicators, such as the price earnings ratio, to ascertain whether the boom in financial assets has become a bubble.
4. **Overzealous expansion** – during benign times, the optimism of various economic agents who have been successful due to the booming market conditions reaches levels of 'irrational exuberance' and people embark on unsustainable projects and developments. For example, a cement manufacturing company trebles its capacity at the peak of the construction boom. As the boom subsides and normality returns the company will face the perennial problem of excess capacity. Usually such expansion and projects would be supported by lenders and banks, which then find the project unviable with frequent delay in debt servicing, restructuring and ultimately credit losses.
5. **Inflationary pressures** – can also be the result of excess credit flows. As the purchasing power increases with easy availability of credit, the inflationary pressures in the economy are unleashed.

The above are just a few instances and not exclusive, i.e. the list is expandable. The impact of unbridled credit creation is that, in the initial stages all economic participants benefit, however soon creates economic imbalances in myriad ways in addition to the situations explained above. If these imbalances are sufficiently large, banking and economic crises follow as the worries about the quality of credit assets held by banks and financial institutions raise questions as to their solvency.

## 24.5 CREDIT BUBBLE EXPLOSION

The unbridled credit expansion or credit creation cannot continue *ad infinitum.* Ultimately the credit flow slackens and the over-leveraged economic players find themselves in trouble as they attempt to reduce leverage. Moreover, the lenders also find that a significant portion of the credit assets are not worth the book value or are not recoverable, forcing many into bankruptcy. A spate of bankruptcies (of both lenders and borrowers) is the end result of unbridled credit expansion.

Wise central banks act before such economic imbalances attain serious proportions. Nonetheless, sometimes central banks also misread the symptoms and act late, by which time the imbalances have reached serious proportions. They attempt to put brakes on credit expansion through policy measures such as a hike in interest rates or open market operations.

With the days of easy credit over, the over-leveraged economic agents are forced to unwind the leverage. The task of de-leverage is not an easy one – especially for economic agents involved in financial and real estate activities. As the over-leveraged entities attempt to unwind and offload various asset classes, a sharp drop in asset values follows. This is exacerbated as other market participants also join in the selling spree before the market values of various asset classes drop further. Another reason for the drop in market prices is that at this stage, there will be very few buyers, as business confidence reaches a low ebb.

The boom conditions and the confidence of the economic agents wane. Banks and lenders become concerned about their credit portfolio and the decision takers in the banks begin to seriously worry about the looming doubtful debts and decline in the repayment capacity of counterparties. The decline in the values of collateral is yet another concern. As the banking sector becomes risk averse, it not only refuse to lend further, but will attempt to recall and cancel existing credit lines, exacerbating the issues.

Capacity expansions and developments would have been undertaken by various economic agents during the benign times, expecting a steady stream of increasing demand. However, they soon realize that they will face the problems of over-capacity and under-utilization. The strategies and growth plans drawn up during the good times will no longer be valid. Usually these expansions would be partly funded by the easily available credit. In such cases, credit losses become unavoidable for banks and financial intermediaries.

Overall, the major consequences of bursting of credit bubble are:

1. **Post bubble it is hard for asset prices to recover to the historic highs of the bubble**: The stock market index (Nikkei) that touched 38,957 in December 1989 has not reached that level even after 22 years. Similarly, it took decades for the Dow Jones Index to reach its 1929 peak in the US. After burning their fingers in the crash, many investors will be cautious about the same asset class and may even warn their children.
2. **Weakened banking sector**: Banks are shaken up since many of them become financially weak as they are saddled with a large percentage of 'non-performing' credit assets (i.e. loans that had to be written off). This leads to closure of several banks or merger with stronger ones.
3. **Risk averse behaviour**: Generally, banks become risk averse with reduced credit risk appetite, curtailing lending in the economy. The net worth is eroded due to a fall in asset values mainly because of the stock market/real estate crash The resultant drop in credit growth will impact economic growth.

4. **De-leveraging**: Many over-leveraged investors and the public curtail consumption and spending, as they try de-leveraging. It is pertinent to note that in most economies private consumption is the largest component of GDP. Lower consumer spending translates into lower demand for goods and services. This in turn will result in a drop in business activities leading to more shutdowns and more unemployment. For example unemployment after the 1929 US economic crash reached 25% in the early 1930s.
5. **Deflation**: A drop in demand can lead to deflation, causing a drop in prices, translating into losses for businesses. This will lead to further shutdowns and more unemployment and less economic confidence. This can become a vicious circle.
6. **Low level of business confidence**: Businessmen, who experienced the trauma of economic collapse and witnessed the drying up of demand and non-payment by debtors, are hesitant about taking risky decisions. They are reluctant to borrow and expand, questioning whether the hard pressed consumers will buy more. Again lower economic activity with predictable consequences.
7. **Fear of another banking collapse**: People become fearful of the banks' collapse as in the case of the Japanese public. They bought gold or invested in United States/Japanese treasury securities instead of bank deposits, reducing the funds available to banks.
8. **Slower credit growth**: Credit growth slows, impacting economic growth as banks become reluctant to lend, while economic participants are disinclined to borrow sincce many of them will be busy de-leveraging.

As the result of interaction between the various consequences discussed above, economic recession may set in.

The list mentioned above is just for guidance. The Japanese banking crisis of the 1990s, the savings and loans crisis during the late 1980s and the Far East Asian Crisis in 1997–98 are some of the recent economic crises where credit expansion had a significant role. The US Great Depression that started in 1929 also bore the hallmark of over-leverage. We will discuss the credit expansion that caused the 2008 Credit Crisis shortly.

One of the best ways to avoid a credit bubble is to have prudent and intelligent credit risk management by all economic agents, especially banks and financial intermediaries. Also a strong central bank is required with powerful tools of oversight authority to avoid credit bubbles.

## CASE STUDY

Long Term Capital Management (LTCM) was a financial intermediary, engaged in intelligent financial speculation (although the term speculation may be disputed). The credit flow into financial speculation activities through LTCM was lopsided, which brought the US economy and other economies to the brink of an economic collapse.

### Launch of Financial Titanic

LTCM was a financial intermediary (hedge fund) promoted in 1994 by John Meriwether, ex-Vice Chairman of Solomon Brothers and an expert in fixed income arbitrage. Co-promoters included financial wizards Myron Scholes and Robert Merton, who won the Nobel Prize in 1997. Both of them played important roles in the development of the 'Black–Scholes–Merton' model of option pricing. LTCM's main strategy was to arbitrage the price/yield differences of debt of near identical maturities while they also took exposures in equities and derivatives. They relied on high leverage and they were confident of managing the risks through complex mathematical models such as Value at Risk (VaR). On the basis of their complex computer models, the firm believed they identified highly correlated long and short positions and hence the net risk was small. Accordingly, the firm used its computer models and extensive databases to identify pairs of financial assets whose values had temporarily diverged, which LTCM expected to converge over time as the maturity dates became nearer. LTCM bought under-priced assets and shorted the over-priced identical assets and then waited for the prices to converge. LTCM's convergence strategy required extensive leverage, because the price differences between the two assets tended to be small. LTCM strategy worked fine during the initial years and achieved ROE as high as 40–50%.

**Collapse of LTCM**

In August 1998, Russia devalued its currency (Rouble) and partially defaulted on $40 billion of its debt. This sovereign default caused panic and investors around the globe sought safer avenues, resulting in a flight to quality. Instead of the convergence, divergence of spreads occurred, which caused massive losses for LTCM. Russian bonds accounted for only a small percentage of the LTCM portfolio, however, the 'collapse of confidence' in the financial system resulted in the flight to safety (mainly to US treasury bonds) and accordingly the value of quality assets soared, hurting LTCM strategies.

LTCM had a relatively high leverage of 28x (on an equity of $4.7billion) excluding the derivative exposure of more than $1 trillion. Most of the derivatives were of the over-the-counter (OTC) type. It is reported that on the day of Russian default the LTCM suffered losses in its various positions such that it wiped out most of the capital.

As the positions went against LTCM, the margin calls from brokers went up dramatically and LTCM did not have enough liquidity or access to additional capital, which anyway was not easy to come by given the market conditions which prevailed then. There was a systemic fear that if LTCM tried to offload its assets to raise liquidity, it would have led to a further drop in prices, which in turn would have affected the positions of other players in the financial system, creating a vicious circle of a drop in asset or security prices. The counterparties (banks and financial intermediates) who lent moneys to LTCM became panicky and a default by LTCM loomed large. A default would have caused a chain reaction of defaults across the US banking system and possibly in other countries which were linked to US.

**Rescue**

Realizing the seriousness of the situation and the threat it posed to the US economy, the US Fed brought together the creditor banks of LTCM who bought into the equity of LTCM and took control and avoided the crisis. In September 1998, the banks injected $3.6 billion of new capital into LTCM in return for 90% of its equity and oversaw the orderly unwinding of its portfolio. LTCM counterparties were lucky as they were rescued from the disaster by a Fed sponsored bail out. Only LTCM equity holders suffered, although they can console themselves with the profitable initial years when LTCM returned $2.7 billion of the fund's capital back to investors, which exceeded their initial investment.

**Lessons**

Among the lessons learned were the following:

- Application of exceptionally high leverage (i.e. borrowings) in an attempt to earn magnified returns from transactions with thin margins is highly risky – even if it is employed under the guidance of financial geniuses who won Nobel Prizes. When this strategy is employed by large banks and FIs, it can threaten the financial system itself.
- Uncontrolled and unmonitored OTC derivatives are a systemic risk.
- Whilst financial models are welcome, how far they are reliable is questionable.[4]

Despite these lessons, the FIs which failed in 2008 repeated the same mistakes that were made by LTCM a decade earlier:

1. **Bear Stearns**: Applied exceptionally high leverage and also engaged in excessive risk taking in sub-prime assets through the hedge funds it formed and over-reliance on financial models. The mistakes of Bear Stearns were fundamentally the same as the errors of LTCM.
2. **AIG**: Undertook reckless risks by insuring credit assets (mainly through CDS) worth more than $400bn for thin margins – i.e. CDS premiums were inadequate for the risks underwritten.
3. **Lehman Brothers**: More or less the same mistakes of Bear Stearns. High leverage with exposure to sub-prime assets driven by faulty modelling with significant off-balance sheet OTC derivatives of $800 billion.

Merrill Lynch, Washington Mutual, CitiBank, Wachovia, Halifax Bank of Scotland and many other institutions that failed or merged with stronger entities or sought bailouts from governments displayed some or all of the mistakes of LTCM. They all under-estimated or ignored risks in the blind pursuit of short-term profits and bonuses.

It seems that many have taken the wrong lesson from the LTCM fiasco. They seem to have confidence that if the Fed could go in and bail out LTCM, then they will bail out all banks and financial institutions in dire straits.

## ✍ QUESTIONS/EXERCISES

1. How does credit expansion help economic growth? Please elaborate.
2. One of your friends says that 'all economic growth involves credit expansion; however all credit expansion may not involve economic growth'. Do you agree with this view? Please elaborate.

[4]It is worth mentioning that during the heyday of credit risk models in many financial institutions and banks, it was tough to override the ratings provided by the system/model.

3. Why is confidence in the banking system of the utmost importance for the smooth functioning of the economy?
4. Explain why banks and financial intermediaries rely on retail deposits and the inter-bank money market as funding sources.
5. What are the major end uses of credit offered by banks and financial institutions?
6. What do you mean by credit bubbles?
7. What are the consequences of credit bubbles?
8. Explain the steps to be taken to control credit bubbles.

# 25
# 2008 Credit Crisis

The growing importance of credit in the modern world and increasing debt in the economic systems in various countries highlights the need for robust credit risk analysis and management. As we discussed earlier, the banking and monetary system depends upon confidence. Billions of dollars are transferred in the inter-bank market every day as the banks and financial institutions adjust their liquidity requirements and positions. If there is any worry about the strength of financial intermediaries, it will cause enormous problems, resulting in risk averse behaviour and consequently a flight to quality. The collapse of confidence in the system is equivalent to a financial earthquake.

On 15 September 2008, the financial giant Lehman Brothers, which had existed for over 160 years, filed for bankruptcy and this resulted in a financial earthquake, the consequences of which reverberated across the world. Let us examine in detail how the 2008 US Credit Crisis unfolded, the contribution of US housing market and how it became a global credit crisis.

## 25.1 CREDIT ASSET – PRIME VS. SUB-PRIME

Prime credit means giving loans to creditworthy customers. As we have discussed in earlier chapters, banks and FIs commit considerable resources to study and identify creditworthy borrowers. A creditworthy customer is one with a sound financial position and good cash flows which ensures timely repayment of credit facilities. Sub-prime credit refers to the credit exposure to customers who are not creditworthy and may have a weak financial position and unreliable cash flows.

Then why should one lend to sub-prime customers? After discussing in the initial chapters the various methods to be deployed to identify creditworthy borrowers, it is perplexing that banks and FIs lend to sub-prime customers. In fact, perfect business sense is to lend only to prime customers because even if you lend to prime borrowers, you still carry the risk of credit loss (see the discussion on PD and EL in earlier part of this book).

The main driver for sub-prime lending is social factors or government policy. In India or the US or any other country, the government comes out with policies that facilitate the flow of credit to the disadvantaged sectors in society, through several schemes sponsored or promoted by government. For example in 2002 the US President issued 'America's Homeownership Challenge'[1] to the real estate and mortgage finance industries to join in their effort to provide more housing to deprived sections of US society.

In some cases, banks and FIs show their willingness to underwrite sub-prime assets (usually based on a security) because of higher pricing. For example, suppose that on a $2 billion portfolio comprising different credit assets, the Board (of Directors) has laid down a policy that the actual loss should not exceed 1.5% of the portfolio. By prudent risk management, the portfolio management team has reduced the loss to 0.5%. In this case, higher risks may be attempted to enhance returns or yields. The Head of Credit can advise the front line to

[1] http://georgewbush-whitehouse.archives.gov/news/releases/2002/06/20020617.html.

cautiously identify some risky assets with higher returns (to maximize return) provided the overall probability of loss does not exceed 1.5%. Accordingly, sometimes sub-prime assets are added given their attractive return characteristics compared to the prime credit assets. However, it is evident that too many sub-prime assets increase the riskiness of the portfolio and hence are not advisable.

## 25.2 SECURITIZATION

As we discussed in Chapter 18, securitization is a revolutionary financial innovation in credit portfolio management. Both prime and sub-prime credit assets began to be securitized, based on a 'originate to distribute' model. A bank or financial institution studies the borrower and the underlying collateral (if any) and originates the loan, which is then securitized. Whilst the originating banks receive various type of fee income, it is not exposed to credit risk, once sold off. The basic idea is that loan 'origination' is decoupled from 'holding' of credit assets. The credit risk is borne by the buyer of the securities – securitized loans. Securitized financial products were a big success. It created a win-win situation for all parties involved as demonstrated below:

- **Mortgage brokers**, who make referrals to bank, earned commission or referral income.
- **Banks**, who study the loan application and grant credit facilities, earn interest as long as they hold it in their balance sheet. When they sell the credit assets, they earn fee income.
- **Investment banks**, who buy the loans from banks and securitize the loans, earn fee income (and interest income if they hold it in their balance sheet for some period).
- **Rating agencies**, who rate the securitized credit assets, earn fee income.
- **Credit insurers**, who usually provide CDS protection, earn insurance premium.
- **Trustees and custodians**, who keep the collateral security, of securitized mortgages, earn fee income.
- **Advisors** (lawyers and accountants), earn fee income.
- **Final investors** earn a higher income, compared to other products in the market. Moreover, due to financial innovation (CDO tranches), final investors have the option to select various levels of risk, based on their risk appetite.

### 25.2.1 Higher Risk Appetite

From 2000 onwards, the US Fed reduced the interest rates sharply to stimulate the economy. The US Fed rate was just 1% in 2003. Many large investors such as pension funds who traditionally invested in gilt edged securities searched for alternative sources given the low interest yield on treasury securities. Realizing the huge potential for high yield bonds and securities, the investment banks focused on securitizing mortgages and marketed products such as CDOs and similar asset backed securities to the investors.

As the supply of prime mortgages was insufficient, the focus shifted to sub-prime assets, which also had relatively higher yields. Steadily sub-prime mortgages increasingly formed part of CDOs. Sub-prime mortgages which constituted less than 5% of the CDOs in 1999 exceeded 20% by 2006. This reflected the higher risk appetite exhibited by US banks, who in turn never intended to hold these assets (also known as 'toxic' assets) as they operated on an 'originate to distribute' model. This in fact exposed the weakness of securitization. If the banks and financial intermediaries held these assets on the balance sheet, they sought the protection of CDS, which were provided by insurers, who seemed to have lacked understanding of the true nature of credit risk.

Given the demand for securitized assets from the yield hungry investors in the low interest rate regime, the investment banks, brokers and financial intermediaries were busy packaging the mortgage loans (increasingly sub-prime loans) into CDOs and other mortgage backed securities. They mixed prime and sub-prime assets and created tranches (or buckets or segments) based on risk profile. The senior tranche, as we have seen earlier (Chapter 18), was perceived to be of low risk and to improve marketability, and usually was rated AAA by the rating agencies. The major investors included pension funds, banks, hedge funds, investment companies, sovereign wealth funds, HNWIs and various cross-sections of investors across the US and the world. The sale of securitized assets resulted in immediate cash flows which were again redeployed into real estate. The resultant multiplier effect of the securitization process enabled the banks to expand loans in the US rapidly.

Whilst hindsight shows it was imprudent to underwrite high risk[2] assets to such an extent, the financial institutions justified creation of more and more sub-prime assets as they believed that sophisticated financial engineering, financial innovations and modelling enabled them to manage risks. Moreover, misplaced confidence reposed on the ever-increasing real estate prices in the US. For example, for a period lasting nearly a decade preceding 2006, real estate in the US had mostly moved in one direction, i.e. upwards. It is stated that many risk and financial models did not even factor in the possible downturn in US housing markets or did not make the scenario harsh enough, reflecting the complacency which crept into the risk management systems. All this reflected appalling apathy about risk standards.

Many academics and practitioners have pointed out that the reason for the rapid increase in RMBS, CDOs, etc. is also explained by the profit motive. By originating and selling the loans, banks and financial institutions enhanced their current income by way of fees instead of waiting for the interest income, which accrues over time. Higher current income also ensured fat bonuses for the top management of several banks, which influenced policy making skewed towards more risk taking. Another incentive was to meet capital adequacy norms by selling off loans and thereby reducing risk weighted assets in the bank's books.

### 25.2.2 Availability of CDS

As discussed in Chapter 19, Credit Default Swaps (CDS) have features of insurance. However unlike insurance, CDS can also be used as a speculation tool, i.e. naked CDS. During the crisis, several hedge funds and other financial intermediaries speculated with CDS and bought CDS protection on an obligor (company or country) without any credit exposure. Whilst CDS were bought by genuine institutions that had underlying credit assets, the largest group who bought CDS was speculators.[3] CDS also gave confidence to the financial intermediaries, banks (now hardly distinguishable from investment banks thanks to the repeal of Glass–Steagall Act) and their SPVs that in case of any problem with the underlying sub-prime credit asset, they could recover the value from the CDS seller.

It is stated that one of the reasons why Bear Stearns was bailed out was because of the massive credit default swaps (stated to exceed $1 trillion) on its books. In case of the collapse of Bear Stearns the banks and institutions who bought CDS from Bear Stearns would lose the

[2] It is pertinent to note that securitization was working fine, benefiting all parties until sub-prime assets entered the scene.

[3] Some conspiracy theorists argue that there was a vested interest in creating a crisis to benefit from long positions in CDS.

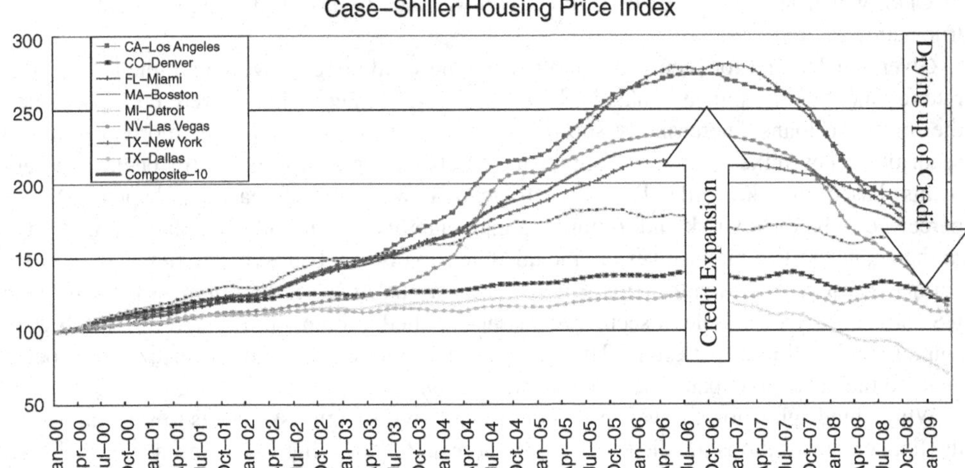


**Figure 25.1** Case–Shiller Housing Price Index (i) Major Cities in the US and (ii) Composite Index
Source: Case–Shiller – S&P Dow Jones

hedge protection and would have suffered billions of dollars in losses, triggering a 'confidence crisis' in the financial system. As we have seen in Chapter 24, the financial sector and banking are all about confidence.

After the Lehman collapse, the same thing happened to AIG, which was among the biggest credit derivative players and sold CDS protection massively. Later, as the housing bubble got into trouble, various credit assets linked to the real estate sector collapsed, impacting the various classes of securitized assets; AIG found the obligations under CDS unbearable and suffered huge losses. AIG had to be bailed out. The collapse of AIG would have brought unbearable suffering to the US and the global economy. AIG was one of the preferred re-insurance companies in the world.

Overall, we can conclude that naked CDS, moral hazard and misuse of credit derivatives also had a role to play in the 2008 Credit Crisis.

## 25.3 US HOUSING BUBBLE[4]

Figure 25.1 shows the boom and decline of US house prices during the 2000–09 period.

The cheap credit policy is a period of low interest rates and usually it spurs residential and commercial mortgages to acquire properties. All asset classes gain upward momentum when credit is cheap because it is the intention of the cheap credit policy to trigger economic activity. During the early 2000s, the US faced a minor recession and as a countermeasure, the US Fed introduced a cheap credit policy and slashed interest rates which touched a low of 1% by 2003.

[4] Whilst we cover the US Housing Bubble, it is pertinent to note that the economic activities reaching 'bubble level' were also noticed in other countries as well. For example, Spain also had a construction boom that resulted in massive surplus capacity. Similarly there was a bubble in certain commodities. For example, the price of crude oil and steel zoomed in 2008 aided by artificial and speculative (besides normal) demand resulting in both commodities touching record highs during mid-2008; however there was an inevitable correction thereafter.

During this period, in 2002, as we discussed earlier in this chapter, the US government had embarked upon 'America's Homeownership Challenge' to increase home ownership. Government sponsored entities such as the Fannie Mae and Freddie Mae corporations also played a role in the expansion of the secondary mortgage market by securitizing mortgages in the form of mortgage backed securities (MBS) allowing lenders to reinvest their assets into more lending.

Prime and sub-prime lending increased the demand for housing during the bubble formation years. The US ownership rate increased rapidly from the late 1990s to 2004/2005. This demand fuelled a sharp rise in housing prices between 1997 and 2006. In other words, easy availability of cheap mortgages propelled housing demand which drove house prices up. The demand for houses was derived from various sources. People bought houses to live in, for renting out, for investment purposes (i.e. to resell for a higher price) or as vacation or second or third homes. Motivated by the demand and increasing housing prices, the builders were busy building and renovating. Several homeowners took advantage of the low interest environment and took out second mortgages against the increased property values of their homes. This amount was either used for consumption or for buying another house.

The collective decisions of banks to deploy a significant part of the credit creation on real estate mortgages (both prime and sub-prime) contributed to a credit fuelled bubble formation in the sector, which gradually impacted the financial system of the country. The availability of OTC derivatives offering insurance on credit risk (mainly CDS) and the easy availability of 'investment grade' ratings from the rating agencies also played a vital role in the growth of securitization at an unprecedented speed and scale. In some cases, it is reported that the sub-prime loans were originated solely for the purpose of securitizing them—the 'originate to distribute' model. This increase in risk does not seem to have been detected by or to have deterred CDS sellers, rating agencies or investors.

Given the massive credit creation power directed to real estate, the supply of houses and residential units increased in line with demand. The boom in the real estate market resulted in sky rocketing house prices, which attained unsustainable levels in 2005. In May 2005, Allan Greenspan,[5] US Fed Governor, acknowledged the situation by stating that the housing market is in state of 'froth' and that the 'red-hot housing market is becoming a little too exuberant for its own good'. As housing prices reached unsustainable levels, there was natural apprehension on the part of buyers, influencing their buy decisions. Moreover, the rampant construction activity triggered by the boom had always carried the risk of supply gradually exceeding demand.

As we have seen in Chapter 24, during the course of fundamentally supported credit expansion, the underlying activity sometimes gets detached from the basics and acquires speculative features. This transformation often goes unnoticed by most of the economic agents, who would logically justify further expansion. Accordingly, although 'froth' in the real estate markets was recognized by the US Fed, it was emphasized that there was no indication of any nationwide housing bubble. The general opinion was that there could be localized bubbles in the country (US) and some speculation, in particular in second homes. Given the optimism in the overall economy, this clearly shows that even the central bank (or regulators) would

[5] Allan Greenspan is considered as being among the longest serving and able Central Bank Governors in the world, although he faced criticism for prolonging a low-interest rate regime during early 2000s. Under his guidance the US enjoyed a prolonged period of benign economic conditions. Many point out that the Global Financial Crisis occurred after he quit the position as Fed Governor and that had he been in charge, he might have handled the situation differently – probably a repeat of the LTCM rescue in Lehman's case.

find it tough to judge the situation. Whilst we have the benefit of hindsight now, the task of separation of the formation of a bubble from fundamentally driven growth is an intricate exercise.

Even corporate business decisions were influenced and attracted by the US property boom. For example HSBC, lacking exposure to the 'lucrative' US property finance market, acquired Household International in 2003, which was hailed as a strategic move. However by 2006 the lax lending practices and a house price crash pushed HSBC's US subsidiary into a den of financial troubles.

## 25.4 ROLE OF OTC DERIVATIVES

CDS, one of the popular credit derivatives, is an OTC derivative. There are two kinds of derivative contracts: exchange traded and Over-The-Counter (OTC). Let us distinguish between exchange traded and OTC derivatives (see Table 25.1).

It is evident that OTC derivatives are riskier than exchange traded derivatives. The advantage of exchange traded derivative contracts is that the counterparty risk is almost non-existent as the contracts are monitored and managed by a 'clearing house or corporation' through appropriate risk containment measures. A clearing house undertakes counterparty risk containment measures which include capital adequacy requirements of counterparties, monitoring of counterparty performance and track record, stringent margin requirements and position limits based on capital and close monitoring of counterparty positions. Since no exchange or clearing house is involved, OTC derivatives are subject to significant counterparty risk. Hence, counterparty credit risk measures such as PD, LGD and EL are relevant.

OTC derivatives are privately negotiated between two parties, without going through an exchange. All derivatives which are not traded or settled through an exchange or clearing-house can be classified as OTC derivatives. About 70% of the derivatives market is comprised of OTC derivatives. The OTC derivatives market is the largest market for derivatives.

Products such as swaps (e.g. CDS and IRS), forward rate agreements and exotic options are OTC derivatives. The major concern on OTC derivatives is that they are largely unregulated. The OTC market is mainly made up of banks and other highly sophisticated institutions, such as large corporates, financial intermediaries and hedge funds. Whilst exchange traded

**Table 25.1** Comparison Between OTC and Exchange Traded Derivatives

| Exchange Traded Derivatives | OTC Derivatives |
|---|---|
| Standardized contracts | Non standardized contracts privately negotiated between two parties |
| Derivatives exchange acts as an intermediary to all related parties to the derivative contract | No derivative exchange or clearing house |
| All exchange traded derivative contracts attract initial margins and maintenance margins depending upon the fluctuations in the underlying | Margins are not strictly enforced or enforceable in the absence of a central clearing house |
| Nil counterparty risk | Counterparty risk exists |

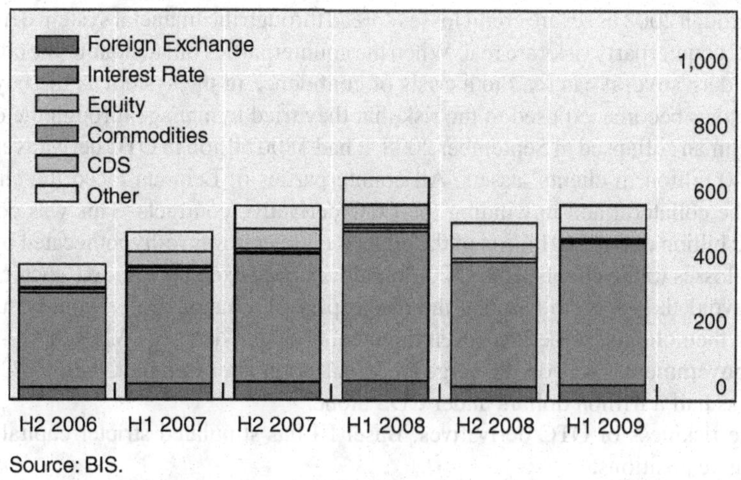


**Figure 25.2** Notional Amounts of OTC Derivatives Outstanding

derivatives are of low risk as far as settlement is concerned, OTC derivatives carry a significant risk in this regard.

### 25.4.1 Reasons for Popularity of OTC Derivatives

Despite the presence of counterparty risks, OTC derivatives are popular because they offer flexibility in implementing various strategies and managing risks. Based on OTC derivatives, many institutions manage currency/interest rate risks and apply sophisticated strategies such as 120/20 funds,[6] protected capital structures, various types of arbitrages or guaranteed returns or simply hedge their portfolios. Dynamic asset allocation and risk management or hedging is possible with swaps, forwards, futures and options. For e.g. CDS was used to take long or short positions in credit assets.

### 25.4.2 Complexity and Opaqueness – the Hallmark of OTC Derivatives

Since OTC derivatives are outside exchange or clearing houses, the margin requirements or collateral is controlled as per the contractual agreements. However, flexibility is often matched by complexity and opaqueness. The OTC derivative documentation is often found to be deficient. However, ISDA have recently been focusing increasingly on documentation. OTC derivatives are prevalent in global markets as is evident from the chart in Figure 25.2.

IRS was the largest OTC derivative and constituted about 72% of total OTC derivatives with a notional exposure of $605 trillion as at 30 June 2009. This was followed by Forex derivatives.

[6] A hedge fund strategy of simultaneous long and short positions in different equities.

### 25.4.3 Systemic Risk and OTC Derivatives

Although OTC derivatives play an important role in the global economy this aggravated the problems during the US credit crisis. The financial crisis which began in August 2007 and escalated through 2008 as severe credit losses spread through the financial system demonstrated that the OTC counterparty risks are real. When the counterparties fail to honour the commitment under OTC derivative, it can lead to a crisis of confidence in the system as the buyers of the OTC derivatives become exposed to the risk that they tried to manage through the derivative!

When Lehman collapsed in September 2008, it had $800 billion in OTC derivatives exposure and held $40 billion in clients' assets. All counterparties of Lehman faced the challenge of retrieving the collateral and unwinding the OTC derivative contracts. This was complicated because $22 billion out of $40 billion of the clients' collateral was re-hypothecated by Lehman, resulting in losses to the clients. Had OTC derivatives been exchange traded, such cases could have been avoided. It was evident that the bankruptcy of a major dealer would cause serious problems to their clients, sometimes even threatening their existence. When AIG – bailed out by the US government – was on the verge of default soon after Lehman, their OTC derivative exposure was half a trillion dollars under CDS alone.

Given the riskiness of OTC derivatives, Basel III has stipulated stricter capital norms on OTC derivative positions.

## 25.5 ROLE OF RATING AGENCIES

Thanks to the second Basel Accord, the rating agencies can influence RWAs in banks. Failures of ratings on structured securities are also highlighted as a facilitating factor contributing to the 2008 Credit Crisis. Credit rating agencies played a pivotal role in the development of the structured finance market such as CDOs. Many institutional investors and banks considered that even the most complex, innovative or opaque debt instrument could be sold as long as long as it received an investment grade rating.

The securitized debt had a few fundamental differences with the traditional corporate debt, which the rating agencies usually rated. The major differences are outlined below:

- Unlike the corporate debt rating,[7] which is usually undertaken by the rating agencies at the request of the borrower, the securitized products rating requests were mainly from the sellers (originators) of securitized debt who wanted to profit from such sale.
- The corporate debt, which was rated, would have been reflected in the leverage of the balance sheets of respective lenders. However, the securitized products did not usually reflect in the sellers' (originators') balance sheet.
- The securitized debt structure is often viewed as more complex than traditional corporate debt. Securitized debt had multiple counterparties, besides underwriters, originators, OTC derivatives, insurers, etc.

It seems that the fundamental differences between the corporate debt rating and securitized debt rating were not given adequate consideration. Given the lower transparency and greater complexity of these innovative products, heavy reliance was placed by market participants on rating agencies.

[7] Moreover, corporate debt credit risk analysis follows a different methodology from retail credit risk analysis. Securitization was heavily focused on retail products such as mortgages.

One of the reasons for the growth of CDOs and similar products linked to sub-prime mortgages was the availability of 'investment grade' ratings. The appetite for highly rated structured securities, combined with the belief that housing prices would remain robust and that the associated risks would also be transferred from the originator, resulted in relaxed credit underwriting standards.

However, once the housing downturn started, the rating agencies, who awarded high ratings to these securities, began to downgrade them, resulting in lowered valuations. The unprecedented speed and scale of the losses suffered by investors was a major contributor to the crisis. No wonder many questioned whether the rating system for such securities was fundamentally flawed. The defence raised by the rating agencies is that their rating is a 'point in time' and that they may alter that opinion at any time without notice. Most of the ratings contains following clause (or equivalent), acting as a disclaimer.

> ... Under the terms of the rating agreement, the ratings are subject to review or withdrawal by XYZ Rating Agency at any time **without notice**, if in XYZ's sole opinion any information (or lack of information) warrants such action. In terms of 'shelf life' the rating is considered a **'point in time' rating** ...

## 25.6 WHY DID THE BUBBLE BURST?

The reasons why the US housing bubble exploded are many. The main factor is that the bubble had run its normal course. The US house prices reached unrealistic levels measured by price to rent ratio or any other prudent measure and, accordingly, incremental demand was tapering away from 2006 onwards. During the ten year period preceding 2006, US house prices had risen sharply. Around the same time US interest rates[8] were hiked by the Fed, partly to curtail the massive credit availability in the system. US Fed rates touched 5.25% in June 2006 from the low of 1% three years earlier.

Higher interest rates had their impact. They reduced the mortgage off-take as the cost of mortgages shot up. Most of the existing mortgages were based on varying/flexible/teaser interest rates and accordingly the borrowing costs on existing mortgages increased. Sub-prime borrowers were hard hit resulting in foreclosures. Since house prices dropped sharply as supply exceeded demand, lenders found the underlying asset values insufficient to cover the outstanding, even in prime assets.

The downturn in the housing market prompted a collapse of the US sub-prime mortgage industry, which offered loans to individuals with poor credit or no cash for a down payment. When the mortgage was extended to sub-prime borrowers, the main comforting factor for the lenders was the expectation that the house value would act as cushion.

US house prices peaked in 2005–06 and thereafter the drop began. By September 2008, average US housing prices had declined by more than 20% from 2006 levels. Households with negative equity on their homes (i.e. the situation where the mortgage value exceeds the house value) increased. During this situation, even prime borrowers had an incentive to 'walk away' from their mortgages and leave their homes for creditors to repossess.

[8] It is argued that inflation levels in the US remained subdued in the boom years due to cheaper imports facilitated by the addition of capacity in low cost emerging markets such as China. Absence of inflation was one of the main reasons why US interest rates remained low. Low US treasury interest rates resulted in investors searching for alternative sources for yield, including commodities. This, along with the demand for commodities led by China, drove commodity prices up and rekindled inflation fears.

## 25.7 CONSEQUENCES

The housing crisis deepened with defaults on both sub-prime and prime mortgages. With the collapse of housing prices, delinquency rates soared. These were higher in the areas which boomed faster than the US national average, such as California and Florida. The default rate of sub-prime borrowers exceeded 20% and this level of substantial default impacted the mortgage portfolio and, consequently, the structured products created out of them. Foreclosures increased sharply with the default from both prime and sub-prime borrowers. Cash flows (interest and instalment receipts) into the CDO and other mortgage backed securities reduced sharply. Instead the custodians held the unsold inventory of houses.

The investors in CDOs, RMBS and similar products did not receive timely interest while even the principal repayments became doubtful. The valuation of such structured products dropped sharply in the secondary market and in some cases there were no buyers left for such products in that market. As a result of the panic, even the good structured products were affected with liquidity implications.

Several Wall Street and global financial institutions had taken exposure to the securitized sub-prime mortgages during the boom years. The drop in values of CDOs and other MBS products exacerbated the losses of the financial institutions. A brief outline of the financial disorder caused by the housing market is given below.

### 25.7.1 2007

Around 25 sub-prime lending firms (including the largest sub-prime lender in the US, New Century Financial Corporation) declared bankruptcy during early 2007. These bankruptcies shook the financial markets. The Dow Jones Industrial Average lost more than 400 points (3%) on 27 February 2007.

Two large hedge funds (run by Bear Stearns, one of the top investment banks in the US) with exposure to sub-prime assets collapsed in May 2007 and had to write off more than 90% of the amount invested. A few European banks (such as BNP Paribas) declared in August 2007 that they also held mortgage backed securitized assets in their investment portfolio and could not value them in the absence of any secondary market. It showed the distrust the MBS suffered during this period.

Inter-bank lending and liquidity become tighter and Northern Rock (UK) which was heavily reliant on wholesale funding, found refinancing tough. Moreover it faced a run on deposits and sought emergency support from the UK central bank in September 2007. The US Fed began reducing interest rates to 4.75% (from 5.25%) in September 2007. The interest rate reductions continued till December 2008.

4Q2007 was a nightmare for several financial institutions as they had to declare substantial losses as a consequence of the bursting of the sub-prime and housing bubble. For example Citigroup and Merrill Lynch reported losses of $18.1 billion and $11.5 billion respectively for 4Q2007. European counterparts such as UBS also reported substantial losses.

### 25.7.2 2008

During February 2008, the UK government nationalized Northern Rock while in March 2008 Bear Stearns, facing losses and a liquidity crisis, was taken over by JP Morgan in a Fed initiated deal. On 7 September 2008, the US government took over US Federal mortgage insurers Fannie Mae and Freddie Mac, as they were reeling under losses. On 15 September 2008, Lehman filed for bankruptcy, triggering a chain reaction in the financial system. (i) Merrill Lynch was taken over by Bank of America while (ii) the US government provided a $85 million lifeline to the American Insurance Group (AIG). To calm the nervous financial markets, the US Treasury announced a $700 billion rescue plan. (iii) On 21 September 2008, Goldman Sachs and Morgan Stanley converted themselves into banking companies, ending the era of independent investment banks. (iv) Washington Mutual became bankrupt and was taken over by JP Morgan towards the end of September 2008. (v) Wachovia was acquired by Wells Fargo early in October 2008. (vi) The US Fed announced $900 billion short-term funds to the US financial sector to avoid a liquidity freeze. Stock markets dropped sharply.

To calm the depositors many European nations guaranteed the depositors and European central banks took steps to safeguard banks. G-7 and G-20 leaders gathered to discuss the issues as IMF predicted a global economic slowdown. In the UK, during September 2008, soon after the Lehman crash, Lloyds TSB announced that it would take over HBOS, reeling under the financial crisis (the acquisition was completed during January 2009). German Bank Bayern LB suffered significant losses due to their exposure to sub-prime linked securities. During September/October 2008 Iceland's Financial Authority took over the country's three largest banks – Glitnir, Landsbanki and Kaupthing – which faced liquidity troubles as they were heavily reliant on wholesale funding. Moreover they faced a run on deposits in the UK. Although many banks in different countries (including ICICI Bank in India) had exposure to sub-prime linked securities, they were able to withstand this as such investments were not significant.

### 25.7.3 2009

Unemployment in the US touched 9%, as the economic recession set in. Iceland plunged into political crisis as its government collapsed. The US declared more stimulus and attempted to revamp its financial regulatory systems with more capital and liquidity requirements for its banking system. G-20 met to coordinate a worldwide action plan to meet the problems caused by the US sub-prime crisis and its aftershocks. Greece plunged into economic crisis causing Euro fluctuations. Two Bahrain banks – The International Banking Corporation (TIBC) and Awal Bank – owned by prominent Saudi business groups collapsed, which in turn resulted in defaults by the respective groups as well. Dubai World, a leading conglomerate of the Middle East, sought a moratorium on repayments on its $25 billion debt. The fear of crisis in other European nations such as Ireland, Spain and Portugal spread. A European sovereign debt crisis loomed large.

The above list of events is not comprehensive, but it does highlight how a credit crisis cascades through various layers of different economies: 2009 was a year of recession in the world with many nations witnessing negative economic growth.

## 25.8 IMPACT OF THE LEHMAN COLLAPSE

Lehman was one of the top five investment banks with operations in more than 120 countries. Lehman managed its operations with a leverage exceeding 20x, excluding its off-balance sheet liabilities. Lehman suffered massive losses as it was forced to hold on to large positions in illiquid sub-prime assets. Lehman was unable to raise sufficient liquidity by offloading its sub-prime linked assets to meets its commitments and consequently was unable to refinance its leverage as many lenders lost confidence. Although Lehman tried for a 'Bear Stearns' style rescue, it did not work out. Finally, Lehman became the largest bankruptcy in US history. When it filed for bankruptcy, Lehman reportedly had a debt of $770 billion against which they had an asset base of c. $640 billion. As we mentioned earlier, in addition Lehman had OTC derivatives of $800 billion as off-balance sheet liabilities.

Lehman's collapse had far reaching implications. Investor sentiment became nervous resulting in sharp falls in stock markets, triggering a flight to safety. If one of the top five investment banks is not safe, who is safe? It resulted in the disappearance of pure investment banking. Goldman Sachs and other remaining prominent investment banks became commercial banks to enjoy state protection. Soon after the fall of Lehman, AIG, among the biggest issuers of CDS was on the verge of bankruptcy. 'Who else is insolvent?' was the biggest question on Wall Street. Fearing further bankruptcies as a chain reaction, the US government decided to bail out AIG and the ailing banking sector. During September 2008 alone, the US government committed $700 billion under the Troubled Asset Relief Program (TARP) to stabilize financial markets. Brushing aside criticisms, Ben Bernanke stated that 'if no intervention, there will not be any economy' which highlighted the importance of the banking system to the economy.

By September/October 2008, the housing crisis in the US had become a full blown banking or financial sector crisis. The US government had to pump more than a trillion dollars into the economic system, under various packages. This questioned the logic of sending Lehman into bankruptcy in the first place, which could have survived had the US government supported it at much lesser cost.

Another interesting aspect is the speed with which US economic troubles affected other countries. Twenty years ago, the sub-prime crisis would have caused major problems for US banks only. However, in recent years the financial markets have become interlinked in different ways, including the trading of structured finance products based on residential mortgages in the US. Thus securitization resulted in a considerable amount of US mortgage debt ending up on the balance sheets of banks and other investors outside the US. Accordingly, when the housing market slumped in the US, the damage spread worldwide. The impact was severe to those with (i) a large exposure to US mortgage debt, or to property markets, via securitization and/or (ii) high leverage.

## 25.9 HOUSING CRISIS TO CREDIT CRISIS TO ECONOMIC CRISIS

Banking crisis and credit crisis are synonymous as lending activity and banking activity in the economy fall. Banks are essential to facilitate the exchange of goods and services in the economy besides acting as the intermediary between savers and investors. Figure 25.3 captures how the housing crisis became a banking or credit crisis, which in turn led to a full blown economic crisis and highlights the interlinking between financial markets and the real economy.

Housing foreclosures reduced the cash flow into banks, i.e. debt servicing on mortgages. This in turn impacted the values of CDOs and other MBS widely held by banks and other financial intermediaries (such as investment banks, hedge funds, pension funds and mutual funds). As the banking and financial sector incurred losses, they were required to seek additional funds (i.e. recapitalization) or reduce balance sheet size. Since getting additional funds is tough in

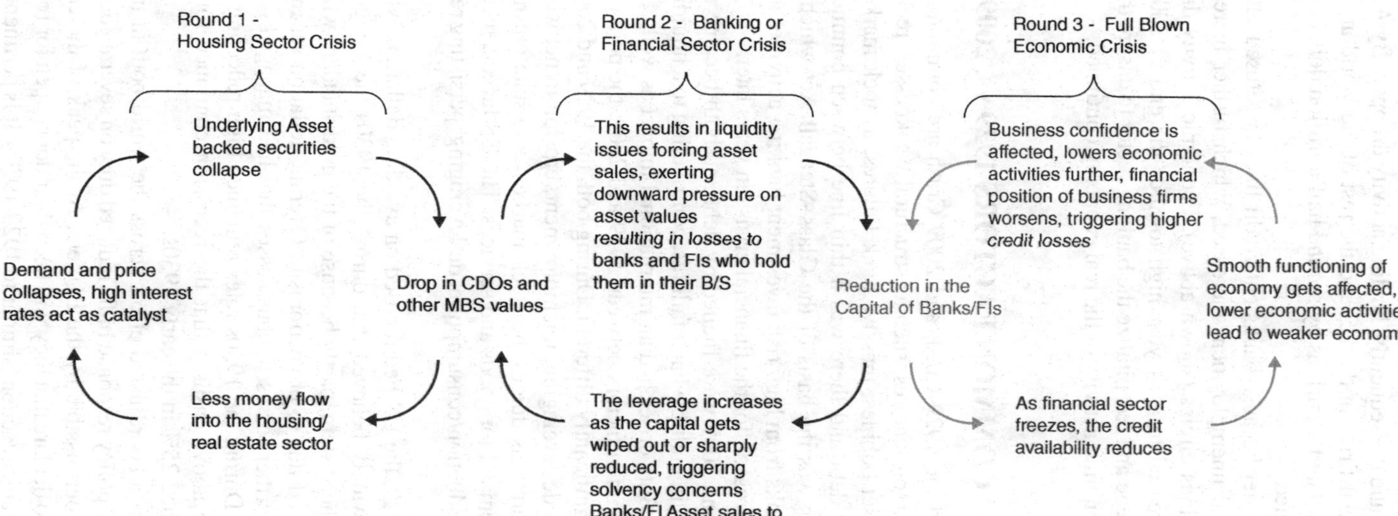


**Figure 25.3** Interconnected Nature of Real Economy and Financial Sector

such conditions, they usually reduced the size of the balance sheet. This had two impacts: (i) it further reduced security prices – i.e. there was a drop in financial markets – and (ii) it reduced the risk appetite of banks and consequently, lending activity dropped. By August 2008, before the Lehman crash, financial firms in the US and the rest of the world are estimated to have written down sub-prime related securities by around half a trillion dollars. After the Lehman crash the situation worsened.

As lending reduced, either because banks cut credit lines or refused further lending, economic activity slowed and unemployment increased, which further increased foreclosures. This exacerbated the vicious circles (shown above). Economic activity dropped and unemployment in the US increased to a 14 year high towards the end of 2008. Finally the US government had to intervene and recapitalize the banking sector to ensure that the lending was unaffected so that the economic activity in the real economy continued.

## 25.10 COMMON FACTORS 1929 vs. 2009

Many factors that caused the 1929 Crash and 2009 Crash are common. The downturns in 1929 and 2009 have common features, such as structural weaknesses, reckless lending, high leverage, speculation, asset bubbles, massive bank failures, a stock market crash, etc. Both bubbles were fuelled by debt and there was a thin line between commercial banking and investment banking. This was the basis of the Glass–Steagall Act which separated deposit accepting commercial banks from high risk investment banking activities and its scrapping in 1999 is often cited as the reason for the financial crisis ten years later.

The bubbles in 1929 and 2009 were fuelled by debt and both became uncontrollable and ultimately burst, resulting in multiple bank failures, contributing to a liquidity crisis and credit squeeze in the economy. Both crises had an international impact as well.

Although there are common factors between 1929 and 2009, the policy measures adopted to face the crises were significantly different. During both the 1929 and 2009 crises consumer spending dropped due to de-leveraging, unemployment, erosion in net worth due to a fall in asset values, which in turn was due to the stock market/real estate crash. Lower consumer spending meant lower demand for goods and services. The US faced a recession – increasing unemployment, lower production/consumption, de-leveraging, persisting real estate problems, bad loans, etc.

However, unlike in 1929, the US Fed focused on avoiding deflation, which was perceived as the real threat. It is widely believed that during the 1930s the US government/Fed did not inject liquidity into the system, partly because of the gold standard which prevailed then. International trade dropped due to protectionism. Overall, deflation set in causing a drop in prices, translating into further losses for businesses that had managed to survive, resulting in more unemployment. During the 1930s rates remained high reflecting the higher risks in the economy. All of the above ensured that the recession continued for a decade and the unemployment rate reached 25% in the early 1930s.

During 2009 there was a coordinated effort across the world both in monetary and fiscal policies. For example as a policy response India reduced duty on several goods, the UK reduced VAT to the lowest level permissible by the EU, etc. At the peak of the crisis G-7 and G-20 leaders met many times to declare that they will keep their doors open for foreign goods, which is expected to avert any panic reaction, similar to 1929/1930s. It is pertinent to note that global economies have links to the US, which accounts for about 25% of the world economy. For example China (manufacturing), India (BPOs/IT) and the Middle East (oil) have significant exports to the US economy in their respective areas of relative advantage.

## 25.11 LESSONS OF THE 2008 CREDIT CRISIS

We have discussed in the Case Study in Chapter 24 how LTCM's collapse nearly threatened the entire US economy. Despite the forewarning in the form of LTCM, the FIs which failed in 2008 had repeated the same mistakes. The Lehman collapse impacted other counterparties and triggered panic in the financial system causing a few more high profile banking bankruptcies and consequent aftershocks, which reverberated across several economies around the world. Among the lessons learned were the following:

1. **Avoid too much leverage**
   LTCM relied on very high leverage of around 30x, excluding the off-balance sheet derivative liabilities. High leverage became a huge problem when the market became volatile. John Maynard Keynes, whose economic theories post Great Depression are collectively known as Keynesian theories, has remarked that 'markets can stay irrational longer than you can stay liquid', which is an ideal warning for all business organizations that depend on leverage. Unlike a highly leveraged entity, a firm that depends more on own equity can hold on till the market recovers. High leverage is extremely dangerous because a small negative move in the markets can have a huge impact.
   Unfortunately, most of the investment banks did not take this lesson seriously and continued to employ strategies based on high leverage, which unravelled ten years later, in 2008.
2. **Avoid too much reliance on external ratings**
   Whilst the external rating agencies provide a sense check of the internal credit rating, never replace the internal rating results with the external ratings. This is especially true for banks. Even though the Basel Accords suggest external ratings for RWA calculations, a comprehensive internal rating of corporate borrowers is to be undertaken internally. Another important aspect is not to assume that ratings are always correct; always bear in mind that there can be a margin for error and, as evidenced in the 2008 crisis, good ratings can change quickly. It may be noted that given the reputation of a few external rating agencies, it may be a challenge for the credit risk department to provide a lower rating; however, application of the proper credit risk analysis and management techniques along with good communication skills ought to overcome this challenge. In other words, conduct an in-depth credit risk analysis and explain the findings with logic and tact.
3. **Never let a financial institution become 'too big to fail'**
   There was a misplaced belief that the larger and more diversified an institution is, the lower the risk of failure. If a financial institution becomes too big, it is a systemic risk because usually it is interconnected with the financial system of the country or across the globe due to its gigantic size. Hence, the near collapse of LTCM was a warning that large financial institutions and banks are not 'too big to fail' but too big a risk for the system/economy. LTCM grew too large with interconnections with a multitude of counterparties (brokers, lenders, clients, etc.) who all panicked when the creditworthiness of LTCM became questionable in a crisis. A default by LTCM would have triggered further defaults in the system.

Despite the near disaster of LTCM, the belief in 'too big to fail' continued in the US and many bank CEOs tried to create 'financial supermarkets' offering all kinds of financial products from simple deposits to hedge funds. Finally, with the 2008 debacle the underlying folly of this belief is now widely accepted. There is a paradigm shift and most authorities believe that banks and FIs should not become 'too big' but be of manageable size and 'large enough to fail' without significant systemic risks.

4. **Beware of flaws in risk models**

   Many financial intermediaries relied on VaR and similar models based on the assumption of normal distribution to study the risks related to credit, equity, derivatives and related markets. However, as many critics of the risk models pointed out, the financial markets are anything but normal. It is stated that the crisis events that impacted LTCM were shown by the risk models to be extremely rare events (tail events) and assigned the probability as a once in a thousand years occurrence. In reality, extreme tail incidents are more common than predicted by these models. Model risk and parameter risks were evident.

   Despite the well-known limitations of 'financial models' much reliance has continued to be placed on the faulty risk models. For example, Citigroup's risk models[9] on Collateralized Debt Obligations (CDO) never accounted for the possibility (even as a worst case scenario) of a national housing downturn and the prospect that millions of homeowners could default on their mortgages. No wonder the faulty risk models exacerbated the 2008 financial crisis.

5. **Give more importance to liquidity risk**

   This risk can be broken down into two: (a) funding risk and (b) asset liquidity risk. Many firms do the stress test of liquidity and have contingency plans, which fall short when the crisis happens. In view of the mounting problems due to the adverse performance of its strategies given Russian sovereign debt default in 1998, LTCM required immediate liquidity to meet its obligations. Under-estimating liquidity needs was evident in LTCM.

   Unfortunately, most of the banks and investment banks did not take this lesson seriously. The lack of liquidity hastened the rapid collapse of major firms such as Bear Stearns, Lehman Brothers, Northern Rock, Wachovia and Washington Mutual in 2008.

6. **Close monitoring of opaque and illiquid over-the-counter (OTC) derivatives**

   Most FIs have massive off-balance sheet liabilities largely in the form of OTC derivatives. In a crisis scenario, the unwinding of these OTC derivative contracts is not easy. Absence of an active secondary market is yet another problem. This may result in inappropriate valuation – say under-valuation of derivative liabilities and over-valuation of derivative assets. This was highlighted by Warren Buffett in his letter to shareholders in 2003. He described the issues they faced while trying to unwind the derivatives of General Re Securities, a subsidiary of General Re Reinsurance Company, which was bought by Warren Buffett's Berkshire Hathaway. The CEOs and traders who created such complex OTC derivatives might have left the company after earning bonuses.

   Despite the warnings, opaque OTC derivatives continue to multiply in the financial system. More than 70% of global derivatives are traded OTC. It is stated that these derivatives were necessary to put in place several strategies and financial innovation instruments as well as managing risks. Whilst this may be true, clearing and settlement through an appropriate regulatory body or oversight of these OTC derivatives would have lessened the impact of the 2008 crisis.

[9] http://www.nytimes.com/2008/11/23/business/23citi.html?pagewanted=4&_r=1.

7. **Strengthen regulatory oversight**

Regulatory authorities are supposed to monitor the risk taking activities of the financial system in the country, as the banking system is crucial to the economy. Ever since the barter system was replaced by a monetary/banking based system to facilitate exchange of goods and services, failure of the banks stifles the smooth flow of goods and services. Banks, sometimes driven solely by the profit motive, apply lax credit standards risking public deposits, hence the reason for regulatory controls on banks. However, banking collapses repeatedly prove that some banks are fallible by extending credit without sufficient credit risk due diligence, as US regulators emphasized faith in 'self-regulation of banks' driven by market forces.

Despite the clear signs that the financial system was too critical to be left to 'market forces' the US authorities repealed the Glass–Steagall Act in 1999. Soon after the 1929 economic crash, US congress separated commercial banking and investment banking (Glass–Steagall Act) thus restricting the deposit taking banks from engaging in high risk investment banking. The Glass–Steagall Act of 1933, enacted based on the hard lessons of the Great Depression, prohibited consolidation of commercial banks, investment banks, securities firms and insurance companies under one umbrella. The logic was that it could result in deposits from the public being channelled into riskier investments, which was often undertaken by investment banks, etc. Thus the banks who accepted deposits from the public were allowed only to extend commercial loans and advances, the bulk of which were retained in their own books. On the other hand investment banks engaged in riskier transactions and dabbled in equity (both trading and investments) and marketable bonds (both trading and investments) and similar transactions. Scrapping the Glass–Steagall Act in 1999 allowed banks to take more risks and engage in investment banking as well. Supporters of the scrapping of the Glass–Steagall Act believed that risk management systems had vastly improved since 1930s and hence the Act was no longer relevant, which shows that one of the key lessons of LTCM was ignored.

After the repeal of the Glass–Steagall Act, more risk taking was allowed in the financial system of the US through the Commodities Futures Modernization Act of 2000 which resulted in the creation of more unregulated derivatives. The second Basel Accord allowed more leverage to those banks with sophisticated risk management systems, which included debatable VaR based systems. Although the LTCM catastrophe cast doubt over the ability of the market to 'self-regulate', the US regulators seem to have continued this 'false' belief, reportedly under pressure from the lobbyists, and allowed more and more high and complex risk taking in the financial system.

The events that encouraged the build-up of the crisis in 2008 show that the lessons of LTCM were ignored. Instead LTCM-like failures multiplied and tested the US financial system in 2008. With many of the US banks functioning like investment banks with their own hedge funds, no wonder LTCM-style failures extended to banks as well.

8. **In-depth credit risk evaluation is needed even for traded credit assets**

It may be noted that traded credit assets have a peculiar position. Traditional credit assets, which are not tradable, are illiquid and are accounted for on an accrual basis in the banking book, where rigorous credit risk analysis and management are undertaken. In a pure traded asset, which is held in the portfolio for a short period, the market risks are monitored and regularly reviewed. Examples include equities, foreign exchange, government bonds and their derivatives such as options and futures.

When the credit assets began to trade massively due to financial innovation, it gave rise to a peculiar problem. How to manage the associated risks? What is the main risk of a traded credit asset – is it a credit risk or a market risk? Immediately preceding the 2008 crisis, the credit risk departments of most of the financial intermediaries held the view that the underlying risk of such assets was market risk as they sat in the trading book. But it is reported that the market risk team believed that the underlying risk was essentially credit risk. However, the 2008 crisis has shown that this is a dangerous approach and all credit assets – whether held in the books short term or long term – must be subjected to strict credit risk analysis. Theoretically, banks and financial institutions will not lend to a poorly rated customer even for a day. Then why should the tradable credit assets issued by such entities be held in the trading book?

## QUESTIONS/EXERCISES

1. Explain the reasons for the housing sector boom in the US prior to 2006.
2. What was the role played by CDS in the 2008 Credit Crisis?
3. What is the reason for the popularity of OTC derivative transactions? Explain how it adds to systemic risks.
4. One of your friends stated that the rating agencies have played a significant role in aiding and abetting the housing sector boom in the US prior to 2006. Do you agree? Please elaborate.
5. Explain how the housing sector crisis became a banking/financial sector crisis. Is it true that when the entire the banking sector is in crisis a credit crisis is unavoidable? Please elaborate.
6. Explain how a credit crisis can lead to a full-blown economic crisis.
7. Explain the similarities between the 1929 Great Crash and the 2008 Credit Crisis.
8. What are the lessons learned from the 2008 Credit Crisis? Please elaborate.

# Bibliography

Allen, Linda and Saunders, Anthony (2003) 'A Survey of Cyclical Effects in Credit Risk Measurement Models', BIS Working Papers, no 126, Basel.

Altman, Edward I., 'Managing Credit Risk: A challenge for the new millennium', Stern School of Business, December 2001.

Altman, Edward I., Resti, Andrea and Sironi, Andrea, 'The Link between Default and Recovery Rates: Effects on the pro-cyclicality of regulatory capital ratios, BIS Working Papers, Basel, July 2002.

Antonov, Ivo: 'Quantitative vs. Judgmental Credit Risk-rating Systems', *The Journal of Lending & Credit Risk Management*, February 2000.

Baldoni, Robert J., 'Risk Management: Journey or destination?' *Cross Currents* (An Ernst & Young Financial Services Industry quarterly) 2001.

Bangia, Anil, Diebold, Francis X. and Schuermann, Til, 'Ratings Migration and the Business Cycle, With Applications to Credit Portfolio Stress Testing', Wharton Financial Institutions Center Working Papers, 2000.

Basel Committee on Banking Supervision, 2010, The New Basel Accord (Basel, Switzerland: Bank for International Settlements).

Bernanke, Ben (Federal Reserve Governor, USA) 'Five Questions about the Federal Reserve and Monetary Policy', Speech delivered at the Economic Club of Indiana, Indianapolis, Indiana, 1 October 2012.

Bernanke, Ben S., Semiannual Monetary Policy Report to the Congress – 17 July 2012.

Berrada, Tony, Gibson, Rajna and Mougeot, Nicolas, 'Systematic Credit Risk and Asset Pricing: Empirical study on the US stock market' – based on research that has been partially supported by the Swiss National Fund for Scientific Research, January 2001.

Borio, C. and Lowe, P., 'Asset Prices, Financial and Monetary Stability: Exploring the nexus', BIS Working Papers no 114, Basel, July 2002.

*Business Week*, 14 June 1999, 'Bulletproof Banker'.

*Business Week*, 27 July 2001, 'We Wanted to Be Held Accountable'.

*Business Week*, 21 August 2001, 'Enron'.

*Business Week*, 11 January 2002, 'Accounting Fraud on the Rise'.

*Business Week*, 29 June 2002, 'To Expense or Not to Expense'.

Cai, Fang, 'Was There Front Running During the LTCM Crisis?' International Finance Discussion Papers (Board of Governors of the Federal Reserve System), February 2003.

Carey, Mark, 'A Guide to Choosing Absolute Bank Capital Requirements', International Finance Discussion Papers (Board of Governors of the Federal Reserve System), May 2002.

Chandra, Prassanna, *Financial Management – Theory & Practice* (Tata McGraw Hill).

Conway, Tom and Davis, Peter O., 'Falling Dominoes – The Impact of Credit-Triggered Risk', *Contingencies* (Bimonthly) November/December 2002.

Dell, J.C., Kunkle, J.W., Streeter, W. et al., 'Rating Approach to Project Finance', Fitch IBCA, Duff & Phelps Special Report, 26 April 2001.

Falkenstein, Eric, 'The Risk Manager of the Future: Scientist or poet?' *The RMA Journal*, February 2001.

Geski, Terry, 'CMS Interactive – Basics of credit modeling', *Financial Times*, October 2002.

Gibson, Michael S., 'Credit Derivatives and Risk Management', *Federal Reserve Bank of Atlanta, Economic Review*, Fourth Quarter 2007.

Gordy, Michael, 'A Comparative Anatomy of Credit Risk Models, *Journal of Banking and Finance*, 24 January 2000.

Greenspan, Allan (Federal Reserve Board) Semi Annual Report to the Congress, 27 February 2002.

Greenspan, Allan (Federal Reserve Governor, USA), 'The US Economy', Speech delivered at Independent Community of Bankers of America (Hawaii, 2002).

Greenspan, Allan (Federal Reserve Governor, USA): 'Corporate Governance', Speech delivered at Stern School of Business, New York University, New York, 2002.

Gupta, N.D., 'Enterprise Governance and Risk Management', *The Chartered Accountant*, ICAI, May 2003.

Henke Sabine, Burghof, Hans-Peter and Rudolph, Bernd, 'Credit Securitization and Credit Derivatives: Financial Instruments and the Credit Risk Management of Middle Market Commercial Loan Portfolios', CFS Working Papers Nr 1998/07.

International Accounting Standard (IAS) 39 – Derivative Accounting.

Jácome, Luis I. and Nier, Erlend W., 'Macroprudential Policy: Protecting the whole', International Monetary Fund website (2011).

Jalan, Bimal (Former RBI Governor), 'India & Globalization', Convocation Address of Indian Statistical Institute, Kolkota, 2002.

Jalan, Bimal (Former RBI Governor), 'Indian Banking and Finance – Managing New Challenges', Speech delivered at Banking Economists Conference, 2002.

James, Christopher, 'RAROC Based Capital Budgeting and Performance Evaluation: A case study of bank capital allocation', Wharton Financial Institutions Center Working Papers, 1996.

Jobst, Norbert J. and Zenios, Stavros A., 'Extending Credit Risk (pricing) Models for the Simulation of Portfolios of Interest Rate and Credit Risk Sensitive Securities', Wharton Financial Institutions Center Working Papers.

Joel Bessis, *Risk Management in Banks* (2nd edn, John Wiley & Sons Ltd, 2002).

Jokivuolle, Esa and Peura, Samu: 'A Value-at-Risk Approach to Banks' Capital Buffers: An application to the new Basel Accord', Bank of Finland Discussion Papers, 2001.

Keay, John, *The Honourable Company – A History of the English East India Company* (Harper Collins, 1993).

Kelly, John, 'A New Interpretation of Information Rate', published in the *Bell System Technical Journal* (1956).

Lehman Brothers Audited Accounts 2006 and 2007.

Lehman Brothers International (Europe) – In Administration Joint Administrators' Progress Report (2011).

Loretan, Mico and English, William B., 'Evaluating "Correlation Breakdowns" during Periods of Market Volatility', Board of Governors of the Federal Reserve System International Finance Working Paper No. 658, February 2000.

Lowe, P. 'Credit Risk Measurement and Procyclicality', BIS Working Papers no 116, Basel, September 2002.

MacLean, Leonard C., Thorp, Edward O. and Ziemba, William T., *The Kelly Capital Growth Investment Criterion: Theory and Practice* (World Scientific Publishing Co, 2010).

MacLeany, Leonard C., Thorp, Edward O. and Ziemba William T., 'How Does the Fortune's Formula-Kelly Capital Growth Model Perform?' (11 January 2011).

Merton, Robert, 'On the Pricing of Corporate Debt: The risk structure of interest rates', *Journal of Finance*, 1974.

Mogul, Sanir S., 'APV – The Preferred DCF Approach', *The Chartered Accountant*, ICAI, July 2002.

Moody's Rating Migration and Credit Quality Correlation, 1920–1996 – Moody's Special Comment. Global Credit Research (1997).

New York Times, 'Citigroup Saw No Red Flags Even as It Made Bolder Bets' November 2008.

Oak, Brian, Off-Balance Sheet Leases: Capitalization and Ratings Implications – Moody's Special Comment. Global Credit Research (August 1999).

Parasuraman, N.R., 'Ascertaining the Divisional Project Beta for Project Evaluation – The Play Method – A Discussion', *The Chartered Accountant*, ICAI, November 2002.

Pathak, Gaurav, Bidrupane. Pramod, and Goli, Rajesh, 'The Role of Credit Default Swaps in Precipitating the Current Global Crisis' (2007).

Porter, Michael 'How Competitive Forces Shape Strategy' *Harvard Business Review* No. 79208 (1980).

Poundstone, William, *Fortunes Formula –The Untold Story of Scientific Betting System* (Hill & Wang, 2006).

Purkayasta, Subir 'Insurance Needs in Project Finance', *The Chartered Accountant*, ICAI, June 2002.

Radelet, S. and Sachs, J.D., 'The East Asian Financial Crisis: Diagnosis, remedies, prospects' (1998) 28(1) *Brookings Papers on Economic Activity* 1–74.

Rowe, David, 'Integrated Credit Risk Management – Are You Ready?' *RISK Magazine*, June 2002.

Rutter Associates, Results from the 2002 Survey of Credit Portfolio Management Practices (with the sponsorship of the International Association of Credit Portfolio Managers (IACPM), the International Association of Swaps and Derivatives Association (ISDA) and the Risk Management Association (RMA)).

Saavedra, Cecile b. (Managing Director S&P), 'Establishment of an Efficient Credit Rating System', Bangkok, June 2001, ADBI Workshop.

Saunders, A. and Allen, L., *Credit Risk Measurement: New Approaches to Value at Risk and Other Paradigms* (2nd edn, John Wiley & Sons Ltd, 2002).

Schwager, Jack D., *Hedge Fund Wizards* (John Wiley & Sons Ltd, 2012).

Shri G.P., Muniappan, 'Management Challenges in Banking', Address by Deputy Governor, Reserve Bank of India at the NIBM Annual Day Celebrations, 6 January 2003.

Taillon, Roger B. (Analyst, S&P) 'Accounting for Impaired Assets in Bank Credit Analysis' – published in Ratings Direct, July 2002, Standard & Poor's.

Thorp, Dr Edward O., *Mathematics of Gambling* (Lyle Stuart, 1985).

Tudela, Merxe and Young, Garry: 'A Merton-model Approach to Assessing the Default Risk of UK Public Companies', Bank of England Working Papers 194, 2003.

UAE Central Bank – Banking Circulars, Dubai Statistics Centre, 2011.

Varotto, Simon, 'Basel III and Beyond: Regulating and supervising banks in the post-crisis era' (2011).

White, Gerald, Sodhi, Ashwin Paul and Fried, Dov, *The Analysis and Use of Financial Statements* (2nd edn, John Wiley & Sons Ltd, 2001).

Wilson, Thomas C., 'Portfolio Credit Risk', *Economic Policy Review*, October 1998.

Zeng, Bin and Zhang, Jing, *Measuring Credit Correlations: Equity Correlations Are Not Enough!* (KMV LLC, 2002).

# Index